Lecture Notes in Computer Science   14659

The series Lecture Notes in Computer Science (LNCS), including its subseries Lecture Notes in Artificial Intelligence (LNAI) and Lecture Notes in Bioinformatics (LNBI), has established itself as a medium for the publication of new developments in computer science and information technology research, teaching, and education.

LNCS enjoys close cooperation with the computer science R & D community, the series counts many renowned academics among its volume editors and paper authors, and collaborates with prestigious societies. Its mission is to serve this international community by providing an invaluable service, mainly focused on the publication of conference and workshop proceedings and postproceedings. LNCS commenced publication in 1973.

Jeremy Gibbons · Dale Miller
Editors

Functional and Logic Programming

17th International Symposium, FLOPS 2024
Kumamoto, Japan, May 15–17, 2024
Proceedings

Editors
Jeremy Gibbons (iD)
Department of Computer Science, Wolfson
Building
Oxford University
Oxford, UK

Dale Miller (iD)
Campus de l'École Polytechnique
Inria Saclay
Palaiseau, France

ISSN 0302-9743   ISSN 1611-3349 (electronic)
Lecture Notes in Computer Science
ISBN 978-981-97-2299-0   ISBN 978-981-97-2300-3 (eBook)
https://doi.org/10.1007/978-981-97-2300-3

This Springer imprint is published by the registered company Springer Nature Singapore Pte Ltd.
The registered company address is: 152 Beach Road, #21-01/04 Gateway East, Singapore 189721, Singapore

Paper in this product is recyclable.

Preface

This volume contains the papers presented at the 17th International Symposium on Functional and Logic Programming (FLOPS 2024), held during May 15–17, 2024 in Kumamoto, Japan.

Writing down detailed computational steps is not the only way of programming. The alternative, being used increasingly in practice, is to start by writing down the desired properties of the result. The computational steps are then (semi-)automatically derived from these higher-level specifications. Examples of this declarative style include functional and logic programming, program transformation and rewriting, and extracting programs from proofs of their correctness.

FLOPS aims to bring together practitioners, researchers, and implementers of declarative programming, to discuss mutually interesting results and common problems: theoretical advances, their implementations in language systems and tools, and applications of these systems in practice. The scope includes all aspects of the design, semantics, theory, applications, implementations, and teaching of declarative programming. FLOPS specifically aims to promote cross-fertilization between theory and practice and among different styles of declarative programming.

FLOPS has a long tradition. Previous meetings were held at Fuji Susono (1995), Shonan Village (1996), Kyoto (1998), Tsukuba (1999), Tokyo (2001), Aizu (2002), Nara (2004), Fuji Susono (2006), Ise (2008), Sendai (2010), Kobe (2012), Kanazawa (2014), Kochi (2016), Nagoya (2018), Akita (online, 2020), and Kyoto (online, 2022).

The call for papers resulted in 34 abstract submissions, of which 28 were finally submitted as full papers. The subsequent reviewing process was double-blind. Each submission was reviewed by at least three reviewers, either Program Committee (PC) members or external referees. After careful and thorough discussions, the PC accepted seven regular research papers, seven system descriptions, and one declarative pearl. The program also included four invited talks by Lennart Augustsson (Epic Games), Youyou Cong (Tokyo Institute of Technology), Katsumi Inoue (National Institute of Informatics), and Yuliya Lierler (University of Nebraska). Katsumi Inoue provided an extended abstract, which is included in these proceedings.

We would like to thank all invited speakers and authors for their contributions. We are grateful to all PC members and external reviewers for their hard work and to EasyChair for their conference management system, which made our work of organizing FLOPS 2024 much easier. We thank the local co-organizers, Shin-ya Katsumata and Naohiko Hoshino, who did a great job setting up the conference and ensuring everything ran smoothly.

Finally, we would like to thank our sponsors, the KDDI Foundation and the Japan Software Science Society Special Interest Group on Programming and Programming

Languages (JSSST-SIGPPL), for their continued support. We acknowledge the cooperation of ACM SIGPLAN and the Asian Association for Foundation of Software (AAFS). .

March 2024   Jeremy Gibbons
                                                              Dale Miller

Organization

General Chair

Shin-ya Katsumata   National Institute of Informatics, Japan

Organizing Chair

Naohiko Hoshino   Sojo University, Japan

Programme Committee Chairs

Jeremy Gibbons   University of Oxford, UK
Dale Miller   Inria Saclay, France

Steering Committee

Michael Codish   Ben Gurion University of the Negev, Israel
John Gallagher   Roskilde University, Denmark
Jeremy Gibbons   University of Oxford, UK
Atsushi Igarashi   Kyoto University, Japan
Michael Hanus   Christian-Albrechts-Universität zu Kiel, Germany
Yukiyoshi Kameyama   University of Tsukuba, Japan
Shin-ya Katsumata   National Institute of Informatics, Japan
Andy King   University of Kent at Canterbury, UK
Oleg Kiselyov   Tohoku University, Japan
Dale Miller   Inria Saclay, France
Keisuke Nakano   Tohoku University, Japan
Konstantinos Sagonas   Uppsala University, Sweden
Martin Sulzmann   Karlsruhe University of Applied Sciences, Germany
Eijiro Sumii   Tohoku University, Japan
Makoto Tatsuta   National Institute of Informatics, Japan

Programme Committee

Sandra Alves	University of Porto, Portugal
Matteo Cimini	University of Massachusetts Lowell, USA
Maribel Fernández	King's College London, UK
Carsten Fuhs	Birkbeck, University of London, UK
Robert Glück	University of Copenhagen, Denmark
Patricia Johann	Appalachian State University, USA
Yukiyoshi Kameyama	University of Tsukuba, Japan
Ekaterina Komendantskaya	Heriot-Watt University, UK
Annie Liu	Stony Brook University, USA
Anil Madhavapeddy	University of Cambridge, UK
Aart Middeldorp	University of Innsbruck, Austria
Akimása Morihata	University of Tokyo, Japan
Gopalan Nadathur	University of Minnesota, USA
Carlos Olarte	Université Sorbonne Paris Nord, France
Andreas Rossberg	Independent, Germany
João Saraiva	University of Minho, Portugal
Alexis Saurin	Centre National de la Recherche Scientifique, France
Paul Tarau	University of North Texas, USA
Tachio Terauchi	Waseda University, Japan
Alwen Tiu	Australian National University, Australia
Kanae Tsushima	National Institute of Informatics, Japan

Additional Reviewers

Matthew Castellana	Francisco Ribeiro
Samuel Frontull	Sofia Santos
José Nuno Macedo	Yi Tong

Abstracts of Invited Talks

Verse: A New Functional Logic Language

Lennart Augustsson

Epic Games

Abstract. Verse is a new functional-logic language. It has several unusual features and this talk will give a brief overview of the language and what makes it different from most other languages. Among other things, Verse has deterministic choice, and choice is very much a first class construct. The talk will also show a core calculus for Verse and how we can use rewrite rules to give a semantics for the language.

Continuations from Three Angles

Youyou Cong

Tokyo Institute of Technology

Abstract. Continuations represent the rest of the computation. This simple yet powerful concept attracted me to programming languages research a decade ago, and since then, I have been studying continuations from different angles. In this talk, I will present three pieces of my work on continuations, focusing on applications, theory, and learning, respectively.

Verification of Refactoring in Answer Set Programming

Yuliya Lierler

University of Nebraska

Abstract. Answer set programming is a declarative programming paradigm for the development of knowledge intensive applications, especially those that involve combinatorial search. It is rooted in work on the semantics of logic programs, so that syntactically answer set programs are reminiscent of those of Prolog. Yet, the systems that process these programs, and the art of programming in this style, differ from classical Prolog. The process of creating an answer set program involves

1. representing a domain in the language of an answer set solver—a system for processing logic programs,
2. making that representation safe for grounding—a process of eliminating variables of the program by substituting object constants, and
3. tuning the representation to facilitate search efficiency.

The processes involved in making the representation safe and efficient fall into the so-called refactoring, which is a common software engineering practice. In this talk, we will discuss answer set programming and its practices, as well as the proof assistant system called Anthem, which is designed for the purpose of facilitating proofs of correctness of the refactoring process. Examples will be used to illustrate the key concepts of answer set programming the operation of Anthem, and its logical foundations based on the relationship between logic programs under the answer set semantics and the process of converting logic programs into first-order logic formulas called completion.

Contents

Extended Abstract

Algebraic Connection Between Logic Programming and Machine Learning (Extended Abstract)

Katsumi Inoue[✉][iD]

National Institute of Informatics,
2-1-2 Hitotsubashi, Chiyoda-ku, Tokyo 101-8430, Japan
inoue@nii.ac.jp

Abstract. There have been attempts to connect machine learning and symbolic reasoning, providing interfaces between them. This work focuses on our original approach to integrate machine learning and symbolic reasoning, in the context of algebraic approaches to logic programming. We here realize logical reasoning using algebraic methods, in which algebraic data structures such as matrices and tensors are used to represent logical formulas. These reasoning methods are robust against noise, while allowing for high parallelism and scalable computation. Algebraic logic programming has been applied to fixponit computation, abduction, answer set programming and inductive logic programming.

Keywords: Logic Programming · Machine Learning · Linear Algebra · Answer Set Programming · Abduction · Inductive Logic Programming · Neurosymbolic AI

1 Introduction

Reasoning and learning are two fundamental components in artificial intelligence (AI), which are complementary to each other. Reasoning is based on logic and makes decisions based on existing knowledge, while learning acquires new knowledge and improves the performance through experience. Reasoning and learning are also interconnected and can enhance each other as a robust AI system that tackles complex tasks. The interplay between reasoning and learning becomes more and more important in generative AI with the growing use of *large language models* (LLMs), and one would expect that LLMs can do a good job in inferring and thinking, given a query in natural language. In this context, however, current LLMs have limitations in correct reasoning, and then active research areas have been highlighted in improving the model's ability to reason within LLMs as well as extending LLMs to perform correct reasoning, e.g., [17].

On the other hand, there have been attempts to connect deep learning and logical reasoning without involving natural language processing. The research field called *neurosymbolic AI* has attracted much attention [3], many of which

J. Gibbons and D. Miller (Eds.): FLOPS 2024, LNCS 14659, pp. 3–9, 2024.
https://doi.org/10.1007/978-981-97-2300-3_1

provide interfaces between low-level perception by neural networks and high-level symbolic reasoning. All such research directions somehow involve integration of machine learning and symbolic reasoning.

Here, we will present our original approach to integrate machine learning and symbolic reasoning, which provides a foundation for realizing a series of intelligent behaviors—recognition, learning, and inference—on a common mathematical ground. As a first step toward connecting machine learning and symbolic reasoning, we focus on realization of *symbolic reasoning with algebraic methods*. Algebraic data structures have been used in machine learning, so we consider that it should be easier to connect symbolic reasoning and machine learning within such a common numeric field. Using algebraic data structures such as matrices and tensors to represent logical formulas and constraints, we can exploit sparse methods of linear algebraic computation and optimization methods in continuous space. We then aim to realize reasoning schemes that are robust against noise, while allowing for high parallelism and scalable computation. Algebraic data structures are further integratable with neural systems in real domains.

Various symbolic reasoning and learning methods have been realized in such algebraic manners. These include: Tarskian semantics [20], Datalog evaluation [21], fixponit computation of logic programs [10,13,18,19], computation of satisfiable assignments in SAT [24,25], abduction [12,14,23], answer set programming [27–29], and inductive reasoning for propositional programs [7,15,16,22,26] and first-order logic programs [5]. These are broadly classified in two methods: *linear algebraic* methods (Sect. 2) and *differentiable* methods (Sect. 3).

2   Linear Algebraic Approaches to Logic Programming

Sakama, Inoue and Sato have defined notable relations between logic programming and linear algebra and have proposed algorithms to compute logic programs numerically using tensors [18,19]. A common principle in this approach is to formulate logical formulas as vectors/matrices/tensors, and linear algebraic operations are applied on these elements for computation of logic programming.

Suppose that P is a propositional logic program and H is the propositional atoms (the Herbrand base). We construct a *program matrix* M_P for the program P in a way that the rules in P are represented as multiple row vectors in M_P: each row in M_P corresponds to the if-and-only-if rule defining each head atom from H in P, and each column represents the existence of a literal from H in the body of rules. For an interpretation $I \subseteq H$, we associate a vector v_I such that an atom $a \in H$ has the value 1 in v_I if $a \in I$; otherwise a has the value 0 in v_I. Then, the *immediate consequences* J of I with respect to P [30]:

$$J = T_P(I) = \{ h \in H \mid (h \leftarrow b_1, \ldots, b_m) \in P \text{ and } \{b_1, \ldots, b_m\} \subseteq I \}$$

can be represented using the matrix-vector product:

$$v_J = \theta(M_P \cdot v_I),$$

where θ is a binary thresholding function for vectors [19].

For a simple example, suppose $H = \{p, q, r\}$, and let P be a program consisting of a single rule $p \leftarrow q \wedge r$ and I be the Herbrand interpretation $\{q, r\}$ (in which p is false and q and r are true). Then, $T_P(I) = \{p\}$, which is the immediate consequences of $(p \leftarrow q \wedge r) \wedge (q \wedge r)$. This is computed as the matrix-vector product:

$$
M_P \cdot v_I = \begin{array}{c} \\ p \\ q \\ r \end{array} \begin{array}{c} \begin{array}{ccc} p & q & r \end{array} \\ \begin{pmatrix} 0 & 1/2 & 1/2 \\ 0 & 0 & 0 \\ 0 & 0 & 0 \end{pmatrix} \end{array} \cdot \begin{array}{c} p \\ q \\ r \end{array}\begin{pmatrix} 0 \\ 1 \\ 1 \end{pmatrix} = \begin{array}{c} p \\ q \\ r \end{array}\begin{pmatrix} 1 \\ 0 \\ 0 \end{pmatrix}
$$

Here, the value $1/2$ is chosen for the row p with columns q and r, since each literal q, r contributes the same amount of information to deduce p. When P is a definite logic program, starting from the *initial vector* v_0 associated with the facts in P, the least fixpoint $v_{k+1} = \theta(M_P \cdot v_k) = v_k$ $(k \geq 0)$ yields the least model of P [19,30]. Stable models [8] of normal logic programs can be computed in a similar way, but several interpretation vectors corresponding to guesses of stable models can be given at once as an *initial matrix* [19]. Alternatively, supported models [1] of normal logic programs have been computed with a *dualized program* in [27]. The computational complexity of converting logic programs into matrices by these methods is analyzed and a linear-time algorithm is proposed in [11].

Algebraic computation of logic programs can maximally exploit the *sparsity* of program matrices, and scalability can be further enhanced by parallelism using GPU computation. In fact, Nguyen, Inoue and Sakama [13] have analyzed the sparsity level of program matrices and have employed sparse representation for scalable model computation of logic programs, resulting in an order of magnitude faster than state-of-the-art solvers. As another technique that can be useful with this representation, we can realize *partial evaluation* (1-step unfolding) *in parallel* by self-multiplication of the program matrix M_P, i.e., $M_P \cdot M_P = M_P{}^2$, which would then lead to an exponential speedup by unfolding it repeatedly: $M_P{}^2 \cdot M_P{}^2 = M_P{}^4, M_P{}^8, M_P{}^{16}, M_P{}^{32}, \ldots$ [10].

Nguyen, Inoue and Sakama [12] have applied the linear algebraic method to propositional *abduction* by considering an *abductive matrix*, which is just the transpose of a program matrix. Given an observation vector, the matrix-vector product is computed as a 1-step explanation vector. This process and minimal hitting set computation are repeatedly alternated until a vector consisting of only abducible literals is found. Sparse representation is shown to be effective for abduction too. Partial evaluation has also been applied to abduction in [14].

For first-order logic programs, Sato illustrated tensorized quantification to formalize Tarskian semantics of first-order logic in vector spaces [20], and realized efficient computation of Datalog programs by translating them into matrices with binary predicates and converting linear recursion into linear matrix equations [21]. Sato, Inoue and Sakama [23] introduced matrix-based abduction in Datalog programs and applied it to relation discovery (*predicate invention*) in knowledge graphs. In contrast to the linear algebraic methods for propositional cases, these studies exploit a matrix to represent a binary predicate with a finite domain.

Although the deductive and abductive techniques in this section are not directly connected to machine learning, the essential ideas to represent logic programs as tensors and matrices and to transform logical reasoning to numeric computation can be the basis of the differentiable methods in Sect. 3.

3   Differentiable Approaches to Logic Programming

Linear algebraic representation of logic programs by program matrices in Sect. 2 can be exploited for computation in more numeric ways using continuous optimization. A common principle in this approach is abstracted by *cost minimization of a differentiable function* with a parameter tensor [24].

Suppose that P is a propositional logic program. For deduction, our goal is to seek a particular interpretation that satisfies the conditions for stable or supported models. To this end, we consider a vector x in a continuous domain rather than a Boolean domain. Then, we define a loss function $L(x)$ with respect to x such that $L(x) = 0$ iff x is an intended model of P. Else, if L is continuous, the gradient of loss is computed: $\frac{\partial L(x)}{\partial x}$. Stochastic gradient descent or Newton's method is then used to compute a minimum x of L. At the end of computation, x is thresholded to a binary vector representing a logical solution.

Using the differentiable method, we obtain several computational advantages. First, the robustness to noise is obtained by continuity. Second, the scalability is expected by multi-core/GPU parallelism. Third, it is easy to integrate the method with neural learning systems. In fact, continuous optimization is typically used in learning model parameters in continuous domains.

The differentiable semantics of answer set programming (ASP) was proposed by Aspis *et al.* [2] for computing supported models by adopting the form of program matrices in [18]. This method has been more elaborated in [29]. Computing stable models is enabled by further putting constraints on supported models, which are embedded in the loss function [28].

Similar techniques can be applied to SAT by constructing a matrix M_S for a set S of propositional clauses and associating a vector x_I for an assignment I. To compute a satisfiable assignment of S, local search is performed with minimizing the loss L^S such that $L^S(x_I) = 0$ iff $\theta'(M_S \cdot x_I)$ is an $\mathbf{1}$-vector [24,25].

Now, cost minimization can be used to induce a program matrix from pairs of input and output vectors. That is, given a set of interpretation pairs (I, J) such that $J = T_P(I)$, a program P is constructed as a real-valued matrix M_P such that the loss L is minimized by computing the distance between $L(x_I)$ and $x_J = \theta(M_P \cdot x_I)$. This is a matricized version of *learning from interpretation transition* (LFIT) [9] in inductive logic programming (ILP). Boolean networks can be differentiably computed from state transitions in this way, and an unprecedented scale (with 10^4 genes) of AND/OR Boolean networks were constructed in [26]. In a more general setting, a differentiable LFIT (D-LFIT) has been designed to provide robust and scalable learning of propositional normal logic programs [7].

Differentiable learning of logic programs has also been realized by matrix representations that are different from program matrices in Sect. 2. Evans and

Grefenstette [4] proposed ∂ILP, which uses program templates to generate the set of candidate clauses. Phua and Inoue learned the class of logic programs instead of learning a single program, and used LSTM for a differentiable LFIT (δLFIT) [15] and then applied transformers to its improvement δLFIT+ [16]. Sato and Inoue have learned a program matrix in DNF instead of CNF by cost minimization that corresponds to a logic-based ReLU neural network [22].

Finally, first-order rule learning is possible by ∂ILP [4] when a program size is limited. D-LFIT has been extended to perform first-order ILP from mislabeled and noisy data [5], enabling scalable rule learning based on sampling [6].

Beyond improvements and applications of the methods presented above, our next goal is to deeply combine the two approaches in Sects. 2 and 3 into one, by extending differentiable methods to obtain knowledge from raw data and by exploiting matrix-based computation for more correct reasoning, for example. Another direction is to explore new methods for commonsense reasoning by connecting these algebraic methods with LLMs.

Acknowledgements. This work has been supported by JSPS KAKENHI Grant Number JP21H04905 and JST CREST Grant Number JPMJCR22D3. I would like to thank all members related to these projects for their continuous supports and long years of discussions.

References

1. Apt, K.R., Blair, H.A., Walker, A.: Towards a theory of declarative knowledge. In: Minker, J. (ed.) Foundations of Deductive Databases and Logic Programming, pp. 89–148. Morgan Kaufmann (1988)
2. Aspis, Y., Broda, K., Russo, A., Lobo, J.: Stable and supported semantics in continuous vector spaces. In: Proceedings of the 17th International Conference on Principles of Knowledge Representation and Reasoning (KR 2020), pp. 59–68 (2020)
3. d'Avila Garcez, A., Lamb, L.C.: Neurosymbolic AI: the 3rd wave. Artif. Intell. Rev. **56**(11), 12387–12406 (2023)
4. Evans, R., Grefenstette, E.: Learning explanatory rules from noisy data. J. Artif. Intell. Res. **61**, 1–64 (2018)
5. Gao, K., Inoue, K., Cao, Y., Wang, H.: Learning first-order rules with differentiable logic program semantics. In: Proceedings of the 31st International Joint Conference on Artificial Intelligence (IJCAI 2022), pp. 3008–3014 (2022)
6. Gao, K., Inoue, K., Cao, Y., Wang, H.: A differentiable first-order rule learner for inductive logic programming. Artif. Intell. **331**, 104108 (2024). https://doi.org/10.1016/j.artint.2024.104108
7. Gao, K., Wang, H., Cao, Y., Inoue, K.: Learning from interpretation transition using differentiable logic programming semantics. Mach. Learn. **111**(1), 123–145 (2022)
8. Gelfond, M., Lifschitz, V.: The stable model semantics for logic programming. In: Proceedings of the 5th International Conference on Logic Programming (ICLP 1988), pp. 1070–1080 (1988)
9. Inoue, K., Ribeiro, T., Sakama, C.: Learning from interpretation transition. Mach. Learn. **94**(1), 51–79 (2014)

10. Nguyen, H.D., Sakama, C., Sato, T., Inoue, K.: An efficient reasoning method on logic programming using partial evaluation in vector spaces. J. Log. Comput. **31**(5), 1298–1316 (2021)
11. Nguyen, T.Q., Inoue, K.: On converting logic programs into matrices. In: Proceedings of the 15th International Conference on Agents and Artificial Intelligence (ICAART 2023), pp. 405–415 (2023)
12. Nguyen, T.Q., Inoue, K., Sakama, C.: Linear algebraic computation of propositional horn abduction. In: Proceedings of the 33rd IEEE International Conference on Tools with Artificial Intelligence (ICTAI 2021), pp. 240–247 (2021)
13. Nguyen, T.Q., Inoue, K., Sakama, C.: Enhancing linear algebraic computation of logic programs using sparse representation. N. Gener. Comput. **40**(1), 225–254 (2022)
14. Nguyen, T., Inoue, K., Sakama, C.: Linear algebraic abduction with partial evaluation. In: Hanus, M., Inclezan, D. (eds.) PADL 2023. LNCS, vol. 13880, pp. 197–215. Springer, Cham (2023). https://doi.org/10.1007/978-3-031-24841-2_13
15. Phua, Y.J., Inoue, K.: Learning logic programs from noisy state transition data. In: Kazakov, D., Erten, C. (eds.) ILP 2019. LNCS (LNAI), vol. 11770, pp. 72–80. Springer, Cham (2020). https://doi.org/10.1007/978-3-030-49210-6_7
16. Phua, Y.J., Inoue, K.: Learning logic programs using neural networks by exploiting symbolic invariance. In: Katzouris, N., Artikis, A. (eds.) ILP 2021. LNCS, vol. 13191, pp. 203–218. Springer, Cham (2022). https://doi.org/10.1007/978-3-030-97454-1_15
17. Qiao, S., et al.: Reasoning with language model prompting: a survey. In: Proceedings of the 61st Annual Meeting of the Association for Computational Linguistics (ACL 2023), pp. 5368–5393 (2023)
18. Sakama, C., Inoue, K., Sato, T.: Linear algebraic characterization of logic programs. In: Li, G., Ge, Y., Zhang, Z., Jin, Z., Blumenstein, M. (eds.) KSEM 2017. LNCS (LNAI), vol. 10412, pp. 520–533. Springer, Cham (2017). https://doi.org/10.1007/978-3-319-63558-3_44
19. Sakama, C., Inoue, K., Sato, T.: Logic programming in tensor spaces. Ann. Math. Artif. Intell. **89**(12), 1133–1153 (2021)
20. Sato, T.: Embedding Tarskian semantics in vector spaces. In: Proceedings of the AAAI-17 Workshop on Symbolic Inference and Optimization, pp. 937–943 (2017)
21. Sato, T.: A linear algebraic approach to Datalog evaluation. Theory Pract. Logic Program. **17**(3), 244–265 (2017)
22. Sato, T., Inoue, K.: Differentiable learning of matricized DNFs and its application to Boolean networks. Mach. Learn. **112**(8), 2821–2843 (2023)
23. Sato, T., Inoue, K., Sakama, C.: Abducing relations in continuous spaces. In: Proceedings of the 27th International Joint Conference on Artificial Intelligence (IJCAI 2018), pp. 1956–1962 (2018)
24. Sato, T., Kojima, R.: Logical inference as cost minimization in vector spaces. In: El Fallah Seghrouchni, A., Sarne, D. (eds.) IJCAI 2019. LNCS (LNAI), vol. 12158, pp. 239–255. Springer, Cham (2020). https://doi.org/10.1007/978-3-030-56150-5_12
25. Sato, T., Kojima, R.: MatSat: a matrix-based differentiable SAT solver. CoRR, abs/2108.06481 (2021)
26. Sato, T., Kojima, R.: Boolean network learning in vector spaces for genome-wide network analysis. In: Proceedings of the 18th International Conference on Principles of Knowledge Representation and Reasoning (KR 2021), pp. 560–569 (2021)
27. Sato, T., Sakama, C., Inoue, K.: From 3-valued semantics to supported model computation for logic programs in vector spaces. In: Proceedings of the 12th Inter-

national Conference on Agents and Artificial Intelligence (ICAART 2020), pp. 758–765 (2020)

28. Sato, T., Takemura, A., Inoue, K.: Towards end-to-end ASP computation. CoRR, abs/2306.06821 (2023)

29. Takemura, A., Inoue, K.: Gradient-based supported model computation in vector spaces. In: Gottlob, G., Inclezan, D., Maratea, M. (eds.) LPNMR 2022. LNCS, vol. 13416, pp. 336–349. Springer, Cham (2022). https://doi.org/10.1007/978-3-031-15707-3_26

30. van Emden, M.H., Kowalski, R.A.: The semantics of predicate logic as a programming language. J. ACM **23**(4), 733–742 (1976)

Rewriting

ACGtk: A Toolkit for Developing and Running Abstract Categorial Grammars

Maxime Guillaume[1,2], Sylvain Pogodalla[1(✉)], and Vincent Tourneur[1]

[1] Université de Lorraine, CNRS, Inria, LORIA, 54000 Nancy, France
{maxime.guillaume,sylvain.pogodalla,vincent.tourneur}@inria.fr
[2] YSEOP, Lyon, France

Abstract. Abstract categorial grammars (ACGs) is an expressive grammatical framework whose formal properties have been extensively studied. While it can provide its own account, as a grammar, of linguistic phenomena, it is known to encode several grammatical formalisms, including context-free grammars, but also mildly context-sensitive formalisms such as tree-adjoining grammars or m-linear context-free rewriting systems for which parsing is polynomial. The ACG toolkit we present provides a compiler, `acgc`, that checks and turns ACGs into representations that are suitable for testing and parsing, used in the `acg` interpreter. We illustrate these functionalities and discuss implementation features, in particular the Datalog reduction on which parsing is based, and the magic set rewriting techniques that can further be applied.

Keywords: Abstract Categorial Grammars · Natural Language Processing · OCaml · Datalog

1 Introduction

Abstract categorial grammars [5, ACGs] is an expressive grammatical framework, designed to account both for the syntax and the semantics of natural languages. ACGs derive from type-theoretic grammars in the tradition of [3,22,24]. While they can provide their own account of linguistic phenomena, they can also be considered as a framework in which several grammatical formalisms may be encoded [6,10,25], including context-free grammars, but also mildly context-sensitive formalisms such as tree-adjoining grammars [12,13] or m-linear context-free rewriting systems [30,31] for which parsing is polynomial. Its formal properties have been extensively studied [10,16,18,28].

The definition of an ACG is based on a small set of mathematical primitives from type theory, λ-calculus, and linear logic. These primitives combine via simple composition rules, offering ACGs a good flexibility. In particular, ACGs generate languages of linear λ-terms, which generalize both string and tree languages, but also allow for using higher-order logic to express semantic representations.

J. Gibbons and D. Miller (Eds.): FLOPS 2024, LNCS 14659, pp. 13–30, 2024.
https://doi.org/10.1007/978-981-97-2300-3_2

A key feature of ACGs is to provide the user direct control over the parse structures of the grammar, the *abstract language*, defined over an abstract vocabulary (i.e., a higher-order signature), which can be seen as the set of admissible parse structures of the grammar. Such structures are later on interpreted by a morphism, the *lexicon*, to get the *object language*, defined over an object vocabulary (i.e., a higher-order signature). The process of recovering an abstract structure from an object term is called *ACG parsing* and consists in inverting the lexicon.

In this article, we present the ACG toolkit, ACGtk, which provides a compiler, `acgc`, that checks and turns ACGs into representations that are suitable for testing and parsing, used in the `acg` interpreter. It is implemented in OCaml and distributed under a free license. We illustrate its functionalities and discuss implementation features, in particular the Datalog reduction on which parsing is based, and the magic set rewriting techniques that can further be applied.

2   Abstract Categorial Grammars

The syntax we use in ACGtk to define grammars is very faithful to their mathematical definitions we introduce next. In order to illustrate the definitions, concepts, and functionalities, we elaborate on an example made very simple on purpose. More involved ones were for instance proposed in [23,25]. Formal definitions are illustrated with examples of ACGtk source listings, to be compiled using `acgc` (as in Grammar 1), and with ACGtk commands, to be run with `acg` (as in Commands 1).[1]

Definition 1 (Types). *Let A be a set of atomic types. The set $\mathscr{T}(A)$ of implicative types built upon A is defined with the following grammar:*

$$\mathscr{T}(A) ::= A \mid \mathscr{T}(A) \to \mathscr{T}(A) \mid \mathscr{T}(A) \Rightarrow \mathscr{T}(A)$$

where $\to$ is the linear implication and $\Rightarrow$ is the intuitionistic implication. They are usually denoted by $\multimap$ and $\to$, resp. However, because ACGtk use the ASCII `->` (or UTF-8 $\to$) and the ASCII `=>` (or UTF-8 $\Rightarrow$) arrows, we use this notation in this article.

Definition 2 (Higher-Order Signatures). *A higher-order signature Σ is a triple $\Sigma = \langle A, C, \tau \rangle$ where:*

- *A is a finite set of atomic types;*
- *C is a finite set of constants;*
- *$\tau : C \to \mathscr{T}(A)$ is a function assigning types to constants.*

As for the implication that comes with the two linear and intuitionistic flavors, the λ-terms also feature two abstractions: the linear one (`lambda` in ASCII and λ° in UTF-8) and the regular one (`Lambda` in ASCII and λ in UTF-8).

---

[1] Grammars and command files used in this article are available at https://inria.hal.science/hal-04479621/file/acg-examples.zip.

Definition 3 (λ-Terms). *Let X be an infinite countable set of λ-variables. The set $\Lambda(\Sigma)$ of λ-terms built upon a higher-order signature $\Sigma = \langle A, C, \tau \rangle$ is inductively defined as follows (the typing rules are provided in Appendix A):*

- *if $c \in C$ then $c \in \Lambda(\Sigma)$;*
- *if $x \in X$ then $x \in \Lambda(\Sigma)$;*
- *if $x \in X$ and $t \in \Lambda(\Sigma)$ and x occurs free in t exactly once, then $\lambda^{\circ} x.t \in \Lambda(\Sigma)$ (linear abstraction);*
- *if $x \in X$ and $t \in \Lambda(\Sigma)$, then $\lambda x.t \in \Lambda(\Sigma)$ (abstraction);*
- *if $t, u \in \Lambda(\Sigma)$ then $(t\,u) \in \Lambda(\Sigma)$.*

Example 1 (Trees). Let us assume a ranked alphabet $A_1 = \{\,John, Mary, saw, everyone, NP_1, Vt_1, S_2, VP_2\,\}$ with the arity given by the subscript (the arity is 0 if there is no subscript). Trees such as the ones of Fig. 1 can be expressed using this alphabet.

A signature describing the trees that can be built over this ranked alphabet is $\mathsf{Trees} = \langle \{\tau\}, \{\,John, Mary, saw, everyone, NP_1, Vt_1, S_2, VP_2\}, \tau_{\mathrm{trees}} \rangle$, with

$$\tau_{\mathrm{trees}} = \begin{cases} John \mapsto \tau & NP_1 \mapsto \tau \to \tau \\ Mary \mapsto \tau & Vt_1 \mapsto \tau \to \tau \\ saw \mapsto \tau & VP_2 \mapsto \tau \to \tau \to \tau \\ everyone \mapsto \tau & S_2 \mapsto \tau \to \tau \to \tau \end{cases}$$

Grammar 1 shows how such a signature is declared in ACGtk. For instance, in such a signature, the trees of Fig. 1 are encoded by:

$$t_{1a} = S_2(NP_1\,John)(VP_2(Vt_1\,saw)NP_1\,Mary)) : \tau$$
$$t_{1b} = S_2(NP_1\,John)(Vt_1\,saw) : \tau$$

The interpreter **acg** can check they are well typed, as Commands 1 shows.

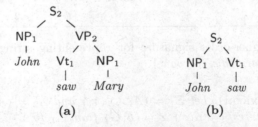

(a)   (b)

Fig. 1. Sample of trees built over the ranked alphabet A_1 of Example 1

Example 2 (Strings). Strings build over an alphabet T are encoded in a higher-order signature $\Sigma_{str} = \langle \{o\}, T, \tau_{\mathrm{str}} \rangle$ where for all $s \in T, \tau_{\mathrm{str}}(s) = o \to o$. It is then easy to check that if we define the type $\sigma \stackrel{\triangle}{=} o \to o$, the infix operator $+ \stackrel{\triangle}{=} \lambda x\,y.\lambda^{\circ} z.x(y\,z)$ and the empty string $\epsilon \stackrel{\triangle}{=} \lambda^{\circ} x.x$, $+$ is associative and ϵ neutral for $+$.

```
signature Trees =
  τ          : type;                John, Mary, saw, everyone : τ;
  NP₁, Vt₁ : τ → τ;                 S₂, VP₂              : τ → τ → τ;
end
```

Grammar 1: A higher-order signature for representing the trees that can be built over the ranked alphabet A_1 of Example 1

```
ACGtk>"S₂ (NP₁ John) (VP₂ (Vt₁ saw) (NP₁ Mary)) : τ" | check signature = Trees
1 term computed.
ACGtk>"S₂ (NP₁ John) (Vt₁ saw) : τ" | check signature = Trees
1 term computed.
ACGtk>"S₂ (NP₁ John) (VP₂ (Vt₁ saw)) : τ" | check signature = Trees
[ERROR] Type error: line 1, characters 16-28:
The type of this expression is "τ" but is used with type "τ → τ".
```

Commands 1: Checking well-formedness and well-typedness of a term against a signature

So we can define a string signature Strings corresponding to the yields of the trees built over the ranked alphabet A_1 as in Grammar 2 (a string constant is introduced for each symbol of arity 0, while the other symbols are not present anymore). The string $John + saw + Mary$ will then be represented by the term $\lambda^\circ z.John(saw(Mary\,z))$.

```
signature Strings =
  o          : type;
  σ = o → o : type;                John, Mary, saw, everyone  : σ;
  ε = λ°x.x  : σ;                  infix+ = λxy. λ°z.x (y z) : σ → σ → σ;
end
```

Grammar 2: A higher-order signature for representing strings built over the alphabet {John, Mary, saw, everyone}

Definition 4 (Lexicon). *Let* $\Sigma_1 = \langle A_1, C_1, \tau_1 \rangle$ *and* $\Sigma_2 = \langle A_2, C_2, \tau_2 \rangle$ *be two higher-order signatures, a lexicon* $\mathscr{L} = \langle F, G \rangle$ *from* Σ_1 *to* Σ_2 *is such that:*

- $F : A_1 \rightarrow \mathscr{T}(A_2)$. *We also note* $F : \mathscr{T}(A_1) \rightarrow \mathscr{T}(A_2)$ *its homomorphic extension;*
- $G : C_1 \rightarrow \Lambda(\Sigma_2)$. *We also note* $G : \Lambda(\Sigma_1) \rightarrow \Lambda(\Sigma_2)$ *its homomorphic extension;*
- F *and* G *are such that for all* $c \in C_1$, $\vdash_{\Sigma_2} G(c) : F(\tau_1(c))$ *is provable.*

We also use $\mathscr{L}$ *instead of* F *or* G.

The lexicon is the interpreting device of ACGs. If $\mathscr{L}(t) = u$, also denoted by $t := u$, we say that u is the *interpretation* or the *realization* of t.

Example 3 (Relating the signature Trees *and the signature* Strings*).* We can now relate the signature Trees and the signature Strings with the lexicon Yield to interpret the trees built over the ranked alphabet as strings. The lexicon we use is defined in Grammar 3. Note that the lexicon satisfies the condition ensuring that the type of the interpretation of a constant is the interpretation of the type of the constant.

It is then straightforward to check that the term $t_{1a} = \mathsf{S}_2(\mathsf{NP}_1\,John)$ $(\mathsf{VP}_2(\mathsf{Vt}_1\,saw)(\mathsf{NP}_1\,Mary)) : \tau$ is interpreted as the string $John + saw + Mary = \lambda^\circ z.John(saw(Mary\,z))$.

```
lexicon Yield (Rules) : Strings =
    τ          := σ;              John       := John;              Mary := Mary;
    saw        := saw;            everyone := everyone;
    NP₁, Vt₁ := λ°x. x;          S₂, VP₂    := λ°x y. x + y;
end
```

Grammar 3: A lexicon for interpreting the trees as strings

The formal definition of ACGs is not used as such in ACGtk because it's enough to have a lexicon (hence two signatures) and an abstract type A in order to parse an (object) term and get an (abstract) term, if any, of type A. The `parse` command of the `acg` interpreter requires these two parameters (see Sect. 4). But for the sake of completeness, we provide here the definitions of ACGs and of the languages they generate.

Definition 5 (Abstract Categorial Grammar and vocabulary). *An abstract categorial grammar is a quadruple* $\mathscr{G} = \langle \Sigma_1, \Sigma_2, \mathscr{L}, S \rangle$ *where:*

- $\Sigma_1 = \langle A_1, C_1, \tau_1 \rangle$ *and* $\Sigma_2 = \langle A_2, C_2, \tau_2 \rangle$ *are two higher-order signatures.* Σ_1 *(resp.* Σ_2*) is called the* abstract vocabulary *(resp. the* object vocabulary*) and* $\Lambda(\Sigma_1)$ *(resp.* $\Lambda(\Sigma_2)$*) is the set of* abstract terms *(resp. the set of* object terms*).*
- $\mathscr{L} : \Sigma_1 \to \Sigma_2$ *is a lexicon.*
- $S \in \mathscr{T}(A_1)$ *is the* distinguished type *of the grammar.*

Definition 6 (Abstract and Object Languages). *Given an ACG* $\mathscr{G}$*, and* S *its distinguished type, the* abstract language *of* $\mathscr{G}$ *is defined by*

$$\mathcal{A}(\mathscr{G}) = \{t \in \Lambda(\Sigma_1) \mid \vdash_{\Sigma_1} t : S \text{ is derivable}\}$$

The object language *of* $\mathscr{G}$ *is defined by*

$$\mathcal{O}(\mathscr{G}) = \{u \in \Lambda(\Sigma_2) \mid \exists t \in \mathcal{A}(\mathscr{G}) \text{ such that } u = \mathscr{L}(t)\}$$

Parsing with an ACG $\mathscr{G}$ any term u that is built over the object vocabulary of $\mathscr{G}$ amounts to finding the abstract terms $t \in \mathcal{A}(\mathscr{G})$ such that $u = \mathscr{L}(t)$. In other words, ACG parsing is morphism inversion.

3   Properties

3.1   Expressive Power

Two parameters are useful to describe the hierarchy of ACGs with respect to their expressive power: the *order* and the *complexity* of an ACG.

Definition 7 (Order and complexity of an ACG, and ACG hierarchy). *The order of a type α, $ord(\alpha)$, is defined inductively on α as follows:*

$$ord(a) = 1$$
$$ord(\alpha \rightarrow \beta) = \max(ord(\alpha) + 1, ord(\beta))$$
$$ord(\alpha \Rightarrow \beta) = \max(ord(\alpha) + 1, ord(\beta))$$

The order *of an ACG is the maximum of the orders of its abstract constants. The* complexity *of an ACG is the maximum of the orders of the interpretations by the lexicon of its abstract atomic types.*

We call second-order ACGs *the set of ACGs whose order is at most 2. $ACG_{(n,m)}$ denotes the set of ACGs whose order is at most n and whose complexity is at most m.*

Second-order ACGs are a particular class of interest because of its polynomial parsing property [27]. Table 1, from [25], sums up some of the formal properties of second-order ACGs.

Table 1. The hierarchy of second-order ACGs

	String language	Tree language
$ACG_{(1,n)}$	finite	finite
$ACG_{(2,1)}$	regular	regular
$ACG_{(2,2)}$	context-free	linear context-free
$ACG_{(2,3)}$	non-duplicating macro well-nested multiple context-free	$\subset$ 1-visit attribute grammar
$ACG_{(2,4)}$	mildly context-sensitive (multiple context-free)	tree-generating hyperedge replacement gram.
$ACG_{(2,4+n)}$	$ACG_{(2,4)}$	$ACG_{(2,4)}$

ACGtk implements parsing of second-order ACGs that are almost linear, i.e., terms in which variables occur exactly once, except for variables of atomic type that occur at least once, but possibly several times.

Higher-order ACGs can generate languages that are NP-complete [28,32]. In general, the problem of parsing with higher-order ACGs is equivalent to the open problem of provability in multiplicative exponential linear logic [9,32]. Even if there is a semi-complete algorithm for parsing with such grammars (see Sect. 3.3), it is currently not implemented in ACGtk. However, the interpretation of terms is available for any ACG (not only second-order ones).

3.2 ACG Composition

Because both abstract and object languages are sets of λ-terms, ACGs have built-in support for *grammar composition*. Two ways of composing ACGs are available:

- ACGs can be composed by making the abstract structures of a grammar the object structures of another ACG. This corresponds to the *applicative* composition paradigm (function composition of the lexicons) of [5] and is illustrated in Fig. 2 by $\mathscr{L}_{Derive}$ (from $\Lambda(\Sigma_{Rules})$ to $\Lambda(\Sigma_{Trees})$) and $\mathscr{L}_{Yield}$ (from $\Lambda(\Sigma_{Trees})$ to $\Lambda(\Sigma_{str})$).
- ACGs can also be composed by having a shared abstract vocabulary. Two terms of the two object languages are related if they share a common abstract structure. This corresponds to the *transductive* composition paradigm of [5] and is typically used to relate a surface form (e.g., as a string) and a semantic form (e.g., as a logical formula) through a common parse structure. This composition is illustrated in Fig. 2 by $\mathscr{L}_{Yield} \circ \mathscr{L}_{Derive}$ and $\mathscr{L}_{Semantics}$ that share the same abstract vocabulary, Σ_{Rules}.

This composition ability makes ACG a modular framework.

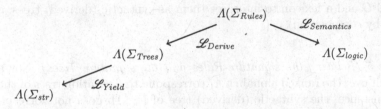

Fig. 2. An example of ACG composition. The structures are the ones used as examples in the article

Example 4 (Encoding a context-free grammar). Let $G = \langle T, N, P, S \rangle$ be the context-free grammar such that:

- the set of terminals T is $\{John, Mary, saw, everyone\}$,
- the set of non terminals N is $\{S, S', NP, VP, Vt\}$ (S' will be used when computing the semantic representation associated to a tree, see Sect. 3.2),

– the set of production rules P is $\{\rho_i \mid 0 \le i \le 6\}$ where:

$$
\begin{array}{llll}
\rho_0 = & \text{S}' \to \text{S} & \rho_4 = & \text{NP} \to \textit{Mary} \\
\rho_1 = & \text{S} \to \text{NP VP} & \rho_5 = & \text{NP} \to \textit{everyone} \\
\rho_2 = & \text{VP} \to \text{Vt NP} & \rho_6 = & \text{Vt} \to \textit{saw} \\
\rho_3 = & \text{NP} \to \textit{John} & &
\end{array}
$$

A signature describing the derivation trees of this context-free grammar is Rules $= \langle \{\text{S}, \text{S}', \text{NP}, \text{VP}, \text{Vt}\}, \{\rho_i \mid 0 \le i \le 6\}, \tau \rangle$ where:

$$
\tau = \begin{cases}
\rho_0 : \text{S} \to \text{S}' & \rho_4 : \text{NP} \\
\rho_1 : \text{NP} \to \text{VP} \to \text{S} & \rho_5 : \text{NP} \\
\rho_2 : \text{Vt} \to \text{NP} \to \text{VP} & \rho_6 : \text{Vt} \\
\rho_3 : \text{NP} &
\end{cases}
$$

Grammar 4 shows how such a signature is declared in ACGtk.

```
signature Rules =
  S, S', NP, VP, Vt : type;                          ρ₀ : S → S';
  ρ₁               : NP → VP → S;                     ρ₂ : Vt → NP → VP;
  ρ₃, ρ₄, ρ₅        : NP;                              ρ₆ : Vt;
end
lexicon Derive (Rules) : Trees =
            S, S', NP, VP, Vt := τ;                  ρ₀ := λ°x. x;
  ρ₁ := λ°l r. S₂ l r;     ρ₂ := λ°l r. VP₂ l r;      ρ₃ := NP₁ John
  ρ₄ := NP₁ Mary           ρ₅ := NP₁ everyone         ρ₆ := Vt₁ saw
end
lexicon CFG = Yield << Derive
```

Grammar 4: A higher-order signature for representing the derivation trees of the CFG G and a lexicon to interpret them as syntactic (derived) trees, and as strings (by composition)

Example 5 (Relating the signature Rules and the signature Trees). Not all the trees built over the ranked alphabet A_1 correspond to derivation trees of the CFG G. For instance, the syntactic (derived) tree of Fig. 1b does not correspond to any derivation tree of G. By relating the signature Rules and Trees, we are able to discriminate between trees corresponding to actual derivations (admissible parse structures) and the other ones. The lexicon we use is defined in Grammar 4.[2]

It is then straightforward to check that $\rho_1 \rho_3 (\rho_2 \rho_6 \rho_4) : \text{S}$ is interpreted as the term $t_{1a} = \text{S}_2(\text{NP}_1 \textit{John})(\text{VP}_2(\text{Vt}_1 \textit{saw})(\text{NP}_1 \textit{Mary}))$ of type τ (tree). This term can in turn be interpreted by the lexicon Yield to get the term $\textit{John} + \textit{saw} + \textit{Mary}$ as Commands 2 shows.

---

[2] This might seem an overkill when dealing with context-free grammars, as the derivation trees are taken to be the syntactic trees. However, when encoding tree-adjoining grammars, it is not the case anymore and such a composed architecture is indeed used in [25].

Grammar 4 also shows how to define a new lexicon CFG as the composition $\mathscr{L}_{CFG} = \mathscr{L}_{Yield} \circ \mathscr{L}_{Rules}$.

ACGtk>"$\rho_1\,\rho_3\,(\rho_2\,\rho_6\,\rho_4)$: S" | **realize lexicons** = Derive
Term : S_2 (NP_1 John) (VP_2 (Vt_1 saw) (NP_1 Mary)) : τ
1 term computed.
ACGtk>"S_2 (NP_1 John) (VP_2 (Vt_1 saw) (NP_1 Mary)) : τ"| **realize lexicons** = Yield
Term : $\lambda^o z$. John (saw (Mary z)) : $o \to o$
1 term computed.

Commands 2: Different interpretations of a term representing a context-free derivation of G

Example 6 (Providing a semantic interpretation to the context-free derivations of G). We now introduce a signature to build logical terms and a new lexicon Semantics that shares its abstract vocabulary, Rules, with Derive (Grammar 5). It is beyond the scope of this article to explain why these semantic interpretations are meaningful, but they correspond to the ones of [2] that provide a continuation based semantics to natural language expressions.

For instance, the term $t_6 = \rho_0(\rho_1\rho_3(\rho_2\rho_6\rho_4))$: S' is interpreted by Semantics as the term $t_{sem} = \text{see}\,j\,m : t$. This allows us to relate, by the transductive composition mode, the string $John + saw + Mary$, which is the interpretation of t_6 by $\mathscr{L}_{CFG} = \mathscr{L}_{Yield} \circ \mathscr{L}_{Rules}$, to the logical term t_{sem}. The same holds for $John + saw + everyone$ and $\forall x.\text{see}\,j\,x$.

Commands 3 illustrates these relations using the **parse** command in both direction (i.e., from strings to logical representations and from logical representations to strings). The ACGs we defined indeed are second order and parsing is available.

3.3 Parsing with Abstract Categorial Grammars and Datalog Reduction

Parsing with ACGs had first been studied as linear higher-order matching, for which several complexity results were established [4,7]. However, [14] showed how parsing of second-order ACGs reduces to Datalog querying, grounding parsing algorithms and optimization techniques on well-established fields, such as database and logic programming, and offering a general method for getting efficient tabular parsing algorithms [17]. This method applies whatever the object language: representing strings, trees, but also any kind of (almost linear) λ-terms as exemplified in Commands 3. This also allows for deriving algorithms with specific properties such as prefix correctness in a general way.[3] ACGtk implements the Datalog reduction with acgc and Datalog evaluation in acg to parse object terms as illustrated by Fig. 3.

---

[3] For a n^6 prefix-correct Earley recognizer for TAGs, see [15].

```
signature Logic =
  e, t : type;                                      j, m      : e;
  see : t → e → t;                                  binder ∃ : (e ⇒ t) → t;
end
lexicon Semantics (Rules) : Logic =
  S'  := t;                    ρ₀ := λ°P. P (λ°p. p);        ρ₃ := λ°P. P j;
  S   := (t → t) → t;          ρ₄ := λ°P. P m;              ρ₅ := λ°P. ∀ x. P x;
  NP  := (e → t) → t;          ρ₆ := λ°R. R saw;
  VP  := ((e → t) → t) → t;    Vt := ((e → e → t) → t) → t;
  ρ₁  := λ°s v. λ°p. v (λ°P. s (λ°x. p (P x)));
  ρ₂  := λ°v o. λ°s. v (λ°R. o (λ°y. s (λ°x. R x y)));
end
```

Grammar 5: A higher-order signature for representing higher-order logical formulas

```
ACGtk>" ρ₀ (ρ₁ ρ₃ (ρ₂ ρ₆ ρ₄)) : S'" | realize lexicons = CFG, Semantics
Term : λ°z. John (saw (Mary z)) : o → o
Term : see j m : t
2 terms computed.
ACGtk>" John + saw + Mary : σ" | parse lexicon = CFG type = S' |
        realize lexicons = Semantics
Parsing time: 76.6μs
Parse forest building time: 6.31μs
Term : see j m : t
1 term computed.
ACGtk>" John + saw + everyone : σ" | parse lexicon = CFG type = S' |
        realize lexicons = Semantics
Parsing time: 76.6μs
Parse forest building time: 6.31μs
Term : ∀ x.see j x : t
1 term computed.
ACGtk>" see j m : t" | parse lexicon = Semantics type = S' |
        realize lexicons = CFG
Parsing time: 76μs
Parse forest building time: 5.27μs
Term : λ°z. John (saw (Mary z)) : o → o
1 term computed.
ACGtk>" ∀x.see j x : t" | parse lexicon = Semantics type = S' |
        realize lexicons = CFG
Parsing time: 74.7μs
Parse forest building time: 4.48μs
Term : λ°z. John (saw (everyone z)) : o → o
1 term computed.
```

Commands 3: Illustration of the transductive composition mode

Because we are interested in parse structures, and not only in membership, not only do we need the answer to the query corresponding to an object term to parse, but also the *Datalog derivations* (and all of them) that prove the query. Then, any Datalog derivation uniquely determines an abstract term, hence the abstract terms corresponding to the term being parsed. Standard engines, to our knowledge, either do not provide proof trees or do so only partially for debugging purposes and explainability. Therefore, ACGtk relies on our own implementation of a Datalog prover that enumerates all the possible derivations.

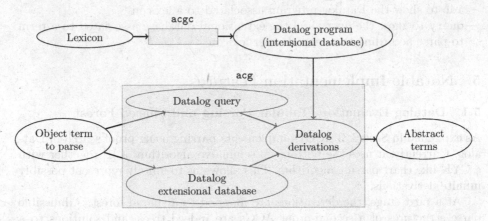

Fig. 3. Parsing process

For higher-order ACGs, [8] shows a similar reduction of ACG parsing to linear logic programming, leading to a semi-complete parsing algorithm (i.e., if the algorithm returns a solution, the term to parse belongs to the object language), not yet implemented.

4   ACGtk

ACGtk is implemented in OCaml, an efficient and expressive functional programming language (the object-oriented features are not used, though). This language provides some features that ease the implementation of the structures and algorithms of ACGtk, such as algebraic data types with pattern matching, an efficient compiler with tail-call optimization, a fast garbage collector.

It is also fully integrated with its development environment: using libraries provided by the OCaml package manager (opam), using the Dune build system, etc. It provides two pieces of software: acgc and acg.

The Grammar Compiler: acgc The main feature of acgc is to provide binary representations (including the associated Datalog reductions for the lexicons) of ACGs. Grammars are parsed, terms are statically type-checked against signatures and lexicon interpretations. Separate compilation is supported, so that different grammars may be coded in different source files.

The Interpreter: acg It provides a simple command language to use and test grammars. The most useful commands are:

- check to check well-formedness and well-typedness against a signature
- realize to interpret a term according to a lexicon
- parse to parse a term according to a second-order lexicon
- list-terms to (randomly or not) list terms of a given type built over a signature (including higher-order ones)
- idb to show the Datalog program associated to a lexicon
- query to show the query and the extensional database associated to a term to parse according to a second-order lexicon

5. Notable Implementation Features

5.1 Datalog Evaluation, Tabular Parsing and Shared Forest

As explained in Sect. 3.3, ACGtk implements parsing using proof search in Datalog. Currently, it uses the bottom-up seminaive algorithm of [1] together with a CYK-like chart parsing algorithm. This allows us to finitely represent possibly infinite derivations.

At a next stage, the derivations are mapped to a shared forest. Admissible parse structures of a second-order ACGs are indeed trees, and solutions to a parsing problem are therefore represented by forests that are shared in order to keep a finite representation of the possibly infinite set of solutions. Enumerating the solutions corresponds to traversing the forest. However, if we want the enumeration to be sorted according to a metric associated to the trees, we need to be able to easily move from the computation of a solution to the computation of another one for which the metric is better. To this end, we implemented a (purely applicative) forest context data structure that behaves with respect to the forest data structures similarly to how zippers [11] behave with respect to trees.

A forest is a list of forest trees, the latter being trees whose children are forests themselves. Consequently, the context of a forest tree needs to keep track: (i) of its context in the forest, i.e., the list of alternatives it belongs to, (ii) of the context of the forest it belongs to as a child in the children list, (iii) of its upper context in the parent-children relation. Such a structure is enough to suspend and resume walks in the forest on demand. Sharing is an orthogonal feature and is currently implemented using relative path in the forest (but other solutions, for instance with association tables, or dictionaries, could be used).

The metric we currently use involves the size and the depth of the abstract terms, i.e., the number of nodes and the depth of the parse trees. The whole framework is, however, ready to have metrics based on weighted grammars inferred from corpora.

5.2 Magic Set Rewriting

We also introduced the ability to use magic set rewriting techniques [1,29] as an experimental feature for acgc and acg. Magic set techniques are logical rewriting techniques used to optimize query evaluation in deductive databases. These methods simulate the selection pushing that is characteristic of top-down query processing algorithms within a bottom-up evaluation framework. Programs are transformed into larger ones that include additional intensional database predicates. These extra predicates make the evaluation focus on those parts of the database that are relevant to the query, thus avoiding unnecessary computations.

In the context of ACGs, the evaluation of rewritten programs leads to an Earley style parsing algorithm. For small grammars, it proves to be very efficient on large sentences as Fig. 4 shows for parsing strings of the mildly context-sensitive language $\{a^n b^n c^n d^n\}$ with n ranging from 1 to 94.[4]

However, Datalog programs (intensional databases) resulting from ACG transformation are usually large compared to the extensional databases corresponding to the terms to parse, a somewhat different situation of what happens for usual databases. Magic set rewriting strengthens this contrast because it makes the number of rules increase (Fig. 4c shows the effect on parsing time of small sentences). We did not yet run extensive experiments with large ACG grammars, first because of their unavailability, and second because of optimization issues (in particular related to size and space) in the current implementation of the rewriting algorithm (not the parsing algorithm).

6 Related Work

Available symbolic parsers (possibly augmented with stochastic models for pruning search space) for natural language processing are usually dedicated to a specific grammar formalism, often tweaked to fit a specific extension of that formalism. See for instance Partage for tree-adjoining grammars, TuLiPA for tree-adjoining grammars and mildly context-sensitive variants such as multi-component tree-adjoining grammars with tree tuples, OpenCCG or NLTK for combinatory categorial grammars, the Babel-System, DELPH-IN tools, or Enju for HPSG. Moreover, getting semantic representations also usually requires using additional tools to process the parsing output, or targets a specific semantic representation language.

From a theoretical perspective, the flexibility provided by the ACG framework and its architecture (often coined as *synchronous* or *parallel* grammars) is shared by other formalisms. For instance, Interpreted Regular Tree Grammars [21] that also consider parsing by morphism inversion and is implemented in Alto. However, this formalism is not well suited to deal with semantics represented with logical formulas. To parse a term t indeed requires that the set of trees that are interpreted as t is regular. To parse a logical representation based

---

[4] Each parsing time is an average of 100 time measures for each length using 1 core on an Intel® Core™ i7-3520M CPU, 2.90 GHz, 16 GB RAM laptop.

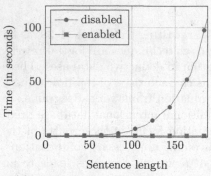

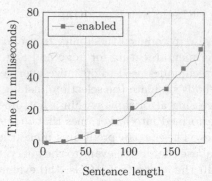

(a) Comparing the parsing time with and without magic set rewriting enabled

(b) Focus on parsing time with magic set rewriting enabled

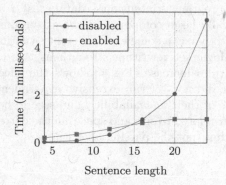

(c) Comparing the parsing time with and without magic set rewriting enabled for short sentences

Fig. 4. Parsing time of sentences $a^n b^n c^n d^n$ (length $= 4n$)

on λ-calculus would mean to represent all terms that are β-equivalent to the term we want to parse by a regular tree grammar. It is not clear how it can be done.

Another related approach is Grammatical Framework [26] and its implementation GF. The type system of GF is based on dependent type theory and is not as flexible as ACG for composing grammars. However, GF is also considered as a programming language for grammar applications, and a lot of solutions have been developed to address grammatical (instead of software) engineering issues. It has been extensively used to develop grammars for many languages (38 languages so far) and is an important source of inspiration for features to add to ACGtk.

Finally, Applicative Abstract Categorial Grammars [19] and its conceptual simplification, Transformational Semantics [20] also come with an implementation in form of a domain-specific language embedded in Haskell.[5] It focuses more specifically on structure transformations that are needed to derive difficult semantic phenomena.

7   Conclusion

ACGtk provides an environment to develop, test, and use ACGs. It is used to implement syntax-semantics interface models for natural languages, possibly using complex composition architectures. It is implemented in a functional language, using interesting data structures such as zippers, and also implements a Datalog prover and optimization related techniques.

Directions for further developments are threefold:

- To integrate recent theoretical work on ACGs (mainly feature structures and weighted grammars).
- To improve the grammatical engineering facilities (for instance introducing functors).
- To use different optimization techniques, either related to Datalog evaluation (e.g., with precedence graph) or to the OCaml language (parallel programming).

A   Typing Rules

Let $\Sigma = \langle A, C, \tau \rangle$ be a higher-order signature. The typing rules for terms of $\Lambda(\Sigma)$ use sequents of the form $\Gamma; \Delta \vdash_\Sigma t : \alpha$ where Γ is a *non-linear* context assigning types to variables and Δ is a *linear* context assigning types to variables. Whenever Δ is empty, e.g., in the (const.), the (var.) and the (app.) rules, such a sequent is written $\Gamma; \vdash_\Sigma t : \alpha$.

$$\frac{c \in C}{\Gamma; \vdash_\Sigma c : \tau(c)} \text{ (const.)}$$

$$\frac{}{\Gamma; x : \alpha \vdash_\Sigma x : \alpha} \text{ (lin. var.)} \qquad \frac{}{\Gamma, x : \alpha; \vdash_\Sigma x : \alpha} \text{ (var.)}$$

$$\frac{\Gamma; \Delta, x : \alpha \vdash_\Sigma t : \beta}{\Gamma; \Delta \vdash_\Sigma \lambda^\circ x.t : \alpha \to \beta} \text{ (lin. abs.)}$$

$$\frac{\Gamma; \Delta_1 \vdash_\Sigma t : \alpha \to \beta \quad \Gamma; \Delta_2 \vdash_\Sigma u : \alpha}{\Gamma; \Delta_1, \Delta_2 \vdash_\Sigma t\,u : \beta} \text{ (lin. app.) if } \mathrm{dom}(\Delta_1) \cap \mathrm{dom}(\Delta_2) = \emptyset$$

$$\frac{\Gamma, x : \alpha; \Delta \vdash_\Sigma t : \beta}{\Gamma; \Delta \vdash_\Sigma \lambda x.t : \alpha \Rightarrow \beta} \text{ (abs.)} \qquad \frac{\Gamma; \Delta \vdash_\Sigma t : \alpha \Rightarrow \beta \quad \Gamma; \vdash_\Sigma u : \alpha}{\Gamma; \Delta \vdash_\Sigma t\,u : \beta} \text{ (app.)}$$

---

[5] https://okmij.org/ftp/gengo/transformational-semantics/.

References

1. Abiteboul, S., Hull, R., Vianu, V.: Foundations of Databases. Assison-Wesley (1995). http://webdam.inria.fr/Alice/pdfs/all.pdf
2. Barker, C.: Continuations and the nature of quantification. Nat. Lang. Semant. **10**(3), 211–242 (2002). https://doi.org/10.1023/A:1022183511876, https://cb125.github.io/Papers/barker-continuations.pdf
3. Curry, H.B.: Some logical aspects of grammatical structure. In: Jakobson, R. (ed.) Structure of Language and its Mathematical Aspects: Proceedings of the Twelfth Symposium in Applied Mathematics, pp. 56–68. American Mathematical Society (1961). https://doi.org/10.1090/psapm/012
4. Groote, P.: Linear higher-order matching is NP-complete. In: Bachmair, L. (ed.) RTA 2000. LNCS, vol. 1833, pp. 127–140. Springer, Heidelberg (2000). https://doi.org/10.1007/10721975_9
5. de Groote, P.: Towards abstract categorial grammars. In: Proceedings of 39th Annual Meeting of the Association for Computational Linguistics, pp. 148–155 (2001). https://doi.org/10.3115/1073012.1073045. ACL anthology: P01-1033
6. de Groote, P.: Tree-adjoining grammars as abstract categorial grammars. In: Proceedings of the Sixth International Workshop on Tree Adjoining Grammars and Related Frameworks (TAG+6), pp. 145–150. Università di Venezia (2002). ACL anthology: W02-2220
7. Groote, P.: Proof-search in implicative linear logic as a matching problem. In: Parigot, M., Voronkov, A. (eds.) LPAR 2000. LNAI, vol. 1955, pp. 257–274. Springer, Heidelberg (2000). https://doi.org/10.1007/3-540-44404-1_17
8. de Groote, P.: Abstract categorial parsing as linear logic programming. In: Proceedings of the 14th Meeting on the Mathematics of Language (MoL 2015), pp. 15–25. Association for Computational Linguistics, Chicago (2015). HAL open archive: hal-01188632. ACL anthology: W15-2302
9. de Groote, P., Guillaume, B., Salvati, S.: Vector addition tree automata. In: Proceedings of the Nineteenth Annual IEEE Symposium on Logic in Computer Science (LICS 2004), pp. 64–73. Turku, Finland, France (2004). https://inria.hal.science/inria-00100081. Colloque avec actes et comité de lecture. internationale
10. de Groote, P., Pogodalla, S.: On the expressive power of abstract categorial grammars: representing context-free formalisms. J. Log. Lang. Inf. **13**(4), 421–438 (2004). https://doi.org/10.1007/s10849-004-2114-x. HAL open archive: inria-00112956
11. Huet, G.: The zipper. J. Funct. Program. **7**(5), 549–554 (1997). https://doi.org/10.1017/S0956796897002864
12. Joshi, A.K., Levy, L.S., Takahashi, M.: Tree adjunct grammars. J. Comput. Syst. Sci. **10**(1), 136–163 (1975). https://doi.org/10.1016/S0022-0000(75)80019-5
13. Joshi, A.K., Schabes, Y.: Tree-adjoining grammars. In: Rozenberg, G., Salomaa, A.K. (eds.) Handbook of Formal Languages, vol. 3, chap. 2, pp. 69–123. Springer, Heidelberg (1997). https://doi.org/10.1007/978-3-642-59126-6_2
14. Kanazawa, M.: Parsing and generation as datalog queries. In: Proceedings of the 45th Annual Meeting of the Association of Computational Linguistics (ACL 2007), pp. 176–183. Association for Computational Linguistics, Prague (2007). ACL anthology: P07-1023
15. Kanazawa, M.: A prefix-correct earley recognizer for multiple context-free grammars. In: Gardent, C., Sarkar, A. (eds.) Proceedings of the Ninth International Workshop on Tree Adjoining Grammars and Related Formalisms (TAG+9),

pp. 49–56. University of Tübingen, Tübingen, Germany (2008). ACL anthology: W08-2307

16. Kanazawa, M.: Second-order abstract categorial grammars as hyperedge replacement grammars. J. Log. Lang. Inf. **19**(2), 137–161 (2009). https://doi.org/10.1007/s10849-009-9109-6

17. Kanazawa, M.: Parsing and generation as datalog query evaluation. IfCoLog J. Log. Their Appl. **4**(4), 1103–1211 (2017). http://www.collegepublications.co.uk/downloads/ifcolog00013.pdf#page=307. Special Issue Dedicated to the Memory of Grigori Mints

18. Kanazawa, M., Salvati, S.: Generating control languages with abstract categorial grammars. In: Penn, G. (ed.) Proceedings of the 12th conference on Formal Grammar (FG 2007). CSLI Publications (2007). https://makotokanazawa.ws.hosei.ac.jp/publications/control.pdf

19. Kiselyov, O.: Applicative abstract categorial grammar. In: Kanazawa, M., Moss, L.S., de Paiva, V. (eds.) NLCS 2015. Third Workshop on Natural Language and Computer Science. EPiC Series in Computing, vol. 32, pp. 29–38. EasyChair (2015). https://doi.org/10.29007/s2m4

20. Kiselyov, O.: Applicative abstract categorial grammars in full swing. In: Otake, M., Kurahashi, S., Ota, Y., Satoh, K., Bekki, D. (eds.) JSAI-isAI 2015. LNCS, vol. 10091, pp. 66–78. Springer, Cham (2017). https://doi.org/10.1007/978-3-319-50953-2_6, https://okmij.org/ftp/gengo/applicative-symantics/AACG1.pdf

21. Koller, A., Kuhlmann, M.: A generalized view on parsing and translation. In: Proceedings of the 12th International Conference on Parsing Technologies, pp. 2–13. Association for Computational Linguistics, Dublin (2011). ACL anthology: W11-2902

22. Lambek, J.: The mathematics of sentence structure. Am. Math. Monthly **65**(3), 154–170 (1958). https://doi.org/10.2307/2310058

23. Maskharashvili, A.: Discourse modeling with abstract categorial grammars. Ph.D. thesis, Université de Lorraine (2016). HAL open archive: tel-01412765

24. Montague, R.: The proper treatment of quantification in ordinary English. In: Hintikka, J., Moravcsik, J., Suppes, P. (eds.) Approaches to Natural Language. Synthese Library, vol. 49, pp. 221–242. Springer, Dordrecht (1973). https://doi.org/10.1007/978-94-010-2506-5_10

25. Pogodalla, S.: A syntax-semantics interface for tree-adjoining grammars through abstract categorial grammars. J. Lang. Modell. **5**(3), 527–605 (2017). https://doi.org/10.15398/jlm.v5i3.193. HAL open archive: hal-01242154

26. Ranta, A.: Grammatical Framework: Programming with Multilingual Grammars. CSLI Studies in Computational Linguistics. CSLI Publications (2011)

27. Salvati, S.: Problèmes de filtrage et problèmes d'analyse pour les grammaires catégorielles abstraites. Ph.D. thesis, Institut National Polytechnique de Lorraine (2005)

28. Salvati, S.: Encoding second order string ACG with deterministic tree walking transducers. In: Wintner, S. (ed.) Proceedings of The 11th conference on Formal Grammar (FG 2006), pp. 143–156. FG Online Proceedings, CSLI Publications, Malaga (2006). http://cslipublications.stanford.edu/FG/2006/salvati.pdf

29. Ullman, J.D.: Principles of Database and Knowledge-Base Systems: Volume II: The New Technologies. W. H. Freeman & Co., New York (1990)

30. Vijay-Shanker, K., Weir, D.J., Joshi, A.K.: Characterizing structural descriptions produced by various grammatical formalisms. In: Proceedings of the 25th Annual Meeting of the Association for Computational Linguistics (ACL 1987), Stanford,

CA, pp. 104–111 (1987). https://doi.org/10.3115/981175.981190. ACL anthology: P87-1015

31. Weir, D.J.: Characterizing mildly context-sensitive grammar formalisms. Ph.D. thesis, University of Pennsylvania (1988). http://users.sussex.ac.uk/~davidw/resources/papers/dissertation.pdf

32. Yoshinaka, R., Kanazawa, M.: The complexity and generative capacity of lexicalized abstract categorial grammars. In: Blache, P., Stabler, E., Busquets, J., Moot, R. (eds.) LACL 2005. LNCS (LNAI), vol. 3492, pp. 330–346. Springer, Heidelberg (2005). https://doi.org/10.1007/11422532_22

Term Evaluation Systems with Refinements: First-Order, Second-Order, and Contextual Improvement

Koko Muroya[1]([✉])[iD] and Makoto Hamana[2][iD]

[1] RIMS, Kyoto University, Kyoto, Japan
kmuroya@kurims.kyoto-u.ac.jp
[2] Kyushu Institute of Technology, Kitakyushu, Japan
hamana@cs.gunma-u.ac.jp

Abstract. For a programming language, there are two kinds of term rewriting: run-time rewriting ("evaluation") and compile-time rewriting ("refinement"). Whereas refinement resembles general term rewriting, evaluation is commonly constrained by Felleisen's evaluation contexts. While evaluation specifies a programming language, refinement models optimisation and should be validated with respect to evaluation. Such validation can be given by Sands' notion of contextual improvement. We formulate evaluation in a term-rewriting-theoretic manner for the first time, and introduce Term Evaluation and Refinement Systems (TERS). We then identify sufficient conditions for contextual improvement, and provide critical pair analysis for local coherence that is the key sufficient condition. As case studies, we prove contextual improvement for a computational lambda-calculus and its extension with effect handlers.

Keywords: term rewriting · evaluation contexts · critical pair analysis

1 Introduction

Term rewriting is a general model of computation. The ecosystem of a functional programming language utilizes two types of term rewriting: run-time rewriting, which we shall refer to as *evaluation*, and compile-time rewriting, referred to as *refinement*. Run-time evaluation specifies operational semantics of the language. It can only happen in a particular order, usually deterministically. On the other hand, compile-time refinement models optimisation. It can happen anywhere, nondeterministically. The difference between evaluation and refinement, as kinds of term rewriting, can be summarised in terms of *contexts*, cf. Fig. 1. Evaluation $\rightarrow_{\mathcal{E}}$ uses a rewrite rule $l \rightarrow r$ inside a Felleisen's *evaluation context* [8,9] $E \in Ectx$ only; this is a new kind of restriction from the rewriting theoretic point of view. In contrast, refinement $\Rightarrow_{\mathcal{R}}$ uses a rewrite rule $l \Rightarrow r$ inside an *arbitrary* context $C \in Ctx$; this resembles general term rewriting.

J. Gibbons and D. Miller (Eds.): FLOPS 2024, LNCS 14659, pp. 31–61, 2024.
https://doi.org/10.1007/978-981-97-2300-3_3

$$\frac{(l \to r) \in \mathcal{E} \quad E \in Ectx}{E[l\theta] \to_{\mathcal{E}} E[r\theta]} \qquad \frac{(l \Rightarrow r) \in \mathcal{R} \quad C \in Ctx}{C[l\theta] \Rightarrow_{\mathcal{R}} C[r\theta]}$$

Fig. 1. Evaluation and refinement relations, where θ is a substitution

From the viewpoint of rewriting theory, the roles of evaluation and refinement are rather unusual. It is evaluation that *specifies* (the behaviour of) a programming language as operational semantics. Evaluation is not simply a deterministic restriction of refinement. Refinement which models optimisation should be *validated* with respect to evaluation. Indeed, compiler optimisation is meant to preserve evaluation results and improve time efficiency of evaluation. This preservation and improvement deserve formal validation.

Such validation can be provided as *observational equivalence* [22], and its quantitative variant, *contextual improvement* [27]. Observational equivalence $t \cong u$ asserts that two terms t and u cannot be distinguished by any context C; formally, if $C[t]$ terminates, $C[u]$ terminates with the same evaluation result, and vice versa. Contextual improvement additionally asserts that $C[u]$ terminates with no more evaluation steps than $C[t]$. This is a suitable notion to validate refinement which models optimisation.

Whereas the theory of refinement, which resembles general term rewriting, has been deeply developed, evaluation seems to be a new kind of restricted rewriting and it lacks a general theory from the perspective of term rewriting. This prevents useful ideas and techniques of term rewriting from transferring from refinement to evaluation. In recent work [23] on a proof methodology of observational equivalence, it is informally observed that a rewriting technique can be useful for proving observational equivalence and contextual improvement. This methodology informally employs critical pair analysis, a fundamental technique in rewriting theory. The idea is that $t \cong u$ holds if replacing t with u (which means applying a refinement rule $t \Rightarrow u$) in any program does not conflict with any evaluation rule $l \to r$.

This paper aims at formalising this connection between observational equivalence proofs and critical pair analysis. In doing so, we introduce a new rewriting-theoretic formalisation of evaluation. Our contributions are:

- introducing a new formalisation of *term evaluation systems (TES)*, and its combination with refinement, dubbed *term evaluation and refinement systems (TERS)*, in both first-order and second-order settings,
- identifying sufficient conditions for contextual improvement that include a notion of *local coherence*,
- establishing critical pair analysis for local coherence, and
- demonstrating TERS with examples including a computational lambda-calculus and its extension with effect handlers.

The key concepts of our development are evaluation contexts, *values* and local coherence. Evaluation contexts are treated axiomatically. Values specify *successful* results of evaluation; not all normal forms of evaluation are deemed successful. Such distinction of values has been studied in second-order rewriting [14]. Finally, local coherence is a notion from the rewriting literature; it is namely a sufficient condition for confluence in equational rewriting [3,15]. We exploit the notion for TERS instead of equational rewriting[1].

1.1   Examples of TES and TERS

The standard left-to-right call-by-value lambda-calculus is a TES. Terms t, t' including values v are defined as below, and the call-by-value evaluation strategy is specified using evaluation contexts E and one evaluation rule $\rightarrow$:

$$v ::= \lambda x.t, \quad t, t' ::= x \mid v \mid t\,t', \quad E ::= \square \mid E\,t \mid v\,E, \quad (\lambda x.t)\,v \rightarrow t[v/x].$$

Values v appearing in this specification play a significant role. The definition of evaluation contexts notably includes the clause $v\,E$ where the left subterm v is restricted to values. This ensures the left-to-right evaluation of application $t\,t'$; the right subterm t' can be evaluated only after the left subterm t has been evaluated to a value. Additionally, the redex $(\lambda x.t)\,v$ restricts the right subterm v to values. This ensures the call-by-value evaluation of application.

A simplified computational lambda-calculus λ_{ml*} [26] is a TERS. Its terms are either values v, v' or computations p, p', and its evaluation (which has been studied [7]) is specified using evaluation contexts E and two evaluation rules $\rightarrow$:

$$v, v' ::= x \mid \lambda x.p, \quad p, p' ::= \mathtt{return}(v) \mid \mathtt{let}\ x = p\ \mathtt{in}\ p' \mid v\,v',$$
$$E ::= \square \mid \mathtt{let}\ x = E\ \mathtt{in}\ p, \quad (\lambda x.p)\,v \rightarrow p[v/x], \quad \mathtt{let}\ x = \mathtt{return}(v)\ \mathtt{in}\ p \rightarrow p[v/x].$$

We can observe that evaluation contexts constrain where evaluation rules can be applied, namely in the subterm p of $\mathtt{let}\ x = p\ \mathtt{in}\ p'$. Again, values in evaluation rules assure the call-by-value evaluation of application and let-binding.

Originally, the calculus λ_{ml*} is specified by equations rather than evaluation. Directed equations can be seen as the following five refinement rules $\Rightarrow$:

$$(\lambda x.p)\,v \Rightarrow p[v/x], \quad \mathtt{let}\ x = \mathtt{return}(v)\ \mathtt{in}\ p \Rightarrow p[v/x],$$
$$\lambda x.v\,x \Rightarrow v, \quad \mathtt{let}\ x = p\ \mathtt{in}\ \mathtt{return}(x) \Rightarrow p,$$
$$\mathtt{let}\ x_1 = (\mathtt{let}\ x_2 = p_2\ \mathtt{in}\ p_1)\ \mathtt{in}\ p_3 \Rightarrow \mathtt{let}\ x_2 = p_2\ \mathtt{in}\ \mathtt{let}\ x_1 = p_1\ \mathtt{in}\ p_3.$$

While the first two rules represent β-conversion, the third one represents η-conversion. The fourth one removes the trivial let-binding, and the last one flattens let-bindings. We can observe that the last three rules *simplify* terms.

We now have a TERS of λ_{ml*} which has both evaluation and refinement. We are now interested in whether refinement is *valid* with respect to evaluation. Our goal here is namely to prove contextual improvement: that is, for any refinement $t \Rightarrow_{\mathcal{R}} u$ and any context $C \in Ctx$, if evaluation of $C[t]$ terminates, then evaluation of $C[u]$ terminates with no more evaluation steps.

---

[1] TERS is *not* equational rewriting. Refinement is compile-time rewriting, and we do not evaluate modulo refinement.

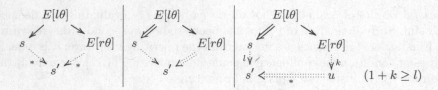

Fig. 2. Joinability for confluence, commutation and local coherence

To prove contextual improvement, we would need to analyse how each evaluation step interferes with the refinement $t \Rightarrow_{\mathcal{R}} u$. This amounts to analyse how each evaluation rule $l \to r$ can *conflict with* each refinement rule $l' \Rightarrow r'$. This is what exactly critical pair analysis is targeted at.

Critical pair analysis is usually for proving *confluence*, which is a fundamental property of term rewriting. It firstly enumerates the situation where two rewrite rules conflict with each other. It then checks if the two conflicting rewritings can be *joined*. This is illustrated in Fig. 2 (left), where the joining part is depicted in dashed arrows, and '$*$' means an arbitrary number of rewriting.

In our development, we exploit critical pair analysis for proving contextual improvement, and more specifically for proving *local coherence*. The analysis is targeted at conflicts between evaluation $\to$ and refinement $\Rightarrow$. We analyse if these conflicts can be *joined* using evaluation and refinement; see Fig. 2 (right). To ensure improvement, our notion of local coherence asserts that the joining part satisfies the inequality $1 + k \geq l$ about the number of evaluation steps.

To prove the joinability for local coherence, we need to be careful with evaluation contexts. We need to show that the $1 + k$ evaluation steps $E[l\theta] \to_{\mathcal{E}} E[r\theta] \xrightarrow{k}_{\mathcal{E}} u$ can be *simulated* by the l evaluation steps $s \xrightarrow{l}_{\mathcal{E}} s'$. Naively, this can be done by showing that the evaluation rule $l \to r$ can also be applied to the term s. This, however, involves making sure that the rule $l \to r$ can be applied *inside an evaluation context*. This is not a trivial issue; the evaluation context E might be modified by the refinement $E[t] \Rightarrow_{\mathcal{R}} s$. This modification should be "mild", and more precisely, refinement should not turn an evaluation context into a non-evaluation context (see Definition 12 (2)).

Note that local coherence can be seen as a generalisation of *commutation* [30]; see Fig. 2 (middle). Commutation is the case where $k = 0$, $l = 1$, and allowing only one step of refinement $\Rightarrow_{\mathcal{R}}$ instead of $\xrightarrow{*}_{\mathcal{R}}$.

2   Preliminaries

Let $\mathbb{N}$ be the set of natural numbers. For any $n \in \mathbb{N}$, let $[n]$ denote the set $\{1, \ldots, n\}$ (mind the starting point); for example, $[0] = \varnothing$, $[1] = \{1\}$, $[2] = \{1, 2\}$. We write $\overline{A}$ for a sequence $A_1, \ldots, A_n$, and $|\overline{A}|$ for its length (i.e. n).

Given a binary relation $\to$ on a set S, let $\xrightarrow{*}$ denote the reflexive and transitive closure of $\to$. For any $k \in \mathbb{N}$, $\xrightarrow{k}$ denotes the k-fold composition of $\to$. An element

$x \in S$ is a *normal form* (with respect to $\to$), if there exists no element $x' \in S$ such that $x \to x'$. Let $\mathsf{NF}(\to)$ denote the set of normal forms with respect to $\to$.

3 First-Order Term Evaluation and Refinement Systems

Evaluation and Refinement. Let Σ be a *signature*. Each element $f \in \Sigma$ comes with an *arity* $n \in \mathbb{N}$; we write $f \colon n$. (First-order) terms are defined by the grammar $t ::= x \mid f(t_1, \ldots, t_n)$ where x is a variable and $f \colon n$. Let T_Σ be the set of terms. A term is *closed* if it has no occurrence of variables.

A *position* of a term is given by a (possibly empty) sequence of positive numbers, in the usual manner. Concatenation of sequences p, q is denoted by pq or $p.q$. Let $Pos(t)$ be the set of all positions in a term t. We write $s[t]_p$ for the term that is obtained by replacing the sub-term of s at the position p with t. We write $s|_p$ for the sub-term of s at the position p.

A *substitution* θ is given by a sequence $\{x_1 \mapsto t_1, \ldots, x_k \mapsto t_k\}$ where $x_1, \ldots, x_k$ are distinct variables. We write $\mathsf{subst}\,\theta$ when θ is a substitution. Let $t\theta$ denote the term where all occurrences of $x_1, \ldots, x_k$ in t are replaced by $t_1, \ldots, t_k$, respectively. We call $t\theta$ an *instance* of t.

A *context* is a term that involves exactly one *hole* $\square$. Let Ctx be the set of contexts. Let $C[t]$ denote the term where the hole $\square$ of $C \in Ctx$ is replaced by t. A set $\mathcal{C}$ of contexts is *closed under substitutions* if $C \in \mathcal{C}$ implies $C\theta \in \mathcal{C}$ for any $\mathsf{subst}\,\theta$, and *closed under composition* if $C, C' \in \mathcal{C}$ implies $C[C'] \in \mathcal{C}$. The set $\mathcal{C}$ is *inductive* if any $C \in \mathcal{C}$ is $\square$ or of the form $f(t_1, \ldots, t_{i-1}, C', t_{i+1}, \ldots, t_n)$ such that $C' \in \mathcal{C}$ and $f(t_1\theta, \ldots, t_{i-1}\theta, \square, t_{i+1}\theta, \ldots, t_n\theta) \in \mathcal{C}$ for any $\mathsf{subst}\,\theta$.

Term evaluation systems (TES) can now be defined, as the standard term rewriting with the new restriction imposed by means of *evaluation contexts*.

Definition 1 (TES). A *term evaluation system* is a tuple $(\Sigma, \mathcal{E}, Ectx, Val)$ consisting of

- a signature Σ,
- a set $\mathcal{E}$ of *evaluation rules*, where $(l \to r) \in \mathcal{E}$ with $l, r \in \mathrm{T}_\Sigma$, such that (i) every free variable occurring in r also occurs in l and (ii) l is not a variable,
- a set $Ectx \subseteq Ctx$ of *evaluation contexts* that is closed under substitutions, closed under composition and inductive, and
- a set $Val \subseteq \mathsf{NF}(\to_\mathcal{E})$ of *values* that satisfies (i) $v \in Val$ implies $v\theta \in Val$ for any $\mathsf{subst}\,\theta$, and (ii) it comes with an equivalence relation $=_{Val} \subseteq Val \times Val$, where:
- the *evaluation relation* $\to_\mathcal{E} \subseteq \mathrm{T}_\Sigma \times \mathrm{T}_\Sigma$ is defined in Fig. 1.

Values specify which normal forms of $\to_\mathcal{E}$ are regarded as *successful* results. For example, in a TES for arithmetics, a term $x + y$ is a normal form but it is not deemed a successful result. The equivalence relation $=_{Val}$ specifies *observations* of these results in terms of equivalence classes. For example, when the syntactic equality $\equiv$ is used, each value $v \in Val$ becomes a distinct observation. On the other hand, when the total relation $\top$ is used, values are all identified; this means that successful termination is the only possible observation.

The evaluation relation $\to_\mathcal{E}$ is closed under evaluation contexts in $Ectx$. It is also closed under substitutions, thanks to $Ectx$ being inductive.

Each TES can be equipped with refinement, which resembles general, unrestricted, term rewriting.

Definition 2 (TERS). A *term evaluation and refinement system* is a tuple $(\Sigma, \mathcal{E}, \mathcal{R}, Ectx, Val)$ consisting of

- A TES $(\Sigma, \mathcal{E}, Ectx, Val)$, and
- a set $\mathcal{R}$ of *refinement rules* where $(l \Rightarrow r) \in \mathcal{R}$ with $l, r \in T_\Sigma$, such that (i) every free variable occuring in r also occurs in l and (ii) l is not a variable.
- The *refinement relation* $\Rightarrow_\mathcal{R} \subseteq T_\Sigma \times T_\Sigma$ is defined by the inference rule in Fig. 1.

We often simply write a TES $(\mathcal{E}, Val)$ and a TERS $(\mathcal{E}, \mathcal{R}, Val)$. The refinement relation $\Rightarrow_\mathcal{R}$ is closed under substitutions, and closed under arbitrary contexts in Ctx.

The following example is from the literature on context-sensitive rewriting.

Example 3 (Nats [20, Ex. 8.19]). Let **Nats** be the TERS defined as follows.

Signature Σ	nats: 0, inc: 1, hd: 1, tl: 1, ':': 2, s: 1, 0: 0
Values *Val*	$V ::= 0 \mid s(V)$
Evaluation contexts *Ectx*	$E ::= \square \mid hd(E) \mid tl(E) \mid inc(E)$
Evaluation rules $\mathcal{E}$	**Refinement rule** $\mathcal{R}$
nats $\to 0 : inc(nats)$	$tl(inc(nats)) \Rightarrow inc(tl(nats))$
$inc(x : y) \to s(x) : inc(y)$	
$hd(x : y) \to x$	
$tl(x : y) \to y$	

We define $=_{Val}$ by the syntactic equality $\equiv$, to allow each value to be observed separately. The refinement rule is reversed, compared to the original one [20, Ex. 8.19], so that it induces improvement; see Sect. 4 for details.

Joinability and Improvement. Evaluation is constrained by means of evaluation contexts, usually to have the evaluation relation $\to_\mathcal{E}$ deterministic. Bridging the gap between evaluation and refinement, we are interested in *joinability up to* $\mathcal{R}$ defined as follows. The joinability is quantitative with an extra constraint on the number of evaluation steps.

Definition 4 (Peaks, joinability).

- An $\mathcal{E}$-*peak* is given by a triple (s_1, t, s_2) such that $t \to_\mathcal{E} s_1$ and $t \to_\mathcal{E} s_2$.
- An $(\mathcal{R}, \mathcal{E})$-*peak* is given by a triple (s_1, t, s_2) such that $t \Rightarrow_\mathcal{R} s_1$ and $t \to_\mathcal{E} s_2$.
- An $\mathcal{E}$-peak (s_1, t, s_2) is *trivial* if $s_1 \equiv s_2$ holds.
- An $(\mathcal{R}, \mathcal{E})$-peak (s_1, t, s_2) is *joinable up to* $\mathcal{R}$ if there exist $k, l \in \mathbb{N}$ and u_1, u_2 such that $s_1 \xrightarrow{k}_\mathcal{E} u_1$, $s_2 \xrightarrow{l}_\mathcal{E} u_2$, $1 + l \geq k$ and $u_2 \xrightarrow{*}_\mathcal{R} u_1$.

Definition 5 (Rewriting properties).

- A TES $(\mathcal{E}, Val)$ is *deterministic* if every $\mathcal{E}$-peak (s_1, t, s_2) is trivial.
- A TERS $(\mathcal{E}, \mathcal{R}, Val)$ is *locally coherent* if every $(\mathcal{R}, \mathcal{E})$-peak is joinable up to $\mathcal{R}$.

We say a TERS $(\mathcal{E}, \mathcal{R}, Val)$ is deterministic if $(\mathcal{E}, Val)$ is deterministic. We also simply say an $(\mathcal{R}, \mathcal{E})$-peak is *joinable*, omitting "up to $\mathcal{R}$."

We formalise the key concept that relates evaluation with refinement in TERS. It is the so-called *(contextual) improvement* [27]: that is, any refinement $t \Rightarrow_\mathcal{R} s$ cannot be distinguished by evaluation $\rightarrow_\mathcal{E}$ inside any contexts, and the refinement cannot increase the number of evaluation steps that are needed for termination. Observation is made according to the set Val of values and its associated equivalence relation $=_{Val}$.

Definition 6 (Value-invariance, improvement).

- A TERS $(\mathcal{E}, \mathcal{R}, Val)$ is *value-invariant* if, for any $v \in Val$ and $s \in T_\Sigma$, $v \Rightarrow_\mathcal{R} s$ implies $s \in Val$ and $v =_{Val} s$.
- For a TERS $(\mathcal{E}, \mathcal{R}, Val)$, $\mathcal{R}$ is *improvement* w.r.t. $\mathcal{E}$ if, for any $k \in \mathbb{N}$, $v \in Val$, $t \Rightarrow_\mathcal{R} s$ and any $C \in Ctx$ such that $C[t], C[s]$ are closed terms, $C[t] \xrightarrow{k}_\mathcal{E} v$ implies $C[s] \xrightarrow{m}_\mathcal{E} v'$ for some $m \in \mathbb{N}$ and $v' \in Val$ such that $v =_{Val} v'$ and $k \geq m$.

Improvement is notoriously difficult to directly prove, because of the universal quantification over all contexts. The following is our first main theorem providing a rewriting-theoretic sufficient condition for improvement, for deterministic TERS.

Theorem 7 (Sufficient condition for improvement: first-order version). *If a TERS $(\mathcal{E}, \mathcal{R}, Val)$ is deterministic, value-invariant and locally coherent, then the set $\mathcal{R}$ of refinement rules is improvement w.r.t. the set $\mathcal{E}$ of evaluation rules.*

This theorem requires to prove determinism, value-invariance and local coherence. When a TERS is orthogonal, determinism boils down to showing that each term can be uniquely decomposed into an evaluation context and a redex. In typical TERS, the equivalence relation $=_{Val}$ on values can be decided by simply comparing head symbols. This makes it easy to verify value-invariance. We will show that local coherence can be shown by critical pair analysis in Sect. 4.

4   Critical Pair Analysis for Local Coherence

Critical Pairs. The definition of critical pairs is standard; it resembles the definition of critical pairs for commutation [30]. Note that critical pairs are generated by two kinds of overlaps, due to asymmetry of $(\mathcal{R}, \mathcal{E})$-peaks.

Definition 8 (Unifiers)

- A *unifier* between t and u is a substitution θ such that $t\theta = u\theta$.

– A *most general unifier* between t and u is given by a unifier θ between t and u such that, for any unifier σ between t and u, there exists a substitution σ' such that $\sigma = \theta\sigma'$.

Definition 9 (Overlaps). Let $\mathcal{X}_1, \mathcal{X}_2 \in \{\mathcal{R}, \mathcal{E}\}$. Given rules $(l_1 \twoheadrightarrow_1 r_1) \in \mathcal{X}_1$, $(l_2 \twoheadrightarrow_2 r_2) \in \mathcal{X}_2$ and a substitution θ, a quadruple $(l_1 \twoheadrightarrow_1 r_1, l_2 \twoheadrightarrow_2 r_2, p, \theta)$ is an $(\mathcal{X}_1, \mathcal{X}_2)$-*overlap* if it satisfies the following.

– The rules $l_1 \twoheadrightarrow_1 r_1$ and $l_2 \twoheadrightarrow_2 r_2$ do not have common variables.
– If $p = \varepsilon$, the rules $l_1 \twoheadrightarrow_1 r_1$ and $l_2 \twoheadrightarrow_2 r_2$ are not variants of each other.
– The sub-term $l_1|_p$ is not a variable, where p is a position of l_1.
– The substitution θ is a most general unifier between $l_1|_p$ and l_2.

Definition 10 (Critical pairs).

– The *critical pair* generated by an $(\mathcal{R}, \mathcal{E})$-overlap $(l_1 \Rightarrow r_1, l_2 \to r_2, p, \theta)$ is an $(\mathcal{R}, \mathcal{E})$-peak $(r_1\theta, l_1\theta, (l_1\theta)[r_2\theta]_p)$.
– The *critical pair* generated by an $(\mathcal{E}, \mathcal{R})$-overlap $(l_1 \to r_1, l_2 \Rightarrow r_2, p, \theta)$ is an $(\mathcal{R}, \mathcal{E})$-peak $((l_1\theta)[r_2\theta]_p, l_1\theta, r_1\theta)$.

Lemma 11. If a critical pair (t_1, s, t_2) is joinable, then for any substitution θ, $(t_1\theta, s\theta, t_2\theta)$ is a joinable $(\mathcal{R}, \mathcal{E})$-peak.

Critical Pair Theorem. To obtain the so-called critical pair theorem, we need to impose extra conditions on TERS that are summarised below.

Definition 12 (Well-behaved TERS). A TERS $(\Sigma, \mathcal{E}, \mathcal{R}, Ectx, Val)$ is *well-behaved* if it satisfies the following.

1. For any $C_1, C_2 \in Ctx$, if $C_1[C_2] \in Ectx$ then $C_1, C_2 \in Ectx$.
2. For any $E \in Ectx$ and $C' \in Ctx$, if $E \Rightarrow_\mathcal{R} C'$ then $C' \in Ectx$.
3. For any $(l \Rightarrow_\mathcal{R} r) \in \mathcal{R}$ and any variable x, the following holds.
   (a) The variable x appears at most once in l, and at most once in r.
   (b) Let p be the position of x in l. For the position q of x in r, if $l[\square]_p \in Ectx$ then $r[\square]_q \in Ectx$.
4. For any $(l \to_\mathcal{E} r) \in \mathcal{E}$, any variable x appears at most once in l.

The condition (1) is usually satisfied by inductively-defined evaluation contexts. The condition (2) was already discussed in Sect. 1.1. The other conditions are rather technical (see Sect. A.3 for some details), but these are easy to verify.

Theorem 13 (Critical pair theorem). *A well-behaved TERS is locally coherent if and only if every critical pair is joinable.*

The Example. The TERS **Nats** in Example 3 is deterministic, value-invariant and locally coherent (Proposition 29 in Appendix). By Theorem 7, its refinement $\mathcal{R}$ is *improvement* w.r.t. its evaluation $\mathcal{E}$. In the proof of local coherence, we observe that the TERS **Nats** has one critical pair; it is joinable as in Fig. 3. The direction of refinement, which we reversed compared to the original [20], is crucial. Refinement must not increase the number of evaluation steps.

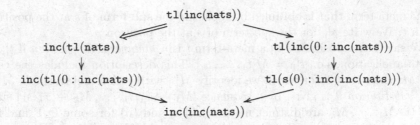

Fig. 3. Joinability of the critical pair

5 Second-Order Term Evaluation and Refinement Systems

Next we extend our framework to the second-order setting. By second-order we mean to use second-order abstract syntax [10,12], i.e. syntax with variable binding and metavariables. It allows us to formally deal with higher-order term languages as in second-order algebraic theories [11] and second-order computation systems [13,14].

Meta-terms. In addition to the countably infinite set X of variables, let Z be a countably infinite set of *metavariables*. Each element $M \in Z$ comes with an *arity* $m \in \mathbb{N}$; we write $M \colon m$. Let $\equiv$ denote the syntactic equality on metavariables. Let Σ be a *signature*, each of whose element $f \in \Sigma$ comes with a sequence $\langle n_1, \ldots, n_l \rangle$ of natural numbers called a *binding arity*; we write $f \colon \langle n_1 \ldots, n_l \rangle$.

Let M_Σ denote the set of *meta-terms* defined using the signature Σ, the set X of variables and the set Z of metavariables. A judgement $\Theta \rhd \Gamma \vdash t$ consists of a set Θ of metavariables, a set Γ of variables, and a meta-term t. A *well-formed* meta-term is a meta-term t such that a judgement $\Theta \rhd \Gamma \vdash t$ is derivable by formation rules below for some Θ, Γ. We assume that meta-terms are well-formed.

$$\frac{x \in \Gamma}{\Theta \rhd \Gamma \vdash x} \qquad \frac{(M \colon m) \in \Theta \quad \{\Theta \rhd \Gamma \vdash t_i\}_{i \in [m]}}{\Theta \rhd \Gamma \vdash M[t_1, \ldots, t_m]}$$

$$\frac{(f \colon \langle n_1, \ldots, n_l \rangle) \in \Sigma \quad \{\Theta \rhd \Gamma, \overline{x_i} \vdash t_i\}_{i \in [l]} \quad \{|\overline{x_i}| = n_i\}_{i \in [l]}}{\Theta \rhd \Gamma \vdash f(\overline{x_1}.t_1, \ldots, \overline{x_l}.t_l)}$$

In a meta-term $f(\overline{x_1}.t_1, \ldots, \overline{x_l}.t_l)$, each $\overline{x_i}.t_i$ introduces bound variables $\overline{x_i}$. We assume the α-equivalence for bound variables. A meta-term $M[t_1, \ldots, t_m]$ is called a *meta-application*. The arguments $t_1, \ldots, t_m$ can be seen as explicit substitution for variables; when a meta-term s substitutes the metavariable M, free variables of s gets substituted by $t_1, \ldots, t_m$. A *term* is a meta-term that contains no meta-application. A term is *closed* if it has no occurrence of variables.

A *position* of a meta-term is given by a (possibly empty) sequence of positive numbers. Let $Pos(t)$ be the set of all positions in a meta-term t. We write $s[t]_p$

for the meta-term that is obtained by replacing the sub-term of s at the position p with t. We write $s|_p$ for the sub-term of s at the position p.

We say that a position p in a meta-term t is a *metavariable position* if $t|_p$ is a meta-application, i.e., $t|_p = M[t_1, \ldots, t_n]$. This description includes the case $t|_p = M$ where $n = 0$, for which we identify $M[\,]$ with just a metavariable M.

A *substitution* θ is given by a sequence $[M_1 \mapsto \overline{x_1}.s_1, \ldots, M_k \mapsto \overline{x_k}.s_k]$ such that: (i) $M_1, \ldots, M_k$ are distinct metavariables, and (ii) for some Θ, Γ and for each $i \in [k]$, $(M_i : |\overline{x_i}|) \in Z$ and $\Theta \vartriangleright \Gamma, \overline{x_i} \vdash s_i$ hold. We call $\Theta \vartriangleright \Gamma$ a *support* of θ, and write $\mathsf{subst}_{\Theta \vartriangleright \Gamma}\,\theta$ when θ is a substitution with a support $\Theta \vartriangleright \Gamma$. We sometimes simply write $\mathsf{subst}\,\theta$, omitting the support. Given a meta-term $\Theta, M_1 : |\overline{x_1}|, \ldots, M_k : |\overline{x_k}| \vartriangleright \Gamma \vdash t$, a meta-term $t\theta$ is defined by

$$x\theta = x \qquad (f(\overline{x_1}.t_1, \ldots, \overline{x_l}.t_l))\theta = f(\overline{x_1}.t_1\theta, \ldots, \overline{x_l}.t_l\theta)$$

$$(M[t_1, \ldots, t_m])\theta = \begin{cases} s_i\{(x_i)_1 \mapsto t_1\theta, \ldots, (x_i)_m \mapsto t_m\theta\} & (\exists i \in [k].\ M \equiv M_i) \\ M[t_1\theta, \ldots, t_m\theta] & (\text{otherwise}) \end{cases}$$

The meta-term $s_i\{(x_i)_1 \mapsto t_1\theta, \ldots, (x_i)_m \mapsto t_m\theta\}$ is the result of standard (capture-avoiding) substitution for variables. We call $t\theta$ an *instance* of t.

A meta-term is a *higher-order pattern* if each occurrence of meta-application has the form $M[x_1, \ldots, x_m]$ such that $x_1, \ldots, x_m$ are distinct bound variables.

A *context* C is a meta-term that involves exactly one *hole* $\square$. A context is *flat* if any prefix of the position of the hole is not a metavariable position; e.g. $f(x.\square)$ is a flat context, but $M[\square]$ and $M[f(x.\square)]$ are not flat contexts. Let Ctx be the set of contexts. Let $C[t]$ denote the term where the hole $\square$ of $C \in Ctx$ is replaced by t. A set $\mathcal{C}$ of contexts is *closed under substitutions* if $C \in \mathcal{C}$ implies $C\theta \in \mathcal{C}$ for any $\mathsf{subst}\,\theta$, and *closed under composition* if $C, C' \in \mathcal{C}$ implies $C[C'] \in \mathcal{C}$. The set $\mathcal{C}$ is *inductive* if any $C \in \mathcal{C}$ is $\square$ or of the form $f(t_1, \ldots, t_{i-1}, C', t_{i+1}, \ldots, t_n)$ such that $C' \in \mathcal{C}$ and $f(t_1\theta, \ldots, t_{i-1}\theta, \square, t_{i+1}\theta, \ldots, t_n\theta) \in \mathcal{C}$ for any $\mathsf{subst}\,\theta$.

Syntax Classes. We introduce a notion of syntactic classification for terms, typically used for distingushing values and non-values, following [14]. In *loc. cit.*, the call-by-value lambda-calculus (dubbed λ_{value}-calculus) involves the following two syntax classes of values and non-values.

$$\textbf{Values} \quad V ::= x \mid \lambda x.M \qquad \textbf{Non-values} \quad P ::= M\,N$$

This also specifies two special names V, P of metavariables that are used for values and non-values. In general, we define a set *Sclass* of names for *syntax classes*. Each syntax class is associated with a BNF grammar to define a set of meta-terms. Every metavariable is either associated with a syntax class and called "<syntax class name> metavariable", or not associated and called *general metavariable*. Moreover, we assume a default syntax class **value** to denote values.

For example, in the case of λ_{value}-calculus, we define *Sclass* = {**values** $V ::= x \mid \lambda x.M$, **non-values** $P ::= M\,N$}. The metavariable V is called a value metavariable, and M is a general metavariable.

Substitutions must also be consistent with syntax classes. A substitution þis *valid* if for each assignment $(M \mapsto \overline{x}.s) \in \theta$, M and s's syntax class are the same, or if M is a general metavariable then s can be arbitrary. We write valid θ when θ is a valid substitution.

Composition of valid substitutions is again valid, under the assumption that each syntax class is closed under substitution: that is, for each syntax class, if a meta-term t is included then $t\theta$ is also included, where θ is a substitution.

Evaluation and Refinement. Second-order TES and TERS can now be defined, in an analogous way to the first-order setting.

Definition 14 (Second-order TES). A *second-order term evaluation system* is a tuple $(\Sigma, \mathcal{E}, Ectx, Sclass)$ consisting of

- a signature Σ,
- a set $\mathcal{E}$ of *evaluation rules*, where $(l \rightarrow r) \in \mathcal{E}$ with $l, r \in M_\Sigma$, such that (i) every free metavariable occuring in r also occurs in l and (ii) l is not a variable nor a metavariable,
- a set $Ectx \subseteq Ctx$ of flat contexts, called *evaluation contexts*, that is closed under substitutions, closed under composition and inductive, and
- a set $Sclass$ of syntax classes that includes a *value* class (V, Val) that satisfies (i) $Val \subseteq \mathsf{NF}(\rightarrow_\mathcal{E})$, (ii) $v \in Val$ implies $v\theta \in Val$ for any valid θ, and (iii) it comes with an equivalence relation $=_{Val} \subseteq Val \times Val$ where:
- the *evaluation relation* $\rightarrow_\mathcal{E} \subseteq M_\Sigma \times M_\Sigma$ is defined in Fig. 1 where θ is valid.

The evaluation relation $\rightarrow_\mathcal{E}$ is closed under evaluation contexts in $Ectx$. It is closed under substitutions, thanks to $Ectx$ being an inductive set of flat contexts.

Definition 15 (Second-order TERS). A *second-order term evaluation and refinement system* is a tuple $(\Sigma, \mathcal{E}, \mathcal{R}, Ectx, Sclass)$ consisting of

- A second-order TES $(\Sigma, \mathcal{E}, Ectx, Sclass)$, and
- a set $\mathcal{R}$ of *refinement rules* where $(l \Rightarrow r) \in \mathcal{R}$ with $l, r \in M_\Sigma$, such that (i) every free metavariable occuring in r also occurs in l and (ii) l is not a variable nor a metavariable.
- The *refinement relation* $\Rightarrow_\mathcal{R} \subseteq M_\Sigma \times M_\Sigma$ is defined in Fig. 1 where θ is valid.

The refinement relation $\Rightarrow_\mathcal{R}$ is closed under arbitrary contexts in Ctx. It is not closed under substitutions per se, but it satisfies the following: $t \Rightarrow_\mathcal{R} u$ implies $t\theta \stackrel{*}{\Rightarrow}_\mathcal{R} u\theta$ for any valid θ.

We also assume that the lhs of every rule is a Miller's higher-order pattern [21] to make unification decidable.

Joinability and Improvement. The definitions of peaks, joinability (see Definition 4), rewriting properties (Definition 5), and improvement (Definition 6) are inherited from the first-order case. Finally, the first main theorem (Theorem 7) also holds in the second-order setting:

Theorem 16 (Sufficient condition for improvement: second-order version). *If a second-order TERS $(\Sigma, \mathcal{E}, \mathcal{R}, Ectx, Sclass)$ is deterministic, value-invariant and locally coherent, then $\mathcal{R}$ is improvement w.r.t. $\mathcal{E}$.*

Signature Σ $\lambda\colon \langle 1 \rangle$, $@\colon \langle 0,0 \rangle$, let: $\langle 0,1 \rangle$, return: $\langle 0 \rangle$

Syntax class *Sclass*

  Values $V, V' ::= x \mid \lambda x.P$

  Computations $P, P' ::= \mathtt{return}(V) \mid \mathtt{let}(P, x.P') \mid V\, V'$

Evaluation contexts *Ectx* $E ::= \square \mid \mathtt{let}(E, x.P)$

Evaluation rules $\mathcal{E}$

$(\lambda x.P[x])\, V \to P[V]$ (1)

$\mathtt{let}(\mathtt{return}(V), x.P[x]) \to P[V]$ (2)

Refinement rules $\mathcal{R}$

$(\lambda x.P[x])\, V \Rightarrow P[V]$ (r1)

$\mathtt{let}(\mathtt{return}(V), x.P[x]) \Rightarrow P[V]$ (r2)

$\lambda x.V\, x \Rightarrow V$ (r3)

$\mathtt{let}(P, x.\mathtt{return}(x)) \Rightarrow P$ (r4)

$\mathtt{let}(\mathtt{let}(P_1, x_1.P_2[x_1]), x_2.P_3[x_2]) \Rightarrow \mathtt{let}(P_1, x_1.\mathtt{let}(P_2[x_1], x_2.P_3[x_2]))$ (r5)

Fig. 4. The TERS $\mathbf{Comp}\lambda_{ml*}$

Examples. In the remainder of this section, we present three examples of TERS.

Example 17 (Left-to-right call-by-value lambda-calculus). A TERS $\mathbf{CBV}\lambda$ of the left-to-right call-by-value lambda-calculus is defined as follows, where t is a term, v is a value, M is a general metavariable, and V is a value metavariable. We use syntactic sugar $\lambda x.t \equiv \lambda(x.t), t\, u \equiv @(t, u)$.

Signature Σ	$\lambda\colon \langle 1 \rangle$, $@\colon \langle 0,0 \rangle$
Syntax class *Sclass*	values $V ::= \lambda x.t$
Evaluation contexts *Ectx*	$E ::= \square \mid E\, t \mid v\, E$
Evaluation rules $\mathcal{E}$	**Refinement rules** $\mathcal{R}$
$(\lambda x.M[x])\, V \to M[V]$	$(\lambda x.M[x])\, V \Rightarrow M[V]$
	$\lambda x.V\, x \Rightarrow V$

We define $=_{Val}$ by the total relation $\top$, namely $\lambda x.t =_{Val} \lambda y.u$ for arbitrary $t, u \in \mathrm{M}_\Sigma$. This means that we observe only termination (since $Val \subseteq \mathsf{NF}(\to_\mathcal{E})$), identifying all values.

Example 18 (A simplified computational lambda-calculus λ_{ml*} [7, 26]). A notion of evaluation for Sabry and Wadler's computational lambda-calculus λ_{ml*} [26] has been studied [7]. A TERS $\mathbf{Comp}\lambda_{ml*}$ of the computational lambda-calculus is defined in Fig. 4. We use syntactic sugar $\lambda x.t \equiv \lambda(x.t), t\, u \equiv @(t, u)$. We define $=_{Val}$ by the total relation $\top$. This means we observe only termination (since $Val \subseteq \mathsf{NF}(\to_\mathcal{E})$), identifying all values.

Signature Σ

true: $\langle 0 \rangle$, false: $\langle 0 \rangle$, fun: $\langle 1 \rangle$, @: $\langle 0, 0 \rangle$, return: $\langle 0 \rangle$, op_1: $\langle 0, 1 \rangle$, op_2: $\langle 0, 1 \rangle$,
$handler_1$: $\langle 1, 2 \rangle$, $handler_0$: $\langle 1 \rangle$, do: $\langle 0, 1 \rangle$, if: $\langle 0, 0, 0 \rangle$, with` handle: $\langle 0, 0 \rangle$

Syntax class *Sclass*

functions $F ::= x \mid \mathtt{fun}(x.P)$

values $V ::= \mathtt{true} \mid \mathtt{false} \mid F \mid H$

handlers $H ::= \mathtt{handler}_1(x.P, x.k.P_1) \mid \mathtt{handler}_0(x.P)$

computations $P, P_1, P_2 ::= \mathtt{return}(V) \mid \mathtt{op}(V, y.P) \mid \mathtt{do}(P_1, x.P_2)$
$\mid \mathtt{if}(V, P_1, P_2) \mid F\ V \mid \mathtt{with`\ handle}(H, P)$

Evaluation contexts *Ectx* $E ::= \square \mid \mathtt{do}(E, x.\Gamma) \mid \mathtt{with\ handle}(H, E)$

Evaluation rules $\mathcal{E}$ where $i \in [2]$

$\mathtt{do}(\mathtt{return}(V), x.P[x]) \to P[V]$ $\hfill (1)$

$\mathtt{do}(\mathtt{op}_i(V, y.P_1[y]), x.P_2[x]) \to \mathtt{op}_i(V, y.\mathtt{do}(P_1[y], x.P_2[x]))$ $\hfill (2)$

$\mathtt{if}(\mathtt{true}, P_1, P_2) \to P_1$ $\hfill (3)$

$\mathtt{if}(\mathtt{false}, P_1, P_2) \to P_2$ $\hfill (4)$

$\mathtt{fun}(x.P[x])\ V \to P[V]$ $\hfill (5)$

In the following three rules, $h_1 \equiv \mathtt{handler}_1(x.P[x], x.k.P_1[x, k])$.

$\mathtt{with`\ handle}(h_1, \mathtt{return}(V)) \to P[V]$ $\hfill (6)$

$\mathtt{with`\ handle}(h_1, \mathtt{op}_1(V, y.P'[y])) \to P_1[V, \mathtt{fun}(y.P'[y])]$ $\hfill (7)$

$\mathtt{with`\ handle}(h_1, \mathtt{op}_2(V, y.P'[y])) \to \mathtt{op}_2(V, y.\mathtt{with`\ handle}(h_1, P'[y]))$ $\hfill (8)$

In the following two rules, $h_0 \equiv \mathtt{handler}_0(x.P[x])$.

$\mathtt{with`\ handle}(h_0, \mathtt{return}(V)) \to P[V]$ $\hfill (9)$

$\mathtt{with`\ handle}(h_0, \mathtt{op}_i(V, y.P'[y])) \to \mathtt{op}_i(V, y.\mathtt{with`\ handle}(h_0, P'[y]))$ $\hfill (10)$

Refinement rules $\mathcal{R}$

$\mathtt{do}(P, x.\mathtt{return}(x)) \Rightarrow P$ $\hfill (\mathrm{r}3)$

$\mathtt{do}(\mathtt{do}(P_1, x_1.P_2[x_1]), x_2.P_3[x_2]) \Rightarrow \mathtt{do}(P_1, x_1.\mathtt{do}(P_2[x_1], x_2.P_3[x_2]))$ $\hfill (\mathrm{r}4)$

$\mathtt{fun}(x.F\ x) \Rightarrow F$ $\hfill (\mathrm{r}9)$

$\mathtt{with`\ handle}(\mathtt{handler}_0(x.P[x]), P') \Rightarrow \mathtt{do}(P', x.P[x])$ $\hfill (\mathrm{r}13)$

Fig. 5. The TERS **Hndl**

Example 19 (Effect handlers [25]). A TERS **Hndl** is defined in Fig. 5, where V, V_1, V_2 are value metavariables, H is a handler metavariable, and $P, P_1, P_2, \ldots$ are computation metavariables.

We only consider two operations op_1, op_2 and two handlers: $handler_1$ for catching the first operation op_1 and $handler_0$ for catching no operation, for simplicity. We change the evaluation rule (7) to be the so-called *shallow handling*; the original, *deep handling*, rule [25] can be accommodated to a TERS, but this TERS would not be well-behaved[2].

---

[2] More specifically, the metavariable P_1 would appear twice in the rhs of the original rule of the evaluation rule (7).

We also select the refinement rules that do not correspond to an evaluation rule and those whose lhs is a Miller's higher-order pattern[3]. The refinement rules are numbered according to the original presentation [25, Fig. 7].

We define $=_{Val}$ for the TERS **Hndl** as follows, where v is any value.

$$x =_{Val} v \qquad \mathbf{true} =_{Val} \mathbf{true} \qquad \mathbf{false} =_{Val} \mathbf{false} \qquad \mathbf{fun}(x.p) =_{Val} \mathbf{fun}(x'.p')$$

$$\mathbf{handler}_1(x.p, x.k.p_1) =_{Val} \mathbf{handler}_1(x'.p', x'.k'.p_1')$$

$$\mathbf{handler}_0(x.p) =_{Val} \mathbf{handler}_0(x'.p')$$

This means that we distinguish each ground type value (i.e. boolean value), and observe merely termination for other values (i.e. functions and handlers), although the TERS **Hndl** is untyped.

6 Second-Order Critical Pair Analysis for Local Coherence

Critical Pairs. The following definitions are analogous to those of first-order TERS. The definition of critical pairs is again standard, akin to commutation.

Definition 20 (Unifiers).

- A *unifier* between t and u is a valid substitution θ such that $t\theta = u\theta$.
- A *most general unifier* between t and u is given by a unifier θ between t and u such that, for any unifier σ between t and u, there exists a valid substitution σ' such that $\sigma = \theta\sigma'$.

Definition 21 (Overlaps). Let $\mathcal{X}_1, \mathcal{X}_2 \in \{\mathcal{R}, \mathcal{E}\}$. Given rules $(l_1 \twoheadrightarrow_1 r_1) \in \mathcal{X}_1$, $(l_2 \twoheadrightarrow_2 r_2) \in \mathcal{X}_2$ and a substitution θ, a quadruple $(l_1 \twoheadrightarrow_1 r_1, l_2 \twoheadrightarrow_2 r_2, p, \theta)$ is an $(\mathcal{X}_1, \mathcal{X}_2)$-*overlap* if it satisfies the following.

- The rules $l_1 \twoheadrightarrow_1 r_1$ and $l_2 \twoheadrightarrow_2 r_2$ do not have common variables or metavariables.
- If $p = \varepsilon$, the rules $l_1 \twoheadrightarrow_1 r_1$ and $l_2 \twoheadrightarrow_2 r_2$ are not variants of each other.
- The sub-term $l_1|_p$ is not a meta-application, where p is a position of l_1.
- The substitution θ is a most general unifier between $l_1|_p$ and l_2.

Definition 22 (Critical pairs).

- The *critical pair* generated by an $(\mathcal{R}, \mathcal{E})$-overlap $(l_1 \Rightarrow r_1, l_2 \rightarrow r_2, p, \theta)$ is an $(\mathcal{R}, \mathcal{E})$-peak $(r_1\theta, l_1\theta, (l_1\theta)[r_2\theta]_p)$.
- The *critical pair* generated by an $(\mathcal{E}, \mathcal{R})$-overlap $(l_1 \rightarrow r_1, l_2 \Rightarrow r_2, p, \theta)$ is an $(\mathcal{R}, \mathcal{E})$-peak $((l_1\theta)[r_2\theta]_p, l_1\theta, r_1\theta)$.

Lemma 23. If a critical pair (t_1, s, t_2) is joinable, then for any valid substitution θ, $(t_1\theta, s\theta, t_2\theta)$ is a joinable $(\mathcal{R}, \mathcal{E})$-peak.

---

[3] The refinement rule (7) in [25, Fig. 7] is the only refinement rule whose lhs is not a Miller's higher-order pattern.

To obtain the so-called critical pair theorem, TERS need to be well-behaved again. The following conditions are similar to the first-order case (see Definition 12), except for the last two conditions which ensure that evaluation and refinement are consistent with syntax classes.

Definition 24 (Well-behaved TERS). A TERS $(\Sigma, \mathcal{E}, \mathcal{R}, Ectx, Sclass)$ is *well-behaved* if it satisfies the following.

1. For any $C_1, C_2 \in Ctx$, if $C_1[C_2] \in Ectx$ then $C_1, C_2 \in Ectx$.
2. For any $E \in Ectx$ and $C' \in Ctx$, if $E \Rightarrow_{\mathcal{R}} C'$ then $C' \subset Ectx$.
3. For any $(l \Rightarrow_{\mathcal{R}} r) \in \mathcal{R}$ and any metavariable N that is not a value metavariable, the following holds.
    (a) The metavariable N appears at most once in l, and at most once in r.
    (b) Let p be the position of N in l. For the position q of N in r, if $l[\square]_p \in Ectx$ then $r[\square]_q \in Ectx$.
4. For any $(l \rightarrow_{\mathcal{E}} r) \in \mathcal{E}$, any metavariable N appears at most once in l.
5. For any $(l \Rightarrow_{\mathcal{R}} r) \in \mathcal{R}$ and any valid θ, if $l\theta$ belongs to a class then $r\theta$ belongs to the same class.
6. For any $(l \rightarrow_{\mathcal{E}} r) \in \mathcal{R}$ and any valid θ, if $l\theta$ belongs to a class then $r\theta$ belongs to the same class.

Theorem 25 (Critical pair theorem). *A well-behaved TERS is locally coherent if and only if every critical pair is joinable.*

The Three Examples. The TERSs **CBV**λ, **Comp**λ_{ml*} and **Hndl** are deterministic, value-invariant and locally coherent (Proposition 34, Proposition 35 & Proposition 36 in Appendix). By Theorem 7, every refinement $\mathcal{R}$ in the examples is *improvement* w.r.t. the corresponding evaluation $\mathcal{E}$.

7   Related Work

Unlike general term rewriting (i.e., refinement), evaluation that uses Felleisen's evaluation contexts has received little attention in the rewriting literature. As an exception, Faggian et al. [6,7] studied evaluation for specific simplified computational lambda-calculi including λ_{ml*}. They proved that refinement implies observational equivalence, crucially using the fact that refinement is confluent in these calculi. In contrast, we study evaluation for general TERS. We identify sufficient conditions (e.g. local coherence) for contextual improvement, not relying on confluence of refinement.

In the first-order setting, Lucas' *context-sensitive rewriting* [20] is capable of restricting where rewriting may happen, by means of a *replacement map* $\mu \colon \Sigma \rightarrow \mathbb{N}^*$. It is possible to encode any replacement map into evaluation contexts. For example, a replacement map $\mu(\texttt{if}) = \{1\}$ specifies that only the first argument (i.e. the guard t of $\texttt{if}(t, s_1, s_2)$) can be rewritten. This can be encoded into evaluation contexts as $E ::= \square \mid \texttt{if}(E, s_1, s_2)$. Another example is $\mu(+) = \{1, 2\}$ that specifies both of the two arguments of $+$ can be rewritten. This can be encoded as $E ::= \square \mid E + t \mid t + E$. Every context-sensitive rewriting system can be simulated by a first-order TES in this way. Advantages of TERS are that (1) TES can also control the evaluation order easily (e.g. the left-to-right evaluation of function application), and (2) we have also formulated second-order TES with refinements as TERS.

Another term-rewriting alternative to evaluation contexts is *rewriting strategies* [16] that provide a way of determinising rewriting. Evaluation typically comes with a convenient inductive structure, which is lacking in strategies.

There is rich literature on methodologies for proving observational equivalence [1,18,24,28]. Some methodologies have been applied to effect handlers [4,5]. We provide a novel term-rewriting-theoretic methodology centred around local coherence and critical pair analysis.

Our methodology is partly automatable, thanks to the fact that critical pair analysis for second-order computation systems can be automated [13,14]. Our prototype analyzer based on this technology could automatically check the join-ablity of all the critical pairs in the examples (see Appendix B for **Hndl**). There are few works on automating observational equivalence proofs for functional programs. Known examples, including the tool SyTeCi [17], are based on or inspired by algorithmic game semantics [2].

This work is targeted at contextual improvement, a quantitative variant of observational equivalence. There is relatively limited literature on proof methodologies for contextual improvement. A coinductive approach based on applicative bisimulation has been used for space improvement [29] and time improvement [19]. This line of work, however, does not come with any form of automation.

8   Conclusion and Future Work

We formalised evaluation from the term-rewriting perspective, and introduced TERS in both first-order and second-order settings. To validate refinement (which models optimisation) with respect to evaluation, we employed the concept of contextual improvement, and identified sufficient conditions for it. The key condition is local coherence, for which we developed critical pair analysis. We demonstrated TERS with examples including λ_{ml*} and its extension with effect handlers.

This work contributes to bridging the gap between general term rewriting and evaluation, by introducing TERS. We are interested in bringing more term-rewriting techniques and insights to evaluation; for example to check if a TERS is deterministic, and if refinement implies observational equivalence instead of contextual improvement.

Acknowledgement. The authors are supported by JSPS, KAKENHI Project No. 20H04164, Japan. K.M. is also supported by JSPS, KAKENHI Project No. 22K17850, Japan.

A   Omitted Proofs

A.1   Proofs for Sect. 3 and Sect. 4

Theorem 26 (Theorem 7: sufficient condition for improvement). *If a TERS is deterministic, value-invariant and locally coherent, then it supports improvement.*

Proof. Take arbitrary $k \in \mathbb{N}$ and $t, u \in T_\Sigma$ such that $t \Rightarrow_{\mathcal{R}} u$ and $t \xrightarrow{k}_{\mathcal{E}} v \in Val$. We first prove that $t \Rightarrow_{\mathcal{R}} u$ and $t \xrightarrow{k}_{\mathcal{E}} v$ imply $u \xrightarrow{m}_{\mathcal{E}} v'$, $v =_{Val} v'$ and $k \geq m$, for any $k \in \mathbb{N}$, by induction on k.

Base Case. When $k = 0$, we have $t = v$. Because the TERS $(\mathcal{E}, \mathcal{R})$ is value-invariant, we have $u \in Val$ and $v =_{Val} u$. We can take $m = 0$.

Inductive Case. When $k > 0$, there exists $t' \in T_\Sigma$ such that $t \rightarrow_{\mathcal{E}} t' \xrightarrow{k-1}_{\mathcal{E}} v$. Because the TERS $(\mathcal{E}, \mathcal{R})$ is locally coherent, the $(\mathcal{R}, \mathcal{E})$-peak (u, t, t') is joinable up to $\mathcal{R}$; namely there exist $t'', u' \in T_\Sigma$ and $l, m, n \in \mathbb{N}$ such that $t' \xrightarrow{l}_{\mathcal{E}} t''$, $u \xrightarrow{n}_{\mathcal{E}} u'$, $t'' \overset{m}{\Rightarrow}_{\mathcal{R}} u'$ and $1 + l \geq n$. Because the TERS $(\mathcal{E}, \mathcal{R})$ is deterministic, t'' must appear in the sequence $t' \xrightarrow{k-1}_{\mathcal{E}} v$, and hence $t \rightarrow_{\mathcal{E}} t' \xrightarrow{l}_{\mathcal{E}} t'' \xrightarrow{k-l-1}_{\mathcal{E}} v$. We prove that we have the following situation:

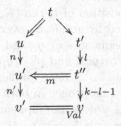

namely that there exist $n' \in \mathbb{N}$ and $v' \in Val$ such that $u' \xrightarrow{n'}_{\mathcal{E}} v'$ and $v =_{Val} v'$, by induction on $m \in \mathbb{N}$.

- *Base case.* When $m = 0$, $t'' = u'$. We can take $n' = k - l - 1$ and $v' = v$. Because $1 + l \geq n$, we have $k \geq n + n'$.
- *Inductive case.* When $m > 0$, we have $t'' \overset{m-1}{\Rightarrow}_{\mathcal{R}} u'' \Rightarrow_{\mathcal{R}} u'$ for some $u'' \in T_\Sigma$. By I.H. on $m - 1$, we have $u'' \xrightarrow{n''}_{\mathcal{E}} v''$ such that $v'' =_{Val} v$ and $k - l - 1 \geq n''$. Furthermore, by I.H. of the outer induction on n'', we have $u' \xrightarrow{n'}_{\mathcal{E}} v'$ such that $v'' =_{Val} v'$ and $n'' \geq n'$. We finally have $k \geq n + n'$.

As a result, we have $u \xrightarrow{n+n'}_{\mathcal{E}} v'$ such that $v =_{Val} v'$ and $k \geq n + n'$. We can take $m = n + n'$.

Secondly, because $\Rightarrow_{\mathcal{R}}$ is closed under any contexts, $t \Rightarrow_{\mathcal{R}} u$ implies $C[t] \Rightarrow_{\mathcal{R}} C[u]$ for any $C \in Ctx$. Therefore, $t \Rightarrow_{\mathcal{R}} u$ and $C[t] \xrightarrow{k}_{\mathcal{E}} v$ imply $C[u] \xrightarrow{m}_{\mathcal{E}} v'$ such that $k \geq m$ and $v =_{Val} v'$, for any $v \in Val$.   □

Lemma 27 (Lemma 11**).** If a critical pair (t_1, s, t_2) is joinable, then for any substitution θ, $(t_1\theta, s\theta, t_2\theta)$ is a joinable $(\mathcal{R}, \mathcal{E})$-peak.

Proof. We have a joinable $(\mathcal{R}, \mathcal{E})$-peak (t_1, s, t_2). Since refinement and evaluation are closed under substitution, $(t_1\theta, s\theta, t_2\theta)$ is also a joinable $(\mathcal{R}, \mathcal{E})$-peak. $\square$

Theorem 28 (Theorem 13**: Critical pair theorem).** *A well-behaved TERS is locally coherent if and only if every critical pair is joinable.*

Proof. The "only if" part is straightforward. In the following, we prove the "if" part.

Take an arbitrary $(\mathcal{R}, \mathcal{E})$-peak (t_1, s, t_2). Our goal is to prove that this $(\mathcal{R}, \mathcal{E})$-peak is joinable. Since $s \Rightarrow_{\mathcal{R}} t_1$, there exist $p \in Pos(s)$, $(l \Rightarrow r) \in \mathcal{R}$ and subst θ such that $s|_p = l\theta$, $t_1 = s[r\theta]_p$ and $s[\square]_p \in Ctx$. We prove that the $(\mathcal{R}, \mathcal{E})$-peak (t_1, s, t_2) is joinable, by induction on the length of the position p.

Base Case. When $|p| = 0$, i.e. $p = \varepsilon$, we have $s = l\theta$ and $t_1 = r\theta$. Because $l\theta \rightarrow_{\mathcal{E}} t_2$, there exist $p' \in Pos(l\theta)$, $(l' \rightarrow r') \in \mathcal{E}$ and subst θ' such that $(l\theta)|_{p'} = l'\theta'$, $t_2 = (l\theta)[r'\theta']_{p'}$ and $(l\theta)[\square]_{p'} \in Ectx$. We have an $(\mathcal{R}, \mathcal{E})$-peak $P = (r\theta, l\theta, (l\theta)[r'\theta']_{p'})$.

- If $p' = \varepsilon$, and $l \Rightarrow r$ and $l \rightarrow r$ are variants of each other, we have $r\theta = r'\theta'$ and the $(\mathcal{R}, \mathcal{E})$-peak P is joinable.
- Otherwise, there are two possibilities.
  - If p' is a non-variable position of l, the $(\mathcal{R}, \mathcal{E})$-peak P is an instance of the critical pair generated by an $(\mathcal{R}, \mathcal{E})$-overlap.
  - Otherwise, there exist sequences q_1, q_2 and a variable y such that: $q_1 \in Pos(l)$, $l|_{q_1} = y$, $q_2 \in Pos(y\theta)$, and $p' = q_1 q_2$. Because of the condition (1) of Definition 12, $(l\theta)[\square]_{p'} \in Ectx$ implies $l[\square]_{q_1}, y\theta[\square]_{q_2} \in Ectx$. The variable y must appear at most once in both l and r, due to the condition (3a) of Definition 12. If y does not appear in r, the $(\mathcal{R}, \mathcal{E})$-peak P is joinable by applying the rule $l \Rightarrow r$ to t_2. Otherwise, i.e. if y appears once in r, the rule $l' \rightarrow r'$ can be applied to t_1 thanks to the condition (3b) of Definition 12, and the rule $l \Rightarrow r$ can be applied to t_2. These two applications yield the same result. Therefore, we can conclude that the $(\mathcal{R}, \mathcal{E})$-peak P is joinable.

Inductive Case. When $|p| > 0$, we have $p = ip_t$ for some positive number i and some sequence p_t. We have $s = f(\overline{x_1}.u_1, \ldots, \overline{x_i}.u_i, \ldots, \overline{x_k}.u_k)$, $l\theta = u_i|_{p_t}$. We have an $(\mathcal{R}, \mathcal{E})$-peak

$$P' = (f(\overline{x_1}.u_1, \ldots, \overline{x_i}.u_i[r\theta]_{p_t}, \ldots, \overline{x_k}.u_k), f(\overline{x_1}.u_1, \ldots, \overline{x_i}.u_i, \ldots, \overline{x_l}.u_l), t_2).$$

By $s \rightarrow_{\mathcal{E}} t_2$, there exist $p' \in Pos(s)$, $(l' \rightarrow r') \in \mathcal{E}$ and subst θ' such that $s|_{p'} = l'\theta'$, $t_2 = s[r'\theta']_{p'}$ and $s[\square]_{p'} \in Ectx$. We proceed by case analysis on $p' \in Pos(s)$.

- When $p' = \varepsilon$, we have $s = l'\theta'$ and $t_2 = r'\theta'$.

- If p is a non-variable position of l', the $(\mathcal{R}, \mathcal{E})$-peak P' is an instance of the critical pair generated by an $(\mathcal{E}, \mathcal{R})$-overlap.
- Otherwise, there exist sequences q_1, q_2 and a variable y such that: $q_1 \in Pos(l')$, $l'|_{q_1} = y$, $q_2 \in Pos(y\theta')$, and $p = q_1 q_2$. The variable y appears at most once in l', due to the condition (4) of Definition 12. We can apply the rule $l' \to r'$ to t_1. We can also apply the rule $l \Rightarrow r$ to t_2, as many times as y appears in r'. These applications of $l' \to r'$ and $l \Rightarrow r$ yield the same result. The $(\mathcal{R}, \mathcal{E})$-peak P' is therefore joinable.

- When $p' \neq \varepsilon$, i.e. $p' = i' p'_t$ for some positive number i' and some sequence p'_t, there are two possibilities.
  - When $i' = i$, by I.H., we have a joinable $(\mathcal{R}, \mathcal{E})$-peak

  $$Q = (u_i[r\theta]_{p_t}, u_i, u_i[r'\theta']_{p'_t}).$$

  Because $f(\ldots, \overline{x_i}.u_i[\square]_{p_t}, \ldots) \in Ectx$, we have $f(\ldots, \overline{x_i}.\square, \ldots) \in Ectx$ too, thanks to the condition (1) of Definition 12. Therefore, joinability of the $(\mathcal{R}, \mathcal{E})$-peak Q implies joinability of the $(\mathcal{R}, \mathcal{E})$-peak P'.
  - When $i' \neq i$, we can assume that $i' < i$ without loss of generality. The $(\mathcal{R}, \mathcal{E})$-peak

  $$P' = (f(\ldots, \overline{x_{i'}}.u_{i'}, \ldots, \overline{x_i}.u_i[r\theta]_{p_t}, \ldots),$$
  $$f(\ldots, \overline{x_{i'}}.u_{i'}, \ldots, \overline{x_i}.u_i, \ldots),$$
  $$f(\ldots, \overline{x_{i'}}.u_{i'}[r'\theta']_{p'_t}, \ldots, \overline{x_i}.u_i, \ldots))$$

  is joinable (to $f(\ldots, \overline{x_{i'}}.u_{i'}[r'\theta']_{p'_t}, \ldots, \overline{x_i}.u_i[r\theta]_{p_t}, \ldots)$), thanks to the condition (2) of Definition 12.

$$\square$$

A.2   The TERS Nats

Proposition 29. The TERS **Nats** is deterministic, value-invariant and locally coherent.

Proof. The TERS **Nats** is deterministic, because evaluation rules concern distinct symbols.

To prove value-invariance, we assume $v \Rightarrow_{\mathcal{R}} u$ for some $v \in Val$ and $u \in T_\Sigma$. It must hold that $v = s^n(0)$, and in this case, the refinement $v \Rightarrow_{\mathcal{R}} u$ is impossible. The TERS **Nats** is trivially value-invariant.

To prove local coherence, we use Theorem 13. We first show that the TERS **Nats** is well-behaved. The condition (1) of Definition 24 is trivially satisfied. As for the condition (2), each evaluation context $E \in Ectx$ never includes the constant **nats**, and hence the refinement rule cannot be applied to $E[t]$ to obtain $C'[t]$. Therefore the condition (2) is trivially satisfied. The other conditions of well-behavedness are easy to check. We then show that any critical pair is join-able. There is only one critical pair, and it is indeed joinable as follows.

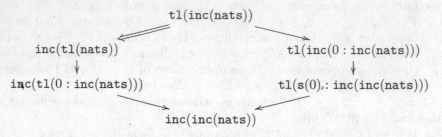

$$\mathtt{tl(inc(nats))}$$

$$\mathtt{inc(tl(nats))}$$

$$\mathtt{tl(inc(0:inc(nats)))}$$

$$\mathtt{inc(tl(0:inc(nats)))}$$

$$\mathtt{tl(s(0),:inc(inc(nats)))}$$

$$\mathtt{inc(inc(nats))}$$

□

A.3   On Linearity Conditions

For a TERS to be well-behaved, its evaluation rules must be left-linear, and its refinement rules must be linear (see Definition 12). Here we observe that relaxing these linearity conditions, with a reasonable set of evaluation contexts and values, leads to non-joinable $(\mathcal{R}, \mathcal{E})$-peaks that are not instances of a critical pair.

Let a TERS $\mathcal{E}_\mathsf{S}$ be defined as follows.

Signature Σ $\qquad\qquad +: 2,\ -: 2,\ \overset{?}{\equiv}: 2,\ \mathsf{s}: 1,\ 0: 0$

Values Val $\qquad\qquad\qquad V ::= 0 \mid \mathsf{s}(V)$

Evaluation contexts $Ectx$ $\;\; E ::= \square \mid \mathsf{s}(E) \mid E + t \mid E - t \mid v - E$

Evaluation rules $\mathcal{E}$ $\qquad$ **Refinement rule** $\mathcal{R}$

$0 + x \to x \qquad\qquad\qquad x - x \Rightarrow 0$

$\mathsf{s}(x) + y \to \mathsf{s}(x + y) \qquad\quad 0 \Rightarrow x - x$

$0 - x \to 0$

$\mathsf{s}(x) - \mathsf{s}(y) \to x - y$

$x \overset{?}{\equiv} x \to 0$

We define $=_{Val}$ by the syntactic equality $\equiv$. The operation $\overset{?}{\equiv}$ checks syntactic equality.

The non-left-linear refinement rule $x - x \Rightarrow 0$ induces the following non-joinable $(\mathcal{R}, \mathcal{E})$-peak.

$$(\mathsf{s}(x) + y) - (\mathsf{s}(x) + y)$$

$$0 \qquad\qquad\qquad\qquad \mathsf{s}(x + y) - (\mathsf{s}(x) + y)$$

In the term $\mathsf{s}(x + y) - (\mathsf{s}(x) + y)$, the sub-term $\mathsf{s}(x) + y$ cannot be evaluated, because $\mathsf{s}(x + y)$ is not a value.

The non-right-linear refinement rule $0 \Rightarrow x - x$ induces the following non-joinable $(\mathcal{R}, \mathcal{E})$-peak.

$$0$$

$$0 - 0 \longrightarrow 0$$

This $(\mathcal{R}, \mathcal{E})$-peak is not joinable with respect to our definition of joinability (see Definition 4). The bottom term $0 - 0$ must not take more evaluation steps than the top term 0.

Finally, the non-left-linear evaluation rule $x \overset{?}{\equiv} x \to 0$ induces the following non-joinable $(\mathcal{R}, \mathcal{E})$-peak.

$$(\mathsf{s}(x) + y) \overset{?}{\equiv} (\mathsf{s}(x) + y)$$

$$\mathsf{s}(x + y) \overset{?}{\equiv} (\mathsf{s}(x) + y) \qquad\qquad\qquad\qquad 0$$

In the term $\mathsf{s}(x + y) \overset{?}{\equiv} (\mathsf{s}(x) + y)$, the sub-term $\mathsf{s}(x) + y$ cannot be evaluated, because $\mathsf{s}(x + y)$ is not a value.

A.4 Proofs for Sect. 5 and Sect. 6

Lemma 30 (Lemma 23). If a critical pair (t_1, s, t_2) is joinable, then for any valid substitution θ, $(t_1\theta, s\theta, t_2\theta)$ is a joinable $(\mathcal{R}, \mathcal{E})$-peak.

Proof. We have a joinable $(\mathcal{R}, \mathcal{E})$-peak (t_1, s, t_2). Because evaluation is closed under valid substitutions, and refinement satisfies $t \Rightarrow_\mathcal{R} u \implies t\theta \overset{*}{\Rightarrow}_\mathcal{R} u\theta$, $(t_1\theta, s\theta, t_2\theta)$ is also a joinable $(\mathcal{R}, \mathcal{E})$-peak.   □

Theorem 31 (Theorem 25: Critical pair theorem). *A well-behaved TERS is locally coherent if and only if every critical pair is joinable.*

Proof. The "only if" part is straightforward. In the following, we prove the "if" part.

Take an arbitrary $(\mathcal{R}, \mathcal{E})$-peak (t_1, s, t_2). Our goal is to prove that this $(\mathcal{R}, \mathcal{E})$-peak is joinable. Since $s \Rightarrow_\mathcal{R} t_1$, there exist $p \in Pos(s)$, $(l \Rightarrow r) \in \mathcal{R}$ and valid θ such that $s|_p = l\theta$, $t_1 = s[r\theta]_p$ and $s[\square]_p \in Ctx$. We prove that the $(\mathcal{R}, \mathcal{E})$-peak (t_1, s, t_2) is joinable, by induction on the length of the position p.

Base Case. When $|p| = 0$, i.e. $p = \varepsilon$, we have $s = l\theta$ and $t_1 = r\theta$. Because $l\theta \to_\mathcal{E} t_2$, there exist $p' \in Pos(l\theta)$, $(l' \to r') \in \mathcal{E}$ and valid θ' such that $(l\theta)|_{p'} = l'\theta'$, $t_2 = (l\theta)[r'\theta']_{p'}$ and $(l\theta)[\square]_{p'} \in Ectx$. We have an $(\mathcal{R}, \mathcal{E})$-peak $P = (r\theta, l\theta, (l\theta)[r'\theta']_{p'})$.

- If $p' = \varepsilon$, and $l \Rightarrow r$ and $l \to r$ are variants of each other, we have $r\theta = r'\theta'$ and the $(\mathcal{R}, \mathcal{E})$-peak P is joinable.
- Otherwise, because $(l\theta)[\square]_{p'} \in Ectx$ is a flat context, every prefix of p' but p' itself is not a metavariable position in $l\theta$.
  - If p' is a non-metavariable position of l, the $(\mathcal{R}, \mathcal{E})$-peak P is an instance of the critical pair generated by an $(\mathcal{R}, \mathcal{E})$-overlap.
  - Otherwise, There exist sequences q_1, q_2, a metavariable N and a sequence $\overline{y}$ such that: $q_1 \in Pos(l)$, $l|_{q_1} = N[\overline{y}]$, $q_2 \in Pos((N[\overline{y}])\theta)$, and $p' = q_1 q_2$. Because of the condition (1) of Definition 24, $(l\theta)[\square]_{p'} \in Ectx$ implies $l[\square]_{q_1}, (N[\overline{y}])\theta[\square]_{q_2} \in Ectx$. In particular, the latter means that $(N[\overline{y}])\theta \notin$

$\mathsf{NF}(\to_{\mathcal{E}})$, and hence N is not a value metavariable. The metavariable N must appear at most once in both l and r, due to the condition (3a) of Definition 24. If N does not appear in r, the $(\mathcal{R},\mathcal{E})$-peak P is joinable by applying the rule $l \Rightarrow r$ to t_2. Otherwise, i.e. if N appears once-in r, the rule $l' \to r'$ can be applied to t_1 thanks to the condition (3b) of Definition 24, and the rule $l \Rightarrow r$ can be applied to t_2, thanks to the condition (6) of Definition 24. These two applications yield the same result. Therefore, we can conclude that the $(\mathcal{R},\mathcal{E})$-peak P is joinable.

Inductive Case. When $|p| > 0$, we have $p = ip_t$ for some positive number i and some sequence p_t. We have either $s = f(\overline{x_1}.u_1, \ldots, \overline{x_i}.u_i, \ldots, \overline{x_k}.u_k)$ or $s = M[u_1, \ldots, u_i, \ldots, u_k]$, such that $l\theta = u_i|_{p_t}$.

Firstly, assume that we have an $(\mathcal{R},\mathcal{E})$-peak

$$P' = (f(\overline{x_1}.u_1, \ldots, \overline{x_i}.u_i[r\theta]_{p_t}, \ldots, \overline{x_k}.u_k), \, f(\overline{x_1}.u_1, \ldots, \overline{x_i}.u_i, \ldots, \overline{x_l}.u_l), \, t_2).$$

By $s \to_{\mathcal{E}} t_2$, there exist $p' \in Pos(s)$, $(l' \to r') \in \mathcal{E}$ and valid θ' such that $s|_{p'} = l'\theta'$, $t_2 = s[r'\theta']_{p'}$ and $s[\Box]_{p'} \in Ectx$. We proceed by case analysis on $p' \in Pos(s)$.

- When $p' = \varepsilon$, we have $s = l'\theta'$ and $t_2 = r'\theta'$.
  - If p is a non-metavariable position of l', the $(\mathcal{R},\mathcal{E})$-peak P' is an instance of the critical pair generated by an $(\mathcal{E},\mathcal{R})$-overlap.
  - Otherwise, there exist sequences q_1, q_2 and a metavariable M such that: $q_1 \in Pos(l')$, $l'|_{q_1} = M[\overline{y}]$, $q_2 \in Pos(M[\overline{y}]\theta')$, and $p = q_1 q_2$. The metavariable M appears at most once in l', due to the condition (4) of Definition 24. We can apply the rule $l' \to r'$ to t_1. The substitution θ' is valid, thanks to the condition (5) of Definition 24. We can also apply the rule $l \Rightarrow r$ to t_2 as many times as M appears in r'. These applications of $l' \to r'$ and $l \Rightarrow r$ yield the same result. The $(\mathcal{R},\mathcal{E})$-peak P' is therefore joinable.
- When $p' \neq \varepsilon$, i.e. $p' = i'p'_t$ for some positive number i' and some sequence p'_t, there are two possibilities.
  - When $i' = i$, by I.H., we have a joinable $(\mathcal{R},\mathcal{E})$-peak $Q = (u_i[r\theta]_{p_t}, u_i, u_i[r'\theta']_{p'_t})$. Because $f(\ldots, \overline{x_i}.u_i[\Box]_{p_t}, \ldots) \in Ectx$, we have $f(\ldots, \overline{x_i}.\Box, \ldots) \in Ectx$ too, thanks to the condition (1) of Definition 24. Therefore, joinability of the $(\mathcal{R},\mathcal{E})$-peak Q implies joinability of the $(\mathcal{R},\mathcal{E})$-peak P'.
  - When $i' \neq i$, we can assume that $i' < i$ without loss of generality. The $(\mathcal{R},\mathcal{E})$-peak

$$P' = (f(\ldots, \overline{x_{i'}}.u_{i'}, \ldots, \overline{x_i}.u_i[r\theta]_{p_t}, \ldots), \, f(\ldots, \overline{x_{i'}}.u_{i'}, \ldots, \overline{x_i}.u_i, \ldots),$$
$$f(\ldots, \overline{x_{i'}}.u_{i'}[r'\theta']_{p'_t}, \ldots, \overline{x_i}.u_i, \ldots))$$

is joinable (to $f(\ldots, \overline{x_{i'}}.u_{i'}[r'\theta']_{p'_t}, \ldots, \overline{x_i}.u_i[r\theta]_{p_t}, \ldots)$), thanks to the condition (2) of Definition 24.

Secondly, assume that we have an $(\mathcal{R}, \mathcal{E})$-peak

$$P' = (M[u_1, \ldots, u_i[r\theta]_{p_t}, \ldots, u_k], \; M[u_1, \ldots, u_i, \ldots, u_l], \; t_2).$$

By $s \to_{\mathcal{E}} t_2$, there exist $p' \in Pos(s)$, $(l' \to r') \in \mathcal{E}$ and valid θ' such that $s|_{p'} = l'\theta'$, $t_2 = s[r'\theta']_{p'}$ and $s[\square]_{p'} \in Ectx$. We proceed by case analysis on $p' \in Pos(s)$.

- When $p' = \varepsilon$, $M[u_1, \ldots, u_k] = l'\theta'$. Because l' is a higher-order pattern, this is impossible.
- When $p' \neq \varepsilon$, the proof is the same as the case for the $(\mathcal{R}, \mathcal{E})$-peak

$$P' = (f(\overline{x_1}.u_1, \ldots, \overline{x_i}.u_i[r\theta]_{p_t}, \ldots, \overline{x_k}.u_k), \; f(\overline{x_1}.u_1, \ldots, \overline{x_i}.u_i, \ldots, \overline{x_l}.u_l), \; t_2).$$

$\square$

A.5   The TERS CBVλ and Hndl

We will use a sufficient condition for a TES to be deterministic, namely *decisiveness*.

Definition 32 (decisiveness). A TES $(\Sigma, \mathcal{E}, Ectx, Val)$ is *decisive* if each $t \in T_\Sigma$ satisfies either of the following:

1. $t \in Val$,
2. there uniquely exist $(l \to r) \in \mathcal{E}$, subst θ and $E \in Ectx$ such that $t = E[l\theta]$,
3. there uniquely exist a variable x and $E \in Ectx$ such that $t = E[x]$.

Proposition 33 (sufficient condition for determinism). If a TES is decisive, then it is deterministic.

Proof. Let $t \to_{\mathcal{E}} s_1$ and $t \to_{\mathcal{E}} s_2$. Because the TES is decisive, t satisfies either the three conditions in Definition 32. Since the left-hand side of each evaluation rule is not a variable, to make the evaluation $t \to_{\mathcal{E}} s_1$ and $t \to_{\mathcal{E}} s_2$ happen, only the case (2) is possible. In this case, both s_1 and s_2 must be $E[r\theta]$. $\square$

Proposition 34. The TERS **CBVλ** is deterministic, value-invariant and locally coherent.

Proof. The TERS **CBVλ** is deterministic, because it is decisive.
   To prove value-invariance, we assume $\lambda x.t \Rightarrow_{\mathcal{R}} u$. There are two possible cases.

- When $u = \lambda x.t'$ for some t' such that $t \Rightarrow_{\mathcal{R}} t'$, we have $\lambda x.t =_{Val} \lambda x.t'$.
- When $t = \lambda x.(\lambda y.t') \; x$, it must be that $u = \lambda y.t'$, and we have $\lambda x.(\lambda y.t') \; x =_{Val} \lambda y.t'$.

Therefore the TERS **CBV**λ is value-invariant.

To prove local coherence, we use Theorem 13.

Firstly, the TERS **CBV**λ is well-behaved. The condition (1) of Definition 24 is trivially satisfied. We can show that the condition (2) is satisfied by straightforward induction on $E \in Ectx$. The condition (6) is satisfied, because any instance of the lhs of the evaluation rule never belongs to a syntax class (i.e. the value class). The condition (5) is also satisfied; the second refinement rule always turns a value into a value. The other conditions of well-behavedness are easy to check.

We then show that any critical pair is joinable. There are two critical pairs, which are for the second refinement rule (the η-rule) and the evaluation rule. These critical pairs are joinable as follows.

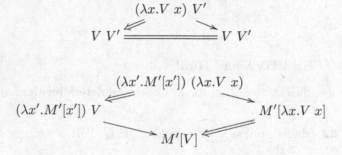

$\square$

Proposition 35. The TERS **Comp**λ_{ml*} is deterministic, value-invariant and locally coherent.

Proof. Firstly, the TERS **Comp**λ_{ml*} is deterministic, because the two evaluation rules consume different head symbols. Secondly, the TERS is value-invariant, thanks to the equivalence $=_{Val}$ being the total order.

To prove local coherence, we use Theorem 13.

The TERS **Comp**λ_{ml*} is well-behaved. The condition (1) of Definition 24 is trivially satisfied. We can show that the condition (2) is satisfied by induction on $E \in Ectx$ as follows.

– When $E = \square$, no refinement rule applies to x, so this case is impossible.
– When $E = \texttt{let}(E', x.P)$, we have $\texttt{let}(E'[t], x.P) \Rightarrow_{\mathcal{R}} C'[t]$. There are four possibilities.
  • If $E'[z] \Rightarrow_{\mathcal{R}} C''[z]$ such that $C' = \texttt{let}(C'', x.P)$, we have $C'' \in Ectx$ by I.H., and hence $C' \in Ectx$.
  • If $P \Rightarrow_{\mathcal{R}} P'$ such that $C' = \texttt{let}(E', x.P')$, we have $C' \in Ectx$.
  • If the refinement rule (r4) is applied at the root position of $E[z]$, we have $\texttt{let}(E'[z], x.\texttt{return}(x)) \Rightarrow_{\mathcal{R}} E'[z]$. We have $C' = E' \in Ectx$.
  • If the refinement rule (r5) is applied at the root position of $E[z]$, we have $\texttt{let}(\texttt{let}(E''[z], x.P[x]), y.P'[y]) \Rightarrow_{\mathcal{R}} \texttt{let}(E''[z], x.\texttt{let}(P[x], y.P'[y]))$. We have $C' = \texttt{let}(E'', x.\texttt{let}(P[x], y.P'[y])) \in Ectx$.

The conditions (6) and (5) are also satisfied; note that instances of $P[V]$ are all computations. The other conditions of well-behavedness are easy to check.

We finally show that any critical pair is joinable. There are the following three critical pairs, which are all joinable. In the following, arrows $\to$, $\Rightarrow$ are labelled by a number that indicates which evaluation/refinement rule is applied.

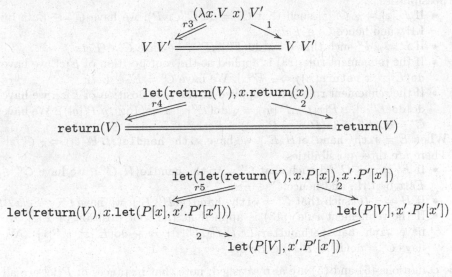

□

Proposition 36. The TERS **Hndl** is deterministic, value-invariant and locally coherent.

Proof. Firstly, to establish that the TERS **Hndl** is deterministic, we show that, for any $t \in \mathrm{M}_\Sigma$, if $t = E[l\theta] = E'[l'\theta']$ for some $E, E' \in Ectx$, $(l \to r), (l' \to r') \in \mathcal{E}$ and valid θ, θ', then the decomposition is unique, namely $E = E'$ and the rules $l \to r$, $l' \to r'$ are variants of each other. This can be proved by induction on $E \in Ectx$.

- When $E = \square$, we have $t = l\theta$. By definition of evaluation rules, $E' = \square$ must hold, and $l \to r$ and $l' \to r'$ must be variants.
- When $E = \mathtt{do}(E', x.P)$, we have $t = \mathtt{do}(E'[l\theta], P)$. By I.H., $E'[l\theta]$ is the only possible decomposition. The meta-term t itself cannot be an instance of any lhs of evaluation rules. Therefore, the decomposition $E[l\theta]$ is unique.
- When $E = \mathtt{with\_handle}(H, E')$, we have $t = \mathtt{with\_handle}(H, E'[l\theta])$. The proof is the same as the previous case.

Consequently, the TERS **Hndl** is deterministic.

Secondly, by definition of $=_{Val}$, the TERS **Hndl** is value-invariant. In particular, the refinement rule (r9) turns a function into a variable or a function; the original function is identified with the resulting variable or function by $=_{Val}$.

To prove local coherence, we use Theorem 13.

The TERS **Hndl** is well-behaved. The condition (1) of Definition 24 is trivially satisfied. We can show that the condition (2) is satisfied by induction on $E \in Ectx$ as follows.

- When $E = \square$, no refinement rule applies to x, so this case is impossible.
- When $E = \mathtt{do}(E', x.P)$, we have $\mathtt{do}(E'[z], x.P) \Rightarrow_{\mathcal{R}} C'[z]$. There are four possibilities.
  - If $E'[z] \Rightarrow_{\mathcal{R}} C''[z]$ such that $C' = \mathtt{do}(C'', x.P)$, we have $C'' \in Ectx$ by I.H., and hence $C' \in Ectx$.
  - If $P \Rightarrow_{\mathcal{R}} P'$ such that $C' = \mathtt{do}(E', x.P')$, we have $C' \in Ectx$.
  - If the refinement rule (r3) is applied at the root position of $E[z]$, we have $\mathtt{do}(E'[z], x.\mathtt{return}(x)) \Rightarrow_{\mathcal{R}} E'[z]$. We have $C' = E' \in Ectx$.
  - If the refinement rule (r4) is applied at the root position of $E[z]$, we have $\mathtt{do}(\mathtt{do}(E''[z], x.P[x]), y.P'[y]) \Rightarrow_{\mathcal{R}} \mathtt{do}(E''[z], x.\mathtt{do}(P[x], y.P'[y]))$. We have $C' = \mathtt{do}(E'', x.\mathtt{do}(P[x], y.P'[y])) \in Ectx$.
- When $E = \mathtt{with\_handle}(H, E')$, we have $\mathtt{with\_handle}(H, E'[z]) \Rightarrow_{\mathcal{R}} C'[z]$. There are three possibilities.
  - If $E'[z] \Rightarrow_{\mathcal{R}} C''[z]$ such that $C' = \mathtt{with\_handle}(H, C'')$, we have $C'' \in Ectx$ by I.H., and hence $C' \in Ectx$.
  - If $H \Rightarrow_{\mathcal{R}} H'$ such that $C' = \mathtt{with\_handle}(H', E')$, we have $C' \in Ectx$.
  - If the refinement rule (r13) is applied at the root position of $E[z]$, we have $\mathtt{with\_handle}(\mathtt{handler}_0(x.P[x]), E'[z]) \Rightarrow_{\mathcal{R}} \mathtt{do}(E'[z], x.P[x])$. We have $C' = \mathtt{do}(E', x.P[x]) \in Ectx$.

The conditions (6) and (5) are also satisfied; note that instances of $P[V]$ are all computations. The other conditions of well-behavedness are easy to check.

We finally show that any critical pair is joinable. There are the following seven critical pairs, which are all joinable. In the following, arrows $\to$, $\Rightarrow$ are labelled by a number that indicates which evaluation/refinement rule is applied, and we set $h_0 \equiv \mathtt{handler}_0(x.P[x])$, and $i \in [2]$.

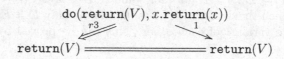

$$\mathtt{do}(\mathtt{return}(V), x.\mathtt{return}(x))$$
$$\mathtt{return}(V) =\!\!=\!\!=\!\!=\!\!=\!\!=\!\!=\!\!=\!\!=\!\!=\!\!= \mathtt{return}(V)$$

(r3, 1)

$$\mathtt{do}(\mathtt{op}_i(V, y.P[y]), x.\mathtt{return}(x))$$
$$\mathtt{op}_i(V, y.P[y]) \xleftarrow{\ \ r3\ \ } \mathtt{op}_i(V, y.\mathtt{do}(P[y], x.\mathtt{return}(x)))$$

(r3, 2)

$$\mathtt{do}(\mathtt{do}(\mathtt{return}(V), x.P[x]), x'.P'[x'])$$
$$\mathtt{do}(\mathtt{return}(V), x.\mathtt{do}(P[x], x'.P'[x'])) \qquad \mathtt{do}(P[V], x'.P'[x'])$$
$$\mathtt{do}(P[V], x'.P'[x'])$$

(r4, 1, 1)

$$do(do(op_i(V, x.P[x]), y.P_2[y]), z.P_3[z])$$

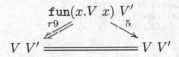

$$do(op_i(V, x.P[x]), y.do(P_2[y], z.P_3[z])) \quad do(op_i(V, x.do(P[x], y.P_2[y])), z.P_3[z])$$

$$op_i(V, x.do(P[x], y.do(P_2[y], z.P_3[z]))) \stackrel{r4}{\Longleftarrow} op_i(V, x.do(do(P[x], y.P_2[y]), z.P_3[z]))$$

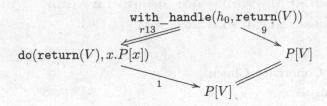

$$fun(x.V\ x)\ V'$$

$$V\ V' =\!=\!=\!=\!=\!=\!=\!= V\ V'$$

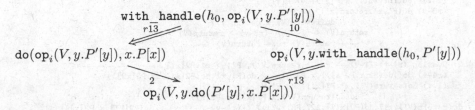

$$with\_handle(h_0, return(V))$$

$$do(return(V), x.P[x]) \qquad\qquad P[V]$$

$$P[V]$$

$$with\_handle(h_0, op_i(V, y.P'[y]))$$

$$do(op_i(V, y.P'[y]), x.P[x]) \qquad\qquad op_i(V, y.with\_handle(h_0, P'[y]))$$

$$op_i(V, y.do(P'[y], x.P[x]))$$

$\square$

B   Critical Pair Analysis of Hndl by Our Prototype Analyzer

B.1   Definition of TERS Hndl

```
sigh = [signature|
  true : T
  false : T
  fun : (T -> T) -> T
  app : T,T -> T
  return : T -> T
  op1 : T, (T -> T) -> T
  op2 : T, (T -> T) -> T
  handler1 : (T -> T), (T,T -> T) -> T
  handler0 : (T -> T) -> T
  do : T, (T -> T) -> T
  if : T,T,T -> T
  with : T,T -> T
|]

evals = [rule|
  (1-v) do(return(V),x.P[x]) => P[V]
```

```
(2-1-v) do(op1(V, y.P1[y]), x.P2[x]) => op1(V, y.do(P1[y],x.P2[x]))
(2-2-v) do(op2(V, y.P1[y]), x.P2[x]) => op2(V, y.do(P1[y],x.P2[x]))
(3-v) if(true, P1, P2) => P1
(4-v) if(false, P1, P2) => P2
(5-v) fun(x.P[x])@V => P[V]
(6-v) with(handler1(x.P[x],x.k.P1[x,k]), return(V)) => P[V]
(7-v) with(handler1(x.P[x],x.k.P1[x,k]),op1(V,y.P'[y])) => P1[V,fun(y.P'[y])]
(8-v) with(handler1(x.P[x],x.k.P1[x,k]),op2(V,y.P'[y])) =>
          op2(V,y.with(handler1(x.P[x],x.k.P1[x,k]),P'[y]))
(9-v)   with(handler0(x.P[x]),return(V)) => P[V]
(10-1-v) with(handler0(x.P[x]),op1(V,y.P'[y])) =>
          op1(V,y.with(handler0(x.P[x]),P'[y]))
(10-2-v) with(handler0(x.P[x]),op2(V,y.P'[y])) =>
          op2(V,y.with(handler0(x.P[x]),P'[y]))
|]


refis = [rule|
(r3-v) do(P,x.return(x)) => P
(r4-v) do(do(P1,x.P2[x]),x.P3[x]) => do(P1, x1.do(P2[x1],x2.P3[x2]))
(r9-v) fun(x.V@x) => V
(r13-v) with(handler0(x.P[x]),P') => do(P',x.P[x])
|]
```

B.2 Local Coherence Check

```
*Ex> lcoh evals refis

1: Overlap (1-v)-(r3-v)--- P'|-> return(V), P|-> z1.return(z1) ----------------
   (1-v) |do(return(V),x.P[x])| => P[V]
   (r3-v) do(P',x'.return(x')) => P'
                        do(return(V),x.return(x))
                  return(V) <-(1-v)-∧-(r3-v)-> return(V)
                  ---> return(V) =OK= return(V) <---

2: Overlap (r4-v)-(1-v)--- P1|-> return(V'), P'|-> z1.P2[z1] -------------------
   (r4-v) do(|do(P1,x.P2[x])|,x.P3[x]) => do(P1,x1.do(P2[x1],x2.P3[x2]))
   (1-v) do(return(V'),x'.P'[x']) => P'[V']
                        do(do(return(V'),x.P2[x]),x.P3[x])
do(return(V'),x17.do(P2[x17],x27.P3[x27])) <-(r4-v)-∧-(1-v)-> do(P2[V'],x.P3[x])
        ---> do(P2[V'],x27.P3[x27]) =OK= do(P2[V'],x.P3[x]) <---

3: Overlap (2-1-v)-(r3-v)--- P'|-> op1(V,y.P1[y]), P2|-> z1.return(z1) --------
   (2-1-v) |do(op1(V,y.P1[y]),x.P2[x])| => op1(V,y.do(P1[y],x.P2[x]))
   (r3-v) do(P',x'.return(x')) => P'
                        do(op1(V,y.P1[y]),x.return(x))
op1(V,y14.do(P1[y14],x14.return(x14))) <-(2-1-v)-∧-(r3-v)-> op1(V,y.P1[y])
---> op1(V,y14.do(P1[y14],x14.return(x14))) =OK= op1(V,y.P1[y]) <---

4: Overlap (r4-v)-(2-1-v)--- P1|-> op1(V',y'.P1'[y']), P2'|-> z1.P2[z1] -------
   (r4-v) do(|do(P1,x.P2[x])|,x.P3[x]) => do(P1,x1.do(P2[x1],x2.P3[x2]))
   (2-1-v) do(op1(V',y'.P1'[y']),x'.P2'[x']) => op1(V',y'.do(P1'[y'],x'.P2'[x']))
                  do(do(op1(V',y'.P1'[y']),x.P2[x]),x.P3[x])
do(op1(V',y'.P1'[y']),x121.do(P2[x121],x1.P3[x1])) <-(r4-v)-∧-(2-1-v)->
do(op1(V',yd.do(P1'[yd],xd.P2[xd])),x.P3[x])
---> op1(V',y23.do(P1'[y23],x23.do(P2[x23],x1.P3[x1]))) =OK=
op1(V',y26.do(do(P1'[y26],xd.P2[xd]),x26.P3[x26])) <---

5: Overlap (2-2-v)-(r3-v)--- P'|-> op2(V,y.P1[y]), P2|-> z1.return(z1) --------
   (2-2-v) |do(op2(V,y.P1[y]),x.P2[x])| => op2(V,y.do(P1[y],x.P2[x]))
   (r3-v) do(P',x'.return(x')) => P'
                        do(op2(V,y.P1[y]),x.return(x))
op2(V,y33.do(P1[y33],x33.return(x33))) <-(2-2-v)-∧-(r3-v)-> op2(V,y.P1[y])
---> op2(V,y33.do(P1[y33],x33.return(x33))) =OK= op2(V,y.P1[y]) <---

6: Overlap (r4-v)-(2-2-v)--- P1|-> op2(V',y'.P1'[y']), P2'|-> z1.P2[z1] -------
   (r4-v) do(|do(P1,x.P2[x])|,x.P3[x]) => do(P1,x1.do(P2[x1],x2.P3[x2]))
   (2-2-v) do(op2(V',y'.P1'[y']),x'.P2'[x']) => op2(V',y'.do(P1'[y'],x'.P2'[x']))
```

```
                do(do(op2(V',y'.P1'[y']),x.P2[x]),x.P3[x])
do(op2(V',y'.P1'[y']),x140.do(P2[x140],x240.P3[x240))) <-(r4-v)-∧-(2-2-v)->
do(op2(V',yd.do(P1'[yd],xd.P2[xd])),x.P3[x])
---> op2(V',y42.do(P1'[y42],x42.do(P2[x42],x240.P3[x240]))) =OK=
op2(V',y45.do(do(P1'[y45],xd.P2[xd]),x45.P3[x45])) <---


7: Overlap (5-v)-(r9-v)--- P|-> z1.app(V',z1) ---------------------------------
   (5-v) |fun(x.P[x])|@V => P[V]
   (r9-v) fun(x'.app(V',x')) => V'
                          app(fun(x.app(V',x)),V)
              app(V',V) <-(5-v)-∧-(r9-v)-> app(V',V)
                 ---> app(V',V) =OK= app(V',V) <---


8: Overlap (9-v)-(r13-v)--- P'|-> z1.P[z1], Pd'|-> return(V) ------------------
   (9-v) |with(handler0(x.P[x]),return(V))| => P[V]
   (r13-v) with(handler0(x'.P'[x']),Pd') => do(Pd',x'.P'[x'])
              with(handler0(x.P[x]),return(V))
                 P[V] <-(9-v)-∧-(r13-v)-> do(return(V),xd66.P[xd66])
                 ---> P[V] =OK= P[V] <---


9: Overlap (10-1-v)-(r13-v)--- P'|-> z1.P[z1], Pd'|-> op1(V,y.Pd[y]) ----------
   (10-1-v) |with(handler0(x.P[x]),op1(V,y.Pd[y]))| => op1(V,y.with(handler0(x.P[x]),Pd[y]))
   (r13-v) with(handler0(x'.P'[x']),Pd') => do(Pd',x'.P'[x'])
              with(handler0(x.P[x]),op1(V,y.Pd[y]))
op1(V,y72.with(handler0(x72.P[x72]),Pd[y72])) <-(10-1-v)-∧-(r13-v)->
do(op1(V,y.Pd[y]),xd73.P[xd73])
---> op1(V,y72.with(handler0(x72.P[x72]),Pd[y72])) =OK=
op1(V,y76.do(Pd[y76],x76.P[x76])) <---


10: Overlap (10-2-v)-(r13-v)--- P'|-> z1.P[z1], Pd'|-> op2(V,y.Pd[y]) ----------
   (10-2-v) |with(handler0(x.P[x]),op2(V,y.Pd[y]))| => op2(V,y.with(handler0(x.P[x]),Pd[y]))
   (r13-v) with(handler0(x'.P'[x']),Pd') => do(Pd',x'.P'[x'])
              with(handler0(x.P[x]),op2(V,y.Pd[y]))
op2(V,y86.with(handler0(x86.P[x86]),Pd[y86])) <-(10-2-v)-∧-(r13-v)->
do(op2(V,y.Pd[y]),xd87.P[xd87])
---> op2(V,y86.with(handler0(x86.P[x86]),Pd[y86])) =OK=
op2(V,y90.do(Pd[y90],x90.P[x90])) <---

#Joinable! (Total 10 CPs)
YES
```

In the proof of Proposition 36, op_1 and op_2 were summed in op_i, so the number of critical pairs in the proof matches this output.

References

1. Abramsky, S.: The Lazy Lambda-Calculus, pp. 65–117. Addison Wesley (1990)
2. Abramsky, S.: Algorithmic game semantics: a tutorial introduction. In: NATO Advanced Study Institute 2001, pp. 21–47 (2001)
3. Aoto, T., Toyama, Y.: A reduction-preserving completion for proving confluence of non-terminating term rewriting systems. Log. Methods Comput. Sci. 8(1) (2012). https://doi.org/10.2168/LMCS-8(1:31)2012
4. Biernacki, D., Lenglet, S., Polesiuk, P.: A complete normal-form bisimilarity for algebraic effects and handlers. In: Ariola, Z.M. (ed.) 5th International Conference on Formal Structures for Computation and Deduction, FSCD 2020, Paris, France, 29 June–6 July 2020 (Virtual Conference). LIPIcs, vol. 167, pp. 7:1–7:22. Schloss Dagstuhl - Leibniz-Zentrum für Informatik (2020). https://doi.org/10.4230/LIPICS.FSCD.2020.7
5. Biernacki, D., Piróg, M., Polesiuk, P., Sieczkowski, F.: Handle with care: relational interpretation of algebraic effects and handlers. Proc. ACM Program. Lang. 2(POPL), 8:1–8:30 (2018).https://doi.org/10.1145/3158096

6. Faggian, C., Guerrieri, G., de'Liguoro, U., Treglia, R.: On reduction and normalization in the computational core. Math. Struct. Comput. Sci. **32**(7), 934–981 (2022). https://doi.org/10.1017/S0960129522000433

7. Faggian, C., Guerrieri, G., Treglia, R.: Evaluation in the computational calculus is non-confluent. In: 10th International Workshop of Confluence, IWC 2021, pp. 31–36 (2021). http://www.lix.polytechnique.fr/iwc2021/papers/IWC_2021_paper_6.pdf

8. Felleisen, M.: lambda-V-CS: an extended lambda-calculus for scheme. In: Chailloux, J. (ed.) Proceedings of the 1988 ACM Conference on LISP and Functional Programming, LFP 1988, Snowbird, Utah, USA, 25–27 July 1988, pp. 72–85. ACM (1988). https://doi.org/10.1145/62678.62686

9. Felleisen, M.: The theory and practice of first-class prompts. In: Ferrante, J., Mager, P. (eds.) Conference Record of the Fifteenth Annual ACM Symposium on Principles of Programming Languages, San Diego, California, USA, 10–13 January 1988, pp. 180–190. ACM Press (1988). https://doi.org/10.1145/73560.73576

10. Fiore, M.: Second-order and dependently-sorted abstract syntax. In: Proceedings of LICS 2008, pp. 57–68 (2008)

11. Fiore, M., Mahmoud, O.: Second-order algebraic theories. In: Hliněný, P., Kučera, A. (eds.) MFCS 2010. LNCS, vol. 6281, pp. 368–380. Springer, Heidelberg (2010). https://doi.org/10.1007/978-3-642-15155-2_33

12. Hamana, M.: Free Σ-monoids: a higher-order syntax with metavariables. In: Chin, W.-N. (ed.) APLAS 2004. LNCS, vol. 3302, pp. 348–363. Springer, Heidelberg (2004). https://doi.org/10.1007/978-3-540-30477-7_23

13. Hamana, M.: How to prove decidability of equational theories with second-order computation analyser SOL. J. Funct. Program. **29**, e20 (2019). https://doi.org/10.1017/S0956796819000157

14. Hamana, M., Abe, T., Kikuchi, K.: Polymorphic computation systems: theory and practice of confluence with call-by-value. Sci. Comput. Program. **187**, 102322 (2020). https://doi.org/10.1016/J.SCICO.2019.102322

15. Huet, G.P.: Confluent reductions: Abstract properties and applications to term rewriting systems: abstract properties and applications to term rewriting systems. J. ACM **27**(4), 797–821 (1980). https://doi.org/10.1145/322217.322230

16. Huet, G.P., Lévy, J.: Computations in orthogonal rewriting systems. In: Lassez, J., Plotkin, G.D. (eds.) Computational Logic - Essays in Honor of Alan Robinson, pp. 395–443. The MIT Press (1991)

17. Jaber, G.: SyTeCi: automating contextual equivalence for higher-order programs with references. Proc. ACM Program. Lang. **4**(POPL), 59:1–59:28 (2020). https://doi.org/10.1145/3371127

18. Koutavas, V., Levy, P., Sumii, E.: From applicative to environmental bisimulation. Elect. Notes in Theor. Comput. Sci. **276**, 215–235 (2011). https://doi.org/10.1016/j.entcs.2011.09.023

19. Dal Lago, U., Gavazzo, F.: Effectful normal form bisimulation. In: Caires, L. (ed.) ESOP 2019. LNCS, vol. 11423, pp. 263–292. Springer, Cham (2019). https://doi.org/10.1007/978-3-030-17184-1_10

20. Lucas, S.: Context-sensitive rewriting. ACM Comput. Surv. **53**(4), 78:1–78:36 (2021). https://doi.org/10.1145/3397677

21. Miller, D.: A logic programming language with lambda-abstraction, function variables, and simple unification. J. Log. Comput. **1**(4), 497–536 (1991). https://doi.org/10.1093/logcom/1.4.497

22. Morris, J.H., Jr.: Lambda-calculus models of programming languages. Ph.D. thesis, Massachusetts Institute of Technology (1969)

23. Muroya, K.: Hypernet semantics of programming languages. Ph.D. thesis, University of Birmingham (2020). https://etheses.bham.ac.uk/id/eprint/10433/

24. Plotkin, G.D.: Lambda-definability and logical relations (1973). Memorandum SAI-RM-4

25. Pretnar, M.: An introduction to algebraic effects and handlers. Invited tutorial paper. In: Ghica, D.R. (ed.) The 31st Conference on the Mathematical Foundations of Programming Semantics, MFPS 2015, Nijmegen, The Netherlands, 22–25 June 2015. Electronic Notes in Theoretical Computer Science, vol. 319, pp. 19–35. Elsevier (2015). https://doi.org/10.1016/J.ENTCS.2015.12.003

26. Sabry, A., Wadler, P.: A reflection on call-by-value. In: Harper, R., Wexelblat, R.L. (eds.) Proceedings of the 1996 ACM SIGPLAN International Conference on Functional Programming, ICFP 1996, Philadelphia, Pennsylvania, USA, 24–26 May 1996, pp. 13–24. ACM (1996). https://doi.org/10.1145/232627.232631

27. Sands, D.: Total correctness by local improvement in the transformation of functional programs. ACM Trans. Program. Lang. Syst. 18(2), 175–234 (1996). https://doi.org/10.1145/227699.227716

28. Statman, R.: Logical relations and the typed lambda-calculus. Inf. Control 65(2/3), 85–97 (1985). https://doi.org/10.1016/S0019-9958(85)80001-2

29. Sumii, E.: A bisimulation-like proof method for contextual properties in untyped lambda-calculus with references and deallocation. Theor. Comput. Sci. 411(51-52), 4358–4378 (2010). https://doi.org/10.1016/J.TCS.2010.09.009

30. Toyama, Y.: Commutativity of Term Rewriting Systems, pp. 393–407. North-Holland (1988)

A Complete Dependency Pair Framework for Almost-Sure Innermost Termination of Probabilistic Term Rewriting

Jan-Christoph Kassing(✉)[iD], Stefan Dollase[iD], and Jürgen Giesl(✉)[iD]

LuFG Informatik 2, RWTH Aachen University, Aachen, Germany
kassing@cs.rwth-aachen.de, giesl@informatik.rwth-aachen.de

Abstract. Recently, we adapted the well-known dependency pair (DP) framework to a *dependency tuple* framework in order to prove almost-sure innermost termination (iAST) of probabilistic term rewrite systems. While this approach was *incomplete*, in this paper, we improve it into a *complete* criterion for iAST by presenting a new, more elegant definition of DPs for probabilistic term rewriting. Based on this, we extend the probabilistic DP framework by new *transformations*. Our implementation in the tool AProVE shows that they increase its power considerably.

1 Introduction

Termination of term rewrite systems (TRSs) has been studied for decades and TRSs are used for automated termination analysis of many programming languages. One of the most powerful techniques integrated in essentially all current termination tools for TRSs is the *dependency pair* (DP) framework [2,15, 16,21] which allows modular proofs that apply different techniques in different sub-proofs.

In [8,9], term rewriting was extended to the probabilistic setting. Probabilistic programs describe randomized algorithms and probability distributions, with applications in many areas. In the probabilistic setting, there are several notions of "termination". A program is *almost-surely terminating* (AST) if the probability of termination is 1. A strictly stronger notion is *positive AST* (PAST), which requires that the expected runtime is finite. While numerous techniques exist to prove (P)AST of imperative programs on numbers (e.g., [1,4,10,14,19,22–24,30–33]), there are only few automatic approaches for programs with complex non-tail recursive structure [7,11,12]. The approaches that are also suitable for algorithms on recursive data structures [6,29,35] are mostly specialized for specific data structures and cannot easily be adjusted to other (possibly user-defined) ones, or are not yet fully automated. In contrast, our goal is a fully automatic termination analysis for (arbitrary) probabilistic TRSs (PTRSs).

Funded by the Deutsche Forschungsgemeinschaft (DFG, German Research Foundation) - 235950644 (Project GI 274/6-2) and DFG Research Training Group 2236 UnRAVeL.

J. Gibbons and D. Miller (Eds.): FLOPS 2024, LNCS 14659, pp. 62–80, 2024.
https://doi.org/10.1007/978-981-97-2300-3_4

Up to now, only two approaches for automatic termination analysis of PTRSs were developed [3,25]. In [3], orderings based on interpretations were adapted to prove PAST. However, already for non-probabilistic TRSs such a direct application of orderings is limited in power. To obtain a powerful approach, one should combine such orderings in a modular way, as in the DP framework.

Indeed, in [25], we adapted the DP framework to the probabilistic setting in order to prove innermost AST (iAST), i.e., AST for rewrite sequences which follow the innermost evaluation strategy. However, in contrast to the DP framework for ordinary TRSs, the probabilistic *dependency tuple* (DT) framework in [25] is *incomplete*, i.e., there are PTRSs which are iAST but where this cannot be proved with DTs. In this paper, we introduce a new concept of probabilistic DPs and a corresponding new rewrite relation. In this way, we obtain a novel *complete* criterion for iAST via DPs while maintaining soundness for all processors that were developed in the probabilistic DT framework of [25]. Moreover, our improvement allows us to introduce additional more powerful "transformational" probabilistic DP processors which were not possible in the framework of [25].

We recapitulate the DP framework for non-probabilistic TRSs in Sect. 2. Then, we present our novel ADPs (*annotated dependency pairs*) for probabilistic TRSs in Sect. 3. In Sect. 4, we show how to adapt the processors from the framework of [25] to our probabilistic ADP framework. In addition, our framework allows for the definition of new processors which *transform* ADPs. As an example, in Sect. 5 we adapt the *rewriting processor* to the probabilistic setting, which benefits from our new, more precise rewrite relation. The implementation of our approach in the tool AProVE is evaluated in Sect. 6. We refer to [26] for all proofs.

2 The DP Framework

We assume familiarity with term rewriting [5] and recapitulate the DP framework with its core processors (see e.g., [2,15,16,21] for details). We regard finite TRSs $\mathcal{R}$ over a finite signature Σ and let $\mathcal{T}(\Sigma, \mathcal{V})$ denote the set of terms over Σ and a set of variables $\mathcal{V}$. We decompose $\Sigma = \mathcal{D} \uplus \mathcal{C}$ such that $f \in \mathcal{D}$ if $f = \text{root}(\ell)$ for some $\ell \to r \in \mathcal{R}$. The symbols in $\mathcal{D}$ are called *defined symbols*. For every $f \in \mathcal{D}$, we introduce a fresh *annotated symbol* $f^{\#}$ of the same arity.[1] Let $\mathcal{D}^{\#}$ be the set of all annotated symbols and $\Sigma^{\#} = \mathcal{D}^{\#} \uplus \Sigma$. For any $t = f(t_1, \ldots, t_n) \in \mathcal{T}(\Sigma, \mathcal{V})$ with $f \in \mathcal{D}$, let $t^{\#} = f^{\#}(t_1, \ldots, t_n)$. For every rule $\ell \to r$ and every (not necessarily proper) subterm t of r with defined root symbol, one obtains a *dependency pair* (DP) $\ell^{\#} \to t^{\#}$. $\mathcal{DP}(\mathcal{R})$ denotes the set of all dependency pairs of $\mathcal{R}$. As an example, consider $\mathcal{R}_{\text{ex}} = \{(1), (2)\}$ with its dependency pairs $\mathcal{DP}(\mathcal{R}_{\text{ex}}) = \{(3), (4)\}$. To ease readability, we often write F instead of $f^{\#}$, etc.

$$f(s(x)) \to c(f(g(x))) \quad (1) \qquad F(s(x)) \to F(g(x)) \quad (3)$$

$$g(x) \to s(x) \quad (2) \qquad F(s(x)) \to G(x) \quad (4)$$

---

[1] The symbols $f^{\#}$ were called *tuple symbols* in the original DP framework [16] and also in [25], as they represent the tuple of arguments of the original defined symbol f.

The DP framework uses *DP problems* $(\mathcal{P}, \mathcal{R})$ where $\mathcal{P}$ is a (finite) set of DPs and $\mathcal{R}$ is a TRS. A (possibly infinite) sequence $t_0, t_1, t_2, \ldots$ with $t_i \xrightarrow{i}_{\mathcal{P},\mathcal{R}} \circ \xrightarrow{*}_{\mathcal{R}} t_{i+1}$ for all i is an (innermost) $(\mathcal{P}, \mathcal{R})$-*chain* which represents subsequent "function calls" in evaluations. Here, "$\circ$" denotes composition and steps with $\xrightarrow{i}_{\mathcal{P},\mathcal{R}}$ are called **p**-*steps*, where $\xrightarrow{i}_{\mathcal{P},\mathcal{R}}$ is the restriction of $\rightarrow_{\mathcal{P}}$ to rewrite steps where the used redex is in $\mathrm{NF}_{\mathcal{R}}$ (the set of normal forms w.r.t. $\mathcal{R}$). Steps with $\xrightarrow{i}{}^{*}_{\mathcal{R}}$ are called **r**-*steps* and are used to evaluate the arguments of an annotated function symbol. So an infinite chain consists of an infinite number of **p**-steps with a finite number of **r**-steps between consecutive **p**-steps. For example, $\mathsf{F}(\mathsf{s}(x)), \mathsf{F}(\mathsf{s}(x)), \ldots$ is an infinite $(\mathcal{DP}(\mathcal{R}_{\mathsf{ex}}), \mathcal{R}_{\mathsf{ex}})$-chain, as $\mathsf{F}(\mathsf{s}(x)) \xrightarrow{i}_{\mathcal{DP}(\mathcal{R}_{\mathsf{ex}}), \mathcal{R}_{\mathsf{ex}}} \mathsf{F}(\mathsf{g}(x)) \xrightarrow{i}{}^{*}_{\mathcal{R}_{\mathsf{ex}}} \mathsf{F}(\mathsf{s}(x))$. Throughout the paper, we restrict ourselves to innermost rewriting ("$\xrightarrow{i}_{\mathcal{R}}$"), because our adaption of DPs to the probabilistic setting relies on this evaluation strategy.[2]

A DP problem $(\mathcal{P}, \mathcal{R})$ is called *innermost terminating* (iTerm) if there is no infinite innermost $(\mathcal{P}, \mathcal{R})$-chain. The main result on DPs is the *chain criterion* which states that there is no infinite sequence $t_1 \xrightarrow{i}_{\mathcal{R}} t_2 \xrightarrow{i}_{\mathcal{R}} \ldots$, i.e., $\mathcal{R}$ is iTerm, iff $(\mathcal{DP}(\mathcal{R}), \mathcal{R})$ is iTerm. The DP framework is a *divide-and-conquer* approach, which applies *DP processors* to transform DP problems into simpler sub-problems. A *DP processor* Proc has the form $\mathrm{Proc}(\mathcal{P}, \mathcal{R}) = \{(\mathcal{P}_1, \mathcal{R}_1), \ldots, (\mathcal{P}_n, \mathcal{R}_n)\}$, where $\mathcal{P}, \mathcal{P}_1, \ldots, \mathcal{P}_n$ are sets of DPs and $\mathcal{R}, \mathcal{R}_1, \ldots, \mathcal{R}_n$ are TRSs. A processor Proc is *sound* if $(\mathcal{P}, \mathcal{R})$ is iTerm whenever $(\mathcal{P}_i, \mathcal{R}_i)$ is iTerm for all $1 \leq i \leq n$. It is *complete* if $(\mathcal{P}_i, \mathcal{R}_i)$ is iTerm for all $1 \leq i \leq n$ whenever $(\mathcal{P}, \mathcal{R})$ is iTerm.

So given a TRS $\mathcal{R}$, one starts with the initial DP problem $(\mathcal{DP}(\mathcal{R}), \mathcal{R})$ and applies sound (and preferably complete) DP processors repeatedly until all sub-problems are "solved" (i.e., sound processors transform them to the empty set). This yields a modular framework for termination proofs, as different techniques can be used for different sub-problems $(\mathcal{P}_i, \mathcal{R}_i)$. The following three theorems recapitulate the three most important processors of the DP framework.

The (innermost) $(\mathcal{P}, \mathcal{R})$-*dependency graph* is a control flow graph that indicates which DPs can be used after each other in a chain. Its set of nodes is $\mathcal{P}$ and there is an edge from $\ell_1^{\#} \rightarrow t_1^{\#}$ to $\ell_2^{\#} \rightarrow t_2^{\#}$ if there exist substitutions σ_1, σ_2 such that $t_1^{\#}\sigma_1 \xrightarrow{i}{}^{*}_{\mathcal{R}} \ell_2^{\#}\sigma_2$ and $\ell_1^{\#}\sigma_1, \ell_2^{\#}\sigma_2 \in \mathrm{NF}_{\mathcal{R}}$. Any infinite $(\mathcal{P}, \mathcal{R})$-chain corresponds to an infinite path in the dependency graph, and since the graph is finite, this infinite path must end in some strongly connected component (SCC).[3] Hence, it suffices to consider the SCCs of this graph independently.

---

[2] Moreover, already in the non-probabilistic setting, the restriction to innermost rewriting makes termination analysis with DPs substantially more powerful, e.g., by allowing the application of additional techniques like *usable rules* and *rewriting* of DPs [15,16]. Indeed, we also adapt these techniques in our novel ADP framework for probabilistic rewriting. Nevertheless, we conjecture that ADPs are also suitable for an adaption to analyze full instead of innermost AST, and we will investigate that in future work.

[3] Here, a set $\mathcal{P}'$ of DPs is an *SCC* if it is a maximal cycle, i.e., it is a maximal set such that for any $\ell_1^{\#} \rightarrow t_1^{\#}$ and $\ell_2^{\#} \rightarrow t_2^{\#}$ in $\mathcal{P}'$ there is a non-empty path from $\ell_1^{\#} \rightarrow t_1^{\#}$ to $\ell_2^{\#} \rightarrow t_2^{\#}$ which only traverses nodes from $\mathcal{P}'$.

Theorem 1 (Dep. Graph Processor). *For the SCCs $\mathcal{P}_1, ..., \mathcal{P}_n$ of the $(\mathcal{P}, \mathcal{R})$-dependency graph, $\mathrm{Proc_{DG}}(\mathcal{P}, \mathcal{R}) = \{(\mathcal{P}_1, \mathcal{R}), ..., (\mathcal{P}_n, \mathcal{R})\}$ is sound and complete.*

Example 2 (Dependency Graph). Consider the TRS $\mathcal{R}_{\mathrm{ffg}} = \{(5)\}$ with $\mathcal{DP}(\mathcal{R}_{\mathrm{ffg}}) = \{(6), (7), (8)\}$. The $(\mathcal{DP}(\mathcal{R}_{\mathrm{ffg}}), \mathcal{R}_{\mathrm{ffg}})$-dependency graph is on the right.

$$\mathsf{F}(\mathsf{f}(\mathsf{g}(x))) \to \mathsf{F}(\mathsf{g}(\mathsf{f}(\mathsf{g}(\mathsf{f}(x))))) \quad (6)$$

$$\mathsf{f}(\mathsf{f}(\mathsf{g}(x))) \to \mathsf{f}(\mathsf{g}(\mathsf{f}(\mathsf{g}(\mathsf{f}(x))))) \quad (5) \qquad \mathsf{F}(\mathsf{f}(\mathsf{g}(x))) \to \mathsf{F}(\mathsf{g}(\mathsf{f}(x))) \quad (7)$$

$$\mathsf{F}(\mathsf{f}(\mathsf{g}(x))) \to \mathsf{F}(x) \quad (8)$$

While the exact dependency graph is not computable in general, there exist several techniques to over-approximate it automatically, see, e.g., [2,16,21]. In our example, $\mathrm{Proc_{DG}}(\mathcal{DP}(\mathcal{R}_{\mathrm{ffg}}), \mathcal{R}_{\mathrm{ffg}})$ yields the DP problem $(\{(8)\}, \mathcal{R}_{\mathrm{ffg}})$.

The next processor removes rules that cannot be used for right-hand sides of dependency pairs when their variables are instantiated with normal forms.

Theorem 3 (Usable Rules Processor). *Let $\mathcal{R}$ be a TRS. For any $f \in \Sigma^\#$ let $\mathrm{Rules}_{\mathcal{R}}(f) = \{\ell \to r \in \mathcal{R} \mid \mathrm{root}(\ell) = f\}$. For any $t \in \mathcal{T}(\Sigma^\#, \mathcal{V})$, its usable rules $\mathcal{U}_{\mathcal{R}}(t)$ are the smallest set such that $\mathcal{U}_{\mathcal{R}}(x) = \varnothing$ for all $x \in \mathcal{V}$ and $\mathcal{U}_{\mathcal{R}}(f(t_1, ..., t_n)) = \mathrm{Rules}_{\mathcal{R}}(f) \cup \bigcup_{i=1}^n \mathcal{U}_{\mathcal{R}}(t_i) \cup \bigcup_{\ell \to r \in \mathrm{Rules}_{\mathcal{R}}(f)} \mathcal{U}_{\mathcal{R}}(r)$. The usable rules for the DP problem $(\mathcal{P}, \mathcal{R})$ are $\mathcal{U}(\mathcal{P}, \mathcal{R}) = \bigcup_{\ell^\# \to t^\# \in \mathcal{P}} \mathcal{U}_{\mathcal{R}}(t^\#)$. Then $\mathrm{Proc_{UR}}(\mathcal{P}, \mathcal{R}) = \{(\mathcal{P}, \mathcal{U}(\mathcal{P}, \mathcal{R}))\}$ is sound but not complete.*[4]

$\mathrm{Proc_{UR}}(\{(8)\}, \mathcal{R}_{\mathrm{ffg}})$ yields the problem $(\{(8)\}, \varnothing)$, i.e., it removes all rules, because the right-hand side of (8) does not contain the defined symbol f.

A *polynomial interpretation* Pol is a Σ-algebra which maps every function symbol $f \in \Sigma$ to a polynomial $f_{\mathrm{Pol}} \in \mathbb{N}[\mathcal{V}]$ over the variables $\mathcal{V}$ with coefficients from $\mathbb{N}$, see [28]. $\mathrm{Pol}(t)$ denotes the *interpretation* of a term t by the Σ-algebra Pol. An arithmetic inequation like $\mathrm{Pol}(t_1) > \mathrm{Pol}(t_2)$ *holds* if it is true for all instantiations of its variables by natural numbers. The reduction pair processor[5] allows us to use *weakly monotonic* polynomial interpretations that do not have to depend on all of their arguments, i.e., $x \geq y$ implies $f_{\mathrm{Pol}}(..., x, ...) \geq f_{\mathrm{Pol}}(..., y, ...)$ for all $f \in \Sigma^\#$. The processor requires that all rules and DPs are weakly decreasing and it removes those DPs that are strictly decreasing.

Theorem 4 (Reduction Pair Processor). *Let $\mathrm{Pol} : \mathcal{T}(\Sigma^\#, \mathcal{V}) \to \mathbb{N}[\mathcal{V}]$ be a weakly monotonic polynomial interpretation. Let $\mathcal{P} = \mathcal{P}_\geq \uplus \mathcal{P}_>$ with $\mathcal{P}_> \neq \varnothing$ such that:*

---

[4] See [15] for a complete version of this processor. It extends DP problems by an additional set to store the left-hand sides of all rules (including the non-usable ones) to determine whether a rewrite step is innermost. We omit this here for readability.

[5] In this paper, we only regard the reduction pair processor with polynomial interpretations, because for most other classical orderings it is not clear how to extend them to probabilistic TRSs, where one has to consider "expected values of terms".

(1) For every $\ell \to r \in \mathcal{R}$, we have $\mathrm{Pol}(\ell) \geq \mathrm{Pol}(r)$.
(2) For every $\ell^\# \to t^\# \in \mathcal{P}$, we have $\mathrm{Pol}(\ell^\#) \geq \mathrm{Pol}(t^\#)$.
(3) For every $\ell^\# \to t^\# \in \mathcal{P}_>$, we have $\mathrm{Pol}(\ell^\#) > \mathrm{Pol}(t^\#)$.

Then $\mathrm{Proc}_{\mathrm{RP}}(\mathcal{P}, \mathcal{R}) = \{(\mathcal{P}_\geq, \mathcal{R})\}$ is sound and complete.

For $(\{(8)\}, \varnothing)$, one can use the reduction pair processor with the polynomial interpretation that maps $f(x)$ to $x + 1$ and both $F(x)$ and $g(x)$ to x. Then, $\mathrm{Proc}_{\mathrm{RP}}(\{(8)\}, \varnothing) = \{(\varnothing, \varnothing)\}$. As $\mathrm{Proc}_{\mathrm{DG}}(\varnothing, \ldots) = \varnothing$ and all processors used are sound, this means that there is no infinite innermost chain for the initial DP problem $(\mathcal{DP}(\mathcal{R}_{\mathrm{ffg}}), \mathcal{R}_{\mathrm{ffg}})$ and thus, $\mathcal{R}_{\mathrm{ffg}}$ is innermost terminating.

3 Probabilistic Annotated Dependency Pairs

In this section we present our novel adaption of DPs to the probabilistic setting. As in [3,9,13,25], the rules of a probabilistic TRS have finite multi-distributions on the right-hand sides. A finite *multi-distribution* μ on a set $A \neq \varnothing$ is a finite multiset of pairs $(p : a)$, where $0 < p \leq 1$ is a probability and $a \in A$, with $\sum_{(p:a) \in \mu} p = 1$. $\mathrm{FDist}(A)$ is the set of all finite multi-distributions on A. For $\mu \in \mathrm{FDist}(A)$, its *support* is the multiset $\mathrm{Supp}(\mu) = \{a \mid (p:a) \in \mu \text{ for some } p\}$.

A pair $\ell \to \mu \in \mathcal{T}(\Sigma, \mathcal{V}) \times \mathrm{FDist}(\mathcal{T}(\Sigma, \mathcal{V}))$ such that $\ell \notin \mathcal{V}$ and $\mathcal{V}(r) \subseteq \mathcal{V}(\ell)$ for every $r \in \mathrm{Supp}(\mu)$ is a *probabilistic rewrite rule*. A *probabilistic TRS* (PTRS) is a finite set of probabilistic rewrite rules. As an example, consider the PTRS $\mathcal{R}_{\mathrm{rw}}$ with the rule $g(x) \to \{1/2 : g(g(x)), \; 1/2 : x\}$, which corresponds to a symmetric random walk. Let $g^2(x)$ abbreviate $g(g(x))$, etc.

A PTRS $\mathcal{R}$ induces a *rewrite relation* $\to_{\mathcal{R}} \subseteq \mathcal{T}(\Sigma, \mathcal{V}) \times \mathrm{FDist}(\mathcal{T}(\Sigma, \mathcal{V}))$ where $s \to_{\mathcal{R}} \{p_1 : t_1, \ldots, p_k : t_k\}$ if there is a position π of s, a rule $\ell \to \{p_1 : r_1, \ldots, p_k : r_k\} \in \mathcal{R}$, and a substitution σ such that $s|_\pi = \ell\sigma$ and $t_j = s[r_j\sigma]_\pi$ for all $1 \leq j \leq k$. We call $s \to_{\mathcal{R}} \mu$ an *innermost* rewrite step (denoted $s \xrightarrow{i}_{\mathcal{R}} \mu$) if $\ell\sigma \in \mathrm{ANF}_{\mathcal{R}}$, where $\mathrm{ANF}_{\mathcal{R}}$ is the set of all *terms in argument normal form w.r.t.* $\mathcal{R}$, i.e., $t \in \mathrm{ANF}_{\mathcal{R}}$ iff $t' \in \mathrm{NF}_{\mathcal{R}}$ for all proper subterms t' of t.

To track all possible rewrite sequences (up to non-determinism) with their probabilities, we *lift* $\xrightarrow{i}_{\mathcal{R}}$ to *(innermost) rewrite sequence trees* (RSTs). An (innermost) $\mathcal{R}$-*RST* is a tree whose nodes v are labeled by pairs (p_v, t_v) of a probability p_v and a term t_v such that the edge relation represents a probabilistic innermost rewrite step. More precisely, $\mathfrak{T} = (V, E, L)$ is an (innermost) $\mathcal{R}$-*RST* if (1) (V, E) is a (possibly infinite) directed tree with nodes $V \neq \varnothing$ and directed edges $E \subseteq V \times V$ where $vE = \{w \mid (v, w) \in E\}$ is finite for every $v \in V$, (2) $L : V \to (0,1] \times \mathcal{T}(\Sigma, \mathcal{V})$ labels every node v by a probability p_v and a term t_v where $p_v = 1$ for the root $v \in V$ of the tree, and (3) for all $v \in V$: if $vE = \{w_1, \ldots, w_k\} \neq \varnothing$, then $t_v \xrightarrow{i}_{\mathcal{R}} \{\frac{p_{w_1}}{p_v} : t_{w_1}, \ldots, \frac{p_{w_k}}{p_v} : t_{w_k}\}$. For any innermost $\mathcal{R}$-RST $\mathfrak{T}$ we define $|\mathfrak{T}|_{\mathrm{Leaf}} = \sum_{v \in \mathrm{Leaf}} p_v$, where Leaf is the set of $\mathfrak{T}$'s leaves. An RST $\mathfrak{T}$ is *innermost almost-surely terminating* (iAST) if $|\mathfrak{T}|_{\mathrm{Leaf}} = 1$. Similarly, a PTRS $\mathcal{R}$ is *iAST* if all innermost $\mathcal{R}$-RSTs are iAST. While $|\mathfrak{T}|_{\mathrm{Leaf}} = 1$ holds for every finite RST $\mathfrak{T}$, for infinite RSTs $\mathfrak{T}$ we may have $|\mathfrak{T}|_{\mathrm{Leaf}} < 1$, and even $|\mathfrak{T}|_{\mathrm{Leaf}} = 0$ if $\mathfrak{T}$ has no leaf at all. This notion is equivalent to the notions of AST in [3,25], where one uses a lifting to multisets instead of trees. For example, the infinite

$\mathcal{R}_{rw}$-RST $\mathfrak{T}$ on the side has $|\mathfrak{T}|_{\text{Leaf}} = 1$. In fact, $\mathcal{R}_{rw}$ is iAST, because $|\mathfrak{T}|_{\text{Leaf}} = 1$ holds for all innermost $\mathcal{R}_{rw}$-RSTs $\mathfrak{T}$.

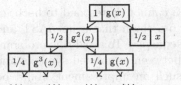

As shown in [25], to adapt the DP framework in order to prove iAST of PTRSs, one has to regard all DPs resulting from the same rule *at once*. Otherwise, one would not be able to distinguish between the DPs of the TRS with the rule $\mathsf{a} \to \{1/2 : \mathsf{b}, 1/2 : \mathsf{c}(\mathsf{a},\mathsf{a})\}$ which is iAST and the rule $\mathsf{a} \to \{1/2 : \mathsf{b}, 1/2 : \mathsf{c}(\mathsf{a},\mathsf{a},\mathsf{a})\}$, which is not iAST. For that reason, in the adaption of the DP framework to PTRSs in [25], one constructs *dependency tuples* (DTs) whose right-hand sides combine the right-hand sides of all dependency pairs resulting from one rule. However, a drawback of this approach is that the resulting chain criterion is not complete, i.e., it allows for chains that do not correspond to any rewrite sequence of the original PTRS $\mathcal{R}$.

Example 5. Consider the PTRS $\mathcal{R}_{\text{incpl}}$ with the rules

$$\mathsf{a} \to \{1 : \mathsf{f}(\mathsf{h}(\mathsf{g}),\mathsf{g})\} \qquad (9) \qquad \mathsf{h}(\mathsf{b}_1) \to \{1 : \mathsf{a}\} \qquad (11)$$

$$\mathsf{g} \to \{1/2 : \mathsf{b}_1, 1/2 : \mathsf{b}_2\} \qquad (10) \qquad \mathsf{f}(x,\mathsf{b}_2) \to \{1 : \mathsf{a}\} \qquad (12)$$

and the $\mathcal{R}_{\text{incpl}}$-RST below. So a can be rewritten to the normal form $\mathsf{f}(\mathsf{h}(\mathsf{b}_2),\mathsf{b}_1)$ with probability $1/4$ and to the terms $\mathsf{f}(\mathsf{a},\mathsf{b}_1)$ and a that contain the redex a with a probability of $1/4 + 1/4 = 1/2$. In the term $\mathsf{f}(\mathsf{a},\mathsf{b}_2)$, one can rewrite the

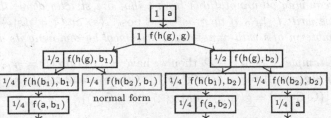

subterm a, and if that ends in a normal form, one can still rewrite the outer f which will yield a again. So to over-approximate the probability of non-termination, one could consider the term $\mathsf{f}(\mathsf{a},\mathsf{b}_2)$ as if one had two occurrences of a. Then this would correspond to a random walk where the number of a symbols is decreased by 1 with probability $1/4$, increased by 1 with probability $1/4$, and kept the same with probability $1/2$. Such a random walk is AST, and since a similar observation holds for all $\mathcal{R}_{\text{incpl}}$-RSTs, $\mathcal{R}_{\text{incpl}}$ is iAST (we will prove iAST of $\mathcal{R}_{\text{incpl}}$ with our new ADP framework in Sect. 4 and 5).

In contrast, the DT framework from [25] fails on this example. As mentioned, the right-hand sides of DTs combine the right-hand sides of all dependency pairs resulting from one rule. So the right-hand side of the DT for (9) contains the term $\mathsf{com}_4(\mathsf{F}(\mathsf{h}(\mathsf{g}),\mathsf{g}),\mathsf{H}(\mathsf{g}),\mathsf{G},\mathsf{G})$, where com_4 is a special compound symbol of arity 4. However, here it is no longer clear which occurrence of the annotated symbol G corresponds to which occurrences of g. Therefore, when rewriting an occurrence of G, in the "chains" of [25] one may also rewrite arbitrary occurrences of g simultaneously. (For that reason, in [25] one also couples the DT together with its original rule.) In particular, [25] also allows a simultaneous rewrite step of all underlined symbols in $\mathsf{com}(\mathsf{F}(\mathsf{h}(\mathsf{g}),\underline{\mathsf{g}}),\mathsf{H}(\underline{\mathsf{g}}),\underline{\mathsf{G}},\mathsf{G})$ even though the underlined

G cannot correspond to both underlined g symbols. As shown in [26], this leads to a chain that is not iAST and that does not correspond to any $\mathcal{R}_{\mathsf{incpl}}$-rewrite sequence. To avoid this problem, one would have to keep track of the connections between annotated symbols and the corresponding original subterms. However, such an improvement would become very complicated in the formalization of [25].

Therefore, in contrast to [25], in our new notion of DPs, we annotate defined symbols directly in the original rewrite rule instead of extracting annotated subterms from its right-hand side. This makes the definition easier, more elegant, and more readable, and allows us to solve the incompleteness problem of [25].

Definition 7 (Annotations). *Let* $t \in \mathcal{T}\left(\Sigma^{\#}, \mathcal{V}\right)$ *be an* annotated *term and for* $\Sigma' \subseteq \Sigma^{\#}$, *let* $\mathrm{pos}_{\Sigma'}(t)$ *be all positions of* t *with symbols from* Σ'. *For a set of positions* $\Phi \subseteq \mathrm{pos}_{\mathcal{D} \cup \mathcal{D}^{\#}}(t)$, *let* $\#_{\Phi}(t)$ *be the variant of* t *where the symbols at positions from* Φ *in* t *are annotated and all other annotations are removed. Thus,* $\mathrm{pos}_{\mathcal{D}^{\#}}(\#_{\Phi}(t)) = \Phi$, *and* $\#_{\varnothing}(t)$ *removes all annotations from* t, *where we often write* $\flat(t)$ *instead of* $\#_{\varnothing}(t)$. *We extend* $\flat$ *to multi-distributions, rules, and sets of rules by removing the annotations of all occurring terms. We write* $\#_{\mathcal{D}}(t)$ *instead of* $\#_{\mathrm{pos}_{\mathcal{D}}(t)}(t)$ *to annotate all defined symbols in* t, *and* $\#_{\varepsilon}(t)$ *instead of* $\#_{\{\varepsilon\}}(t)$ *to annotate just the root symbol of* t. *Moreover, let* $\flat_{\pi}^{\uparrow}(t)$ *result from removing all annotations from* t *that are strictly above the position* π. *Finally, we write* $t \trianglelefteq_{\#} s$ *if there is a* $\pi \in \mathrm{pos}_{\mathcal{D}^{\#}}(s)$ *and* $t = \flat(s|_{\pi})$, *i.e.,* t *results from a subterm of* s *with annotated root symbol by removing its annotation.*

Example 8. So if $g \in \mathcal{D}$, then we have $\#_{\{1\}}(g(g(x))) = \#_{\{1\}}(G(G(x))) = g(G(x))$, $\#_{\mathcal{D}}(g(g(x))) = \#_{\{\varepsilon,1\}}(g(g(x))) = G(G(x))$, and $\flat(G(G(x))) = g(g(x))$. Moreover, $\flat_1^{\uparrow}(G(G(x))) = g(G(x))$ and $g(x) \trianglelefteq_{\#} g(G(x))$.

Next, we define the *canonical annotated dependency pairs* for a given PTRS.

Definition 9 (Canonical Annotated Dependency Pairs). *For a rule* $\ell \to \mu = \{p_1 : r_1, \ldots, p_k : r_k\}$, *its canonical* annotated dependency pair *(ADP) is*

$$\mathcal{DP}(\ell \to \mu) \;=\; \ell \to \{p_1 : \#_{\mathcal{D}}(r_1), \ldots, p_k : \#_{\mathcal{D}}(r_k)\}^{\mathsf{true}}$$

The canonical ADPs of a PTRS $\mathcal{R}$ *are* $\mathcal{DP}(\mathcal{R}) = \{\mathcal{DP}(\ell \to \mu) \mid \ell \to \mu \in \mathcal{R}\}$.

Example 10. For $\mathcal{R}_{\mathsf{rw}}$, the canonical ADP for $g(x) \to \{{}^1\!/{}_2 : g(g(x))), {}^1\!/{}_2 : x\}$ is $g(x) \to \{{}^1\!/{}_2 : G(G(x)), {}^1\!/{}_2 : x\}^{\mathsf{true}}$ instead of the (complicated) DT from [25]:

$$\mathcal{DT}(\mathcal{R}_{\mathsf{rw}}) = \{\langle G(x), g(x)\rangle \to \{{}^1\!/{}_2 : \langle \mathsf{com}_2(G(g(x)), G(x)), g^2(x)\rangle, {}^1\!/{}_2 : \langle \mathsf{com}_0, x\rangle\}\}$$

So the left-hand side of an ADP is just the left-hand side of the original rule. The right-hand side of the ADP results from the right-hand side of the original rule by replacing all $f \in \mathcal{D}$ with $f^{\#}$. Moreover, every ADP has a flag $m \in \{\mathsf{true}, \mathsf{false}\}$ to indicate whether this ADP may be used for an **r**-step at a position below the next **p**-step. (This flag will later be modified by our usable rules processor.) In general, we work with the following rewrite systems in our new framework.

Definition 11 (Annotated Dependency Pairs, $\stackrel{i}{\hookrightarrow}_{\mathcal{P}}$). *An ADP has the form $\ell \to \{p_1 : r_1, \ldots, p_k : r_k\}^m$, where $\ell \in \mathcal{T}(\Sigma, \mathcal{V})$ with $\ell \notin \mathcal{V}$, $m \in \{\mathsf{true}, \mathsf{false}\}$, and for all $1 \le j \le k$ we have $r_j \in \mathcal{T}(\Sigma^\#, \mathcal{V})$ with $\mathcal{V}(r_j) \subseteq \mathcal{V}(\ell)$.*

Let $\mathcal{P}$ be a finite set of ADPs (a so-called ADP problem). An annotated term $s \in \mathcal{T}(\Sigma^\#, \mathcal{V})$ rewrites with $\mathcal{P}$ to $\mu = \{p_1 : t_1, \ldots, p_k : t_k\}$ (denoted $s \stackrel{i}{\hookrightarrow}_{\mathcal{P}} \mu$) if there is a rule $\ell \to \{p_1 : r_1, \ldots, p_k : r_k\}^m \in \mathcal{P}$, a substitution σ, and a position $\pi \in \mathrm{pos}_{\mathcal{D} \cup \mathcal{D}^\#}(s)$ such that $\flat(s|_\pi) = \ell\sigma \in \mathsf{ANF}_{\mathcal{P}}$, and for all $1 \le j \le k$ we have

$$
\begin{aligned}
t_j &= \quad s[r_j\sigma]_\pi & \text{if } \pi \in \mathrm{pos}_{\mathcal{D}^\#}(s) \text{ and } m = \mathsf{true} & \qquad \textbf{(pr)} \\
t_j &= \flat_\pi^\uparrow(\ s[r_j\sigma]_\pi) & \text{if } \pi \in \mathrm{pos}_{\mathcal{D}^\#}(s) \text{ and } m = \mathsf{false} & \qquad \textbf{(p)} \\
t_j &= \quad s[\flat(r_j)\sigma]_\pi & \text{if } \pi \notin \mathrm{pos}_{\mathcal{D}^\#}(s) \text{ and } m = \mathsf{true} & \qquad \textbf{(r)} \\
t_j &= \flat_\pi^\uparrow(\ s[\flat(r_j)\sigma]_\pi) & \text{if } \pi \notin \mathrm{pos}_{\mathcal{D}^\#}(s) \text{ and } m = \mathsf{false} & \qquad \textbf{(irr)}
\end{aligned}
$$

To highlight the position π of the redex, we also write $s \stackrel{i}{\hookrightarrow}_{\mathcal{P}, \pi} t$. Again, $\mathsf{ANF}_{\mathcal{P}}$ is the set of all terms in argument normal form w.r.t. $\mathcal{P}$.

Rewriting with $\mathcal{P}$ can be seen as ordinary term rewriting while considering and modifying annotations. In the ADP framework, we represent all DPs resulting from a rule as well as the original rule by just one ADP. So for example, the ADP $\mathsf{g}(x) \to \{1/2 : \mathsf{G}(\mathsf{G}(x)), 1/2 : x\}^{\mathsf{true}}$ for the rule $\mathsf{g}(x) \to \{1/2 : \mathsf{g}(\mathsf{g}(x)), 1/2 : x\}$ represents both DPs resulting from the two occurrences of g on the right-hand side, and the rule itself (by simply disregarding all annotations of the ADP).

As in the classical DP framework, our goal is to track specific reduction sequences where (1) there are **p**-steps where the root symbol of the redex is annotated and a DP is applied, and (2) between two **p**-steps there can be several **r**-steps where rules are applied below the position of the next **p**-step.

A step of the form **(pr)** in Definition 11 can represent both **p**- and **r**-steps. All annotations are kept during this step except for annotations of the subterms that correspond to variables of the applied rule. These subterms are always in normal form due to the innermost evaluation strategy and we erase their annotations in order to handle rewriting with non-left-linear rules correctly. A **(pr)**-step at position π plays the role of an **r**-step for terms in multi-distributions where one later rewrites an annotated symbol at a position above π, and for all other terms it plays the role of a **p**-step. As an example, for a PTRS $\mathcal{R}_{\mathsf{ex2}}$ with the rules $\mathsf{g}(x, x) \to \{1 : \mathsf{f}(x)\}$ and $\mathsf{f}(\mathsf{a}) \to \{1 : \mathsf{f}(\mathsf{b})\}$, we have the canonical ADPs $\mathsf{g}(x, x) \to \{1 : \mathsf{F}(x)\}^{\mathsf{true}}$ and $\mathsf{f}(\mathsf{a}) \to \{1 : \mathsf{F}(\mathsf{b})\}^{\mathsf{true}}$, and we can rewrite $\mathsf{G}(\mathsf{F}(\mathsf{b}), \mathsf{f}(\mathsf{b})) \stackrel{i}{\hookrightarrow}_{\mathcal{DP}(\mathcal{R}_{\mathsf{ex2}})} \{1 : \mathsf{F}(\mathsf{f}(\mathsf{b}))\}$ using the first ADP. Here, we have $\pi = \varepsilon$, $\flat(s|_\varepsilon) = \mathsf{g}(\mathsf{f}(\mathsf{b}), \mathsf{f}(\mathsf{b})) = \ell\sigma$ where σ instantiates x with the normal form $\mathsf{f}(\mathsf{b})$, and $r_1 = \mathsf{F}(x)$.

A step of the form **(r)** rewrites at the position of a non-annotated defined symbol. So this represents an **r**-step and thus, we remove all annotations from the right-hand side r_j. As an example, we have $\mathsf{G}(\mathsf{F}(\mathsf{b}), \mathsf{f}(\mathsf{a})) \stackrel{i}{\hookrightarrow}_{\mathcal{DP}(\mathcal{R}_{\mathsf{ex2}})} \{1 : \mathsf{G}(\mathsf{F}(\mathsf{b}), \mathsf{f}(\mathsf{b}))\}$ using the ADP $\mathsf{f}(\mathsf{a}) \to \{1 : \mathsf{F}(\mathsf{b})\}^{\mathsf{true}}$.

A step of the form **(p)** represents a **p**-step. Thus, we remove all annotations above the position π, because no **p**-steps are possible above π. So if $\mathcal{P}$ contains $\mathsf{f}(\mathsf{a}) \to \{1 : \mathsf{F}(\mathsf{b})\}^{\mathsf{false}}$, then $\mathsf{G}(\mathsf{F}(\mathsf{b}), \mathsf{F}(\mathsf{a})) \stackrel{i}{\hookrightarrow}_{\mathcal{P}} \{1 : \mathsf{g}(\mathsf{F}(\mathsf{b}), \mathsf{F}(\mathsf{b}))\}$.

Finally, a step of the form (**irr**) is an **r**-step that is irrelevant for proving iAST, because due to $m = \mathsf{false}$, afterwards there cannot be a **p**-step at a position above. For example, if $\mathcal{P}$ again contains $\mathsf{f(a)} \to \{1 : \mathsf{F(b)}\}^{\mathsf{false}}$, then $\mathsf{G(F(b), f(a))} \xhookrightarrow{i}_{\mathcal{P}}$ $\{1 : \mathsf{g(F(b), f(b))}\}$. Such (**irr**)-steps are needed to ensure that all rewrite steps with $\mathcal{R}$ are also possible with the ADP problems $\mathcal{P}$ that result from $\mathcal{DP}(\mathcal{R})$ when applying ADP processors. So for all these ADP problems $\mathcal{P}$, we have $\flat(t) \in \mathsf{ANF}_{\mathcal{R}}$ iff $t \in \mathsf{ANF}_{\mathcal{P}}$ for all $t \in \mathcal{T}\left(\Sigma^{\#}, \mathcal{V}\right)$, i.e., the innermost evaluation strategy is not affected by the application of ADP processors. This is different from the classical DP framework, where the usable rules processor reduces the number of rules. This may result in new redexes that are allowed for innermost rewriting. Thus, the usable rules processor in our new ADP framework is *complete*, whereas in [15], one has to extend DP problems by an additional component to achieve completeness of this processor (see Footnote 4).

Now, $s \xrightarrow{i}_{\mathcal{R}} \{p_1 : t_1, \ldots, p_k : t_k\}$ essentially[6] implies $\#_{\mathcal{D}}(s) \xhookrightarrow{i}_{\mathcal{DP}(\mathcal{R})} \{p_1 : \#_{\mathcal{D}}(t_1), \ldots, p_k : \#_{\mathcal{D}}(t_k)\}$, and we got rid of any ambiguities in the rewrite relation that led to incompleteness in [25]. While our ADPs are much simpler than the DTs of [25], due to their annotations they still contain all information that is needed to define the required DP processors.

Instead of chains of DPs, in the probabilistic setting one works with *chain trees* [25], where **p**- and **r**-steps are indicated by P- and R-nodes in the tree. Chain trees are defined analogously to RSTs, but the crucial requirement is that every infinite path of the tree must contain infinitely many steps of the forms (**pr**) or (**p**). Thus, in our setting $\mathfrak{T} = (V, E, L, P)$ is a $\mathcal{P}$-*chain tree* (CT) if

1. (V, E) is a (possibly infinite) directed tree with nodes $V \neq \varnothing$ and directed edges $E \subseteq V \times V$ where $vE = \{w \mid (v, w) \in E\}$ is finite for every $v \in V$.
2. $L : V \to (0, 1] \times \mathcal{T}\left(\Sigma^{\#}, \mathcal{V}\right)$ labels every node v by a probability p_v and a term t_v. For the root $v \in V$ of the tree, we have $p_v = 1$.
3. $P \subseteq V \setminus \mathsf{Leaf}$ (where Leaf are all leaves) is a subset of the inner nodes to indicate whether we use (**pr**) or (**p**) for the next rewrite step. $R = V \setminus (\mathsf{Leaf} \cup P)$ are all inner nodes that are not in P, i.e., where we rewrite using (**r**) or (**irr**).
4. For all $v \in P$: if $vE = \{w_1, \ldots, w_k\}$, then $t_v \xhookrightarrow{i}_{\mathcal{P}} \{\frac{p_{w_1}}{p_v} : t_{w_1}, \ldots, \frac{p_{w_k}}{p_v} : t_{w_k}\}$ using Case (**pr**) or (**p**).
5. For all $v \in R$: if $vE = \{w_1, \ldots, w_k\}$, then $t_v \xhookrightarrow{i}_{\mathcal{P}} \{\frac{p_{w_1}}{p_v} : t_{w_1}, \ldots, \frac{p_{w_k}}{p_v} : t_{w_k}\}$ using Case (**r**) or (**irr**).
6. Every infinite path in $\mathfrak{T}$ contains infinitely many nodes from P.

Let $|\mathfrak{T}|_{\mathsf{Leaf}} = \sum_{v \in \mathsf{Leaf}} p_v$. We define that $\mathcal{P}$ is iAST if $|\mathfrak{T}|_{\mathsf{Leaf}} = 1$ for all $\mathcal{P}$-CTs $\mathfrak{T}$. So Conditions 1–5 ensure that the chain tree corresponds to an RST and Condition 6 requires that one may only use finitely many **r**-steps before the next

---

[6] We have $\#_{\mathcal{D}}(s) \xhookrightarrow{i}_{\mathcal{DP}(\mathcal{R})} \{p_1 : t'_1, \ldots, p_k : t'_k\}$ where t'_j and $\#_{\mathcal{D}}(t_j)$ are the same up to some annotations of subterms that are $\mathcal{DP}(\mathcal{R})$-normal forms. The reason is that as mentioned above, annotations of the subterms (in normal form) that correspond to variables of the rule are erased. So for example, rewriting $\mathsf{G(F(b), F(b))}$ with $\mathcal{DP}(\mathcal{R}_{\mathsf{ex2}})$ yields $\{1 : \mathsf{F(f(b))}\}$ and not $\{1 : \mathsf{F(F(b))}\}$.

p-step. This yields a chain criterion as in the non-probabilistic setting, where (in contrast to the chain criterion of [25]) we again have "iff" instead of "if".

Theorem 12 (Chain Criterion). $\mathcal{R}$ *is iAST iff* $\mathcal{DP}(\mathcal{R})$ *is iAST.*

Our chain criterion is complete ("only if"), because ADPs only add annotations to rules. Hence, every $\mathcal{DP}(\mathcal{R})$-CT can be turned into an $\mathcal{R}$-RST by omitting all annotations. So in contrast to [25], the step from the original PTRS to ADPs does not affect the "potential power" of the approach. Moreover, in the future this may also allow the development of techniques to *disprove* iAST within the ADP framework. To prove soundness ("if"), one has to show that every $\mathcal{R}$-RST can be simulated by a $\mathcal{DP}(\mathcal{R})$-CT. As mentioned, all proofs can be found in [26].

4 The ADP Framework

Our new (probabilistic) ADP framework again applies processors to transform an ADP problem into simpler sub-problems. An *ADP processor* Proc has the form $\text{Proc}(\mathcal{P}) = \{\mathcal{P}_1, \ldots, \mathcal{P}_n\}$, where $\mathcal{P}, \mathcal{P}_1, \ldots, \mathcal{P}_n$ are ADP problems. Proc is *sound* if $\mathcal{P}$ is iAST whenever $\mathcal{P}_i$ is iAST for all $1 \leq i \leq n$. It is *complete* if $\mathcal{P}_i$ is iAST for all $1 \leq i \leq n$ whenever $\mathcal{P}$ is iAST. For a PTRS $\mathcal{R}$, one starts with the canonical ADP problem $\mathcal{DP}(\mathcal{R})$ and applies sound (and preferably complete) ADP processors repeatedly until the ADPs contain no annotations anymore. Such an ADP problem is trivially iAST. The framework again allows for modular termination proofs, since different techniques can be applied on each sub-problem $\mathcal{P}_i$.

We now adapt the processors from [25] to our new framework. The (innermost) $\mathcal{P}$-*dependency graph* is a control flow graph between ADPs from $\mathcal{P}$, indicating whether an ADP α may lead to an application of another ADP α' on an annotated subterm introduced by α. This possibility is not related to the probabilities. Hence, we can use the *non-probabilistic variant* $\text{np}(\mathcal{P}) = \{\ell \to \flat(r_j) \mid \ell \to \{p_1 : r_1, \ldots, p_k : r_k\}^{\text{true}} \in \mathcal{P}, 1 \leq j \leq k\}$, which is an ordinary TRS over the signature Σ. Note that for $\text{np}(\mathcal{P})$ we only need to consider rules with the flag true, since only such rules can be used at a position below the next **p**-step.

Definition 13 (Dependency Graph). *The* $\mathcal{P}$-*dependency graph has the nodes* $\mathcal{P}$ *and there is an edge from* $\ell_1 \to \{p_1 : r_1, \ldots, p_k : r_k\}^m$ *to* $\ell_2 \to \ldots$ *if there are substitutions* σ_1, σ_2 *and a* $t \trianglelefteq_\# r_j$ *for some* $1 \leq j \leq k$ *such that* $t^\# \sigma_1 \xrightarrow{i}{}^*_{\text{np}(\mathcal{P})} \ell_2^\# \sigma_2$ *and both* $\ell_1 \sigma_1$ *and* $\ell_2 \sigma_2$ *are in* $\text{ANF}_\mathcal{P}$.

So there is an edge from an ADP α to an ADP α' if after a step of the form (**pr**) or (**p**) with α at position π there may eventually come another step of the form (**pr**) or (**p**) with α' on or below π. Hence, for every path in a $\mathcal{P}$-CT from a P-node where an annotated subterm $f^\#(\ldots)$ is introduced to the next P-node where the subterm $f^\#(\ldots)$ at this position is rewritten, there is a corresponding edge in the $\mathcal{P}$-dependency graph. Since every infinite path in a CT contains infinitely many nodes from P, every such path traverses a cycle of the dependency graph infinitely often. Thus, it suffices to consider the SCCs of the dependency graph separately. In our framework, this means that we remove the annotations from all rules except those that are in the SCC that we want to analyze. As in [25], to automate the following two processors, the same over-approximation techniques as for the non-probabilistic dependency graph can be used.

Theorem 14 (Probabilistic Dependency Graph Processor). *For the SCCs $\mathcal{P}_1, \ldots, \mathcal{P}_n$ of the $\mathcal{P}$-dependency graph, $\mathrm{Proc}_{\mathrm{DG}}(\mathcal{P}) = \{\mathcal{P}_1 \cup \flat(\mathcal{P} \setminus \mathcal{P}_1), \ldots, \mathcal{P}_n \cup \flat(\mathcal{P} \setminus \mathcal{P}_n)\}$ is sound and complete.*

Example 15. Consider the PTRS $\mathcal{R}_{\mathsf{incpl}}$ from Example 5 with the canonical ADPs

$$\mathsf{a} \to \{1 : \mathsf{F}(\mathsf{H}(\mathsf{G}), \mathsf{G})\}^{\mathsf{true}} \quad (13) \qquad \mathsf{h}(\mathsf{b}_1) \to \{1 : \mathsf{A}\}^{\mathsf{true}} \quad (15)$$
$$\mathsf{g} \to \{1/2 : \mathsf{b}_1, 1/2 : \mathsf{b}_2\}^{\mathsf{true}} \quad (14) \qquad \mathsf{f}(x, \mathsf{b}_2) \to \{1 : \mathsf{A}\}^{\mathsf{true}} \quad (16)$$

The $\mathcal{DP}(\mathcal{R}_{\mathsf{incpl}})$-dependency graph can be seen on the right. As (14) is not contained in the only SCC, we can remove all annotations from (14). However, since (14) already does not contain any annotations, here the dependency graph processor does not change $\mathcal{DP}(\mathcal{R}_{\mathsf{incpl}})$.

To remove the annotations of *non-usable* terms like G in (13) that lead out of the SCCs of the dependency graph, one can apply the *usable terms processor*.

Theorem 16 (Usable Terms Processor). *Let $\ell_1 \in \mathcal{T}(\Sigma, \mathcal{V})$ and $\mathcal{P}$ be an ADP problem. We call $t \in \mathcal{T}(\Sigma^{\#}, \mathcal{V})$ with $\mathrm{root}(t) \in \mathcal{D}^{\#}$ usable w.r.t. ℓ_1 and $\mathcal{P}$ if there are substitutions σ_1, σ_2 and an $\ell_2 \to \mu_2 \in \mathcal{P}$ where μ_2 contains an annotated symbol, such that $\#_\varepsilon(t)\sigma_1 \overset{\mathsf{i}}{\to}^*_{\mathrm{np}(\mathcal{P})} \ell_2^{\#} \sigma_2$ and both $\ell_1\sigma_1$ and $\ell_2\sigma_2$ are in $\mathrm{ANF}_{\mathcal{P}}$. Let $\flat_{\ell,\mathcal{P}}(s)$ result from s by removing the annotations from the roots of all its subterms that are not usable w.r.t. ℓ and $\mathcal{P}$, i.e., $\mathrm{pos}_{\mathcal{D}^{\#}}(\flat_{\ell,\mathcal{P}}(s)) = \{\pi \in \mathrm{pos}_{\mathcal{D}^{\#}}(s) \mid s|_\pi \text{ is usable w.r.t. } \ell_1 \text{ and } \mathcal{P}\}$. The transformation that removes the annotations from the roots of all non-usable terms in the right-hand sides of ADPs is $\mathcal{T}_{\mathrm{UT}}(\mathcal{P}) = \{\ell \to \{p_1 : \flat_{\ell,\mathcal{P}}(r_1), \ldots, p_k : \flat_{\ell,\mathcal{P}}(r_k)\}^m \mid \ell \to \{p_1 : r_1, \ldots, p_k : r_k\}^m \in \mathcal{P}\}$. Then $\mathrm{Proc}_{\mathrm{UT}}(\mathcal{P}) = \{\mathcal{T}_{\mathrm{UT}}(\mathcal{P})\}$ is sound and complete.*

So for $\mathcal{DP}(\mathcal{R}_{\mathsf{incpl}})$, $\mathrm{Proc}_{\mathrm{UT}}$ replaces (13) by $\mathsf{a} \to \{1 : \mathsf{F}(\mathsf{H}(\mathsf{g}), \mathsf{g})\}^{\mathsf{true}}$ (13′).

As in Theorem 3 of the ordinary DP framework, the idea of the *usable rules processor* remains to find rules that cannot be used below steps at annotations in right-hand sides of ADPs when their variables are instantiated with normal forms.

Theorem 17 (Prob. Usable Rules Processor). *For an ADP problem $\mathcal{P}$ and $f \in \Sigma^{\#}$, let $\mathrm{Rules}_{\mathcal{P}}(f) = \{\ell \to \mu^{\mathsf{true}} \in \mathcal{P} \mid \mathrm{root}(\ell) = f\}$. For any $t \in \mathcal{T}(\Sigma^{\#}, \mathcal{V})$, its usable rules $\mathcal{U}_{\mathcal{P}}(t)$ are the smallest set with $\mathcal{U}_{\mathcal{P}}(x) = \varnothing$ for all $x \in \mathcal{V}$ and $\mathcal{U}_{\mathcal{P}}(f(t_1, \ldots, t_n)) = \mathrm{Rules}_{\mathcal{P}}(f) \cup \bigcup_{i=1}^n \mathcal{U}_{\mathcal{P}}(t_i) \cup \bigcup_{\ell \to \mu^{\mathsf{true}} \in \mathrm{Rules}_{\mathcal{P}}(f), r \in \mathrm{Supp}(\mu)} \mathcal{U}_{\mathcal{P}}(\flat(r))$, otherwise. The usable rules for $\mathcal{P}$ are $\mathcal{U}(\mathcal{P}) = \bigcup_{\ell \to \mu^m \in \mathcal{P}, r \in \mathrm{Supp}(\mu), t \trianglelefteq_{\#} r} \mathcal{U}_{\mathcal{P}}(t^{\#})$. Then $\mathrm{Proc}_{\mathrm{UR}}(\mathcal{P}) = \{\mathcal{U}(\mathcal{P}) \cup \{\ell \to \mu^{\mathsf{false}} \mid \ell \to \mu^m \in \mathcal{P} \setminus \mathcal{U}(\mathcal{P})\}\}$ is sound and complete, i.e., we turn the flag of all non-usable rules to false.*

Example 18. For our ADP problem $\{(13'), (14), (15), (16)\}$, (16) is not usable because neither f nor F occur below annotated symbols on right-hand sides. Hence, Proc_{UR} replaces (16) by $f(x, b_2) \to \{1 : A\}^{\text{false}}$ $(16')$. As discussed after Definition 11, in contrast to the processor of Theorem 3, our usable rules processor is complete since we do not remove non-usable rules but only set their flag to false.

Finally, we adapt the reduction pair processor. Here, (1) for every rule with the flag true (which can therefore be used for r-steps), the expected value must be weakly decreasing when removing the annotations. Since rules can also be used for p-steps, (2) we also require a weak decrease when comparing the annotated left-hand side with the expected value of all annotated subterms in the right-hand side. Since we sum up the values of the annotated subterms of each right-hand side, we can again use *weakly monotonic* interpretations. As in [3, 25], to ensure "monotonicity" w.r.t. expected values we have to restrict ourselves to interpretations with multilinear polynomials, where all monomials have the form $c \cdot x_1^{e_1} \cdot \ldots \cdot x_n^{e_n}$ with $c \in \mathbb{N}$ and $e_1, \ldots, e_n \in \{0, 1\}$. The processor then removes the annotations from those ADPs where (3) in addition there is at least one right-hand side r_j whose annotated subterms are strictly decreasing.[7]

Theorem 19 (Probabilistic Reduction Pair Processor). *Let* Pol : $\mathcal{T}(\Sigma^{\#}, \mathcal{V}) \to \mathbb{N}[\mathcal{V}]$ *be a weakly monotonic, multilinear polynomial interpretation. Let* $\mathcal{P} = \mathcal{P}_{\geq} \uplus \mathcal{P}_{>}$ *with* $\mathcal{P}_{>} \neq \varnothing$ *such that:*

(1) For every $\ell \to \{p_1 : r_1, \ldots, p_k : r_k\}^{\text{true}} \in \mathcal{P}$, *we have*
$\text{Pol}(\ell) \geq \sum_{1 \leq j \leq k} p_j \cdot \text{Pol}(\flat(r_j))$.
(2) For every $\ell \to \{p_1 : r_1, \ldots, p_k : r_k\}^m \in \mathcal{P}$, *we have*
$\text{Pol}(\ell^{\#}) \geq \sum_{1 \leq j \leq k} p_j \cdot \sum_{t \trianglelefteq_{\#} r_j} \text{Pol}(t^{\#})$.
(3) For every $\ell \to \{p_1 : r_1, \ldots, p_k : r_k\}^m \in \mathcal{P}_{>}$, *there exists a* $1 \leq j \leq k$ *with*
$\text{Pol}(\ell^{\#}) > \sum_{t \trianglelefteq_{\#} r_j} \text{Pol}(t^{\#})$.
If $m = \text{true}$, *then we additionally have* $\text{Pol}(\ell) \geq \text{Pol}(\flat(r_j))$.

Then $\text{Proc}_{\text{RP}}(\mathcal{P}) = \{\mathcal{P}_{\geq} \cup \flat(\mathcal{P}_{>})\}$ *is sound and complete.*

Example 20. In Sect. 5, we will present a new *rewriting processor* and show how the ADP $(13')$ can be transformed into

$a \to \{1/4 : f(H(b_1), b_1), 1/4 : f(h(b_2), b_1), 1/4 : F(H(b_1), b_2), 1/4 : F(h(b_2), b_2)\}^{\text{true}}$ $(13'')$

---

[7] In addition, the corresponding non-annotated right-hand side $\flat(r_j)$ must be at least weakly decreasing. The reason is that in contrast to the original DP framework, we may now have nested annotated symbols and thus, we have to ensure that they behave "monotonically". So we have to ensure that $\text{Pol}(A) > \text{Pol}(B)$ also implies that the measure of $F(A)$ is greater than $F(B)$. Every term r is "measured" as $\sum_{t \trianglelefteq_{\#} r} \text{Pol}(t^{\#})$, i.e., $F(A)$ is measured as $\text{Pol}(F(a)) + \text{Pol}(A)$. Hence, in this example we must ensure that $\text{Pol}(A) > \text{Pol}(B)$ implies $\text{Pol}(F(a)) + \text{Pol}(A) > \text{Pol}(F(b)) + \text{Pol}(B)$. For that reason, we also have to require $\text{Pol}(a) \geq \text{Pol}(b)$.

For the resulting ADP problem $\{(13''), (14), (15), (16')\}$ with

$$\mathsf{g} \to \{1/2 : \mathsf{b}_1, 1/2 : \mathsf{b}_2\}^{\mathsf{true}} \ (14) \quad \mathsf{h}(\mathsf{b}_1) \to \{1 : \mathsf{A}\}^{\mathsf{true}} \ (15) \quad \mathsf{f}(x, \mathsf{b}_2) \to \{1 : \mathsf{A}\}^{\mathsf{false}} \ (16')$$

we use the reduction pair processor with the polynomial interpretation that maps A, F, and H to 1 and all other symbols to 0, to remove all annotations from the a-ADP $(13'')$, because it contains the right-hand side $\mathsf{f}(\mathsf{h}(\mathsf{b}_2), \mathsf{b}_1)$ without annotations and thus, $\mathrm{Pol}(\mathsf{A}) = 1 > \sum_{t \trianglelefteq_{\#} \mathsf{f}(\mathsf{h}(\mathsf{b}_2), \mathsf{b}_1)} \mathrm{Pol}(t^{\#}) = 0$. Another application of the usable terms processor removes the remaining A-annotations from (15) and $(16')$. Since there are no more annotations left, this proves iAST of $\mathcal{R}_{\mathsf{incpl}}$.

Finally, in proofs with the ADP framework, one may obtain ADP problems $\mathcal{P}$ that have a non-probabilistic structure, i.e., every ADP has the form $\ell \to \{1 : r\}^m$. Then the *probability removal processor* allows us to switch to ordinary DPs.

Theorem 21 (Probability Removal Processor). *Let $\mathcal{P}$ be an ADP problem where every ADP in $\mathcal{P}$ has the form $\ell \to \{1 : r\}^m$. Let $\mathrm{dp}(\mathcal{P}) = \{\ell^{\#} \to t^{\#} \mid \ell \to \{1 : r\}^m \in \mathcal{P}, t \trianglelefteq_{\#} r\}$. Then $\mathcal{P}$ is iAST iff the non-probabilistic DP problem $(\mathrm{dp}(\mathcal{P}), \mathrm{np}(\mathcal{P}))$ is iTerm. So the processor $\mathrm{Proc}_{\mathsf{PR}}(\mathcal{P}) = \varnothing$ is sound and complete iff $(\mathrm{dp}(\mathcal{P}), \mathrm{np}(\mathcal{P}))$ is iTerm.*

5   Transforming ADPs

Compared to the DT framework for PTRSs in [25], our new ADP framework is not only easier, more elegant, and yields a complete chain criterion, but it also has important practical advantages, because every processor that performs a rewrite step benefits from our novel definition of rewriting with ADPs (whereas the rewrite relation with DTs in [25] was an "incomplete over-approximation" of the rewrite relation of the original TRS). To illustrate this, we adapt the *rewriting* processor from the original DP framework [16] to the probabilistic setting, which allows us to prove iAST of $\mathcal{R}_{\mathsf{incpl}}$ from Example 5. Such transformational processors had not been adapted in the probabilistic DT framework of [25]. While one could also adapt the rewriting processor to the setting of [25], then it would be substantially weaker, and we would fail in proving iAST of $\mathcal{R}_{\mathsf{incpl}}$. We refer to [26] for our adaption of the remaining transformational processors from [16] (based on *instantiation*, *forward instantiation*, and *narrowing*) to the probabilistic setting.

In the non-probabilistic setting, the rewriting processor may rewrite a redex in the right-hand side of a DP if this does not affect the construction of chains. To ensure that, the usable rules for this redex must be non-overlapping (NO). If the DP occurs in a chain, then this redex is weakly innermost terminating, hence by NO also terminating and confluent, and thus, it has a unique normal form [20].

In the probabilistic setting, to ensure that the probabilities for the normal forms stay the same, in addition to NO we require that the rule used for the rewrite step is linear (L) (i.e., every variable occurs at most once in the left-hand side and in each term of the multi-distribution μ on the right-hand side) and non-erasing (NE) (i.e., each variable of the left-hand side occurs in each term of $\text{Supp}(\mu)$).

Definition 22 (Rewriting Processor). *Let $\mathcal{P}$ be an ADP problem with $\mathcal{P} = \mathcal{P}' \uplus \{\ell \to \{p_1 : r_1, \ldots, p_k : r_k\}^m\}$. Let $\tau \in \text{pos}_\mathcal{D}(r_j)$ for some $1 \le j \le k$ such that $r_j|_\tau \in \mathcal{T}(\Sigma, \mathcal{V})$, i.e., there is no annotation below or at the position τ. If $r_j \hookrightarrow_{\mathcal{P},\tau}^{\text{true}} \{q_1 : e_1, \ldots, q_h : e_h\}$, where $\hookrightarrow_{\mathcal{P},\tau}^{\text{true}}$ is defined like $\hookrightarrow_{\mathcal{P},\tau}^{i}$ but the used redex $r_j|_\tau$ does not have to be in $\text{ANF}_\mathcal{P}$ and the applied rule from $\mathcal{P}$ must have the flag $m = \text{true}$, then we define*

$$\text{Proc}_r(\mathcal{P}) = \Big\{ \mathcal{P}' \cup \{ \ell \to \{p_1 : \flat(r_1), \ldots, p_k : \flat(r_k)\}^m, $$
$$\ell \to \{p_1 : r_1, \ldots, p_k : r_k\} \setminus \{p_j : r_j\}$$
$$\cup \{p_j \cdot q_1 : e_1, \ldots, p_j \cdot q_h : e_h\}^m \} \Big\}$$

In the non-probabilistic DP framework, one only transforms the DPs by rewriting, but the rules are left unchanged. But since our ADPs represent both DPs and rules, when rewriting an ADP, we add a copy of the original ADP without any annotations (i.e., this corresponds to the original rule which can now only be used for (r)-steps). Another change to the rewriting processor in the classic DP framework is the requirement that there exists no annotation below τ. Otherwise, rewriting would potentially remove annotations from r_j. For the soundness of the processor, we have to ensure that this cannot happen.

Theorem 23 (Soundness[8] of the Rewriting Processor). Proc_r *as in Definition 22 is sound if one of the following cases holds:*

1. $\mathcal{U}_\mathcal{P}(r_j|_\tau)$ *is NO, and the rule used for rewriting $r_j|_\tau$ is L and NE.*
2. $\mathcal{U}_\mathcal{P}(r_j|_\tau)$ *is NO, and all its rules have the form $\ell' \to \{1 : r'\}^{\text{true}}$.*
3. $\mathcal{U}_\mathcal{P}(r_j|_\tau)$ *is NO, $r_j|_\tau$ is a ground term, and $r_j \hookrightarrow_{\mathcal{P},\tau}^{i} \{q_1 : e_1, \ldots, q_h : e_h\}$ is an innermost step.*

We refer to [26] for a discussion on the requirements L and NE in the first case. The second case corresponds to the original rewrite processor where all usable rules of $r_j|_\tau$ are non-probabilistic. In the last case, for any instantiation only a single innermost rewrite step is possible for $r_j|_\tau$. The restriction to innermost rewrite steps is only useful if $r_j|_\tau$ is ground. Otherwise, an innermost step on $r_j|_\tau$ might become a non-innermost step when instantiating $r_j|_\tau$'s variables.

The rewriting processor benefits from our ADP framework, because it applies the rewrite relation $\hookrightarrow_\mathcal{P}$. In contrast, a rewriting processor in the DT framework of [25] would have to replace a DT by *multiple* new DTs, due to the ambiguities in their rewrite relation. Such a rewriting processor would fail for $\mathcal{R}_{\text{incpl}}$ whereas with the processor of Theorem 23 we can now prove that $\mathcal{R}_{\text{incpl}}$ is iAST.

---

[8] For completeness in the non-probabilistic setting [16], one uses a different definition of "non-terminating" (or "infinite") DP problems. In future work, we will examine if such a definition would also yield completeness of Proc_r in the probabilistic case.

Example 24. After applying the usable terms and the usable rules processor to $\mathcal{DP}(\mathcal{R}_{\text{incpl}})$, we obtained:

$$\mathsf{a} \to \{1 : \mathsf{F}(\mathsf{H}(\mathsf{g}), \mathsf{g})\}^{\text{true}} \qquad (13') \qquad\qquad \mathsf{h}(\mathsf{b}_1) \to \{1 : \mathsf{A}\}^{\text{true}} \qquad (15)$$

$$\mathsf{g} \to \{1/2 : \mathsf{b}_1, 1/2 : \mathsf{b}_2\}^{\text{true}} \qquad (14) \qquad\qquad \mathsf{f}(x, \mathsf{b}_2) \to \{1 : \mathsf{A}\}^{\text{false}} \qquad (16')$$

Now we can apply the rewriting processor on $(13')$ repeatedly until all gs are rewritten and replace it by the ADP $\mathsf{a} \to \{1/4 : \mathsf{F}(\mathsf{H}(\mathsf{b}_1), \mathsf{b}_1), 1/4 : \mathsf{F}(\mathsf{H}(\mathsf{b}_2), \mathsf{b}_1), 1/4 : \mathsf{F}(\mathsf{H}(\mathsf{b}_1), \mathsf{b}_2), 1/4 : \mathsf{F}(\mathsf{H}(\mathsf{b}_2), \mathsf{b}_2)\}^{\text{true}}$ as well as several resulting ADPs $\mathsf{a} \to \ldots$ without annotations. Now in the subterms $\mathsf{F}(\ldots, \mathsf{b}_1)$ and $\mathsf{H}(\mathsf{b}_2)$, the annotations are removed from the roots by the usable terms processor, as these subterms cannot rewrite to annotated instances of left-hand sides of ADPs. So the a-ADP is changed to $\mathsf{a} \to \{1/4 : \mathsf{f}(\mathsf{H}(\mathsf{b}_1), \mathsf{b}_1), 1/4 : \mathsf{f}(\mathsf{h}(\mathsf{b}_2), \mathsf{b}_1), 1/4 : \mathsf{F}(\mathsf{H}(\mathsf{b}_1), \mathsf{b}_2), 1/4 : \mathsf{F}(\mathsf{h}(\mathsf{b}_2), \mathsf{b}_2)\}^{\text{true}}$ $(13'')$. Then we use the reduction pair processor as in Example 20 to prove iAST for $\mathcal{R}_{\text{incpl}}$.

6   Conclusion and Evaluation

We developed a new ADP framework, which advances our work in [25] into a *complete* criterion for almost-sure innermost termination by using annotated DPs instead of dependency tuples, which also simplifies the framework substantially. Moreover, we adapted the *rewriting* processor of the classic DP framework to the probabilistic setting. We also adapted the other transformational processors of the non-probabilistic DP framework, see [26]. The soundness proofs for the adapted processors are much more involved than in the non-probabilistic setting, due to the more complex structure of chain trees. However, the processors themselves are analogous to their non-probabilistic counterparts, and thus, existing implementations of the processors can easily be adapted to their probabilistic versions.

We implemented our new contributions in our termination prover AProVE [17] and compared the new probabilistic ADP framework with transformational processors (ADP) to the DT framework from [25] (DT) and to AProVE's techniques for ordinary non-probabilistic TRSs (AProVE-NP), which include many additional processors and which benefit from using separate dependency pairs instead of ADPs or DTs. For the processors in Sect. 4, we could re-use the existing implementation of [25] for our ADP framework. The main goal for probabilistic termination analysis is to become as powerful as termination analysis in the non-probabilistic setting. Therefore, in our first experiment, we considered the non-probabilistic TRSs of the *TPDB* [34] (the benchmark set used in the annual *Termination and Complexity Competition (TermComp)* [18]) and compared ADP and DT with AProVE-NP, because at the current *TermComp*, AProVE-NP was the most powerful tool for termination of ordinary non-probabilistic TRSs. Clearly, a TRS can be represented as a PTRS with trivial probabilities, and then (innermost) AST is the same as (innermost) termination. While both ADP and DT have a probability removal processor to switch to the classical DP framework for such problems, we disabled that processor in this experiment. Since ADP and DT can only deal with innermost evaluation, we used the benchmarks from the "TRS Innermost" and "TRS Standard" categories of the *TPDB*, but only considered innermost evaluation for all examples. We used a timeout of 300 s for each example. The "TRS Innermost" category contains 366 benchmarks, where APROVE-NP proves innermost termination for 293, DT is able to prove it for 133 (45% of APROVE-NP), and for ADP this number rises to 159 (54%). For the 1512 benchmarks from the "TRS Standard" category, APROVE-NP can prove innermost termination for 1114, DT for 611 (55% of APROVE-NP), and ADP for 723 (65%). This shows that the transformations are very important for automatic termination proofs as we get around 10% closer to APROVE-NP's results in both categories.

As a second experiment, we extended the PTRS benchmark set from [25] by 33 new PTRSs for typical probabilistic programs, including some examples with complicated probabilistic structure. For instance, we added the following PTRS $\mathcal{R}_{qsrt}$ for probabilistic quicksort. Here, we write r instead of $\{1 : r\}$ for readability.

$$\text{rotate}(\text{cons}(x, xs)) \rightarrow \{1/2 : \text{cons}(x, xs),\ 1/2 : \text{rotate}(\text{app}(xs, \text{cons}(x, \text{nil})))\}$$
$$\text{qsrt}(xs) \rightarrow \text{if}(\text{empty}(xs),\ \text{low}(\text{hd}(xs), \text{tl}(xs)),\ \text{hd}(xs),\ \text{high}(\text{hd}(xs), \text{tl}(xs)))$$
$$\text{if}(\text{true}, xs, x, ys) \rightarrow \text{nil} \qquad \text{empty}(\text{nil}) \rightarrow \text{true} \qquad \text{empty}(\text{cons}(x, xs)) \rightarrow \text{false}$$
$$\text{if}(\text{false}, xs, x, ys) \rightarrow \text{app}(\text{qsrt}(\text{rotate}(xs)),\ \text{cons}(x,\ \text{qsrt}(\text{rotate}(ys))))$$
$$\text{hd}(\text{cons}(x, xs)) \rightarrow x \qquad \text{tl}(\text{cons}(x, xs)) \rightarrow xs$$

The rotate-rules rotate a list randomly often (they are AST, but not terminating). Thus, by choosing the first element of the resulting list, one obtains random pivot elements for the recursive calls of qsrt in the second if-rule. In addition to the rules above, $\mathcal{R}_{qsrt}$ contains rules for list concatenation (app), and rules such that $\text{low}(x, xs)$ ($\text{high}(x, xs)$) returns all elements of the list xs that are smaller (greater or equal) than x, see [26]. In contrast to the quicksort example in [25], proving iAST of the above rules requires transformational processors to instantiate and rewrite the empty-, hd-, and tl-subterms in the right-hand side of the qsrt-rule. So while DT fails for this example, ADP can prove iAST of $\mathcal{R}_{qsrt}$.

90 of the 100 PTRSs in our set are iAST, and DT succeeds for 54 of them (60 %) with the technique of [25] that does not use transformational processors. Adding the new processors in ADP increases this number to 77 (86 %), which demonstrates their power for PTRSs with non-trivial probabilities. For details on our experiments and for instructions on how to run our implementation in APROVE via its *web interface* or locally, see: https://aprove-developers.github.io/ProbabilisticADPs/.

On this website, we also performed experiments where we disabled individual transformational processors of the ADP framework, which shows the usefulness of each new processor. In addition to the ADP and DT framework, an alternative technique to analyze PTRSs via a direct application of interpretations was presented in [3]. However, [3] analyzes PAST (or rather *strong* AST), and a comparison between the DT framework and their technique can be found in [25]. In future work, we will adapt more processors of the DP framework to the probabilistic setting. Moreover, we work on analyzing AST also for full instead of innermost rewriting and already developed criteria when iAST implies full AST [27].

References

1. Agrawal, S., Chatterjee, K., Novotný, P.: Lexicographic ranking supermartingales: an efficient approach to termination of probabilistic programs. Proc. ACM Program. Lang. **2**(POPL) (2017). https://doi.org/10.1145/3158122
2. Arts, T., Giesl, J.: Termination of term rewriting using dependency pairs. Theor. Comput. Sci. **236**(1–2), 133–178 (2000). https://doi.org/10.1016/S0304-3975(99)00207-8
3. Avanzini, M., Dal Lago, U., Yamada, A.: On probabilistic term rewriting. Sci. Comput. Program. **185** (2020). https://doi.org/10.1016/j.scico.2019.102338
4. Avanzini, M., Moser, G., Schaper, M.: A modular cost analysis for probabilistic programs. Proc. ACM Program. Lang. **4**(OOPSLA) (2020). https://doi.org/10.1145/3428240
5. Baader, F., Nipkow, T.: Term Rewriting and All That. Cambridge University Press (1998). https://doi.org/10.1017/CBO9781139172752
6. Batz, K., Kaminski, B.L., Katoen, J.-P., Matheja, C., Verscht, L.: A calculus for amortized expected runtimes. Proc. ACM Program. Lang. **7**(POPL) (2023). https://doi.org/10.1145/3571260
7. Beutner, R., Ong, L.: On probabilistic termination of functional programs with continuous distributions. In: Freund, S.N., Yahav, E. (eds.) PLDI 2021, pp. 1312–1326 (2021). https://doi.org/10.1145/3453483.3454111
8. Bournez, O., Kirchner, C.: Probabilistic rewrite strategies applications to ELAN. In: Tison, S. (ed.) RTA 2002. LNCS, vol. 2378, pp. 252–266. Springer, Heidelberg (2002). https://doi.org/10.1007/3-540-45610-4_18
9. Bournez, O., Garnier, F.: Proving positive almost-sure termination. In: Giesl, J. (ed.) RTA 2005. LNCS, vol. 3467, pp. 323–337. Springer, Heidelberg (2005). https://doi.org/10.1007/978-3-540-32033-3_24
10. Chatterjee, K., Fu, H., Novotný, P.: Termination analysis of probabilistic programs with martingales. In: Barthe, G., Katoen, J.-P., Silva, A. (eds.) Foundations of Probabilistic Programming, pp. 221–258. Cambridge University Press (2020). https://doi.org/10.1017/9781108770750.008
11. Dal Lago, U., Grellois, C.: Probabilistic termination by monadic affine sized typing. In: Yang, H. (ed.) ESOP 2017. LNCS, vol. 10201, pp. 393–419. Springer, Heidelberg (2017). https://doi.org/10.1007/978-3-662-54434-1_15
12. Dal Lago, U., Faggian, C., Della Rocca, S.R.: Intersection types and (positive) almost-sure termination. Proc. ACM Program. Lang. **5**(POPL) (2021). https://doi.org/10.1145/3434313
13. Faggian, C.: Probabilistic rewriting and asymptotic behaviour: on termination and unique normal forms. Log. Methods Comput. Sci. **18**(2) (2022). https://doi.org/10.46298/lmcs-18(2:5)2022
14. Ferrer Fioriti, L.M., Hermanns, H.: Probabilistic termination: soundness, completeness, and compositionality. In: Rajamani, S.K., Walker, D. (eds.) POPL 2015, pp. 487–501 (2015). https://doi.org/10.1145/2676726.2677001

15. Giesl, J., Thiemann, R., Schneider-Kamp, P.: The dependency pair framework: combining techniques for automated termination proofs. In: Baader, F., Voronkov, A. (eds.) LPAR 2005. LNCS, vol. 3452, pp. 301–331. Springer, Heidelberg (2005). https://doi.org/10.1007/978-3-540-32275-7_21

16. Giesl, J., Thiemann, R., Schneider-Kamp, P., Falke, S.: Mechanizing and improving dependency pairs. J. Autom. Reason. 37(3), 155–203 (2006). https://doi.org/10.1007/s10817-006-9057-7

17. Giesl, J., et al.: Analyzing program termination and complexity automatically with AProVE. J. Autom. Reason. 58(1), 3–31 (2017). https://doi.org/10.1007/s10817-016-9388-y

18. Giesl, J., Rubio, A., Sternagel, C., Waldmann, J., Yamada, A.: The termination and complexity competition. In: Beyer, D., Huisman, M., Kordon, F., Steffen, B. (eds.) TACAS 2019. LNCS, vol. 11429, pp. 156–166. Springer, Cham (2019). https://doi.org/10.1007/978-3-030-17502-3_10

19. Giesl, J., Giesl, P., Hark, M.: Computing expected runtimes for constant probability programs. In: Fontaine, P. (ed.) CADE 2019. LNCS, vol. 11716, pp. 269–286. Springer, Cham (2019). https://doi.org/10.1007/978-3-030-29436-6_16

20. Gramlich, B.: Abstract relations between restricted termination and confluence properties of rewrite systems. Fundam. Informaticae 24, 2–23 (1995)

21. Hirokawa, N., Middeldorp, A.: Automating the dependency pair method. Inf. Comput. 199(1–2), 172–199 (2005). https://doi.org/10.1016/j.ic.2004.10.004

22. Huang, M., Fu, H., Chatterjee, K., Goharshady, A.K.: Modular verification for almost-sure termination of probabilistic programs. Proc. ACM Program. Lang. 3(OOPSLA) (2019). https://doi.org/10.1145/3360555

23. Kaminski, B.L., Katoen, J.-P., Matheja, C., Olmedo, F.: Weakest precondition reasoning for expected runtimes of randomized algorithms. J. ACM 65, 1–68 (2018). https://doi.org/10.1145/3208102

24. Kaminski, B.L., Katoen, J.-P., Matheja, C.: Expected runtime analysis by program verification. In: Barthe, G., Katoen, J.-P., Silva, A. (eds.) Foundations of Probabilistic Programming, pp. 185–220. Cambridge University Press (2020). https://doi.org/10.1017/9781108770750.007

25. Kassing, J.C., Giesl, J.: Proving almost-sure innermost termination of probabilistic term rewriting using dependency pairs. In: Pientka, B., Tinelli, C. (eds.) CADE 2023. LNCS, vol. 14132, pp. 344–364. Springer, Cham (2023). https://doi.org/10.1007/978-3-031-38499-8_20

26. Kassing, J.-C., Dollase, S., Giesl, J.: A complete dependency pair framework for almost-sure innermost termination of probabilistic term rewriting. CoRR abs/2309.00344 (2023). https://doi.org/10.48550/arXiv.2309.00344

27. Kassing, J.-C., Frohn, F., Giesl, J.: From innermost to full almost-sure termination of probabilistic term rewriting. In: In: Kobayashi, N., Worrell, J. (eds.) FoSSaCS 2024. LNCS, vol. 14575, pp. 206–228. Springer, Cham (2024). Long version available at CoRR abs/2310.06121. https://doi.org/10.48550/arXiv.2310.06121

28. Lankford, D.S.: On Proving Term Rewriting Systems are Noetherian. Memo MTP-3, Mathematics Department, Louisiana Technical University, Ruston, LA (1979). http://www.ens-lyon.fr/LIP/REWRITING/TERMINATION/Lankford_Poly_Term.pdf

29. Leutgeb, L., Moser, G., Zuleger, F.: Automated expected amortised cost analysis of probabilistic data structures. In: Shoham, S., Vizel, Y. (eds.) CAV 2022. LNCS, vol. 13372, pp. 70–91. Springer, Cham (2022). https://doi.org/10.1007/978-3-031-13188-2_4

30. McIver, A., Morgan, C., Kamiński, B.L., Katoen, J.-P.: A new proof rule for almost-sure termination. Proc. ACM Program. Lang. **2**(POPL) (2018). https://doi.org/10.1145/3158121

31. Meyer, F., Hark, M., Giesl, J.: Inferring expected runtimes of probabilistic integer programs using expected sizes. In: Groote, J.F., Larsen, K.G. (eds.) TACAS 2021. LNCS, vol. 12651, pp. 250–269. Springer, Cham (2021). https://doi.org/10.1007/978-3-030-72016-2_14

32. Moosbrugger, M., Bartocci, E., Katoen, J.P., Kovács, L.: Automated termination analysis of polynomial probabilistic programs. In: Yoshida, N. (ed.) ESOP 2021. LNCS, vol. 12648, pp. 491–518. Springer, Cham (2021). https://doi.org/10.1007/978-3-030-72019-3_18

33. Ngo, V.C., Carbonneaux, Q., Hoffmann, J.: Bounded expectations: resource analysis for probabilistic programs. In: Foster, J.S, Grossman, D. (eds.) PLDI 2018, pp. 496–512 (2018). https://doi.org/10.1145/3192366.3192394

34. Termination Problem Data Base. https://github.com/TermCOMP/TPDB

35. Wang, D., Kahn, D.M., Hoffmann, J.: Raising expectations: automating expected cost analysis with types. Proc. ACM Program. Lang. **4**(ICFP) (2020). https://doi.org/10.1145/3408992

Algebra

Tabulation with Zippers

Marcos Viera[1]([envelope]) [ID], Alberto Pardo[1] [ID], and João Saraiva[2] [ID]

[1] Instituto de Computación, Universidad de la República, Montevideo, Uruguay
{mviera,pardo}@fing.edu.uy
[2] Department of Informatics and HASLab/INESC TEC, University of Minho,
Braga, Portugal
saraiva@di.uminho.pt

Abstract. Tabulation is a well-known technique for improving the efficiency of recursive functions with redundant function calls. A key point in the application of this technique is to identify a suitable representation for the table. In this paper, we propose the use of zippers as tables in the tabulation process. Our approach relies on a generic function `zipWithZipper`, that makes strong use of lazy evaluation to traverse two zippers in a circular manner. The technique turns out to be particularly efficient when the arguments to recursive calls are closely situated within the function domain. For example, in the case of natural numbers this means function calls on fairly contiguous values. Likewise, when dealing with tree structures, it means functions calls on immediate sub-trees and parent nodes. This results in a concise and efficient zipper-based embedding of attribute grammars.

Keywords: Zipper · Tabulation · Generics · Attribute Grammars

1 Introduction

The evaluation of recursive functions may require multiple computations of identical function calls. A classical example of this behaviour is the recursive definition of the Fibonacci function as show in Fig. 1a. Although this definition is simple and easy to understand, it is very inefficient due to the repeated computation of identical recursive calls; a call to `fib n` requires two evaluations of `fib(n-2)`, three evaluations of `fib(n-3)`, and so on.

One possible solution to improve this inefficiency is the use of *tabulation* [2], a well-known technique that uses a bottom-up scheme in which function calls are computed once and stored in a *table* for future reuse. Function calls in the program code are then changed by lookups in the table. In Fig. 1b we present a tabulation-based version of `fib`, where we rely on lists to model the table.

In this case the table `fibTab` is given by a list of suspensions, each one corresponding to the computation of a Fibonacci number. Recursive calls in the original function definition are replaced by requests to other positions in the table by using list indexing (!!). The necessary sharing of the table in order to avoid multiple recomputations of its entries is achieved thanks to lazy evaluation and a circular definition of the table. In fact, the suspended computations stored

J. Gibbons and D. Miller (Eds.): FLOPS 2024, LNCS 14659, pp. 83–98, 2024.
https://doi.org/10.1007/978-981-97-2300-3_5

```
                                    tab_fib n = fibTab !! n
                                      where fibTab = map (fibm fibTab) [0..]
    fib 0 = 0                               fibm _ 0 = 0
    fib 1 = 1                               fibm _ 1 = 1
    fib n = fib (n−1) + fib (n−2)           fibm t n = t !! (n−1) + t !! (n−2)

            (a) Recursive                          (b) Tabulation-based
```

Fig. 1. Fibonacci

in the table entries form a sort of dependency graph in such a way that the request of certain position of the table triggers the evaluation of the other entries (computations) it depends on. Lazy evaluation ensures that, once an entry is evaluated, its value is available without the need for recomputation.

Despite the use of tabulation, a drawback of `tab_fib` is the use of a list for implementing the table, as list indexing requires to traverse the list from the beginning each time an element is required. This implies that each call to `tab_fib` causes multiple traversals through the list to pick up the values that are required for the computation of the different positions. Using an array instead of a list improves efficiency by allowing direct access to any position.

Fibonacci turns out to be a good motivating example to show the power of tabulation, but on the other hand it relies on a simple, linear data structure to model the table. There are algorithms, however, that require more elaborated tables to be used with tabulation. Indeed, several algorithms may use an underlying inductive structure, for example a tree, to store values on the nodes so that they can be reused in future computations.

In this paper we focus on the design of the table. Our aim is to provide a generic and efficient solution for the table design and manipulation that can be uniformly used in many applications of the tabulation technique. Concretely, the generic solution we propose is to represent the table as a *zipper* [5], a data structure that provides efficient navigation through tree structures, allowing to move *left*, *right*, *up*, or *down* within a tree.

Once we have the table represented as a zipper, our technique provides the ways to move along the table in order to build the suspensions that are stored in the table and reflect the outcomes of the original function. The assembly of the table is carried out by a function, called `zipWithZipper`, which performs a sort of `zipWith` between the table (the zipper) and the (virtual) structure of function arguments that is traversed by the original function to compute each particular result (e.g. the list of naturals that Fibonacci traverses when called on a certain argument n). Again, a sophisticated use of lazy evaluation and circularity proves to be an essential aspect to achieve an effective and elegant solution.

In the case of Fibonacci, the solution based on a zipper looks as follow:

```
tab_fib_Z n = focusL (fibTab !> n)
  where fibTab = zipWithZipperL fibm fibTab [0..]
        fibm _ 0 = 0
        fibm _ 1 = 1
        fibm z n = focusL (z <! 1) + focusL (z <! 2)
```

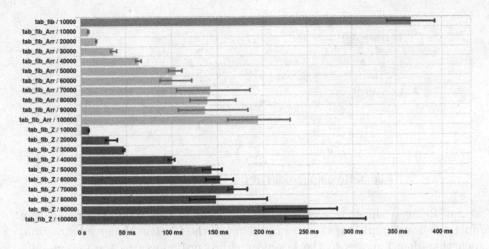

Fig. 2. Performance of the Zipper-based Fibonacci

where the operators (`<!`) and (`!>`) make it possible to move left and right (resp.) on the zipper a given number of times. Function `focusL` returns the zipper focus, while `zipWithZipperL` (introduced in Sect. 3) denotes the particular case of `zipWithZipper` where the construction of the table is performed by zipping a zipper that navigates on a list and a list of indexes.

It is interesting to mention that, as shown in Fig. 2, the zipper-based version of Fibonacci is competitive even with the array-based implementation.

The rest of the paper is structured as follows. In Sect. 2 we show how this technique can be applied to optimize functions that navigate through tree-shaped terms, delving into a concise and efficient embedding of *Attribute Grammars*. In Sect. 3, we introduce the function `zipWithZipper`, which forms the backbone of the technique. We also provide some generic instances of the function, that we use in Sect. 4 to implement a complete example of Attribute Grammar. In Sect. 5 we analyze the performance of the programs obtained using this technique, identifying some cases when it is worth using it and others where it is not. Finally, we discuss related work and conclude.

2   Zipper Tabulation of Functions on Trees

Zippers are mostly used to navigate tree-shaped terms. This leads us to the question whether we can take advantage of the tabulation technique using zippers in the context of functions on trees.

As an example, let us consider a solution to the classical *repmin* problem, where a zipper is used to navigate through the tree. The goal of *repmin* is to transform a binary leaf tree containing integers into a structurally identical tree, where all leaves are replaced by the original's tree minimum value.

Given a datatype representing binary leaf trees:

```
data Tree = Leaf Int | Fork Tree Tree
```

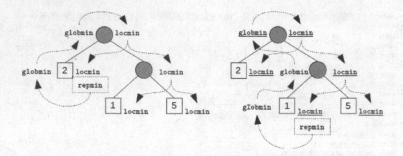

Fig. 3. Recomputations of the Zipper-based repmin

we can define a zipper to navigate through trees of this type. The navigation functions downT, upT, leftT and rightT move the focus in the given direction, such that downT moves to the left-most child, upT moves to the parent, and leftT and rightT move to the left and right sibling (resp.) if they exist. With the function focusT we get the subtree currently being visited.

The following code implements a zipper-based solution to *repmin*:

```
repmin z = case focusT z of
  (Leaf _)   → Leaf (globmin z)
  (Fork _ _) → Fork (repmin (downT z)) (repmin ((rightT . downT) z))

globmin z = if isTopT z then locmin z else globmin (upT z)

locmin z = case focusT z of
  (Leaf x)   → x
  (Fork _ _) → min (locmin (downT z)) (locmin ((rightT . downT) z))
```

Function repmin computes a new tree with the same shape as the original one, but replacing the value of each leaf by the global minimum. The (global) minimum of the original tree is computed bottom-up by locmin, and distributed top-down by globmin. Notice the use of the zipper functions to navigate to the children in repmin and locmin, and to the parent in the case of globmin.

This implementation implies plenty of recomputations of the functions locmin and globmin. In Fig. 3 we show the function calls to compute repmin to the tree Fork (Leaf 2) (Fork (Leaf 1) (Leaf 5)) at the leaf with value 2 (left) and at the leaf with value 5 (right). We underlined the function calls that are recomputed in the latter, which are a major source of inefficiency. The idea is then to apply a technique like the one applied to Fibonacci in order to avoid those re-computations.

In Fibonacci the table was indexed by a sequence of integers and therefore could be implemented with a list. In contrast, in this case we want to store computations on each node of a tree. To do so let us define a type TTree to represent the table, which is isomorphic to the original tree but with values attached at every node.

```
data TTree t = TLeaf t | TFork (TTree t) (TTree t) t
```

Now, using a function zipWithZipperT (introduced in Sect. 3), which zips a zipper that navigates on trees of type TTree with a tree of type Tree, we

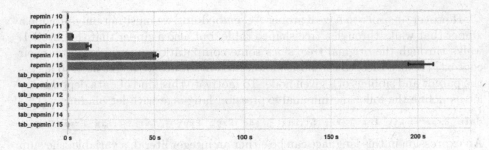

Fig. 4. Performance of the tabulated repmin

can implement a tabulation-based version of *repmin* (following the same receipt applied to Fibonacci), which generates a table with the suspended computations and uses the zipper to navigate through it:

```
repmin t = focusRmin rmTab
  where rmTab = zipWithZipperT (app (gmin,lmin,rmin)) rmTab t

      rmin z (Leaf _)   = Leaf (focusGmin  z)
      rmin z (Fork _ _) = Fork ((focusRmin . downT) z)
                               ((focusRmin . rightT . downT) z)

      gmin z _          = if isTopT z then focusLmin  z
                                      else (focusGmin . upT) z

      lmin _ (Leaf x)   = x
      lmin z (Fork _ _) = min ((focusLmin . downT)  z)
                              ((focusLmin . rightT . downT) z)
```

In this case we have three mutually recursive functions instead of just one. Consequently, each node of the table stores a triple of computations (one corresponding to each function). Functions `focusRmin`, `focusGmin` and `focusLmin`, get the focus and project the desired component of the triple. With `app` we define a function that takes a triple of functions (`gmin`,`lmin`,`rmin`) and applies each one to a zipper and a tree.

In this new version of *repmin*, we avoid all duplicated computations, resulting in a significant improvement in efficiency. Figure 4 presents the execution times of both versions of *repmin* for complete trees with depths ranging from 10 to 15. While the former grows exponentially, the latter presents times that are relatively negligible.

2.1 Efficient Zipper-Based Attribute Grammars

Some readers may have already noticed that we have the ingredients to define an embedding of *Attribute Grammars* [6,7]. Indeed, the zipper-based version coincides with the zipper-based AG embedding proposed in [11]. Attribute Grammars are a formalism used to define and compute attributes of nodes in a tree-like structure. Attributes can be categorized as *inherited* and *synthesized*, where the former propagate values downwards the tree, and can be seen as arguments of the (evaluator) functions, while the latter compute values upwards the tree, and correspond to results of the (evaluator) function. In the case of *repmin*, `repmin` and `locmin` are synthesized attributes, while `globmin` is an inherited attribute.

However, in order to have a proper AG embedding we must not only provide a zipper that walks through a tree-shaped table, but also a zipper that (in parallel) walks through the original tree, since some computations may depend on their context. For instance, to compute an inherited attribute we might need to access the parent and siblings of a given node. To motivate this kind of data dependency let us define the following minimal expression language with let bindings:

```
data Expr = Lit Int | Var String | Add Expr Expr | Let String Expr Expr
```

An expression in this language can be either an integer literal, a variable, the sum of two expressions or a let expression. We define the evaluation semantics in terms of two attributes: a synthesized attribute, *eval*, that contains the value obtained by evaluating the expression and an inherited attribute, *env*, that distributes the variable environment, adding the bindings defined on let expressions.

```
eval zt ze = case focusE ze of
    (Lit x)    → x
    (Var v)    → (slookup v . focusEnv) zt
    (Add _ _)  → focusEval (zt .$ 1) + focusEval (zt .$ 2)
    (Let _ _ _) → focusEval (zt .$ 3)

env zt ze
  | isTopE ze = []
  | otherwise = case ((focusE . parentE) ze, parent zt) of
    (Let x _ _,zp) → if ze .? 3
                     then (x,focusEval (zp .$ 2)) : focusEnv zp
                     else focusEnv zp
    (_         ,zp) → focusEnv zp
```

Function `eval` implements the attribute of the same name. The arguments `zt` and `ze` are both zippers, the former for the table and the latter for the expression. By getting the focus of `ze` we obtain the node and thus determine the kind of expression we are evaluating. For literals, the result is simply their value. In case we use the value of an attribute, we get it from `zt`. The operator (`.$`) navigates to the given child, and (`.?`) returns true if the given child exists. For addition, the result is the sum of the *eval* attributes of the subexpressions, whereas for `let` the result is the *eval* attribute of the third subexpresion. In case of variables, we have to search the value of the variable in the environment *env*.

For the *env* attribute we have to analyze the zipper of the expression. If we are at the top, then we return the empty environment. Otherwise, the environment to return depends on the parent. If the parent is a let expression, and we are computing the environment of the third subexpression (`ze .? 3`), then the resulting environment is the inherited *env* of the parent extended with the new binding, which associates the variable x with the value of *eval* for the second subexpression. In any other case the environment is just inherited from the parent.

Finally we "tie the knot", as we did in the previous examples. In this case we use a version of `zipWithZipper` that navigates through two zippers in parallel.

```
semExpr :: Expr → Int
semExpr e = focusEval tab
  where tab = zipWithZipper (app (eval, env)) tab (toZipper e)
```

Notice that this version of `zipWithZipper` is more general than the previous ones, in the sense that all the previous examples could have been written following this same approach, by just applying the function to get the focus in the cases we do not need the zipper. For example, `tab_fib_Z` (shown in Sect. 1) can be rewritten as follows (assume `fm` is some function):

```
tab_fib_Z n = focus ( fibTab !> n )
  where fibTab = zipWithZipper fibm' fibTab [0 ..]
        fibm' z zn = fm z (focusL zn)
        ...
```

3 Zip with Zipper

In this section, we develop the `zipWithZipper` function to traverse two zippers in parallel, potentially circularly. We demonstrate specific implementations to identify common patterns before generalizing it.

In Sect. 1 we used `zipWithZipperL` to zip a zipper with a list, while constructing the resulting zipper. This function can be implemented as follows:

```
zipWithZipperL :: (ZipperL a → b → c) → ZipperL a → [b] → ZipperL c
zipWithZipperL f _ []      = emptyL
zipWithZipperL f z (x:xs) = consL (f z x) $
                              zipWithZipperL f ((fromJust . rightL) z) xs
```

where `emptyL` represents the zipper corresponding to the empty list, whereas `consL` returns a new zipper which has (`f z x`) as focus.

Notice that, unlike in previous sections, the navigation function `rightL` now returns the zipper as part of a `Maybe` type. In previous examples, we did not want to introduce the noise of using error handling, but from now on, we will use safe versions. The use of `fromJust` makes the function partial, as it is only defined in cases where the length of the path through the list zipper (`ZipperL`) is greater than or equal to the length of the list (`x:xs`). That is not a problem in the context in which we use the function, as the zipper is constructed in a circular manner from the list. Therefore, we say that the list traversal *guides* the zipper traversal. It would indeed be a problem if we attempt to inspect the zipper before building it. For instance, by defining the second equation in the following way we would have made the function total:

```
zipWithZipperL f z (x:xs) = consL (f z x) zs
  where zs = maybe [] (λz' → zipWithZipperL f z' xs) (rightL z)
```

but would not allow circularity, since we have to inspect the zipper we are constructing in order to determine if the `rightL` movement returns `Just` or `Nothing`, generating thus a loop. However, if we want to be total anyway, allowing the use of `zipWithZipperL` for contexts other than our own, a possible solution is to change (`fromJust . rightL`) by (`maybe z id . rightL`), using for the last calls the same zipper `z`. Notice that in doing so we are not inspecting the zipper while traversing, we are just generating suspended computations that will provide the function `f` access to a specific place in the zipper when necessary.

Now, let us analyze `zipWithZipperT`, which was the function we used in Sect. 2 to implement *repmin*.

```
zipWithZipperT :: (ZipperTTree a → Tree → b) → ZipperTTree a → Tree
                    → ZipperTTree b
zipWithZipperT f z t@(Leaf _)  = toZipperT $ TLeaf (f z t)
zipWithZipperT f z t@(Fork l r) = toZipperT $ TFork (fromZipperT zl')
                                                    (fromZipperT zr')
                                                    (f z t)
      where zl = (fromJust . downT)  z
            zr = (fromJust . rightT) zl
            zl' = zipWithZipperT f zl l
            zr' = zipWithZipperT f zr r
```

Like in the case of lists, here it is the traversal on the tree that guides the recursion. For the resulting zipper we are just generating computations that will navigate through it once needed by the function **f**. In fact, both **zipWithZipperL** and **zipWithZipperT** have the same structure: they recursively produce new zippers for the children of the third argument and combine them in a new zipper with the result of applying **f** to the actual zipper and value.

As we explained at the end of Sect. 2, a more general version of this last function can be defined by using a zipper (**ZipperTree**) instead of a tree (**Tree**).

```
zipWithZipperTZ :: (ZipperTTree a → ZipperTree → b) → ZipperTTree a
                     → ZipperTree → ZipperTTree b
zipWithZipperTZ f z zt = case children zt of
  []     → toZipperT $ TLeaf (f z zt)
  [l,r] → toZipperT $ TFork (fromZipperT zl') (fromZipperT zr')
                             (f z zt)
      where zl = (fromJust . downT)  z
            zr = (fromJust . rightT) zl
            zl' = zipWithZipperTZ f zl l
            zr' = zipWithZipperTZ f zr r

children z  = maybe [] g (downT z)
   where g z' = [z', (fromJust . rightT) z']
```

With function **children** we obtain either the list of zippers pointing to the (two) children or, in the case of a leaf, the empty list. Thus, we use the navigation functions (**downT** and **rightT**) of the second zipper to guide the recursion.

3.1   zipWithZipper

We have already observed that the various versions of **zipWithZipper** essentially perform the same operation: recursion over the children of the second structure, providing a way to navigate the corresponding children in the first structure, and combining the results with the result of applying function **f** to both structures. This leads us to a unified implementation, where the variations that may occur depending on the zipper used will be implemented as class instances.

The class **Zipper** contains the minimal interface we require of a zipper: a way to construct a zipper from a structure, and four navigation functions.

```
class Zipper z where
  type Root z
  toZipper :: Root z → z
  up, down, left, right :: z → Maybe z

class Zipper z ⇒ CombineZipper z where
  type Info z
  combine :: Info z → [z] → z
```

The associated type `Root z` is the type of the structure we want to navigate with the zipper `z`. Note that, despite being present in all zippers, the class does not include functions for retrieving or modifying the focus. This is due to two reasons: firstly, we do not need them for implementing `zipWithZipper`, and secondly, their types can vary among different zippers. For example, the type of the focus in a generic zipper does not have to be the same as the type of the root.

The class `CombineZipper` represents a zipper we can construct by the combination of some information (`Info`) with a list of zippers representing the substructures (i.e. the children).

Based on these two classes and the pattern we identified in the previous subsection, we can define a generic version of `zipWithZipper`:

```
zipWithZipper :: (CombineZipper z, Zipper z')
                 ⇒ (z → z' → Info z) → z → z' → z
zipWithZipper f z zt = combine (f z zt) (zipWith ($) fzs zs)
  where fzs = mapZipper (flip (zipWithZipper f)) zt
        zs  = (fromJust . down) z : map (fromJust . right) zs

mapZipper :: Zipper z ⇒ (z → b) → z → [b]
mapZipper f z  = maybe [] g (down z)
  where g z' = f z' : maybe [] g (right z')
```

As mentioned before, we combine the result of applying `f` to the actual zippers with the recursive calls to the children. With `mapZipper` we apply the recursive call to all the immediate children of the zipper `zt`, obtaining a list of functions `fzs`. The functions in `fzs` will then be applied to the corresponding elements of the list `zs`, which is the (potentially infinite) list of zippers that are obtained by descending one level in zipper z. This list contains the zipper with the focus on the first child of z's focus, the focus on the second child, and so on. Sharing makes that navigation to each element of the list starts from the previous one and not each time from the root.

3.2   Tying the Knot

Finally, we can also abstract the tabulation process.

```
tabulate :: (CombineZipper z, Zipper z')
            ⇒ (z → a) → (z → z' → Info z) → Root z' → a
tabulate get f x = get tab
  where tab = zipWithZipper f tab (toZipper x)
```

3.3   A Generic Zipper Instance of `zipWithZipper`

Now that we have a general interface for zippers and a corresponding implementation of `zipWithZipper` based on it, we can define some useful instances. The Generic Zipper [1] is a zipper implementation based on the *Scrap your Boilerplate* [8–10] framework which operates over any[1] possibly heterogeneous tree-shaped type. Thus, if we provide an instance of our `Zipper` class for the

---

[1] Provided the type is an instance of `Data`.

Generic Zipper, we can then use our approach for any structure. The instance is immediate:

```
instance Data t ⇒ Zipper (GZ.Zipper t)  where
  type Root (GZ.Zipper t) = t

  toZipper = GZ.toZipper
  up       = GZ.up
  down     = GZ.down '
  left     = GZ.left
  right    = GZ.right
```

3.4   A Generic Table

In the examples of Sect. 2 we had to define new datatypes, isomorphic to the original trees, in order to represent the tables. This can be done in a more generic way, by representing the tables with a Rose Tree.

```
data Rose t = Node t [Rose t]
```

This is somehow related to *type erasure* [9], where the generic function gmapQ is used to render terms as trees, preserving their shapes. In our case the work is done by the zipWithZipper function.

The instance of Zipper for Rose presents no surprises. The context stores the left and right siblings of the focus and the context of the parent.

```
data ZipperRose a = ZR (Rose a) (CtxR a)
data CtxR a       = TopR | CtxR [Rose a] a (CtxR a) [Rose a]

instance Zipper (ZipperRose t) where
  type Root (ZipperRose t) = Rose t
  ...
```

Then, for instance, to go left we obtain the focus from the list of left siblings and store the former focus in the list of right siblings. To go down involves moving the focus to the first element of the list of children of the node, and store the rest as right siblings on the context. To go up we restore the Node based on the information of the context.

The CombineZipper instance is also straightforward.

```
instance CombineZipper (ZipperRose m)  where
  type Info (ZipperRose m) = m

  combine m zs = toZipper (Node m (map fromZipperR zs))

fromZipperR :: ZipperRose a → Rose a
fromZipperR (ZR t TopR) = t
fromZipperR z           = (fromZipperR . fromJust . up) z
```

4   The Expression Language Revisited

Now that we have all the ingredients defined, we use them in a more complex example that involves heterogeneous trees. We extend the expression language of Sect. 2 now allowing let expressions to include a list of bindings. Additionally, we divided the Expr type in four different types.

```
data Prog = Prog Expr
data Expr = EAtom Atom | EAdd Expr Expr | ELet [Bind] Expr
data Atom = Lit Int | Var String
data Bind = Bind String Expr
```

We do not need to define new instances of `Zipper` and `CombineZipper` to implement this example. We use the defined instances for `GZ.Zipper` and `ZipperRose`, which are generic. We only need to derive the `Data` instances for the expression datatypes and define the different *focus* functions in order to provide type information to select the instances. For instance, `focus` is just:

```
focus :: Typeable a ⇒ GZ.Zipper t → Maybe a
focus = GZ.getHole
```

Concerning the attributes, the synthesized attribute *attEval* for expression evaluation is defined in the following way.

```
attEval = close $ evalP `ext` evalE `ext` evalA

evalP zt zp  = do p ← focus zp
                  return $ case p of
                     Prog _  → focusEval (zt .$ 1)

evalE zt ze  = do e ← focus ze
                  return $ case e  of
                     EAtom _  → focusEval (zt .$ 1)
                     EAdd _ _ → focusEval (zt .$ 1) + focusEval (zt .$ 2)
                     ELet _ _ → focusEval (zt .$ 2)

evalA zt za  = do a ← focus za
                  return $ case a  of
                     Lit x → x
                     Var v → (slookup v . focusIEnv) zt
```

We use the Maybe monad in order to be able to define the different possible alternatives for the attribute. Since the `focus` function will return `Nothing` in case the type of the element in the focus does not coincide with the expected type, we can implement all the alternatives in different functions, in a modular way, and combine them using the `Alternative` instance of `Maybe`. This is performed by the `ext` function, that also applies the two alternative functions to both zippers. Once we have all the definitions, we `close` the attribute, assuming that it will produce a `Just` value.

```
ext f g z t = f z t <|> g z t
close f z t = fromJust (f z t)
```

Inherited attributes like *attIEnv* are computed from the parent to the children. The function `parents` is used to go up in both the zipper of the expression and the zipper of the tables, and get the focus of the first one, to distinguish the different cases.

```
attIEnv = close $ iEnvP `ext` iEnvE `ext` iEnvL `ext` iEnvCpy

iEnvP zt z = do (Prog _,_) ← parents z zt
                return [ ]

iEnvE zt z = do (p,ztp) ← parents z zt
                return $ case p of
                   ELet _ _ → if z .? 2 then focusSEnv ztp
                                        else focusIEnv ztp
                   _        → focusIEnv ztp
```

```
iEnvL zt z = do (p,ztp) ← parents z zt
                return $ case (p  :: [Bind]) of
                _ : _ → if z .? 2 then focusSEnv (ztp .$ 1)
                                  else focusIEnv ztp

iEnvCpy zt _ = return $ (focusIEnv . parent) zt
```

In case of a let expression, the inherited environment is distributed unchanged to the list of bindings, while a new environment (*senv*) produced by the bindings is distributed to the sub-expression. The behaviour is similar for the cons of binding lists, meaning that the expressions in new bindings can use the bindings previously defined.

The synthesized environment attribute *sEnv* is defined to collect the bindings in the list.

```
attSEnv = close $ sEnvE 'ext' sEnvL 'ext' sEnvB

sEnvE zt ze = do e ← focus ze
                 return $ case e  of
                     ELet _ _ → focusSEnv (zt .$ 1)

sEnvL zt zl = do l ← focus zl
                 return $ case l  :: [Bind]  of
                 _ : _ → focusSEnv (zt .$ 2)
                 []    → focusIEnv zt

sEnvB zt zb = do b ← focus zb
                 return $ case b  of
                     Bind x _ → (x, focusEval (zt .$ 2)) : focusIEnv zt
```

We start at the end of the list (case []) with the inherited environment *ienv*, and then on each cons we add the new binding.

Finally, we define the semantic function using **tabulate**.

```
semProg p  = tabulate focusEval (app (attEval , attIEnv , attSEnv)) p
```

5   Performance

In this section we analyze the performance of zipper-based tabulation in different scenarios, and compare it with existing alternatives. The idea is to identify cases where it is worth using this technique and cases where it is not.

In Sect. 1 we showed that the execution time of zipper-based versions of functions like Fibonacci is comparable to the obtained using arrays. An elegant aspect of lazy tabulation is that it enables the construction of a data structure consisting of deferred computations, activating only the necessary ones when demanded. This facilitates the representation of functions that utilize "future" computations (i.e., accessing values further ahead in the table) as long as the dependencies between computations are non-circular. We show a function called *Foobonacci* that exhibits these characteristics.

```
foo n | n <= 6          = 1
      | n 'mod' 5 == 0 = foo (n−8)
      | n 'mod' 5 == 1 = foo (n−9)
      | otherwise       = foo (n+1) + foo (n+2)
```

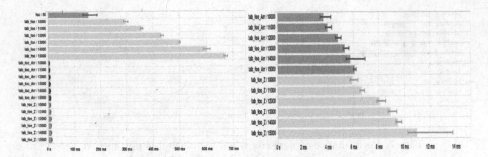

Fig. 5. Performance of Foobonacci

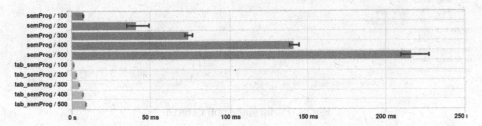

Fig. 6. Performance of `semProg` when tabulation is needed

In Fig. 5, it can be seen that also in the case of Foobonacci the zipper version presents much better times than those using lists. We are still quite competitive with the array version, which performs better but it has the flaw that it cannot be produced trivially, since some care has to be taken when choosing the array boundaries. This is an important advantage of using zippers compared to arrays: there is no need to set bounds, allowing us to work with (potentially) infinite structures.

With respect to tree traversals, we have shown in Fig. 4 of Sect. 2, that in the case of *repmin* avoiding duplicated computations has an important gain in performance.

Of course, the use of tabulation also has its costs. On the one side we can observe in Fig. 6 the comparison of execution times of a tabulated and a non-tabulated version of `semProg` (from Sect. 4) when the expression represents a program with the form: `let x1 = 1 ... xn = n in x1 + ... + xn`. In the non-tabulated version, every occurrence of a variable involves recomputing the environment, thus the tabulated version performs significantly better. On the other hand, in expressions where no recomputations are needed, like `let x1 = 1 ... xn = n in 1 ... + n`, the non-tabulated version clearly outperforms the tabulated one (see Fig. 7). However, it is important to note that for similar expressions the worst case for the non-tabulated version is approximately 200ms, whereas for the tabulated version is of around 3ms. So, the cost associated with tabulation is worth paying in order to avoid worse performance issues.

The zipper-based approach is useful when long list searches can be substituted by short zipper traversals in the neighbourhood of the focus. In other cases,

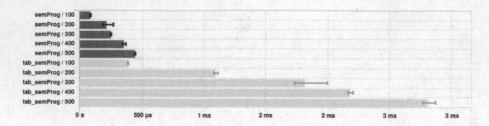

Fig. 7. Performance of `semProg` when tabulation is not needed

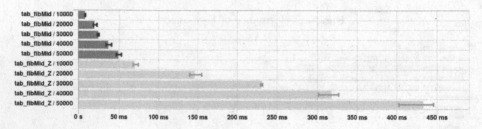

Fig. 8. Performance of `fibMid`

the cost of using a zipper is not justified. To illustrate this, we define another Fibonacci-like function that instead of calling the recursion with $n-1$ and $n-2$ it halves n. Figure 8 shows the results.

```
fibMid 0 = 0
fibMid 1 = 1
fibMid n = fib (n 'div' 2) + fib (n 'div' 2 -1)
```

Another case where it does not seem wise to use the zipper-based approach is when tabulation involves a matrix, since the zipper is not an efficient structure to move through it. For instance, if the matrix is implemented as a list of rows, moving up and down involves moving all along the actual row to the left and then back right in the upper row. A well-known example of such case is the *knapsack problem*, which involves finding the maximum profit obtained by introducing some subset of n objects with given weights (ws) and profits (ps) in a knapsack with capacity c.

```
knapsack 0 c = 0
knapsack n c | c<ws!n    = knapsack (n-1) c
             | otherwise = max (knapsack (n-1) c)
                               (knapsack (n-1) (c-ws!n) + ps!n)
```

We show in Fig. 9 the times of executing `snackpack` with 100 objects, respective weights [1..100], profits [100..1], and capacity 500. It is clearly more efficient to use a list of lists as table than to use a zipper of them.

6   Related Work

Tabulation is a well-known and commonly used optimization technique in the context of dynamic programming. Our work is based on what Bird [2] called

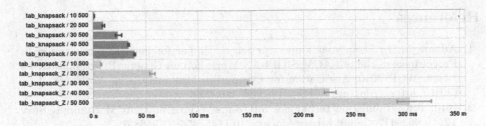

Fig. 9. Performance of knapsack

exact tabulation, in contrast to a more fine grained tabulation technique based on the analysis of the dependency graph. Pareja-Flores et. al. [12] proposed a transformation tactic to convert recursive functions into tabulated ones based on arrays. In the case of exact tabulation (that they call total tabulation), it corresponds to the technique we showed in the introduction. In our work we adapted the standard tabulation technique to be used with zippers as tables, changing from absolute to relative addressing on the tables. To deal with the genericity of the tables we introduced the classes Zipper and CombineZipper and a function zipWithZipper to construct them. Based on a different approach, Bird [3] investigated the systematic derivation of tabulation versions for recursive functions that satisfy certain conditions. Similar to us he put the focus of his analysis on the tree structure one can form with the successive arguments to the recursive calls.

The use of zippers to embed attribute grammars in a functional setting is proposed in [11] as the ZipperAG embedding, which has been extended with memoization to avoid attribute re-computations [4]. In those works a set of domain-specific zipper-based combinators were introduced to express attribute grammars. Our zipper-based tabulation technique offers for free the expressiveness of those AG combinators. As we showed in Sects. 2 and 4 we can express AGs directly in our setting without having to introduce AG specific combinators/notation. In our embedding attributes have to be *closed* in order to be evaluated and stored in the table, while ZipperAG implements the attribute calls as function applications. On the other hand, ZipperAG needs to model attribute computations as computations in the State monad in order to perform memoization.

7   Conclusions

We have adapted the tabulation technique to be used with zippers as tables. It showed to be particularly useful to represent recursive functions whose recursive calls are performed on closely situated arguments within the function domain. We have also defined generic instances of the needed ingredients in order to avoid having to define boilerplate code. This technique can also be applied to avoid duplicated computations of functions that use the zipper to traverse tree-shaped terms. This delves to a concise and efficient zipper-based embedding of attribute grammars.

References

1. Adams, M.D.: Scrap your zippers: a generic zipper for heterogeneous types. In: Proceedings of the 6th ACM SIGPLAN Workshop on Generic Programming, pp. 13–24. WGP 2010, Association for Computing Machinery, New York, NY, USA (2010). https://doi.org/10.1145/1863495.1863499
2. Bird, R.S.: Tabulation techniques for recursive programs. ACM Comput. Surv. **12**(4), 403–417 (1980). https://doi.org/10.1145/356827.356831
3. Bird, R.S.: Zippy tabulations of recursive functions. In: Audebaud, P., Paulin-Mohring, C. (eds.) MPC 2008. LNCS, vol. 5133, pp. 92–109. Springer, Heidelberg (2008). https://doi.org/10.1007/978-3-540-70594-9_7
4. Fernandes, J.P., Martins, P., Pardo, A., Saraiva, J., Viera, M.: Memoized zipper-based attribute grammars and their higher order extension. Sci. Comput. Program. **173**, 71–94 (2019). https://doi.org/10.1016/j.scico.2018.10.006
5. Huet, G.P.: The zipper. J. Funct. Program. **7**(5), 549–554 (1997). https://doi.org/10.1017/s0956796897002864
6. Knuth, D.E.: Semantics of Context-free Languages. Math. Syst. Theory **2**(2), 127–145 (1968). https://doi.org/10.1007/BF01692511, correction: Math. Syst. Theory **5**(1), 95–96 (1971)
7. Knuth, D.E.: The genesis of attribute grammars. In: Deransart, P., Jourdan, M. (eds.) Attribute Grammars and their Applications. LNCS, pp. 1–12. Springer, Heidelberg (1990). https://doi.org/10.1007/3-540-53101-7_1
8. Lämmel, R., Jones, S.P.: Scrap your boilerplate: a practical design pattern for generic programming. In: Proceedings of the 2003 ACM SIGPLAN International Workshop on Types in Languages Design and Implementation, pp. 26–37. TLDI 2003, Association for Computing Machinery, New York, NY, USA (2003). https://doi.org/10.1145/604174.604179
9. Lämmel, R., Jones, S.P.: Scrap more boilerplate: reflection, zips, and generalised casts. SIGPLAN Not. **39**(9), 244–255 (2004). https://doi.org/10.1145/1016848.1016883
10. Lämmel, R., Jones, S.P.: Scrap your boilerplate with class: extensible generic functions. In: Proceedings of the Tenth ACM SIGPLAN International Conference on Functional Programming, pp. 204–215. ICFP 2005. Association for Computing Machinery, New York, NY, USA (2005). https://doi.org/10.1145/1086365.1086391
11. Martins, P., Fernandes, J.P., Saraiva, J., Van Wyk, E., Sloane, A.: Embedding attribute grammars and their extensions using functional zippers. Sci. Comput. Program. **132**(P1), 2–28 (2016). https://doi.org/10.1016/j.scico.2016.03.005
12. Pareja, C., Pena, R., Velázquez-Iturbide, J.Á.: A tabulation transformation tactic using haskell arrays. In: Alpuente, M., Sessa, M.I. (eds.) 1995 Joint Conference on Declarative Programming, GULP-PRODE'95, Marina di Vietri, Italy, September 11-14, 1995, pp. 485–496 (1995)

Declarative Pearl: Rigged Contracts

Alexander Vandenbroucke[1] and Tom Schrijvers[2]

[1] London, UK
alexander.vandenbroucke@sc.com
[2] KU Leuven, Leuven, Belgium
tom.schrijvers@kuleuven.be

Abstract. Over 20 years ago, Peyton Jones et al. embarked on an adventure in financial engineering with their functional pearl on "Composing Contracts". They introduced a combinator library—a domain-specific language—for precisely describing complex financial contracts and a formal denotational semantics for computing their value, for which they briefly sketched an implementation.

This paper reworks the design of their library to make the central datatype of contracts less ad-hoc by giving it a well-understood algebraic structure: the semiring. Then, interpreting a contract's worth as a generic semiring homomorphism directly gives rise to a natural semantics for contracts, of which computing the (monetary) value is but one instance.

Keywords: semiring · financial contract · domain-specific language

1 Introduction

Consider the following contract from "Composing Contracts" [6]:

```
C The right to choose on 30 June 2000 between:
  C1 Both of:  C11 Receive $100 on 29 Jan 2001.
               C12 Pay $105 on 1Feb 2002.
  C2 An option exercisable on 15 Dec 2000 to choose one of:
    C21 Both of:  C211 Receive $100 on 29 Jan 2001.
                  C212 Pay $106 on 1 Feb 2002.
    C22 Both of:  C221 Receive $100 on 29 Jan 2001.
                  C222 Pay $112 on 1 Feb 2003.
```

This simplified contract is representative of those that commonly occur in the finance industry. A key insights is that larger contracts, such as C, are created by composing smaller contracts, such as C1 and C2.

The finance industry employs an extensive vocabulary for describing specific forms of financial contracts (swaps, futures, caps, floors, American options, and European options, to list but a few). As Peyton Jones et al. [6] say "Treating each of these individually is like having a large catalogue of prefabricated components. The trouble is that someone will soon want a contract that is not in

© The Author(s), under exclusive license to Springer Nature Singapore Pte Ltd. 2024
J. Gibbons and D. Miller (Eds.): FLOPS 2024, LNCS 14659, pp. 99–114, 2024.
https://doi.org/10.1007/978-981-97-2300-3_6

the catalogue." The benefit of realising and exploiting the compositional nature of contracts is that we can describe and reason about a vast class of complex contracts with only a small set of primitive combinators. Indeed, with only ten combinators, Peyton Jones et al. manage to express a wide variety of contracts.

The design of a combinator library can be helped immensely by relying on algebraic abstractions (e.g., [8]). Therefore, a natural question is if there is a suitable abstraction for financial contracts. This paper focuses on such an abstraction: the semiring (also called a *rig*). A semiring is a set equipped with two operations and two identities for those operations, satisfying certain axioms. Semirings capture a large variety of concepts, e.g., natural, integer and real numbers, polynomials, gradients, probabilities, and tropical semirings.

The key idea of this paper is that contracts also form a semiring. The two primary ways of combining contracts ("Choose between" and "Both Of") are associative and commutative. Both operations have identities, the first of which is the second's annihilator. Finally, "Both Of" distributes over "Choose Between".

To give a precise meaning to the monetary value of a contract, Peyton Jones et al. [6] define a denotational semantics of the combinators in terms of so-called "value processes", i.e., time-varying probabilistic processes. Here too, we can take inspiration from mathematics, by reimagining the semantics as a *universal semiring homomorphism*, i.e. a structure-preserving function from contracts to any semiring (equipped with inverses). In other words, the contract semiring is the initial object with respect to such semirings. In essence, this defines a family of correct-by-construction interpretations for contracts where the particular interpretation depends on the targeted semiring. Thus, we can instantiate new interpretations for contracts, simply by plugging in semirings from the literature. Notably, the tropical semiring coincides with the original semantics.

We make the following changes to Peyton Jones et al. [6]'s contract library: (1) a new annihilator contract, **expired**; (2) a new combinator **both**, that replaces **and**; and (3) a small change to the meaning of *expiry date* and the related **truncate**-primitive. These changes make contracts into a semiring, without losing expressivity. Reviewer 1 characterizes them as follows: "*Computationally, they are every bit as reasonable as the originals, syntactically they are no harder, and semantically they are much more understandable and satisfying.*"

Moreover, we give a universal definition of a homomorphism from contracts to any semiring that has a multiplicative group, i.e., whose multiplicative operation is invertible. Assuming that such a semiring admits a useful financial model, this definition *subsumes* the original denotational semantics. This paper is written in Literate Haskell, but a more complete implementation of the combinator library is available at https://github.com/tschrijv/RiggedContracts.

2   The Contract Library

This section presents the contract combinator library, which is inspired by—but not identical to—that of Peyton Jones et al. Our running example contract is the *zero-coupon bond*, one of the simplest contracts in the finance industry:

```
zcb :: Time -> Double -> Currency -> Contract obs
c0 = zcb (date "21 Apr 2020") 100 EUR
```

Contract c0 entitles its holder to receive 100 EUR on the April 21, 2020. The zcb function takes a time, a Double amount and a Currency; and it returns a value of type (Contract obs).[1] A Currency is a sum type of different currencies, e.g.:

```
data Currency = EUR | GBP | ...
```

We assume a given function date :: String -> Time that turns a textual representation of a date into a value of the type Time, which is defined in Sect. 3.1.

2.1 Acquisition Date and Expiry Date

To give a precise description of the contract combinators, we must first define two technical notions: the *acquisition time*[2] and the *expiry date*. For the purposes of this paper, a contract is a legally binding agreement between the holder of the contract and another party. *Acquiring* a contract means that the holder enters into a legally binding agreement with the other party, with legal consequences for both parties that stem from the rights and obligations it mentions. These consequences depend on the *acquisition time*, the time at which the contract is acquired. For example, the contract c0 above is worth a lot less if it is acquired on the 22nd of April, 2020 than if it is acquired on the 19th of the same month, because obligations and rights before the acquisition time have no effect.

Complementary to the acquisition time is the contract's *expiry date*. The expiry date is defined as *the earliest point in time at which a contract can no longer be acquired*. This differs subtly from the concept of a *horizon* as defined by Peyton Jones et al. [6], which is *the latest time at which it can be acquired*. We use the term "expiry date" rather than "horizon" to emphasise this distinction. This small—but crucial—difference is necessary to equip contracts with a semiring (see Sects. 3.2 and 4.3). A contract's expiry date is an innate property that is completely specified by its definition (see Fig. 1). However, a contract's consequences may extend well beyond its expiry date. Consider a contract that confers "the right to decide on Dec 26, 2020 whether or not to acquire contract C". This contract must be acquired before Dec 26, 2020—its expiry date—but the underlying contract C may have consequences much later than Dec 26, 2020. This kind of contract is called an *option*.

Figure 1 describes each primitive contract combinator in an informal manner.[3] The relevant parts of the description that differ from Peyton Jones et al.'s due to our definition of the expiry date are underlined.

2.2 Discount Bonds

To illustrate the combinator library, let us reconsider the zero-coupon bond, zcb, which, it turns out, is not a primitive. It is defined as follows:

---

[1] The meaning of the obs parameter is explained in Sect. 2.2.
[2] Also called the acquisition *date*.
[3] Backquotes turn a function into an infix operator, e.g., x `f` y = f x y.

`expired :: Contract obs`

> This contract expires at the *epoch*, the first moment in time. Because the contract is always expired, it is not acquirable.

`zero :: Contract obs`

> `zero` is a contract that may be acquired at any time. It conveys neither rights nor obligations, and never expires.

`one :: Currency -> Contract obs`

> `(one k)` is a contract that immediately pays the holder one unit of the currency `k`. The contract never expires.

`give :: Contract obs -> Contract obs`

> To acquire `(give c)` is to acquire all `c`'s rights as obligations and vice versa. It expires when the underlying contract expires.

`both :: Contract obs -> Contract obs -> Contract obs`

> If you acquire `both c1 c2`, then you immediately acquire both `c1` and `c2` unless either `c1` or `c2` has expired, in which case you acquire neither. The composite contract expires when either `c1` or `c2` expires.

`or :: Contract obs -> Contract obs -> Contract obs`

> If you acquire `(c1 'or' c2)` then you must immediately acquire `c1` or `c2` (*but not both*). If either has expired, that one cannot be acquired. When both have expired, the compound contract has expired.

`truncate :: Time -> Contract obs -> Contract obs`

> `(truncate t c)` is exactly like `c` except that its expiry date is the earlier of `t` and the expiry date of `c`. Notice that `truncate` limits only the *possible acquisition dates* of `c`; it does not truncate `c`'s rights or obligations, which may extend beyond `t`.

`thereafter :: Contract obs -> Contract obs`

> If you acquire `(c1 'thereafter' c2)` and `c1` has not expired, then you must acquire `c1`. If `c1` has expired and `c2` has not, you must acquire `c2`. The compound contract expires when `c1` and `c2` expire. (Called "**then**" in the original paper, a reserved Haskell keyword.)

`scale :: obs -> Contract obs -> Contract obs`

> If you acquire `(scale o c)`, then you immediately acquire a contract just like `c`, except that all rights and obligations of `c` are multiplied by the value of the observable `o` at the moment of acquisition. The scaled contract expires when the underlying contract expires.

`get :: Contract obs -> Contract obs`

> If you acquire `(get c)` then you must acquire `c` just before it expires. The new contract expires when the underlying contract expires.

`anytime :: Contract obs -> Contract obs`

> If you acquire `(anytime c)` then you must acquire `c`, but you can do so at any time (from the acquisition of `(anytime c)` onwards) before `c` expires. The new contract expires when the underlying contract expires.

Fig. 1. Contract Combinators

```
zcb :: Time -> r -> Currency -> Contract (Time -> r)
zcb time amount currency = scaleK amount (get (truncate time (one currency)))
```

At its core is the one contract:

```
one :: Currency -> Contract obs
```

Acquiring (one EUR) at any time immediately gives you €1. However, suppose instead that we want to receive €100 at a specific time, and not earlier. First, to fix the time, we combine get and truncate, to get a contract that gives you €1 at a specific time t:

```
get (truncate t (one EUR))
```

The truncate combinator trims (one EUR)'s expiry date to t, so that it can only be acquired before t, and get forces truncate t (one EUR) to be acquired at the last possible moment, i.e. *just before* t. The combined effect is the desired one, namely that by acquiring this contract at any time before t, the holder will receive one euro at t.

Second, to receive €100, not €1, we must scale up the contract by a factor of 100. This scaling is achieved with the auxiliary combinator scaleK, which builds on the primitive combinator scale:

```
scaleK :: r -> Contract (Time -> r) -> Contract (Time -> r)
scaleK x c = scale (const x) c
```

The contract (scale obs c), when acquired at time t, scales all the rights and obligations of c by the value of the *observable* obs at time t. Observables are time-varying quantities like a particular stock price, interest rate, or even temperature. For simplicity, this paper represents observables as functions of type (Time -> r). The scaleK combinator simply uses a constant function, i.e. scales with a constant factor.

2.3   Composing Contracts

So far, we have seen combinators that create new contracts by modifying a single contract in some way (e.g., truncating its expiry date or scaling its value). Another way to create contracts is by composing several into a larger contract. A straightforward way of combining two contracts c1 and c2 is by creating a new contract that confers the rights and obligations of both c1 and c2. This is accomplished by the both combinator (see Fig. 1):

```
both :: Contract obs -> Contract obs -> Contract obs
```

Upon acquiring both c1 c2, you must immediately acquire both c1 and c2, unless either c1 or c2 has expired, in which case you acquire *neither*. The compound contract expires when either c1 or c2 expires. For example, the following is a contract that entitles you to receive €100 at time t1, and €100 more at t2:

```
both (zcb t1 100 EUR) (zcb t2 100 EUR)
```

Another way to combine contracts is to introduce a choice between two contracts: upon acquiring the contract (c1 'or' c2) you must immediately acquire either c1 (if it has not expired) or c2 (if it has not expired), but not both. The compound contract expires when both c1 and c2 have expired. This operator is commutative: choosing between c1 and c2 is equivalent to choosing between c2 and c1.

For example, the following contract entitles you to receive €100 at time t1, or €200 at time t2:

```
zcb t1 100 EUR 'or' zcb t2 200 EUR
```

The available choices are determined by the acquisition time: if you acquire the contract above after t1, but before t2, only the second contract is still available. You cannot choose to do nothing.

Nevertheless, the option to do nothing is useful to have, and it is captured by the zero contract, which confers neither rights nor obligations. For example, it allows a style of contract, called a *European option* that bestows the right to decide, at a particular time, whether or not to acquire some underlying contract:

```
european :: Time -> Contract obs -> Contract obs
european t c = get (truncate t (c 'or' zero))
```

We see that we first introduce a choice between acquiring c and doing nothing (zero). Next, we truncate the expiry date of the choice to t and use get to enforce that the choice is made just before t.

Recall that contracts are agreements between *two* parties. Thus, it seems rather unfair that the one combinator only pays the holder, and not the other party. This situation is reversed by the give combinator: (give c) is the contract c, with the rights and obligations reversed. For example, the following is a contract whose holder receives €100 at time t1, and *pays* €200 at time t2:

```
both (zcb t1 100 EUR) (give (zcb t2 200 EUR))
```

Note that give also changes who makes the choices. E.g., in the following,

```
give (european t1 (give (zcb t2 200 EUR)))
```

the other party decides whether the holder of the contract receives €200.

Both vs. And. Instead of both, we could define a similar combinator and: if you acquire (c1 'and' c2), you acquire both c1 (unless it has expired) and c2 (unless it has expired), and the compound contract expires only when both c1 and c2 have expired. That is, one contract expiring does not prevent you from acquiring the other contract. The both combinator enforces a stronger tie between two contracts: For instance, suppose contract c1 obliges the holder to pay a certain amount, and c2 obliges the holder to receive a certain amount, then (both c1 c2) ensures that no money is received (c2) without the required payment (c1). On the other hand, (c1 'and' c2) may seem more flexible.

However, unlike in Peyton Jones et al.'s library, where and is defined as a primitive, in our library, the behaviour of and can instead be recovered from both and or by acquiring (both c1 c2) before it expires, or afterwards picking up the remaining contract with (c1 'or' c2):

```
and :: Contract obs -> Contract obs -> Contract obs
c1 'and' c2 = (both c1 c2) 'thereafter' (c1 'or' c2)
```

The `thereafter` combinator (see Fig. 1) composes contracts sequentially: it blocks the acquisition of a contract until another contract has expired. More precisely: if you acquire (c1 'thereafter' c2), you must acquire c1, *unless* c1 has expired, in which case you must acquire c2. Consider, for instance:

```
zcb t1 200 EUR 'thereafter' zcb t4 300 EUR
```

If it is acquired before t1, it entitles you to receive €200 on t1. If it is acquired on or after t1, but before t4, it entitles you to receive €300 on t4.

Choosing When. The `or` combinator allows the holder to choose which of two contracts to acquire. Conversely, the `anytime` combinator allows the holder to choose *when* to acquire a contract. More precisely, if you acquire (`anytime` c), then you *must* acquire c, but you are free to do so at any time after the acquisition date and before c expires. This allows the contract language to express an *American option*. Unlike the European option, an American option not only allows you to decide whether to acquire an underlying contract, but also *when* to do so (within a specific time interval):

```
american :: Time -> Time -> Contract obs -> Contract obs
american t1 t2 c = beforeT1 'thereafter' afterT1 where
   beforeT1 = get (truncate t1 afterT1)
   afterT1  = anytime (truncate t2 (zero 'or' c))
```

There are two parts to this contract. The first part, `beforeT1`, prevents the acquisition of c *until* t1: if the option is acquired before t1, all it does is ensure you acquire `afterT1` at t1. Otherwise, if the option is acquired after t1, `afterT1` is acquired directly. This contract then allows you to choose whether and when to acquire c—until t2, when the option expires.

3 Instant Semiring, Just Add Expired

Having introduced all the necessary combinators, we now recall the definition of a semiring and then explain how to equip contracts with a semiring structure.

3.1 Definition of a Semiring

A semiring is an algebraic structure defined as follows:

Definition 1 (Semiring). *A semiring* $(R, +, \times, 0, 1)$ *is a set R equipped with two operations $+$ and $\times$ and elements $0, 1 \in R$ such that $+$ and $\times$ are associative, with identities 0 and 1, respectively. Additionally, $+$ is commutative, 0 is the annihilator for $\times$, and $\times$ distributes over $+$ on the left and right.*

That is, + and × are *monoids* (they are associative and each have a neutral element). Additionally, + *commutes*, but × does not have to. For instance, square-matrix multiplication is a semiring, even though matrix multiplication is not commutative (unless the matrices are invertible). Annihilation and distributivity ensure that + and × are compatible.

In Haskell, we capture semirings in the following `Semiring` type class:

```
class Semiring r where               instance Semiring Double where
  nil   :: r                           nil   = 0
  unit  :: r                           unit  = 1
  plus  :: r -> r -> r                 plus  = (+)
  times :: r -> r -> r                 times = (*)
```

Numeric Semirings. The natural numbers, integers and real numbers form semirings, with their standard notions of addition and multiplication. For instance, we can define the above instance for `Double`.[4]

Tropical Semirings. A more exotic variant of a semiring is the Tropical Semiring. The *max(resp. min)-tropical semiring* consists of the real number line extended with negative (resp. positive) infinity. Addition is defined by taking the maximum of its arguments, and multiplication is addition of the extended real numbers. In Haskell, we provide a slightly more general definition:

```
data Max a = NegInfty | Max a    deriving (Eq,Ord,Show,Functor)
data Min a = Min a     | PosInfty deriving (Eq,Ord,Show,Functor)

instance (Ord a, Semiring a) => Semiring (Max a) where
  nil  = NegInfty
  unit = Max nil
  plus = max
  Max a 'times' Max b = Max (a 'plus' b)
  _ 'times' _         = NegInfty
-- instance Semiring Min omitted for brevity
```

Time Semiring. The natural numbers extended with positive infinity possess an alternative semiring, by setting + to max and × to min. This proves to be a convenient definition of time:

```
data Time = Finite Int | Infinite deriving (Eq,Ord,Show)

instance Semiring Time where
  nil  = epoch     ; unit  = Infinite
  plus = max       ; times = min
```

Thus, `Time` is an ordered series of discrete points, beginning at the `epoch`, and extending infinitely into the future.

---

[4] In reality, floating point numbers such as `Double` do violate semiring axioms due to rounding errors. Here, we stick with `Double`s for simplicity.

```
epoch :: Time
epoch = Finite 0

previous :: Time -> Maybe Time
previous (Finite t) | t > 0 = Just (Finite (t - 1))
previous _             = Nothing
```

Every point in time has a previous time, except epoch and Infinite. The major implication is that a contract that expires at the epoch is unobtainable, since a contract must be acquired *strictly before* its expiry date.

3.2   The Contract Semiring

The contract combinators or and both form a semiring. The former is +, the latter ×. From their informal descriptions, it is quite easy to see that both operators are associative and commutative, and that both distributes over or. These properties can be proved formally using the semantics defined in Sect. 4.

The identity contract for both is zero. Intuitively, acquiring (both c zero) acquires exactly the rights and obligations of c, with exactly the same expiry date, since zero has neither rights nor obligations, and has an infinite expiry date. Symbolically,

$$\text{both c zero} = \text{c.}$$

The identity for or is the contract expired, which expires at the epoch, meaning that actually obtaining expired is impossible. To see why this is the neutral element, consider that upon acquiring (c 'or' expired), one must acquire either c or expired. Because expired expires at the epoch, the only permissible option is to acquire c, symbolically,

$$\text{c 'or' expired} = \text{c.}$$

Additionally, expired annihilates any other contract with respect to both: because (both expired c) expires when the most short-lived contract expires, it expires when expired does, at the epoch. But this exactly matches the definition of expired, symbolically,

$$\text{both c expired} = \text{expired.}$$

These four combinators give rise to the following semiring instance:

```
instance Semiring (Contract obs) where
  nil  = expired    ; unit  = zero
  plus = or         ; times = both
```

3.3   Beyond Semirings: Groups

A group is a fundamental algebraic concept which captures the notion that a binary operator is invertible. In particular, it is useful to formalise the idea that some contracts cancel each other, for example (one EUR) and (give (one EUR)). Formally, a group is defined as:

Definition 2 (Group). *A group* $(R, +, 0, -)$ *is a monoid* $(R, +, 0)$ *equipped with an operation* $(-) : R \rightarrow R$ *such that for all* $a \in R$: $a + -a = 0 = -a + a$.

Groups pervade mathematics. For instance, integer or real addition form groups with negation, and real multiplication forms a group with the reciprocal, to give but two straightforward examples. Generally, two kinds of groups can be distinguished in a semiring, depending on whether they arise from the additive operator $(+)$ or from the multiplicative operator $(\times)$.

For example, the natural numbers have neither additive nor multiplicative inverses; the integers have an additive inverse, but no multiplicative inverse; and the rationals have both, as do the reals. Tropical semirings do not have an additive group, but they have a multiplicative one, which is the additive group of the underlying semiring. The `Time` semiring has no groups.

Formally, these groups are defined as follows:

Definition 3. *Let* $(R, +, \times, 0, 1)$ *be a semiring.*

- *The semiring has an* additive group *if there exists an additive inverse* $(-)$ *such that* $(R, +, 0, -)$ *is a group.*
- *The semiring has a* multiplicative group *if there exists a multiplicative inverse* $(\cdot)^{-1}$ *such that* $(R \backslash \{0\}, \times, 1, (\cdot)^{-1})$ *is a group.*
- *A semiring that has an additive group is called a* ring. *(For this reason a semiring is sometimes also called a* rig, *i.e. a ring without* negatives.*)*
- *A semiring with both an additive and a multiplicative group is called a* field.

Notice that an additive group has all of R as its underlying set, but a multiplicative group only has R without 0. This situation is analogous to the real numbers and other fields, where division by zero is undefined.

The `Contract` semiring has a (multiplicative) group: the inverse of a contract c is the contract (`give c`), which reverses the rights and obligations of the two parties. Indeed, if one party acquires c, the other party acquires (`give c`) at the same time. Note that `give` changes the primary actor of a contract: if one party makes a choice (e.g. c1 'or' c2) in c, the other party is entitled to make that choice in (`give c`). This means that acquiring (`both c (give c)`) is equivalent to acquiring `zero`, since acquiring (`give c`) cancels out the rights and obligations of any contract c that is not `expired`.[5]

In Haskell, we define the type classes `Additive` and `Multiplicative` for semirings with an additive and multiplicative group, respectively:

```
class Semiring r => Additive r        where neg :: r -> r
class Semiring r => Multiplicative r  where inv :: r -> r
instance Multiplicative (Contract obs) where inv = give
```

Section 4.4 and below also need instances for `Double` and `Max` (`Max` has a multiplicative group if the underlying semiring has an additive group).[6]

---

[5] `give` need not cancel out `expired`, since the annihilator of the semiring is excluded from the multiplicative group.

[6] The partial `inv` is acceptable since the annihilator, `NegInfty`, need not be invertible.

```
instance Additive Double        where neg = negate
instance Multiplicative Double where inv = recip
instance (Ord r, Additive r) => Multiplicative (Max r) where
  inv (Max x) = Max (neg x)
```

All is now in place to formally define the denotational semantics of a contract.

4   Denotational Semantics: Expiry Date and Worth

This section presents the denotational semantics of the contract language as implemented in Haskell, using a *deep embedding* [4]. In this style of embedding, the abstract syntax tree of the contract language is explicitly reified as a Haskell data type Contract that has a constructor for each primitive:

```
data Contract obs
  = Zero
  | Both (Contract obs) (Contract obs)
  | Or (Contract obs) (Contract obs)
  | Give (Contract obs)
  | Truncate Time (Contract obs)
  | Thereafter (Contract obs) (Contract obs)
  | One Currency
  | Scale obs (Contract obs)
  | Get (Contract obs)
  | Anytime (Contract obs)
```

Observe that expired is not a primitive, it can be defined as:

```
expired = truncate epoch zero
```

The appendix derives this equation from the denotational semantics using straightforward equational reasoning. The denotational semantics itself consists of two distinct parts: a contract's *expiry date* and its *worth* (e.g., monetary value).

4.1   A Contract's Expiry Date

The expiry function in Fig. 2 calculates the earliest point at which its argument contract can no longer be acquired. The definition has a case for each constructor of Fig. 1. Moreover, the expiry date of expired is:

$$
\begin{aligned}
\text{expiry expired} &= \text{expiry (truncate epoch zero)} \\
&= \text{min (expiry zero) epoch} \\
&= \text{epoch} \qquad\qquad\qquad\qquad\qquad\qquad \text{(E1)}
\end{aligned}
$$

Recall that Time is a semiring, where nil is epoch, unit is Infinity, times is the minimum, and plus is the maximum. Then, looking at Equation (E1) and lines 2, 3 and 4 in Fig. 2, it follows that expiry preserves the semiring structure:

```
1   expiry :: Contract obs -> Time
2   expiry Zero                 = Infinite
3   expiry (Both c1 c2)         = min (expiry c1) (expiry c2)
4   expiry (Or c1 c2)           = max (expiry c1) (expiry c2)
5   expiry (Give c)             = expiry c
6   expiry (Truncate t c)       = min (expiry c) t
7   expiry (Thereafter c1 c2)   = max (expiry c1) (expiry c2)
8   expiry (One c)              = Infinite
9   expiry (Scale o c)          = expiry c
10  expiry (Get c)              = expiry c
11  expiry (Anytime c)          = expiry c
```

Fig. 2. Expiry Date

it (recursively) maps the nil, unit, times and plus of the contract semiring to their counterparts in the Time semiring. Such a structure-preserving function is called a (semiring) *homomorphism*. Because it preserves the compositional nature of its argument, a homomorphism enables modular equational reasoning about contracts.

4.2   The Bottom Line

As a rule, a contract is acquired because it is worth something to its holder. How much depends on the real-world financial context and the time at which it is acquired. This value is computed by the function worth (Fig. 3). The main work is done by the local function go (lines 11–23). By design, go only returns non-nil values *before the contract's expiry date*, and nil ever after:

$$\text{go c t} = \text{nil} \Leftarrow \text{t} \geq \text{expiry c} \tag{W1}$$

Before the contract expiry date, go satisfies the following properties:

$$\text{go expired t} = \text{nil} \tag{W2}$$
$$\text{go zero t} = \text{unit} \tag{W3}$$
$$\text{go (both c1 c2) t} = \text{go c1 t 'times' go c2 t} \tag{W4}$$
$$\text{go (c1 'or' c2) t} = \text{go c1 t 'plus' go c2 t} \tag{W5}$$
$$\text{go (give c) t} = \text{inv (go c t)} \tag{W6}$$

Equations (W2–W6) state that go is a *multiplicative* semiring homomorphism. That is, the worth of a contract is always interpreted in a generic multiplicative semiring, such that go preserves the contract's semiring structure (W2–W5) and multiplicative inverses (W6). Equation (W2) is somewhat redundant: it follows from Equation (W1) that go maps expired to nil.

```
1    data Financial r obs =
2      Financial { exch  :: Currency -> Time -> r
3               , disc  :: Time -> r -> Time -> r
4               , snell :: (Time -> r) -> Time -> r
5               , eval  :: obs -> Time -> r -> r      }
6
7    worth :: Multiplicative r => Financial r obs -> Contract obs -> Time -> r
8    worth (Financial exch disc snell eval) = go where
9       go c                     time | time >= expiry c = nil
10      go Zero                  time = unit
11      go (Both c1 c2)          time = go c1 time 'times' go c2 time
12      go (Or c1 c2)            time = go c1 time 'plus' go c2 time
13      go (Give c)              time = inv (go c time)
14      go (Truncate t c)        time = go c time
15      go (Thereafter c1 c2)    time | time < expiry c1 = go c1 time
16                                    | otherwise       = go c2 time
17      go (One k)               time = exch k time
18      go (Scale o c)           time = eval o time (go c time)
19      go (Get c)               time | Just t <- horizon c = disc t (go c t) time
20                                    | otherwise = nil
21      go (Anytime c)           time | Just t <- horizon c = snell (go c) time
22                                    | otherwise = nil
23      horizon = previous . expiry
```

Fig. 3. Worth

Implementation. Let us now look at each line of go in detail. *Line 9* implements Equation (W1). *Lines 10–13* implement Equations (W3–W6). In *Line 14* the worth of truncate t c is simply the worth of c, because line 9 has already checked that time is less than the expiry date. In *Lines 15 and 16* the worth of (c1 'thereafter' c2) is the worth of c1 if time has not yet passed the expiry date of c1, otherwise it is the worth of c2.

So far, all the cases have been nicely generic. However, to define the remaining cases, we must introduce a financial model into our abstract mathematics. This model consists of the data type Financial, which contains all the finance-specific know-how. This knowledge is expressed in a specific currency k', for instance exch k t is the value, expressed in k' of one unit of currency k, at time t. There are some properties that the components exch, disc and snell must satisfy. For brevity, we refer the interested reader to the original [6] for their definitions. The meaning of these components is best explained by their usage in lines 17–23. For instance, *line 17* says that the worth of obtaining one unit of a specific currency k is exch k t, the value at time t of one unit of k expressed in the financial model's currency k'. Next, *line 18* defines the worth of (scale o c) by evaluating the *observable* o at time and multiplying it with the c's worth at time. This scaling operation is captured by the function eval.

The last two cases are identical to the version in the original paper: The penultimate case computes the worth of (get c) (*line 19*), which is the value of the contract c when it is acquired (t), but discounted to the current time

(time). The function `disc` models this style of interest evolution: given a time t and a value v at time t', (`disc t' v t`) is the interest-rate discounted value of v at time t expressed in currency k'.

The final case computes the worth of (`anytime c`) (*line 21*). Upon acquiring (`anytime c`), the primary party *must* acquire c, but they can do so at any time between the acquisition and the expiry date of c. The idea is that it allows one to choose to acquire c when it is most valuable, possibly based on exchange and interest rates, share prices, etc. Determining the optimal time to acquire c is complicated, and requires finding the *snell-envelope* of c (*line 21*). The implementation of `disc` and `snell` is beyond the scope of this paper. The original paper briefly sketches one possible implementation in Haskell.

4.3   Comparison with the Original

There are two main difference between the original library and ours. Firstly, as mentioned in Sect. 2.3, their **and** combinator is less expressive than our **both** combinator. Secondly, the original library cannot express the **expired** contract,[7] which has no horizon, and, as a consequence, lacks the corresponding semantic notion: the **nil** of the semiring. Lacking this notion, their worth function is partial; it is simply undefined where ours is **nil**.

4.4   Executable Semantics

The code presented in Fig. 3 is a denotational semantics; its primary purpose is to give a precise, formal, and generic specification. That being said, the fact that the semantics is executable also provides a straightforward implementation, albeit not a terribly realistic one, performance-wise.

The most immediately obvious application is to simply compute the value of a contract. This is accomplished by the max-tropical semiring over real numbers, `Max Double`. By plugging the definition of `plus` and `times` for `Max` into Fig. 3 it is easy to see that the `or` of two contracts is the maximum value of either contract, and that `both` simply sums the values. The worths of `expired` and `zero` are $-\infty$ and 0, respectively. (It is helpful to think of $-\infty$ as "undefined".) The remaining cases in Fig. 3 are determined by the financial model, `static`:

```
static :: Currency -> Double -> Financial (Max Double) (Time -> Double)
```

This simplistic model assumes time-invariant exchange and interest rates. The full implementation of `static` can be found in the supplementary implementation.

Figure 4a shows the value at the epoch of progressively later ZCBs yielding €100 (with a fixed interest rate of 7% per time step). Note that more interest accrues if a contract is acquired longer before its expiry date, until the expiry date

---

[7] For instance, their `truncate epoch zero` is not equal to our `expired`, because it can still be acquired at the epoch.

n	(worth s7eur cn t0)	ρ
0	$-\infty$	N/A
1	100	0
2	93	-0.87
3	86.49	-1.63
4	80.44	-2.29

(a) Value of cn at the epoch.

c	(worth s0eur c t0)
both c1 c2'	300
c1 'and' c2'	300
both c0 c2'	$-\infty$
c0 'and' c2'	200

(b) Compare the behaviour of both vs. and.

Fig. 1. Examples of contracts under the max-tropical semiring. Assume $n \in [0,4]$, tn = Finite n, cn = zcb tn 100 EUR, cn' = zcb tn 200 EUR, s7eur = static EUR 0.07, and S0eur = static EUR 0.00.

is reached and the value of the contract is $-\infty$. ρ is the derivative with respect to a 1% change in the interest rate, computed via automatic differentiation [1].

Figure 4b once more demonstrates the difference between both and and (the interest rate is held at 0% to make the difference more obvious). Since neither c1 nor c2' has expired, both combinators behave the same, summing the values of both contracts. However, since c0 has expired, (both c0 c2') is $-\infty$, while (c0 'and' 'c2') is equivalent to the remaining contract, c2'.

5   Conclusion

This paper has investigated the compositional nature of financial contracts from the perspective of abstract algebra, and equipped them with a semiring structure.

The advantages are threefold: First, semirings have straightforward axioms and properties, and admit a natural formulation of the denotational semantics as a semiring homomorphism. This theory is beneficial for equational reasoning, as is briefly demonstrated in the appendix, and it means that if the target domain satisfies the axioms, the semantics is correct, at least for the compositional part.

Second, the aim of defining a contract semiring leads directly to the both combinator, which seems slightly more powerful than the and combinator of Peyton Jones et al. [6], in the sense that it allows more contracts to be expressed in the language directly. To clarify this point, consider that it is always possible to define a contract that behaves like (both c1 c2) by using features from the host language (Haskell): simply trim the expiry dates of c1 and c2 to the earlier of the dates of c1 and c2. Such tricks are not needed when both is a primitive, meaning that the intent of the contract is captured more precisely.

Third, formulating contracts in terms of semirings may reveal new applications inspired by semirings from the literature, such as those for automatic differentiation[8] [1,2,7], probabilities [3], polynomials, and Kleene-Algebras [5].

Acknowledgments. We are grateful for the helpful feedback of the anonymous reviewers. Part of this work was funded by FWO project 3E221387.

---

[8] See the code repository for a gradient-based semantics.

Disclosure of Interests. The authors have no competing interests.

Appendix: Deriving Expired

Let us derive the implementation of `expired` from the semantics:

> worth m k expired t
>
> [(W2): semiring homomorphism preserves `nil`]
>
> = nil
>
> [(W1): `nil` = worth m k c t ⇐ t ≥ expiry c]
>
> = worth m k (truncate t' c) t if t ≥ expiry (truncate t' c)
>
> [t' ≥ min (expiry c) t' = expiry (truncate t' c)]
>
> = worth m k (truncate t' c) t if t ≥ t'
>
> [instantiate t' = epoch; t ≥ epoch]
>
> = worth m k (truncate epoch c) t
>
> [instantiate c = zero]
>
> = worth m k (truncate epoch zero) t

The choice of `zero` for c in the derivation is immaterial; any contract would do. Moreover, there are other forms of contracts that behave like `expired`. For instance, (`get zero`) is also `nil` everywhere, because the getting a contract with an infinite expiry date is ill-defined, i.e., `nil`. The definition above is preferable because it relies only on the non-finance specific part of the semantics.

References

1. van den Berg, B., Schrijvers, T., McKinna, J., Vandenbroucke, A.: Forward- or reverse-mode automatic differentiation: what's the difference? Sci. Comput. Program. **231**, 103010 (2024)
2. Elliott, C.: The simple essence of automatic differentiation. Proc. ACM Program. Lang. **2**(ICFP), 70:1–70:29 (2018)
3. Erwig, M., Kollmansberger, S.: Functional pearls: probabilistic functional programming in Haskell. J. Funct. Program. **16**(1), 21–34 (2006)
4. Gibbons, J., Wu, N.: Folding domain-specific languages: deep and shallow embeddings (functional pearl). In: Proceedings of the 19th ACM SIGPLAN International Conference on Functional Programming. p. 339-347. ICFP '14, Association for Computing Machinery, New York, NY, USA (2014). https://doi.org/10.1145/2628136. 2628138
5. Kozen, D.: Kleene algebra with tests. ACM Trans. Program. Lang. Syst. **19**(3), 427–443 (1997)
6. Peyton Jones, S.L., Eber, J., Seward, J.: Composing contracts: an adventure in financial engineering, functional pearl. In: ICFP. pp. 280–292. ACM (2000)
7. Rall, L.B.: Automatic Differentiation: Techniques and Applications. Lecture Notes in Computer Science, vol. 120. Springer, Heidelberg (1981). https://doi.org/10. 1007/3-540-10861-0
8. Yorgey, B.A.: Monoids: theme and variations *(functional pearl)*. In: Haskell, pp. 105–116. ACM (2012)

Applications

System Description: DeepLLM, Casting Dialog Threads into Logic Programs

Paul Tarau(✉) iD

University of North Texas, Denton, USA
paul.tarau@unt.edu

Abstract. We automate deep step-by step reasoning in an LLM dialog thread by recursively exploring alternatives (OR-nodes) and expanding details (AND-nodes) up to a given depth. Starting from a single succinct task-specific initiator we steer the automated dialog thread to stay focussed on the task by synthesizing a prompt that summarizes the depth-first steps taken so far.

Our algorithm is derived from a simple recursive descent implementation of a Horn Clause interpreter, except that we accommodate our logic engine to fit the natural language reasoning patterns LLMs have been trained on. Semantic similarity to ground-truth facts or oracle advice from another LLM instance is used to restrict the search space and validate the traces of justification steps returned as focussed and trustable answers. At the end, the unique minimal model of a generated Horn Clause program collects the results of the reasoning process.

As applications, we sketch implementations of consequence predictions, causal explanations, recommendation systems and topic-focussed exploration of scientific literature.

Keywords: automation of LLM dialog threads · recursive task-focused steering of LLM interactions · logic-programming driven LLM reasoning · LLM-based algorithmic information retrieval · context-driven LLM prompt synthesis

1 Introduction

Interaction with today's high-end LLMs like ChatGPT, GPT-4 [3,19], Claude-2 [1] and Bard [9] allows the patient and prompt-savvy user to steer the interaction toward fulfillment of a well-specified information seeking goal. The resulting dialog thread can be labor intensive and assumes solid prompt engineering skills to keep the LLM focussed on the task while digging as deep as needed into details.

This raises the obvious question: can we get back the simplicity of a one-shot query and automatically manage the navigation in the answer-space of the dialog thread?

We start by planning out the key steps of our proposed solution. Clearly, we need first an elaboration or refinement process that reduces a given task to

© The Author(s), under exclusive license to Springer Nature Singapore Pte Ltd. 2024
J. Gibbons and D. Miller (Eds.): FLOPS 2024, LNCS 14659, pp. 117–134, 2024.
https://doi.org/10.1007/978-981-97-2300-3_7

a sequence of subtasks. We call this conjunctive elaboration into subtasks an *AND-step*. Next, we will need a dual, disjunctive elaboration, as a generation of alternative ways to make progress on the task. We call this an *OR-step*. To advance into more detail we can rely on a recursive process that alternates these two steps up to the desired depth.

This brings us to the key topic of this paper: an algorithm that extracts a salient set of answers, by zooming into the desired level of detail, from a single, succinct human prompt. To this end, we automate step-by step reasoning in an LLM dialog thread to explore recursively alternatives (OR-steps) and expand details (AND-steps) up to a given depth.

Our approach will follow closely the SLD-resolution algorithm for pure Horn Clause logic [13,14]. Restriction to Horn Clauses is motivated by the fact that LLMs are genuinely "constructive" and known not to be comfortable with negation [11,15], limiting one's interest in either classical negation or negation-as-failure under a closed-world assumption as present in ASP systems [8,21] or in Prolog [27].

This makes the use of a conventional logic programming language unnecessary as Python's coroutining generators are expressive enough for succinctly implementing a simplified SLD-resolution algorithm [23]. Another departure from logic programming as we know it, is that we will need to "unformalize" the underlying logic to more easily interoperate with the LLMs. In fact, LLMs do have a limited ability to generate correct logic forms of simple sentences [28]. But their training is based mostly on completion of natural language sentences and they are more in their element with the reasoning steps humans express in natural language.

Thus, instead of trying to force LLMs to use logic formalisms they are not yet comfortable with, we accommodate our logic engine to fit natural language reasoning, goal driven planning, task decomposition and association patterns with minimal task-specific prompt engineering.

This brings us to the key features of our approach:

- SLD-resolution's clause selection via unification is replaced by LLM-driven dynamic clause head creation with an option of focusing by proximity of embeddings to ground truth facts
- as dialog units are sentences, the underlying logic is propositional
- client-side management (via the API) of the LLM's memory is based on the equivalent of a *goal stack*, as used in logic-programming implementations like [22,23], and a *goal trace* recording our steps on the current search path
- instead of variable bindings, answers are traces of justification steps clearly explaining where they are derived from
- when their depth-limit is reached, the items on the goal stack are interpreted as "abducibles", statements that can be hypothetically assumed and then checked against "integrity constraints" [6,12].
- our depth-bounded refinement steps support compilation of the dialog threads to a Horn Clause program to be explored with logic programming solvers
- modular, task specific, customizable prompt engineering primitives are aggregated together for "AND-step" and "OR-step" prompts

- normalized semantic similarity measures of embeddings can be made available when generating probabilistic logic programs
- sentences in authoritative documents or collections seen as "ground-truth facts" can be used to select abducibles via semantic similarity or advice of an LLM-based oracle

Overall, our approach exploits synergies between structured prompt engineering, logic-guided recursion over LLM queries and semantic search in an embeddings vector store.

Applications are built by customizing prompts, LLM models and recursion level, resulting in automatically generated detailed, "hallucination-free" answers, crisper and more accurate than what one can obtain after lengthy interactions with conventional search engines or Chat-GPT style dialog agents.

Among potential applications we will overview the following:

- consequence predictions and causal explanations with full justification traces
- recommendation closely focussed on an initial preference seed
- actionable step-by-step advice on practical "how to repair" problems
- topic-focussed scientific literature keyphrase and key concept generation

The rest of the paper is organized as follows: Sect. 2 sketches the architecture of our implemented system. Section 3 introduces Interactors – designed by aggregating components needed for interacting with LLM APIs. Section 4 describes Recursors – our programs steering the LLMs dialog threads while focusing on the task at hand over multiple levels of nested OR-steps and AND-steps. Section 5 describes Refiners, specializations of Recursors checking against ground-truth facts using semantic distances to abducible facts as well as several LLM-based oracle agents. Section 6 describes our propositional Horn Clause model generator that extracts the set of true facts inferred from the logic program generated by our Recursors and Refiners. Section 7 shows how task-specific applications are built simply by adjusting the AND-step, OR-step and oracle prompts. Section 8 discusses variations on the main theme of the paper and possible future extensions. Section 9 discusses related work and Sect. 10 concludes the paper.

Note : The system has been fully implemented[1] and it is deployed online[2].

2   System Architecture

We start with a quick overview of an implemented system architecture and a sketch of its execution flows, as shown in Fig. 1.

Starting from a succinct prompt (typically a nominal phrase describing the task) an Interactor will call the LLM via its API, driven by a Recursor that analyzes the LLM responses and activates new LLM queries as it proceeds to refine the information received up to a given depth. Refiners are Recursor subclasses

---

[1] code at https://github.com/ptarau/recursors.
[2] demo at https://deepllm.streamlit.app.

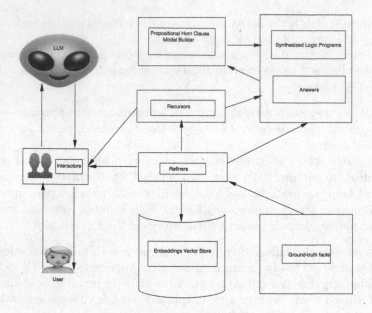

Fig. 1. System Architecture

that rely on semantic search in an Embeddings Store containing ground-truth facts as well as on oracles implemented as specialized Interactors that ask the LLM for advice on deciding the truth of, or the rating of hypotheses. Besides returning a stream of answers, Recursors and Refiners compile their reasoning steps to a propositional Horn Clause program available for inspection by the user or subject for execution and analysis with logic programming tools (in particular, with our Model builder – a fast Propositional Horn Clause theorem prover).

3   Interactors

Setting up the interaction mechanism with LLMs via an API is a multi-faceted process involving several orthogonal aspects.

We will overview here our interactor Agent class managing the dialog with LLMs centered around OpenAI's `gpt-4` and `gpt-3.5-turbo` models [3,19], but able also to accommodate smaller footprint, locally running LLMs models like LLaMA 2 [25], that provide an OpenAI compatible API.

An interactor is put together by designing Prompter, Tuner, Tracker and Talker components.

Tuner. The Tuner is a wrapper around the LLM's API, managing the API parameters and the settings of the interaction.

Prompters. Prompters are patterns expressed as Python dictionaries from which substitution of $-variables with data provided at various recursion levels will generate actual prompts to be sent to the LLMs.

Here is an overview of our Prompters' key features and use cases:

- a Prompter is a dictionary of prompt templates for aggregated, task specific OR and AND prompt generators or decision oracles
- on top of them we build a collection of task specific parametric prompt templates
- AND and OR prompt templates for a given task are designed together to facilitate their experimental fine-tuning
- prompt templates instantiate one-shot instructions to the LLM that enforce focussed, succinct answers
- possible post-processors (algorithmic or implemented as "verifier" LLM oracles) can be used to discard answers when the LLM disobeys the instructions either in requested syntactic form or in content.

We will show next a few prompt template examples. Note as the LLMs (in this case GPT-3.5 and GPT-4) and their APIs evolve, minor edits might be needed to adjust them to the changes.

Example 1. *AND-OR prompt patterns for causal reasoning*

```
causal_prompter = dict(
    name='causal',
    and_p="""We need causal explanations in this context: "$context"
    Generate 3-5 explanations of 2-4 words each for the causes of "$g".
    Itemize your answer, one reason for "$g" per line.
    No explanations needed, just the 2-4 words noun phrase,
    nothing else.
    Your answer should not contain ":" or "Cause".
    """,
    or_p="""We need causal explanations in this context: "$context"
    Generate 2-3 alternative explanations citing facts that might
    cause "$g".
    Itemize your answer, one noun phrase per line.
    No explanations needed, just the noun phrase, nothing else.
    Avoid starting your sentence with the word "Alternative".
    Your answer should not contain ":" .
    Your answer should avoid the words "Causes" and "causes" ."""
)
```

Note that the $context *and current goal* $g *parameters will specialize the pattern for each of the uses of its* and_p *and* or_p *components in the recursive descent process. Note also the "petty" avoidance remarks in the prompt that we had to use to ensure that the answer returned by the LLM matches the expected output structure, given that after parsing, it has to provide the inputs of the next recursive step.*

Example 2. *Oracle pattern used to filter hypotheses generated by a Recursor*

```
decision_prompter = dict(
    name='oracle',
    decider_p="""
    You play the role of an oracle that decides if "$g" is relevant for
    our interest in "$context".
    Your answer should be "True" or "False" expressing agreement or
    disagreement with the relevance of "$g".
    """
)
```

The pattern is used to decide about adequacy of a given subtask or alternative in a given context. With a similar rater oracle we request ratings on a scale of 100 if we want to generate a probabilistic logic program to be analyzed with tools like Problog [5, 18].

Tracker. The Tracker is managing API messages, contexts and API costs. It ensures that answers to questions already answered by the LLM are cached and reused to save costs and ensure full determinism and replicability. It also handles the on-demand migrations from an Interactor's short-term memory to its long-term memory. While the short-term memory is kept small enough to fit in the LLMs message size, both memories are dictionaries used to retrieve available cached answers. As a special case, Trackers also enable spilling of the full content of the short-term memory to the long-term memory when a fresh dialog thread is needed for a change of topic or focus.

Talker. The Talker is a component managing the overall interaction with the LLM. It implements the Interactor's high level **ask** method that encapsulates the details of applying the appropriate prompt template to a given question, activates mechanisms to trim the context to a size acceptable to the LLM, activates conversion of the content of the short-term memory to the message format the LLM expects. It also activates possible application-specific post-processing of the LLM's answers and manages the retrying of the completion request if the API is temporarily unresponsive.

4 Recursors

Recursors implement the central idea of this paper: automatically focusing a dialog thread with an LLM, while exploring a given topic in depth.

4.1 Synthesizing the Logic Program on Recursive Descent

Starting from a succinct initiator goal, the Recursor performs a recursive descent guided by task specific Prompters. At each step, the OR-prompter asks the LLM to generate alternative ways to fulfill the current goal. Then, for each alternative, the LLM is asked to expand it to a sequence of task specific subgoals, guided by the AND-prompter. The AND and the OR prompter templates are activated with information about the current context and the current goal. The context is a linearization of a chronologically ordered trace that accumulates the previously expanded goals. The presence of this context, serving as the *short term dialog memory* of the otherwise stateless LLM API, steers the generative process to stay focussed on the task.

At a given step, the effect of the OR-prompter expanding the head h in a series of alternatives $a_1, \ldots, a_n$ can be described as a set of binary Horn Clauses of the form:

$h : - a_1.$

$h : - a_2.$

$\ldots$

$h : - a_m.$

more concisely expressed with a disjunctive body as:

$h : - a_1; a_2 ; \ldots ; a_m.$

On the other other hand, the result of an AND-prompter can be described as a set of Horn clauses of the form:

$h : - b_1, b_2, \ldots, b_n.$

When a depth limit is reached, the remaining unexplored goals on the goal stack are considered as *abducibles* [6,12], i.e., hypotheses to be assumed until integrity constraints might invalidate them, a process that, like in Logic Programming, results in backtracking to explore other possibilities. Should some of them fail, the presence of the OR-nodes at each recursive step ensures that plenty of choices remain available, despite possible failures.

A simple way to select abducibles is to check the semantic distance of their embeddings to embeddings in a set of *ground-truth facts*. For efficiency, a few nearest neighbors of each abducible are fetched from the vector embeddings store (see Subsect. 5.1) and their average distance to the ground truth is used to decide if the abducible is assumed as a hypothesis. A summary of the sentences extracted from the ground-truth facts can be used as an explanation supporting the abducible. This can be seen as an instant constraints-driven filtering operation that results in eagerly omitting the assumption of the irrelevant abducibles as hypotheses.

Besides returning a stream of answers, we also generate a propositional Horn Clause program to be further explored with logic programming tools.

At the end, a minimal model [13] of the remaining rules can be obtained with a SAT solver, although our implementation prefers a fast direct algorithm (see Sect. 6), given that Horn Clause satisfiability is polynomial [7].

4.2 The Unfolder

Our implementation of the depth limited recursive descent encapsulates the unfolding of AND-nodes and OR-nodes. An Unfolder instance contains two Interactor Agents, one for each node type, initialized with their jointly designed prompter dictionary described in Sect. 3. The agents are activated with the `ask_and` and `ask_or` methods and are also responsible for persisting past LLM interactions in appropriately named unique disk caches. By alternating the creation of AND-nodes and OR-nodes we will reshape the resulting dialog thread as a propositional Horn Clause program.

4.3 The AndOrExplorer

The process of building the propositional Horn Clause program is encapsulated in the AndOrExplorer class, that handles:

- the invention of clause heads by an OR-node induced by a given goal
- the invention of clause bodies by an AND-node induced by the clause head.

The AndOrExplorer implements its recursive descent by relying directly on the Python-stack and emulating Prolog's backtracking via Python's `yield`-based coroutining mechanism. It returns the trace of expanded goals (and invented clause heads) for each successful "proof step", assuming all facts at the depth limit as abducibles, subject to future validation by independent Oracle Agents.

The clause invention step is sketched by the following Python code snippet:

```
def new_clause(self, g, trace, topgoal):
    or_context = to_context(trace, topgoal)
    hs = self.unf.ask_or(g, or_context)      # invent the clause heads
    and_context = to_context((g, trace), topgoal)
    for h in hs:
        bs = self.unf.ask_and(h, and_context)  # invent their bodies
        yield (h, bs)
```

The `or_context` is built from the generic OR-pattern instantiated to the specifics of the step in the `trace` of the goals expanded so far on this resolution branch. Note that `topgoal` is also passed to the context builder to help focus on the original goal that has started the recursive descent. It is responsible for the generation of the list of clause heads `hs`. For each clause head `h` in `hs`, a clause body `bs` is generated by the AND-node prompter. Finally each clause is yielded as a pair `(h, bs)`.

Besides its `resume`, `persist` and `costs` methods the `AndOrExplorer` defines also an `appraise` method meant to be overridden by its refiner subclasses.

4.4 The SVO Relation Extractor

The relation Extractor class invokes the LLM to decompose facts inferred from the Horn Clause program into <Subject, Verb, Object> triplets, usable for knowledge representation tasks. It also shows them in the `streamlit` Web app[3] using the `pyvis` graph visualizer.

---

[3] https://deepllm.streamlit.app/.

4.5   The Logic Programming Connection

The recursive descent algorithm is implemented as a generator of answers (traces of steps included) to the initiator goal, in a way similar to Prolog's SLD-resolution algorithm operating on Horn Clauses. In fact, its Python implementation has been derived as a simplification of the Natlog [23] Horn Clause interpreter, where clause selection via the unification algorithms is replaced by synthesis of a clause head by an OR-node. Then, given the clause head, the body of the clause is generated by the LLM as an AND-node expansion of the synthesized clause head.

Instead of the `true` or `fail` answer generated by a Prolog system running the propositional Horn Clause program, the complete trace of goals generated by the LLM and "solved" by our recursor is returned as an "explanation" of the "reasoning steps" taken in the process. In fact, the resulting Horn Clauses are also "compiled" on the fly to a Prolog program that could be independently explored with a Prolog, Datalog or ASP system. However, given the presence of loops (as the LLM might come back in the recursive process to things it has already seen), we use instead of Prolog a low polynomial-time model builder that is insensitive to the presence of loops [7].

5   Refiners

Refiners are extensions of Recursors evaluating AND-nodes and OR-nodes against ground-truth facts in the embeddings store or via *decision* or *rating* LLM-oracles (see Subsect. 5.3).

In the first case, normalized semantic distances between embeddings of a goal hitting a depth limit and ground-truth facts are used. If close enough to a ground-truth fact, the "abducible" goal becomes a clause head and the ground-truth fact becomes the body of a newly generated clause. If not close enough to any ground-truth fact, the goal becomes the head of a clause marked for failure when compiled to the Prolog program by having as body the atom `fail`.

Alternatively, abducibles can be evaluated by an oracle – another LLM instance that judges their relevance to the task in the current context, for instance against embeddings of ground truth statements stored in a vector store.

5.1   The Embeddings Vector Store

We build a simple `numpy`-based vector store supporting efficiently ground-truth collections of fact embeddings obtained via the LLM's API. The ground-truth facts store is then used to find the K nearest neighbors of a given query and also to return cosine distances, usable as probabilities to decide what hypotheses can be assumed during the recursive descent as "abducible" facts, subject to filtering via evaluation of integrity constraints. Adopting scalable vector stores or databases can support the use of a knowledge base possibly derived from very large document collections.

5.2   Filtering with Semantic Distance to Ground-Truth Facts

By using the ground-truth facts in our embeddings store the simplest way to appraise if a given goal is "on topic" is to compute its semantic distance to its nearest neighbor in the store, as shown in the following code snippet:

```
def appraise(self, g, _trace, _topgoal):
    rates, neighbors = self.store.qa(g, top_k=1)
    rate, neighbor = float(rates[0]), neighbors[0]
    return rate > self.threshold:
```

The method `qa` that queries the store passes the goal `g` and the request for a single nearest neighbor `top_k`.

A more elaborate technique relies on k nearest neighbors fetched from the store that would collectively "champion" the goal if their (weighted) average semantic distance to the goal is below a threshold, fixed in advance or dynamically computed or machine-learned form past appraisals.

The mechanism can also be extended to continuously check for staying close in terms of semantic distance to the ground-truth facts.

Alternatively, the semantic distances (interpreted as probabilities) can be used to annotate clause heads as part of a probabilistic logic program to be evaluated later.

Oracles can also be used to implement *continual appraising*: at each step they can check reasonable closeness to ground truth and task at hand. In particular, they can mark confidence level for each rated step and then select overall highest only.

5.3   Refining Decisions with LLM-Based Oracles

In the absence of a set of ground-truth facts relevant to a given initiator goal, the LLM itself can be asked to make True/False decisions or generate ratings.

The LLM-Based True/False Decider. The following code snippet delegates the steering to focus on a given context (in this case the initiator goal that has started the recursive descent). In this case, the `appraise` method instantiates the oracle prompt pattern shown in Subsect. 3.

```
def appraise(self, g, trace, topgoal):
    advice = just_ask(self.oracle, g=g, context=topgoal)
    return 'True.' == advice
```

More elaborate refiners can use the depth-first path `trace` or an LLM-generated summary thereof instead of `topgoal`.

The LLM-Based Rater. The Rater queries the LLM asking for a score on the 0 to 100 scale that is next converted into a probability. Like the Decider oracle, it uses the goal at hand and its context. For both oracles, the prompter can be configured to ask for an explanation sentence or paragraph to be adopted as ground-truth in case of favorable True/False decision or high enough confidence level.

5.4   Toward Trustable Generative AI

Both oracle types, in concert with the focussed reasoning steps enforced by casting AND/OR steps into a propositional Horn clause program provide a principled approach toward trustable generative AI, an often expressed requirement for wide adoption of today's LLMs in medical, educational, defense and several other business applications as well as likely subjects of upcoming government regulations [10].

6   The Model Builder: A Propositional Horn Clause Satisfiability Solver

It is not unusual to have loops in the propositional Horn Clause program connecting the LLM generated items by our recursors and refiners. As that would create problems with Prolog's depth-first execution model, we implement a simple low-polynomial complexity propositional satisfiability checker and model builder along the lines of [7].

The model builder works by propagating truth from facts to rules until a fix point is reached. Given a Horn Clause $h : -b_1, b_2, ..., b_n$, when all b_i are known to be true (i.e., in the model), h is also added to the model. If integrity constraints (Horn clauses of the form $false : -b_1, b_2, ..., b_n$) have also been generated by the oracle agents monitoring our refiners, in the advent that all $b_1, b_2, ..., b_n$ end up in the model, $b_1, b_2, ..., b_n$ implying $false$ signals a contradiction and thus unsatisfiability of the Horn formula associated to the generated program. However as the items generated by our recursive process are not necessarily expressing logically connected facts (e.g., they might be just semantic similarity driven associations), turning on or off this draconian discarding of the model is left as an option for the application developer. Also, the application developer can chose to stop as soon as a proof of the original goal emerges, in a way similar to goal-driven ASP-solvers like [2], irrespectively to unrelated contradictions elsewhere in the program.

7   Applications

A good hint on deciding which recursor or refiner is the most appropriate for developing an application, is the closeness of its atomic steps to processes of human problem solving that are similar to logic inferences, e.g., by sharing a

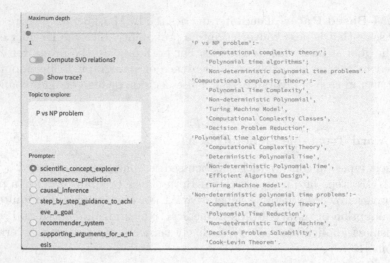

Fig. 2. Exploring the P vs. NP problem

similar underlying boolean algebra, lattice or preordered set structure. Besides causal reasoning or consequence prediction most goal-oriented tasks (e.g., planning) fit this structure. It is also good to be aware that when exploring the causes or the consequences of an initial state of the world, technological development, military, political or judicial decision, it is likely that the LLM will generate a richer model than if it explores names of movies, books or songs in a recommender system, where titles are often overlapping semantically with unrelated embeddings. In the former, restricting the model with a stricter oracle can even out spurious facts. In the latter, being aware that the LLMs will work better on very well known movies or books than when asking for recommendations similar to a relatively new or niche product, can guide the scope of the application.

When developing an application that, starting from a keyphrase of a scientific paper or the name of a scientific domain (e.g., as shown in Fig. 2 with the system exploring the P vs. NP problem), an oracle set up to filter out less specific concepts from encompassing more general domain can help with the return of more salient results. In this case a second oracle, filtering out generic methodological boilerplate concepts, shared by virtually all scientific domains will be also useful to give more focussed results. Similar refinements can also be used when focusing on predicting consequences of a (likely counterfactual) result (e.g., as shown in Fig. 3).

In the case of requesting expert advice on practical common tasks (e.g., actionable step-by-step advice on how to repair something), the oracle can filter out advice to contact the manufacturer or seek the advice of an expert nearby, when the point is to receive the actual steps need to solve the problem. This can also be implemented by a set of negative ground facts for which a refiner can try to maximize average semantic distances or a post-processor that rejects choices containing words or keyphrases in a blacklist.

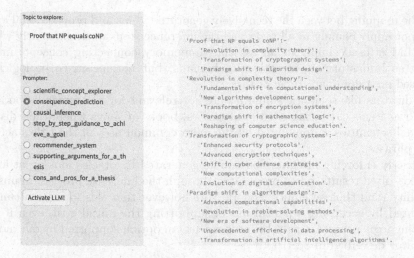

Fig. 3. Exploring consequences of the NP=coNP hypothesis

Another kind of application of significant practical value is to use a set of generated models to benchmark newcomer LLMs' performance against established best in their class like, at the time of writing this paper, OpenAI's GPT-4. This can be achieved with something as simple as the Jaccard distance between the inferred models at a given depth and it can be fine-tuned to the specific task the LLMs are planned to be used for. Related to this, when transferring from strong LLMs like GPT-4 to weaker ones, it can be useful to train the Reinforcement Learning loop rewards to be based on how many hits the weaker LLM gets when recursing on a relatively small collection of "critically important topics" automatically collected from the stronger LLM, thus providing a novel, potentially very effective transfer learning mechanism.

The generated Prolog programs, models and execution traces are available online at: https://github.com/ptarau/recursors/tree/main/examples.

8   Discussion on Limitations and Variations on the Theme

8.1   Limitations

We will next overview some of the limitations we have experienced when testing (the current implementation of) our recursors and refiners when on several target applications.

First, let us note that recursors are obviously not needed when one-shot detailed descriptions of common processes (e.g., cooking recipes, tell a joke, write a haiku) are available directly from the LLM. They are also unnecessary for help from the LLM to write a news story, a bio, an essay, a resume or an add, where interactive fine-tuning of the LLM's in-context learning by the user is a clear requirement.

The mapping between the recursively generated items and propositional logic does not apply equally to all tasks and the inference steps work differently when the LLM is used simply as an associative-memory connecting concepts interesting as brainstorming incentives to humans, but not meant to be logically focussed on a dominant topic or task.

Indicators like semantic similarity are not relevant for recommendation systems over items consisting of titles of movies, books or songs where their distributional semantics is dominated by the more common uses of the title's actual word phrases.

Strictly enforcing integrity constraints generated by oracles looking at local contexts often results, when propagated through the inference process, in unsatisfiability (and thus an empty model). Note however that this limitation can be alleviated by accepting a partial model supporting the initial goal, even if the resulting logic program might be inconsistent, an option supported by our model generator described in Sect. 6.

There's increased sensitivity to prompts during deeper recursive thought-to-thought steps. In this case, careful prompt engineering is needed as recursors can easily induce "butterfly effects" - small variations in wording of the prompt can drastically change the resulting model.

8.2 Future Work Directions

Once the key idea of the paper for steering LLMs to generate a stream of items focussed on the initiator goal is implemented, several "variations on the theme" can be tried out relatively easily by overriding methods in Prompters, Recursors and Refiners.

Granularity Refiners. At a higher granularity one can work with sentences/statements instead of noun phrases, sometime a more natural match to the underlying propositional logic.

At a lower granularity, one might want to use SVO triplets that LLMs are quite good at decomposing a sentence into. The generated SVO triplets can then serve as building blocks for Description Logics or Datalog programs.

Question Generators. Answers to LLM-generated how+wh-questions for a given goal can be used as expansions to new goals simply by re-engineering our AND-OR Prompters.

Generalizers. Inductive Logic Programming techniques can be used to generalize the resulting propositional or triplet clauses by sharing common SVO fragments, possibly in combination with Prolog-rules describing the ground-truth background knowledge.

Diversifiers and Harmonizers. To further restrict unwanted "hallucinatory" generation twists *diversifiers* for OR-nodes and *harmonizers* for AND-nodes can be expressed as additional integrity constraints. A diversifier will work by ensuring no two OR-nodes are too close semantically while a harmonizer will ensure that no two AND-nodes are too far semantically. Both could be implemented with help of semantic distances in the embeddings vector store.

Extend Implementation Techniques. One can implement recursors by relying on bare completion-only LLMs (e.g., GPT3) as their usual question-answering fine-tunings (e.g., ChatGPT) can be emulated with minor prompt engineering efforts.

To limit the scope of decider and rater oracles, one can preprocess the ground-truth facts into k-means clusters, and restrict oracle search to the cluster closest to the initiator goal.

Extend the Power of the Underlying Logic Language. It is possible to use SAT-based ASP solvers [21] or Prolog-based CASP systems [2] to take advantage of failed LLM returns rejected by our oracles, to enhance the ability of the LLMs to reason with negative information in a principled way as well as with negative ground-truth facts meant to avoid extending into semantically close but distinct domains during the recursive descent.

9   Related Work

The major disruption brought by the often near-human quality of generative AI [3, 19, 25] is quickly changing the landscape of query-driven information retrieval, moving the emphasis from traditional search engines to human-friendly dialog threads. However, the effectiveness of actionable information extraction is often hindered by the slower partner in this interaction – the human that needs to understand, evaluate and validate each step. In this context, our work emphasizes the full automation of this retrieval process, starting from a succinct query term. Thus, we are back to the one-shot simplicity of "short question by human → arbitrarily deep, elaborated answer from the AI", steered to stay focussed on the actual query. As a side effect of this automation, our approach preempts most of the usual problems with hallucinations, lack of factuality and bias that LLMs are often blamed for.

Our recursive descent algorithm shares with work on "Chain of Thought" prompting of LLMs [17, 26] and with step by step [16] refinement of the dialog threads the goal of extracting more accurate information from the interaction. However our process aims to fully automate the dialog thread while also ensuring validation of the results with help of ground-truth watching oracles and independent LLM-based agents. Our approach shares with tools like LangChain [4] the idea of piping together multiple instances of LLMs, computational units, prompt templates and custom agents, except that we fully automate the process without the need to manually stitch together the components.

By contrast to "neuro-symbolic" AI [20], where the neural architecture is closely intermixed with symbolic steps, in our approach the neural processing is encapsulated in the LLMs and accessed via a declarative, high-level API. This reduces the semantic gap between the neural and symbolic sides as their communication happens at a much higher, fully automated and directly explainable level.

In [28] LLMs are cleverly used to generate Prolog code snippets with an enhanced CASP [2] semantics. This allows hand-building of useful applications like a conversational AutoConcierge bot, recommending local restaurants. By contrast, our method is generic, and "no code" applications consist simply in queries with possible minor prompt engineering, as we adapt logic programming to think in terms familiar to LLMs, rather than adapting LLMs to generate application specific code snippets.

Also within Logic Programming, in relation with probabilistic approaches [5], our abducibles acquire probabilities from normalized vector distances to ground truths, usable to automate generation of probabilistic logic programs, thus sharing objectives with typical neuro-symbolic approaches like [18]. Finally, we share with [24] the idea to use a custom logic solver (an Intuitionistic Propositional Theorem prover, in that case) to synthesize abducibles (the Propositional Horn Clause model generator in our case).

10   Conclusion

We have automated deep step-by step reasoning in LLM dialog threads up to a given depth, by recursively descending from a single succinct initiator phrase, while staying focussed on the task at hand. In the process, we have made LLMs function as de facto logic programming engines that mimic Horn Clause resolution. However, instead of trying to parse sentences into logic formulas, we have accommodated our logic engine to fit the natural language reasoning patterns LLMs have been trained on.

Semantic similarity to ground-truth facts and oracle advice from another LLM instance has been used to restrict the search space and validate the traces of justification steps returned as answers. This has resulted in focussed, controllable output, enabling deep investigations into details of specific scientific domains as well as expert-level causal reasoning or consequence predictions. As such, our approach streamlines key use cases of LLMs as focussed information seeking tools and enables practical application back-ends simply by customizing prompt templates.

By casting the LLM dialog into a precise logic frame and by filtering the LLMs reasoning via semantic closeness to ground-truth facts, we have devised a method to extract hallucination-free focussed knowledge expressed as a logic program that encapsulates trustable AI in a clearly expressed and easily verifiable framework.

References

1. Anthropic: Claude-2 (2023). https://claude.ai/chats/. Accessed 02 Oct 2023
2. Arias, J., Carro, M., Salazar, E., Marple, K., Gupta, G.: Constraint answer set programming without grounding (2018)
3. Brown, T., et al.: Language models are few-shot learners. In: Larochelle, H., Ranzato, M., Hadsell, R., Balcan, M., Lin, H. (eds.) Advances in Neural Information Processing Systems, vol. 33, pp. 1877–1901. Curran Associates, Inc. (2020). https://doi.org/10.48550/arXiv.2005.14165
4. Chase, H.: LangChain (2022). https://github.com/hwchase17/langchain
5. De Raedt, L., Kimmig, A., Toivonen, H.: ProbLog: a probabilistic prolog and its application in link discovery. In: IJCAI, vol. 7, pp. 2462–2467 (2007). https://doi.org/10.5555/1625275.1625673
6. Denecker, M., Kakas, A.: Abduction in logic programming. In: Kakas, A.C., Sadri, F. (eds.) Computational Logic: Logic Programming and Beyond. LNCS, vol. 2407, pp. 402–36. Springer, Heidelberg (2002). https://doi.org/10.1007/3-540-45628-7_16
7. Dowling, W.F., Gallier, J.H.: Linear-time algorithms for testing the satisfiability of propositional horn formulae. J. Log. Program. 1(3), 267–284 (1984). https://doi.org/10.1016/0743-1066(84)90014-1
8. Gelfond, M., Lifschitz, V.: The stable model semantics for logic programming. In: Kowalski, R.A., Bowen, K.A. (eds.) Logic Programming, Proceedings of the Fifth International Conference and Symposium, Seattle, Washington, USA, August 15–19 1988, vol. 2, pp. 1070–1080. MIT Press (1988)
9. GoogleAI: Bard (2023). https://bard.google.com/. Accessed 23 June 2023
10. Hacker, P., Engel, A., Mauer, M.: Regulating ChatGPT and other large generative AI models, pp. 1112–1123. FAccT 2023, Association for Computing Machinery, New York, NY, USA (2023). https://doi.org/10.1145/3593013.3594067
11. Hossain, M.M., Holman, L., Kakileti, A., Kao, T.I., Brito, N.R., Mathews, A.A., Blanco, E.: A Question-Answer Driven Approach to Reveal Affirmative Interpretations from Verbal Negations (2022)
12. Kakas, A.C., Kowalski, R.A., Toni, F.: Abductive logic programming. J. Log. Comput. 2(6), 719–770 (1992). http://dblp.uni-trier.de/db/journals/logcom/logcom2.html#KakasKT92
13. Kowalski, R., Emden, M.V.: The semantics of predicate logic as a programming language. JACM 23(4), 733–743 (1976). https://doi.org/10.1145/321250.321253
14. Kowalski, R.A.: Predicate logic as programming language. In: Rosenfeld, J.L. (ed.) Information Processing, Proceedings of the 6th IFIP Congress 1974, Stockholm, Sweden, August 5–10, 1974, pp. 569–574. North-Holland (1974)
15. Levy, M.G.: Chatbots Don't Know What Stuff Isn't (2023). https://www.quantamagazine.org/ai-like-chatgpt-are-no-good-at-not-20230512/
16. Lightman, H., et al.: Let's verify step by step (2023)
17. Ling, Z., et al.: Deductive verification of chain-of-thought reasoning (2023)
18. Manhaeve, R., Dumancic, S., Kimmig, A., Demeester, T., De Raedt, L.: Deepproblog: neural probabilistic logic programming. In: Advances in Neural Information Processing Systems, vol. 31 (2018)
19. Ouyang, L., et al.: Training language models to follow instructions with human feedback (2022). https://doi.org/10.48550/ARXIV.2203.02155, https://arxiv.org/abs/2203.02155

20. Sarker, M.K., Zhou, L., Eberhart, A., Hitzler, P.: Neuro-symbolic artificial intelligence: current trends (2021). https://doi.org/10.48550/ARXIV.2105.05330, https://arxiv.org/abs/2105.05330

21. Schaub, T., Woltran, S.: Special issue on answer set programming. KI **32**(2-3), 101–103 (2018). https://doi.org/10.1007/s13218-018-0554-8

22. Tarau, P.: A Hitchhiker's guide to reinventing a prolog machine. In: Rocha, R., Son, T.C., Mears, C., Saeedloei, N. (eds.) Technical Communications of the 33rd International Conference on Logic Programming (ICLP 2017). OpenAccess Series in Informatics (OASIcs), vol. 58, pp. 10:1–10:16. Schloss Dagstuhl–Leibniz-Zentrum fuer Informatik, Dagstuhl, Germany (2018). https://doi.org/10.4230/OASIcs.ICLP.2017.10, http://drops.dagstuhl.de/opus/volltexte/2018/8453

23. Tarau, P.: Natlog: a lightweight logic programming language with a neuro-symbolic touch. In: Formisano, A., (eds.) et al Proceedings 37th International Conference on Logic Programming (Technical Communications) , 20–27th September 2021 (2021). https://doi.org/10.4204/EPTCS.345.27

24. Tarau, P.: Abductive reasoning in intuitionistic propositional logic via theorem synthesis. Theory Pract. Logic Program. **22**(5), 693–707 (2022). https://doi.org/10.1017/S1471068422000254

25. Touvron, H., et al.: Llama: open and efficient foundation language models (2023)

26. Wei, J., et al.: Chain-of-thought prompting elicits reasoning in large language models (2023)

27. Wielemaker, J., Schrijvers, T., Triska, M., Lager, T.: SWI-Prolog. Theory Pract. Logic Program. **12**, 67–96 (2012). https://doi.org/10.1017/S1471068411000494

28. Zeng, Y., Rajasekharan, A., Padalkar, P., Basu, K., Arias, J., Gupta, G.: Automated interactive domain-specific conversational agents that understand human dialogs (2023)

A Constraint-Based Mathematical Modeling Library in Prolog with Answer Constraint Semantics

François Fages(✉) ⓘ

Inria Saclay, Palaiseau, France
`Francois.Fages@inria.fr`

Abstract. Constraint logic programming emerged in the late 80's as a highly declarative class of programming languages based on first-order logic and theories with decidable constraint languages, thereby subsuming Prolog restricted to equality constraints over the Herbrand's term domain. This approach has proven extremely successful in solving combinatorial problems in the industry which quickly led to the development of a variety of constraint solving libraries in standard programming languages. Later came the design of a purely declarative front-end constraint-based modeling language, MiniZinc, independent of the constraint solvers, in order to compare their performances and create model benchmarks. Beyond that purpose, the use of a high-level modeling language such as MiniZinc to develop complete applications, or to teach constraint programming, is limited by the impossibility to program search strategies, or new constraint solvers, in a modeling language, as well as by the absence of an integrated development environment for both levels of constraint-based modeling and constraint solving. In this paper, we propose to solve those issues by taking Prolog with its constraint solving libraries, as a unified relation-based modeling and programming language. We present a Prolog library for high-level constraint-based mathematical modeling, inspired by MiniZinc, using subscripted variables (arrays) in addition to lists and terms, quantifiers and iterators in addition to recursion, together with a patch of constraint libraries in order to allow array functional notations in constraints. We show that this approach does not come with a significant computation time overhead, and presents several advantages in terms of the possibility of focussing on mathematical modeling, getting answer constraints in addition to ground solutions, programming search or constraint solvers if needed, and debugging models within a unique modeling and programming environment.

Keywords: constraint logic programming · algebraic modeling languages · answer constraints · MiniZinc · meta-predicates · constraint solving · constraint simplification · attributed variables · ISO-Prolog

1 Introduction

Jean-Baptiste Fourier is very well-known for his numerous contributions to mathematics and physics, but much less known for being the father of what is called

© The Author(s), under exclusive license to Springer Nature Singapore Pte Ltd. 2024
J. Gibbons and D. Miller (Eds.): FLOPS 2024, LNCS 14659, pp. 135–150, 2024.
https://doi.org/10.1007/978-981-97-2300-3_8

today Constraint Programming. In two lectures at the French Academy of Sciences given in 1823 and 1824, he considered the example of determining the region where a given weight can be placed on a triangular table with constraints on the maximum forces that can be exerted on each leg, in order to promote a general problem solving method based on, first, modeling the problem at hand with inequalities over real numbers, and second, solving them by applying general purpose simplification rules a.k.a. Fourier Motzkin's elimination rules today. Quoting him, "the advantage of this method consists in that it is sufficient, in all cases, to express the conditions of the question, which is easy, and to then combine these expressions, by means of general rules which are always the same; and we thus form the solution which could only have been reached by a series of very complicated reasonings". Furthermore, he mentions that these simplification rules presented for linear inequalities apply as well to non-linear inequalities a.k.a. interval arithmetic: "if the conditions are expressed by non-linear inequalities, the question does not change its nature, and can still be treated by the same principles.". In his second lecture, he considers the optimisation problem and describes a method for moving from vertices to vertices of the feasible region polyhedron, in order to improve the cost up to its optimal value, a.k.a the geometrical interpretation of the Simplex algorithm [9].

In the realm of Linear Programming today, several Algebraic Modeling Languages such as OPL, AMPL, Mosel, etc. have been defined as input modeling languages with a syntax near to mathematical notations for optimization problems, using indices, sets, algebraic expressions and data handling variables. Then external solvers interfaced with these modeling languages can be called to actually solve the problem instances defined by the model and a dataset.

In the realm of Constraint Programming, MiniZinc is a similarly high-level constraint-based modeling language to model constraint satisfaction and optimization problems in a solver-independent way [12,16]. A MiniZinc model is usually transformed in a FlatZinc model in which the high-level constructs have been eliminated and replaced by a flat constraint satisfaction problem that can be solved by a variety of constraint solvers parsing FlatZinc syntax. This is the way for instance SICStus-Prolog is interfaced with FlatZinc as a general purpose constraint solver to solve problems modeled in MiniZinc [11]. Because of the importance of global constraints, several of them are defined in MiniZinc, kept in FlatZinc, and handled by the constraint solver, either directly as global constraints if they are implemented as such, or by decomposition into basic constraints supported by the constraint solver.

Because of the importance of search in constraint programming, MiniZinc contains some predefined common search heuristic options that are kept in FlatZinc for their possible interpretation by the constraint solvers, in addition to solver specific annotations in the MiniZinc model that are similarly kept in FlatZinc [12]. Nevertheless, the absence of programming constructs in a modeling language like MiniZinc limits the search strategies that can be tried to solve a complex problem, which may finally lead to abandon the high-level modeling approach in favor of a lower level constraint programming language.

Furthermore, when it comes to teaching constraint-based modeling and algorithms for decision making, there is a need to teach constraint solving algorithms and program them as well. The recourse to a modeling language like MiniZinc makes it possible to focus on the declarative modeling aspects but cannot be used to show the implementation of constraint solvers, nor implement new constraints. Because of its roots in first-order logic, Prolog should be a natural choice to address these needs as both a programming language in its own right, and a modeling language based on relations a.k.a. constraints. Nevertheless the historical focus on list data structure, and the definition of meta-predicates before the advent of constraint logic programming, make of Prolog a poor modeling language for complex constraint satisfaction problems, moreover exhibiting incompatibilities of use between some standard meta-predicates and constraint solving libraries.

In this paper we propose solutions to those issues by presenting a general purpose mathematical modeling library[1] in Prolog, based on bounded quantifiers and arrays for subscripted variables, which is essentially compatible with MiniZinc models and obviously Prolog programming facilities for programming search, constraint solvers, and using external interfaces.

The next section contains a motivating example for modeling the N-queens problem and breaking all the symmetries of that placement problem on a square (i.e. with respect to the 8 elements of the dihedral group of isometries of order 4). The recourse to mathematical notations made possible with our modeling library using subscripted variables and bounded quantifiers rather than lists and recursion, marks a striking gain in declarativity for engineers and students in engineering schools more acquainted to mathematical notations than programming structures. We provide some performance figures which show that this is achieved with no computation time overhead.

In Sect. 3 we compare our modeling library in Prolog to the solver-independent constraint-based modeling language MiniZinc [12,16]. We show the large compatibility between both modeling languages, and describe the advantages of the Prolog library approach in terms of ability to compute answer constraints, not just ground solutions, a definite advantage of constraint logic programming [8] illustrated there with Fourier's example, as well as to program search and debug models in a unique modeling and programming environment.

In Sect. 4 we describe the main predicates of our modeling library for arrays and iterator meta-predicates for answer constraint semantics. The development of such a library raises however a number of subtle issues that cannot be solved with standard Prolog meta-predicates that have been designed before the advent of constraints. This leads us to make a proposal for extending the specification of the behaviour of ISO-Prolog meta-predicates to attributed variables, in the realm of Prolog answer constraint semantics. Finally, we conclude on the importance of keeping the development of Prolog systems in both perspectives of a relation-based declarative programming language and a constraint-based mathematical modeling language.

---

[1] The Prolog libraries presented here form a pack named modeling, currently available for SWI-Prolog at https://lifeware.inria.fr/wiki/Main/Software#modeling.

2   Motivating Example

2.1   List Recursion Versus Array Iteration in the N-Queens Problem

The N-queens puzzle consists in placing N queens on an $N \times N$ chessboard such that they do not attack each other, i.e. no pair of queens is on the same line or diagonal. This is a classical example used in constraint programming to illustrate the power of the active use of constraints to prune the search tree when they are posted in advance in the paradigm of "constrain and generate", by opposition to pure backtracking "generate and test" programs limited to small size problems. This makes it possible for instance to place by search 100 queens in 0.25 s CPU time on a standard laptop, a performance out of reach of search methods without active use of constraints to filter the domains of all variables during search.

The standard definition of this problem by Prolog clauses with constraints over the integers uses a list of N variables representing the queens (say per column as in Fig. 1) with a finite domain of possible values in the interval [1, N] (representing their position in the rows) and posts the no-attack constraints by double recursion on that list of variables, before enumerating the values in the domain of the variables (predicate labeling/2 with ff first-fail smallest-domain variable and-choice heuristics), as follows:

```
:- use_module(library(clpfd)).

queens(N, Queens):-
  length(Queens, N),
  Queens ins 1..N,
  safe(Queens),
  labeling([ff], Queens).

safe([]).
safe([QI | Tail]) :-
  noattack(Tail, QI, 1),
  safe(Tail).

noattack([], _, _).
noattack([QJ | Tail], QI, D) :-
  QI #\= QJ,
  QI #\= QJ + D,
  QI #\= QJ - D,
  D1 #= D + 1,
  noattack(Tail, QI, D1).
```

The double recursion on the lists of queens and of their successor queens on the right, is standard in Prolog where the list data structure is promoted, mainly for historical reasons including comparison to Lisp, and where most built-in predicates are defined on lists.

In algebraic modeling languages however, mathematical notations using subscripted variables, with iteration over subscripts instead of recursion, are usually

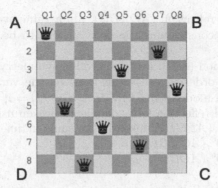

Fig. 1. Placement of 8 queens on a 8×8 chessboard with no two queens in the same column, row or diagonal, modeled as a constraint satisfaction problem, with 8 variables $Q_1, \ldots, Q_8$, representing the queens say in each column, taking integer values in the interval $[1, 8]$ representing the rows where they are placed.

preferred for better declarativity. This is what offers our mathematical modeling library in Prolog. The double list recursion for posting the constraints between each pair of queens in the program above can thus be replaced by iteration on the indices of an array of decision variables as follows:

```
:- use_module(modeling).

queens(N, Queens):-
  int_array(Queens, [N], 1..N),
  for_all([I in 1..N-1, D in 1..N-I],
          (Queens[I] #\= Queens[I+D],
           Queens[I] #\= Queens[I+D]+D,
           Queens[I] #\= Queens[I+D]-D)),
  satisfy(Queens).
```

Compared to the previous Prolog program using lists and recursion, the advantage in terms of declarativity of the constraint-based model using subscripted variables should be clear, at least for engineers or students more familiar with mathematical notations than programming structures.

2.2 Breaking Symmetries in the N-Queens Problem

The gain in declarativity becomes even more striking however, when it comes to breaking all symmetries of the chessboard square with respect of the 8 isometries of the dihedral group of order 4 for a square [A, B, C, D] as in Fig. 1, using lexicographic ordering constraints [17], namely

- the reflection symmetry $(AB)(CD)$ around the vertical axis, a variable symmetry in the model of Fig. 1 which can be eliminated here by constraining the first variable to be less than the last;

- the horizontal axis reflection $(AD)(BC)$, i.e. a value symmetry that can be
eliminated here by constraining the first variable to be less or equal to the
mid row value;
- the diagonal reflection (BD), a variable-value symmetry that can be broken
by a lexicographic ordering constraint between the variables of the primal
model and the dual model defined by $D_i = j \Leftrightarrow Q_j = i$;
- the second diagonal reflection (AC), similarly broken using a dual model;
- the rotation by 90° $(ABCD)$ broken in the same manner;
- the rotation by 180° $(AC)(BD)$;
- the rotation by 270° $(ADCB)$;
- (the identity).

These symmetry breaking constraints can be added to the model using lexicographic ordering `lex_leq/2` constraints on arrays as follows:

```
sym_elim(N, Queens) :-
  Queens[1] #< Queens[N], % vertical reflection symmetry
  Queens[1] #=< (N+1)//2, % horizontal reflection symmetry

  int_array(Dual, [N], 1..N),
  for_all([I, J] in 1..N, Queens[I] #= J #<==> Dual[J] #= I),
  lex_leq(Queens, Dual), % first diagonal reflection

  int_array(SecondDiagonal, [N], 1..N),
  for_all(I in 1..N, SecondDiagonal[I] #= N + 1 - Dual[N+1-I]),
  lex_leq(Queens, SecondDiagonal),

  int_array(R90, [N], 1..N),
  for_all(I in 1..N, R90[I] #= Dual[N+1-I]),
  lex_leq(Queens, R90),   % rotation symmetry by 90 degrees

  int_array(R180, [N], 1..N),
  for_all(I in 1..N, R180[I] #= N + 1 - Queens[N+1-I]),
  lex_leq(Queens, R180),

  int_array(R270, [N], 1..N),
  for_all(I in 1..N, R270[I] #= N + 1 - Dual[I]),
  lex_leq(Queens, R270).
```

Implementing arrays in ISO-Prolog is straightforward using term meta-
predicates `functor/3` and `arg/3`, and reading/writing cells by unification (backtrackable and non-backtrackable assignments using `setarg/3` or `nb_setarg/3`
are also possible but not considered here).

On the other hand, implementing bounded quantifiers and iteration meta-
predicates like `for_all/2` above raises some issues with the existing ISO-Prolog
meta-predicates which have been defined for the provability semantics of Prolog,
before the advent of the answer constraint semantics of Constraint Logic Programming [8]. This justifies a new implementation of control meta-predicates
compatible with constraint solving libraries in Prolog, and probably the definition of a second level of normalization for ISO-Prolog with attributed variables
for constraint handling. These aspects are discussed in Sect. 4.3.

2.3 Performance Figures

Table 1. CPU time in seconds and reported number of logical inferences in SWI-Prolog for solving various variants of the N-queens problem, compared between the recursive program on lists and the mathematical model using subscripted variables and quantifiers. The last benchmark simply shows the logarithmic versus linear access times in large datasets represented by arrays versus lists.

Benchmark	CPU time in seconds	Nb logical inferences
100-queens first solution		
math model	0.373	4,552,518
list program	0.298	4,472,406
all-distinct math model	3.611	63,565,626
all-distinct list program	3.470	63,502,308
8-queens all 92 solutions		
math model	0.041	757,835
list program	0.042	757,303
all-distinct math model	0.297	4,025,643
all-distinct list program	0.289	4,012,622
8-queens all 12 non-symmetrical sol.		
math model	0.045	667,850
list program	0.048	664,708
all-distinct math model	0.125	1,471,542
all-distinct list program	0.128	1,509,989
10^2 accesses in an array of size 10^2	0.000	301
in a list of size 10^2	0.000	544
10^3 accesses in an array of size 10^3	0.001	3,001
in a list of size 10^3	0.003	4,144
10^4 accesses in an array of size 10^4	0.005	30,001
in a list of size 10^4	0.161	40,001
10^5 accesses in an array of size 10^5	0.027	300,001
in a list of size 10^5	13.615	400,001
10^6 accesses in an array of size 10^6	0.148	3,000,001
in a list of size 10^6	1567.177	4,000,144

We report here some performance figures obtained with our modeling library in SWI-Prolog version 9.0.4, including the `clpfd` library of constraints over integer variables, on a MacBook Pro 2,3 GHz Quad-Core Intel Core i7 32 GB 3733 MHz.

Table 1 shows the absence of significant difference in computation time between the execution of our models based on arrays and universal quantifiers for iterations, and the Prolog programs based on lists and list recursions.

On the other hand, the speed-up due to logarithmic access in an array versus linear access in a list (which does not occur in the list based model of the N-queens problem) begins to show up from size 1000 in pure cell access problems.

3 Comparison to MiniZinc Modeling Language

3.1 Types

Compared to MiniZinc, the writing of the N-queens model is very similar:

```
int: n = 8;
array [1..n] of var 1..n: queens;
constraint forall (i in 1..n-1, d in 1..n-i)
                   (queens[i] != queens[i+d] /\
                    queens[i] != queens[i+d] + d /\
                    queens[i] != queens[i+d] - d);
solve satisfy;
```

Type declarations are necessary in MiniZinc to overload operators and constraint predicates over the four constraint domains considered in MiniZinc: the integers, the Booleans, the real numbers (floating points) and the domain of finite sets of integers.

This is not implemented in our modeling library in Prolog since constraint predicate symbols are currently not overloaded. More specifically

- constraint predicates over integers and Booleans values 0/1 of library clpfd are prefixed and distinguished by the # symbol,
- constraints over real numbers are distinguished by enclosing between curly brackets in the clpr library used,
- constraints on finite sets are currently not implemented.

It is worth noting however that prescriptive typing and type inference are possible in Prolog, as demonstrated for instance in [4] using a powerful system of subtyping constraints [2]. This could be used to parse MiniZinc models and type check mixed MiniZinc-Prolog programs.

3.2 Programming Search

The search procedure is the second most important component of constraint programming techniques to solve hard combinatorial problems. For that reason, MiniZinc offers the possibility to provide a limited set of search annotations, which can be interpreted by the solvers, for specifying and-choice heuristics (e.g. first-fail principle), or-choice heuristics (e.g. best-first criterions) and also some search strategies such as dichotomic search.

Of course, such search options cannot cover all needs for controlling search. In [10], it is however shown how some more elaborated search strategies such as Limited Discrepancy Search [7] can be specified by constraints in the model.

In [13], a solver-independent language is proposed to control search in MiniZinc with a limited set of instructions to execute each time a solution is found. This is illustrated by the implementation of Large Neighborhood Search (LNS), an important strategy for optimization problems.

In [15], search combinators are proposed to specify general search instructions to execute at each choice point in the model. This requires interaction with the solver at each node of the search tree which is hardly supported by constraint solvers implemented in a different programming language.

The capability to program search at that level of granularity can however make a decisive difference in hard combinatorial problems. For instance, in disjunctive scheduling, it can be worth spending time to determine the best mutual exclusion constraint to select for the next choice point, in order to prune the search tree by constraint propagation, instead of just duplicating the real search space with a bad selection. Sophisticated strategies, including looking-ahead techniques for determining that most informative disjunctive constraint by trying them all may thus become necessary to implement.

This requires the recourse to a programming language which is possible with a programming library-based approach to modeling, like here in Prolog, a natural choice for relation-based modeling, and not possible with a pure modeling language approach like MiniZinc or other algebraic modeling languages, beyond a limited set of search annotations.

3.3   Answer Constraint Semantics in Fourier's Example

Thanks to the computed answer constraint semantics of the class of constraint logic programming languages [8], and of Prolog with its constraint-solving libraries, the execution of MiniZinc models directly in our modeling library in Prolog makes it possible to obtain much more informative answer constraints, compared to the ground solutions obtained with MiniZinc solvers.

This can be illustrated by the example given by Fourier in his lecture on constraint-based modeling and solving for systems of linear inequalities [9]. He took the problem of placing a given weight P at unknown coordinates (X, Y) on an isocele triangular table with a maximum force F exerted on each of the 3 legs (see Fig. 2).

By assuming that the triangle table has leg 1 at coordinates $(0, 0)$, leg 2 at coordinates $(20, 0)$ and leg 3 at coordinates $(0, 20)$, simple moment equilibrium equations give the following model:

```
fourier(P, X, Y, F):-
    float_array(Forces, [3], 0..F),
    {Force[1]+Force[2]+Force[3] = P},
    {P*X = 20*Force[2]},
    {P*Y = 20*Force[3]}.

?- fourier(3, X, Y, 1).
X = Y, Y = 6.666666666666667.
```

```
?- fourier(3.1, X, Y, 1).
false.

?- fourier(2, X, Y, 1).
{Y=20.0-10.0*_A-10.0*_B, X=10.0*_B, _=2.0-_A-_B, _B=<1.0, _A=<1.0}.

?- fourier(2, X, Y, 1), maximize(X).
X = 10.0,
{Y=10.0-10.0*_A, _=1.0-_A, _A=<1.0, _A>=0.0}.

?- fourier(2, X, Y, 1), maximize(X+Y).
X = Y, Y = 10.0.
```

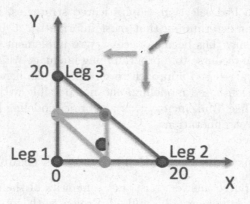

Fig. 2. Example given by Fourier to illustrate a general purpose constraint-based modeling method, applied to the placement of a weight on a triangular table with limit constraints on the forces exerted on its legs 1, 2, 3, together with a general purpose method for solving systems of linear inequalities over the real numbers. The inner triangle represents the validity domain of the placement of a weight of 2 units. This triangle is symbolically represented by the computed answer constraint for the query `fourier(2, X, Y, 1)`.

For a weight of 3 units, a single point is returned as unique solution. Interestingly, for the placement of a weight of 2 units maximizing its coordinate along the X axis, the value 10 is found for X together with one constraint on Y and A which defines the vertical segment where the weight can be placed. Similarly, the computed answer constraints returned for the placement of a weight of 2 units without optimization criterion define symbolically the validity domain depicted by the inner triangle in Fig. 2. It is worth noting that the computed answer constraint set semantics are a quite unique advantage of the constraint logic programming paradigm, compared to other declarative modeling languages that are usually interfaced to solvers restricted to compute ground solutions and not constraints.

3.4   Model Debuging and Visualization in a Unique IDE

In our modeling library approach in Prolog, a MiniZinc model can be executed in two ways:

- either by parsing the MiniZinc syntax and interpreting it directly by the predicates of our library,
- or by parsing the FlatZinc model generated by the MiniZinc compiler which is the standard way of evaluating backend MiniZinc constraint solvers.

A FlatZinc parser has been developed for SICStus Prolog which shows excellent performance on MiniZinc challenge competitions [16].

On the other hand, the advantage of parsing MiniZinc syntax in a Prolog system has already been demonstrated in a system like Eclipse [1]. Making it available in a library for standard Prolog systems is however a significant contribution to factorize system development efforts, and use the single Integrated Development Environment (IDE) of Prolog to debug MiniZinc models.

For instance, the general purpose search tree visualization and interaction library CLPGUI, developed for constraint logic programming [5], can be used here to visualize, and restore states in, the search tree developed by our modeling library in Prolog. This is illustrated in Fig. 3 in the model above for enumerating all 92 solutions of the 8 queens problem.

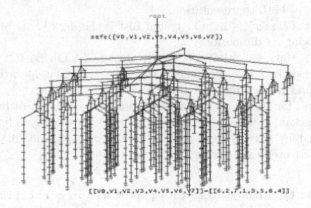

Fig. 3. Visualization of the search tree for enumerating all the 92 solutions of the 8-queens problem in Prolog with constraints, using the interactive graphical visualization system CLPGUI of [5]. This illustrates the good job of constraints for pruning the search tree in this example. Indeed, after around 5 choice points with a limited number of possible values, the branches of the search tree become linear and lead to one solution.

From the point of view of a modeler, or of a teacher, this is a very useful tool that is difficult to implement without a unique declarative programming/modeling IDE. For the same reasons, model debugging is greatly facilitated by the absence of a first transformation of the model to a FlatZinc model, followed by a second transformation to an external constraint solver which can create runtime errors difficult to recover.

4   Modeling Library

4.1   Subscripted Variables with Library arrays.pl

Subscripted variables, i.e. arrays, are not normalized in ISO-Prolog but can be easily represented by terms with functor array. Multidimensional arrays are then represented by arrays of arrays. On top of that, library modeling.pl defines predicates for defining arrays of Booleans, integers or real number with domain constraints. The main predicates defined in library arrays.pl are:

array(?Array, ?Dimensions) true if Array is an array of dimension Dimensions. Either creates an array of given dimensions, or returns the list of dimensions of a given array, or checks the relation.

cell(+Array, +Indices, ?Cell). true if Cell is the cell or subarray cell of a given array at given indices (integer or list of integers). Throws an error if the indices are out of range of the array. The cell is read and written by unification. The functional notation syntax Array[Indices] is also authorized in constraints to denote the cell of an array without having to introduce an existentially quantified variable for that, e.g. with the quantifier meta-predicates described below.

array_list(?Array, ?List). true if List is the flat list of all elements in Array. Either creates a one-dimensional array, or the list of array cells, or checks the consistency of both representation.

array_lists(?Array, ?List). true if List is the list of lists of elements in the array following its dimensions.

tensor(+A, +Op, +B, +Rel, ?C) equivalent to (A Op B) Rel C, where A, B, C are arrays or lists of same dimensions, Op is a binary operation executed element-wise, and Rel a binary predicate.

Furthermore, for the sake of generality outside the scope of our modeling library, backtrackable and non-backtrackable imperative array cell assignments are also defined by extra-logical predicates set_cell/3 and nb_set_cell/3 using ISO-Prolog predicate setarg/3.

4.2   Bounded Quantification Meta-predicates in quantifiers.pl

Iteration with subscripted variables is more natural to implement using quantifiers on the indices rather than recursion. To this end, we introduce the following general-purpose meta-predicates to quantify variables either universally or existentially, and distinguish them from context variables in goals:

for_all(+Args, +Goal) calls Goal for all the arguments specified in Args, i.e. calls the conjunction Goal(Arg1), ..., Goal(ArgN). The list of arguments Args is a list of universally quantified variables given with a finite domain (either finite interval of integers or list of terms), plus possibly a deterministic condition goal, using expressions of the form Args in Domain where Condition.

exists(+Vars, +Goal) to make a list of variables renamed-apart and local to the goal.

let(+Bindings, +Goal) to additionally apply a binding constraint =, =.., in, #=, #<, #>, #=<, #>= between an existentially quantified variable and a term, possibly using Array[Indices] functional notation for array cells.

list_of(+Vars, ?List) to build the list of terms specified in Args.

The introduction of those meta-predicates in our modeling library is justified by the fact that ISO-Prolog meta-predicates bagof/3, setof/3, findall/3 have been introduced before the advent of constraint logic programming, and of the implementation of constraint solvers based on attributed variables, at a time focussing on the provability semantics of Prolog.

Indeed, in his seminal paper [19], David Warren introduced an extra logical meta-predicate to collect information across branches of the search tree. Paraphrasing him, the extension takes the form of a new built-in predicate: setof(X,P,S) to be read as: *"The set of instances of X such that P is provable is S"*. This is achieved with a special mechanism introduced in the WAM [18] for copying and memorizing terms in a list across backtracking. The non deterministic goal P can thus be used as a *generator of the instances* to be checked for satisfiability.

This mechanism has been used to introduce various meta-predicates for higher-order programming in Prolog [14]. Those meta-predicates thus refer to the provability semantics of Prolog, not the answer constraint semantics. Similarly, meta-predicates forall/3, foreach/3 found in several Prolog dialects have no normalized behaviour with respect to attributed variables and constraints.

In the success set semantics of a universal quantifier for goals, it is not clear whether the successful bindings should be kept across backtracking. On the other hand, in the answer constraint semantics, it is clear that the computed answer constraints should be added conjunctively to the store of constraints. This is precisely what is achieved by our for_all/2 meta-predicate that generates instances of the goal by iteration, unlike for example the forall/2 predicate of SWI-Prolog that generates instances by backtracking:

```
?- L=[X, Y], forall(member(V, L), V=a).
L = [X, Y].
```

```
?- L=[X, Y], for_all(V in L, V=a).
L = [a, a],
X = Y, Y = a.
```

4.3   Interface to Constraint Solvers with Library clp.pl

We also found it useful to create a front-end interface to existing libraries for solving constraints over the real numbers, integers and booleans, for several reasons. First, this front-end library makes it possible to use evaluable expressions and Array[Indices] functional notation in constraints and in the definitions of variable domains. Second, global constraints on lists of variables can now undifferently accept arrays instead of lists.

Beyond that, some questions arise concerning the answer constraint semantics and the copying or not by Prolog meta-predicates of the constraints attached to the variables. For constraint libraries using attributed variables, this amounts to the question of whether those meta-predicates should copy the attributes or not, in particular the constraint propagator attributes.

In the answer constraint semantics, the answer is clearly yes, and this is what is done for instance in SWI-Prolog and Scryer-Prolog. There is however currently a side effect concerning the duplication of the constraint propagators, e.g.

```
?- L=[A, B], L ins 1..2, A #=< B, bagof(W, member(W, L), L2).
L = L2, L2 = [A, B],
A in 1..2,
B#>=A,
B#>=A,
B#>=A,
B in 1..2.
```

This is patched in our library clp.pl by making a set union instead of concatenating the constraint propagators attached to two variables when they are unified. In this respect, it is worth noting that the set union of constraint propagators should not be implemented by maintaining the constraint propagation attributes sorted, since that could severely affect the scheduling and performance of constraint propagators.

Furthermore, a more efficient and more general solution would be to consider the simplification of constraints on two variables that get unified. This is not usually done in constraint programming and global constraint solvers, e.g.

```
?- L=[X, Y], L ins 1..3, all_distinct(L), X=Y.
L = [Y, Y],
X = Y,
Y in 1..3,
all_distinct([Y, Y]).
```

Symbolic simplification of constraints is however instrumental in SMT solvers or in Constraint Handling Rules (CHR) [6]. This has been shown responsible for drastic performance improvement in some contexts, for instance in [2,3] for solving subtyping constraints using CHR, with better performance than dedicated algorithms in CAML, thanks to the constraint simplifications performed by CHR immediately upon unification of two variables.

4.4   Proposal for a Second-Level of Normalization of ISO-Prolog

Because of the importance of constraint-based methods in many applications of Prolog, and because of the numerous implementations of constraint solvers in Prolog libraries using attributed variables, we propose to specify the behaviour of ISO-Prolog predicates with respect to attributed variables in a new level 2 norm for ISO-Prolog.

More specifically, we mainly propose to open discussion to:

1. normalize attributed variables;

2. specify the copying or not of attributed variables in ISO-Prolog predicates `findall/3`, `bagof/3`, `setof/3`;
3. define meta-predicates compatible with constraint answer semantics;
4. normalize predicates for arrays.

5   Conclusion

Last year was the 50th year of Prolog, and this remarkable longevity for a programming language was clearly recognized as a mark of the fundamental importance of the relational programming paradigm based on first-order Horn clause logic and constraints in decidable theories. It also showed the need to transmit knowledge to new generations of Prolog system developpers, teachers and users, and unite the Prolog community with new momentum.

The development of our constraint-based mathematical modeling library in Prolog aims at going in that direction from the triple points of view of the users, by providing a higher-level modeling library with full programming features; of the teachers, by providing a unique environment for both constraint-based modeling and programming; and of the system developpers, by factorizing library development efforts, and providing use cases of standard predicates and libraries that require some corrections and probably a normalization effort.

On-going work concerns the addition of a MiniZinc parser to our modeling library in order to directly execute and debug MiniZinc models in a single modeling/programming environment, compare performances using the large database of MiniZinc models, compute answer constraints not just ground solutions for getting more declarative answers, and stop being blocked from programming search for hard decision making problems.

Acknowledgments. I am grateful to my students at Ecole Polytechnique for their interest in my courses on Constraint Programming including practical work that evolved over the years from Prolog to MiniZinc and now back to Prolog; to Mathieu Hemery and Sylvain Soliman for their participation in the teaching and fruitful discussions; to Guy-Alain Narboni for his vision of the importance of the Prolog heritage and the organization of the 50th year of Prolog in Paris; to Markus Triska, Ulrich Neumerkel and Christian Jendreiko for their organization of the Scryer Meetup in Dusseldorf; and to the reviewers for their comments.

References

1. Apt, K., Wallace, M.: Constraint Logic Programming Using Eclipse. Cambridge University Press, Cambridge (2006)
2. Coquery, E., Fages, F.: TCLP: overloading, subtyping and parametric polymorphism made practical for CLP. In: Stuckey, P.J. (ed.) ICLP 2002. LNCS, vol. 2401, p. 480. Springer, Heidelberg (2002). https://doi.org/10.1007/3-540-45619-8_42
3. Coquery, E., Fages, F.: Subtyping constraints in quasi-lattices. In: Pandya, P.K., Radhakrishnan, J. (eds.) FSTTCS 2003. LNCS, vol. 2914, pp. 136–148. Springer, Heidelberg (2003). https://doi.org/10.1007/978-3-540-24597-1_12

4. Fages, F., Coquery, E.: Typing constraint logic programs. J. Theory Pract. Log. Program. **1**(6), 751–777 (2001)
5. Fages, F., Soliman, S., Coolen, R.: CLPGUI: a generic graphical user interface for constraint logic programming. J. Constraints Spec. Issue User-Interact. Constraint Satisfaction **9**(4), 241–262 (2004). https://doi.org/10.1023/B:CONS.0000049203.53383.c1
6. Frühwirth, T.W.: Constraint Handling Rules. Cambridge University Press, Cambridge (2009)
7. Harvey, W.D., Ginsberg, M.L.: Limited discrepancy search. In: IJCAI 1995: Proceedings of the 14th International Joint Conference on Artificial Intelligence, pp. 607–613. Morgan Kaufmann Publishers Inc., San Francisco (1995)
8. Jaffar, J., Lassez, J.L.: Constraint logic programming. In: Proceedings of the 14th ACM Symposium on Principles of Programming Languages, Munich, Germany, pp. 111–119. ACM (1987)
9. Lassez, J.L., Maher, M.J.: On Fourier's algorithm for linear arithmetic constraints. J. Autom. Reason. **9**, 373–379 (1992)
10. Martinez, T., Fages, F., Soliman, S.: Search by constraint propagation. In: Proceedings of the 17th International Conference on Principles and Practice of Declarative Programming, PPDP 2015, pp. 173–183. ACM (2015). https://doi.org/10.1145/2790449.2790527
11. Carlsson, M., et al.: Sicstus 4.2.3 (2012). https://sicstus.sics.se/
12. Nethercote, N., Stuckey, P.J., Becket, R., Brand, S., Duck, G.J., Tack, G.: MiniZinc: towards a standard CP modelling language. In: Bessiére, C. (ed.) CP 2007. LNCS, vol. 4741, pp. 529–543. Springer, Heidelberg (2007). https://doi.org/10.1007/978-3-540-74970-7_38
13. Rendl, A., Guns, T., Stuckey, P.J., Tack, G.: MiniSearch: a solver-independent meta-search language for MiniZinc. In: Pesant, G. (ed.) CP 2015. LNCS, vol. 9255, pp. 375–392. Springer, Cham (2015). https://doi.org/10.1007/978-3-319-23219-5_27
14. Sagonas, K., Warren, D.S.: Efficient execution of HiLog in WAM-based prolog implementations. In: Sterling, L. (ed.) Proceedings of the 12th International Conference on Logic Programming, pp. 349–363. MIT Press (1995)
15. Schrijvers, T., Tack, G., Wuille, P., Samulowitz, H., Stuckey, P.J.: Search combinators. Constraints **18**(2), 269–305 (2013)
16. The Zinc Team: MiniZinc web page (2023). http://www.minizinc.org/
17. Walsh, T.: General symmetry breaking constraints. In: Benhamou, F. (ed.) CP 2006. LNCS, vol. 4204, pp. 650–664. Springer, Heidelberg (2006). https://doi.org/10.1007/11889205_46
18. Warren, D.: An abstract Prolog instruction set. Technical note 309, SRI International, Menlo Park (1983)
19. Warren, D.H.D.: Higher-order extension to PROLOG: are they needed? In: Machine Intelligence, vol. 10, pp. 441–454 (1982)

Grants4Companies: Applying Declarative Methods for Recommending and Reasoning About Business Grants in the Austrian Public Administration (System Description)

Björn Lellmann[1]([⊠])(iD), Philipp Marek[2], and Markus Triska[1]

[1] Bundesministerium für Finanzen, Vienna, Austria
{bjoern.lellmann,markus.triska}@bmf.gv.at
[2] Bundesrechenzentrum GmbH, Vienna, Austria
philipp.marek@brz.gv.at

Abstract. We describe the methods and technologies underlying the application *Grants4Companies*. The application uses a logic-based expert system to display a list of business grants suitable for the logged-in business. To evaluate suitability of the grants, formal representations of their conditions are evaluated against properties of the business, taken from the registers of the Austrian public administration. The logical language for the representations of the grant conditions is based on S-expressions. We further describe a Proof of Concept implementation of reasoning over the formalised grant conditions. The proof of concept is implemented in Common Lisp and interfaces with a reasoning engine implemented in Scryer Prolog. The application has recently gone live and is provided as part of the *Business Service Portal* by the Austrian Federal Ministry of Finance.

Keywords: Applications · Expert systems · S-Expressions · Common Lisp · Scryer Prolog

1 Introduction

Business grants are an important tool for steering and supporting the economy. In addition, they can be used to quickly react to and counter crises. However, the search for suitable business grants can be a challenge for companies and businesses in Austria. This is due to the large number of available business grants from a multitude of different providers. While there are dedicated search engines, companies and businesses often are simply not aware of the existence of grants on a specific topic, and hence cannot use these engines in a targeted search.

As an additional tool for providing targeted information about potentially interesting business grants to businesses the application *Grants4Companies* was

© The Author(s), under exclusive license to Springer Nature Singapore Pte Ltd. 2024
J. Gibbons and D. Miller (Eds.): FLOPS 2024, LNCS 14659, pp. 151–164, 2024.
https://doi.org/10.1007/978-981-97-2300-3_9

introduced. The application is part of the Austrian *Unternehmensservicepor-tal* (USP)[1] and is productive since November 2022 with around 50 visits per month on average. The application uses data about available grants from the Austrian *Transparenzportal*[2] to formalise formal grant conditions, e.g., on the type of business or the location of the head office. Data sources within the public administration are queried and used to evaluate these formalised criteria, to display a list of grants ordered according to the feasibility of applying - i.e. whether the business fulfils the criteria or doesn't fulfil the criteria; a third category contains grants for which the available information is not sufficient to decide.

While the application in the USP is written in Java[3], we have also implemented a Proof of Concept (PoC) for testing out new features, which we describe in more detail in this article. In particular, this PoC contains a reasoning engine for reasoning about the formalised grant conditions themselves. The main features of the PoC are implemented in Common Lisp while the reasoning engine is implemented in Scryer Prolog[4], following the Lean Methodology [1] for implementing proof search in logical calculi using Prolog's backtracking mechanism. The PoC is of interest for two reasons: First, it combines implementations in Common Lisp and Scryer Prolog to leverage the strengths of each programming language. Second, it provides an example and showcase for the use of declarative programming languages in public administration. To the best of our knowledge, such examples are currently rather rare.

The source code for the reasoning engine complete with examples of business grants with their conditions is available under https://github.com/blellmann/g4c-reasoner. While there is no openly accessible web interface, the reasoning engine can be loaded into the *Scryer Playground*[5], the freely accessible web interface for Scryer Prolog, and used for running evaluations.

In the remainder of the article we first give a brief overview of the development history (Sect. 2), followed by a description of the productive implementation of *Grants4Companies* (Sect. 3) and the technical details underlying the representation of the grants as well as their evaluation (Sect. 4). We then provide details about the PoC implementation (Sect. 5) including the implementation of the reasoning engine and the interface between the Common Lisp implementation and the Prolog reasoner, before concluding with an outlook (Sect. 6). We do not include any benchmark results or comparisons regarding efficiency of the reasoning engine here, since the focus of the implementation is on correctness instead of maximal efficiency, and it is part of a PoC implementation. Since the examples of grants are taken from the official productive data set, we chose to keep the original formulation of the examples and several concepts of the

---

[1] The official Austrian portal for interaction between businesses and public administration. See https://www.usp.gv.at/en/ueber-das-usp/index.html.
[2] The official Austrian data base containing (amongst other information) data about the available grants. See https://transparenzportal.gv.at.
[3] Due to interoperability concerns with existing libraries.
[4] See https://www.scryer.pl.
[5] See https://play.scryer.pl.

representation language in German, providing additional explanations in English. The technical terms from Austrian legislation can of course be adapted to other languages.

2   Development History

To assess the basic feasibility of the approach, we started with a pilot project, using Common Lisp for rapid prototyping. Grants were expressed as Lisp forms, a natural representation when working with Lisp. The pilot was successful, and also served as an illustration and internal tool for communicating the approach we planned. Already in this phase of the project, particular care was taken to explain in the UX that company data would only be processed with explicit user consent, and no data would be stored permanently by the planned service. In order to demonstrate the key concepts without any legal concerns, the pilot did not use any real company data, but only a fixed set of imaginary test companies.

For the production version of our service, we replaced the Common Lisp engine with a Java-based implementation to align the engine with architectural principles of surrounding IT services, and we retained the representation of grants as Lisp forms. As a result, the Lisp-based pilot can still be seamlessly used on the production data of the formalised grants to quickly prototype and assess additional features, while the Java-based Lisp parser and evaluation engine can also be used in other IT-services that require a Java implementation for architectural or other reasons. Only the production version of the service has access to real company data, and explicit consent of the company is required.

An additional component is the Prolog-based reasoner described in Sect. 5.1. This component can be used independently of the production environment to reason about grants, and is freely provided in a public repository. This component can reason with the productive formalised grants. Since the reasoning concerns only logical relations between the grants themselves, no company data is used by the reasoner.

3   Grants4Companies Overview

While the main focus of this article is the presentation of the PoC implementation of extended features for *Grants4Companies*, for context we briefly describe the productive application. *Grants4Companies* is an application in the Austrian *Unternehmensserviceportal* (USP)[6]. The USP is Austria's main digital portal for the interaction between public administration and businesses with currently more than 600.000 registered businesses and more than 120 integrated applications. It also acts as identity provider for the businesses.

After logging into the USP and starting the application *Grants4Companies*, businesses consent to the use of their data from registers of public administration in line with the GDPR [10]. Following this consent, the application fetches

---

[6] See https://www.usp.gv.at/en/index.html.

available data about the companies from registers of public administration. Currently the data sources are the *Unternehmensregister* and the *Firmenbuch*, the data used concerns, e.g., information about the geographic location of the business, its legal type, or the area of business following the Austrian version of the NACE-classification[7]. The extension to further registers is planned. Companies are then presented with a list of grants, ordered according to whether the formal grant criteria are satisfied by the company, not satisfied, or cannot be sufficiently evaluated based on the available data. The latter option caters for potential unavailability of necessary data from the registers, due to lack of coverage or also maintenance downtime of the registers. The results can be filtered and sorted according to the evaluation result, categories of the grants, or application date. A screenshot of the productive version is shown in Fig. 11.

The architecture of *Grants4Companies* follows that of classical knowledge based systems, with a clear separation between the knowledge base, i.e., grant definitions including the formalised grant criteria, and evaluation engine. The evaluation engine of the productive version of *Grants4Companies* is implemented in Java. The knowledge base contains currently 45 grants which were formalised manually. The details of the formal language used for representing the grants will be considered in Sect. 4.1. The knowledge base is stored in a GIT repository to keep track of historical data, and enable version control, reproducibility and data sharing. This knowledge base is shared with the PoC implementation.

4   Representation and Evaluation of the Grant Conditions

The knowledge base containing the grants with their formalised grant conditions is based on data about Austrian grants contained in the Austrian *Transparenzportal*[8], a portal provided by the Austrian Ministry of Finance, where funding agencies are to enter grants and the granted funding. For the PoC and the initial productive version of *Grants4Companies*, a number of grants were formalised manually by us, the current knowledge base contain 45 grants. In the future this might be extended following a rules as code approach [6], e.g., using tools like *POTATO* [5,8] for automatically suggesting formalised grant conditions based on the natural language descriptions provided by the funding agencies.

4.1   Representation of the Grants

The grant conditions are formalised as quantifier-free logical formulae. The language contains predicates for expressing properties of the businesses related to location, legal form, classification of business activity, etc. Examples of *atomic formulae* with their intended semantics are given in Fig. 1. For ease of use by Austrian funding agencies, these predicates are formulated in German and

---

[7] See   https://ec.europa.eu/eurostat/statistics-explained/index.php?title=Glossary: Statistical_classification_of_economic_activities_in_the_European_Community _(NACE).

[8] See https://transparenzportal.gv.at/tdb/tp/startpage (in German).

Atomic Formula	Intended semantics
Betriebsstandort-in(L)	The business has a location in one of the areas/regions specified in the list L
Rechtsform-in(L)	The legal form of the business is one of those in the list L
ÖNACE-in(L)	The business activity classification falls under one of the areas in the list L

Fig. 1. Examples of atomic formulae and their intended semantics

often take a list as argument. *Complex formulae* are built from the atomic formulae as well as $\top, \bot$ as usual using the standard propositional connectives $\neg, \vee, \wedge, \rightarrow$. At the current state there was no need for quantifiers, these might be added in the future. Working in a quantifier-free language has the benefit of a greatly reduced complexity for the reasoning tasks, of course. For the sake of referring to commonly used concepts, the language also contains *defined concepts*. On the logical level, these are given as pairs $(\eth, D)$ consisting of the name $\eth$ of the concept, which can be used like an atomic formula, and its definition D, i.e., a formula not containing $\eth$. The definition might contain other defined concepts, absence of cycles is assumed to be ensured externally. E.g., the concept of a legal person is introduced as the an abbreviation with name G4c/Grants_Gv.At:Ist-Juristische-Person for the formula Rechtsform-in(L), where $L = $ [Genossenschaft, Verein, ...] is a list of the legal forms which count as legal persons in Austria. Naming the definitions in the style of packages makes it possible to differentiate between concepts with the same name from different funding agencies, e.g., general funding conditions specific to the funding agencies.

On a technical level, the language used for representing the logical formulae is based on the Lisp-syntax of *S-expressions* [2, 102]. In particular, the logical formulae formalising the grant conditions are represented in prefix notation as lists, where the first element is the logical connective and the following elements are its arguments. E.g., a formula $\neg A \wedge (B \vee C)$ is represented as the S-expression (and (neg A) (or B C)). Predicates are represented by (Common Lisp) symbols. E.g., the predicate Betriebsstandort-in represents the fact that the business has a location in one of a list of certain areas given by their *Gemeindekennzahl*, the Austrian identification number for municipalities. To enable restriction also on a regional or county level, also prefixes of these identification numbers are covered. E.g., the atomic formula (Betriebsstandort-in 2 617 60101) represents the assertion that the business has a site in the county Carinthia, the region East Styria, or the municipality of the city of Graz.

The full representation of a grant also contains in addition to the formalised grant conditions also its name, metadata about application dates and links to the full description on the Transparenzportal, as well as the natural language description of the grant conditions. The latter are included as Lisp comments

```
(def-concept gv.at:natürliche-oder-juristische-Person
  (OR
    (Rechtsform-in :Einzelunternehmen)
    (gv.at:Ist-Juristische-Person)))
```

Fig. 2. The definition of the concept `gv.at:natürliche-oder-juristische-Person`. The formula captures the condition that the applicant is a natural person, i.e., the legal form of the company is that of a sole trader (`:Einzelunternehmen`), or a legal person (captured by the defined formula `gv.at:Ist-Juristische-Person`).

interspersed with the formalised conditions in the spirit of literate programming [4]. This allows to have human-readable explanations collected and used for explaining the evaluation of a grant. An example of a grant in this representation is given in Fig. 3. Defined concepts $(\eth, D)$ are represented as (`def-concept` $\eth$ D). An issue that came up right from the beginning is having one concept in multiple different implementations. A clause specifying that the company has to be a small or medium enterprise (SME, in German "*Der Antragsteller muss ein KMU sein*") is used in many grants; sadly there are three different definitions for this term, one from the federal government in Austria, one from the EU, and one from the FFG[9]. As mentioned, this ambiguity is solved via package names - there are simply three functions, `GV.AT:IS-KMU`, `FFG:IS-KMU`, and `EU:IS-KMU`. This enables the use of different interpretations of the same natural language term depending on the source of the regulation. An example of a defined concept is given in Fig. 2.

4.2   Evaluation of the Grants

Evaluating whether the formal conditions of a grant apply for a specific business essentially corresponds to checking, whether the business is a model of the logical formula representing these conditions. Here the business is identified with its properties given by the data about the business available. The atomic formulae are chosen to directly correspond to data fields from specific registers and hence their evaluation is rather straightforward. Complex formulae are evaluated according to their main logical connectives. Names $\eth$ for defined concepts $(\eth, D)$ are unpacked into their definition D and then evaluated.

Of course not all the data required to evaluate whether a company satisfies the formalised eligibility criteria of a grant is necessarily always available. While data like *location* of a company needs to be provided before it is officially recognized, e.g., the (Ö)NACE classification[10] of the economic activities of Austrian businesses is not complete. In particular, for a sizeable number of companies the ÖNACE-classification has not yet been assigned. In addition, the connection to a specific register might drop out temporarily due to maintenance work.

---

[9] The *Österreichische Förderagentur für wirtschaftsnahe Forschung, Entwicklung und Innovation*, in English *Austrian Research Promotion Agency*.

[10] https://www.statistik.at/en/databases/classification-database.

```
(define-grant ("Umweltschutz- und Energieeffizienzförderung - Förderung
  sonstiger Energieeffizienzmanahmen Villach"
   (:href "https://transparenzportal.gv.at/tdb/tp/leistung/1052703.html")
   (:transparenzportal-ref-nr 1052703)
   (:Fördergebiet :Umwelt)
   (gültig-von "2019-01-01"))
  "Unter der Berücksichtigung der Verwendung erneuerbarer Energieträger
   sowie der Umsetzung der Intention der Umweltschutz- und
   Energieeffizienzrichtlinie im Bereich privater Haushalte fördert die
   Stadt Villach folgende Energieeffizienzmanahmen."
  ;; Voraussetzungen
  ;;
  ;; - Förderungswerber/innen können natürliche oder juristische Personen
  ;;   sein. Bei juristischen Personen hat die firmenmäige bzw.
  ;;   statutenkonforme Unterfertigung des Antrages auf Gewährung einer
  ;;   Förderung durch den Vertretungsbefugten zu erfolgen.
  (AND
    (GV.AT:natürliche-oder-juristische-Person)
    ;; - Die Förderungswerber haben bei der Antragstellung zu erklären,
    ;;   dass für die beantragten Förderungen keine weiteren Förderungen
    ;;   von anderen Stellen beantragt wurden.
    ;; - Ein Förderungsansuchen muss spätestens innerhalb von 8 Monaten
    ;;   nach Umsetzung der Manahme/n bzw. Kaufdatum bei der Stadt
    ;;   Villach einlangen
    ;; - Die Förderung wird nur für die sach- und fachgerechten Umsetzung
    ;;   der Manahme (Einbau) im Stadtgebiet von Villach gewährt.
    (OR
      (Unternehmenssitz-in 20201)
      (Betriebsstandort-in 20201)))))
```

Fig. 3. Example grant, TP-Nr.1052703. The grant provides funding for increasing energy efficiency. It is applicable to natural and legal persons (`GV.AT:natürliche-oder-juristische-Person`) in the city of Villach (the `Unternehmenssitz` or a `Betriebsstandort` has to be in the municipal identification number 20201). Some other conditions cannot be checked automatically based on the data about the company available within public administration and hence are not formalised (e.g., that the request for funding has to be submitted at most 8 months after implementing the measures for increasing energy efficiency).

To cover these eventualities, the evaluation is done in a three-valued logic, which allows a third truth value of *unknown* next to *true* and *false*. The logical connectives then propagate the truth value *unknown* upwards, whenever no definite evaluation to *true* or *false* is possible. To be precise, we use (so far quantifier-free) *strong Kleene-Logic* K_3, considered, e.g., in [3]. The truth tables for the logical connectives are given in Fig. 5. This ensures that grants which have been evaluated for a company to *true* or *false* while some of their atomic components are evaluated to *unknown* are evaluated with the same result

```
förderung("G4c/Grants_Umweltschutz- Und Energieeffizienzförderung
 - Förderung Sonstiger Energieeffizienzmanahmen Villach",
  förderkriterien(
    (
      df( "G4c/Grants_Gv.At:Natürliche-Oder-Juristische-Person" )
    and
      (
        at( unternehmenssitz_in( [ 20201 ] ) )
      or
        at( betriebsstandort_in( [ 20201 ] ) )
      )
    )
  )
).
```

Fig. 4. Example grant in Prolog syntax, TPPNr#1052703. For the original formulation of this particular grant, see Fig. 3

¬		∧	⊥	u	⊤		∨	⊥	u	⊤		→	⊥	u	⊤
⊥	⊤		⊥	⊥	⊥	⊥		⊥	⊥	u	⊤		⊥	⊤	⊤	⊤
u	u		u	⊥	u	u		u	u	u	⊤		u	u	u	⊤
⊤	⊥		⊤	⊥	u	⊤		⊤	⊤	⊤	⊤		⊤	⊥	u	⊤

Fig. 5. The truth tables for 3-valued strong Kleene logic K_3. The truth values *false*, *unknown*, *true* are represented by ⊥, u and ⊤, respectively.

when additional data becomes available and some of the atomic components are no longer evaluated as *unknown*. Range-based reasoning for numeric operations would also be possible, and is planned as future work.

As a further potential next step, the symbolic representation also allows for some easy optimizations – for commutative connectives/operations (like AND, OR, possibly in the future also numerical addition via +), we could reorder the arguments before evaluating. By moving the subformula with the highest probability for a negative result to the front, a short-cutting evaluation could quickly discard grant/company pairs, allowing for mass assessments: given a newly proposed grant, how many companies in Austria will (be able to) apply? This reordering is not implemented yet, though.

5   PoC: Extensions and Interfaces

The PoC also contains an implementation of the evaluation of grant conditions based on company data. However, for the purpose of this article we concentrate on the functionality which goes beyond that of the productive system. In particular, the representation of grant conditions as logical formulae opens the possibility to not just evaluate the conditions based on business data, but to also reason *about* the conditions themselves. Interesting questions here are in particular consistency, useful for discovering mistakes in the formalisation of grant conditions, and logical implication, useful for finding unintended overlap between multiple grants in the same area. To enable such reasoning, we implemented backwards proof search in a Gentzen-style sequent calculus (see, e.g., [9] for the proof-theoretic background). Following the Lean-methodology [1] we make use of Prolog's backtracking mechanism to perform the proof search.

We use Scryer Prolog due to its strong conformance to the Prolog ISO standard, which will ease future cooperations with other organizations and public administrations. In addition, the system is freely available and allows inspection of its entire source code, which works towards our aim of providing full transparency and explainability of all computed results.

5.1   Symbolic Reasoning over Grants

The Proof-of-Concept has the ability to connect one or more *Scryer Prolog*[11] sessions to the web frontend, providing a convenient REPL that is pre-loaded with some known facts and the transpiled grant forms (see Fig. 4). We included a prototypical implementation of logical reasoning over the formalised eligibility criteria in the form of a *sequent calculus*, specifically a G3-style calculus for classical (propositional) logic (see, e.g. [9]), extended to cover basic facts about atomic statements and the defined concepts. We use reasoning in classical logic and not the three-valued logic used for evaluating the grants, because reasoning about the logical properties of grant conditions is independent of the data available for particular businesses. A calculus for the three-valued logic used could be implemented, e.g., following [7]. However, this would be useful mainly for reasoning about which grants are shown to the business with which evaluation.

As usual, *sequents* are of the form $A_1, \ldots, A_n \Rightarrow B_1, \ldots, B_m$ with $n, m \geq 0$ and are interpreted as the logical formula $A_1 \wedge \cdots \wedge A_n \to B_1 \vee \cdots \vee B_m$. The standard logical rules are given in Fig. 6. Basic knowledge about implications between atomic statements is included in the form of (rather simple) *ground sequents*, and defined concepts are included in the form of separate left- and right rules for each defined concept. The ground sequents and rules for unpacking the defined concepts are given in Fig. 7. Cut-free completeness of the calculus follows from an extension of [9, Thm.4.6.1] to the calculus with defined formulae, noting that the set of ground sequents is closed under substitutions (because no variables occur), contraction and basic cuts. In order to avoid unnecessary repetitions, in the implementation the rules are given as facts about the term `rule(Name, Prem_List/PF)`, where `Name` is the name of the rule, `Prem_List` is the list of premisses and `PF` is the principal formula of the rule, i.e., a sequent with exactly one formula on the left or right hand side. The provability predicate is given by `prov2//2`, which is true if the first argument is a derivable sequent, and the second argument a term describing a corresponding derivation. Examples are given in Fig. 8. The auxiliary predicate `merge_sequent_list//3`

---

[11] See www.scryer.pl.

$$\overline{\Gamma, A \Rightarrow A, \Delta} \qquad \overline{\Gamma, \bot \Rightarrow \Delta} \; {}^{\bot}L \qquad \overline{\Gamma \Rightarrow \top, \Delta} \; {}^{\top}R$$

$$\frac{\Gamma \Rightarrow A, \Delta}{\Gamma, \neg A \Rightarrow \Delta} \; \neg L \qquad \frac{\Gamma, A \Rightarrow \Delta}{\Gamma \Rightarrow \neg A, \Delta} \; \neg R$$

$$\frac{\Gamma, A, B \Rightarrow \Delta}{\Gamma, A \wedge B \Rightarrow \Delta} \; \wedge L \qquad \frac{\Gamma \Rightarrow A, \Delta \quad \Gamma \Rightarrow B, \Delta}{\Gamma \Rightarrow A \wedge B, \Delta} \; \wedge R$$

$$\frac{\Gamma, A \Rightarrow \Delta \quad \Gamma, B \Rightarrow \Delta}{\Gamma, A \vee B \Rightarrow \Delta} \; \vee L \qquad \frac{\Gamma \Rightarrow A, B\Delta}{\Gamma \Rightarrow A \vee B, \Delta} \; \vee R$$

$$\frac{\Gamma, B \Rightarrow \Delta \quad \Gamma \Rightarrow A, \Delta}{\Gamma, A \rightarrow B \Rightarrow D} \; \rightarrow L \qquad \frac{\Gamma, A \Rightarrow B, \Delta}{\Gamma \Rightarrow A \rightarrow B, \Delta} \; \rightarrow R$$

Fig. 6. The sequent rules of the propositional part of calculus G3

$$\frac{}{\Gamma, \mathsf{unternehmenssitz\_in}(L_1) \Rightarrow \mathsf{unternehmenssitz\_in}(L_2), \Delta} \quad \begin{array}{l} \forall x \in L_1 \exists y \in L_2: \\ y \text{ is prefix of } x \end{array}$$

$$\frac{}{\Gamma, \mathsf{betriebsstandort\_in}(L_1) \Rightarrow \mathsf{betriebsstandort\_in}(L_2), \Delta} \quad \begin{array}{l} \forall x \in L_1 \exists y \in L_2: \\ y \text{ is prefix of } x \end{array}$$

$$\frac{}{\Gamma, \mathsf{oenace\_in}(L_1) \Rightarrow \mathsf{oenace\_in}(L_2), \Delta} \quad \begin{array}{l} \forall x \in L_1 \exists y \in L_2: \\ y \text{ is prefix of } x \end{array}$$

$$\frac{}{\Gamma, \mathsf{rechtsform\_in}(L_1) \Rightarrow \mathsf{rechtsform\_in}(L_2), \Delta} \; L_1 \subseteq L_2$$

$$\frac{\Gamma, D \Rightarrow \Delta}{\Gamma, \eth \Rightarrow \Delta} \; (\eth, D)_L \qquad \frac{\Gamma \Rightarrow D, \Delta}{\Gamma \Rightarrow \eth, \Delta} \; (\eth, D)_R$$

Fig. 7. The ground sequents and definition rules used in the calculus. In the definition rules the pair $(\eth, D)$ is a defined concept.

is true if the first argument contains a list $\Gamma_1 \Rightarrow \Delta_1, ..., \Gamma_n \Rightarrow \Delta_n$ of premisses, i.e., sequents, the second argument contains a sequent $\Sigma \Rightarrow \Pi$, and the third argument contains the list of premisses merged with this sequent, i.e., $\Gamma_1, \Sigma \Rightarrow \Pi, \Delta_1, ..., \Gamma_n, \Sigma \Rightarrow \Pi, \Delta_n$. Since the rules of the calculus are invertible, we could introduce prolog cuts ! after the goals `rule(Rule_name, ...)` to increase efficiency – this would not influence completeness wrt. derivability of sequents. However, since this *would* limit the number of derivations found, and to preserve monotonicity of the program, we refrain from doing so.

The result of querying for logical implication between the formalised eligibility conditions of two grants is shown in Fig. 9. The prolog variable `Tree` is instantiated with a term for the derivation of the result abbreviated here for the sake of better readability.

The terms representing derivations can also be converted into human-readable form in a formalised natural language using Prolog's Definite Clause Grammars. The result is a string containing html-code which can be displayed in a browser, see Fig. 10.

```
rule(andL, [[A,B]=>[]] / and(A,B)=>[]).
rule(andR, [ [] => [A], [] => [B] ] / [] => and(A,B)).

prov2(Gamma => Delta, der(Rule_name, Gamma => Delta, [Fml] => [],
New_prems_ders)) :-
    select(Fml,Gamma,Omega),
    rule(Rule_name,Prems / Fml => []),
    merge_sequent_list(Prems, Omega => Delta, New_Prems),
    maplist(prov2,New_Prems, New_prems_ders).

prov2(Gamma => Delta, der(Rule_name, Gamma => Delta, [] => [Fml],
New_prems_ders)) :-
    select(Fml, Delta, Pi),
    rule(Rule_name, Prems / [] => Fml),
    merge_sequent_list(Prems,Gamma => Pi, New_prems),
    maplist(prov2, New_prems, New_prems_ders).
```

Fig. 8. Examples of the Prolog code for rules of the sequent calculus.

5.2   Interface Between Lisp and Prolog

To enable the reasoning functionality from within the Lisp-part of the PoC, the prolog prover is called and its output on `std_out` interpreted. For this, the implementation of a basic interface was necessary.

Conversion from Grant-Code in Lisp-Syntax to Prolog. Since the formalised grant conditions are given in the syntax of S-Expressions, they need to be converted to Prolog terms. While there is an existing project that transpiles S-expressions to ISO Prolog[12], it didn't fit our usecase; this library only allows batch processing and not the desired interactive querying, the already-parsed internal grant structure isn't supported, and a few special-cases demand a non-verbatim translation. In our implementation, negation and the typical infix operators `AND` and `OR` get printed out with parenthesis, to ensure the right precedence – the Prolog side ignores superfluous parens anyway.

Parsing Prolog Output. Custom parsing of Prolog output provides a nice special case: At the beginning of an output block, one or more lines containing a string beginning with the sequence `<html>` are recognized and displayed verbatim; this way a human-readable version of the derivations can be created in Prolog by nesting `<div>`s as necessary. Some CSS provided by the POC is then used by the browser to provide a nice visual display. Regular prolog output is parsed via the `ESRAP` library.

---

[12] https://github.com/cl-model-languages/cl-prolog2.

```
% förderung(F1, förderkriterien(K1)),
  förderung(F2, förderkriterien(K2)),
  dif(K1, K2),
  prov2([K1] => [K2], Tree),
  !.
F1 = "Per-Bundesland/Steiermark_Beratungskostenzuschuss-Für-Gastronomie-
      /Hotelleriebetriebe-In-Der-Steiermark",
K1 = ( df("Gv.At_Natürliche-Oder-Juristische-Person")
      or
      at(rechtsform_in(["Offene-Gesellschaft","Kommanditgesellschaft"]))
     )
     and
     ( at(önace_in(["55"]))
      or
      at(önace_in(["56"]))
     )
     and
     ( at(unternehmenssitz_in(["Land-Stmk"]))
      or
      at(betriebsstandort_in(["Land-Stmk"]))
     ),
F2 = "Per-Bundesland/Steiermark_Förderung-Zur-Wirtschaftsinitiative-
      Nachhaltigkeit-Steiermark",
K2 = at(unternehmenssitz_in(["Land-Stmk"]))
     or
     at(betriebsstandort_in(["Land-Stmk"])),
Tree = der(andL,...).
```

Fig. 9. Reasoning over grants. The query is shown at the top. The variables F1 and F2 are instantiated with the names of grants, such that the conditions K1 of the first one imply the conditions K2 of the second one. The variable Tree is instantiated with the derivation witnessing provability of the sequent K1 ⇒ K2, abbreviated here for the sake of space.

Fig. 10. HTML output of a Prolog reasoning.

Grants4Companies - Förderungsvorschläge für Unternehmen

Die folgende Liste enthält Vorschläge von Förderungen, welche für Ihr Unternehmen potenziell passen. Die Voraussetzungen für den Erhalt einer Unternehmensförderung gliedern sich dabei in rein formale Förderkriterien, welche automatisiert auswertbar sind, und zusätzliche nicht automatisiert auswertbare Bedingungen wie die positive Bewertung eines eingebrachten Projektantrages. Förderungen, für welche Ihr Unternehmen die rein formalen Förderkriterien erfüllt, werden Ihnen mit dem Hinweis „Automatisiert auswertbare Förderkriterien treffen zu" angezeigt. Förderungen, für welche nicht alle zur Bewertung der formalen Förderkriterien notwendigen Unternehmensdaten vorliegen, werden mit dem Hinweis „Förderkriterien treffen potenziell zu" angezeigt. Förderungen, bei denen mindestens ein formales Förderkriterium nicht erfüllt ist, werden mit dem Hinweis „Förderkriterien treffen nicht zu" angezeigt.

Für weitergehende Informationen zu den einzelnen Förderungen folgen Sie bitte den jeweils angegebenen Verweisen auf die Seiten der zuständigen Förderstellen bzw. das Transparenzportal. Zur Beantragung einer Förderung wenden Sie sich bitte an die jeweiligen Förderstellen. Beachten Sie dabei, dass sich aus der Anzeige einer Förderung mit dem Hinweis „Automatisiert auswertbare Förderkriterien treffen zu" kein Anspruch auf die Gewährung dieser Förderung ergibt.

| Förderkriterium ⌄ | Kategorie ⌄ | Gültigkeitszeitraum ⌄ | | Sortierreihenfolge ⌄ |

Ausgewählte Filter: ⊘ Trifft zu ×   ⊘ Trifft potenziell zu ×   ⊘ Trifft nicht zu ×   Wirtschaft ×   Derzeit aktiv ×

6 Förderungen gefunden

Innovationsförderung Villach   ⌄

Die Innovationsförderung stellt eine Unterstützung für Unternehmer/innen zur Förderung innovativer Vorhaben dar.

⊘ Automatisiert auswertbare Förderkriterien treffen zu

gültig bis
unbegrenzt

Standort- und Infrastrukturunterstützungen Villach   ⌄

Die Stadt Villach fördert Aktivitäten, Angebote, und Investitionen, die den Wirtschaftsstandort wettbewerbsfähiger und lebenswerter gestalten. Basis für die Leistung sind individuelle Förderverträge und Finanzierungsvereinbarungen.

⊘ Automatisiert auswertbare Förderkriterien treffen zu

gültig bis
unbegrenzt

Allgemeine Investitionsförderung Villach   ⌄

Die Wirtschaftsförderung der Stadt Villach hat zum Ziel, eine wachstumsfördernde, beschäftigungsschaffende sowie ökologisch verträgliche Wirtschaftsentwicklung zu sichern, die regionale Wertschöpfung anzuheben, die Wettbewerbsfähigkeit zu verbessern und die zentralörtliche Funktion der...

⊘ Förderkriterien treffen potenziell zu

gültig bis
unbegrenzt

Beratungskostenzuschuss für Gastronomie-/Hotelleriebetriebe in der Steiermark   ⌄

Unterstützung von bestehenden Gastronomie- und Hotelleriebetrieben für Beratungen von grundlegender Bedeutung (Umstrukturierung, Marktanalyse, betriebswirtschaftliche Durchleuchtung, usw.)

⊗ Förderkriterien treffen nicht zu

gültig bis
unbegrenzt

Fig. 11. The productive version of *Grants4Companies*. This figure shows the main page with a short description at the top and the list of grants. The grants are sorted with the applicable ones shown at the top of the list, the not applicable ones at the bottom, and the ones requiring further data for a conclusive evaluation in the middle. The list can be filtered, e.g., according to the topic of the grant, in this case "economy" ("Wirtschaft").

6   Conclusion and Outlook

We presented *Grants4Companies*, an application in the Austrian public administration, which uses declarative methods to recommend business grants based on the data available for the businesses from sources in the public administration. We also presented the Proof of Concept implementation of logical reasoning over the formalised grant conditions, implemented in Common Lisp and Scryer Prolog. A main interest here lies in the fact that the PoC implementation uses declarative and logical methods in the context of an application, which is already live in public administration.

In terms of future work we are steadily extending the list of covered grants, and are considering automatised rules extraction methods (e.g., [5,8]) for speeding up this process. Extending the coverage of the grants will necessitate the extension of the logical language and hence the reasoning mechanisms to further concepts and also towards (limited) reasoning with natural numbers. We envisage the resulting tool to become a possible basis for systematic analyses of the Austrian landscape of business grants by stakeholders in funding agencies and public administration.

References

1. Beckert, B., Posegga, J.: Logic programming as a basis for lean automated deduction. J. Log. Program. **28**(3), 231–236 (1996). https://doi.org/10.1016/0743-1066(96)00054-4. https://www.sciencedirect.com/science/article/pii/0743106696000544
2. Belzer, J., Holzman, A., Kent, A.: Encyclopedia of Computer Science and Technology: Volume 10 - Linear and Matrix Algebra to Microorganisms: Computer-Assisted Identification. Taylor & Francis (1978)
3. Kleene, S.C.: Introduction to Metamathematics. North-Holland, Amsterdam (1952)
4. Knuth, D.: Literate programming. Comput. J. **27**(2), 97–111 (1984)
5. Kovács, A., Gémes, K., Iklódi, E., Recski, G.: Potato: explainable information extraction framework. In: Proceedings of the 31st ACM International Conference on Information & Knowledge Management, CIKM 2022, pp. 4897-4901. Association for Computing Machinery, New York (2022). https://doi.org/10.1145/3511808.3557196
6. Mowbray, A., Chung, P., Greenleaf, G.: Representing legislative rules as code: reducing the problems of 'scaling up'. Comput. Law Secur. Rev. **48**, 105772 (2023)
7. Multlog: Analytic proof systems for strong Kleene logic K_3 (2022). pdf generated by MULTLOG, v.1.16a. https://logic.at/multlog. https://logic.at/multlog/kleene.pdf
8. Recski, G., Lellmann, B., Kovács, A., Hanbury, A.: Explainable rule extraction via semantic graphs. In: ASAIL 2021. CEUR Workshop Proceedings, pp. 24–35 (2021)
9. Troelstra, A.S., Schwichtenberg, H.: Basic Proof Theory. Cambridge Tracts In Theoretical Computer Science, vol. 43, 2nd edn. Cambridge University Press, Cambridge (2000)
10. European Union: Regulation (EU) 2016/679 of the European parliament and of the council of 27 April 2016 on the protection of natural persons with regard to the processing of personal data and on the free movement of such data, and repealing directive 95/46/EC (general data protection regulation). OJL (2016)

Program Analysis

Inferring Non-failure Conditions
for Declarative Programs

Michael Hanus(✉) 🆔

Institut für Informatik, Kiel University, Kiel, Germany
mh@informatik.uni-kiel.de

Abstract. Unintended failures during a computation are painful but frequent during software development. Failures due to external reasons (e.g., missing files, no permissions) can be caught by exception handlers. Programming failures, such as calling a partially defined operation with unintended arguments, are often not caught due to the assumption that the software is correct. This paper presents an approach to verify such assumptions. For this purpose, non-failure conditions for operations are inferred and then checked in all uses of partially defined operations. In the positive case, the absence of such failures is ensured. In the negative case, the programmer could adapt the program to handle possibly failing situations and check the program again. Our method is fully automatic and can be applied to larger declarative programs. The results of an implementation for functional logic Curry programs are presented.

1 Introduction

The occurrence of failures during a program execution is painful but still frequent when developing software systems. The main reasons for such failures are

- external, i.e., outside the control of the program, like missing files or access rights, unexpected formats of external data, etc.
- internal, i.e., programming errors like calling a partially defined operation with unintended arguments.

External failures can be caught by exception handlers to avoid a crash of the entire software system. Internal failures are often not caught since they should not occur in a correct software system. In practice, however, they occur during software development and even in deployed systems which results in expensive debugging tasks. For instance, a typical internal failure in imperative programs is dereferencing a pointer variable whose current value is the null pointer (due to this often occurring failure, Tony Hoare called the introduction of null pointers his "billion dollar mistake"[1]).

Although null pointer failures cannot occur in declarative programs, such programs might contain other typical programming errors, like failures due to incomplete pattern matching. For instance, consider the following operations (shown in Haskell syntax):

---

[1] http://qconlondon.com/london-2009/speaker/Tony+Hoare.

ⓒ The Author(s), under exclusive license to Springer Nature Singapore Pte Ltd. 2024
J. Gibbons and D. Miller (Eds.): FLOPS 2024, LNCS 14659, pp. 167–187, 2024.
https://doi.org/10.1007/978-981-97-2300-3_10

```
head :: [a] → a                tail :: [a] → [a]
head (x:xs) = x                tail (x:xs) = xs
```

In a correct program, it must be ensured that `head` and `tail` are not evaluated on empty lists. If we are not sure about the data provided at run time, we can check the arguments of partial operations before the application. For instance, the following code snippet defines an operation to read a command together with some arguments from standard input (the operation `words` breaks a string into a list of words separated by white spaces) and calls an operation `processCmd` with the input data:

```
readCmd = do putStr "Input a command:"
             s <- getLine
             let ws = words s
             case null ws of True  → readCmd
                             False → processCmd (head ws) (tail ws)
```

By using the predicate `null` to check the emptiness of a list, it is ensured that `head` and `tail` are not applied to an empty list in the `False` branch of the case expression.

In this paper we present a fully automatic tool which can verify the non-failure of this program. Our technique is based on analyzing the types of arguments and results of operations in order to ensure that partially defined operations are called with arguments of appropriate types. The principle idea to use type information for this purpose is not new. For instance, one can express restrictions on arguments of operations with *dependent types*, as in Agda [35], Coq [10], or Idris [11], or *refinement types*, as in LiquidHaskell [39,40]. Since one has to prove that these restrictions hold during the construction of programs, the development of such programs becomes harder [38]. Another alternative, proposed in [20], is to annotate operations with *non-fail conditions* and verify that these conditions hold at each call site by an external tool, e.g., an SMT solver [34]. In this way, the verification is fully automatic but requires user-defined annotations and, in some cases, also the verification of post-conditions or contracts to state properties about result values of operations [21].

The main idea of this work is to *infer* non-fail conditions of operations. Since the inference of precise conditions is undecidable in general, we approximate them by *abstract types*, e.g., finite representations of sets of values. Hence, our contributions are:

1. We define a *call type* for each operation. If the actual arguments belong to the call type, the operation is reducible with some rule.
2. For each operation, we define *in/out types* to approximate its input/output behavior.
3. For each call to an operation g occurring in a rule defining f, we check, by considering the call structure and in/out types, whether the call type of g is satisfied. If this is not the case, the call type of f is refined and we repeat the checks with the refined call type.

At the end of this process, each operation has some correct call type which ensures that it does not fail on arguments belonging to its call type. Note that the call type might be empty on always failing operations. To avoid empty call types, one can modify the program code so that a different branch is taken in case of a failure.

In order to make our approach accessible to various declarative languages, we formulate and implement it in the declarative multi-paradigm language Curry [25]. Since Curry extends Haskell by logic programming features and there are also methods to transform logic programs into Curry programs [22], our approach can also be applied to purely functional or logic programs. A consequence of using Curry is the fact that programs might compute with failures, e.g., it is not an immediate programming error to apply `head` and `tail` to possibly empty lists. However, subcomputations involving such possibly failing calls must be encapsulated so that it can be checked whether such a computation has no result (this corresponds to exception handling in deterministic languages). If this is done, one can ensure that the overall computation does not fail even in the presence of encapsulated logic (non-deterministic) subcomputations.

The paper is structured as follows. After sketching the basics of Curry in the next section, we introduce call types and their abstraction in Sect. 3. Section 4 defines in/out types and methods to approximate them. The main Sect. 5 presents our method to infer and check call types for all operations in a program. We evaluate our approach in Sect. 6 before we conclude with a discussion of related work. More details as well as correctness results and their proofs can be found in [23].

2   Functional Logic Programming and Curry

The declarative language Curry [25] amalgamates features from functional programming (demand-driven evaluation, strong typing, higher-order functions) and logic programming (computing with partial information, unification, constraints), see [6,19] for surveys. The syntax of Curry is close to Haskell [36]. In addition to Haskell, Curry applies rules with overlapping left-hand sides in a (don't know) non-deterministic manner (where Haskell always selects the first matching rule) and allows *free (logic) variables* in conditions and right-hand sides of defining rules. The operational semantics is based on an optimal lazy evaluation strategy [4].

Curry is strongly typed so that a Curry program consists of data type definitions (introducing *constructors* for data types) and *functions* or *operations* on these types. As an example, we show the definition of two operations: the list concatenation "++" and an operation `dup` which returns some number having at least two occurrences in a list:[2]

---

[2] Note that Curry requires the explicit declaration of free variables, as x in the rule of `dup`, to ensure checkable redundancy, except for anonymous variables, denoted by an underscore.

$$P ::= D_1 \ldots D_m \qquad \text{(program)}$$
$$D ::= f(x_1, \ldots, x_n) = e \qquad \text{(function definition)}$$
$$e ::= x \qquad \text{(variable)}$$
$$\mid \quad c(x_1, \ldots, x_n) \qquad \text{(constructor application)}$$
$$\mid \quad f(x_1, \ldots, x_n) \qquad \text{(function call)}$$
$$\mid \quad e_1 \ or \ e_2 \qquad \text{(disjunction)}$$
$$\mid \quad let \ x_1, \ldots, x_n \ free \ in \ e \qquad \text{(free variables)}$$
$$\mid \quad let \ x = e \ in \ e' \qquad \text{(let binding)}$$
$$\mid \quad case \ x \ of \ \{p_1 \to e_1; \ldots; p_n \to e_n\} \qquad \text{(case expression)}$$
$$p ::= c(x_1, \ldots, x_n) \qquad \text{(pattern)}$$

Fig. 1. Syntax of the intermediate language FlatCurry

```
(++) :: [a]  →  [a]  →  [a]    dup :: [Int]  →  Int
[]       ++ ys = ys            dup xs | xs == _ ++ [x] ++ _ ++ [x] ++ _
(x:xs) ++ ys = x : (xs ++ ys)        = x      where x free
```

Since dup might deliver more than one result for an argument, e.g., dup [1,2,2,1] yields 1 and 2, it is also called a *non-deterministic operation*. Such operations, which are interpreted as mappings from values into sets of values [18], are an important feature of contemporary functional logic languages. To express failing computations, there is also a predefined operation failed which has no value.

Curry has more features than described so far.[3] Due to these numerous features, language processing tools for Curry (compilers, analyzers,...) often use an intermediate language where the syntactic sugar of the source language has been eliminated and the pattern matching strategy is explicit. This intermediate language, called FlatCurry, has also been used, apart from compilers, to specify the operational semantics of Curry programs [1] or to implement a modular framework for the analysis of Curry programs [24]. Since we will use FlatCurry to describe and implement our inference method, we sketch the structure of FlatCurry programs.

Figure 1 summarizes the abstract syntax of FlatCurry. A FlatCurry program consists of a sequence of function definitions (we omit data type definitions here), where each function is defined by a single rule. Patterns in source programs are compiled into case expressions, overlapping rules are joined by explicit disjunctions, and arguments of constructor and function calls are variables (introduced in left-hand sides, let expressions, or patterns). We will write $\mathcal{F}$ for the set of defined operations and $\mathcal{C}$ for the set of constructors of a program. In order to provide a simple definition of our inference method, we assume that FlatCurry programs satisfy the following properties:

– All variables introduced in a rule (parameters, free variables, let bindings, pattern variables) have unique identifiers.

---

[3] Conceptually, Curry is intended as an extension of Haskell although not all extensions of Haskell are actually supported.

- For the sake of simplicity, let bindings are non-recursive, i.e., all recursion is introduced by functions (although our implemented tool supports recursive bindings).
- The patterns in each case expression are non-overlapping and cover all data constructors of the type of the discriminating variable. Hence, if this type contains n constructors, there are n branches without overlapping patterns. This can be ensured by adding missing branches with failure expressions (`failed`).

Usually, the front end of a Curry compiler transforms source programs into such a form [3,7]. For instance, the operation `head` is transformed into the FlatCurry definition

```
head(zs) = case zs of { x:xs  →  x ; []  →  failed }
```

3   Call Types and Abstract Types

We consider a computation as *non-failing* if it does not stop due to a pattern mismatch or a call to `failed`. In order to infer conditions on arguments of operations so that the evaluation of an operation does not fail, we will analyze the rules of each operation.[4] For instance, the operation `head` is not defined on empty lists so that the condition for a non-failing evaluation of `head` is the non-emptiness of the argument list. Sometimes the exact condition requires more advanced descriptions. Consider the operation

```
lastTrue [True]    = True
lastTrue (x:y:ys) = lastTrue (y:ys)
```

The evaluation of a call `lastTrue` l does not fail if the argument list l ends with `True`. Although such lists could be finitely described using regular types [15], such a description is impossible for arbitrary operations. For instance, if some branch in a condition of an operation causes a failure but the condition of the branch contains a function call, the failure is only relevant if the function call terminates. Due to the undecidability of the halting problem, we cannot hope to infer exact non-failure conditions.

Due to this general problem, we *approximate* non-failure conditions so that the evaluation of a call with arguments satisfying the non-failure condition is non-failing. However, there might be successfully evaluable calls which do not satisfy the inferred non-failure condition.

In order to support different structures to approximate non-failure conditions, we do not fix a language for call types but assume that there is a domain $\mathcal{A}$ of *abstract types*. Elements of this domain describe sets of concrete *data terms*, i.e., terms consisting of data constructors only. There are various options for such abstract types, like depth-k abstractions [37] or regular types [15]. The latter

---

[4] Note that we do not consider external failures of operations, like file access errors, since they need to be handled differently.

have been used to infer success types to analyze logic programs [17], whereas depth-k abstractions were used in the abstract diagnosis of functional programs [2] or in the abstraction of term rewriting systems [8,9]. Since regular types are more complex and computationally more expensive, we use depth-k abstractions in our examples. In this domain, denoted by A_k, subterms exceeding the given depth k are replaced by a specific constant ($\top$) that represents any term. Since the size of this domain is quickly growing for $k > 1$, we use $k = 1$ in examples, i.e., terms are approximated by their top-level constructors. As we will see, this is often sufficient in practice to obtain reasonable results. Nevertheless, our technique and implementation is parametric over the abstract type domain.

If $\mathcal{C}$ is the set of data constructors, *depth-1 types* can be simply described by the set

$$\mathcal{A}_1 = \{D \subseteq \mathcal{C} \mid \text{all constructors of } D \text{ belong to the same type}\} \cup \{\top\}$$

Hence, each element of $\mathcal{A}_1$ is either a set of data constructors of the same type or $\top$. The latter denotes the set of all data terms when no type information is available.

Following the framework of abstract interpretation [14], the meaning of abstract values is specified by a concretization function γ. For $\mathcal{A}_1$, γ is defined by

$$\begin{aligned} \gamma(\top) &= \{t \mid t \text{ is a data term}\} \\ \gamma(D) &= \{t \mid t = c(t_1, \ldots, t_n) \text{ is a data term with } c \in D\} \end{aligned}$$

Thus, $\varnothing$ is the bottom element of this domain w.r.t. the standard ordering defined by $a \sqsubseteq \top$ for any a, and $a_1 \sqsubseteq a_2$ if $a_1 \subseteq a_2$.

In the following, we present a framework for the inference of call types which is parametric over the abstract domain $\mathcal{A}$. Thus, we assume that $\mathcal{A}$ is a lattice with an ordering $\sqsubseteq$, greatest lower bound ($\sqcap$) and least upper bound ($\sqcup$) operations, a least or bottom element $\bot$, and a greatest or top element $\top$. Furthermore, for each n-ary data constructor c, there is an *abstract constructor application* c^α which maps abstract values $a_1, \ldots, a_n$ into an abstract value a such that $c(t_1, \ldots, t_n) \in \gamma(a)$ for all $t_1 \in \gamma(a_1), \ldots, t_n \in \gamma(a_n)$. For the domain $\mathcal{A}_1$, this can be defined by $c^\alpha(x_1, \ldots, x_n) = \{c\}$ (it could also be defined by $c^\alpha(x_1, \ldots, x_n) = \top$ but this yields less precise approximations).

We use $\mathcal{A}$ to specify *call types* or *non-failure conditions* for operations. Let f be a unary operation (the extension to more than one argument is straightforward). A call type $C \in \mathcal{A}$ is *correct* for f if the evaluation of $f(t)$ is non-failing for any $t \in \gamma(C)$. For instance, the depth-1 type $\{:\}$ is correct for the operations head or tail defined above.

In order to verify the correctness of call types for a program, we have to check whether each call of an operation satisfies its call type. Since this requires the analysis of conditions and other operations (see the operation readCmd defined in Sect. 1), we will approximate the input/output behavior of operations, as described next.

4   In/Out Types

To provide a fully automatic inference method for call types, we need some knowledge about the behavior of auxiliary operations. For instance, consider the operation

```
null []     = True
null (x:xs) = False
```

This operation is used in the definition of readCmd (see Sect. 1) to ensure that head and tail are applied to non-empty lists. In order to verify this property, we have to infer that, if "null ws" evaluates to False, the argument is a non-empty list.

For this purpose, we associate an in/out type to each operation. An *in/out type io* for an n-ary operation f is a set of elements containing a sequence of $n + 1$ abstract types:

$$io \subseteq \{a_1 \cdots a_n \hookrightarrow a \mid a_1, \ldots, a_n, a \in \mathcal{A}\}$$

The first n components of each element approximate input values (where we write ε if $n = 0$) and the last component approximate output values associated to the inputs. An in/out type io is *correct* for f if, for each value t' of $f(t_1, \ldots, t_n)$, there is some $a_1 \cdots a_n \hookrightarrow a \in io$ such that $t_i \in \gamma(a_i)$ $(i = 1, \ldots, n)$ and $t' \in \gamma(a)$.

In/out types are disjunctions of possible input/output behaviors of an operation. For instance, a correct in/out type of null is $\{\{[]\} \hookrightarrow \{True\}, \{:\} \hookrightarrow \{False\}\}$ (w.r.t. $\mathcal{A}_1$). Another trivial and less precise in/out type is $\{\top \hookrightarrow \top\}$.

In/out types allow also to express non-terminating operations. For instance, a correct in/out type for the operation loop defined by

```
loop = loop
```

is $\{\varepsilon \hookrightarrow \varnothing\}$. The empty type in the result indicates that this operation does not yield any value.

Similarly to call types, we approximate in/out types since the inference of precise in/out types is intractable in general. For this purpose, we analyze the definition of each operation and associate patterns to result values. Result values are based on general information about the abstract result types of operations. Therefore, we assume that there is a mapping $R : \mathcal{F} \to \mathcal{A}$ which associates to each defined function $f \in \mathcal{F}$ an abstract type $R(f) \in \mathcal{A}$ approximating the possible values to which f (applied to some arguments) can be evaluated. For instance, $R(\text{loop}) = \varnothing$, $R(\text{null}) = \{False, True\}$, and $R(\text{head}) = \top$ (w.r.t. the domain $\mathcal{A}_1$). Approximations for R can be computed in a straightforward way by a fixpoint computation. Using the Curry analysis framework CASS [24], this program analysis can be defined in 20 lines of code—basically a case distinction on the structure of FlatCurry operations.

Our actual approximation of in/out types is defined by the rules in Fig. 2. A sequence $o_1, \ldots, o_n$ of objects is abbreviated by $\overline{o_n}$. We use a *type environment* Γ which maps variables into abstract types. We denote by $\Gamma[x \mapsto e]$ the environment Γ' with $\Gamma'(x) = e$ and $\Gamma'(y) = \Gamma(y)$ for all $x \neq y$. The judgement $\Gamma \vdash e : \{\overline{\Gamma_k} \hookrightarrow a_k\}$ is interpreted as "the evaluation of the expression e in the context Γ yields a new context Γ_i and result value of abstract type a_i,

Var	$\Gamma \vdash x : \{\Gamma \hookrightarrow \Gamma(x)\}$	(x variable)
Cons	$\Gamma \vdash c(x_1,\ldots,x_n) : \{\Gamma \hookrightarrow c^\alpha(\Gamma(x_1),\ldots,\Gamma(x_n))\}$	(c constructor)
Func	$\Gamma \vdash f(x_1,\ldots,x_n) : \{\Gamma \hookrightarrow R(f)\}$	(f operation)

$$\text{Or} \qquad \frac{\Gamma \vdash e_1 : io_1 \quad \Gamma \vdash e_2 : io_2}{\Gamma \vdash e_1 \text{ or } e_2 : io_1 \cup io_2}$$

$$\text{Free} \qquad \frac{\Gamma[\overline{x_n \mapsto \top}] \vdash e : io}{\Gamma \vdash \text{let } x_1,\ldots,x_n \text{ free in } e : io}$$

$$\text{Let} \qquad \frac{\Gamma[x \mapsto \top] \vdash e' : io}{\Gamma \vdash \text{let } x = e \text{ in } e' : io}$$

$$\text{Case} \qquad \frac{\Gamma_1 \vdash e_1 : io_1 \quad \ldots \quad \Gamma_n \vdash e_n : io_n}{\Gamma \vdash \text{case } x \text{ of } \{p_1 \to e_1; \ldots; p_n \to e_n\} : io_1 \cup \ldots \cup io_n}$$

where $p_i = c_i(\overline{x_{n_i}})$ and $\Gamma_i = \Gamma[x \mapsto c_i^\alpha(\overline{\top}), \overline{x_{n_i} \mapsto \top}]$

Fig. 2. Approximation of in/out types

for some $i \in \{1,\ldots,k\}$." To infer an in/out type io of an operation f defined by $f(x_1,\ldots,x_n) = e$, we derive the judgement $\{\overline{x_n \mapsto \top}\} \vdash e : \{\overline{\Gamma_k \hookrightarrow a_k}\}$ and return the in/out type

$$io = \{\Gamma_i(x_1)\cdots\Gamma_i(x_n) \hookrightarrow a_i \mid i = 1,\ldots,k\}$$

Thus, we derive an in/out type without any restriction on the arguments.

Let us consider the inference rules in more detail. In the case of variables or applications, the type environment is not changed and the approximated result is returned, e.g., the abstract type of the variable (rule Var), the abstract representation of the constructor (rule Cons), or the approximated result value of the operation (rule Func). Rule Or combines the results of the different branches. Rules Free and Let add the new variables to the type environment with most general types. Although one could refine these types, we try to keep the analysis simple since this seems to be sufficient in practice.

The most interesting rule is Case. The results from the different branches are combined, but inside each branch, the type of the discriminating variable x is refined to the constructor of the branch. For instance, consider the operation

```
null(zs) = case zs of { []  → True ; (x:xs)  → False }
```

If we analyze the in/out type with our rules, we start with the type environment $\Gamma_0 = \{zs \mapsto \top\}$. Inside the branch, Γ_0 is refined to $\Gamma_1 = \{zs \mapsto \{[]\}\}$ and $\Gamma_2 = \{zs \mapsto \{:\}, x \mapsto \top, xs \mapsto \top\}$, respectively, so that the in/out type (w.r.t. $\mathcal{A}_1$) derived for `null` is $\{\{[]\} \hookrightarrow \{True\}, \{:\} \hookrightarrow \{False\}\}$.

In our implementation, we keep in/out types in a normalized form where different pairs with identical input types are joined by the least upper bound of their output types. Moreover, the in/out types of failed branches are omitted so that we obtain

```
head : {{:} ↪ ⊤}
tail : {{:} ↪ ⊤}
```

5   Inference and Checking of Call Types

Based on the pieces introduced in the previous sections, we can present our method to infer and verify call types for all operations in a given program. Basically, our method performs the following steps:

1. The in/out types for all operations are computed (see Sect. 4).
2. Initial call types for all operations are computed by considering the left-hand sides or case structure of their defining rules.
3. These call types are abstracted w.r.t. the abstract type domain.
4. For each call to an operation g occurring in a rule defining operation f, we check, by considering the call structure and in/out types, whether the call type of g is satisfied.
5. If some operation cannot be verified due to unsatisfied call type restrictions, its call type is refined by considering the additional call-type constraints due to operations called in its right-hand side, and start again with step 4.

This fixpoint computation terminates if the abstract type domain is finite (which is the case for depth-k types) or it is ensured that there are only finitely many refinements for each call type in step 5 (which could be ensured by widening steps in infinite abstract domains [14]). In the worst case, an empty call type might be inferred for some operation. This does not mean that this operation is not useful but one has to encapsulate its use with some safeness check.

In the following, we describe these steps in more detail.

5.1   Initial Call Types

Concrete call types are easy to derive by considering the structure of case expressions in the transformed FlatCurry program. If all constructors of some data type are covered in non-failed branches of some case construct, there is no call type restriction due to this pattern matching. Otherwise, the call type restriction consists of those constructors occurring in non-failed branches. For instance, the operation null has no call type restriction, whereas the operations head and tail have failed branches for the empty list so that the call type restriction could be expressed by the set of terms

$$\{t_1{:}t_2 \mid t_1, t_2 \text{ are arbitrary terms}\}$$

As already discussed, we map such sets into a finite representation by using abstract types. Hence, the *abstract call type* of an n-ary operation is a sequence of elements of $\mathcal{A}$ of length n. We say that such a type is *trivial* if all elements in this sequence are $\top$. In case of the abstract type domain $\mathcal{A}_1$, the set above is abstracted to $\{:\}$, thus, it is non-trivial. Since the derivation of concrete call types and their abstraction is straightforward, we omit further details here.

5.2   Call Type Checking

We assume that two kinds of information are given for each operation f:

$$\text{Var}_{nf} \qquad \Delta, z = x \vdash \{(z, \{\varepsilon \mapsto \Delta(x)\}, \varepsilon)\}$$

$$\text{Cons}_{nf} \qquad \Delta, z = c(x_1, \ldots, x_n) \vdash \{(z, \{\top^n \hookrightarrow c^\alpha(\overline{\Delta(x_n)})\}, x_1 \ldots x_n)\}$$

$$\text{Func}_{nf} \qquad \frac{CT(f) = a_1 \ldots a_n \quad \Delta(x_i) \sqsubseteq a_i \ (i = 1, \ldots, n)}{\Delta, z = f(x_1, \ldots, x_n) \vdash \{(z, IO(f), x_1 \ldots x_n)\}}$$

$$\text{Or}_{nf} \qquad \frac{\Delta, z = e_1 \vdash \Delta_1 \quad \Delta, z = e_2 \vdash \Delta_2}{\Delta, z = e_1 \ or \ e_2 \vdash \Delta_1 \cup \Delta_2}$$

$$\text{Free}_{nf} \qquad \frac{\Delta \cup \{x_1 :: \top, \ldots, x_n :: \top\}, z = e \vdash \Delta'}{\Delta, z = let \ x_1, \ldots, x_n \ free \ in \ e \vdash \Delta'}$$

$$\text{Let}_{nf} \qquad \frac{\Delta, x = e \vdash \Delta' \quad \Delta \cup \Delta', z = e' \vdash \Delta''}{\Delta, z = let \ x = e \ in \ e' \vdash \Delta''}$$

$$\text{Case}_{nf} \qquad \frac{\Delta_{r_1}, z = e_{r_1} \vdash \Delta'_{r_1} \quad \ldots \quad \Delta_{r_k}, z = e_{r_k} \vdash \Delta'_{r_k}}{\Delta, z = case \ x \ of \ \{p_1 \to e_1; \ldots; p_n \to e_n\} \vdash \Delta'_{r_1} \cup \ldots \cup \Delta'_{r_k}}$$

where $p_i = c_i(\overline{x_{n_i}})$, $\Delta_i = (\Delta \wedge [x \mapsto c_i]) \cup \{x_1 :: \top, \ldots, x_{n_i} :: \top\}$,
and $r_1, \ldots, r_k$ are the reachable branches (i.e., $\Delta_{r_j}(x) \neq \bot$)

Fig. 3. Call type checking

- An in/out type $IO(f)$ approximating the input/output behavior of f.
- An abstract call type $CT(f)$ specifying the requirements to evaluate f without failure.

$IO(f)$ can be computed as shown in Sect. 4. $CT(f)$ can be approximated as discussed above, but we have to show that all calls to f actually satisfy these requirements. This is the purpose of the inference system shown in Fig. 3.

As discussed in Sect. 4, it is important to have information about the input/output behavior of operations. Therefore, we introduced the notion of in/out types. Now we use this information to approximate values of variables occurring in program rules and pass this information through the rules during checking time. For this purpose, we use *variable types* which are triples of the form $(z, io, x_1 \ldots x_n)$ where $z, x_1, \ldots, x_n$ are program variables and io is an in/out type for an n-ary operation. This is interpreted as: z might have some value of the result type a for some $a_1 \ldots a_n \hookrightarrow a \in io$ and, in this case, $x_1, \ldots, x_n$ have values of type $a_1, \ldots, a_n$, respectively. For instance, the variable type

$$(z, \{\{[]\} \hookrightarrow \{\text{True}\}, \{:\} \hookrightarrow \{\text{False}\}\}, \ xs)$$

expresses that z might have value True and xs is an empty list, or z has value False and xs is a non-empty list. Since we approximate values, we abstract a set of variable environments with concrete values for variables to a set of variable types. If such a set contains only one triple for some variable and the io component is a one-element set, we can use it for definite reasoning. To have a more compact notation for the abstract type of a program variable, we denote by $x :: a$ the triple $(x, \{\varepsilon \mapsto a\}, \varepsilon)$.

Now we have a closer look at the rules of Fig. 3. This inference system derives judgements of the form $\Delta, z = e \vdash \Delta'$ containing sets of variable types Δ, Δ', a variable z, and an expression e. This is interpreted as "if Δ holds, then the expression e evaluates without a failure and, if z is bound to the result of this evaluation, Δ' holds". To check the call type $a_1 \ldots a_n$ of an operation f defined by $f(x_1, \ldots, x_n) = e$, we try to derive the judgement

$$\{x_1 :: a_1, \ldots, x_n :: a_n\}, z = e \vdash \Delta$$

for some fresh variable z. Thus, we assign the call types as initial values of the parameters and analyze the right-hand side of the operation.

Keeping the interpretation of variable types in mind, the inference rules are not difficult to understand. $\Delta(x)$ denotes the least upper bound of all abstract type information about variable x available in Δ, which is defined by

$$\Delta(x) = \bigsqcup \{a \mid (x, \{\ldots, a_1 \ldots a_n \hookrightarrow a, \ldots\}, \ldots) \in \Delta\}$$

Rule Var_{nf} is immediate since the evaluation of a value cannot fail so that we set the result z to the abstract type of x. Rule Cons_{nf} adds the simple condition that z is bound to the constructor c after the evaluation ($\top^n = \top \ldots \top$ is a sequence of n $\top$ elements). Rule Func_{nf} is the first interesting rule. The condition states that the abstract arguments of the function must be smaller than the required call type so that the concrete values are in a subset relationship. If the requirements on call types hold, the operation is evaluable and we connect the results and the arguments with the in/out type of the operation. The rules for disjunctions and free variable introduction are straightforward. In rule Let_{nf}, the result of analyzing the local binding is used to analyze the expression. We finally discuss the most important rule for case selections.

In rule Case_{nf}, $\Delta \wedge [x \mapsto c_i]$ denotes the set of variable types Δ modified by the definite binding of x to the constructor c_i. This means that, if Δ contains a triple (x, io, xs), all result values in io which are incompatible to c_i are removed. After this modification of Δ, it may happen that $\Delta(x)$ is the empty type, i.e., there is no concrete value which x can have so that this branch is *unreachable*. Therefore, the right-hand side of this branch need not be analyzed so that rule Case_{nf} does not consider them. For the remaining reachable branches, the right-hand side is analyzed with the modified set of variable types so that the value in the specific branch value is considered.

As an example, we check the simple operation

```
f(x) = let y = null(x) in case y of True   → True
                                    False  → head(x)
```

For the abstract type domain $\mathcal{A}_1$, the in/out type of `null` is

$$IO(\mathtt{null}) = \{\{[]\} \hookrightarrow \{\mathtt{True}\}, \{:\} \hookrightarrow \{\mathtt{False}\}\}$$

and the abstract call type of `head` is $\{:\}$. When we check the right-hand side of the definition of `f`, we start the checking of the `case` (after having checked the `let` binding) with the set of variable types

$$\Delta_1 = \{(\mathtt{x}, \{\varepsilon \hookrightarrow \top\}, \varepsilon),\ (\mathtt{y}, \{\{[]\} \hookrightarrow \{\mathtt{True}\}, \{:\} \hookrightarrow \{\mathtt{False}\}\}, \mathtt{x})\}$$

The check of the first case branch is immediate. For the second case branch, we modify the previous set of variable types to $\Delta_2 = \Delta_1 \wedge [\mathtt{y} \mapsto \mathtt{False}]$ so that we have

$$\Delta_2 = \{(\mathtt{x}, \{\varepsilon \hookrightarrow \top\}, \varepsilon),\ (\mathtt{y}, \{\{:\} \hookrightarrow \{\mathtt{False}\}\}, \mathtt{x})\}$$

The definite binding for $\mathtt{y}$ implies a definite binding for $\mathtt{x}$ so that Δ_2 is equivalent to

$$\Delta_3 = \{(\mathtt{x}, \{\varepsilon \hookrightarrow \{:\}\}, \varepsilon),\ (\mathtt{y}, \{\{:\} \hookrightarrow \{\mathtt{False}\}\}, \mathtt{x})\}$$

Hence, if we check the call "$\mathtt{head(x)}$" w.r.t. Δ_3, the abstract argument type is $\Delta_3(\mathtt{x}) = \{:\}$ so that the call type of $\mathtt{head}$ is satisfied.

As we have seen in this example, sets of variable types should be kept in a simplified form in order to deduce most precise type information. For instance, the definite bindings of variables, like $(\mathtt{y}, \{\{:\} \hookrightarrow \{\mathtt{False}\}\}, \mathtt{x})$, should be propagated to get a definitive binding for $\mathtt{x}$. Although this is not explicitly stated in the inference rules, we assume that it is always done whenever sets of variable types are modified.

5.3 Iterated Call Type Checking

Consider the operation

```
hd(x) = head(x)
```

Applying the inference rules of Fig. 3 is not successful: the initial abstract call type for $\mathtt{hd}$ is $\top$ so that the call type requirement for $\mathtt{head}$ is not satisfied.

In order to compute call types for all operations, we try to refine the call type of $\mathtt{hd}$. For this purpose, we collect the requirements on variables for unsatisfied call types during the check of an operation. If such a required type is on some variable occurring in the left-hand side of an operation, the call type of the operation is restricted and the operation is checked again. In case of the operation $\mathtt{hd}$, the failure in the call $\mathtt{head(x)}$ leads to the requirement that $\mathtt{x}$ must have the abstract type $\{:\}$ so that we check $\mathtt{hd}$ again but with this new call type—which is now successful.

There are also cases where such a refinement is not possible. For instance, consider the slightly modified example

```
hdfree(x) = let y free in head(y)
```

Since the type restriction $\{:\}$ on variable $\mathtt{y}$ can not be obtained by restricting the call type of $\mathtt{hdfree}$, we assume the most restricted call type $CT(\mathtt{hdfree}) = \{\}$. This means that any call to $\mathtt{hdfree}$ might fail so that one has to encapsulate calls to $\mathtt{hdfree}$ with some safeness check.

This strategy leads to an iterated analysis of call types. In each iteration, either all call types can be verified or the call type of some operation becomes more restricted. This iteration always terminates if one can ensure finitely many refinements of call types (which is the case for depth-k types).

For an efficient computation of this fixpoint computation, it is reasonable to use call dependencies of operations so that one has to re-check only the more restricted operations and the operations that use them. We have implemented this strategy in our tool and obtained a good improvement compared to the initial naive fixpoint computation. For instance, the prelude of Curry (the base module containing a lot of basic definitions for arithmetic, lists, type classes, etc.) contains 1262 operations (public and also auxiliary operations). After the first iteration, the call types of 14 operations are refined so that 17 operations are reanalyzed in the next iteration. Altogether, the check of the prelude requires five iterations.

5.4   Extensions

Up to now, we presented the analysis of a kernel language. Since application programs use more features, we discuss in the following how to cover all features occurring in Curry programs.

Literals. Programs might contain numbers or characters which are not introduced by explicit data definitions. Although there are conceptually infinitely many literals, their handling is straightforward. A literal can be treated as a 0-ary constructor. Since there are only finitely many literals in each program, the abstract types for a given program are also finite. For instance, consider the operation

```
k 0 = 'a'
k 1 = 'b'
```

The call type of k inferred w.r.t. domain $\mathcal{A}_1$ is $CT(\text{k}) = \{0, 1\}$. Similarly, the in/out type of k is $IO(\text{k}) = \{\{0\} \hookrightarrow \{\text{'a'}\}, \{1\} \hookrightarrow \{\text{'b'}\}\}$.

External Operations. Usually, externally defined primitive operations do not fail so that they have trivial call types. There are a few exceptions which are handled by explicitly defined call types, like the always failing operation `failed`, or arithmetic operations like division.

Higher-Order Operations. Since it is seldom that generic higher-order operations have functional parameters with non-trivial call types, we take a simple approach to check higher-order operations. We assume that higher-order arguments have trivial call types and check this property for each call to a higher-order operation. Thus, a call like "`map head [[1,2],[3,4]]`" is considered as potentially failing. Our practical evaluation shows this assumption provides reasonable results in practice.

Encapsulation. Failures might occur during run time, either due to operations with complex non-failure conditions (e.g., arithmetic) or due to the use of logic programming techniques with search and failures. In order to ensure an overall non-failing application in the presence of possibly failing subcomputations, the programmer has to encapsulate such subcomputations and then analyze its outcome, e.g., branching on the result of the encapsulation. For this purpose, one can use an exception handler (which represents a failing computation as an error value) or some method to encapsulate non-deterministic search (e.g., [5,12,28,29]). For instance, the primitive operation `allValues` returns all the values of its argument expression in a list so that a failure corresponds to an empty list. In order to include such a primitive in our framework, we simply skip the analysis of its arguments. For instance, a source expression like `allValues (head ys)` is not transformed into `let x = head(y) in allValues(x)` (where `x` is fresh), but it is kept as it is. Furthermore, rule $Func_{nf}$ is specialized for `allValues` so that the condition on the arguments w.r.t. the call type is omitted and the in/out type is trivial, i.e., $IO(\texttt{allValues}) = \{\top \hookrightarrow \top\}$. In a similar way, other methods to encapsulate possibly non-deterministic and failing operations, like *set functions* [5], can be handled.

Errors as Failures. The operation `error` is an external operation to emit an error message and terminate the program (if it does not occur inside an exception handler). Since we are mainly interested to avoid internal programming errors, `error` is not considered as a failing operation in the default mode. Thus, if we change the definition of `head` into (as in the prelude of Haskell)

```
head :: [a]  → a
head []      = error "head: empty list"
head (x:xs) = x
```

the inferred call type is $\top$ so that the call "`head []`" is not considered as failing. From some point of view, this is reasonable since the evaluation does not fail but shows a result—the error message.

However, in safety-critical applications we want to be sure that all errors are caught. In this case, we can still use our framework and define the call type of `error` as $\bot$ so that any call to `error` is considered as failing. Moreover, exception handlers can be treated similarly to encapsulated search operators as described above. In order to be flexible with the interpretation of `error`, our tool (see below) provides an option to set one of these two views of `error`.

6   Evaluation

We have implemented the methods described above in a tool[5] written in Curry. In the following we evaluate it by discussing some examples and applying it to various libraries.

---

[5] Available as package https://cpm.curry-lang.org/pkgs/verify-non-fail-1.0.0.html.

First, we compare our approach to a previous tool to verify non-failing Curry programs [20]. In that tool the programmer has to annotate partially defined operations with *non-fail conditions*. Based on these conditions, the tool extracts proof obligations from a program which are sent to an SMT solver. For instance, consider the operation to compute the last element of a non-empty list:

```
last [x]      = x
last (_:x:xs) = last (x:xs)
```

The condition to express the non-failure of this expression must be explicitly defined as a predicate on the argument:

```
last'nonfail xs = not (null xs)
```

This predicate together with the definition of the involved operations are translated to SMT formulas and then checked by an SMT solver, e.g., Z3 [34]. Using our approach, the abstract call type $CT(\texttt{last}) = \{:\}$ is automatically inferred and the definition of last is successfully checked. Actually, we tested our tool on various libraries and could deduce almost all manually written non-fail conditions of [20]. Only in four prelude operations, our tool could not infer these non-fail conditions since they contain arithmetic conditions on integers. We leave it for future work to combine our approach with an SMT solver to enable also successful checks in these cases.

Another interesting example is the operation split from the library Data.List. This operation takes a predicate and a list as arguments and splits this list into sublists at positions where the predicate holds. It is defined in Curry as

```
split :: (a  →  Bool)  →  [a]  →  [[a]]
split _ []                = [[]]
split p (x:xs) | p x      = [] : split p xs
               | otherwise = let (ys:yss) = split p xs
                             in (x:ys):yss
```

Since the pattern in the let expression is translated into partially defined selector functions in FlatCurry, this definition cannot be directly verified by [20] due to missing non-fail conditions for these auxiliary operations. Furthermore, a post-condition on split must be stated and proved. Our method infers all these conditions and verifies the non-failure of split.

If our tool is applied to a Curry module, it infers the in/out types and the call types of all operations defined in this module and then checks all branches and calls whether they might be failing. If this is the case, the call types are refined and the problematic ones are reported to the user. Then the user can decide to either accept the refined call types or modify the program code to handle possible failures so that the call type does not need a refinement.

Table 1 contains the results of checking various Curry libraries with our tool. The "operations" column contains the number of public (exported) operations and the number of all operations defined in the module. Similarly, the following three columns shows the information for public and all operations. The "in/out

Table 1. Inference of call types for some standard libraries

Module	operations	in/out types	initial call types	final call types	final failing	itera-tions	verify time
Prelude	862/1262	605/857	24/32	63/71	45/53	5	969
Data.Char	9/9	0/0	0/0	0/0	0/0	1	272
Data.Either	7/11	5/9	2/2	2/2	0/0	1	113
Data.List	49/87	39/73	7/15	8/16	1/1	2	290
Data.Maybe	8/9	7/8	0/0	0/0	0/0	1	113
Numeric	5/7	0/2	0/0	0/0	0/0	1	273
System.Console.GetOpt	6/47	5/41	0/0	0/0	0/0	1	287
System.IO	32/51	10/12	0/0	0/0	0/0	1	115
Text.Show	4/4	4/4	0/0	0/0	0/0	1	110

types" column shows the numbers of non-trivial in/out types. The initial and final call types are the number of non-trivial call types computed at the beginning and obtained after some iterations (the number of iterations is shown in the next to last column). The "final failing" column contains the number of operations where an empty call type is inferred, i.e., there is no precise information about the required call types. The last column shows the verification time in milliseconds.[6]

As one can see from this table, even quite complex modules, like the prelude, have only a few operations with non-trivial call types that need to be checked. Therefore, the effort to infer and check modules is limited. The higher number of failing operations in the prelude are the various arithmetic division operators and enumeration and parsing operations where a precise call type cannot be inferred.

7   Related Work

The exclusion of run-time failures at compile time is a practically relevant but also challenging issue. Therefore, there are many approaches targeting it so that we can only discuss a few of them. We concentrate on approaches for functional and logic programming, although there are also many in the imperative world. As mentioned in the introduction, the exclusion of dereferencing null pointers is quite relevant there. As an example from object-oriented programming, the Eiffel compiler uses appropriate type declarations and static analysis to ensure that pointer dereference failures cannot occur in accepted programs [30].

In logic programming, there is no common definition of "non-failing" due to different interpretations of non-determinism. Whereas we are interested to exclude any failure in a top-level computation, other approaches, like [13,16], consider a predicate in a logic program as non-failing if at least one answer is

---

[6] We measured the verification time on a Linux machine running Ubuntu 22.04 with an Intel Core i7-1165G7 (2.80 GHz) processor with eight cores.

produced. Similarly to our approach, type abstractions are used to approximate non-failure properties, but the concrete methods are different.

Another notion of failing programs in a dynamically typed programming language is based on success types, e.g., as used in Erlang [27]. Success types over-approximate possible uses of an operation so that an empty success type indicates an operation that never evaluates to some value. Thus, success types can show definite failures, whether we are interested in definite non-failures.

Strongly typed programming languages are a reasonable basis to check run-time failures at compile time, since the type system already ensures that some kind of failures cannot occur ("well-typed programs do not go wrong" [31]). However, failures due to definitions with partial patterns are not covered by a standard type system. Therefore, Mitchell and Runciman developed a checker for Haskell to verify the absence of pattern-match errors due to incomplete patterns [32,33]. Their checker extracts and solves specific constraints from pattern-based definitions. Although these constraints have similarities to the abstract type domain $\mathcal{A}_1$, our approach is generic w.r.t. the abstract type domain so that it can also deal with more powerful abstract type domains.

An approach to handle failures caused by restrictions on number arguments is described in [26]. It is based on generating (arithmetic) constraints which are translated into an imperative program such that the constraints are satisfiable iff the translated program is safe. This enables the inference of complex conditions on numbers, but pattern matching with algebraic data types and logic-oriented subcomputations are not supported.

Another approach to ensure the absence of failures is to make the type system stronger or more expressive in order to encode non-failing conditions in the types. For instance, operations in dependently typed programming languages, such as Coq [10], Agda [35], or Idris [11], must be totally defined, i.e., terminating and non-failing. Such languages have termination checkers but non-fail conditions need to be explicitly encoded in the types. For instance, the definition of the operation `head` in Agda [35] requires, as an additional argument, a proof that the argument list is not empty. Thus, `head` could have the type signature

```
head : {A : Set} → (xs : List A) → is-empty xs == ff → A
```

Therefore, each use of `head` must provide, as an additional argument, an explicit proof for the non-emptiness of the argument list `xs`. Type-checked Agda programs do not contain run-time failures but programming in a dependently typed language is more challenging since the programmer has to construct non-failure proofs.

Refinement types, as used in LiquidHaskell [39,40], are another approach to encode non-failing conditions or more general contracts on the type level. Refinement types extend standard types by a predicate that restricts the set of allowed values. For instance, the applications of `head` to the empty list can be excluded by the following refinement type [39]:

```
head :: {xs : [a] | 0 < len xs} → a
```

The correctness of refinement types is checked by an SMT solver so that they are more expressive than our non-failure conditions. On the other hand, refinement types must be explicitly added by the programmer whereas our goal is to infer non-failure conditions from a standard program. This allows the use of potentially failing operations in encapsulated subcomputations, which is relevant to use logic programming techniques. This aspect is also the motivation for the non-failure checking tool proposed in [20]. As already discussed in Sect. 6, the advantage of our tool is the automatic inference of non-failing conditions which supports an easier application to larger programs.

8   Conclusions

In this paper we proposed a new technique and a fully automatic tool to check declarative programs for the absence of failing computations. In contrast to other approaches, our approach does not require the explicit specification of non-fail conditions but is able to infer them. In order to provide flexibility with the structure of non-fail conditions, our approach is generic w.r.t. a domain of abstract types to describe non-fail conditions. Since we developed our approach for Curry, it is also applicable to purely functional or logic programs. Due to the use of Curry, we do not need to abandon all potentially failing operations. Partially defined operations and failing evaluations are still allowed in logic-oriented subcomputations provided that they are encapsulated in order to control possible failures.

Although the inference of non-fail conditions is based on a fixpoint iteration and might yield, in the worst case, an empty (i.e., always failing) condition, our practical evaluation showed that even larger programs contain only a few operations with non-trivial non-fail conditions which are inferred after a small number of iterations. When a non-trivial non-fail condition is inferred for some operation, the programmer can either modify the definition of this operation (e.g., by adding missing case branches) or control the invocation of this operation by checking its outcome with some control operator.

For future work, we plan to extend our approach to built-in types, like integers, and infer non-failure conditions on such types, like non-negative or positive numbers, and check them using SMT solvers. Furthermore, it is interesting to see whether other abstract domains, e.g., regular types, yield more precise results in application programs.

References

1. Albert, E., Hanus, M., Huch, F., Oliver, J., Vidal, G.: Operational semantics for declarative multi-paradigm languages. J. Symb. Comput. **40**(1), 795–829 (2005). https://doi.org/10.1016/j.jsc.2004.01.001
2. Alpuente, M., Comini, M., Escobar, S., Falaschi, M., Lucas, S.: Abstract diagnosis of functional programs. In: Leuschel, M. (ed.) LOPSTR 2002. LNCS, vol. 2664, pp. 1–16. Springer, Heidelberg (2003). https://doi.org/10.1007/3-540-45013-0_1

3. Antoy, S.: Constructor-based conditional narrowing. In: Proceedings of the 3rd International ACM SIGPLAN Conference on Principles and Practice of Declarative Programming (PPDP 2001), pp. 199–206. ACM Press (2001). https://doi.org/10.1145/773184.773205

4. Antoy, S., Echahed, R., Hanus, M.: A needed narrowing strategy. J. ACM **47**(4), 776–822 (2000). https://doi.org/10.1145/347476.347484

5. Antoy, S., Hanus, M.: Set functions for functional logic programming. In: Proceedings of the 11th ACM SIGPLAN International Conference on Principles and Practice of Declarative Programming (PPDP 2009), pp. 73–82. ACM Press (2009). https://doi.org/10.1145/1599410.1599420

6. Antoy, S., Hanus, M.: Functional logic programming. Commun. ACM **53**(4), 74–85 (2010). https://doi.org/10.1145/1721654.1721675

7. Antoy, S., Hanus, M., Jost, A., Libby, S.: ICurry. In: Hofstedt, P., Abreu, S., John, U., Kuchen, H., Seipel, D. (eds.) INAP/WLP/WFLP -2019. LNCS (LNAI), vol. 12057, pp. 286–307. Springer, Cham (2020). https://doi.org/10.1007/978-3-030-46714-2_18

8. Bert, D., Echahed, R.: Abstraction of conditional term rewriting systems. In: Proceedings of the 1995 International Logic Programming Symposium, pp. 147–161. MIT Press (1995)

9. Bert, D., Echahed, R., Østvold, B.M.: Abstract rewriting. In: Cousot, P., Falaschi, M., Filé, G., Rauzy, A. (eds.) WSA 1993. LNCS, vol. 724, pp. 178–192. Springer, Heidelberg (1993). https://doi.org/10.1007/3-540-57264-3_39

10. Bertot, Y., Castéran, P.: Interactive Theorem Proving and Program Development - Coq'Art: The Calculus of Inductive Constructions. Texts in Theoretical Computer Science. An EATCS Series. Springer (2004). https://doi.org/10.1007/978-3-662-07964-5

11. Brady, E.: Idris, a general-purpose dependently typed programming language: design and implementation. J. Funct. Program. **23**(5), 552–593 (2013). https://doi.org/10.1017/S095679681300018X

12. Braßel, B., Hanus, M., Huch, F.: Encapsulating non-determinism in functional logic computations. J. Funct. Logic Program. **2004**(6) (2004)

13. Bueno, F., López-García, P., Hermenegildo, M.: Multivariant non-failure analysis via standard abstract interpretation. In: Kameyama, Y., Stuckey, P.J. (eds.) FLOPS 2004. LNCS, vol. 2998, pp. 100–116. Springer, Heidelberg (2004). https://doi.org/10.1007/978-3-540-24754-8_9

14. Cousot, P., Cousot, R.: Abstract interpretation: a unified lattice model for static analysis of programs by construction of approximation of fixpoints. In: Proceedings of the 4th ACM Symposium on Principles of Programming Languages, pp. 238–252 (1977). https://doi.org/10.1145/512950.512973

15. Dart, P., Zobel, J.: A regular type language for logic programs. In: Pfenning, F. (ed.) Types in Logic Programming, pp. 157–187. MIT Press (1992)

16. Debray, S., López-García, P., Hermenegildo, M.: Non-failure analysis for logic programs. In: 14th International Conference on Logic Programming (ICLP 1997), pp. 48–62. MIT Press (1997)

17. Gallagher, J.P., Henriksen, K.S.: Abstract domains based on regular types. In: Demoen, B., Lifschitz, V. (eds.) ICLP 2004. LNCS, vol. 3132, pp. 27–42. Springer, Heidelberg (2004). https://doi.org/10.1007/978-3-540-27775-0_3

18. González-Moreno, J., Hortalá-González, M., López-Fraguas, F., Rodríguez-Artalejo, M.: An approach to declarative programming based on a rewriting logic. J. Log. Program. **40**, 47–87 (1999). https://doi.org/10.1016/S0743-1066(98)10029-8

19. Hanus, M.: Functional logic programming: from theory to curry. In: Voronkov, A., Weidenbach, C. (eds.) Programming Logics. LNCS, vol. 7797, pp. 123–168. Springer, Heidelberg (2013). https://doi.org/10.1007/978-3-642-37651-1_6

20. Hanus, M.: Verifying fail-free declarative programs. In: Proceedings of the 20th International Symposium on Principles and Practice of Declarative Programming(PPDP 2018), pp. 12:1–12:13. ACM Press (2018). https://doi.org/10.1145/3236950.3236957

21. Hanus, M.: Combining static and dynamic contract checking for Curry. Fund. Inform. **173**(4), 285–314 (2020). https://doi.org/10.3233/FI-2020-1925

22. Hanus, M.: From logic to functional logic programs. Theory Pract. Logic Program. **22**(4), 538–554 (2022). https://doi.org/10.1017/S1471068422000187

23. Hanus, M.: Inferring non-failure conditions for declarative programs. CoRR abs/2402.12960 (2024). http://arxiv.org/abs/2402.12960

24. Hanus, M., Skrlac, F.: A modular and generic analysis server system for functional logic programs. In: Proceedings of the ACM SIGPLAN 2014 Workshop on Partial Evaluation and Program Manipulation (PEPM 2014), pp. 181–188. ACM Press (2014). https://doi.org/10.1145/2543728.2543744

25. Hanus (ed.), M.: Curry: an integrated functional logic language (vers. 0.9.0) (2016). http://www.curry-lang.org

26. Jhala, R., Majumdar, R., Rybalchenko, A.: HMC: verifying functional programs using abstract interpreters. In: Gopalakrishnan, G., Qadeer, S. (eds.) CAV 2011. LNCS, vol. 6806, pp. 470–485. Springer, Heidelberg (2011). https://doi.org/10.1007/978-3-642-22110-1_38

27. Lindahl, T., Sagonas, K.: Practical type inference based on success typings. In: Proceedings of the 8th International ACM SIGPLAN Conference on Principles and Practice of Declarative Programming (PPDP 2006), pp. 167–178. ACM Press (2006). https://doi.org/10.1145/1140335.1140356

28. López-Fraguas, F., Sánchez-Hernández, J.: A proof theoretic approach to failure in functional logic programming. Theory Pract. Logic Program. **4**(1), 41–74 (2004). https://doi.org/10.1017/S1471068403001728

29. Lux, W.: Implementing encapsulated search for a lazy functional logic language. In: Middeldorp, A., Sato, T. (eds.) FLOPS 1999. LNCS, vol. 1722, pp. 100–113. Springer, Heidelberg (1999). https://doi.org/10.1007/10705424_7

30. Meyer, B.: Ending null pointer crashes. Commun. ACM **60**(5), 8–9 (2017). https://doi.org/10.1145/3057284

31. Milner, R.: A theory of type polymorphism in programming. J. Comput. Syst. Sci. **17**, 348–375 (1978)

32. Mitchell, N., Runciman, C.: A static checker for safe pattern matching in Haskell. In: Trends in Functional Programming, vol. 6, pp. 15–30. Intellect (2007)

33. Mitchell, N., Runciman, C.: Not all patterns, but enough: an automatic verifier for partial but sufficient pattern matching. In: Proceedings of the 1st ACM SIGPLAN Symposium on Haskell (Haskell 2008), pp. 49–60. ACM (2008). https://doi.org/10.1145/1411286.1411293

34. de Moura, L., Bjørner, N.: Z3: an efficient SMT solver. In: Ramakrishnan, C.R., Rehof, J. (eds.) TACAS 2008. LNCS, vol. 4963, pp. 337–340. Springer, Heidelberg (2008). https://doi.org/10.1007/978-3-540-78800-3_24

35. Norell, U.: Dependently typed programming in Agda. In: Koopman, P., Plasmeijer, R., Swierstra, D. (eds.) AFP 2008. LNCS, vol. 5832, pp. 230–266. Springer, Heidelberg (2009). https://doi.org/10.1007/978-3-642-04652-0_5

36. Peyton Jones, S. (ed.): Haskell 98 Language and Libraries-The Revised Report. Cambridge University Press, Cambridge (2003)

37. Sato, T., Tamaki, H.: Enumeration of success patterns in logic programs. Theoret. Comput. Sci. **34**, 227–240 (1984). https://doi.org/10.1016/0304-3975(84)90119-1
38. Stump, A.: Verified Functional Programming in Agda. ACM and Morgan & Claypool (2016). https://doi.org/10.1145/2841316
39. Vazou, N., Seidel, E., Jhala, R.: LiquidHaskell: experience with refinement types in the real world. In: Proceedings of the 2014 ACM SIGPLAN Symposium on Haskell, pp. 39–51. ACM Press (2014). https://doi.org/10.1145/2633357.2633366
40. Vazou, N., Seidel, E., Jhala, R., Vytiniotis, D., Peyton Jones, S.: Refinement types for Haskell. In: Proceedings of the 19th ACM SIGPLAN International Conference on Functional Programming (ICFP), pp. 269–282. ACM Press (2014). https://doi.org/10.1145/2628136.2628161

Being *Lazy* When It *Counts*
Practical Constant-Time Memory Management for Functional Programming

Chun Kit Lam[ID] and Lionel Parreaux[✉][ID]

HKUST, Hong Kong, China
{cklamaq,parreaux}@ust.hk

Abstract. Functional programming (FP) lets users focus on the business logic of their applications by providing them with high-level and composable abstractions. However, both automatic memory management schemes traditionally used for FP, namely tracing garbage collection and reference counting, may introduce latencies in places that can be hard to predict, which limits the applicability of the FP paradigm.

We reevaluate the use of lazy reference counting in single-threaded functional programming with guaranteed constant-time memory management, meaning that allocation and deallocation take only a bounded and predictable amount of time. This approach does not leak memory as long as we use uniform allocation sizes. Uniform allocation sizes were previously considered impractical in the context of imperative programming, but we find it to be surprisingly suitable for FP.

Preliminary benchmark results suggest that our approach is practical, as its performance is on par with Koka's existing state-of-the-art implementation of reference counting for FP, sometimes even outperforming it. We also evaluate the effect of different allocation sizes on application performance and suggest ways of allowing large allocation in non-mission-critical parts of the program via Koka's effect system.

We believe this potentially opens the door to many new industrial applications of FP, such as its use in real-time embedded software. In fact, the development of a high-level domain-specific language for describing latency-critical quantum physics experiments was one of the original use cases that prompted us to initiate this work.

1 Introduction

Functional programming allows software developers to design applications at a very high level of abstraction. It lets them focus on immutability and function composition to design programs in a way that can often be described as "correct by construction".

For example, the *functional reactive programming* (FRP) pattern [10,15,22], as found in popular languages like Haskell and Elm, uses immutable data structures and higher-order functions to let users *declaratively* specify reactive designs, such as animations, graphical user interfaces, and video games.

In practice however, a major problem with FRP, as well as with a number of other functional design patterns, is that it is extremely *memory-intensive*—on

© The Author(s), under exclusive license to Springer Nature Singapore Pte Ltd. 2024
J. Gibbons and D. Miller (Eds.): FLOPS 2024, LNCS 14659, pp. 188–216, 2024.
https://doi.org/10.1007/978-981-97-2300-3_11

each event, the old immutable states of objects that change are discarded and reconstructed from scratch, and new closures are allocated to register actions to be performed when new events occur. This means that typical FRP programs continuously allocate and free lots of memory, which can translate to jerky animations and small pauses in graphical user interface rendering.

Some FRP implementations allow users to avoid needless recomputation by telling parent components whether the state has changed [7]. This enables the runtime to reuse computation results for unaffected parts of the GUI, which reduces memory allocator pressure and makes the program less memory-intensive. However, the effectiveness of this kind of optimization depends not only on the GUI layout design, but also programmer efforts and discipline. Beginner users may not understand the need for such optimization, or may not know for sure if the layout is truly unchanged.

Traditional Memory Management for Functional Programming. Functional programming languages typically rely on some kind of garbage collection for automatic memory management. They often rely on generational, copying garbage collectors [9] to efficiently process short-lived objects while performing tracing garbage collection for older generations.

Reference counting, one of the oldest memory management techniques [5,24], was historically considered less practical than garbage collectors in this context, because frequent reference count updates can have a large performance impact and because reference counting cannot handle cycles [14]. However, there has been a recent surge in the popularity of reference counting for general-purpose memory management. Shahriyar et al. [20] analyzed the overhead of reference counting compared to tracing garbage collectors and introduced several strategies for improving its performance. Ullrich and de Moura [21] showed that destructive updates enabled by precise reference counting can provide significant performance improvements for functional programming languages. Reinking et al. [19] introduced Perceus, an algorithm for precise reference counting with destructive updates and specialization, and implemented the algorithm on Koka, a functional programming language with a type and effect system. These papers showed that functional programming languages using reference counting can have good performance too and can compete with state-of-the-art garbage collectors.

On the other hand, latency is also a key metric for system performance, sometimes even more important than throughput, and it has not been directly addressed by these recent works. Indeed, *eager* forms of reference counting can often lead to garbage collection pauses, sometimes even longer than those of tracing garbage collectors [3]. For example, consider an application that represents a news feed as an infinitely-scrollable view on which various widgets can appear. Imagine that a particular drawing-board widget interacts with user input by letting the user draw shapes in it. Each of these shapes will be represented as some vector-graphics object in a collection of shapes that have been drawn so far, which could grow very large. Thus, when the user finally loses interest and scrolls past the widget, its deallocation in a normal reference counting implementation will require recursively deallocating an unbounded number of vector-graphic objects, which is likely to cause a small pause in the scrolling animation, making it appear jerky.

Constant-Time Memory Management for Functional Programming. In this paper, we revisit the old idea of *lazy* reference counting, which avoids the long delays introduced by cascading deallocations. Our technique works by deferring the deallocation of an object's fields until the memory is needed by further allocations, which can progressively reuse memory by traversing the graph of objects no longer in use. This effectively gives us *constant-time* allocation and deallocation procedures, which we refer to as *constant-time memory management*.

There are naturally a number of limitations and caveats to this approach. First, in order to be truly (non-amortized) constant-time without the possibility of leaking unbounded amounts of memory, we need all allocations to share the same size. While it means that the compiler must *split up* large objects into multiple allocations, we argue that this approach is eminently practical in the context of functional programming languages. Indeed, algebraic data type objects tend to be on the smaller side, and we show that the performance hit associated with splitting larger objects in this context varies from moderate to small or insignificant.

Second, like most reference counting approaches, we do not handle cycles in the reference graph. But we argue that in the context of functional programming, where most data is immutable and tree-like, cycles can normally be avoided. Depending on the compilation strategy and language features, cycles may still be introduced in the presence of laziness, recursive closures, or OCaml-style cyclic values. With a slight loss of expressiveness, it is possible to design pure functional programming languages where cycles cannot be constructed, as exemplified by Lean [21]. We argue that the loss of expressiveness is acceptable. On one hand, while it is true that recursive closures are traditionally implemented through cyclic values, other implementation strategies exist, used for example in languages like Rust and Koka. On the other hand, while some languages use laziness to allow conveniently constructing cyclic values, it is possible to design more restricted languages where laziness is still supported but where cyclic values cannot be constructed. Third, our approach is currently only applicable to sequential mutators. Due to the lazy nature of our approach, it is impossible in general to know the amount of memory actually in use by the program at any given time. This makes some approaches to concurrent memory management with thread-local free lists impractical.

In turn, our approach also has large advantages. While the uniform allocation size does create *internal* fragmentation (which could lead to up to 2x memory usage overhead in the worst case), it also means that we are effectively free from *external* fragmentation, whose worst-case overhead can become vastly higher than 2x, and which often cripples long-running systems in practice, leading to degraded performance and even system failure [17].

We formalized our design, nicknamed CTRC (for *constant-time reference counting*), and implemented it inside the Koka programming language, leveraging its existing reference counting optimizations as well as its type-and-effect system. The allocator adopts the approach of Leijen et al. [13] with page-local free lists to improve memory locality.

Our experimental results show that this approach can achieve throughput comparable with Koka using the state-of-the-art mimalloc allocator, while providing constant-time guarantees for both allocation and deallocation, even for cases with larger objects that require splitting into several allocations. A major advantage of our approach is that it is extremely simple to implement: the basic runtime is about 160 lines of C code (the entirety of which fits into four pages of Appendix B), and does not make use of any existing system allocator beyond the operating system's memory page allocation routines.

This could enable the implementation of efficient automatic memory reclamation for resource-constrained embedded systems, which could have future applications in the domain of hard real-time systems.

Contributions

- Although similar solutions were proposed in the past in slightly different contexts back in 1963 [24], we present a refreshed and practical solution to *constant-time* memory management for functional programming, called CTRC (Sect. 2). CTRC was implemented by adapting the existing Koka runtime system and compiler. Our implementation is extremely simple, which we consider to be a major selling point.
- We formalize this new approach and show that it is sound and prevents memory leaks, in the sense that it does not increase the peak memory usage of programs (Sect. 2.4 and Appendix A). We also show that CTRC can be applied only locally, to those parts of a program that are latency-sensitive.
- We experimentally justify the practicality of CTRC, showing that on our benchmark programs, its space and time overheads are small when compared to Perceus, a state-of-the-art reference-counting implementation (Sect. 3). We also discuss the source of the overhead, and suggest approaches for programmers to reduce the overhead.

2   Presentation of Constant-Time Reference Counting

In this section, we present our basic idea of *constant-time reference counting* for Functional Programming (CTRC).

2.1   Eager and Lazy Reference Counting

Reference counting is typically implemented by attaching an integer reference count to each object, indicating the number of pointers pointing to the current object. When pointers or variables are modified, the reference count of the referred object is updated. As the reference count of an object becomes zero, it is deleted and the reference counts of its fields are decremented. For example, when deallocating a linked list, the reference count of the first node becomes zero, which recursively decrements the subsequent nodes and deletes them. We shall refer to this type of reference counting as *eager* reference counting.

Eager reference counting allows immediate garbage collection with low pause times compared to tracing garbage collectors, as the tracing part is done incrementally by tracking reference counts rather than a separate tracing phase. However, reference counting can still have unbounded pause time as a deallocation event can trigger a chain of deallocation.

By contrast, CTRC performs reference counting *lazily*. Instead of updating reference counts for the fields of deallocated objects immediately, the updates are postponed by storing the deallocated objects in a free list. When there is a new allocation request, the fields of the object are freed as the object allocation is being reused. This breaks the chain of deallocation mentioned previously, making the allocation and deallocation of objects constant-time.

The use of constant-time reference counting mandates using only a single allocation size, as using multiple allocation sizes may result in memory leaks, which we discuss in Sect. 2.2. In general, large objects can always be split up into smaller segments to fit the single allocation size requirement. Although using a constant allocation size was traditionally considered impractical in previous literature, our experiments show that by selecting a suitable size, the space and performance penalty of splitting large objects is limited. While CTRC requires a constant allocation size, there can be cases in which the program requires large contiguous arrays, for example when interacting with graphics APIs. We show that one can make use of an effect system to isolate the parts of a program that need to perform variable-sized memory allocation, while maintaining the constant-time guarantee for all other parts of the program.

2.2   Allocation Size

We now discuss why it is necessary to have a single allocation size for constant-time memory management, overhead associated with this strategy, and criteria for choosing allocation size.

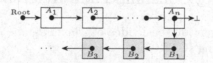

Fig. 1. Linked List with 2 Size Classes.

In the case of having multiple constant allocation sizes, one either has to give up constant time guarantee or potentially suffer from memory leaks [3]. Consider the example shown in Fig. 1, where there are two size classes, with small and large objects denoted by white and pale blue boxes respectively. The last element of the small-object linked list contains a unique reference to a linked list with large objects. Assume that the program loses the unique reference to

A_1 at some point, causing all the small objects A_i and large objects B_i to become unreachable. For normal reference counting schemes, the entire linked list together with the large-object linked list is deallocated. However, for constant time memory management schemes, the collector can only visit and deallocate a bounded number of objects per step. Hence, if the small-object linked list is sufficiently long, the memory collector can only deallocate the small objects, which cannot be used to fulfill allocation for large objects. The allocator has to allocate additional memory to fulfill large object allocations, even though there are unused large object allocations that could be reused, causing a memory leak.

To avoid such an issue, our implementation only allows a single allocation size, and large objects are split into segments.[1] For imperative programming languages, this approach is considered infeasible as it is more common to have arrays and objects with a large number of fields. However, for functional programming languages, it is common to use data structures such as linked lists and other tree-shaped linked data structures, whose nodes are usually small. This makes our approach feasible, as shown by our experiments (Sect. 3).

There are multiple considerations when choosing the allocation size, including memory overhead and architecture-specific details. If the allocation size is a lot larger than the average object size, there will be severe internal fragmentation, which wastes memory and memory bandwidth, which can cause performance degradation. However, if the allocation size is too small, large objects are split into multiple cells, and access to certain fields involves multiple pointer indirections, making the access slow. In addition, each cell has to store metadata such as reference counts, so the overhead increases when large objects are split into multiple cells. One should also consider architecture-specific details, such as the cache line size and alignment requirements when choosing the allocation size. This is to make sure allocations satisfy alignment requirements when packed together, and require minimal cache access when accessing an object.

In our experiments, we choose 32 bytes as the size of each allocation, with a header occupying 8 bytes. The target CPU architecture includes x86-64 and aarch64, which uses 64-byte cache lines. Our objects should align to cache line boundaries to avoid false-sharing, so it is natural to choose 64 bytes as the allocation size. However, our early experiments found that the typical object sizes are small, so using an allocation size of 32 bytes can improve memory and cache utilization, while still being aligned to cache line boundaries.

Let the object size be n bytes, it requires at most $\lceil \frac{n}{16} \rceil$ segment, where every non-leaf segment contains a header and a pointer to the next segment. The worst-case memory usage is four times the optimal memory usage when metadata occupies 8 bytes. However, the actual worst-case memory usage is usually much smaller. For example, if the smallest allocations are 32-bit integers which occupy 4 bytes each, the object size is 12 bytes together with the metadata, and the memory overhead is 2.66 times the optimal memory usage. Note that this worst-case memory usage is independent of the allocation and deallocation pattern, which makes it simple to reason about statically with a tight upper bound.

---

[1] Note that since object sizes are a constant of the program, field accesses still take constant time, even for split objects.

2.3 Implementation in Koka

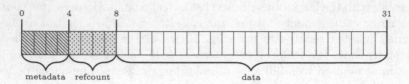

Fig. 2. Cell Data Layout.

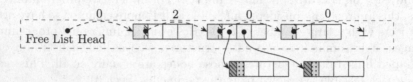

Fig. 3. Free List Layout.

We implemented the CTRC memory management scheme by extending Koka's C runtime and modifying the Koka compiler to split large objects into constant-size segments. In the following, we shall use *cell* to denote a fixed-size memory allocation (32 bytes, including a header of 8 bytes) and *drop* to denote decreasing the reference count of an object and *deallocating* it when the reference count is 0. Figure 2 shows a simplified view of the memory layout for each cell, which consists of a 32-bit metadata, 32-bit reference count `refcount`, and 24 bytes of actual storage which is capable of storing three 64-bit pointers or integers. The metadata encodes information including object type for pattern matching, the number of pointers in the current cell, and additional data for other extensions such as the "eagerly-deallocating-allocation" effect referred to in Sect. 2.5.

The free list is maintained as an intrusive linked list where the 8-byte header acts as the pointer to the next cell. As cells are aligned to 32 bytes boundary, the 5 least significant bits of the free list pointers can be used for storing some of the metadata, which includes information such as the segment's pointer count, that has been replaced by the intrusive pointer and can no longer reside in the object. Note that this does not apply to pointers pointing to live objects, i.e. the normal pointers, as the reference count must be stored in the object and 5 bits are not enough for other metadata. The linked list is maintained with a last-in-first-out (LIFO) order. As the last deallocated cell is likely to reside in the cache, reusing it first can increase the chance of getting a cache hit. Figure 3 shows an example free list layout. The cells inside the red dashed rectangle are inside the free list, note that their headers are different from those outside the free list. Pointers pointing to other free list cells contain metadata, such as the next cell pointer counts on top of the dashed arrows. Pointers pointing to live cells, denoted by solid arrows, are dropped when the free list cell is being reused.

In case the object occupies more than 24 bytes, the compiler splits the object into multiple segments. Each segment occupies a single cell, with pointers pointing to other segments in a tree-like fashion. Note that in our prototype implementation, the objects are split up in a linked-list-like fashion, i.e. each segment can only point to one other segment, for simplicity. The runtime treats each segment inside the free list as individual objects.

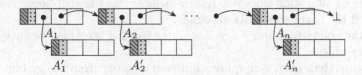

Fig. 4. Linked List Example.

Consider a linked list example, where each node contains a pointer to the next node and 3 64-bit integers. As each node is larger than 32 bytes, it is split into 2 segments. The example memory layout is shown in Fig. 4. The i-th node is split into two segments A_i and A'_i, where A_i contains pointer to A'_i, pointer to the next node A_{i+1}, and 1 64-bit integer. A'_i contains the remaining 2 64-bit integers. When A_1 is deallocated, it is put into the free list. When there is another memory allocation and A_1 is removed from the free list, the allocator puts A'_1 into the free list as A_1 must contain the unique reference to A'_1, A_2 is dropped at this point but not necessarily deallocated as there can still be other references to A_2.

2.4 Soundness and Garbage-Free Guarantee

Due to space limitation, we provide the details of our formalization in Appendix A. We define the "*baseline semantics*" to be the typical operational semantics for untyped lambda calculus with explicit binding, pattern matching, and an interpretation of *dup* and *drop* as *no-op* instructions. The baseline semantics is the observable behavior of the program and is independent of the underlying memory management strategy. We refer to the semantics that manage the heap and perform eager reference counting as the "*eager semantics*". Similarly, we define the semantics of CTRC that perform lazy reference counting as the "*lazy semantics*". In addition to the heap, the lazy semantics also has the concept of a free list, which is a list of dropped cells that can be reused. Instead of getting a fresh memory location in the heap when performing allocation, the lazy semantics attempts to get a cell from the free list and drop its fields when the free list is non-empty. Also, instead of recursively dropping an object when the reference count becomes zero, the lazy semantics keeps the object in the heap and adds it to the free list.

Our formalization reasons about program traces in different semantics. We show that:

1. The eager semantics and lazy semantics both simulate the baseline semantics. This makes sure the behavior is correct when allocation does not return memory that is still being referenced. Also, this provides the notion of time for other parts of the formalization.
2. At any point in the execution, the reference count of an object in the eager semantics x_k is smaller than that in the lazy semantics x_c, i.e. $x_k \leq x_c$.
   This makes sure we never put things that are still being referenced in the free list, so allocation does not return memory that is still being referenced, provided the eager semantics is sound.
3. When the points-to graph is acyclic and the free list is empty, we have $x_k = x_c$ for every object.
   This means that when we require additional memory from the system to fulfill allocation, the current heap is garbage-free, provided that the execution under the eager semantics is garbage-free at this point.

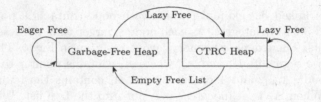

Fig. 5. Relationship between Eager free and Lazy free.

The proof is based on simulation, which means that we do not have to prove the soundness and garbage-free properties for program transformations under the lazy semantics. If the program transformation preserves soundness and garbage-free properties in the eager semantics, the same guarantees hold in the lazy semantics. Figure 5 shows the relationship between the eager and lazy semantics.

2.5   Eagerly-Deallocating-Allocation Effect

While functional programming typically uses small objects, some data structures require large contiguous memory allocation to be efficient, such as B-Trees [6] which benefit from a larger branching factor, and hash tables, which benefit from being able to perform random accesses in an array. However, increasing the fixed allocation size to satisfy these use cases causes a large increase in memory usage, and may impact performance due to worse cache utilization. Ideally, there should be a way of using variable-sized memory together with fixed-size constant-time memory management.

Eagerly-Deallocating-Allocation Effect (EDA), is an extension to CTRC that allows users to use variable-sized memory, without sacrificing the constant-time guarantee for the whole program. The idea is to utilize the effect system to mark parts of the program that perform variable-sized memory allocations which take non-constant time. Users can use the effect system to prohibit calling functions that perform variable-sized memory allocations in timing-sensitive regions of the program. Note that memory deallocation is still constant-time in all cases, and users can still perform read and write operations on those variable-sized allocations from all parts of the program. Only variable-sized allocations take unbounded time, as they deallocate everything in the eager free list to recover space.

The runtime segregates the free list into a lazy free list and an eager free list. The eager free list contains all large allocations and objects that can transitively reach objects in the eager free list. For implementation, one can use 1 bit in the metadata to determine whether or not the object can transitively reach large objects. Deallocation operations put the object into the corresponding free list depending on this bit, and each operation still takes constant time. If there is insufficient memory to satisfy a variable-sized allocation, the allocator first tries to empty the eager free list, and then the lazy free list, to try to get enough space to fulfill the allocation. When both free lists are empty, the system should be garbage-free, so emptying the two free lists can make sure the system does not use more memory than necessary. The eager free list is emptied first to free large allocations, which are more likely to be able to satisfy the large allocation request. For normal fixed-size allocation, the allocator tries to reuse cells in the lazy free list. When the lazy free list is empty, the allocator uses cells in the eager free list, splitting large allocations when necessary. The allocator avoids splitting large allocations when possible, as splitting such allocation to fulfill small allocation requests may cause fragmentation.

3   Preliminary Experiments

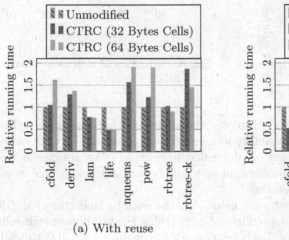
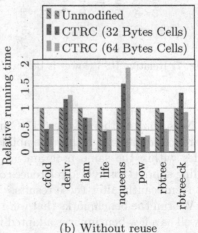

(a) With reuse   (b) Without reuse

Fig. 6. Relative Running Time

In this section, we discuss the initial benchmarks of CTRC, implemented by modifying the compiler and runtime system of Koka, versus Koka with the mimalloc [13] memory allocator.

3.1   Experimental Setup

Our CTRC implementation is extremely simple, the allocator runtime contains about 150 lines of C code that *does not depend on the system memory allocator*. We included the implementation of the allocator in Appendix B, which uses mmap for allocating new pages but can be modified to use memory from a static buffer, and is simple to port to embedded systems. We modified the Koka compiler[2] to limit the size of each allocation and split the object when necessary. In the benchmark, we compare the performance of different cell sizes (32 bytes and 64 bytes) as cell size impacts both the performance and memory usage of the application.

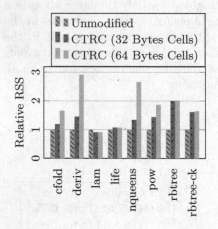

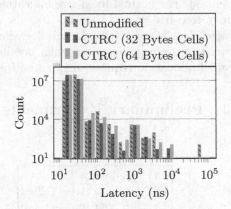

Fig. 7. Relative RSS (lower is better).

Fig. 8. Histogram of statement latencies (Sect. 3.3).

Note that neither of the CTRC implementations used here supports hybrid reference counting, which is the ability to mix different eager and lazy allocation styles within the same program, as described in Sect. 2.5. We anticipate that adding support for hybrid reference counting would be straightforward and would not significantly alter these results.[3]

We run the benchmarks that were included in the work by Reinking et al. [19], as well as a few benchmarks adapted from NoFib [16], a Haskell benchmark suite, that stress memory allocation. Each benchmark is run in a loop 100 times in

---

[2] Commit hash: **b167030**.

[3] The only change needed for hybrid reference counting in the CTRC allocator implementation is the addition of a check for the dirty bit stored in object headers.

Koka, to avoid measuring only the startup and termination overhead of the runtime. All the benchmarks are run on a desktop computer with Intel i5-13600KF with 32 GiB of RAM, running NixOS 23.11 with Linux 6.5.12 Xanmod kernel. The benchmarks are compiled with -O3 optimization using GCC 11.3.0. The benchmark run is pinned on a performance core with `taskset`, with SMT and turbo boost disabled to ensure all the code is run at the same CPU frequency. The relative execution time and memory usages are given in Fig. 6a, Fig. 6b and Fig. 7. By default, Koka compiles with reuse optimization [19] enabled, which reduces the number of deallocations by performing in-place updates when the reference to the data structure is unique. Figure 6b shows the benchmark result in which the reuse optimization is disabled, which demonstrates the performance when such reuse optimization is inapplicable or not implemented, for example when run in an interpreter.

3.2   Performance and Memory Usage

From Fig. 6a, CTRC with a 32-byte cell size has similar performance compared with Koka unmodified, except in the N-queens (nqueens) and red-black tree (rbtree-ck) benchmarks. For nqueens, this is because it mostly uses integer cons lists, where each node only occupies 16 bytes in the 32-byte cell. Every access fetches some unused memory, which under-utilizes the memory bandwidth. This behavior is also apparent in most benchmarks when increasing the cell size from 32 bytes to 64 bytes: these benchmarks run slower in addition to using more memory. For rbtree-ck, the slowness is caused by the compiler splitting the left-child and right-child pointers into two segments. Tree traversal requires one additional pointer indirection, making the running time slower. Switching the cell size to 64 bytes removes the need for pointer indirection, which makes the running time faster in this case.

For the lambda evaluation (lam) and game of life (life) benchmarks, they are significantly faster compared with Koka unmodified because they involve deallocating large collections. For example, the life benchmark allocates and deallocates a large grid, and the lazy deallocation approach used by CTRC provides better temporal locality. CTRC with a 32-byte cell size has on average 8.8M L1 d-cache misses per iteration, while unmodified Koka has on average 26M L1 d-cache misses per iteration for the life benchmark. Similar behavior occurs when the reuse optimization is disabled, because in-place updates become deallocation and allocation of the same large collection, so CTRC becomes faster than unmodified Koka in these cases.

CTRC generally uses more memory compared to the baseline. For some benchmarks, 64-byte cell size can have a relatively high memory overhead because the object size is small (e.g. 16 bytes), wasting the remaining 48 bytes. However, the advantage of CTRC is that the maximal memory overhead can be determined statically, and is independent from the allocation/deallocation pattern.

Programmers can reduce the performance and memory overhead of CTRC by changing the datatypes to pack more data into each cell. For example, instead of using the usual cons list definition, one can use the following:

```
alias i32 = int32
type i32-list
  Nil
  Cons1{h1: i32;                                  t: i32-list}
  Cons2{h1: i32; h2: i32;                         t: i32-list}
  Cons3{h1: i32; h2: i32; h3: i32;                t: i32-list}
  Cons4{h1: i32; h2: i32; h3: i32; h4: i32; t: i32-list}
```

When compiled, the pointer t uses 8 bytes in 64-bit systems, and the maximal of 4 32-bit integer fields occupy 16 bytes in total. Together with the 8-byte metadata per cell, this fully utilizes the 32-byte cell size. Note that these transformations will make the code more complicated, which may cause additional overhead if the program bottleneck is not caused by memory bandwidth limitation or cache misses. For example instead of simply using cons cells to add an element to the start of the list, the code now should check for the variant of the first cell and change the cell type accordingly. Also, the code transformation requires knowing the size of the fields, which may make it hard to apply the optimization for polymorphic types. For example, we can only unroll two fields if the data type used is a pointer instead of 32-bit integers.

There are also opportunities for data structure inlining [8], which is a well-known approach to optimizing program performance and memory footprint. Bruno et al. [4] uses value semantics to determine if data structures are eligible for inlining, where data objects with value semantics are not used for reference comparison and do not require atomic field access. In the context of functional programming, objects automatically have value semantics, so inlining can be applied to most objects except those behind reference cells. The problem is how to pack the objects such that fields accessed together are placed in the same cell, and how to maximize the utilization of cell size, which we leave as future work.

3.3   Latency Measurements

In the context of embedded programming, it is common to implement cooperative scheduling by explicitly yielding program control. This does not require a complicated program runtime and is more efficient, but requires careful coordination to meet latency requirements. Unbounded latency caused by recursive drop is particularly problematic in this scenario, because the programmer may think that every statement in the source language corresponds to a bounded number of steps in the machine execution. As the famous saying goes, "Any sufficiently complicated C or Fortran program contains an [...] implementation of half of Common Lisp", we implemented a simple lambda calculus interpreter to simulate the workload of complicated embedded programs and measured the latency per statement, to simulate the latency of cooperative scheduling. The result is shown in Fig. 8, where "Count" is the number of statements that require a certain amount of time to execute.

From the figure, although most statements have low latency, unmodified Koka can occasionally get latency spikes of around 10 μs or higher, which are caused by deallocating large data structures. The latencies of around 1 μs for unmodified Koka and CTRC are caused by page faults, and are unavoidable when running with virtual memory. This shows that the unbounded latency for eager reference counting can have a measurable impact, and is not only a theoretical problem, while CTRC mitigates the issue of unbounded latency in both memory allocation and deallocation.

4   Related Work and Conclusion

We now discuss related work and conclude.

4.1   Related Work

Reinking et al. [19] introduced a new algorithm for optimizing reference counting with memory reuse and specialization. Their work showed that reference counting can achieve comparable performance with state-of-the-art memory management systems, and sometimes even out-performing in terms of efficiency, while maintaining low memory usage and reasonable pause time. Our implementation is based on their work on the Koka compiler, which benefits from their reference counting optimization. Some of the optimization, such as reuse analysis, becomes more efficient in CTRC due to the constant allocation size guarantee.

Leijen et al. [13] implemented mimalloc, a fast memory allocator developed for Koka and Lean. Their implementation uses free list sharding to increase locality and reduce fragmentation. Free list sharding can be implemented in constant time for our approach, but experiments showed no consistent performance improvement due to worse temporal locality compared with a stack-like approach (LIFO). Our implementation achieves competitive performance when compared with Koka together with mimalloc, and the latter was already shown to be competitive with existing functional programming language implementations like GHC and OCamlc, which uses traditional tracing GC, as well as Swift, which uses reference counting. But while mimalloc is implemented in about 8k lines of code, our prototype implementation just takes around 150 lines of C code due to having fewer features and supporting Unix only.

Lazy reference counting is not a new concept. Back in 1963, Weizenbaum [24] introduced a list processing system that used lazy reference counting, and provided a simple implementation of the processing system in FORTRAN. However, due to various limitations of reference counting, such as the performance impact caused by frequent reference count updates and the inability to deal with cycles, tracing garbage collection is still the preferred way for performing automatic memory management in most high-level languages. Joisha [11, 12] used the idea of lazy reference counting to bound pause time in garbage collection. Instead of immediately collecting all the garbage, the deallocator maintains a list of zombie objects that have a reference count of zero but are yet to be reclaimed. This avoids triggering unbounded pause time when deallocating linked lists. However, as the system uses variable allocation size, the runtime may need to eagerly process all the zombie objects when there is insufficient space to serve certain allocation requests.

Boehm [3] analyzed the upper bound on the memory usage of lazy reference counting when multiple size classes are used. When the maximum and minimum cell size are s_{max} and s_{min} respectively and the number of live object is N, the space bound is $\frac{s_{max}}{s_{min}} N$. This upper bound is not better than using only one size class and promoting all small objects to the largest size class.

Puaut [18] evaluated the performance of various dynamic memory allocation approaches, comparing their analytical worst-case allocation time with their actual observed worst-case allocation time. Those algorithms tend to work well in practice and the observed worst-case allocation time is not too large compared with the average allocation time. However, their analytical worst-case time can be very large due to the variable allocation sizes they support, and are unsuitable for hard real-time applications. On the other hand, our work allows for simple implementation, high throughput, and low analytical worst-case allocation time in the portions of the program that are statically proven by the type system not to have large allocation effects.

Bruno et al. [4] showed that object inlining can provide large improvements to throughput and reduce memory footprint. It may be possible to perform similar object inlining in CTRC to reduce the memory overhead of constant allocation size, and potentially improve performance by improving cache utilization.

Blelloch and Wei [2] gave a wait-free implementation for fixed-size allocation and free that is linearizable. This can potentially be used to implement the concurrency extension of CTRC, which requires balancing the global and thread-local heaps.

Blackburn and McKinley [1] introduced a hybrid garbage collector that combined both generational collector and reference-counting collector for high throughput and low maximum pause time. Their implementation divided the heap into an immortal part, a reference counted space for mature objects and a nursery space for short-lived objects with a high mutation rate. By deferring reference count updates for short-lived objects, the system's throughput can be improved. While they added a *time cap* parameter to limit the time spent on each garbage collection phase, our approach is inherently lazy and does not require tuning such ad hoc parameters. In addition, as shown in Reinking et al. [19], the throughput of reference counting with compile-time optimization is on par with or even better than state-of-the-art garbage collectors, without the complexity of a hybrid garbage collector.

Wan et al. [23] designed a statically-typed language called Real-Time FRP, that statically bounds the time and space cost of each execution step, which avoids unbounded allocation size and infinite recursion in the computation. However, in their formalism, the time cost of allocation and deallocation are not considered, as they only bound the term size. But allocation times can be significant in practice and could make their approach not truly real-time.

4.2   Conclusion

In this paper, we presented CTRC, a lazy reference counting system that provides a constant-time guarantee for memory allocation and deallocation operations. We also presented extensions for supporting a hybrid memory management strategy by utilizing a type-and-effect system, and discussed challenges and potential solutions for handling multithreaded allocation with memory sharing. While extremely concise, our implementation in Koka is competitive with the Koka runtime using mimalloc, a state-of-the-art memory allocator optimized for functional programming languages, which shows that our approach is practical and does not suffer from any significant performance penalty. We would like to experiment with other optimization techniques, such as object inlining [4] and profile-guided optimizations, to further reduce the performance and memory overhead of splitting objects. We leave as future work how to handle multithreaded allocation efficiently.

A   Formalization

In this section, we present the formal operational semantics of CTRC, prove its soundness, and show that it is garbage-free when the free list is empty (and the free list is always used for new allocations when non-empty).

Expressions

$$e ::= x \mid v \mid e\ e \qquad\qquad \text{(variable, value, application)}$$
$$\mid \text{val } x = e; e \qquad\qquad \text{(bind)}$$
$$\mid \text{dup } x;\ e \qquad\qquad \text{(duplicate)}$$
$$\mid \text{drop } x;\ e \qquad\qquad \text{(drop)}$$
$$\mid \text{match } x\ \{\ \overline{p_i \to e_i}^n\ \} \qquad \text{(match expr)}$$
$$v ::= \lambda^{\overline{y_i}^n} x.\ e \qquad\qquad \text{(function capturing } \overline{y_i}^n)$$
$$\mid C\ \overline{v_i}^n \qquad\qquad \text{(constructor of arity } n)$$
$$p ::= C\ \overline{b_i}^n \qquad\qquad \text{(pattern)}$$
$$b ::= x \mid \_ \qquad\qquad \text{(binder or wildcard)}$$

Syntactic Shorthands

$$e_1; e_2 \qquad\qquad ::= \text{val } x = e_1; e_2\ \ x \notin \text{fv}(e_2)$$
$$\lambda x.\ e \qquad\qquad ::= \lambda^{\overline{y_i}^n} x.\ e \qquad \overline{y_i}^n = \text{fv}(e)$$
$$\text{dropf } \lambda^{\overline{y_i}^n} x.\ e ::= \overline{\text{drop } y_i}^n$$
$$\text{dropf } C\ \overline{x_i}^n \quad ::= \overline{\text{drop } x_i}^n$$

Evaluation Judgments

$$e \longrightarrow \qquad\qquad e'\ \text{Baseline Semantics}$$
$$H \mid e \longrightarrow_k \qquad H' \mid e'\ \text{Reference Koka Semantics}$$
$$H; F \mid e \longrightarrow_c H'; F' \mid e'\ \text{New CTRC Semantics}$$

Heap and Free List

$$\textit{(Heap)} \qquad H: \quad x \to (\mathbb{N}^+, v)$$
$$\textit{(Free List)}\ F ::= \varnothing \mid F, x$$

Fig. 9. Syntax of λ^1.

A.1   Syntax

Figure 9 shows the syntax of λ^1 which is the same presented by Reinking et al. [19]. It is an untyped lambda calculus extended with explicit binding, pattern matching, as well as duplicate and drop instructions. Note that the duplicate and drop instructions are added by the compiler into the compiled program and are not written by the user. Constructors with fields $x_1, x_2, \ldots, x_n$ are denoted as $C\ \overline{x_i}^n$. Functions with parameter x, body e, free variables $y_1, y_2, \ldots, y_n$ are denoted as $\lambda^{\overline{y_i}^n} x.\ e$.

$$E ::= \Box \mid E\ e \mid x\ E \mid \text{val } x = E;\ e \qquad \frac{e \longrightarrow e'}{E[e] \longrightarrow E[e']}\text{[EVAL]}$$
$$\mid\ C\ x_1 \ldots x_i\ E\ v_j \ldots v_n$$

(app)	$(\lambda x.\ e)\ v$	$\longrightarrow$	$e[x := v]$
(bind)	$\text{val } x = v;\ e$	$\longrightarrow$	$e[x := v]$
(match)	$\text{match } (C\ \overline{v_i}^n)\{\overline{p_j \rightarrow e_j}^m\}$	$\longrightarrow$	$e_j[\overline{x_i := v_i}^n] \text{ with } p_j = C\ \overline{x_i}^n$
(no-op-1)	$\text{drop } x;\ e$	$\longrightarrow e$	
(no-op-2)	$\text{dup } x;\ e$	$\longrightarrow e$	

Fig. 10. Baseline Semantics.

We also define a few syntactic shorthands to simplify the presentation. We define sequence $e_1; e_2$ as binding e_1 to an unused variable x, functions are written as $\lambda x.\ e$ when the free variables are not important, and define dropf v for functions and constructors. dropf is used for dropping the fields of constructors and free variables of functions. It is a syntactic shorthand because it can be expanded into a fixed number of drops.

There are three different evaluation judgments, corresponding to different operational semantics.

Baseline Semantics The baseline semantics is the typical operational semantics that does not model memory management. Note that the syntax for match expression is modified to match $e\ \{\overline{p_i \rightarrow e_i}^n\}$, as the variable being matched is replaced with a value. The evaluation rules for the baseline semantics are shown in Fig. 10, where the *app* rule is function application, the *bind* rule is variable binding, and the *match* rule is pattern matching. drop and dup instructions are ignored, as the baseline semantics does not model memory management and these two instructions are only for reference counting. In this paper, the baseline semantics serves as the baseline for program behavior, where the other two operational semantics should simulate. The *simulation* relation is shown with the simplified program trace defined below.

Reference Koka Semantics The reference Koka semantics, which we shall later refer to as the *eager* semantics, models memory management with reference counting. The heap H is a mapping from variable to reference count and value. The evaluation judgment $H \mid e \longrightarrow_k H' \mid e'$ reads as follows: given a heap H, the expression e is evaluated to e' with the heap updated to H'. This semantics is discussed in detail below.

New CTRC Semantics The new CTRC semantics, which can also be called the *lazy* semantics, models memory management with lazy reference counting. Instead of just a heap, the semantics also includes a free list F which stores reusable allocations. The evaluation judgment $H; F \mid e \longrightarrow_c H'; F' \mid e'$ reads as follows: given a heap H and free list F, the expression e is evaluated to e', with the heap updated to H' and the free list updated to F'.

A.2   Reference Koka Semantics

$$E ::= \Box \mid E\ e \mid x\ E \mid \text{val}\ x = E;\ e \qquad \dfrac{H \mid e \longrightarrow_k H' \mid e'}{H \mid E[e] \longrightarrow_k H' \mid E[e']}\ \text{[EVAL]}$$
$$\mid\ C\ x_1 \ldots x_i\ E\ v_j \ldots v_n$$

(new_k)	H	$\mid v$	$\longrightarrow_k H, z \mapsto^1 v$	$\mid z$	fresh z
(app_k)	H	$\mid f\ z$	$\longrightarrow_k H$	$\mid \boxed{\text{dup } y_i;^n \text{ drop } f;}\ e[x := z]$	
			with $(f \mapsto^m \lambda \overline{y_i}^n x.\ e) \in H$		
$(match_k)$	H	$\mid \text{match } x\ \{\overline{p_i \to e_i}^n\}$	$\longrightarrow_k H$	$\mid \boxed{\text{dup } y_j;^m \text{ drop } x;}\ e[\overline{x_j := y_j}^n]$	
			with $p_i = C\ \overline{x_i}^n \wedge (x \mapsto^n C\ \overline{y_j}^n) \in H$		
$(bind_k)$	H	$\mid \text{val } x = y;\ e$	$\longrightarrow_k H$	$\mid e[x := y]$	
(dup_k)	$H, x \mapsto^n v$	$\mid \underline{\text{dup } x;}\ e$	$\longrightarrow_k H, x \mapsto^{n+1} v$	$\mid e$	
$(drop_k)$	$H, x \mapsto^{n+1} v$	$\mid \underline{\text{drop } x;}\ e$	$\longrightarrow_k H, x \mapsto^n v$	$\mid e$	if $n \geq 1$
$(free_k)$	$H, x \mapsto^1 v$	$\mid \underline{\text{drop } x;}\ e$	$\longrightarrow_k H$	$\mid \boxed{\text{dropf } v;}\ e$	

Fig. 11. Reference Koka semantics for λ^1.

Figure 11 shows the original[4] Koka reference-counted heap semantics. The evaluation context E uniquely determines where to apply an evaluation step. The $\boxed{boxes}$ are tools we introduced to facilitate the proofs below. When the boxed instructions are removed, the semantics become the baseline semantics without reference counting, so the boxed instructions can be viewed as internal routines of the memory management scheme. Note that drop and dup instructions may be added by the compiler, i.e. they exist statically in the program, and are not boxed. They can also be internal routines of the memory management scheme, which are introduced on the right-hand side of evaluation rules and are boxed. We use a $\underline{dashed}$ box to denote instructions that can either be normal or boxed.

Values are allocated in the heap with rule new_k and evaluated to the variable pointing to the allocation. The freshly allocated variable has a reference count of 1. Function application with rule app_k duplicates the captured values of the function, drop the function allocation itself, and then perform the actual application via substitution. Similarly, for pattern matching, rule $match_k$ duplicates the fields of the constructor, drop the constructor object itself, and substitute the fields to the pattern in the matched case. The $drop_k$ and dup_k rules update the reference count of the target variable. When the reference count reaches 1, the drop instruction instead is evaluated according to $free_k$, which drops the fields of the value and deallocates the allocation.

We define *simplified program trace* as the sequence of program states when executed according to some operational semantics, excluding the heap, free list

---

[4] slightly modified to merge rules related to lambda and constructor for cleaner presentation.

and all steps that have boxed instructions. The simplified program trace corresponds to the execution trace of the baseline semantics, and should be the same for both the reference Koka semantics and the CTRC semantics.

For example, the full program-trace of val $x = C_1$; dup x; val $y = \lambda^x z.\ x$; drop x; drop y; $\lambda x.\ x$ according to the reference Koka semantics is

1.	$\varnothing$	val $x = C_1$; dup x; val $y = \lambda^x z.\ x$; drop x; drop y; $\lambda x.\ x$
2. (new_k)	$u \mapsto^1 C_1$	val $x = u$; dup x; val $y = \lambda^x z.\ x$; drop x; drop y; $\lambda x.\ x$
3. $(bind_k)$	$u \mapsto^1 C_1$	dup u; val $y = \lambda^u z.\ u$; drop u; drop y; $\lambda x.\ x$
4. (dup_k)	$u \mapsto^2 C_1$	val $y = \lambda^u z.\ u$; drop u; drop y; $\lambda x.\ x$
5. (new_k)	$u \mapsto^? C_1, w \mapsto^1 \lambda^u z.\ u$	val $y = w$; drop u; drop y; $\lambda x.\ x$
6. $(bind_k)$	$u \mapsto^2 C_1, w \mapsto^1 \lambda^u z.\ u$	drop u; drop w; $\lambda x.\ x$
7. $(drop_k)$	$u \mapsto^1 C_1, w \mapsto^1 \lambda^u z.\ u$	drop w; $\lambda x.\ x$
8. $(free_k)$	$u \mapsto^1 C_1$	$\boxed{\text{drop } u;}\ \lambda x.\ x$
9. $(free_k)$	$\varnothing$	$\lambda x.\ x$
10. (new_k)	$y \mapsto^1 \lambda x.\ x$	y

Each row above shows the rule used to arrive at the current state, current heap and the resulting expression. The *simplified program trace* contains states 1–7, 9–10. State 8 is excluded from the simplified trace because it contains boxed instructions.

A.3   New CTRC Semantics

We define the operational semantics for constant-time reference-counted heap in Fig. 12, i.e. the *lazy* semantics. The reference count in the heap can now be zero, indicating the value is no longer reachable and is added to the free list. The free list, which is denoted by F, contains a list of memory locations that the program can reuse.

The major differences between the reference Koka semantics and the CTRC semantics are the allocation and deallocation rules. When the free list is empty, allocation requests are met by requesting more memory from the system according to rule new_c, which is the same as the rule new_k in the reference Koka semantics. When the free list is non-empty, however, the first entry in the free list is used to meet the request, and the fields in the original value of the entry are dropped according to the rule $newr_c$, where the r suffix stands for reuse.

For the previous example, the program trace is

1.	$\varnothing$	; $\varnothing$	val $x = C_1$; dup x; val $y = \lambda^x z.\ x$; drop x; drop y; $\lambda x.\ x$
2. (new_c)	$u \mapsto^1 C_1$	; $\varnothing$	val $x = u$; dup x; val $y = \lambda^x z.\ x$; drop x; drop y; $\lambda x.\ x$
3. $(bind_c)$	$u \mapsto^1 C_1$	; $\varnothing$	dup u; val $y = \lambda^u z.\ u$; drop u; drop y; $\lambda x.\ x$
4. (dup_c)	$u \mapsto^2 C_1$	; $\varnothing$	val $y = \lambda^u z.\ u$; drop u; drop y; $\lambda x.\ x$
5. (new_c)	$u \mapsto^2 C_1, w \mapsto^1 \lambda^u z.\ u$	; $\varnothing$	val $y = w$; drop u; drop y; $\lambda x.\ x$
6. $(bind_c)$	$u \mapsto^2 C_1, w \mapsto^1 \lambda^u z.\ u$	; $\varnothing$	drop u; drop w; $\lambda x.\ x$
7. $(drop_c)$	$u \mapsto^1 C_1, w \mapsto^1 \lambda^u z.\ u$	; $\varnothing$	drop w; $\lambda x.\ x$
8. $(free_c)$	$u \mapsto^1 C_1, w \mapsto^0 \lambda^u z.\ u$	; w	$\lambda x.\ x$
9. $(newr_c)$	$u \mapsto^1 C_1, w \mapsto^1 \lambda x.\ x$	; $\varnothing$	$\boxed{\text{drop } u;}\ w$
10. $(free_c)$	$u \mapsto^0 C_1, w \mapsto^1 \lambda x.\ x$	; u	w

Each row above shows the rule used to arrive at the current state, current heap, current free list, and the expression being evaluated. The simplified program trace is the above trace excluding step 9. Note that the full trace for both the eager semantics and the lazy semantics are very similar, except in the last few steps where they treat free and allocation differently. For the eager semantics, step 8 recursively drops the field of w, while the lazy semantics just put w into the free list. The field of w is dropped when there are new allocation requests, which happens in step 9 above. When the states involving boxed instructions are removed, the simplified traces for both semantics are the same and correspond to the baseline semantics.

$$E ::= \Box \mid E\ e \mid v\ E \mid \text{val } x = E;\ e$$
$$\mid\quad C\ x_1 \ldots x_i\ E\ v_j \ldots v_n$$

$$\frac{H; F \mid e \longrightarrow_c H'; F' \mid e'}{H; F \mid E[e] \longrightarrow_c H'; F' \mid E[e']}\ \text{[EVAL]}$$

(new_c)	$H; \varnothing$	$\mid v$	$\longrightarrow_c H, z \mapsto^1 v; \varnothing$	$\mid z$	fresh z
$(newr_c)$	$H, x \mapsto^0 v; F, x$	$\mid v'$	$\longrightarrow_c H, x \mapsto^1 v'; F$	$\mid \boxed{\text{dropf } v;}\ x$	
(app_c)	$H; F$	$\mid f\ z$	$\longrightarrow_c H; F$	$\mid \boxed{\text{dup } y_i;^m \text{drop } f;}\ e[x := z]$	
			with $(f \mapsto^n \lambda \overline{y_i}^n x.\ e) \in H$		
$(match_c)$	$H; F$	$\mid \text{match } x\ \{\overline{p_i \to e_i}^m\}$	$\longrightarrow_c H; F$	$\mid \boxed{\text{dup } y_j;^n \text{drop } x;}\ e[\overline{x_j := y_j}^n]$	
			with $p_i = C\ \overline{x_i}^n \wedge (x \mapsto^n C\ \overline{y_j}^n) \in H$		
$(bind_c)$	$H; F$	$\mid \text{val } x = y;\ e$	$\longrightarrow_c H; F$	$\mid e[x := y]$	
(dup_c)	$H, x \mapsto^n v; F$	$\mid \boxed{\text{dup } x;}\ e$	$\longrightarrow_c H, x \mapsto^{n+1} v; F$	$\mid e$	
$(drop_c)$	$H, x \mapsto^{n+1} v; F$	$\mid \boxed{\text{drop } x;}\ e$	$\longrightarrow_c H, x \mapsto^n v; F$	$\mid e$	if $n \geq 1$
$(free_c)$	$H, x \mapsto^1 v; F$	$\mid \boxed{\text{drop } x;}\ e$	$\longrightarrow_c H, x \mapsto^0 v; F, x$	$\mid e$	

Fig. 12. Constant-time heap semantics for λ^1

A.4   Metatheory

In this section, we prove the correctness of the CTRC semantics. We show that the simplified program trace for the reference Koka semantics and the CTRC semantics are equal. From this, we derive that the CTRC semantics never reuse memory before the reference Koka semantics drop them. By the soundness of the reference Koka semantics, the CTRC is also sound because it cannot cause memory corruption. We then prove that the system is garbage-free when the free list is empty. As CTRC would not request memory from the system when the free list is non-empty, it would not allocate more memory than needed. This property is also one that enables the eager-deallocating-allocation effect extension to work (see Sect. 2.5). At last, we show that each memory instructions of CTRC only perform a statically-bounded number of steps, which provides the constant-time guarantee as promised.

Lemma 1. *The eager semantics and lazy semantics simulate the baseline semantics.*

Proof. Boxed instructions do not add any non-boxed instructions when evaluated, so for the simplified program trace, we can safely remove them from the rules. The resulting rules are the same for both semantics, so their simplified program traces are the same.

With the simulation relation, we can define time in program execution by the position in the simplified trace, i.e. according to the baseline semantics. We denote the reference count of variable x at a certain time when executed according to the eager semantics and the lazy semantics by x_k and x_c respectively.

Lemma 2. *At any point in the program execution, we have $x_k \leq x_c - x_f$, where x_f is the number of times x occurs as a field of variables that are freed in the eager semantics but not reused in the lazy semantics.*

Proof. First, notice that if the proposition holds, the lazy execution never reuses memory before the eager execution deallocates the variable. This is because in order for the lazy execution to reuse memory, it has to execute the new_c rule, whereas the new_k rule of the eager semantics does not deallocate anything. Let x'_k and x'_c be the reference count after this step, we know that $x'_c = 0$ because we deallocate in this step, and $x_k = x'_k$ as the eager semantics do not deallocate in this step, we have $x_k = x'_k \leq x'_c = 0$ so x is already deallocated in the eager execution.

Now we prove the proposition by induction on the evaluation rules.

Case $H = \varnothing$. Initially, the free list and heap are empty, so the proposition holds trivially.

Case new. For allocation expressions, the new_k and $new_c/newr_c$ rules are executed. In both semantics, the newly allocated value has $x_k = x_c = 1$ and is not freed in the eager semantics, so the proposition holds for the newly allocated value.

We now prove that the proposition still holds for all the original fields of the value being reused. Notice that for the original eager semantics, it cannot perform deallocation when evaluating allocation, so f_k is not changed. For $newr_c$, the fields of the old deallocated value *old* are dropped, so reference count f_c for the field f is decremented n times, where n is the number of occurrences of the variable in the fields of the deallocated object. f_f is also decremented by n, because *old* is now reused in the lazy semantics, and its fields no longer contribute to f_f, so the inequality still holds for f.

For other objects y, as the lazy semantics does not perform recursive drop, the reference counts are not being changed. Also, as the eager semantics does not perform reference count update in the case of allocation, except for the newly allocated value, y_f will not change, and the inequality still holds.

Case $free$ For $free_k$ and $free_c$ rules, it is easy to see that $free_k$ decrements the reference count x_k of every field x of the deallocated value by n, while $free_c$ causes x_f to increase by n and no change in x_c. So the proposition still holds for all fields of the deallocated value.

Other cases For other rules, both semantics have the same behavior so they do not affect the invariant.

Corollary 1. *The lazy semantics is sound, i.e. it only reuses garbage that would have been deallocated in the eager semantics.*

We now prove the garbage-free property for this lazy semantics, and the proof also shows that one can perform garbage collection and get to the same state as in the eager semantics.

Lemma 3. *When the points-to graph is acyclic and the free list is empty, $v_k = v_c$.*

Proof. Note that we only have to count the number of drop calls because dups are treated the same in both semantics, and drops are commutative so order does not matter.

By induction on the longest distance from the root set in the points-to graph. If the longest distance is zero, this holds because the reference count can only be n, where n is the number of dup and drop calls, as there are no references to the variable. For the induction case, note that every pointer pointing to the current object has a strictly smaller longest distance, and the induction hypothesis holds for them. If the pointer is from some garbage, by the induction hypothesis the reference count of the garbage is the same as in the eager semantics. Because the eager semantics is garbage-free, the reference count of the garbage has 0 reference count, which should already be dropped and added to the free list. As the free list is empty, the memory is already being reused by the $(newr_c)$ rule and the fields are dropped. Hence, the reference count of the current object is equal to the number of live objects pointing to it, which is the same as in the eager semantics.

Note that the proof requires an acyclic heap, which is also a property required for reference counting to work. For functional programming languages without mutation, with suitable compilation strategy, programs can guarantee to have no reference cycles.

Corollary 2. *Acyclic heaps are garbage-free when the free list is empty.*

The relationship between eager reference counting and lazy reference counting is shown in Fig. 5. The heap is originally garbage-free as there is no allocation. When users perform deallocation, eager deallocation removes all garbage associated with the object, while lazy deallocation turns the heap into the CTRC heap. When the user empties the free list of the CTRC heap, the heap becomes garbage-free again.

Theorem 1 (Constant-time memory management). *Each memory management instruction takes constant time with the CTRC semantics.*

Proof. There are three cases to consider:

Case dup This instruction is evaluated according to dup_c in 1 step.
Case drop This instruction can be evaluated according to $drop_c$ or $free_c$, where both of them can be evaluated in 1 step. $free_c$ requires appending a variable to the free list, which can be implemented in constant time with a linked list.
Case Allocation There are two cases for allocation, depending on whether the free list is empty.

Subcase Empty free list Allocation is evaluated according to rule new_c, which requests memory from the system in 1 step.

Subcase Non-empty free list Allocation reuses an allocation from the free list and drops all its fields according to rule $newr_c$. As we assume the number of fields is statically bounded, and each drop instruction takes a statically-bounded amount of CPU operations, the whole operation takes a statically-bounded amount of CPU operations.

Note that the formalization is different from the actual implementation, we do not distinguish between objects and segments. The compiler is responsible for splitting objects into segments, satisfying the constant size requirement. We do not model this compiler transformation because there can be many different implementations, and our operational semantics do not depend on such details. As the size is bounded, the number of fields of each object is also bounded.

B   CTRC Allocator Source Code

In this appendix, we present our implementation of basic CTRC (without the locality optimization).

The `defer_drop` function is used for deallocating objects, and the `get_block` function is used for allocating new objects.

Header initialization and reference-count updates are handled in the Koka runtime.

```
1   #include "kklib.h"
2   #include <sys/mman.h>
3
4   #define STACK_NODE_PAGES 1ull
5   #define NUM_CELLS_PER_PAGE ((4096 * STACK_NODE_PAGES /
        SMALL_BLOCK) - 1)
6   #define MAGIC_BITS 0xCA
7   #define SPLIT_BIT 0x8
8
9   typedef union ctrc_cell_s {
10    struct {
11      kk_header_t header;
12      uint8_t data[SMALL_BLOCK - 8];
13    };
14    struct {
15      union ctrc_cell_s *next;
16    };
17  } ctrc_cell_t;
18  _Static_assert(sizeof(ctrc_cell_t) == SMALL_BLOCK, "
        ctrc_cell_t???");
19
20  typedef struct ctrc_page_s {
21    ctrc_cell_t *free_ptr;
22    ctrc_cell_t *drop_ptr;
```

```
23    struct ctrc_page_s *next_page;
24    uint64_t free_counter;
25    ctrc_cell_t cells[NUM_CELLS_PER_PAGE];
26  } ctrc_page_t;
27  _Static_assert(sizeof(ctrc_page_t) == 4096 *
        STACK_NODE_PAGES,
28                    "ctrc_page_t???");
29
30  static ctrc_page_t *last_page = NULL;
31
32  static inline void drop_cell(ctrc_cell_t *cell) {
33    // find page
34    size_t page_addr = (size_t)cell & ~(((size_t)
        STACK_NODE_PAGES * 4096) - 1);
35    ctrc_page_t *page = (ctrc_page_t *)page_addr;
36    __builtin_prefetch(page, 1);
37
38    if (kk_unlikely(cell->header._field_idx != MAGIC_BITS)
        )
39      return;
40    kk_ssize_t scan_fsize = cell->header.scan_fsize;
41    // avoid corrupting the pointer part
42    scan_fsize &= (SMALL_BLOCK - 1);
43    bool new_page = page->drop_ptr == NULL && page->
        free_ptr == NULL &&
44                    page->free_counter == 0;
45    if (new_page) {
46      page->next_page = last_page;
47      last_page = page;
48    }
49    if (scan_fsize == 0) {
50      cell->next = page->free_ptr;
51      page->free_ptr = cell;
52    } else {
53      cell->next = (ctrc_cell_t *)((size_t)page->drop_ptr
          | scan_fsize);
54      page->drop_ptr = cell;
55    }
56  }
57
58  void force_free(kk_block_t *block) {
59    // ignore
60    if (kk_unlikely(block->header._field_idx != MAGIC_BITS
        ))
61      return;
62    if (block->header.scan_fsize & SPLIT_BIT) {
63      // splitted object
64      kk_box_t box = kk_block_field(block, 0);
65      kk_assert(kk_box_is_ptr(box));
66      kk_block_t *next_block = kk_ptr_unbox(box);
```

```
67        // ignore other ptrs...
68        next_block->header.scan_fsize &= SPLIT_BIT;
69        drop_cell((ctrc_cell_t *)next_block);
70      }
71      block->header.scan_fsize = 0;
72      drop_cell((ctrc_cell_t *)block);
73    }
74
75    static void drop_fields(kk_block_t *block) {
76      kk_ssize_t scan_fsize = block->header.scan_fsize & (
          SMALL_BLOCK - 1);
77      if (scan_fsize & SPLIT_BIT) {
78        scan_fsize = (scan_fsize & (~SPLIT_BIT)) + 1;
79        if (scan_fsize == 1) {
80          force_free(kk_ptr_unbox(kk_block_field(block, 0)))
          ;
81          return;
82        }
83      }
84      kk_context_t *context = kk_get_context();
85      for (kk_ssize_t i = 0; i < scan_fsize; i++) {
86        kk_box_drop(kk_block_field(block, i), context);
87      }
88    }
89
90    static ctrc_page_t *mmap_cache;
91    static size_t mmap_cache_count = 0;
92    static bool use_htlb = true;
93
94    static ctrc_page_t *alloc_blocks() {
95      if (kk_unlikely(mmap_cache_count-- == 0)) {
96        unsigned long long size =
97          use_htlb ? (32ull * 1024ull * 1024ull) : (64ull
          * 1024ull);
98        mmap_cache =
99          mmap(NULL, size, PROT_WRITE | PROT_READ,
100                 MAP_PRIVATE | MAP_ANONYMOUS | (use_htlb ?
          MAP_HUGETLB : 0), -1, 0);
101        if (kk_unlikely(mmap_cache == MAP_FAILED)) {
102          if (use_htlb) {
103            use_htlb = false;
104            mmap_cache_count++;
105            return alloc_blocks();
106          }
107          fprintf(stderr, "allocation␣error:␣%s\n", strerror
          (errno));
108          exit(1);
109        }
110        madvise(mmap_cache, size, MADV_POPULATE_WRITE |
          MADV_WILLNEED);
```

```
111      mmap_cache_count = size / sizeof(ctrc_page_t) - 1;
112    }
113    ctrc_page_t *page = mmap_cache++;
114    page->drop_ptr = NULL;
115    page->free_ptr = NULL;
116    page->free_counter = NUM_CELLS_PER_PAGE;
117    return page;
118  }
119
120  static ctrc_cell_t *pop_free() {
121    if (kk_unlikely(last_page == NULL)) {
122      ctrc_page_t *page = alloc_blocks();
123      page->next_page = last_page;
124      last_page = page;
125    }
126    ctrc_cell_t *result = last_page->free_ptr;
127    __builtin_prefetch(result, 1);
128    bool need_drop = false;
129    if (result == NULL) {
130      if (last_page->free_counter > 0) {
131        result = &last_page->cells[--last_page->
       free_counter];
132      } else {
133        result = last_page->drop_ptr;
134        size_t next_ptr = (size_t)result->next;
135        result->header.scan_fsize = next_ptr & (
       SMALL_BLOCK - 1);
136        last_page->drop_ptr = (ctrc_cell_t *)(next_ptr &
       ~(SMALL_BLOCK - 1));
137        need_drop = true;
138      }
139    } else {
140      last_page->free_ptr = result->next;
141    }
142    if (kk_unlikely(last_page->drop_ptr == NULL &&
       last_page->free_ptr == NULL &&
143                      last_page->free_counter == 0)) {
144      last_page = last_page->next_page;
145      __builtin_prefetch(last_page, 0);
146    }
147    if (need_drop)
148      drop_fields((kk_block_t *)result);
149    return result;
150  }
151
152  void defer_drop(kk_block_t *block) { drop_cell((
       ctrc_cell_t *)block); }
153
154  kk_block_t *get_block() {
155    kk_block_t *block = (kk_block_t *)pop_free();
```

```
156    block->header._field_idx = MAGIC_BITS;
157    return block;
158  }
```

References

1. Blackburn, S.M., McKinley, K.S.: Ulterior reference counting: fast garbage collection without a long wait. In: Crocker, R., Jr., G.L.S. (eds.) Proceedings of the 2003 ACM SIGPLAN Conference on Object-Oriented Programming Systems, Languages and Applications, OOPSLA 2003, 26–30 October 2003, Anaheim, CA, USA, pp. 344–358. ACM (2003), https://doi.org/10.1145/949305.949336
2. Blelloch, G.E., Wei, Y.: Concurrent fixed-size allocation and free in constant time (2020). https://doi.org/10.48550/ARXIV.2008.04296, https://arxiv.org/abs/2008.04296
3. Boehm, H.J.: The space cost of lazy reference counting. In: Proceedings of the 31st ACM SIGPLAN-SIGACT Symposium on Principles of Programming Languages, POPL 2004, pp. 210–219. Association for Computing Machinery, New York (2004). https://doi.org/10.1145/964001.964019. ISBN 158113729X
4. Bruno, R., Jovanovic, V., Wimmer, C., Alonso, G.: Compiler-assisted object inlining with value fields. In: Freund, S.N., Yahav, E. (eds.) PLDI 2021: 42nd ACM SIGPLAN International Conference on Programming Language Design and Implementation, Virtual Event, Canada, 20–25 June 2021, pp. 128–141. ACM (2021). https://doi.org/10.1145/3453483.3454034
5. Collins, G.E.: A method for overlapping and erasure of lists. Commun. ACM 3(12), 655–657 (1960). https://doi.org/10.1145/367487.367501. ISSN 0001-0782
6. Comer, D.: Ubiquitous B-tree. ACM Comput. Surv. (CSUR) 11(2), 121–137 (1979)
7. Czaplicki, E., Chong, S.: Asynchronous functional reactive programming for GUIs. In: Boehm, H., Flanagan, C. (eds.) ACM SIGPLAN Conference on Programming Language Design and Implementation, PLDI 2013, Seattle, WA, USA, 16–19 June 2013, pp. 411–422. ACM (2013). https://doi.org/10.1145/2491956.2462161
8. Dolby, J.: Automatic inline allocation of objects. In: Chen, M.C., Cytron, R.K., Berman, A.M. (eds.) Proceedings of the ACM SIGPLAN 1997 Conference on Programming Language Design and Implementation (PLDI), Las Vegas, Nevada, USA, 15–18 June 1997, pp. 7–17. ACM (1997). https://doi.org/10.1145/258915.258918
9. Doligez, D., Leroy, X.: A concurrent, generational garbage collector for a multi-threaded implementation of ML. In: Deusen, M.S.V., Lang, B. (eds.) Conference Record of the Twentieth Annual ACM SIGPLAN-SIGACT Symposium on Principles of Programming Languages, Charleston, South Carolina, USA, January 1993, pp. 113–123. ACM Press (1993). https://doi.org/10.1145/158511.158611
10. Elliott, C., Hudak, P.: Functional reactive animation. In: International Conference on Functional Programming (1997). http://conal.net/papers/icfp97/
11. Joisha, P.G.: Compiler optimizations for nondeferred reference: counting garbage collection. In: Proceedings of the 5th International Symposium on Memory Management, ISMM 2006, pp. 150–161. Association for Computing Machinery, New York (2006). https://doi.org/10.1145/1133956.1133976. ISBN 1595932216
12. Joisha, P.G.: Overlooking roots: a framework for making nondeferred reference-counting garbage collection fast. In: Proceedings of the 6th International Symposium on Memory Management, ISMM 2007, pp. 141–158. Association for Computing Machinery, New York (2007). https://doi.org/10.1145/1296907.1296926. ISBN 9781595938930

13. Leijen, D., Zorn, B., de Moura, L.: Mimalloc: free list sharding in action. In: Lin, A.W. (ed.) APLAS 2019. LNCS, vol. 11893, pp. 244–265. Springer, Cham (2019). https://doi.org/10.1007/978-3-030-34175-6_13

14. McBeth, J.H.: Letters to the editor: on the reference counter method. Commun. ACM **6**(9), 575 (1963). https://doi.org/10.1145/367593.367649. ISSN 0001-0782

15. Nilsson, H., Courtney, A., Peterson, J.: Functional reactive programming, continued. In: Proceedings of the 2002 ACM SIGPLAN Workshop on Haskell, Haskell 2002, pp. 51–64. Association for Computing Machinery, New York (2002). https://doi.org/10.1145/581690.581695. ISBN 1581136056

16. Partain, W.: The nofib benchmark suite of Haskell programs. In: Launchbury, J., Sansom, P.M. (eds.) Functional Programming, Glasgow 1992. Workshops in Computing, pp. 195–202. Springer, London (1992). https://doi.org/10.1007/978-1-4471-3215-8_17

17. Powers, B., Tench, D., Berger, E.D., McGregor, A.: Mesh: compacting memory management for C/C++ applications. In: Proceedings of the 40th ACM SIGPLAN Conference on Programming Language Design and Implementation, PLDI 2019, pp. 333–346. Association for Computing Machinery, New York (2019). https://doi.org/10.1145/3314221.3314582. ISBN 9781450367127

18. Puaut, I.: Real-time performance of dynamic memory allocation algorithms. In: 14th Euromicro Conference on Real-Time Systems (ECRTS 2002), 19-21 June 2002, Vienna, Austria, Proceedings, pp. 41–49. IEEE Computer Society (2002). https://doi.org/10.1109/EMRTS.2002.1019184

19. Reinking, A., Xie, N., de Moura, L., Leijen, D.: Perceus: garbage free reference counting with reuse. In: Freund, S.N., Yahav, E. (eds.) PLDI 2021: 42nd ACM SIGPLAN International Conference on Programming Language Design and Implementation, Virtual Event, Canada, 20–25 June 2021, pp. 96–111. ACM (2021). https://doi.org/10.1145/3453483.3454032

20. Shahriyar, R., Blackburn, S.M., Frampton, D.: Down for the count? Getting reference counting back in the ring. In: Proceedings of the 2012 International Symposium on Memory Management, ISMM 2012, pp. 73–84. Association for Computing Machinery, New York (2012). https://doi.org/10.1145/2258996.2259008. ISBN 9781450313506

21. Ullrich, S., de Moura, L.: Counting immutable beans: reference counting optimized for purely functional programming. In: Proceedings of the 31st Symposium on Implementation and Application of Functional Languages, IFL 2019. Association for Computing Machinery, New York (2021). https://doi.org/10.1145/3412932.3412935. ISBN 9781450375627

22. Wan, Z., Hudak, P.: Functional reactive programming from first principles. In: Proceedings of the ACM SIGPLAN 2000 Conference on Programming Language Design and Implementation, PLDI 2000, pp. 242–252. Association for Computing Machinery, New York (2000). https://doi.org/10.1145/349299.349331. ISBN 1581131992

23. Wan, Z., Taha, W., Hudak, P.: Real-time FRP. In: Pierce, B.C. (ed.) Proceedings of the Sixth ACM SIGPLAN International Conference on Functional Programming (ICFP 2001), Firenze (Florence), Italy, 3–5 September 2001, pp. 146–156. ACM (2001). https://doi.org/10.1145/507635.507654

24. Weizenbaum, J.: Symmetric list processor. Commun. ACM **6**(9), 524–536 (1963). https://doi.org/10.1145/367593.367617. ISSN 0001-0782

Metaprogramming

MetaOCaml: Ten Years Later
System Description

Oleg Kiselyov(✉) (iD)

Tohoku University, Sendai, Japan
oleg@okmij.org
https://okmij.org/ftp/

Abstract. MetaOCaml is a superset of OCaml for convenient code generation with static guarantees: the generated code is well-formed, well-typed and well-scoped, by construction. Not only the completed generated code always compiles; code fragments with a variable escaping its scope are detected already during code generation. MetaOCaml has been employed for compiling domain-specific languages, generic programming, automating tedious specializations in high-performance computing, generating efficient computational kernels and embedded programming. It is used in education, and served as inspiration for several other metaprogramming systems.

Most well-known in MetaOCaml are the types for values representing generated code and the template-based mechanism to produce such values, a.k.a., brackets and escapes. MetaOCaml also features cross-stage persistence, generating ordinary and mutually-recursive definitions, first-class pattern-matching and heterogeneous metaprogramming.

The extant implementation of MetaOCaml, first presented at FLOPS 2014, has been continuously evolving. We describe the current design and implementation, stressing particularly notable additions. Among them is a new, efficient, the easiest to retrofit translation from typed code templates to code combinators. Scope extrusion detection unexpectedly brought let-insertion, and a conclusive solution to the 20-year–old vexing problem of cross-stage persistence.

Keywords: metaprogramming · staging · code generation

1 Introduction

(BER) MetaOCaml [15,18] is a superset of OCaml to generate assuredly well-formed, well-scoped and well-typed code using code templates, also known as brackets and escapes (see Sect. 2 for the extended example). If code is successfully generated, it is certain to compile. Not only all variables in it are bound: they are bound as intended (see [13] for the discussion of unintended binding). The guarantees apply not only to the completed code: ill-formed or ill-typed code fragments are rejected already by the type checker. MetaOCaml permits unrestricted manipulation of open code fragments, including storing them in

© The Author(s), under exclusive license to Springer Nature Singapore Pte Ltd. 2024
J. Gibbons and D. Miller (Eds.): FLOPS 2024, LNCS 14659, pp. 219–236, 2024.
https://doi.org/10.1007/978-981-97-2300-3_12

reference cells or memo tables. However, as soon as it is detected that a free variable in such fragment cannot possibly be bound by its intended binder, an exception is raised with a detailed error message.

MetaOCaml has been employed for compiling domain-specific languages [20, 25,32], generic programming [30], automating tedious specializations in high-performance computing [17], modeling of digital signal processing, generating efficient computational kernels [2,9,19] and embedded programming. It is spreading into industry.

MetaOCaml is used in metaprogramming courses at the University of Cambridge and Tsukuba University, and in programming language courses at the University of Montreal, McMaster University, etc. MetaOCaml has had an influence on the design of Scala 3 metaprogramming facilities and Eliom [27], among others. An unexpected application is implementing sophisticated type systems such as session types [21]: fancy (linear, dependent, resource, etc.) types are treated as 'run-time tags' but at a code generation stage. Type errors produce stack traces and can be debugged with an ordinary debugger.

MetaOCaml is being considered for merging into the mainline OCaml, in part due to requests from industry. Preliminary steps are already taken.

The first incarnation of MetaOCaml was described at GPCE 2003 [3]. The current, completely re-designed and re-written version was presented at FLOPS ten years ago [15]. It was called BER MetaOCaml, to distinguish from the original version. The original was unavailable even back then, and has faded by now. The 'BER' qualification has lost its significance, too: it is no longer just about brackets and escapes. Therefore, we shall refer to the sole extant version as MetaOCaml.

Since 2014, MetaOCaml has developed significantly: not only has it kept up with OCaml, it also evolved as a metaprogramming system. Notable milestones include native (native-code, as opposite to bytecode) compilation, offshoring, ordinary and mutually recursive let-insertion, first-class patterns, the conclusive solution to cross-stage persistence. Achieving them required solving long-standing theoretical problems [16,19,24,31]. Here we touch upon hereto unpublished features, also requiring theoretical development, focusing on their design and implementation. More detailed history can be found on the Meta-OCaml home page.[1]

Concretely, the paper makes the following contributions:

1. New, efficient, the easiest to retrofit into the extant type-checker translation from typed code templates to code combinators: Sect. 3;
2. Let-insertion as the evolution of scope extrusion: Sect. 4;
3. The conclusive solution to cross-stage persistence, specifically, implementing cross-stage persistence at all types: Sect. 5.

We start with the brief introduction to staging and MetaOCaml, and finish with the related work in Sect. 6. MetaOCaml is available from Opam,[2] among other sources. The current version is N114.

---

[1] https://okmij.org/ftp/ML/MetaOCaml.html#history.

[2] https://opam.ocaml.org/.

2   Introduction to Staging and MetaOCaml

The standard example to introduce staging – the "Hello World" of metaprogramming – is the specialization of the power function, first described by A.P.Ershov in 1977 [8]. The well-deserved popularity has made the example a cliche, however. This section uses a related example: more realistic and designed to introduce many facilities of MetaOCaml.[3]

Suppose we are writing code for an embedded system with a low-level CPU that has no multiplication instruction (or it is too slow). It is worth then to try to optimize an important particular case: multiplication by a constant, using shifts and addition. For concreteness, let's take the following target OCaml code intended for the device[4]

let x = read_int () in let y = read_int () in 5*(x+1)+y

where read_int is a stand-in for reading a sensor value. For optimization we shall use OCaml as well, now as a metalanguage. To be exact, we shall use MetaOCaml, which adds to OCaml the facility to represent, or quote code, using code templates, or brackets .⟨...⟩.:

let c = .⟨ let x = read_int () in let y = read_int () in 5*(x+1)+y ⟩.

Brackets are akin to string quotation marks "''. In fact, the above code template can be converted to a string and written to a file. Unlike strings, however, code templates have structure: the code within a template must be a well-formed – moreover, well-typed OCaml code. Since the sample enclosed code has the type int, the entire template has the type int code. Code templates like above are values – also called 'code values' – and can be named (bound to variables), passed as arguments and returned from functions. The code within a template is only quoted (and type-checked), but not evaluated. It can be written to a file, compiled and then executed – at a 'future stage', so to speak. In contrast, unquoted MetaOCaml code, which is ordinary OCaml, is executed when the program runs: 'now', at the present stage.

To optimize the constant multiplication in c, we change the template to

let copt = .⟨ let x = read_int () in let y = read_int () in .~(mul 5 .⟨(x+1)⟩.)+y ⟩.

Here, .~ (called 'escape') marks the hole in the template; the escaped expression mul 5 .⟨(x+1)⟩. is evaluated to generate the code to plug into the hole. A template with a hole is no longer a value then. The function mul defined below is a code generator: it takes the known multiplicand (as integer) and the *code* for the other multiplicand (as a code value) and produces the code for the product. The code value .⟨(x+1)⟩. passed as the second argument to mul is open, with the free variable "x". Passing around, splicing, storing in reference cells, etc.,

---

[3] The complete code for the example is available at https://okmij.org/ftp/meta-programming/tutorial/mult.ml.

[4] One may quip that a platform with no support for multiplication unlikely supports OCaml. Later in this section we mention using MetaOCaml for generating C (or Wasm) instead.

open code is the source of MetaOCaml power. In effect, we manipulate (future-stage) variables *symbolically*. Although we can splice variables into larger future-stage expressions, we cannot compare or substitute them, learn their name, or examine the already generated code and take it apart.[5] This pure generativity of MetaOCaml helps maintain hygiene: open code can be manipulated but the lexical scoping is still preserved.[6]

The code generator mul is as follows (the type annotations are optional):

```
let rec mul (n:int) (x:int code) : int code = match n with
  | 0 → .⟨0⟩.
  | 1 → x
  | n when n < 0 → .⟨ − .~(mul (−n) x) ⟩.
  | n when n land 1 = 1 → .⟨ .~x + .~(mul (n−1) x) ⟩.
  | n → let (m,k) = factors_of_two n in .⟨ Int.shift_left .~(mul m x) k ⟩.
```

where factors_of_two n computes the representation of the positive integer n as $m2^k$ with m odd, and returns (m,k) as a pair. Brackets and escapes are also called staging annotations, for a reason: if we erase them from mul, it becomes the ordinary, well-typed OCaml function for correctly, but slowly, multiplying two integers.

Before applying mul to copt, one may want to test it. First, let's see the code mul generates – in a simple context, provided by the so-called eta (which is often used in partial evaluation and called 'the trick' [6]):

```
let eta = fun f → .⟨fun x → .~(f .⟨x⟩.)⟩.
⤳ val eta : (α code → β code) → (α → β) code = <fun>
```

```
eta (mul 5)
⤳ − : (int → int) code = .⟨fun x_1 → x_1 + (Int.shift_left x_1 2)⟩.
```

(shown after ⤳ is the response of the MetaOCaml top-level). The expression eta (mul 5) hence generates the code template of a function. Code values can be printed, which is what we see in the top-level response. The bound variable is renamed: important to ensure hygiene [3].

Code values can also be saved as text into a file, to be compiled as ordinary code. Code values can also be 'run': that is, their code can be compiled, linked in and executed within the generator. It is useful for run-time specialization, and also for testing. For example, we can evaluate Runcode.run (eta (mul 5)) 7 and check that it returns 35 as expected.

Returning to the earlier copt, it evaluates to

```
.⟨let x_1 = read_int () in let y_2 = read_int () in
    ((x_1 + 1) + (Int.shift_left (x_1 + 1) 2)) + y_2⟩.
```

---

[5] At first blush, the inability to examine the generated code seems to preclude any optimizations. Nevertheless, generating optimal code is possible [17,19,22,23].

[6] Unless we store open code in reference cells outside the template that binds the variables. Code generation with effects hence brings in the danger of *scope extrusion*. MetaOCaml takes great pains to detect and report scope extrusion: Sect. 4.

Compared to the original c, it uses only shifts and additions and should be faster. There is a problem: the expression x_1 + 1 is duplicated. The problem can be severe for a complicated expression, or even in a call to an imperative function. To avoid duplication, MetaOCaml lets us bind an expression to a variable, using letl :α code → ((α code →ω code) →ω code) (local let-insertion). We can also use a general, floating let-insertion genlet (exp :α code) :α code to bind exp at the highest possible position determined by data dependencies[7] to a fresh variable, obtaining the code value containing the variable:

.⟨ let x = read_int () in let y = read_int () in .~(letl .⟨(x+1)⟩. (mul 5))+y ⟩.
⤳ .⟨let x_1 = read_int () in let y_2 = read_int () in
    (let t_3 = x_1 + 1 in t_3 + (Int.shift_left t_3 2)) + y_2⟩.

.⟨ let x = read_int () in let y = read_int () in .~(mul 5 (genlet .⟨(x+1)⟩.))+y ⟩.
⤳ .⟨let x_1 = read_int () in let t_2 = x_1 + 1 in let y_3 = read_int () in
    (t_2 + (Int.shift_left t_2 2)) + y_3⟩.

We could have used letl or genlet in the implementation of mul. A better idea is to leave the decision as to what, where and how to let-bind to the user, and merely require the second argument to mul be the code value that is safe to duplicate. MetaOCaml provides a special type α val_code for such code values, which is a subtype of α code. Values of val_code types are produced from literals (with a particular MetaOCaml annotation) or using genletv.[8] Here is the re-written mul:

```
let rec mul (n:int) (x:int val_code) : int code = match n with
  | 0 → .⟨0⟩.
  | 1 → (x :> int code)
  | n when n < 0 → .⟨ − .~(mul (−n) x) ⟩.
  | n when n land 1 = 1 → .⟨ .~(x :> int code) + .~(mul (n−1) x) ⟩.
  | n → (* as before *)
```

to be invoked like mul 5 (.⟨y⟩. [@metaocaml.value]) or mul 5 (genletv .⟨(x+1)⟩..). The invocation mul 5 .⟨(x+1)⟩. does not type check: .⟨(x+1)⟩. is not of the type α val_code; mul 5 (.⟨(x+1)⟩. [@metaocaml.value]) does not type either since x+1 is not syntactically a value.

One might have wished for the optimization to apply to the original c template as it was, without adding mul explicitly by hand. The explicitness is intentional. One has to keep in mind that staging was developed as a push-back against partial evaluators: a magic box that did everything automatically, and sometimes to an impressive result (which could inexplicably change upon a small, seemingly innocent modification). Programmers had no explicit control, or understanding of what it did. Still, the point that MetaOCaml is too explicit stands. It is indeed better thought of as an 'assembler' of metaprogramming. The end users should generate code not with code templates but with abstractions suitable to their domain – as was demonstrated in [19,23]. The explicitness of MetaOCaml has an upside: knowing exactly what code will be produced, with no surprises.

---

[7] There is also a way to specify the desired binding locus [24].

[8] Thus genlet is genletv followed by the upcast to code.

The reader may have noted that an embedded system with no or very slow hardware multiplication would unlikely run OCaml code. Generating OCaml code was not a waste however: since the code is simple (as is often the case), it may be converted to a low-level language such as C, using *offshoring* [19]. For our example code, offshoring produces

```
int fn(){
  int const x_26 = read_int();
  int const t_28 = x_26 + 1;
  int const y_27 = read_int();
  return ((t_28 + (t_28 << 2)) + y_27); }
```

One may quip that GCC will automatically convert multiplication by constants to shifts and additions (at least on x86 platform). However, an embedded platform may not be supported by GCC. In fact, our running example is modeled after two student projects of developing a simple DSL for robot control, using MetaOCaml to generate and then offshore the code. The robot platform was rather peculiar, underpowered and not supported by GCC.[9]

3   Implementing MetaOCaml

MetaOCaml is a programming language system, and hence looks like most other (typed) language systems: the compiler with parsing, type-checking, optimization and code-generation passes producing an executable; the standard library; tools. MetaOCaml is deliberately designed to share, or piggy-back, on the parent OCaml language as much as possible. It is intended to be fully source- and binary-compatible with OCaml.[10] Therefore, MetaOCaml code can use (in source or binary) any OCaml standard or third-party library and any tool. Compiled MetaOCaml code can be linked with any other OCaml code. One may use MetaOCaml as a daily driver for ordinary OCaml development, as the author has been doing for over a decade.

MetaOCaml compiler is also engineered to be a *small* set of patches to the OCaml front-end (parser and type-checker). The OCaml back-end (optimizer and code generator) is reused, *exactly as is*. To this end, MetaOCaml deliberately avoids extending any OCaml compiler data structures.

When it comes to syntax, MetaOCaml only adds three new tokens: two brackets and the escape, which require all but a simple change to the OCaml grammar. The brackets and escapes are parsed into so-called extension nodes of the OCaml AST (a.k.a. Parsetree). One may create them using OCaml's own notation. For example, eta in Sect. 2 could be entered as

---

[9] The robot is based on Daizen's e-Gadget CORE, whose development environment uses MPLAB C compiler for PIC18 MCU by Microchip Technology.

[10] It was not the case for the original MetaOCaml.

```
let eta (f: α code → β code) : (α → β) code =
[%metaocaml.bracket fun x → [%metaocaml.escape f [%metaocaml.bracket x]]]
```

without the bracket-escape syntax. The two notations can be mixed-and-matched. One may design a source-level preprocessor to create the extension nodes from any other syntax for code templates. (So far, no candidates have been proposed however.)

The common approach of implementing quasi-quotation (of which brackets and escapes are an instance), which goes back to Lisp, is translating to code-generating combinators [3,5]. In Lisp, this translation is a source-level, macro-expansion–like transformation. In MetaOCaml, quasi-quotation is typed, however. It may be surprising that a source-to-source translation for brackets and escapes is possible, in principle [16]. No changes to OCaml would be needed then. On the other hand, type errors will be reported in terms of the translated code, which may be confusing. Any translation to code-generating combinators needs to associate variables with their stage, and hence to maintain a variable environment. Handling data types requires type/constructor information. Therefore, a translation to code-generating combinators has to do some amount of type checking anyway. All in all, it seems a better idea to do the translation at or after type checking.

In the original MetaOCaml, the translation to code-generating combinators was post type-checking. A translation before or after type checking is a separate pass, over the entire code. In the current MetaOCaml, the translation is integrated with type checking, avoiding the overhead of a separate pass and of scanning the code outside brackets. The cost of specifically MetaOCaml processing is hence proportional only to the amount of the bracketed code, which is normally a small portion of code base. Furthermore, the current type-checking–integrated translation is designed to be the least invasive, the easiest to retrofit into an existing type-checker, and hence easily portable. Uncannily, the translation is using what feels like only two stages to support multiple. As the warm-up, Sect. 3.1 describes the type-checking of staged programs with brackets and escapes, introducing the notation. Sect. 3.2 presents the modification to translate brackets and escapes away.

3.1   Type-Checking Staged Programs

The present and the following section present the theory of MetaOCaml implementation. They use the standard in theoretical CS mathematical notation and look theoretical. The notation, however, is the *pseudo-code of the actual implementation*. The efficient translation, Sect. 3.2, was first designed in the mathematical notation, to clarify its subtle points. The implementation later transcribed the notation into OCaml code.

We start with the base calculus: it is the utterly standard simply typed lambda calculus with integers, shown merely for the sake of notation, particularly the notation of the typing judgment: $\Gamma \vdash e \Rightarrow e : t$. The notation makes it explicit that type checking is type reconstruction: converting an 'untyped' expression e

Variables	f, x, y, z
Types	$t ::= \text{int} \mid t \to t$
Integer constants	$i ::= 0, 1, \ldots$
Expressions	$e ::= i \mid x \mid e\,e \mid \lambda x.\,e$
Environment	$\Gamma ::= \cdot \mid \Gamma, x{:}t$

Variables	f, x, y, z
Types	$t ::= \text{int} \mid t \to t \mid \texttt{<t>}$
Integer constants	$i ::= 0, 1, \ldots$
Expressions	$e ::= i \mid x \mid e\,e \mid \lambda x.\,e \mid \texttt{<e>} \mid {\sim}e$
Stage	$n, m \geq 0$
Environment	$\Gamma ::= \cdot \mid \Gamma, x^n : t$

Fig. 1. Base calculus: simply-typed lambda calculus with integers (left) and the corresponding staged calculus (right)

to the type-annotated form $e : t$ – or, in terms of the OCaml type checker, converting from Parsetree to Typedtree.

$$\frac{}{\Gamma \vdash i \Rightarrow i : \text{int}} \qquad \frac{x : t \in \Gamma}{\Gamma \vdash x \Rightarrow x : t} \qquad \frac{\Gamma \vdash e \Rightarrow e : t' \to t \quad \Gamma \vdash e' \Rightarrow e' : t'}{\Gamma \vdash e\,e' \Rightarrow (e : (t' \to t)\,e' : t') : t}$$

$$\frac{\Gamma, x : t' \vdash e \Rightarrow e : t}{\Gamma \vdash \lambda x.\,e \Rightarrow (\lambda x{:}t'.\,e : t) : (t' \to t)}$$

We assume that the initial environment Γ_{init} to type check the whole program contains the bindings of the standard library functions such as succ, addition, etc. In the rule for abstraction, one may wonder where does the type t' come from. For the purpose of the present paper, one may consider it a 'guess'. After all, our subject is not type inference, but staging – to which we now turn.

Figure 1 (right) presents the staged calculus: the Base calculus extended with bracket $\texttt{<e>}$ and escape ${\sim}e$ expression forms and code types $\texttt{<t>}$.[11] The calculus (as MetaOCaml) is actually *multi-staged*: brackets may nest arbitrarily, e.g., $\texttt{<<1>>}$. The level of nesting is called *stage*. The present stage, stage 0, is outside of any brackets. An expression at stage 1 or higher is called future-stage. The typing judgment $\Gamma \vdash_n e \Rightarrow e : t$ is now annotated with stage $n \geq 0$. All variable bindings in Γ are also annotated with their stage: $x^n : t$.

The rules for integer constants and application remain the same, modulo replacing $\vdash$ with $\vdash_n$: in general, most typing rules are unaffected by (or, are invariant of) staging. This is a good news for implementation: adding staging to an extant language does not affect the type checker to large extent. Here are the changed and new rules:

$$\frac{x^m : t \in \Gamma}{\Gamma \vdash_n x \Rightarrow x^m : t}\ m \leq n \qquad \frac{\Gamma, x^n : t' \vdash_n e \Rightarrow e : t}{\Gamma \vdash_n \lambda x.\,e \Rightarrow (\lambda x^n{:}t'.\,e : t) : (t' \to t)}$$

$$\frac{\Gamma \vdash_{n+1} e \Rightarrow e : t}{\Gamma \vdash_n \texttt{<e>} \Rightarrow \texttt{<e : t>} : \texttt{<t>}} \qquad \frac{\Gamma \vdash_n e \Rightarrow e : \texttt{<t>}}{\Gamma \vdash_{n+1} {\sim}e \Rightarrow {\sim}(e : \texttt{<t>}) : t}$$

---

[11] The code type in the current MetaOCaml is not pre-defined, but is a library type like Stdlib.Complex.t. Since the set of pre-defined types and values remains the same as in OCaml, binary compatibility is maintained.

The type-checker also annotates variable references with the stage, in addition to the type. A variable bound at stage n may be used at the same stage – or higher (but not lower!). A present-stage variable may appear within brackets: so-called *cross-stage persistence* (or, CSP). As one may expect, bracket increments the stage for its containing expression and escape decrements. Furthermore, escapes must appear within a bracket.

For example, `<<~(<1>)>>` has the type `<<int>>`, the expression `<<λx. ~(f x)>>` is ill-typed but `<<λx. ~(f <x>)>>` is well-typed in an environment where f is bound to a function `<int>` → `<int>` at stage 0.

After a program is type-checked and converted to the type-annotated form (a.k.a., Typedtree), we have to compile it. The type-annotated form contains brackets and escapes, so our compilation has to account for them. One popular approach [3,5] is to post-process the type-annotated expression to eliminate all brackets and escapes. The post-processed Typedtree then has the same form as in the ordinary OCaml; therefore, we can use the OCaml back-end (optimizer and code generator) as it is – which is what MetaOCaml does.

$$\text{lift}_t \quad : t \to \text{<}t\text{>}$$
$$\text{mkid}_t : \text{string} \to \text{<}t\text{>}$$
$$\text{mka} \quad : \text{<}t_2 \to t_1\text{>} \to \text{<}t_2\text{>} \to \text{<}t_1\text{>}$$

$$\text{mkl} \quad : (\text{<}t_2\text{>} \to \text{<}t_1\text{>}) \to \text{<}t_2 \to t_1\text{>}$$
$$\text{mkbr} : \text{<}t\text{>} \to \text{<}\text{<}t\text{>}\text{>}$$
$$\text{mkes} : \text{<}\text{<}t\text{>}\text{>} \to \text{<}t\text{>}$$

Fig. 2. Code-generating combinators, see Sect. 4 for more discussion and possible implementation. Here lift_t is the family indexed by type t, to be discussed in Sect. 5.

Formally, the result of post-processing is the Base calculus enriched with code types (as well as string types and literals) and whose initial environment contains the functions in Fig. 2. These code-generating combinators are the producers of values of the code type. We call this calculus Base_1.

3.2 Optimized Translation of Brackets and Escapes

We now present the optimized translation of Staged expressions that converts brackets and escapes into invocations of code-generating combinators.

Figure 3 presents the translation $\lfloor e : t \rfloor$ of the interior of outer brackets in Staged to the code-generating combinators.[12] As mentioned earlier, we do not have to scan the whole staging program, but only the part within brackets. The interior translation exploits the fact that, surprisingly, the translation does not depend on the exact future stage number. The case for x^0 is discussed in Sect. 5.

---

[12] Performed by trx_translate of `typing/trx.ml`.

$$\lfloor i : \text{int} \rfloor = \text{lift}_{\text{int}}\ i : \texttt{<int>}$$
$$\lfloor x^{m+1} : t \rfloor = x : \texttt{<t>}$$
$$\lfloor x^0 : t \rfloor = \begin{cases} \text{mkid}_t\ \texttt{"x"} : \texttt{<t>} & \text{if } x \in \Gamma_{init} \\ \text{lift}_t\ x : \texttt{<t>} & \text{otherwise} \end{cases}$$
$$\lfloor (e\ e') : t \rfloor = \text{mka}\ \lfloor e \rfloor\ \lfloor e' \rfloor : \texttt{<t>}$$
$$\lfloor \lambda x^{n+1} : t'. e : t \rfloor = \text{mkl}\ (\lambda x : \texttt{<t'>}.\ \lfloor e : t \rfloor) : \texttt{<t'} \to t\texttt{>}$$
$$\lfloor \tilde{\ }(e : \texttt{<t>}) \rfloor = e : \texttt{<t>}$$

Fig. 3. Translation of the interior of outer brackets into Base$_2$.

The typing judgment is now $\Gamma \vdash_n e \Rightarrow e' : t$ where e is an (un-annotated) expression of the Staged calculus and e' is the type-annotated expression of Base$_1$ extended with $\tilde{\ }e$ and stage-annotated variables. (Bindings in Γ are also stage-annotated. For present stage, the annotation may be dropped.) Such extended calculus is called Base$_2$. Quite unexpectedly, Base$_2$ has no need for brackets; it only needs escapes, hence the changes to the OCaml Typedtree are minimal. In fact, there are no changes at all, thanks to Typedtree attributes: an escape is indicated by a dedicated attribute attached to a Typedtree node.

$$\frac{}{\Gamma \vdash_n i \Rightarrow i : \text{int}} \qquad \frac{x^m : t \in \Gamma}{\Gamma \vdash_n x \Rightarrow x^m : t}\ m \leq n$$

$$\frac{\Gamma \vdash_n e \Rightarrow e : t' \to t \quad \Gamma \vdash_n e' \Rightarrow e' : t'}{\Gamma \vdash_n e\ e' \Rightarrow (e : (t' \to t)\ e' : t') : t} \qquad \frac{\Gamma, x^n : t' \vdash_n e \Rightarrow e : t}{\Gamma \vdash_n \lambda x. e \Rightarrow (\lambda x^n : t'. e : t) : (t' \to t)}$$

$$\frac{\Gamma \vdash_1 e \Rightarrow e : t}{\Gamma \vdash_0 \texttt{<e>} \Rightarrow \lfloor e : t \rfloor : \texttt{<t>}} \qquad \frac{\Gamma \vdash_{n+2} e \Rightarrow e : t}{\Gamma \vdash_{n+1} \texttt{<e>} \Rightarrow \tilde{\ }(\text{mkbr}\ \lfloor e : t \rfloor) : \texttt{<t>}}$$

$$\frac{\Gamma \vdash_0 e \Rightarrow e : \texttt{<t>}}{\Gamma \vdash_1 \tilde{\ }e \Rightarrow \tilde{\ }(e : \texttt{<t>}) : t} \qquad \frac{\Gamma \vdash_{n+1} e \Rightarrow e : \texttt{<t>}}{\Gamma \vdash_{n+2} \tilde{\ }e \Rightarrow \tilde{\ }(\text{mkes}\ \lfloor e : \texttt{<t>} \rfloor) : t}$$

Fig. 4. Type-checking and translation of Staged into Base$_2$.

Figure 4 presents the pseudo-code of the optimized translation integrated with type reconstruction. The figure makes it clear how the Base type reconstruction – that is, the Typedtree construction in the ordinary OCaml – has to be modified for staging. Most of the rules (see constant and application rules) are unmodified. We still need to maintain the stage (as a global mutable variable in the current implementation). The rule for lambda (and other binding forms) has to annotate the bound variable with its stage as it is put into the environment. We do it by adding an attribute bearing the stage to the value_description of the variable. The variable rule has to check that the stage of the variable is less than or equal the current stage, and to put the stage-annotated variable into Typedtree. In the implementation, nothing needs to be done for the latter: The

Texp_ident node of the Typedtree carries the value_description taken from the environment, which already has the stage attribute. The only significant changes are the rules for brackets and escapes (represented in Parsetree as extension nodes).

The selective translation $\lfloor - \rfloor$ is indeed done only on the parts of the overall Typedtree that represent future-stage sub-expressions. Therefore, when compiling plain OCaml programs, MetaOCaml imposes *no* overhead: MetaOCaml-specific processing is not even activated.

Proposition. If $\Gamma \vdash_n e \Rightarrow e : t$ in the Staged calculus then $\Gamma \vdash_n e \Rightarrow e' : t$ in the optimized translation.

Proposition. If $\Gamma \vdash_n e \Rightarrow e' : t$, then e' has no nested escapes.

Corollary. If $\Gamma_{init} \vdash_0 e \Rightarrow e' : t$ then e' is strictly a $Base_1$ expression: it contains no escape nodes or stage-annotated bindings. The type reconstruction hence gives the ordinary OCaml Typedtree, which can then be processed by the OCaml back-end as is.

Theorem. If $\Gamma \vdash_0 e \Rightarrow e' : t$ then $\Gamma \vdash \bar{e'} \Rightarrow e' : t$ in $Base_1$ where $\bar{e'}$ is e' with all type annotations removed.

Evaluation. The integrated translation sounds almost too good to be true. The goal of the formalization, and of the main theorem, is to convince that the translation is correct. It is implemented in the current MetaOCaml (version N114) – by literally transcribing the pseudo-code of Fig. 4 into OCaml – resulting in simpler and shorter code. It worked on the first try, passing all tests in the extensive MetaOCaml testing suite. No issues have been reported.

Since the very beginning BER MetaOCaml took pains to make the Typedtree after the translation look exactly as in the plain OCaml. Time has showed that it was wise. We remind that MetaOCaml is designed to use the OCaml back-end as is. The OCaml back-end has been constantly enhanced with new optimizations and facilities (FLambda, Multi-core, to name the biggest). MetaOCaml comes to benefit from these optimizations automatically.

4 Let-Insertion

As we have seen in Sect. 2, let-insertion (particularly, genlet) is useful for effecting sharing and avoiding code duplication. The importance of let-insertion has been recognized early on in partial evaluation [11, §5.5.4]. It is commonly accomplished via continuation-passing (monadic) style [1,4,28] or, more conveniently, via delimited control [12,26]. In fact, the primary motivation for the OCaml delimited control library delimcc [14] was implementing genlet. Surprisingly, genlet turns out realizable in MetaOCaml much simpler, without any delimited control, piggy-backing on what MetaOCaml has had for a decade: detecting scope extrusion.

Detecting scope extrusion (that is, open code whose free variables shall remain unbound) was introduced in version N103 and described in [15]. Here is a brief reminder, using the formalization from the previous section. Figure 2 introduced code-generating combinators, but did not say what they generate. Indeed, how is the type `<t>` realized, what exactly is the code value? As Sect. 2 has hinted, a code value (code template) is essentially a string containing code text. An easier to generate representation is an algebraic data type [3]. An algebraic data type representing code is nothing but the abstract syntax tree (AST), called Parsetree in the OCaml compiler. From the very beginning and up until N103, code values in MetaOCaml were Parsetree.expression values.

In the formalism of Sect. 3.1, the AST corresponding to Base can be described by the following OCaml data type[13]

```
type vname = string
type ast = Int of int | Var of vname | App of ast * ast | Lam of vname * ast
```

The code-generating combinators are then

```
type α code = ast
let mkid (n:vname) : α code = Var n
let mka (e1: (α → β) code) (e2: α code) : β code = App (e1,e2)
let mkl (f: α code → β code) : (α→β) code = let v = gensym () in Lam (v, f (Var v))
```

The function mkl (whose real MetaOCaml name is build_fun_simple) chooses a fresh bound variable name, as explained in [3].

Such simple implementation does not suffice for detecting scope extrusion: we need to keep track of free variables. To this end, version N103 introduced an annotated AST:

```
type annot
type α code = annot * ast
let mkid n = (empty, Var n)
let mka (a1,e1) (a2,e2) = (merge a1 a2, App (e1,e2))
```

where annot is a monoid with the unit empty and the operation merge. Specifically, annot is a set of variable names that are free in the code value. The function mkl, which introduces a new variable name, also dynamically binds it for the dynamic extent of generating its body. It uses a dynamic binding facility

```
val dlet : vname  → (unit → α) → α
val dbound : vname → bool
```

to dynamically bind a given vname for the duration of executing a thunk, and check if vname is dynamically bound. The scope extrusion check is hence the check that each free variable occurs only within the dynamic extent of mkl that introduced it. Concretely,

```
type annot = VSet.t   (* set of variable names *)
let empty = VSet.empty
let merge a1 a2 = if VSet.all dbound a1 && VSet.all dbound a2 then VSet.union a1 a2
                  else error "Scope_extrusion"
```

---

[13] For simplicity, we hereafter restrict ourselves to two stages, as most common. Therefore, the generated code contains no staging annotations.

```
let mkl f = let v = gensym () in
            let (a,c) = dlet v (fun () → f (VSet.singleton v, Var v)) in
            (VSet.remove v a, Lam (v, c))
```

Every code-generating combinator performs the scope extrusion check on its arguments (for mka above, the check is integrated into the merge operation). In reality, MetaOCaml uses a priority heap rather than set; it also takes great pains to generate a detailed error message upon scope extrusion. See [15] for more detail, and also the discussion on lexical scoping in the generated code corresponding to dynamic scoping in the generator.

Turning to let-insertion, recall from Sect. 2 that genlet (exp :α code) :α code binds exp 'somewhere above' to a fresh variable and returns the code value containing the variable. One may say that genlet exp creates a *promise* of a let-binding of a fresh v to exp – so-called 'virtual let-binding' – and returns Var v. This is the key idea of the implementation. The virtual let-binding is carried as yet another annotation to the code value. Concretely, annot is extended to

```
type vbindings = (vname * (annot * ast)) list
and  annot = VSet.t * vbindings
```

The merge function is extended to merge vbindings – checking, as before, for scope extrusion and merging free variable sets. The code generating combinator mka (and many more like it in the actual MetaOCaml) remain unchanged. The let-insertion introduces the virtual binding, which is then propagated (floats) as composite expressions form and their annotations are merged:

```
let genlet exp = let v = gensym () in ((VSet.empty,[(v,exp)]),Var v)
```

The combinator mkl now has to check if any exp$_i$ in list of virtual bindings (v$_i$,exp$_i$) contains the variable that is bound by that mkl. If so, the corresponding virtual binding has to be converted to the real let-binding; it cannot be allowed to float further as scope extrusion occurs otherwise. We see now where exactly the let-binding corresponding to genlet exp will be inserted: right under the closest binder that binds a variable that is free in exp (or at the top level, if exp is closed).

There is a bit more than meets the eye: for example, the exp in genlet exp may itself use genlet, which induces a dependency and an order on let-bindings.

Evaluation. The implementation of let-insertion followed the just presented outline and was relatively short, changing hardly any code, because the code annotation infra-structure was already in place and could be reused. The extension to mutually-recursive let-insertion [24] proved to be just as straightforward. Also straightforward is the explicit control of the insertion locus [24].

Let-insertion proved to be a valuable addition to MetaOCaml, appearing quite often in code bases: see, e.g., the scalar promotion optimization in [19].

5   Cross-Stage Persistence

Looking back to the fragment of mul code from Sect. 2:

let (m,k) = factors_of_two n in .⟨ Int.shift_left .~(mul m x) k ⟩.

we see k appearing inside the bracket but bound outside. The bracket contains one more free variable: Int.shift_left, bound in the OCaml standard library. Program variables appearing in templates are called "cross-stage persistence" (CSP).[14] Cross-stage persistence is ubiquitous: for one, all references to standard library are CSPs.

The example highlights the two varieties of CSP: global, (standard) library identifiers; and locally-bound identifiers. The difference is visible in the translation rules for $\lfloor x^0 : t \rfloor$ in Fig. 3. For our example, the translation to code-generating combinators gives:

let (m,k) = factors_of_two n in mka (mka (mkid "Int.shift_left") (mul m x)) (lift$_{int}$ k)

The generated code will hence include the identifier Int.shift_left, which, when the code is compiled, will be taken to refer to the standard library function – the same function it refers to in the generator. Globally-bound CSPs are hence references to the libraries available at the present stage and assumed available at a future stage: the 'common knowledge' so to speak.[15]

Locally-bound CSPs, in contrast, are by their very nature valid only within their local scope and are not accessible from other code. Their values have to be incorporated into the generated code: somehow represented in AST and eventually converted to text. This lifting, or serialization, is performed by the family of functions lift$_t$ of Fig. 2. Serialization clearly cannot be done the same way for all types. For integers, lift$_{int}$ n is just Int n. Booleans, strings, and other easily serializable values are similar. Users may also define their own lifting functions [17, §3.2.1].

On the other hand, when t is a function, reference, input channel, etc., type, lift$_t$ is a puzzle. It is not clear if such a lifting is possible – or even makes sense. Deepens the puzzle is the polymorphic

let polylift : $\alpha \rightarrow \alpha$ code = fun x → .⟨x⟩.

which has been definable in MetaOCaml since the very beginning. This definition looks like a type-uniform serialization, which is impossible.

The long-standing, vexing puzzle has been finally solved in the latest version of MetaOCaml – using let-insertion. That is, lift$_t$ v for any non-serializable t is implemented essentially as genlet: choosing a fresh identifier cps$_i$ and returning Var"cps$_i$" annotated with a special virtual let-binding of cps$_i$ to v. Unlike the ordinary virtual let-binding, its rhs is not necessarily of code type. It is certain however to contain no free future-stage variable; therefore, it always floats to the very top. For example,

.⟨ .~(let f = fun x → x in .⟨f⟩.) 1⟩.

when translated and evaluated becomes the code value that is the AST

App (Var "csp₁", Int 1)

---

[14] We will take 'CSP' to also abbreviate 'cross-stage–persistent variable'.
[15] A pun on the modal logic of code types [7].

annotated with the special virtual let-binding of csp_1 to fun x → x. Such code value may be thought of as a 'staged-separated' let-binding

let csp_1 = fun x → x in .⟨ csp_1 1 ⟩.

whose binding is in the present-stage but the body is in the future. More constructively, it may be thought of as a pair of the present-stage value fun x → x and the code value .⟨fun csp_1 → csp_1 1⟩.. When such a code value is Runcode.run, the code fun csp_1 → csp_1 1 is compiled and then applied to the first component of the pair (the identity function in our case). One may say that the binding and the body of a stage-separated let-expression are re-united. When a CSP code value is saved into a file, it is saved as a function taking the CSP value as the argument. When eventually invoked, the programmer will have to somehow arrange for the appropriate value (e.g., recomputed, etc.) All in all, in the presence of arbitrary CSP, a code value is a 'staged' closure, over CSPs.

Evaluation. CSPs are ubiquitous: although hardly ever mentioned in staging literature, no practical metaprogramming system may afford to ignore them. The experience has shown that locally-bound CSPs at function types are surprisingly common, in cases of run-code specialization. In earlier versions of MetaOCaml, such CSPs have been supported via a horrible hack, which only worked for bytecode and resulted in printing of non-compilable code. At long last, the problem has been solved.

CSPs are so common that they are used in the MetaOCaml implementation itself. For a simple code template, rather than translating it to the code that builds AST at the generator run-time, we may build the AST at the compilation time. AST is serializable, and lifted as CSP from the compile-time to the generator run-time. The generator then accesses it as a literal constant.

The implementation of MetaOCaml hence uses itself. The code typing/trx.ml that contains the type-checking, translation and code-generation combinators is used both at type-checking and code-generation time. In particular, the CSP implementation is used at both times. One gets the feeling of a self-specializer, familiar from Futamura projections.

6   Related Work

Due to the lack of space we have to refer to [15] for the detailed discussion of related metaprogramming systems.

Here we have to mention the very recent MacoCaml [29]: a macro-processor for OCaml based on code templates. Unlike MetaOCaml but like Template Haskell, Scala 3 or Zig, it generates code at compile-time to be used later in compilation. MacoCaml has to deal with the difficult problem of modules and module abstractions – which MetaOCaml skirts since it does not support code templates with module expressions.[16] On the other hand, MetaOCaml is more than just brackets and escapes.

---

[16] It is not clear if code generation of modules is needed: [10] tried to find a compelling example but ended up implementing all candidates in the ordinary MetaOCaml.

7   Conclusions

Ten years have passed since MetaOCaml was first presented [15]. They have seen its increased use in research, education and even industry. It is hard to tell what the next ten years may bring. There is no shortage of problems to solve, however, with MetaOCaml, and in the further development of MetaOCaml. Among the latter are significant theoretical challenges: unsound interaction of template-based metaprogramming with polymorphism (for which [16] outlined a research program) and GADTs.[17]

Acknowledgments. I am very grateful to the users of MetaOCaml for their interest and encouragement, and also comments and suggestions. I particularly thank Jeremy Yallop for many fruitful discussions and valuable suggestions. Comments by anonymous reviewers are gratefully acknowledged. This work was partially supported by JSPS KAKENHI Grants Numbers 17K12662, 18H03218, 21K11821 and 22H03563.

Disclosure of Interests. The author has no competing interests to declare.

References

1. Bondorf, A.: Improving binding times without explicit CPS-conversion. In: LISP & Functional Programming, pp. 1–10 (1992). https://doi.org/10.1145/141471.141483
2. Bussone, G.: Generating OpenMP code from high-level specifications. Internship report to ENS (2020)
3. Calcagno, C., Taha, W., Huang, L., Leroy, X.: Implementing multi-stage languages using ASTs, Gensym, and Reflection. In: Pfenning, F., Smaragdakis, Y. (eds.) GPCE 2003. LNCS, vol. 2830, pp. 57–76. Springer, Heidelberg (2003). https://doi.org/10.1007/978-3-540-39815-8_4
4. Carette, J., Kiselyov, O.: Multi-stage programming with functors and monads: eliminating abstraction overhead from generic code. Sci. Comput. Program. **76**(5), 349–375 (2011). https://doi.org/10.1016/j.scico.2008.09.008
5. Chen, C., Xi, H.: Meta-programming through typeful code representation. J. Funct. Program. **15**(6), 797–835 (2005). https://doi.org/10.1017/S0956796805005617
6. Danvy, O., Malmkjær, K., Palsberg, J.: Eta-expansion does the trick. ACM Trans. Program. Lang. Syst. **18**(6), 730–751 (1996)
7. Davies, R., Pfenning, F.: A modal analysis of staged computation. J. ACM **48**(3), 555–604 (2001)
8. Ershov, A.P.: On the partial computation principle. IPL: Inf. Process. Lett. **6**(2), 38–41 (1977)
9. Hirohara, K.: Generating GPU kernels from high-level specifications using Meta-OCaml. Tohoku University, Master thesis (2019). (in Japanese)
10. Inoue, J., Kiselyov, O., Kameyama, Y.: Staging beyond terms: prospects and challenges. In: Proceedings of the 2016 ACM SIGPLAN Workshop on Partial Evaluation and Program Manipulation, PEPM, pp. 103–108. ACM (2016). https://doi.org/10.1145/2847538.2847548

---

[17] For more detail on the planned features and challenges, see NOTES.txt in the MetaOCaml distribution.

11. Jones, N.D., Gomard, C.K., Sestoft, P.: Partial Evaluation and Automatic Program Generation. Prentice-Hall, Englewood Cliffs (1993). http://www.itu.dk/people/sestoft/pebook/pebook.html
12. Kameyama, Y., Kiselyov, O., Shan, C.: Shifting the stage: staging with delimited control. J. Funct. Program. **21**(6), 617–662 (2011). https://doi.org/10.1017/S0956796811000256
13. Kameyama, Y., Kiselyov, O., Shan, C.: Combinators for impure yet hygienic code generation. Sci. Comput. Program. **112**(Part 2), 120–144 (2015). https://doi.org/10.1016/j.scico.2015.08.007
14. Kiselyov, O.: Delimited control in OCaml, abstractly and concretely. Theor. Comput. Sci. **435**, 56–76 (2012). https://doi.org/10.1016/j.tcs.2012.02.025
15. Kiselyov, O.: The design and implementation of BER MetaOCaml. In: Codish, M., Sumii, E. (eds.) FLOPS 2014. LNCS, vol. 8475, pp. 86–102. Springer, Cham (2014). https://doi.org/10.1007/978-3-319-07151-0_6
16. Kiselyov, O.: Generating code with polymorphic let: a ballad of value restriction, copying and sharing. EPTCS **241**, 1–22 (2017). https://doi.org/10.4204/EPTCS.241.1
17. Kiselyov, O.: Reconciling Abstraction with High Performance: A MetaOCaml approach. Foundations and Trends in Programming Languages, Now Publishers (2018). https://doi.org/10.1561/2500000038
18. Kiselyov, O.: BER MetaOCaml N114 (2023). https://okmij.org/ftp/ML/MetaOCaml.html
19. Kiselyov, O.: Generating C: heterogeneous metaprogramming system description. Sci. Comput. Program. **231**, 103015 (2023). https://doi.org/10.1016/J.SCICO.2023.103015
20. Kiselyov, O., Biboudis, A., Palladinos, N., Smaragdakis, Y.: Stream fusion, to completeness. In: POPL 2017: Conference Record of the Annual ACM Symposium on Principles of Programming Languages, pp. 285–299. ACM Press, New York (2017). https://doi.org/10.1145/3009837
21. Kiselyov, O., Imai, K.: Session types without sophistry. In: Nakano, K., Sagonas, K. (eds.) FLOPS 2020. LNCS, vol. 12073, pp. 66–87. Springer, Cham (2020). https://doi.org/10.1007/978-3-030-59025-3_5
22. Kiselyov, O., Swadi, K.N., Taha, W.: A methodology for generating verified combinatorial circuits. In: EMSOFT, pp. 249–258 (2004)
23. Kiselyov, O., Taha, W.: Relating FFTW and split-radix. In: Wu, Z., Chen, C., Guo, M., Bu, J. (eds.) ICESS 2004. LNCS, vol. 3605, pp. 488–493. Springer, Heidelberg (2005). https://doi.org/10.1007/11535409_71
24. Kiselyov, O., Yallop, J.: Let (rec) insertion without effects, lights or magic. CoRR abs/2201.00495 (2022). https://doi.org/10.48550/arxiv.2201.00495
25. Krishnaswami, N.R., Yallop, J.: A typed, algebraic approach to parsing. In: Proceedings of the 40th ACM SIGPLAN Conference on Programming Language Design and Implementation, PLDI, pp. 379–393. ACM (2019). https://doi.org/10.1145/3314221.3314625
26. Lawall, J.L., Danvy, O.: Continuation-based partial evaluation. In: LISP & Functional Programming, pp. 227–238 (1994). https://doi.org/10.1145/182409.182483
27. Radanne, G.: Tierless Web programming in ML. Ph.D. thesis, Université Sorbonne Paris Cité, Paris, France (2017)
28. Swadi, K., Taha, W., Kiselyov, O., Pašalić, E.: A monadic approach for avoiding code duplication when staging memoized functions. In: PEPM, pp. 160–169 (2006)

29. Xie, N., White, L., Nicole, O., Yallop, J.: MacoCaml: staging composable and compilable macros. Proc. ACM Program. Lang. **7**(209), 604–648 (2023). https://doi.org/10.1145/3607851
30. Yallop, J.: Staged generic programming. Proc. ACM Program. Lang. **1**(ICFP), 29:1–29:29 (2017). https://doi.org/10.1145/3110273
31. Yallop, J., Kiselyov, O.: Generating mutually recursive definitions. In: Proceedings of the 2019 ACM SIGPLAN Workshop on Partial Evaluation and Program Manipulation, PEPM 2019, pp. 75–81. ACM, New York (2019). https://doi.org/10.1145/3294032.3294078
32. Yallop, J., Xie, N., Krishnaswami, N.: Flap: a deterministic parser with fused lexing. Proc. ACM Program. Lang. **7**(PLDI), 1194–1217 (2023). https://doi.org/10.1145/3591269

An ML-Style Module System for Cross-Stage Type Abstraction in Multi-stage Programming

Takashi Suwa[1,2]($\boxtimes$)(iD) and Atsushi Igarashi[1](iD)

[1] Graduate School of Informatics, Kyoto University, Kyoto, Japan
{tsuwa,igarashi}@fos.kuis.kyoto-u.ac.jp
[2] National Institute of Informatics, Tokyo, Japan

Abstract. We propose *MetaFM*, a novel ML-style module system that enables users to decompose *multi-stage programs* (i.e., programs written in a typed *multi-stage programming* language) into loosely coupled components in a manner natural with respect to type abstraction. The distinctive aspect of MetaFM is that it allows values at different stages to be bound in a single structure (i.e., **struct** $\cdots$ **end**). This feature is crucial, for example, for defining a function and a macro that use one abstract type in common, without revealing the implementation detail of that type. MetaFM also accommodates *functors*, *higher-kinded types*, the **with type**-*construct*, etc. with staging features. For defining semantics and proving type safety, we employ an *elaboration* technique, i.e., type-directed translation to a target language, inspired by the formalization of F-ing Modules. Specifically, we give a set of elaboration rules for converting MetaFM programs into *System $F\omega^{\langle\rangle}$*, a multi-stage extension of System $F\omega$, and prove that the elaboration preserves typing. Additionally, our language supports *cross-stage persistence* (*CSP*), a feature for code reuse spanning more than one stage, without breaking type safety.

Keywords: Staging · Code generation · Macros · Module systems

1 Introduction

1.1 Multi-stage Programming

Program generation is a technique useful for several purposes such as improving performance or enhancing maintainability of programs; it can be used for optimizing programs by exploiting information available only at runtime, and also works as a basis for macros for eliminating so-called boilerplate code. Various studies and implementations provide features for code generation, and their formalizations differ from one another. Among these, a considerable amount of studies have been done for proposing *multi-stage programming* (*MSP*) languages [5, 6, 12, 13, 16, 26, 31–35, 38]. They enable users to write code-generating programs in a less error-prone manner with the aid of their type systems.

J. Gibbons and D. Miller (Eds.): FLOPS 2024, LNCS 14659, pp. 237–272, 2024.
https://doi.org/10.1007/978-981-97-2300-3_13

For a brief introduction to MSP, we use a simple setting similar to *MetaML* [32,33] or $\lambda^{\bigcirc}$ [5,6] here. In addition to ordinary constructs for typed functional languages, two special constructs, *bracket* $\langle e \rangle$ and *escape* $\sim e$, are provided: $e ::= x \mid \lambda x.\, e \mid e\, e \mid \cdots \mid \langle e \rangle \mid \sim e$. Brackets and escapes correspond to (hygienic) quasi-quotes and unquotes in Lisp, respectively. Owing to brackets and escapes, every subpart of expressions has its *stage*; a subexpression inside a bracket has one higher stage than outside, and conversely, a subexpression inside an escape has one lower stage. The lowermost stage is called stage 0, and seen from stage n, subexpressions at stage $(n + 1)$ intuitively represent code fragments used for building the resulting code. One can intuitively understand the notion of stages in a graphical manner like (a) and (b) below, considering that expressions are bumpy; brackets are convex, and escapes are concave.

(a) Bracket   (b) Escape   (c) An example cancellation

The essentials of the evaluation rules are the following: (i) The ordinary (call-by-value) β-reduction is performed *only at stage* 0; expressions inside brackets are not evaluated in a usual sense except for ones inside escapes, since they represent code fragments. (ii) Escape cancels bracket; an expression of the form $\sim\langle e \rangle$ is evaluated to e when e is a "completed" code fragment, i.e., does not contain further escapes. Such code fragments are dubbed as *code values* henceforth. An example evaluation step is shown in (c) above.

After repeated reduction, a program at stage 0 hopefully reaches a code value $\langle e \rangle$, which intuitively corresponds to the end of macro expansion. Then the bracketed expression e is "put down" to stage 0, and the evaluation of the expression starts in turn. Especially when the number of stages is 2, stage 0 is for code generation, and the generated program at stage 1 is for ordinary evaluation.

As an example multi-stage program, let us consider **genpower**, a function that takes a natural number n and produces code for the n-th power function. This function can be implemented like the following:

> **let rec aux n s = if** $n \leq 0$ **then** $\langle 1 \rangle$ **else** $\langle \sim s * \sim (\text{aux } (n-1)\text{ s}) \rangle$
> **let genpower =** $\lambda n.\ \langle \lambda x.\ \sim(\text{aux } n\ \langle x \rangle) \rangle$

The application **genpower** 2 is, for instance, evaluated as follows (which does not precisely conform to the operational semantics but describes overall steps):

$$\underline{\text{genpower } 2} \longrightarrow \langle \lambda x.\ \sim(\underline{\text{aux } 2\ \langle x \rangle}) \rangle \longrightarrow^* \langle \lambda x.\ \sim(\underline{\sim\langle x \rangle} * \sim(\text{aux } (2-1)\ \langle x \rangle)) \rangle$$

$$\longrightarrow \langle \lambda x.\ \sim(x * \sim(\text{aux } \underline{(2-1)}\ \langle x \rangle)) \rangle \longrightarrow \langle \lambda x.\ \sim(x * \sim(\underline{\text{aux } 1\ \langle x \rangle})) \rangle$$

$$\longrightarrow^* \langle \lambda x.\ \sim(x * \sim(x * \sim(\underline{\text{aux } 0\ \langle x \rangle}))) \rangle \longrightarrow^* \langle \lambda x.\ \sim(x * \sim(x * \underline{\sim\langle 1 \rangle})) \rangle$$

$$\longrightarrow \langle \lambda x.\ \underline{\sim\langle x * \sim\langle x * 1 \rangle \rangle} \rangle \longrightarrow^* \langle \lambda x.\ x * (x * 1) \rangle$$

A minimal type system for asserting the safety of staged computation is actually quite concise; it basically suffices to equip types of the form $\langle \tau \rangle$, which is the type for code fragments that will be expressions of type τ at the next stage. For example, genpower is assigned type int → ⟨int → int⟩ since it takes an integer and returns a code value bracketing an expression of type int → int at stage 1. Thanks to such typing, we can assert that programs do not get stuck during code generation and neither does the evaluation of produced code, once code-generating programs are successfully type-checked.

1.2   Point at Issue: Modularity

Although possibly used as an intermediate language to handle the results of some transformations such as those guided by *binding-time analysis* [30], MSP languages are intended to be written by hand as well. As long as written and read directly by users, multi-stage programs are desirably composed of loosely coupled smaller components for code maintainability. To this end, as widely known, ML-family languages such as Standard ML or OCaml conventionally have an encapsulation mechanism called a *module system* [7–9,14,19,21,23,24]. One can naturally expect that such a module system is also useful for MSP.

In this paper, we propose a new module system for the purpose above. Our contributions can be summarized as follows: (1) **Language design**: We design a module system named *MetaFM* that enables us to decompose multi-stage programs in a manner natural with respect to type abstraction. Unlike some existing module systems equipped with staging features [16,26,35], our module system does not assign stages to modules; instead, it allows values at different stages to be bound in the same structure (i.e., **struct** ⋯ **end**). We observe that this language design is crucial for the natural decomposition of multi-stage programs into loosely coupled components, as exemplified in Sects. 2–3. (2) **Reconciliation of staging with full-fledged ML-style modules**: Based on the language design above, we accommodate staging with some advanced features for modules such as higher-order functors, sealing, the **with type**-construct, or higher-kinded types. Our module system also supports *cross-stage persistence* (*CSP*) [33,38], an important staging feature that enables the reuse of one common value at more than one stage. We give semantics to our language through an *elaboration*, i.e., a type-directed translation to a target language, and show that the elaboration is sound, i.e., that any target terms produced by the elaboration are well-typed. (3) **Target type safety**: As a target language, we define *System* $F\omega^{\langle\rangle}$, a multi-stage extension of System $F\omega$ [11,22], and prove its type safety. The language has its own *stage polymorphism* to provide CSP for MetaFM.

On the other hand, our method has the following limitations so far: (a) It does not support the **run**-primitive [13,26,32,34,35], which executes code like (**run** (genpower 3)) 5 ⟶* 125. This is not a severe limitation because **run** is not necessary if one wants to do only compile-time code generation, and may well be covered by some techniques orthogonal to ours, such as $\lambda^{\triangleright}$ [34]. (b) It cannot handle *first-class modules* [20,24,25]. This is perhaps difficult to overcome within our language design because unpacking them can be done only at runtime while modules in our formalization are not staged and considered stage-0. (c) It cannot straightforwardly extend with features that have side effects such as *mutable*

```
module Timestamp :> sig
  type t :: *
  val precedes : t → t → bool
  ...
  ~val gen : string → ⟨t⟩
end = struct
  type t = int
  val precedes ts1 ts2 = ts1 ≤ ts2
  ...
  ~val gen s =
    case parseDatetime s of
    | None → fail "not-a-datetime"
    | Some ts → lift ts
end                                    (a)
```

```
module MakeMap :> (Key : Ord) → sig
  type key = Key.t
  type t :: * → *
  val empty : ∀α. t α
  ...
  ~val gen : ∀α. list (key ∗ α) → ⟨t α⟩
end = fun(Key : Ord) → struct
  type key = Key.t
  type t α = ...
  val empty = ...
  val add k v map = ...
  ...
  ~val gen bindings = ...
end                                    (b)
```

Fig. 1. Example definition of modules in MetaFM

references due to a lack of sophistication in the semantics. We have a promising solution to this issue nonetheless, and discuss it as part of our future work.

The rest of the paper is organized as follows: First, Sect. 2 displays examples that motivate our language design. Section 3 compares related work and ours, and discusses the necessity of the design. Section 4 formalizes the source language, omitting CSP for clarity for the moment. After Sect. 5 defines the target language and proves its type safety, Sect. 6 explains the elaboration rules and proves their soundness. Section 7 extends our language with CSP without breaking the previously proved properties. Finally, Sect. 8 mentions future work and its provisional implementation, and Sect. 9 concludes the paper. Many definitions and proofs are in Appendix due to space limitations.

2   Motivating Examples

To showcase our motivation, consider a module Timestamp that handles absolute timestamps as data of abstract type Timestamp.t, under the two-stage setting, i.e., where we only have stages 0 and 1, which are for compile-time macro expansion and runtime, respectively. The module has, for instance, a predicate precedes of type t → t → bool that takes two timestamps and judges which is earlier. It would be useful if the module provides a macro gen that transforms datetime texts into the corresponding timestamps beforehand like the following:

let hasFlops2024Started =
  Timestamp.precedes ~(Timestamp.gen "2024-05-15T00:09:30+09:00")

In our language, one can implement such Timestamp as shown in Fig. 1(a)[1]. Timestamps are represented by Unix time integers, and functions are imple-

---

[1] We here use a Haskell-like notation for kinds like **type** t :: *. We also write type constructors before type arguments in type-level applications.

mented as simple arithmetics. The macro gen is implemented by using an auxiliary function parseDatetime of type string → option int at stage 0; Although its definition is omitted, parseDatetime parses a text and returns Some ts if the given text is a valid datetime, where ts is the corresponding Unix timestamp, or returns None otherwise. Most importantly, gen does not expose the internal representation of Timestamp.t-typed values, as the ordinary functions do not.

As a side note, two additional constructs excluded from the formalization are used in the example above. One is **fail**, which simply aborts the program when evaluated. Note that allowing the use of **fail** at stage 0 is much less harmful than that at stage 1; such an abort occurs before runtime. The other is **lift** e, which evaluates e to a value v, and "lifts" it to $\langle v \rangle$ for the next stage. We should note here that lifting and CSP are different despite their apparent resemblance, and that one cannot lift arbitrary values; lifting functions, for example, makes variable occurrences in the function body inconsistent as to their stage. It is thus desirable to rule out such lifting, but that topic is out of the scope of this paper.

Another example is shown in Fig. 1(b). We here implement a functor MakeMap for handling (finite) maps, which is equivalent to OCaml's Map.Make; it takes a module Key of signature Ord, which requires Key to have a type Key.t of mapping keys and a comparison function Key.compare of type Key.t → Key.t → int used for efficient access to values, and produces a module that provides a type t α for maps whose keys and values are of type Key.t and α, respectively. We add to the resulting module a macro gen that produces a map from a list of key–value pairs beforehand. Since module expressions are not staged, we do not have any additional difficulty in the reconciliation of functors and staging features. One can use this macro as follows, for instance:

```
module StringMap = MakeMap String
val monthAbbrevToInt s =
    StringMap.find s ~(StringMap.gen [("Jan", 1), . . . , ("Dec", 12)])
```

One important thing here is that Key.compare should be available both at stage 0 and 1 so that both gen and ordinary functions can use it at compile-time and runtime, respectively. Such capability is called *cross-stage persistence* or *CSP* for short [33,38] and is known as one of the vital staging features for practical use. We support it by bindings of the form $\mathbf{val}^{\geq n} X = E$, which defines a value X for any stage n' such that $n' \geq n$. Based on this language design, Ord will be (**sig type** t :: *; $\mathbf{val}^{\geq 0}$ compare : t → t → int **end**), for example.

3   Related Work and Our Approach

There are some existing studies that mix staging features with module systems, though their goals differ from ours: Inoue et al. [16] indicated that by staging modules we can eliminate abstraction overheads due to the use of functors, and then Watanabe et al. [35] and Sato et al. [26] followed the approach and proposed the formalization of such type systems. Despite the difference in the purpose, it is apparently worth considering that we can possibly utilize them for our goal. However, such reuse seems somewhat unsatisfactory; to implement modules equivalent to `Timestamp` (or `MakeMap`) in such languages where only entire modules are staged, one could do one of the following: (1) separate the module into two, i.e., `Timestamp` at stage 1 for ordinary functions, and `GenTimestamp` at stage 0 for defining macros; (2) do basically the same as (1), but define the type for representing timestamps internally in a separate module `TimestampImpl`, and both `Timestamp` and `GenTimestamp` include it; or (3) define `Timestamp` at stage 0, and ordinary functions are bound as code values. Each option has a kind of drawback, unfortunately. First, consider implementing the macro `gen` in `GenTimestamp` based on (1). To assign type $\text{string} \rightarrow \langle\text{Timestamp.t}\rangle$ to the macro, we must provide a "backdoor" function $\lambda x.\ x$ as `Timestamp.make` of type $\text{int} \rightarrow \text{Timestamp.t}$ and leave its application in code fragments produced by `gen`. Things get worse when considering the `MakeMap` example; we cannot even provide such a backdoor so that `GenMakeMap` can use it (at least when functors are *generative*, not *applicative*). Option (2) seems better in that it does not require a backdoor, but it is a kind of expediency; it reveals `TimestampImpl` (or `MapImpl`) to outside and thus requires another mechanism than modules that conceals the implementation. Option (3) is good in terms of modularity, but it makes every occurrence of ordinary values at stage 1 be like $\sim(\text{Timestamp.precedes})$.

Perhaps some of the most similar existing work would be Modular Macros [37] and MacoCaml [36]; the former informally suggests a language design similar to ours by giving some examples, and the latter gives a formalization that supports a subset of that language design. MacoCaml offers structures (i.e., **struct** $\cdots$ **end**) in which both values and macros can be bound, and supports CSP by level-shifting imports $\textbf{import}^{\downarrow}$ inspired by Flatt [10]. Major differences between ours and MacoCaml are that the number of stages in a structure is not limited to two, that the type abstraction by signatures is taken into account, and that functors can be handled. Aside from how semantics is precisely defined, ours can perhaps be seen as an extension of MacoCaml (without mutable references) with functors, higher-kinded types, sealing, the **with type**-construct, etc.

A technical challenge lies in giving semantics to our language and, at the same time, proving that our language is type-safe and does not break type abstraction. Indeed, defining semantics conforming to full-fledged ML-style module systems has long been an issue by itself [4,7,14,15,23,27]. Among the line of studies, F-ing Modules [23,24] elegantly formalizes such semantics through an *elaboration* (i.e., a type-directed translation) to System Fω [11,22]. This approach seems better than giving semantics directly on module expressions in that it does not suffer at all from the *avoidance problem* [4,7,14] caused by locally defined types under the combination of sealing ($X :> S$) and projection ($M.X$).

To define semantics for our language, we follow the elaboration approach taken by F-ing Modules. Specifically, we translate the source language *MetaFM* into *System F$\omega^{\langle\rangle}$*, a multi-stage extension of System Fω. This is in contrast to MacoCaml, which gives semantics directly to module expressions and might well induce the avoidance problem when extending with features of full-fledged ML-style modules such as sealing and projection. Although the elaboration intensively utilizes the existential quantification offered by System $F\omega^{\langle\rangle}$ to demonstrate that type abstraction is properly done, its operational essence is rather simple; in a sense, our elaboration performs the option (3) above internally.

4 Source Language

The following defines the entire syntax for our source language *MetaFM*, where meta-level notations $[\mu]^*$ and $[\mu \mapsto \nu]$ range over the (possibly empty) finite sequences of μ and the finite maps from μ to ν, respectively:

$$
\begin{aligned}
M &::= X \mid M.X \mid \mathbf{struct}\ [B]^*\ \mathbf{end} & S &::= \mathbf{sig}\ [D]^*\ \mathbf{end} \mid (X : S) \to S \\
&\mid \mathbf{fun}(X : S) \to M \mid X\ X \mid X :> S & &\mid S\ \mathbf{with\ type}\ [X]^* X = T \\
B &::= \mathbf{val}^n\ X = E \mid \mathbf{type}\ X = T & D &::= \mathbf{val}^n\ X : T \mid \mathbf{type}\ X :: K \\
&\mid \mathbf{module}\ X = M \mid \mathbf{include}\ M & &\mid \mathbf{module}\ X : S \mid \mathbf{include}\ S \\
E &::= x \mid \lambda x : T.\ E \mid E\ E \mid P \mid \langle E \rangle \mid {\sim}E \mid \cdots & P &::= X \mid M.X \\
T &::= T \to T \mid T\ T \mid P \mid \langle T \rangle \mid \cdots & K &::= * \mid K \to K
\end{aligned}
$$

The metavariables M, S, B, and D stand for modules, signatures, bindings, and declarations, respectively. For brevity, we use the same metavariable X in common for names of values, types, and modules bound as members of structures. The module language is quite similar to that of F-ing Modules [23,24]; modules consist of identifiers X, projections $M.X$, structures $\mathbf{struct}\ B\ \mathbf{end}$, functor abstractions $\mathbf{fun}(X : S) \to M$, functor applications $X_1\ X_2$, and sealing $X :> S$. The sole essential difference is that value bindings $\mathbf{val}^n\ X = E$ and declarations $\mathbf{val}^n\ X : T$ have an annotation n that specifies for which stage the value X is defined. The binding forms ${\sim}\mathbf{val}\ X = E$ and $\mathbf{val}\ X = E$ used in Sect. 1 were actually syntax sugars of $\mathbf{val}^0\ X = E$ and $\mathbf{val}^1\ X = E$, respectively. We do not specify the core language in detail, but both expressions E and types T are equipped with *paths* P to items in structures (e.g. `Timestamp.precedes`). We only formalize *generative* functors (i.e., ones that produce fresh abstract types each time even if applied to the same module); we can perhaps handle *applicative* ones as well in an F-ing Modules-like manner, but omit them for simplicity.

For defining elaboration rules, we employ *semantic signatures* Σ and ξ [23, 24], as internal representations, and make type environments Γ track them:

$$
\begin{aligned}
\Sigma &::= [\![\tau]\!]^n \mid [\![= \tau :: \kappa]\!] \mid \{\!\{R\}\!\} \mid \forall \boldsymbol{b}.\ \Sigma \to \xi & \xi &::= \exists \boldsymbol{b}.\ \Sigma & s &::= n \\
R &::= [l \mapsto \Sigma] & \boldsymbol{b} &::= [\alpha :: \kappa]^* & \Gamma &::= \bullet \mid \Gamma, X : \Sigma \mid \Gamma, \alpha :: \kappa \mid \Gamma, x : \tau^s
\end{aligned}
$$

where n ranges over the set of stage numbers (i.e. the set of natural numbers). Although s ranges over exactly the same set as n for the moment, it will be extended for CSP in Sect. 7. Basically, $[\![\tau]\!]^n$ and $[\![= \tau :: \kappa]\!]$ correspond to value and type items in structures, respectively, and $\{\!\{R\}\!\}$ and $\forall \boldsymbol{b}.\ \Sigma \to \xi$ work respectively as structure and functor signatures. Existentially quantified type variables intuitively correspond to abstract types. For simplicity, we assume that source variables X can be injectively embedded into the set of labels as l_X.

$$\boxed{\Gamma \vdash S \rightsquigarrow \xi}$$

$$\frac{\Gamma \vdash D \rightsquigarrow \exists b.\ R}{\Gamma \vdash \mathbf{sig}\ D\ \mathbf{end} \rightsquigarrow \exists b.\ \{\!| R |\!\}}\ \text{S-Str}$$

$$\frac{\Gamma \vdash S_1 \rightsquigarrow \exists b.\ \Sigma_1 \qquad \Gamma, b, X : \Sigma_1 \vdash S_2 \rightsquigarrow \xi_2}{\Gamma \vdash (X : S_1) \to S_2 \rightsquigarrow \exists \varepsilon.\ \forall b.\ \Sigma_1 \to \xi_2}\ \text{S-Fun}$$

$$\boxed{\Gamma \vdash D \rightsquigarrow \exists b.\ R}$$

$$\frac{}{\Gamma \vdash \varepsilon \rightsquigarrow \exists \varepsilon.\ \varnothing}\ \text{Ds-Nil}$$

$$\frac{\Gamma \vdash D_1 \rightsquigarrow \exists b_1.\ R_1 \qquad \mathrm{dom}\ b_1 \cap \mathrm{domtv}\ \Gamma = \varnothing \qquad \Gamma, b_1, R_1 \vdash D_2 \rightsquigarrow \exists b_2.\ R_2 \qquad \mathrm{dom}\ b_2 \cap \mathrm{dom}\ b_1 = \varnothing \qquad \mathrm{dom}\ R_1 \cap \mathrm{dom}\ R_2 = \varnothing}{\Gamma \vdash D_1 \cdot D_2 \rightsquigarrow \exists (b_1 \cdot b_2).\ R_1 \uplus R_2}\ \text{Ds-Cons}$$

$$\frac{\Gamma \vdash K \rightsquigarrow \kappa}{\Gamma \vdash \mathbf{type}\ X :: K \rightsquigarrow \exists (\alpha :: \kappa).\ \{l_X \mapsto [\![= \alpha :: \kappa]\!]\}}\ \text{D-Type}$$

$$\frac{\Gamma \vdash T :: * \rightsquigarrow \tau}{\Gamma \vdash \mathbf{val}^n\ X : T \rightsquigarrow \exists \varepsilon.\ \{l_X \mapsto [\![\tau]\!]^n\}}\ \text{D-Val}$$

$$\frac{\Gamma \vdash S \rightsquigarrow \exists b.\ \Sigma}{\Gamma \vdash \mathbf{module}\ X : S \rightsquigarrow \exists b.\ \{l_X \mapsto \Sigma\}}\ \text{D-Mod}$$

Fig. 2. Signature elaboration rules (selective; see Fig. 11 for omitted ones)

Figure 2 displays the elaboration rules for the judgment $\Gamma \vdash S \rightsquigarrow \xi$, which converts syntactic signature S into semantic signature ξ. Among the rules, only D-Val is essentially new, compared to those of F-ing Modules [23, 24]; it handles declarations of value items of type τ at stage n by signatures $[\![\tau]\!]^n$.

The set of typing rules for modules and bindings is displayed in Fig. 3. The judgment $\Gamma \vdash M : \xi \rightsquigarrow e$ intuitively states that M is assigned signature ξ under type environment Γ, aside from the elaboration part $\rightsquigarrow e$ for the moment; indeed, one can read the rules just ignoring the portions with a gray background. We explain how the elaboration works later in Sect. 5. While most of the rules are essentially the same as those of F-ing Modules, only B-Val is new; it type-checks the left-hand side E of a binding $\mathbf{val}^n\ X = E$ as an expression at stage n, and assigns signature $[\![\tau]\!]^n$ to the value item X, where τ is the resulting type.

Although we do not fix the core language, Fig. 4 displays foundational or basic rules for judgments such as $\Gamma \vdash^s E : \tau \rightsquigarrow e$. Among the rules, E-Path essentially uses signatures $[\![\tau]\!]^n$ for value items; it limits the occurrence of paths by stage number n as well as by types so that value items are used only at the stage for which they are bound. The rules for staging, i.e., E-Brkt and E-Esc, are fairly standard as an MSP language; an expression of the form $\langle E \rangle$ has a code type $\langle \tau \rangle$ if the subexpression E is assigned the type τ at the next stage, and a subexpression E of $\sim E$ is expected to be of type $\langle \tau \rangle$ at the previous stage.

As is usual with module systems, the rules M-App and M-Seal depend on *signature matching* $\Gamma \vdash \Sigma \leqslant \exists b.\ \Sigma' \uparrow \tau \rightsquigarrow e$, where τ ranges over the set of finite sequences of types. This judgment intuitively asserts that Σ can be a subtype of $\exists b.\ \Sigma'$ when the type variables in b (i.e., abstract types) are respectively instantiated by the types listed in τ. Selected rules for signature matching are shown in Fig. 5. Again, only U-Val is essentially new; the others are exactly the same as the corresponding rules of F-ing Modules.

What we should note lastly is decidability. While most of the rules are syntax-directed, U-Val requires type equivalence $\tau \equiv \tau'$, and U-Match depends on the guess at each τ_i, which makes the decidability of the whole type-checking non-

$$\boxed{\Gamma \vdash M : \xi \rightsquigarrow e}$$

$$\frac{\Gamma \vdash B : \exists \boldsymbol{b}.\ R \rightsquigarrow e}{\Gamma \vdash \textbf{struct } B \textbf{ end} : \exists \boldsymbol{b}.\ \{\!| R |\!\} \rightsquigarrow e} \ \text{M-STR}$$

$$\frac{\Gamma(X) = \Sigma}{\Gamma \vdash X : \exists \varepsilon.\ \Sigma \rightsquigarrow X} \ \text{M-VAR} \qquad \frac{\Gamma \vdash M : \exists \boldsymbol{b}.\ \{\!| R |\!\} \rightsquigarrow e \qquad R(l_X) = \Sigma}{\Gamma \vdash M.X : \exists \boldsymbol{b}.\ \Sigma \rightsquigarrow e \# l_X} \ \text{M-MEM}$$

$$\frac{\Gamma \vdash S_1 \rightsquigarrow \exists \boldsymbol{b}.\ \Sigma_1 \qquad \Gamma, \boldsymbol{b}, X : \Sigma_1 \vdash M_2 : \xi_2 \rightsquigarrow e_2}{\Gamma \vdash \textbf{fun}(X : S_1) \to M_2 : \exists \varepsilon.\ \forall \boldsymbol{b}.\ \Sigma_1 \to \xi_2 \rightsquigarrow \lambda X : \lfloor \Sigma_1 \rfloor.\ e_2} \ \text{M-FUN}$$

$$\frac{\begin{array}{c} \Gamma(X_1) = \forall \boldsymbol{b}_1.\ \Sigma_1 \to \xi_1 \qquad \Gamma(X_2) = \Sigma_2 \\ \boldsymbol{b}_1 = (\alpha_i :: \kappa_i)_{i=1}^m \qquad \Gamma \vdash \Sigma_2 \leqslant \exists \boldsymbol{b}_1.\ \Sigma_1 \uparrow (\tau_i)_{i=1}^m \rightsquigarrow e_0 \end{array}}{\Gamma \vdash X_1\ X_2 : [\tau_m/\alpha_m] \cdots [\tau_1/\alpha_1]\xi \rightsquigarrow X_1\ \tau_1\ \cdots\ \tau_m\ (e_0\ X_2)} \ \text{M-APP}$$

$$\boxed{\Gamma \vdash B : \exists \boldsymbol{b}.\ R \rightsquigarrow e} \quad \text{(omitted; basically concatenates the results for elements)}$$

$$\boxed{\Gamma \vdash B : \exists \boldsymbol{b}.\ R \rightsquigarrow e} \qquad \frac{\Gamma \vdash M : \exists \boldsymbol{b}.\ \Sigma \rightsquigarrow e}{\Gamma \vdash \textbf{module } X = M : \exists \boldsymbol{b}.\ \{l_X \mapsto \Sigma\} \rightsquigarrow \{l_X = e\}} \ \text{B-MOD}$$

$$\frac{\Gamma \vdash^n E : \tau \rightsquigarrow e}{\Gamma \vdash \textbf{val}^n\ X = E : \exists \varepsilon.\ \{l_X \mapsto [\![\tau]\!]^n\} \rightsquigarrow \{l_X = \langle\{\textbf{val} = e\}\rangle^{\times n}\}} \ \text{B-VAL}$$

$$\frac{\Gamma \vdash T :: \kappa \rightsquigarrow \tau \qquad e = \Lambda \alpha :: \kappa \to *.\ \lambda x : \alpha\ \tau.\ x}{\Gamma \vdash \textbf{type } X = T : \exists \varepsilon.\ \{l_X \mapsto [\![= \tau :: \kappa]\!]\} \rightsquigarrow \{l_X = \{\textbf{type} = e\}\}} \ \text{B-TYPE}$$

Fig. 3. Module elaboration rules (selective; see Fig. 10 for omitted ones)

trivial. The former is easy: we can prove that the evident type-level reduction relation on well-kinded types is confluent and strongly normalizing, and can thus check type equivalence by comparing normal forms. The latter requires a more complicated technique, but we can indeed infer each τ_i as discussed in [24].

In the forthcoming two sections, we define a target language, see how the elaboration part $\rightsquigarrow e$ works, and show that e is well-typed in the target language.

5   Target Language and Its Type Safety

This section introduces *System* $F\omega^{\langle\rangle}$, a multi-stage extension of System $F\omega$ [11, 22] used as a target language. The following defines the syntax:

$$e ::= x \mid \lambda x : \tau.\ e \mid e_1\ e_2 \mid \{[l = e]^*\} \mid e\#l \mid \Lambda \alpha :: \kappa.\ e \mid e\ \tau$$
$$\quad \mid \textbf{pack}\ (\tau, e)\ \textbf{as}\ \tau \mid \textbf{unpack}\ (\alpha, x) = e\ \textbf{in}\ e \mid \langle e \rangle \mid \sim e$$
$$\tau ::= \alpha \mid \tau \to \tau \mid \{r\} \mid \Lambda \alpha :: \kappa.\ \tau \mid \tau\ \tau \mid \exists \alpha :: \kappa.\ \tau \mid \forall \alpha :: \kappa.\ \tau \mid \langle \tau \rangle$$
$$\kappa ::= * \mid \kappa \to \kappa \qquad r ::= [l \mapsto \tau] \qquad \gamma ::= \bullet \mid \gamma, x : \tau^s \mid \gamma, \alpha :: \kappa$$

Expressions e have bracket $\langle e \rangle$ and escape $\sim e$ for staging in addition to the standard constructs for typed lambda calculi, record construction $\{l_1 = e_1, \ldots, l_m \doteq e_m\}$ (where the labels are assumed to be pairwise distinct), record projection $e\#l$, type variable abstraction $\Lambda \alpha :: \kappa.\ e$, type application $e\ \tau$, and

$$\boxed{\Gamma \vdash P : \Sigma \rightsquigarrow e}$$

$$\frac{\Gamma(X) = \Sigma}{\Gamma \vdash X : \Sigma \rightsquigarrow X} \text{ P-Var}$$

$$\frac{\Gamma \vdash M : \exists \boldsymbol{b}.\ \Sigma \rightsquigarrow e \qquad \Sigma(X) = \Sigma' \qquad \lfloor \Gamma \rfloor \vdash \lfloor \Sigma' \rfloor :: *}{\Gamma \vdash M.X : \Sigma' \rightsquigarrow \mathbf{unpack}\ (\boldsymbol{b}, x : \lfloor \Sigma \rfloor) = e\ \mathbf{in}\ x\#lx} \text{ P-Mem}$$

$$\boxed{\Gamma \vdash^s E : \tau \rightsquigarrow e}$$

$$\frac{\Gamma \vdash P : \llbracket \tau \rrbracket^n \rightsquigarrow e}{\Gamma \vdash^n P : \tau \rightsquigarrow (\sim^{\times n} e)\#\mathtt{val}} \text{ E-Path} \qquad \frac{\Gamma(x) = \tau^s}{\Gamma \vdash^s x : \tau \rightsquigarrow x} \text{ E-Var}$$

$$\frac{\Gamma \vdash T :: * \rightsquigarrow \tau \qquad \Gamma, x : \tau^s \vdash^s E : \tau' \rightsquigarrow e}{\Gamma \vdash^s (\lambda x : T.\ E) : \tau \to \tau' \rightsquigarrow \lambda x : \tau.\ e} \text{ E-Abs} \qquad \frac{\Gamma \vdash^{s+1} E : \tau \rightsquigarrow e}{\Gamma \vdash^s \langle E \rangle : \langle \tau \rangle \rightsquigarrow \langle e \rangle} \text{ E-Brkt}$$

$$\frac{\Gamma \vdash^s E_1 : \tau' \to \tau \rightsquigarrow e_1 \qquad \Gamma \vdash^s E_2 : \tau' \rightsquigarrow e_2}{\Gamma \vdash^s E_1\ E_2 : \tau \rightsquigarrow e_1\ e_2} \text{ E-App} \qquad \frac{\Gamma \vdash^s E : \langle \tau \rangle \rightsquigarrow e}{\Gamma \vdash^{s+1} \sim E : \tau \rightsquigarrow \sim e} \text{ E-Esc}$$

$$\boxed{\Gamma \vdash T :: \kappa \rightsquigarrow \tau}$$

$$\frac{\Gamma \vdash T :: * \rightsquigarrow \tau}{\Gamma \vdash \langle T \rangle :: * \rightsquigarrow \langle \tau \rangle} \text{ T-Code} \qquad \frac{\Gamma \vdash T_i :: * \rightsquigarrow \tau_i \quad (i \in \{1,2\})}{\Gamma \vdash T_1 \to T_2 :: * \rightsquigarrow \tau_1 \to \tau_2} \text{ T-Fun}$$

$$\frac{\Gamma \vdash P : \llbracket = \tau :: \kappa \rrbracket \rightsquigarrow e}{\Gamma \vdash P :: \kappa \rightsquigarrow \tau} \text{ T-Path} \qquad \frac{\Gamma \vdash T_1 :: \kappa \to \kappa' \rightsquigarrow \tau_1 \qquad \Gamma \vdash T_2 :: \kappa \rightsquigarrow \tau_2}{\Gamma \vdash T_1\ T_2 :: \kappa' \rightsquigarrow \tau_1\ \tau_2} \text{ T-App}$$

Fig. 4. Core language elaboration rules

$$\boxed{\Gamma \vdash \Sigma \leqslant \xi \uparrow \tau \rightsquigarrow e}$$

$$\boxed{\Gamma \vdash \Sigma \leqslant \Sigma' \rightsquigarrow e}$$

$$\frac{\boldsymbol{b} = (\alpha_i :: \kappa_i)_{i=1}^m \qquad \lfloor \Gamma \rfloor \vdash \tau_i :: \kappa_i \quad (\text{for each } i) \qquad \Gamma \vdash \Sigma \leqslant [\tau_i/\alpha_i]_{i=1}^m \Sigma' \rightsquigarrow e}{\Gamma \vdash \Sigma \leqslant \exists \boldsymbol{b}.\ \Sigma' \uparrow (\tau_i)_{i=1}^m \rightsquigarrow e} \text{ U-Match}$$

$$\frac{\Gamma \vdash \tau \leqslant \tau' \rightsquigarrow e}{\Gamma \vdash \llbracket \tau \rrbracket^n \leqslant \llbracket \tau' \rrbracket^n \rightsquigarrow \lambda x : \{\{\mathtt{val} : \tau\}\}^{\times n}.\ \{\{\mathtt{val} = e\ ((\sim^{\times n} x)\#\mathtt{val})\}\}^{\times n}} \text{ U-Val}$$

$$\frac{\forall l \in \mathrm{dom}\ R'.\ \Gamma \vdash R(l) \leqslant R'(l) \rightsquigarrow e_l \qquad \hat{r} = \{l \mapsto e_l\ (x\#l) \mid l \in \mathrm{dom}\ R'\}}{\Gamma \vdash \{\!\{R\}\!\} \leqslant \{\!\{R'\}\!\} \rightsquigarrow \lambda x : \lfloor \{\!\{R\}\!\} \rfloor.\ \{\hat{r}\}} \text{ U-Str}$$

Fig. 5. Signature subtyping rules (selective; see Fig. 12 for omitted ones)

pack/unpack expressions for existential quantification. Higher-kinded types τ consist of type variables α, function types $\tau \to \tau$, record types $\{r\}$, type-level abstractions $\Lambda \alpha :: \kappa.\ \tau$, type-level applications $\tau\ \tau$, existential (resp. universal) quantification $\exists \alpha :: \kappa.\ \tau$ (resp. $\forall \alpha :: \kappa.\ \tau$), and *code types* $\langle \tau \rangle$.

Figure 6 shows the typing rules for $\gamma \vdash^s e : \tau$, which states that e is assigned type τ at stage s under the type environment γ. The judgments $\vdash \gamma$ and $\gamma \vdash \tau :: \kappa$, which are defined in Appendix, assert that γ is well-formed and that τ is assigned the kind κ under γ, respectively. The set of rules is basically a natural integration of System Fω with staging features, but pack/unpack-expressions are allowed only at stage 0. This is just because it suffices for our purpose; we could possibly allow them at arbitrary stages, but we don't have to.

The small-step call-by-value operational semantics of System F$\omega^{\langle \rangle}$ is shown in Fig. 7. The judgment $e \xrightarrow{n} e'$ stands for the reduction of the expression e at stage n. As is usual in multi-stage languages, essential reductions, such as ordinary β-reduction or access to record fields, are defined only at stage 0, and

$$\boxed{\gamma \vdash^s e : \tau} \qquad \dfrac{\gamma \vdash^{s+1} e : \tau}{\gamma \vdash^s \langle e \rangle : \langle \tau \rangle} \qquad \dfrac{\gamma \vdash^s e : \langle \tau \rangle}{\gamma \vdash^{s+1} \sim e : \tau} \qquad \dfrac{\gamma \vdash^s e : \tau' \qquad \tau' \equiv \tau \qquad \gamma \vdash \tau :: *}{\gamma \vdash^s e : \tau}$$

$$\dfrac{\vdash \gamma \qquad \gamma(x) = \tau^s}{\gamma \vdash^s x : \tau} \qquad \dfrac{\gamma, x : \tau^s \vdash^s e : \tau'}{\gamma \vdash^s (\lambda x : \tau.\ e) : \tau \to \tau'} \qquad \dfrac{\gamma \vdash^s e_1 : \tau \to \tau' \qquad \gamma \vdash^s e_2 : \tau}{\gamma \vdash^s e_1\ e_2 : \tau'}$$

$$\dfrac{\gamma \vdash \tau :: \kappa \qquad \gamma \vdash^0 e : [\tau/\alpha]\tau' \qquad \gamma \vdash (\exists \alpha :: \kappa.\ \tau') :: *}{\gamma \vdash^0 (\mathbf{pack}\ (\tau, e)\ \mathbf{as}\ \exists \alpha :: \kappa.\ \tau') : \exists \alpha :: \kappa.\ \tau'}$$

$$\dfrac{\gamma \vdash^0 e_1 : \exists \alpha :: \kappa.\ \tau \qquad \gamma, \alpha : \kappa, x : \tau^0 \vdash^0 e_2 : \tau_2 \qquad \gamma \vdash \tau_2 :: *}{\gamma \vdash^0 \mathbf{unpack}\ (\alpha, x) = e_1\ \mathbf{in}\ e_2 : \tau_2}$$

Fig. 6. Typing rules for System $F\omega^{\langle\rangle}$ (selective; see Fig. 14 for omitted ones)

$$\boxed{e \xrightarrow{n} e'} \qquad \dfrac{e \xrightarrow{n+1} e'}{\lambda x : \tau.\ e \xrightarrow{n+1} \lambda x : \tau.\ e'} \qquad \dfrac{e_1 \xrightarrow{n} e_1'}{e_1\ e_2 \xrightarrow{n} e_1'\ e_2} \qquad \dfrac{e_2 \xrightarrow{n} e_2'}{v_1^{(n)}\ e_2 \xrightarrow{n} v_1^{(n)}\ e_2'}$$

$$\dfrac{}{(\lambda x : \tau.\ e)\ v^{(0)} \xrightarrow{0} [v^{(0)}/x]e} \qquad \dfrac{e_1 \xrightarrow{0} e_1'}{\mathbf{unpack}\ (\alpha, x) = e_1\ \mathbf{in}\ e_2 \xrightarrow{0} \mathbf{unpack}\ (\alpha, x) = e_1'\ \mathbf{in}\ e_2}$$

$$\dfrac{}{\mathbf{unpack}\ (\alpha, x) = \mathbf{pack}\ (\tau, v^{(0)})\ \mathbf{as}\ \tau'\ \mathbf{in}\ e_2 \xrightarrow{0} [v^{(0)}/x][\tau/\alpha]e_2} \qquad \dfrac{}{\sim\langle v^{(1)} \rangle \xrightarrow{1} v^{(1)}}$$

$$\dfrac{e \xrightarrow{0} e'}{\mathbf{pack}\ (\tau, e)\ \mathbf{as}\ \tau' \xrightarrow{0} \mathbf{pack}\ (\tau, e')\ \mathbf{as}\ \tau'} \qquad \dfrac{e \xrightarrow{n+1} e'}{\langle e \rangle \xrightarrow{n} \langle e' \rangle} \qquad \dfrac{e \xrightarrow{n} e'}{\sim e \xrightarrow{n+1} \sim e'}$$

Fig. 7. Operational semantics of System $F\omega^{\langle\rangle}$ (selective; see Fig. 15 for omitted ones)

the cancellation of brackets by escapes happens only at stage 1. Here, values $v^{(0)}$ (resp. $v^{(n)}$) at stage 0 (resp. at stage $n \geq 1$) are defined by the following:

$$v^{(0)} \ ::=\ \lambda x : \tau.\ e \ \mid\ \{[l = v^{(0)}]^*\} \ \mid\ \Lambda \alpha :: \kappa.\ e \ \mid\ \mathbf{pack}\ (\tau, v^{(0)})\ \mathbf{as}\ \tau \ \mid\ \langle v^{(1)} \rangle$$

$$v^{(n)} \ ::=\ x \ \mid\ \lambda x : \tau.\ v^{(n)} \ \mid\ v^{(n)}\ v^{(n)} \ \mid\ \{[l = v^{(n)}]^*\} \ \mid\ v^{(n)}\#l$$

$$\mid\ \Lambda \alpha :: \kappa.\ v^{(n)} \ \mid\ v^{(n)}\ \tau \ \mid\ \langle v^{(n+1)} \rangle \ \mid\ \sim v^{(n-1)} \quad (\text{The last one is for } n \geq 2)$$

We have the following standard type safety properties of System $F\omega^{\langle\rangle}$. Here, we write $\vdash^{\geq n} \gamma$ if all entries in γ of the form $x : \tau^s$ satisfy $s \geq n$. Since the language has type equivalence, we have to take care of the so-called inversion lemma by using an argument similar to the one in Chapter 30 of [22].

Theorem 1 (Preservation). *If $\gamma \vdash^n e : \tau$ and $e \xrightarrow{n} e'$, then $\gamma \vdash^n e' : \tau$.*

Theorem 2 (Progress). *If $\vdash^{\geq 1} \gamma$ and $\gamma \vdash^n e : \tau$, then e is a value at stage n, or there exists e' such that $e \xrightarrow{n} e'$.*

6 Elaboration and Its Soundness

This section explains the elaboration of MetaFM programs into System $F\omega^{\langle\rangle}$, i.e., discusses the $\rightsquigarrow e$ part of the rules in Figs. 3, 4, and 5.

Taking the elaboration part into account, the judgment $\Gamma \vdash^s E : \tau \rightsquigarrow e$ intuitively states that the core language expression E at stage s is translated to the term e at stage s in System $F\omega^{\langle\rangle}$, in addition to typing E. Basically the same holds for the judgment $\Gamma \vdash M : \xi \rightsquigarrow e$; it illustrates that the module M is converted to the term e. What should be noted here is that the resulting terms e of the module elaboration are at stage 0 in System $F\omega^{\langle\rangle}$; through elaboration, we virtually deal with modules as if they were at stage 0. In this sense, particularly, functor applications are resolved by stage-0 computation. Lastly, terms e produced by judgments for signature subtyping such as $\Gamma \vdash \Sigma \leqslant \Sigma' \rightsquigarrow e$ are intuitively "upcast functions" from the subtype to the supertype. This intuition is justified afterwards by Theorem 3. For simplicity, in Figs. 3, 4, and 5, we assume that source variables X can be injectively embedded into the target variables, which is ranged over by x. The figures also use the following syntax sugars as well as let-expressions and pack/unpack-expressions generalized for sequences, the precise definitions of which are shown in Appendix:

$$\langle e \rangle^{\times n} := \underbrace{\langle \cdots \underbrace{\langle e \rangle}_{n} \cdots \rangle}_{n} \qquad \sim^{\times n} e := \underbrace{\sim \cdots \sim}_{n} e \qquad \langle \tau \rangle^{\times n} := \underbrace{\langle \cdots \underbrace{\langle \tau \rangle}_{n} \cdots \rangle}_{n}$$

We embed semantic signatures into System $F\omega^{\langle\rangle}$ types by the following $\lfloor - \rfloor$, and use them for describing the rules and for proving type safety:

$$\lfloor \llbracket \tau \rrbracket^n \rfloor := \langle \{ \mathsf{val} : \tau \} \rangle^{\times n} \qquad \lfloor \llbracket = \tau :: \kappa \rrbracket \rfloor := \{ \mathsf{type} : \forall \alpha :: \kappa \to *.\ \alpha\, \tau \to \alpha\, \tau \}$$

$$\lfloor \{\!| R |\!\} \rfloor := \{ \lfloor R \rfloor \} \qquad \lfloor \{ l_i \mapsto R_i \}_{i=1}^m \rfloor := \{ l_i \mapsto \lfloor R_i \rfloor \}_{i=1}^m$$

$$\lfloor \forall (\alpha_i :: \kappa_i)_{i=1}^m.\ \Sigma \to \xi \rfloor := \forall \alpha_1 :: \kappa_1.\ \cdots\ \forall \alpha_m :: \kappa_m.\ \lfloor \Sigma \rfloor \to \lfloor \xi \rfloor$$

$$\lfloor \exists (\alpha_i :: \kappa_i)_{i=1}^m.\ \Sigma \rfloor := \exists \alpha_1 :: \kappa_1.\ \cdots\ \exists \alpha_m :: \kappa_m.\ \lfloor \Sigma \rfloor \qquad \lfloor \Gamma, \alpha :: \kappa \rfloor := \lfloor \Gamma \rfloor, \alpha :: \kappa$$

$$\lfloor \Gamma, X : \Sigma \rfloor := \lfloor \Gamma \rfloor, X : \lfloor \Sigma \rfloor^0 \qquad \lfloor \Gamma, x : \tau^s \rfloor := \lfloor \Gamma \rfloor, x : \tau^s \qquad \lfloor \bullet \rfloor := \bullet$$

The intuition for the elaboration rules involved in staging is fairly easy; leaving types out of account, B-VAL and E-PATH convert bindings $\mathsf{val}^n X = E$ and variable occurrences X at stage n into $\mathsf{let}\ X = \langle e \rangle^{\times n}$ and $\sim^{\times n} X$ in essence, respectively. The rule U-VAL does similar things for building upcast functions.

Example 1. The elaboration translates `Timestamp` to the following in essence:

$$\mathbf{pack}\ (\mathsf{int}, \{ l_t = \{ \mathsf{type} = \ldots \}, l_{\mathrm{precedes}} = \langle \{ \mathsf{val} = \lambda \mathtt{ts1}.\ \lambda \mathtt{ts2}.\ \mathtt{ts1} \leq \mathtt{ts2} \} \rangle),$$

$$\ldots, l_{\mathrm{gen}} = \{ \mathsf{val} = \lambda \mathtt{ts}.\ \ldots \} \})\ \mathbf{as}\ \exists \alpha :: *.\ \{ l_t : \lfloor \llbracket = \alpha :: * \rrbracket \rfloor,$$

$$l_{\mathrm{precedes}} : \langle \{ \mathsf{val} : \alpha \to \alpha \to \mathsf{bool} \} \rangle), \ldots, l_{\mathrm{gen}} : \{ \mathsf{val} : \mathsf{string} \to \langle \alpha \rangle \} \}$$

Although the translation above suffices for giving semantics that fulfills type safety as shown by the theorems below, we do not assert that resulting terms are evaluated in the same manner as programmers' intuition on source programs. This is a common downside of the elaboration approach, which defines semantics

$$\boxed{e \xrightarrow{n} e'} \qquad \cfrac{e \xrightarrow{0} e'}{e \uparrow n' \xrightarrow{0} e' \uparrow n'} \text{ TE-StgApp} \qquad \cfrac{}{(\Lambda\sigma.\ e) \uparrow n' \xrightarrow{0} [n'/\sigma]e} \text{ TE-StgBeta}$$

$$\boxed{\gamma \vdash^s e : \tau} \qquad \cfrac{\sigma \notin \gamma \qquad \gamma, \sigma \vdash^0 e : \tau}{\gamma \vdash^0 (\Lambda\sigma.\ e) : \forall\sigma.\ \tau} \text{ TT-StgAbs} \qquad \cfrac{\gamma \vdash^0 e : \forall\sigma.\ \tau \qquad \gamma \vdash s}{\gamma \vdash^0 e \uparrow s : [s/\sigma]\tau} \text{ TT-StgApp}$$

$$\cfrac{\sigma \in \gamma \qquad \gamma \vdash^{n+\sigma} e : \tau}{\gamma \vdash^n \langle e \rangle^\sigma : \langle \tau \rangle^\sigma} \text{ TT-BrktVar} \qquad \cfrac{\sigma \in \gamma \qquad \gamma \vdash^n e : \langle \tau \rangle^\sigma}{\gamma \vdash^{n+\sigma} \sim^\sigma e : \tau} \text{ TT-EscVar}$$

Fig. 8. Extension of System $F\omega^{()}$ with stage polymorphism

only through translation[2]. Indeed, our translation sometimes causes a counterintuitive evaluation order due to its naïveness; it does not bind identifiers to values but to code fragments in general. This might be fine for typical items defined by immediate values such as lambda abstractions, but some cases are essentially unsatisfactory. For example, one may expect that $\textbf{val}^1\ \textsf{a} = 1 + 2$ computes $1 + 2$ once and replaces all the occurrences of $\textsf{a}$ with 3 at runtime, but this is not the case; it replaces $\textsf{a}$ with the *expression* $1 + 2$ at compile-time. In a sense, value items for stage ≥ 1 are used in a CBN-like manner. For the same reason, the translation prevents the extension with features that have side effects, such as *mutable references*[3], in a straightforward manner. It may also enlarge the generated code and make it less performant since code fragments are copied to every occurrence. Section 8 discusses possible improvements in the elaboration.

Nonetheless, we have the following theorems that prove that the elaboration is *sound* in the sense that every produced term is well-typed (under some moderate requirements for the core language; see Assumption 5 in Appendix).

Theorem 3 (Soundness of Signature Subtyping). *If* $\Gamma \vdash \Sigma \leqslant \exists b.\ \Sigma' \uparrow (\tau_i)_{i=1}^m \rightsquigarrow e$ *and* $\lfloor \Gamma \rfloor, b \vdash \lfloor \Sigma' \rfloor :: *$, *then* $\lfloor \Gamma \rfloor \vdash^0 e : \lfloor \Sigma \rfloor \rightarrow \lfloor [\tau_i/\alpha_i]_{i=1}^m \Sigma' \rfloor$ *and* $\lfloor \Gamma \rfloor \vdash \tau_i :: \kappa_i$ *for each* i, *where* $b = (\alpha_i :: \kappa_i)_{i=1}^m$.

Theorem 4 (Soundness of Elaboration).

1. $\Gamma \vdash T :: \kappa \rightsquigarrow \tau$ *implies* $\lfloor \Gamma \rfloor \vdash \tau :: \kappa$.
2. $\Gamma \vdash^s E : \tau \rightsquigarrow e$ *implies* $\lfloor \Gamma \rfloor \vdash^s e : \tau$.
3. $\Gamma \vdash P : \Sigma \rightsquigarrow e$ *implies* $\lfloor \Gamma \rfloor \vdash^0 e : \lfloor \Sigma \rfloor$.
4. $\Gamma \vdash D \rightsquigarrow \exists b.\ R$ *(resp.* $\Gamma \vdash \boldsymbol{D} \rightsquigarrow \exists \boldsymbol{b}.\ \boldsymbol{R}$*) implies* $\lfloor \Gamma \rfloor \vdash \lfloor \exists b.\ \{R\} \rfloor :: *$.
5. $\Gamma \vdash B : \exists b.\ R \rightsquigarrow e$ *(resp.* $\Gamma \vdash \boldsymbol{B} : \exists \boldsymbol{b}.\ \boldsymbol{R} \rightsquigarrow e$*) implies* $\lfloor \Gamma \rfloor \vdash^0 e : \lfloor \exists b.\ \{R\} \rfloor$.
6. $\Gamma \vdash S \rightsquigarrow \xi$ *implies* $\lfloor \Gamma \rfloor \vdash \lfloor \xi \rfloor :: *$.   7. $\Gamma \vdash M : \xi \rightsquigarrow e$ *implies* $\lfloor \Gamma \rfloor \vdash^0 e : \lfloor \xi \rfloor$.

---

[2] One exception is Crary's work [3]. It defines a target language as a superset of the source language, and shows observational equivalence between source programs and their corresponding target terms for the first time.

[3] Note that mixing mutable references with staging is challenging by itself for another reason; it easily causes the *scope extrusion* problem [2,18].

7 Extension with Cross-Stage Persistence

As mentioned earlier in Sect. 1, we support *cross-stage persistence* (*CSP*) [13,33, 38] by the following binding (resp. declaration) form, which binds (resp. declares) X as a value available at any stages n' such that $n' \geq n$:

$$B ::= \cdots \mid \mathbf{val}^{\geq n} \, X = E \qquad\qquad D ::= \cdots \mid \mathbf{val}^{\geq n} \, X : T$$

To achieve this, we first extend System $F\omega^{\langle\rangle}$ with *stage variables* σ:

$$s ::= n \mid n \dotplus \sigma \qquad e ::= \cdots \mid \Lambda\sigma.\, e \mid e \uparrow s \mid \langle e \rangle^{\sigma} \mid \sim^{\sigma} e$$

$$v^{(0)} ::= \cdots \mid \Lambda\sigma.\, e \qquad \tau ::= \cdots \mid \forall\sigma.\, \tau \mid \langle \tau \rangle^{\sigma} \qquad \gamma ::= \cdots \mid \gamma, \sigma$$

Intuitively, stage variables work for *"stage polymorphism"* and can be instantiated with an arbitrary natural number k. Stages s can newly be of the form $n \dotplus \sigma$, which stands for any stages greater than or equal to n. Bracket $\langle e \rangle^{\sigma}$ with a stage variable expresses arbitrarily nested brackets and is instantiated to $\langle e \rangle^{\times k}$. We correspondingly have escape $\sim^{\sigma} e$, which can be instantiated to $\sim^{\times k} e$. *Stage abstractions* ($\Lambda\sigma.\, e$) and *stage applications* $e \uparrow s$ perform generalization and instantiation of the stage variables, respectively. For typing, we use *stage-polymorphic types* $\forall\sigma.\, \tau$ and *persistent code types* $\langle e \rangle^{\sigma}$. Figure 8 displays additional rules for extending System $F\omega^{\langle\rangle}$ with the stage polymorphism. The rule TT-BRKTVAR allows brackets with a stage variable σ to be used in "fixed" stages n (as long as σ is valid in that scope), and expressions inside them are regarded as being at "polymorphic" stages $n \dotplus \sigma$. TT-EscVAR does the converse by requiring persistent code types $\langle \tau \rangle^{\sigma}$ to expressions inside escapes with σ. One may see that stage variables are a minimal version of *transition variables* [13,34] or *environment classifiers* [31]. We can keep the stage polymorphism minimal here because we do not have to provide something like $\sigma + \sigma'$ for the elaboration. Most importantly, adding these rules can be done without breaking the type safety of System $F\omega^{\langle\rangle}$, i.e., Theorems 1 and 2.

Now that the target language supports stage polymorphism, we can utilize it to support CSP in MetaFM by extending rules as displayed in Fig. 9. Here, we add a new semantic signature $\llbracket\tau\rrbracket^{\geq n}$ for persistent value items that can be embedded into System $F\omega^{\langle\rangle}$ by using stage-polymorphic types, and Γ newly tracks stage variables for the soundness of the expression elaboration:

$$\Sigma ::= \cdots \mid \llbracket\tau\rrbracket^{\geq n} \qquad\qquad \lfloor \llbracket\tau\rrbracket^{\geq n} \rfloor := \forall\sigma.\, \langle\!\langle \{\mathtt{val} : \tau\} \rangle^{\times n} \rangle^{\sigma}$$

$$\Gamma ::= \cdots \mid \Gamma, \sigma \qquad\qquad \lfloor \Gamma, \sigma \rfloor := \lfloor \Gamma \rfloor, \sigma$$

An essential part of the extended rules lies in those for paths in expressions, i.e., E-PATH, E-PERSINNONPERS, and E-PERSINPERS. These rules permit paths to persistent values to occur at any expressions but prevent definitions of persistent value items from depending on non-persistent ones in order for CSP to work correctly, i.e., we do not allow expressions E of $\mathbf{val}^{\geq n} \, X = E$ to contain paths to non-persistent values. Again, owing to such typing, we successfully extend MetaFM with CSP without breaking the soundness shown by Theorems 3 and 4.

$$\boxed{\Gamma \vdash^s E : \tau \rightsquigarrow e} \qquad \frac{\Gamma \vdash P : [\![\tau]\!]^{\geq n_0} \rightsquigarrow e \qquad n \geq n_0}{\Gamma \vdash^n P : \tau \rightsquigarrow (\sim^{\times n}(e \uparrow (n - n_0)))\#\mathtt{val}} \quad \text{E-PersInNonPers}$$

$$\frac{\sigma \in \Gamma \qquad \Gamma \vdash P : [\![\tau]\!]^{\geq n_0} \rightsquigarrow e \qquad n \geq n_0}{\Gamma \vdash^{n+\sigma} P : \tau \rightsquigarrow (\sim^{\times n} \sim^{\sigma}(e \uparrow ((n - n_0) \dotplus \sigma)))\#\mathtt{val}} \quad \text{E-PersInPers}$$

$$\boxed{\Gamma \vdash B : \exists \boldsymbol{b}.\ R \rightsquigarrow e} \qquad \frac{\sigma \notin \Gamma \qquad \Gamma, \sigma \vdash^{n+\sigma} E : \tau \rightsquigarrow e}{\Gamma \vdash \mathtt{val}^{\geq n} X = E \ : \exists \varepsilon.\ \{l_X \mapsto [\![\tau]\!]^{\geq n}\} \rightsquigarrow \{l_X = \Lambda\sigma.\ \langle\!\langle\{\mathtt{val} = e\}\rangle\!\rangle^{\times n}\rangle^{\sigma}\}} \quad \text{B-ValPers}$$

$$\boxed{\Gamma \vdash D \rightsquigarrow \exists \boldsymbol{b}.\ R} \qquad \frac{\Gamma \vdash T :: * \rightsquigarrow \tau}{\Gamma \vdash \mathtt{val}^{\geq n} X : T \rightsquigarrow \exists \varepsilon.\ \{l_X \mapsto [\![\tau]\!]^{\geq n}\}} \quad \text{D-ValPers}$$

$$\boxed{\Gamma \vdash \Sigma \leqslant \Sigma' \rightsquigarrow e}$$

$$\frac{\Gamma \vdash \tau \leqslant \tau' \rightsquigarrow e \qquad n \leq n_0 \qquad e' = \sim^{\times n_0}\sim^{\sigma'}(x \uparrow ((n_0 - n) \dotplus \sigma'))}{\Gamma \vdash [\![\tau]\!]^{\geq n} \leqslant [\![\tau']\!]^{\geq n_0} \rightsquigarrow \lambda x : \lfloor[\![\tau]\!]^{\geq n}\rfloor.\ \Lambda\sigma'.\ \langle\!\langle\{\mathtt{val} = e\ (e'\#\mathtt{val})\}\rangle\!\rangle^{\times n_0}\rangle^{\sigma'}} \quad \text{U-PersAsPers}$$

$$\frac{\Gamma \vdash \tau \leqslant \tau' \rightsquigarrow e \qquad n \leq n_0 \qquad e' = \sim^{\times n_0}(x \uparrow (n_0 - n))}{\Gamma \vdash [\![\tau]\!]^{\geq n} \leqslant [\![\tau']\!]^{n_0} \rightsquigarrow \lambda x : \lfloor[\![\tau]\!]^{\geq n}\rfloor.\ \langle\!\langle\{\mathtt{val} = e\ (e'\#\mathtt{val})\}\rangle\!\rangle^{\times n_0}} \quad \text{U-PersAsNonPers}$$

Fig. 9. Extension of MetaFM with cross-stage persistence

8   Future Work and Provisional Implementation

Though we have successfully given semantics to our language and proved its type safety, several aspects can be improved further. To remedy the issues pointed out in Sect. 6, we should desirably modify the translation about when to bind value items. Possible solutions would be the following: (1) use the *genlet primitive* [17, 26] for performing *let-insertion* during code generation; or (2) define conversion of programs into a flat list of bindings of the form **val**^{n} $x = e$ with functor applications resolved, by using *static interpretation* (which is dubbed as *SI* here) [1,8,9]. Because the former appears less suitable for proving type safety in that it complicates formal semantics, we have been intensively studying the latter. Our ongoing study is implying that mixing staging features with SI is fine, but the soundness of SI itself seems not so well-established. Elsman [8] first showed the soundness of SI for first-order functors, which is quite sufficient for typical use cases, but it did not support higher-order ones. The SI for Futhark [9] claims its support for higher-order ones, but it seems that its current mechanized proof only covers functors assigned a signature of the form $\forall \varepsilon.\ \Sigma \to \exists \varepsilon.\ \Sigma'$ in essence.

Although its type safety has not yet been proved, we implemented a two-stage version[4] of MetaFM with an SI-based elaboration for SAT_YSF_I [29]. SAT_YSF_I [28] is a statically-typed domain-specific language for typesetting documents where commands for the markup, which are equivalent to control sequences in LaTeX like \section, can be implemented in an OCaml-like manner. Programs in this language are basically functional, but mutable references are exceptionally

---

[4] This is not due to some kind of limitation; just because providing two stages suffices for most use cases. Indeed, very few realistic examples that use more than two stages are known in the literature of multi-stage programming.

used for numbering sections, for example. Because the module system incorporated in SAT$_Y$SF$_I$ appears working fine with mutable references so far, we believe that the SI approach is promising for solving the binding-time issue.

9   Conclusion

We have proposed MetaFM, a module system for decomposing multi-stage programs into loosely coupled components without breaking type abstraction, by defining semantics and proving its type safety through an elaboration to System $F\omega^{\langle\rangle}$. It supports several important features such as sealing, functors, higher-kinded types, or CSP. Further improvements on the elaboration are nonetheless desirable for real-world use, which can probably be done by static interpretation.

Acknowledgments. We thank the anonymous referees for a number of helpful suggestions. This work is supported in part by JSPS KAKENHI Grant Number JP20H00582.

A   An Example Elaboration Involving CSP

Example 2. Consider the following structure:

$$
\begin{aligned}
&\textbf{struct}\\
&\quad \textbf{val}^{\geq 0} \text{ compare i j} = \text{j} - \text{i}\\
&\quad \textbf{val}^{\geq 1} \text{ equal i j} = (\text{compare i j} = 0)\\
&\textbf{end}
\end{aligned}
$$

This will be translated to the following target term:

$\textbf{let } x_1 = \{l_{\text{compare}} = \Lambda\sigma_1.\ \langle\langle\text{val} = \lambda\text{i}.\ \lambda\text{j}.\ \text{j} - \text{i}\rangle\rangle^{\sigma_1}\} \textbf{ in}$

$\textbf{let } x_2 =$

$\quad \textbf{let compare} = x_1\#l_{\text{compare}} \textbf{ in}$

$\quad \{l_{\text{equal}} = \Lambda\sigma_2.\ \langle\langle\{\text{val} = \lambda\text{i}.\ \lambda\text{j}.\ (\sim\sim^{\sigma_2}(\text{compare} \uparrow (1 + \sigma_2)))\#\text{val i j} = 0\}\rangle\rangle^{\sigma_2}\}$

$\textbf{in}$

$\quad \{l_{\text{compare}} = x_1\#l_{\text{compare}}, l_{\text{equal}} = x_2\#l_{\text{equal}}\}$

B   Complete Definitions

This section displays definitions including ones omitted from the text.

- Figure 10: Module elaboration rules (other than the ones for CSP)
- Figure 11: Signature elaboration rules (other than the ones for CSP)
- Figure 12: Signature subtyping rules (other than the ones for CSP)
- Figure 13: Syntax sugars for System $F\omega^{\langle\rangle}$ terms used in elaboration rules
- Figure 14: Typing rules for System $F\omega^{\langle\rangle}$ (without CSP)
- Figure 15: Operational semantics of System $F\omega^{\langle\rangle}$ (without CSP)
- Figure 16: Well-formedness, kinding, and type equivalence in System $F\omega^{\langle\rangle}$
- Figure 17: Type-level parallel reduction relation for System $F\omega^{\langle\rangle}$ types
- Figure 18: Miscellaneous definitions

$$\boxed{\Gamma \vdash M : \xi \leadsto e}$$

$$\frac{\Gamma \vdash B : \exists b.\ R \leadsto e}{\Gamma \vdash \mathbf{struct}\ B\ \mathbf{end} : \exists b.\ \{\!|R|\!\} \leadsto e}\ \text{M-Str}$$

$$\frac{\Gamma(X) = \Sigma}{\Gamma \vdash X : \exists \varepsilon.\ \Sigma \leadsto X}\ \text{M-Var} \qquad \frac{\Gamma \vdash M : \exists b.\ \{\!|R|\!\} \leadsto e \qquad R(l_X) = \Sigma}{\Gamma \vdash M.X : \exists b.\ \Sigma \leadsto e\#l_X}\ \text{M-Mem}$$

$$\frac{\Gamma \vdash S_1 \leadsto \exists b.\ \Sigma_1 \qquad \Gamma, b, X : \Sigma_1 \vdash M_2 : \xi_2 \leadsto e_2}{\Gamma \vdash \mathbf{fun}(X : S_1) \to M_2 : \exists \varepsilon.\ \forall b.\ \Sigma_1 \to \xi_2 \leadsto \lambda X : \lfloor \Sigma_1 \rfloor.\ e_2}\ \text{M-Fun}$$

$$\frac{\begin{array}{c}\Gamma(X_1) = \forall b_1.\ \Sigma_1 \to \xi_1 \qquad \Gamma(X_2) = \Sigma_2 \\ b_1 = (\alpha_i :: \kappa_i)_{i=1}^m \qquad \Gamma \vdash \Sigma_2 \leqslant \exists b_1.\ \Sigma_1 \uparrow (\tau_i)_{i=1}^m \leadsto e_0\end{array}}{\Gamma \vdash X_1\ X_2 : [\tau_m/\alpha_m] \cdots [\tau_1/\alpha_1]\xi \leadsto X_1\ \tau_1\ \cdots\ \tau_m\ (e_0\ X_2)}\ \text{M-App}$$

$$\frac{\Gamma(X_1) = \Sigma_1 \qquad \Gamma \vdash S_2 \leadsto \xi_2 \qquad \Gamma \vdash \Sigma_1 \leqslant \xi_2 \uparrow \boldsymbol{\tau} \leadsto e_0}{\Gamma \vdash (X_1 :> S_2) : \xi_2 \leadsto \mathbf{pack}\ (\boldsymbol{\tau}, e_0\ X_1)\ \mathbf{as}\ \lfloor \xi_2 \rfloor}\ \text{M-Seal}$$

$$\boxed{\Gamma \vdash B : \exists b.\ R \leadsto e} \qquad\qquad \frac{}{\Gamma \vdash \varepsilon : \exists \varepsilon.\ \varnothing \leadsto \{\}}\ \text{Bs-Nil}$$

$$\frac{\begin{array}{c}\Gamma \vdash B_1 : \exists b_1.\ R_1 \leadsto e_1 \qquad \Gamma, b_1, R_1 \vdash B_2 : \exists b_2.\ R_2 \leadsto e_2 \\ \mathrm{dom}\ b_1 \cap \mathrm{domtv}\ \Gamma = \varnothing \qquad \mathrm{dom}\ b_2 \cap \mathrm{dom}\ b_1 = \varnothing \qquad b_1 \cdot b_2 = b = (\alpha_i :: \kappa_i)_{i=1}^m \\ \hat{r} = \{l_X \mapsto x_1\#l_X \mid l_X \in \mathrm{dom}\ R_1\} + \{l_X \mapsto x_2\#l_X \mid l_X \in \mathrm{dom}\ R_2\}\end{array}}{\begin{array}{l}\Gamma \vdash B_1 \cdot B_2 : \exists b.\ R \leadsto \mathbf{unpack}\ (b_1, x_1 : \lfloor \{\!|R_1|\!\} \rfloor) = e_1\ \mathbf{in} \\ \qquad \mathbf{unpack}\ (b_2, x_2 : \lfloor \{\!|R_2|\!\} \rfloor) = \\ \qquad \mathbf{let}\ \{X : \lfloor \Sigma \rfloor = x_1\#l_X \mid (l_X \mapsto \Sigma) \in R_1\}\ \mathbf{in}\ e_2\ \mathbf{in} \\ \qquad \mathbf{pack}\ ((\alpha_i)_{i=1}^m, \{\hat{r}\})\ \mathbf{as}\ \lfloor \exists b.\ \{\!|R_1 + R_2|\!\} \rfloor\end{array}}\ \text{Bs-Cons}$$

$$\boxed{\Gamma \vdash B : \exists b.\ R \leadsto e} \qquad\qquad \frac{\Gamma \vdash M : \exists b.\ \{\!|R|\!\} \leadsto e}{\Gamma \vdash \mathbf{include}\ M : \exists b.\ R \leadsto e}\ \text{B-Incl}$$

$$\frac{\Gamma \vdash^n E : \tau \leadsto e}{\Gamma \vdash \mathbf{val}^n\ X = E : \exists \varepsilon.\ \{l_X \mapsto \llbracket \tau \rrbracket^n\} \leadsto \{l_X = \langle\{\mathbf{val} = e\}\rangle^{\times n}\}}\ \text{B-Val}$$

$$\frac{\Gamma \vdash T :: \kappa \leadsto \tau \qquad e = \Lambda \alpha :: \kappa \to *.\ \lambda x : \alpha\ \tau.\ x}{\Gamma \vdash \mathbf{type}\ X = T : \exists \varepsilon.\ \{l_X \mapsto \llbracket = \tau :: \kappa \rrbracket\} \leadsto \{l_X = \{\mathbf{type} = e\}\}}\ \text{B-Type}$$

$$\frac{\Gamma \vdash M : \exists b.\ \Sigma \leadsto e}{\Gamma \vdash \mathbf{module}\ X = M : \exists b.\ \{l_X \mapsto \Sigma\} \leadsto \{l_X = e\}}\ \text{B-Mod}$$

Fig. 10. Module elaboration rules (other than the ones for CSP)

$$\boxed{\Gamma \vdash S \rightsquigarrow \xi}$$

$$\frac{\Gamma \vdash D \rightsquigarrow \exists \boldsymbol{b}.\ R}{\Gamma \vdash \mathbf{sig}\ D\ \mathbf{end} \rightsquigarrow \exists \boldsymbol{b}.\ \{\!|R|\!\}}\ \text{S-Str}$$

$$\frac{\begin{array}{c}\Gamma \vdash S_1 \rightsquigarrow \exists \boldsymbol{b}.\ \Sigma_1 \\ \Gamma, \boldsymbol{b}, X : \Sigma_1 \vdash S_2 \rightsquigarrow \xi_2\end{array}}{\Gamma \vdash (X : S_1) \rightarrow S_2 \rightsquigarrow \exists \varepsilon.\ \forall \boldsymbol{b}.\ \Sigma_1 \rightarrow \xi_2}\ \text{S-Fun}$$

$$\frac{\Gamma \vdash S \rightsquigarrow \exists(\boldsymbol{b}_1 \cdot (\alpha :: \kappa) \cdot \boldsymbol{b}_2).\ \Sigma \qquad \Sigma(X) = [\![= \alpha :: \kappa]\!] \qquad \Gamma \vdash T :: \kappa \rightsquigarrow \tau}{\Gamma \vdash S\ \mathbf{with\ type}\ X = T \rightsquigarrow \exists(\boldsymbol{b}_1 \cdot \boldsymbol{b}_2).\ [\tau/\alpha]\Sigma}\ \text{S-With}$$

$$\boxed{\Gamma \vdash D \rightsquigarrow \exists \boldsymbol{b}.\ R}$$

$$\frac{}{\Gamma \vdash \varepsilon \rightsquigarrow \exists \varepsilon.\ \varnothing}\ \text{Ds-Nil}$$

$$\frac{\begin{array}{c}\Gamma \vdash D_1 \rightsquigarrow \exists \boldsymbol{b}_1.\ R_1 \qquad \operatorname{dom} \boldsymbol{b}_1 \cap \operatorname{domtv} \Gamma = \varnothing \\ \Gamma, \boldsymbol{b}_1, R_1 \vdash D_2 \rightsquigarrow \exists \boldsymbol{b}_2.\ R_2 \\ \operatorname{dom} \boldsymbol{b}_2 \cap \operatorname{dom} \boldsymbol{b}_1 = \varnothing \qquad \operatorname{dom} R_1 \cap \operatorname{dom} R_2 = \varnothing\end{array}}{\Gamma \vdash D_1 \cdot D_2 \rightsquigarrow \exists(\boldsymbol{b}_1 \cdot \boldsymbol{b}_2).\ R_1 \uplus R_2}\ \text{Ds-Cons}$$

$$\boxed{\Gamma \vdash D \rightsquigarrow \exists \boldsymbol{b}.\ R}$$

$$\frac{\Gamma \vdash S \rightsquigarrow \exists \boldsymbol{b}.\ \Sigma}{\Gamma \vdash \mathbf{module}\ X : S \rightsquigarrow \exists \boldsymbol{b}.\ \{l_X \mapsto \Sigma\}}\ \text{D-Mod}$$

$$\frac{\Gamma \vdash T :: * \rightsquigarrow \tau}{\Gamma \vdash \mathbf{val}^n\ X : T \rightsquigarrow \exists \varepsilon.\ \{l_X \mapsto [\![\tau]\!]^n\}}\ \text{D-Val}$$

$$\frac{\Gamma \vdash S \rightsquigarrow \exists \boldsymbol{b}.\ \{\!|R|\!\}}{\Gamma \vdash \mathbf{include}\ S \rightsquigarrow \exists \boldsymbol{b}.\ R}\ \text{D-Incl}$$

$$\frac{\Gamma \vdash K \rightsquigarrow \kappa}{\Gamma \vdash \mathbf{type}\ X :: K \rightsquigarrow \exists(\alpha :: \kappa).\ \{l_X \mapsto [\![= \alpha :: \kappa]\!]\}}\ \text{D-Type}$$

Fig. 11. Signature elaboration rules (other than the ones for CSP)

$$\boxed{\Gamma \vdash \Sigma \leqslant \xi \uparrow \tau \rightsquigarrow e}$$

$$\frac{\begin{array}{c}\boldsymbol{b} = (\alpha_i :: \kappa_i)_{i=1}^m \qquad \lfloor \Gamma \rfloor \vdash \tau_i :: \kappa_i \quad \text{(for each } i) \\ \Gamma \vdash \Sigma \leqslant [\tau_i/\alpha_i]_{i=1}^m \Sigma' \rightsquigarrow e\end{array}}{\Gamma \vdash \Sigma \leqslant \exists \boldsymbol{b}.\ \Sigma' \uparrow (\tau_i)_{i=1}^m \rightsquigarrow e}\ \text{U-Match}$$

$$\boxed{\Gamma \vdash \Sigma \leqslant \Sigma' \rightsquigarrow e}$$

$$\frac{\begin{array}{c}\forall l \in \operatorname{dom} R'.\ \Gamma \vdash R(l) \leqslant R'(l) \rightsquigarrow e_l \\ \hat{r} = \{l \mapsto e_l\ (x \# l) \mid l \in \operatorname{dom} R'\}\end{array}}{\Gamma \vdash \{\!|R|\!\} \leqslant \{\!|R'|\!\} \rightsquigarrow \lambda x : \lfloor \{\!|R|\!\} \rfloor.\ \{\hat{r}\}}\ \text{U-Str}$$

$$\frac{\Gamma \vdash \tau \leqslant \tau' \rightsquigarrow e}{\Gamma \vdash [\![\tau]\!]^n \leqslant [\![\tau']\!]^n \rightsquigarrow \lambda x : \langle\!\langle \mathbf{val} : \tau \rangle\!\rangle^{\times n}.\ \langle\!\langle \mathbf{val} = e\ ((\sim^{\times n} x) \# \mathbf{val}) \rangle\!\rangle^{\times n}}\ \text{U-Val}$$

$$\frac{\tau \equiv \tau'}{\Gamma \vdash [\![= \tau :: \kappa]\!] \leqslant [\![= \tau' :: \kappa]\!] \rightsquigarrow \lambda x : \lfloor [\![= \tau :: \kappa]\!] \rfloor.\ x}\ \text{U-Type}$$

$$\frac{\begin{array}{c}\operatorname{domtv} \Gamma \cap \operatorname{dom} \boldsymbol{b}' = \varnothing \qquad \Gamma, \boldsymbol{b}' \vdash \Sigma' \leqslant \exists \boldsymbol{b}.\ \Sigma \uparrow (\tau_i)_{i=1}^m \rightsquigarrow e_1 \\ \boldsymbol{b} = (\alpha_i :: \kappa_i)_{i=1}^m \qquad \Gamma, \boldsymbol{b}' \vdash [\tau_i/\alpha_i]_{i=1}^m \xi \leqslant \xi' \rightsquigarrow e_2 \qquad \tau' = \lfloor \forall \boldsymbol{b}.\ \Sigma \rightarrow \xi \rfloor\end{array}}{\Gamma \vdash \forall \boldsymbol{b}.\ \Sigma \rightarrow \xi \leqslant \forall \boldsymbol{b}'.\ \Sigma' \rightarrow \xi' \rightsquigarrow \lambda x' : \tau'.\ \lambda x : \lfloor \Sigma' \rfloor.\ e_2'\ (x'\ \tau_1 \cdots \tau_m\ (e_1\ x))}\ \text{U-Fun}$$

$$\boxed{\Gamma \vdash \xi \leqslant \xi' \rightsquigarrow e}$$

$$\frac{\xi = \exists \boldsymbol{b}.\ \Sigma \qquad \operatorname{domtv} \Gamma \cap \operatorname{dom} \boldsymbol{b} = \varnothing \qquad \Gamma, \boldsymbol{b} \vdash \Sigma \leqslant \xi' \uparrow \tau \rightsquigarrow e}{\Gamma \vdash \xi \leqslant \xi' \rightsquigarrow \lambda x : \lfloor \xi \rfloor.\ \mathbf{unpack}\ (\boldsymbol{b}, x' : \lfloor \Sigma \rfloor) = x\ \mathbf{in}\ \mathbf{pack}\ (\tau, e\ x')\ \mathbf{as}\ \lfloor \xi' \rfloor}\ \text{U-Abs}$$

Fig. 12. Signature subtyping rules (other than the ones for CSP)

$$\langle e \rangle^{\times n} := \underbrace{\langle \cdots \langle}_{n} e \underbrace{\rangle \cdots \rangle}_{n} \qquad \sim^{\times n} e := \underbrace{\sim \cdots \sim}_{n} e$$

$$\textbf{pack } (\varepsilon, e) \textbf{ as } \tau := e \qquad (\textbf{let } x : \tau = e \textbf{ in } e') := (\lambda x : \tau.\ e')\ e$$

$$\textbf{pack } (\tau \cdot \boldsymbol{\tau}, e) \textbf{ as } \exists \alpha :: \kappa.\ \tau' := \textbf{pack } (\tau, \textbf{pack } (\boldsymbol{\tau}, e) \textbf{ as } \tau') \textbf{ as } \exists \alpha :: \kappa.\ \tau'$$

$$(\textbf{let } \{x_i : \tau_i = e_i\}_{i=1}^{m} \textbf{ in } e') := \textbf{let } x_1 : \tau_1 = e_1 \textbf{ in } \cdots \textbf{ let } x_m : \tau_m = e_m \textbf{ in } e'$$
$$(\text{in arbitrary order; where } x_i \notin \mathrm{fv}(e_j) \text{ for each } i \text{ and } j)$$

$$(\textbf{unpack } (\boldsymbol{b}, x : \tau) = e \textbf{ in } e') := \textbf{unpack } (\alpha, x') = e \textbf{ in unpack } (\boldsymbol{b}', x : \tau) = x' \textbf{ in } e'$$
$$(\text{where } \boldsymbol{b} = (\alpha :: \kappa) \cdot \boldsymbol{b}', \text{ and } x' \notin \mathrm{fv}(e'))$$

$$(\textbf{unpack } (\varepsilon, x : \tau) = e \textbf{ in } e') := \textbf{let } x : \tau = e \textbf{ in } e'$$

Fig. 13. Syntax sugars for System $F\omega^{\langle\rangle}$ terms used in elaboration rules

$$\boxed{\gamma \vdash^s e : \tau}$$

$$\frac{\gamma \vdash^{s+1} e : \tau}{\gamma \vdash^s \langle e \rangle : \langle \tau \rangle} \text{ TT-BRKT} \qquad \frac{\gamma \vdash^s e : \langle \tau \rangle}{\gamma \vdash^{s+1} \sim e : \tau} \text{ TT-ESC}$$

$$\frac{\gamma \vdash^s e : \tau' \quad \tau' \equiv \tau \quad \gamma \vdash \tau :: *}{\gamma \vdash^s e : \tau} \text{ TT-TEQ} \qquad \frac{\vdash \gamma \quad \gamma(x) = \tau^s}{\gamma \vdash^s x : \tau} \text{ TT-VAR}$$

$$\frac{\gamma, x : \tau^s \vdash^s e : \tau'}{\gamma \vdash^s (\lambda x : \tau.\ e) : \tau \to \tau'} \text{ TT-ABS} \qquad \frac{\gamma \vdash^s e_1 : \tau \to \tau' \quad \gamma \vdash^s e_2 : \tau}{\gamma \vdash^s e_1\ e_2 : \tau'} \text{ TT-APP}$$

$$\frac{\gamma \vdash^s e_i : \tau_i \quad (\text{for each } i)}{\gamma \vdash^s \{l_1 = e_1, \ldots, l_m = e_m\} : \{l_1 : \tau_1, \ldots, l_m : \tau_m\}} \text{ TT-RCD} \qquad \frac{\gamma \vdash^s e : \{r\}}{\gamma \vdash^s e \# l : r(l)} \text{ TT-PRJ}$$

$$\frac{\alpha \notin \mathrm{domtv}\ \gamma \quad \gamma, \alpha :: \kappa \vdash^s e : \tau}{\gamma \vdash^s (\Lambda \alpha :: \kappa.\ e) : \forall \alpha :: \kappa.\ \tau} \text{ TT-TABS}$$

$$\frac{\gamma \vdash^s e : \forall \alpha :: \kappa.\ \tau' \quad \gamma \vdash \tau :: \kappa}{\gamma \vdash^s e\ \tau : [\tau/\alpha]\tau'} \text{ TT-TAPP}$$

$$\frac{\gamma \vdash \tau :: \kappa \quad \gamma \vdash^0 e : [\tau/\alpha]\tau' \quad \gamma \vdash (\exists \alpha :: \kappa.\ \tau') :: *}{\gamma \vdash^0 (\textbf{pack } (\tau, e) \textbf{ as } \exists \alpha :: \kappa.\ \tau') : \exists \alpha :: \kappa.\ \tau'} \text{ TT-PACK}$$

$$\frac{\gamma \vdash^0 e_1 : \exists \alpha :: \kappa.\ \tau \quad \gamma, \alpha :: \kappa, x : \tau^0 \vdash^0 e_2 : \tau_2 \quad \gamma \vdash \tau_2 :: *}{\gamma \vdash^0 \textbf{unpack } (\alpha, x) = e_1 \textbf{ in } e_2 : \tau_2} \text{ TT-UNPACK}$$

Fig. 14. Typing rules for System $F\omega^{\langle\rangle}$ (without CSP)

$$\boxed{e \xrightarrow{n} e'}$$

$$\frac{e \xrightarrow{n+1} e'}{\lambda x : \tau.\, e \xrightarrow{n+1} \lambda x : \tau.\, e'} \text{ TE-Abs} \qquad \frac{e \xrightarrow{n+1} e'}{\Lambda \alpha :: \kappa.\, e \xrightarrow{n+1} \Lambda \alpha :: \kappa.\, e'} \text{ TE-TAbs}$$

$$\frac{e_1 \xrightarrow{n} e_1'}{e_1\, e_2 \xrightarrow{n} e_1'\, e_2} \text{ TE-App1} \qquad \frac{e_2 \xrightarrow{n} e_2'}{v_1^{(n)}\, e_2 \xrightarrow{n} v_1^{(n)}\, e_2'} \text{ TE-App2} \qquad \frac{e \xrightarrow{n} e'}{e\, \tau \xrightarrow{n} e'\, \tau} \text{ TE-TApp}$$

$$\frac{}{(\lambda x : \tau.\, e)\, v^{(0)} \xrightarrow{0} [v^{(0)}/x]e} \text{ TE-Beta} \qquad \frac{}{(\Lambda \alpha :: \kappa.\, e)\, \tau \xrightarrow{0} [\tau/\alpha]e} \text{ TE-TBeta}$$

$$\frac{e_i \xrightarrow{n} e_i'}{\{l_1 = v_1^{(n)}, \ldots, l_{i-1} = v_{i-1}^{(n)}, l_i = e_i, l_{i+1} = v_{i+1}^{(n)}, \ldots, l_m = v_m^{(n)}\}} \text{ TE-Rcd}$$
$$\xrightarrow{n} \{l_1 = v_1^{(n)}, \ldots, l_{i-1} = v_{i-1}^{(n)}, l_i = e_i', l_{i+1} = v_{i+1}^{(n)}, \ldots, l_m = v_m^{(n)}\}$$

$$\frac{e \xrightarrow{n} e'}{e\#l \xrightarrow{n} e'\#l} \text{ TE-Prj1} \qquad \frac{}{\{l_1 = v_1^{(0)}, \ldots, l_m = v_m^{(0)}\}\#l_i \xrightarrow{0} v_i^{(0)}} \text{ TE-Prj2}$$

$$\frac{e \xrightarrow{0} e'}{\textbf{pack } (\tau, e) \textbf{ as } \tau' \xrightarrow{0} \textbf{pack } (\tau, e') \textbf{ as } \tau'} \text{ TE-Pack}$$

$$\frac{e_1 \xrightarrow{0} e_1'}{\textbf{unpack } (\alpha, x) = e_1 \textbf{ in } e_2 \xrightarrow{0} \textbf{unpack } (\alpha, x) = e_1' \textbf{ in } e_2} \text{ TE-Unpack1}$$

$$\frac{}{\textbf{unpack } (\alpha, x) = \textbf{pack } (\tau, v^{(0)}) \textbf{ as } \tau' \textbf{ in } e_2 \xrightarrow{0} [v^{(0)}/x][\tau/\alpha]e_2} \text{ TE-Unpack2}$$

$$\frac{e \xrightarrow{n+1} e'}{\langle e \rangle \xrightarrow{n} \langle e' \rangle} \text{ TE-Brkt} \qquad \frac{e \xrightarrow{n} e'}{\sim e \xrightarrow{n+1} \sim e'} \text{ TE-Esc1} \qquad \frac{}{\sim \langle v^{(1)} \rangle \xrightarrow{1} v^{(1)}} \text{ TE-Esc2}$$

Fig. 15. Operational semantics of System $F\omega^{\langle \rangle}$ (without CSP)

$\boxed{\vdash \gamma}$ $\qquad \dfrac{}{\vdash \bullet}$ $\qquad \dfrac{\vdash \gamma \quad \alpha \notin \mathrm{domtv}\, \gamma}{\vdash \gamma, \alpha :: \kappa}$ $\qquad \dfrac{\gamma \vdash \tau :: *}{\vdash \gamma, x : \tau^s}$ $\qquad \dfrac{\vdash \gamma \quad \sigma \notin \gamma}{\vdash \gamma, \sigma}$

$\boxed{\gamma \vdash \tau :: \kappa}$ $\qquad \dfrac{\gamma, \alpha :: \kappa \vdash \tau :: \kappa'}{\gamma \vdash (\Lambda\alpha :: \kappa.\, \tau) :: \kappa \to \kappa'}$ $\qquad \dfrac{\gamma \vdash \tau_1 :: \kappa' \to \kappa \quad \gamma \vdash \tau_2 :: \kappa'}{\gamma \vdash \tau_1\, \tau_2 :: \kappa}$

$\dfrac{\vdash \gamma \quad \gamma(x) = \kappa}{\gamma \vdash \alpha :: \kappa}$ $\qquad \dfrac{\gamma \vdash \tau_1 :: * \quad \gamma \vdash \tau_2 :: *}{\gamma \vdash \tau_1 \to \tau_2 :: *}$ $\qquad \dfrac{\gamma \vdash \tau :: *}{\gamma \vdash \langle \tau \rangle :: *}\ \text{TK-Code}$

$\dfrac{\gamma \vdash \tau_i :: * \quad (\text{for each } i)}{\gamma \vdash \{l_1 : \tau_1, \ldots, l_m : \tau_m\} :: *}$ $\qquad \dfrac{\gamma, \alpha :: \kappa \vdash \tau :: *}{\gamma \vdash (\exists\alpha :: \kappa.\, \tau) :: *}$ $\qquad \dfrac{\gamma, \alpha :: \kappa \vdash \tau :: *}{\gamma \vdash (\forall\alpha :: \kappa.\, \tau) :: *}$

$\dfrac{\sigma \notin \gamma \quad \gamma, \sigma \vdash \tau :: *}{\gamma \vdash (\forall\sigma.\, \tau) :: *}\ \text{TK-StgPoly}$ $\qquad \dfrac{\sigma \in \gamma \quad \gamma \vdash \tau :: *}{\gamma \vdash \langle \tau \rangle^\sigma :: *}\ \text{TK-PersCode}$

$\boxed{\tau \equiv \tau'}$ $\quad \dfrac{}{\tau \equiv \tau}$ $\quad \dfrac{\tau_1 \equiv \tau_2}{\tau_2 \equiv \tau_1}$ $\quad \dfrac{\tau_1 \equiv \tau_2 \quad \tau_2 \equiv \tau_3}{\tau_1 \equiv \tau_3}$ $\quad \dfrac{\tau_1 \equiv \tau_1' \quad \tau_2 \equiv \tau_2'}{\tau_1 \to \tau_1' \equiv \tau_2 \to \tau_2'}$

$\dfrac{\tau \equiv \tau'}{\Lambda\alpha :: \kappa.\, \tau \equiv \Lambda\alpha :: \kappa.\, \tau'}$ $\qquad \dfrac{\tau_1 \equiv \tau_1' \quad \tau_2 \equiv \tau_2'}{\tau_1\, \tau_2 \equiv \tau_1'\, \tau_2'}$ $\qquad \dfrac{}{(\Lambda\alpha :: \kappa.\, \tau')\, \tau \equiv [\tau/\alpha]\tau'}$

$\dfrac{\alpha \notin \mathrm{ftv}(\tau)}{\Lambda\alpha :: \kappa.\, \tau\, \alpha \equiv \tau}$ $\qquad \dfrac{\mathrm{dom}\, r = \mathrm{dom}\, r' \quad \forall l \in \mathrm{dom}\, r.\, r(l) \equiv r'(l)}{\{r\} \equiv \{r'\}}$ $\qquad \dfrac{\tau \equiv \tau'}{\langle \tau \rangle^\sigma \equiv \langle \tau' \rangle^\sigma}$

$\dfrac{\tau \equiv \tau'}{\exists\alpha :: \kappa.\, \tau \equiv \exists\alpha :: \kappa.\, \tau'}$ $\quad \dfrac{\tau \equiv \tau'}{\forall\alpha :: \kappa.\, \tau \equiv \forall\alpha :: \kappa.\, \tau'}$ $\quad \dfrac{\tau \equiv \tau'}{\langle \tau \rangle \equiv \langle \tau' \rangle}$ $\quad \dfrac{\tau \equiv \tau'}{\forall\sigma.\, \tau \equiv \forall\sigma.\, \tau'}$

Fig. 16. Well-formedness, kinding, and type equivalence in System $F\omega^{\langle\rangle}$

$\boxed{\tau \Rrightarrow \tau'}$ $\quad \dfrac{}{\tau \Rrightarrow \tau}$ $\quad \dfrac{\tau \Rrightarrow \tau'}{\Lambda\alpha :: \kappa.\, \tau \Rrightarrow \Lambda\alpha :: \kappa.\, \tau'}$ $\quad \dfrac{\tau_1 \Rrightarrow \tau_1' \quad \tau_2 \Rrightarrow \tau_2'}{\tau_1\, \tau_2 \Rrightarrow \tau_2\, \tau_2'}$

$\dfrac{\tau_1 \Rrightarrow \tau_1' \quad \tau_2 \Rrightarrow \tau_2'}{(\Lambda\alpha :: \kappa.\, \tau_1)\, \tau_2 \Rrightarrow [\tau_2'/\alpha]\tau_1'}$ $\qquad \dfrac{\tau_1 \Rrightarrow \tau_1' \quad \tau_2 \Rrightarrow \tau_2'}{\tau_1 \to \tau_2 \Rrightarrow \tau_2 \to \tau_2'}$

$\dfrac{\mathrm{dom}\, r = \mathrm{dom}\, r' \quad \forall l \in \mathrm{dom}\, r.\, r(l) \Rrightarrow r'(l)}{\{r\} \Rrightarrow \{r'\}}$ $\qquad \dfrac{\tau \Rrightarrow \tau'}{\forall\sigma.\, \tau \Rrightarrow \forall\sigma.\, \tau'}$ $\qquad \dfrac{\tau \Rrightarrow \tau'}{\langle \tau \rangle^\sigma \Rrightarrow \langle \tau' \rangle^\sigma}$

$\dfrac{\tau \Rrightarrow \tau'}{\forall\alpha :: \kappa.\, \tau \Rrightarrow \forall\alpha :: \kappa.\, \tau'}$ $\qquad \dfrac{\tau \Rrightarrow \tau'}{\exists\alpha :: \kappa.\, \tau \Rrightarrow \exists\alpha :: \kappa.\, \tau'}$ $\qquad \dfrac{\tau \Rrightarrow \tau'}{\langle \tau \rangle \Rrightarrow \langle \tau' \rangle}$

Fig. 17. Type-level parallel reduction relation for System $F\omega^{\langle\rangle}$ types

$\boxed{\Sigma(\boldsymbol{X})}$ $\quad \Sigma(\boldsymbol{X} \cdot X) := (\Sigma(\boldsymbol{X}))(X)$

$\qquad \{|R|\}(X) := R(l_X)$

$\boxed{\text{dom } \boldsymbol{b}} \qquad \text{dom } \varepsilon := \varnothing$

$\qquad \text{dom}((\alpha :: \kappa) \cdot \boldsymbol{b}) := \{\alpha\} \uplus \text{dom } \boldsymbol{b}$

$\boxed{\text{domtv } \Gamma}$

$\text{domtv}(\Gamma, X : \Sigma) := \text{domtv } \Gamma$

$\text{domtv}(\Gamma, \alpha :: \kappa) := (\text{domtv } \Gamma) \uplus \{\alpha\}$

$\text{domtv}(\Gamma, x : \tau^s) := \text{domtv } \Gamma$

$\quad \text{domtv}(\Gamma, \sigma) := \text{domtv } \Gamma$

$\qquad \text{domtv} \bullet := \varnothing$

$\boxed{\Gamma, \boldsymbol{b} = \Gamma'} \quad \Gamma, \varepsilon := \Gamma$

$\Gamma, ((\alpha :: \kappa) \cdot \boldsymbol{b}) := (\Gamma, \alpha :: \kappa), \boldsymbol{b}$

$\boxed{\gamma_1, \gamma_2 = \gamma}$

$\qquad\qquad \gamma_1, \bullet := \gamma_1$

$\gamma_1, (\gamma_2', x : \tau^s) := (\gamma_1, \gamma_2'), x : \tau^s$

$\gamma_1, (\gamma_2', \alpha :: \kappa) := (\gamma_1, \gamma_2'), \alpha :: \kappa$

$\quad \gamma_1, (\gamma_2', \sigma) := (\gamma_1, \gamma_2'), \sigma$

$\boxed{\text{fsv}(\tau)} \quad \text{(selected)}$

$\quad \text{fsv}(\langle \tau \rangle^\sigma) := \text{fsv}(\tau) \cup \{\sigma\}$

$\quad \text{fsv}(\forall \sigma.\ \tau) := \text{fsv}(\tau) \setminus \{\sigma\}$

$\text{fsv}(\tau_1 \to \tau_2) = \text{fsv}(\tau_1) \cup \text{fsv}(\tau_2)$

$\boxed{\gamma \vdash s} \qquad \dfrac{}{\gamma \vdash n} \qquad \dfrac{\sigma \in \gamma}{\gamma \vdash n \dotplus \sigma}$

$\boxed{s + k} \qquad n + k := (n + k) \qquad \text{(where the last } n + k \text{ is a meta-level integer addition)}$

$\qquad (n \dotplus \sigma) + k := (n + k) \dotplus \sigma \qquad \text{(where } n + k \text{ is a meta-level integer addition)}$

$\boxed{\sigma \in \gamma} \qquad \dfrac{\sigma \in \gamma}{\sigma \in \gamma, x : \tau^s} \qquad \dfrac{\sigma \in \gamma}{\sigma \in \gamma, \alpha :: \kappa} \qquad \dfrac{}{\sigma \in \gamma, \sigma} \qquad \dfrac{\sigma' \neq \sigma \quad \sigma \in \gamma}{\sigma \in \gamma, \sigma'}$

$\boxed{\Gamma, R = \Gamma'} \qquad \Gamma, \varnothing := \Gamma$

$\quad \Gamma, (\{l_X \mapsto \Sigma\} \uplus R) := (\Gamma, X : \Sigma), R \qquad \text{(in arbitrary order)}$

$\boxed{f_1 + f_2 = f} \quad f_1 + f_2 := \{x \mapsto f_1(x) \mid x \in \text{dom } f_1 \setminus \text{dom } f_2\} \uplus f_2$

$\boxed{\Gamma(X)}$

$\quad (\Gamma, X' : \Sigma)(X) := \begin{cases} \Sigma & (\text{if } X' = X) \\ \Gamma(X) & (\text{if } X' \neq X) \end{cases}$

$\quad (\Gamma, \alpha :: \kappa)(X) := \Gamma(X)$

$\quad (\Gamma, x : \tau^n)(X) := \Gamma(X)$

$\quad (\Gamma, \sigma)(X) := \Gamma(X)$

$\boxed{[s'/\sigma]e} \quad \text{(selected)}$

$\quad [s'/\sigma]\langle e \rangle^{\sigma'} := \langle [s'/\sigma]e \rangle^{\sigma'} \qquad (\text{if } \sigma' \neq \sigma)$

$\quad [n/\sigma]\langle e \rangle^\sigma := \langle [s'/\sigma]e \rangle^{\times n}$

$\quad [n \dotplus \sigma'/\sigma]\langle e \rangle^\sigma := \langle\langle [n \dotplus \sigma'/\sigma]e \rangle^{\times n} \rangle^{\sigma'}$

$\quad [s'/\sigma](\sim^{\sigma'} e) := \sim^{\sigma'} [s'/\sigma]e \qquad (\text{if } \sigma' \neq \sigma)$

$\quad [n/\sigma](\sim^\sigma e) := \sim^{\times n} [n/\sigma]e$

$\quad [n \dotplus \sigma'/\sigma](\sim^\sigma e) := \sim^{\times n} \sim^{\sigma'} [n \dotplus \sigma'/\sigma]e$

$\quad [s'/\sigma](\Lambda \sigma'.\ e) := \Lambda \sigma'.\ [s'/\sigma]e \qquad (\text{if } \sigma' \neq \sigma)$

$\boxed{[s'/\sigma]\tau} \quad \text{(selected)}$

$\quad [s'/\sigma]\langle \tau \rangle^{\sigma'} := \langle \tau \rangle^{\sigma'} \qquad (\text{if } \sigma' \neq \sigma)$

$\quad [n/\sigma]\langle \tau \rangle^\sigma := \langle \tau \rangle^{\times n}$

$\quad [n \dotplus \sigma'/\sigma]\langle \tau \rangle^\sigma := \langle\langle \tau \rangle^{\times n} \rangle^{\sigma'}$

$\quad [s'/\sigma](\forall \sigma'.\ \tau) := \forall \sigma'.\ [s'/\sigma]\tau \qquad (\text{if } \sigma' \neq \sigma)$

$\boxed{[s'/\sigma]s} \qquad [s'/\sigma]n := n$

$\quad [s'/\sigma](n \dotplus \sigma') := n \dotplus \sigma' \qquad (\text{if } \sigma' \neq \sigma)$

$\quad [s'/\sigma](n \dotplus \sigma) := s' + n$

Fig. 18. Miscellaneous definitions

C   Proofs for Target Type Safety

Lemma 1 (Substitution of terms). *If $\gamma, x : (\tau')^{s'}, \gamma' \vdash^s e : \tau$ and $\gamma \vdash^{s'} e' : \tau'$, then $\gamma, \gamma' \vdash^s [e'/x]e : \tau$.*

Proof. By straightforward induction on the derivation of $\gamma, x : (\tau')^{s'}, \gamma' \vdash^s e : \tau$.

Lemma 2. (Substitution of types).

1. If $\gamma, \alpha :: \kappa', \gamma' \vdash \tau :: \kappa$ and $\gamma \vdash \tau' :: \kappa'$, then $\gamma, [\tau'/\alpha]\gamma' \vdash [\tau'/\alpha]\tau :: \kappa$.
2. $\tau_1 \equiv \tau_2$ implies $[\tau'/\alpha]\tau_1 \equiv [\tau'/\alpha]\tau_2$.
3. If $\gamma, \alpha :: \kappa', \gamma' \vdash^s e : \tau$ and $\gamma \vdash \tau' :: \kappa'$, then $\gamma, [\tau'/\alpha]\gamma' \vdash^s [\tau'/\alpha]e : \tau$.

Proof. By straightforward induction on the derivation of $\gamma, \alpha :: \kappa', \gamma' \vdash \tau :: \kappa$, $\tau_1 \equiv \tau_2$, and $\gamma, \alpha :: \kappa', \gamma' \vdash^s e : \tau$, respectively.

Lemma 3 (Substitution of stages).

1. If $\gamma, \sigma, \gamma' \vdash s$ and $\gamma \vdash s'$, then $\gamma, [s'/\sigma]\gamma' \vdash [s'/\sigma]s$.
2. $\tau_1 \equiv \tau_2$ implies $[s'/\sigma]\tau_1 \equiv [s'/\sigma]\tau_2$.
3. If $\gamma, \sigma, \gamma' \vdash \tau :: \kappa$ and $\gamma \vdash s'$, then $\gamma, [s'/\sigma]\gamma' \vdash [s'/\sigma]\tau :: \kappa$.
4. If $\gamma, \sigma, \gamma' \vdash^s e : \tau$ and $\gamma \vdash s'$, then $\gamma, [s'/\sigma]\gamma' \vdash^{[s'/\sigma]s} [s'/\sigma]e : [s'/\sigma]\tau$.

Proof. 1. By a case analysis on s and s'.
  – Case $s = n$: Trivially holds.
  – Case $s = n + \sigma'$ and $\sigma' \neq \sigma$: Easy.
  – Case $s = n + \sigma$:
    • Case $s' = n'$: We have $[s'/\sigma]s = (n+n')$, which makes the goal trivial.
    • Case $s' = n' + \sigma'$: By $\gamma \vdash s'$, we have $\sigma' \in \gamma$. Since $[s'/\sigma]s = (n + n') + \sigma'$, we clearly have $\gamma, [s'/\sigma]\gamma' \vdash [s'/\sigma]s$.
2. By straightforward induction on the derivation of $\tau_1 \equiv \tau_2$.
3. By induction on the derivation of $\gamma, \sigma, \gamma' \vdash \tau :: \kappa$.
  – Case $\dfrac{\sigma' \notin \gamma, \sigma, \gamma' \quad \gamma, \sigma, \gamma', \sigma' \vdash \tau' :: *}{\gamma, \sigma, \gamma' \vdash \forall \sigma'.\, \tau' :: *}$ TK-StgPoly: By IH, we first have $\gamma, [s'/\sigma](\gamma', \sigma') \vdash [s'/\sigma]\tau' :: *$, namely $\gamma, [s'/\sigma]\gamma', \sigma' \vdash [s'/\sigma]\tau' :: *$ by $\sigma \neq \sigma'$. This derives $\dfrac{\gamma, [s'/\sigma]\gamma', \sigma' \vdash [s'/\sigma]\tau' :: *}{\gamma, [s'/\sigma]\gamma' \vdash \forall \sigma'.\, [s'/\sigma]\tau' :: *}$ TK-StgPoly.

  – Case $\dfrac{\sigma' \in \gamma, \sigma, \gamma' \quad \gamma, \sigma, \gamma' \vdash \tau' :: *}{\gamma, \sigma, \gamma' \vdash \langle \tau' \rangle^{\sigma'} :: *}$ TK-PersCode: By IH for $\gamma, \sigma, \gamma' \vdash \tau' :: *$, we have $\gamma, [s'/\sigma]\gamma' \vdash [s'/\sigma]\tau' :: *$.
    • Case where $\sigma' \neq \sigma$: Since $[s'/\sigma]\langle \tau' \rangle^{\sigma'} = \langle [s'/\sigma]\tau' \rangle^{\sigma'}$ and either γ or γ' contains σ', we can derive:
      $$\dfrac{\sigma' \in \gamma, [s'/\sigma]\gamma' \quad \gamma, [s'/\sigma]\gamma' \vdash \tau' :: *}{\gamma, [s'/\sigma]\gamma' \vdash [s'/\sigma]\langle \tau' \rangle^{\sigma'} :: *} \text{ TK-PersCode.}$$
    • Case where $\sigma' = \sigma$ and $s' = n$: We have $[s'/\sigma]\langle \tau' \rangle^{\sigma'} = \langle [s'/\sigma]\tau' \rangle^{\times n}$, and we can clearly derive $\gamma, [s'/\sigma]\gamma' \vdash \langle [s'/\sigma]\tau' \rangle^{\times n} :: *$ by repeatedly applying TK-Code.

- Case where $\sigma' = \sigma$ and $s' = n \dotplus \sigma''$: We have $[s'/\sigma](\tau')^{\sigma'} = \langle\!\langle([s'/\sigma]\tau')^{\times n}\rangle^{\sigma''}$ and can derive $\gamma, [s'/\sigma]\gamma' \vdash \langle\!\langle[s'/\sigma]\tau'\rangle^{\times n} :: *$ in the same manner as the previous case. Since we have $\sigma'' \in \gamma$ by $\gamma \vdash s'$, we can derive:

$$\frac{\sigma'' \in \gamma, [s'/\sigma]\gamma' \qquad \gamma, [s'/\sigma]\gamma' \vdash \langle\!\langle[s'/\sigma]\tau'\rangle^{\times n} :: *}{\gamma, [s'/\sigma]\gamma' \vdash \langle\!\langle([s'/\sigma]\tau')^{\times n}\rangle^{\sigma''} :: *} \text{ TK-PersCode.}$$

- The other cases are straightforward.

4. By induction on the derivation of $\gamma, \sigma, \gamma' \vdash^s e : \tau$.

- Case $\dfrac{\sigma' \notin \gamma, \sigma, \gamma' \qquad \gamma, \sigma, \gamma', \sigma' \vdash^0 e' : \tau'}{\gamma, \sigma, \gamma' \vdash^0 (\Lambda\sigma'.\ e') : \forall\sigma'.\ \tau'}$ TT-StgAbs: By IH, we first have

$\gamma, [s'/\sigma](\gamma', \sigma') \vdash^0 [s'/\sigma]e' : [s'/\sigma]\tau'$, namely $\gamma, [s'/\sigma]\gamma', \sigma' \vdash^0 [s'/\sigma]e' : [s'/\sigma]\tau'$ by $\sigma \neq \sigma'$. This enables us to derive:

$$\frac{\sigma' \notin \gamma, [s'/\sigma]\gamma' \qquad \gamma, [s'/\sigma]\gamma', \sigma' \vdash^0 [s'/\sigma]e' : [s'/\sigma]\tau'}{\gamma, [s'/\sigma]\gamma' \vdash^0 [s'/\sigma](\Lambda\sigma'.\ e') : [s'/\sigma](\forall\sigma'.\ \tau')} \text{ TT-StgAbs.}$$

- Case $\dfrac{\gamma, \sigma, \gamma' \vdash^0 e_1 : \forall\sigma_1.\ \tau_1 \qquad \gamma, \sigma, \gamma' \vdash s_2}{\gamma, \sigma, \gamma' \vdash^0 e_1 \uparrow s_2 : [s_2/\sigma_1]\tau_1}$ TT-StgApp: By IH, we have

$\gamma, [s'/\sigma]\gamma' \vdash^0 [s'/\sigma]e_1 : [s'/\sigma](\forall\sigma_1.\ \tau_1)$. We can assume $\sigma_1 \neq \sigma$ w.l.o.g. here, and thus have $[s'/\sigma](\forall\sigma_1.\ \tau_1) = \forall\sigma_1.\ [s'/\sigma]\tau_1$. By 1, from $\gamma, \sigma, \gamma' \vdash s_2$, we have $\gamma, [s'/\sigma]\gamma' \vdash [s'/\sigma]s_2$. Therefore, we can derive:

$$\frac{\gamma, [s'/\sigma]\gamma' \vdash^0 [s'/\sigma]e_1 : \forall\sigma_1.\ [s'/\sigma]\tau_1 \qquad \gamma, [s'/\sigma]\gamma' \vdash [s'/\sigma]s_2}{\gamma, [s'/\sigma]\gamma' \vdash^0 ([s'/\sigma]e_1) \uparrow ([s'/\sigma]s_2) : [[s'/\sigma]s_2/\sigma_1][s'/\sigma]\tau_1} \text{ TT-StgApp,}$$

i.e., we have $\gamma, [s'/\sigma]\gamma' \vdash^0 [s'/\sigma](e_1 \uparrow s_2) : [s'/\sigma]([s_2/\sigma_1]\tau_1)$.

- Case $\dfrac{\sigma' \in \gamma, \sigma, \gamma' \qquad \gamma, \sigma, \gamma' \vdash^{n \dotplus \sigma'} e' : \tau'}{\gamma, \sigma, \gamma' \vdash^n \langle e'\rangle^{\sigma'} : \langle\tau'\rangle^{\sigma'}}$ TT-BrktVar: By IH, we have

$\gamma, [s'/\sigma]\gamma' \vdash^{[s'/\sigma](n \dotplus \sigma')} [s'/\sigma]e' : [s'/\sigma]\tau'$.

  - Case $\sigma' \neq \sigma$: Since $[s'/\sigma](n \dotplus \sigma') = n \dotplus \sigma'$ and either γ or γ' contains σ', we can derive:

$$\frac{\sigma' \in \gamma, [s'/\sigma]\gamma' \qquad \gamma, [s'/\sigma]\gamma' \vdash^{n \dotplus \sigma'} [s'/\sigma]e' : [s'/\sigma]\tau'}{\gamma, [s'/\sigma]\gamma' \vdash^n \langle[s'/\sigma]e'\rangle^{\sigma'} : \langle[s'/\sigma]\tau'\rangle^{\sigma'}} \text{ TT-BrktVar,}$$

    i.e., we have $\gamma, [s'/\sigma]\gamma' \vdash^n [s'/\sigma]\langle e'\rangle^{\sigma'} : [s'/\sigma]\langle\tau'\rangle^{\sigma'}$.

  - Case $\sigma' = \sigma$ and $s' = n'$: We have $[s'/\sigma](n \dotplus \sigma') = (n + n')$, and thus by repeatedly applying TT-Brkt, we can derive:

$$\frac{\dfrac{\gamma, [n'/\sigma]\gamma' \vdash^{n+n'} [n'/\sigma]e' : [n'/\sigma]\tau'}{\vdots} \text{ TT-Brkt}}{\gamma, [n'/\sigma]\gamma' \vdash^n \langle[n'/\sigma]e'\rangle^{\times n'} : \langle[n'/\sigma]\tau'\rangle^{\times n'}} \text{ TT-Brkt},$$

    i.e., we have $\gamma, [n'/\sigma]\gamma' \vdash^{[s'/\sigma]n} [n'/\sigma]\langle e'\rangle^{\sigma'} : [n'/\sigma]\langle\tau'\rangle^{\sigma'}$.

  - Case $\sigma' = \sigma$ and $s' = n' \dotplus \sigma''$: We have $[s'/\sigma](n \dotplus \sigma') = (n + n') \dotplus \sigma''$, and we can derive $\gamma, [s'/\sigma]\gamma' \vdash^{n \dotplus \sigma''} \langle[s'/\sigma]e'\rangle^{\times n'} : \langle[s'/\sigma]\tau'\rangle^{\times n'}$ in the same way as the previous case. Since $\sigma'' \in \gamma$ holds by $\gamma \vdash s'$, we can further derive:

$$\frac{\sigma'' \in \gamma, [s'/\sigma]\gamma' \qquad \gamma, [s'/\sigma]\gamma' \vdash^{n+\sigma''} \langle\!\langle [s'/\sigma]e'\rangle^{\times n'}\rangle : \langle\!\langle [s'/\sigma]\tau'\rangle^{\times n'}\rangle}{\gamma, [s'/\sigma]\gamma' \vdash^n \langle\!\langle [s'/\sigma]e'\rangle^{\times n'}\rangle^{\sigma''} : \langle\!\langle [s'/\sigma]\tau'\rangle^{\times n'}\rangle^{\sigma''}} \text{ TT-BrktVar,}$$

i.e., we have $\gamma, [s'/\sigma]\gamma' \vdash^{[s'/\sigma]n} [s'/\sigma]\langle e'\rangle^{\sigma'} : [s'/\sigma]\langle\tau'\rangle^{\sigma'}$.

– Case $\dfrac{\sigma' \in \gamma, \sigma, \gamma' \qquad \gamma, \sigma, \gamma' \vdash^n e' : \langle\tau\rangle^{\sigma'}}{\gamma, \sigma, \gamma' \vdash^{n+\sigma'} \sim^{\sigma'} e' : \tau}$ TT-EscVar: By IH, we first have

$\gamma, [s'/\sigma]\gamma' \vdash^n [s'/\sigma]e' : [s'/\sigma]\langle\tau\rangle^{\sigma'}$.

• Case $\sigma' \neq \sigma$: Since $[s'/\sigma]\langle\tau\rangle^{\sigma'} = \langle [s'/\sigma]\tau\rangle^{\sigma'}$, we can derive:
$$\frac{\gamma, [s'/\sigma]\gamma' \vdash^n [s'/\sigma]e' : \langle [s'/\sigma]\tau\rangle^{\sigma'}}{\gamma, [s'/\sigma]\gamma' \vdash^{n+\sigma'} \sim^{\sigma'} [s'/\sigma]e' : [s'/\sigma]\tau} \text{ TT-EscVar.}$$

• Case $\sigma' = \sigma$ and $s' = n'$: We have $[s'/\sigma]\langle\tau\rangle^{\sigma'} = \langle [n'/\sigma]\tau\rangle^{\times n'}$, and this enables us to derive:
$$\frac{\gamma, [n'/\sigma]\gamma' \vdash^n [n'/\sigma]e' : \langle [n'/\sigma]\tau\rangle^{\times n'}}{\vdots \qquad\qquad\qquad \text{TT-Esc}}$$
$$\frac{}{\gamma, [n'/\sigma]\gamma' \vdash^{n+n'} \sim^{\times n'} [n'/\sigma]e' : [n'/\sigma]\tau} \text{ TT-Esc},$$
i.e., we have $\gamma, [s'/\sigma]\gamma' \vdash^{[s'/\sigma](n+\sigma')} [s'/\sigma](\sim^{\sigma'} e') : [s'/\sigma]\tau$.

• Case $\sigma' = \sigma$ and $s' = n' + \sigma''$: We have $[s'/\sigma]\langle\tau\rangle^{\sigma'} = \langle\!\langle [n'/\sigma]\tau\rangle^{\times n'}\rangle^{\sigma''}$. Since we have $\sigma'' \in \gamma$ by $\gamma \vdash s'$, we can derive:

$$\frac{\sigma'' \in \gamma, [s'/\sigma]\gamma' \qquad \gamma, [s'/\sigma]\gamma' \vdash^n [s'/\sigma]e' : \langle\!\langle [n'/\sigma]\tau\rangle^{\times n'}\rangle^{\sigma''}}{\gamma, [s'/\sigma]\gamma' \vdash^{n+\sigma''} \sim^{\sigma''} [s'/\sigma]e' : \langle [n'/\sigma]\tau\rangle^{\times n'}} \text{ TT-EscVar}$$
$$\frac{\vdots}{\gamma, [s'/\sigma]\gamma' \vdash^{(n+n')+\sigma''} \sim^{\times n'} \sim^{\sigma''} [s'/\sigma]e' : [n'/\sigma]\tau} \text{ TT-Esc}$$

i.e., we have $\gamma, [s'/\sigma]\gamma' \vdash^{[s'/\sigma](n+\sigma')} [s'/\sigma](\sim^{\sigma'} e') : [s'/\sigma]\tau$.

– Case $\dfrac{\gamma, \sigma, \gamma' \vdash^s e : \tau' \qquad \tau \equiv \tau' \qquad \gamma, \sigma, \gamma' \vdash \tau :: *}{\gamma, \sigma, \gamma' \vdash^s e : \tau}$ TT-TEq: By IH, we

have $\gamma, [s'/\sigma]\gamma' \vdash^{[s'/\sigma]s} [s'/\sigma]e : [s'/\sigma]\tau'$. By 2 and 3, we also have $[s'/\sigma]\tau \equiv [s'/\sigma]\tau'$ and $\gamma, [s'/\sigma]\gamma' \vdash [s'/\sigma]\tau :: *$, respectively. Therefore, we can derive:
$$\frac{\gamma, [s'/\sigma]\gamma' \vdash^{[s'/\sigma]s} [s'/\sigma]e : [s'/\sigma]\tau' \qquad [s'/\sigma]\tau \equiv [s'/\sigma]\tau'}{\gamma, [s'/\sigma]\gamma' \vdash [s'/\sigma]\tau :: *} $$
$$\frac{}{\gamma, [s'/\sigma]\gamma' \vdash^{[s'/\sigma]s} [s'/\sigma]e : [s'/\sigma]\tau} \text{ TT-TEq.}$$

– The other cases are straightforward.

Lemma 4 (Equivalence of the two equivalences). $\tau_1 \equiv \tau_2$ *iff* $\tau_1 \Longleftrightarrow^* \tau_2$.

Proof. Mostly the same as Lemma 30.3.5 of [22].

Lemma 5. $\tau_1 \Rightarrow \tau_1'$ *implies* $[\tau_1/\alpha]\tau \Rightarrow [\tau_1'/\alpha]\tau$.

Proof. By induction on the structure of τ.

Lemma 6. *If* $\tau_1 \Rightarrow \tau_1'$ *and* $\tau_2 \Rightarrow \tau_2'$, *then* $[\tau_1/\alpha]\tau_2 \Rightarrow [\tau_1'/\alpha]\tau_2'$.

Proof. Do the same thing as Lemma 30.3.7 of [22] by using Lemma 5.

Lemma 7 (One-step diamond property). *If* $\tau \Rightarrow \tau_1$ *and* $\tau \Rightarrow \tau_2$, *then there exists* τ' *such that* $\tau_1 \Rightarrow \tau'$ *and* $\tau_2 \Rightarrow \tau'$.

Proof. By induction on the derivation of $\tau \Rightarrow \tau_1$.

- Case $\dfrac{\tau_1' \Rightarrow \tau_1'' \qquad \tau_2' \Rightarrow \tau_2''}{(\Lambda\alpha :: \kappa.\ \tau_1')\ \tau_2' \Rightarrow [\tau_2''/\alpha]\tau_1''}$: The last rule for deriving $\tau \Rightarrow \tau_2$ is one of the following:

  - Case $\dfrac{}{\tau \Rightarrow \tau}$ is trivial.

  - Case $\dfrac{\tau_1' \Rightarrow \tau_1''' \qquad \tau_2' \Rightarrow \tau_2'''}{(\Lambda\alpha :: \kappa.\ \tau_1')\ \tau_2' \Rightarrow [\tau_2'''/\alpha]\tau_1'''}$: By IH, there exist τ_1'''' and τ_2'''' such that $\tau_1'' \Rightarrow \tau_1''''$, $\tau_1''' \Rightarrow \tau_1''''$, $\tau_2'' \Rightarrow \tau_2''''$, and $\tau_2''' \Rightarrow \tau_2''''$. Therefore, by Lemma 6, we have $[\tau_2''/\alpha]\tau_1'' \Rightarrow [\tau_2''''/\alpha]\tau_1''''$ and $[\tau_2'''/\alpha]\tau_1''' \Rightarrow [\tau_2''''/\alpha]\tau_1''''$.

  - Case $\dfrac{(\Lambda\alpha :: \kappa.\ \tau_1') \Rightarrow \tau_0 \qquad \tau_2' \Rightarrow \tau_2'''}{(\Lambda\alpha :: \kappa.\ \tau_1')\ \tau_2' \Rightarrow \tau_0\ \tau_2'''}$: By IH, from $\tau_2' \Rightarrow \tau_2''$ and $\tau_2' \Rightarrow \tau_2'''$, there exists τ_2'''' such that $\tau_2'' \Rightarrow \tau_2''''$ and $\tau_2''' \Rightarrow \tau_2''''$. The last rule for deriving $(\Lambda\alpha :: \kappa.\ \tau_1') \Rightarrow \tau_0$ is either of the following:

    * Case $\dfrac{}{\Lambda\alpha :: \kappa.\ \tau_1' \Rightarrow \Lambda\alpha :: \kappa.\ \tau_1'}$: Since $\tau_0 = \Lambda\alpha :: \kappa.\ \tau_1'$, we can derive $\dfrac{\tau_1' \Rightarrow \tau_1'' \qquad \tau_2''' \Rightarrow \tau_2''''}{\tau_0\ \tau_2''' \Rightarrow [\tau_2''''/\alpha]\tau_1''}$ and, at the same time, have $[\tau_2''/\alpha]\tau_1'' \Rightarrow [\tau_2''''/\alpha]\tau_1''$ by Lemma 5 and $\tau_2'' \Rightarrow \tau_2''''$.

    * Case $\dfrac{\tau_1' \Rightarrow \tau_1'''}{\Lambda\alpha :: \kappa.\ \tau_1' \Rightarrow \Lambda\alpha :: \kappa.\ \tau_1'''}$: By IH, from $\tau_1' \Rightarrow \tau_1''$ and $\tau_1' \Rightarrow \tau_1'''$, there exists τ_1'''' such that $\tau_1'' \Rightarrow \tau_1''''$ and $\tau_1''' \Rightarrow \tau_1''''$. Since $\tau_0 = \Lambda\alpha :: \kappa.\ \tau_1'''$, we can derive $\dfrac{\tau_1''' \Rightarrow \tau_1'''' \qquad \tau_2''' \Rightarrow \tau_2''''}{\tau_0\ \tau_2''' \Rightarrow [\tau_2''''/\alpha]\tau_1''''}$ and, at the same time, have $[\tau_2''/\alpha]\tau_1'' \Rightarrow [\tau_2''''/\alpha]\tau_1''''$ by Lemma 6, $\tau_1'' \Rightarrow \tau_1''''$, and $\tau_2'' \Rightarrow \tau_2''''$.

The other cases are more straightforward.

Lemma 8 (Confluence). *If* $\tau \Rightarrow^* \tau_1$ *and* $\tau \Rightarrow^* \tau_2$, *then there exists* τ' *such that* $\tau_1 \Rightarrow^* \tau'$ *and* $\tau_2 \Rightarrow^* \tau'$.

Proof. By repeated use of Lemma 7.

Lemma 9. *If* $\tau_1 \Longleftrightarrow^* \tau_2$, *then there exists* τ' *such that* $\tau_1 \Rightarrow^* \tau'$ *and* $\tau_2 \Rightarrow^* \tau'$.

Proof. By induction on the "length" of $\tau_1 \Longleftrightarrow^* \tau_2$.

- Case $\tau_1 = \tau_2$ trivially holds by $\tau' := \tau_1$.

- Case $\tau_1 \Leftarrow \tau_0$ and $\tau_0 \Longleftrightarrow^* \tau_2$ (where $\Leftarrow$ means the transposition of $\Rightarrow$): By IH, there exists τ'' such that $\tau_0 \Rightarrow^* \tau''$ and $\tau_2 \Rightarrow^* \tau''$. By Lemma 8, from $\tau_0 \Rightarrow \tau$ and $\tau_0 \Rightarrow^* \tau''$, there exists τ' such that $\tau \Rightarrow^* \tau'$ and $\tau'' \Rightarrow^* \tau'$. By transitivity, from $\tau_2 \Rightarrow^* \tau''$ and $\tau'' \Rightarrow^* \tau'$, we have $\tau_2 \Rightarrow^* \tau'$. Thus, both $\tau_1 \Rightarrow^* \tau'$ and $\tau_2 \Rightarrow^* \tau'$ hold.
- Case $\tau_1 \Rightarrow \tau_0$ and $\tau_0 \Longleftrightarrow^* \tau_2$: Again, there exists τ' such that $\tau_0 \Rightarrow^* \tau'$ and $\tau_2 \Rightarrow^* \tau'$ by IH. Then, by transitivity, from $\tau_1 \Rightarrow \tau_0$ and $\tau_0 \Rightarrow^* \tau'$, we also have $\tau_1 \Rightarrow^* \tau'$.

Corollary 1. *If $\tau_1 \equiv \tau_2$, then there exists τ' such that $\tau_1 \Rightarrow^* \tau'$ and $\tau_2 \Rightarrow^* \tau'$.*

Proof. Immediate from Lemma 4 and Lemma 9.

Lemma 10 (Preservation of forms by reduction on types).

1. *If $\tau_1 \to \tau_2 \Rightarrow^* \tau'$, then there exist τ_1' and τ_2' such that $\tau' = \tau_1' \to \tau_2'$, $\tau_1 \Rightarrow^* \tau_1'$, and $\tau_2 \Rightarrow^* \tau_2'$.*
2. *If $\forall \alpha :: \kappa.\ \tau_1 \Rightarrow^* \tau'$, then there exists τ_1' such that $\tau' = \forall \alpha :: \kappa.\ \tau_1'$ and $\tau_1 \Rightarrow^* \tau_1'$.*
3. *If $\exists \alpha :: \kappa.\ \tau_1 \Rightarrow^* \tau'$, then there exists τ_1' such that $\tau' = \exists \alpha :: \kappa.\ \tau_1'$ and $\tau_1 \Rightarrow^* \tau_1'$.*
4. *If $\{l_1 : \tau_1, \ldots, l_m : \tau_m\} \Rightarrow^* \tau'$, then there exist $\tau_1', \ldots, \tau_m'$ such that $\tau' = \{l_1 : \tau_1', \ldots, l_m : \tau_m'\}$ and $\tau_i \Rightarrow^* \tau_i'$ for each i.*
5. *If $\langle \tau_1 \rangle \Rightarrow^* \tau'$, then there exists τ_1' such that $\tau' = \langle \tau_1' \rangle$ and $\tau_1 \Rightarrow^* \tau_1'$.*

Proof. By straightforward induction on the "length" of reduction sequences.

Lemma 11 (Inversion).

1. *If $\gamma \vdash^s (\lambda x : \tau_1.\ e) : \tau$, $\tau \equiv \tau_1' \to \tau_2'$, and $\gamma \vdash \tau_1' \to \tau_2' :: *$, then we have $\tau_1 \equiv \tau_1'$, $\gamma, x : \tau_1^s \vdash^s e : \tau_2'$, and $\gamma \vdash \tau_1 :: *$.*
2. *If $\gamma \vdash^s (\Lambda \alpha :: \kappa.\ e) : \tau$, $\tau \equiv \forall \alpha :: \kappa'.\ \tau'$, and $\gamma \vdash (\forall \alpha :: \kappa'.\ \tau') :: *$, then we have $\kappa = \kappa'$ and $\gamma, \alpha :: \kappa \vdash^s e : \tau'$.*
3. *If $\gamma \vdash^0 (\mathbf{pack}\ (\tau_1, e)\ \mathbf{as}\ \tau_2) : \tau$, $\tau \equiv \exists \alpha :: \kappa.\ \tau_1'$, and $\gamma \vdash (\exists \alpha :: \kappa.\ \tau_1') :: *$, then we have $\tau \equiv \tau_2$, $\gamma \vdash \tau_1 :: *$, and $\gamma \vdash^0 e : [\tau_1/\alpha]\tau_1'$.*
4. *If $\gamma \vdash^s \{l_1 = e_1, \ldots, l_m = e_m\} : \tau$, $\tau \equiv \{l_1 : \tau_1', \ldots, l_m : \tau_m'\}$, and $\gamma \vdash \{l_1 : \tau_1', \ldots, l_m : \tau_m'\} :: *$, then, for each $i \in \{1, \ldots, m\}$, we have $\gamma \vdash^s e_i : \tau_i'$.*
5. *If $\gamma \vdash^s \langle e \rangle : \tau$, $\tau \equiv \langle \tau_1' \rangle$, and $\gamma \vdash \langle \tau_1' \rangle :: *$, then we have $\gamma \vdash^{s+1} e : \tau_1'$.*
6. *If $\gamma \vdash^0 (\Lambda \sigma.\ e) : \tau$, $\tau \equiv \forall \sigma.\ \tau'$, and $\gamma \vdash (\forall \sigma.\ \tau') :: *$, then we have $\gamma, \sigma \vdash^0 e : \tau'$.*

Proof. By induction on the derivation. We only show 1; the others can be proved in a similar manner. The last rule for deriving $\gamma \vdash^s (\lambda x : \tau_1.\ e) : \tau$ is either TT-TEQ or TT-ABS.

- Case $\dfrac{\gamma \vdash^s (\lambda x : \tau_1.\ e) : \tau' \qquad \tau' \equiv \tau \qquad \gamma \vdash \tau :: *}{\gamma \vdash^s (\lambda x : \tau_1.\ e) : \tau}$ TT-TEQ: Since we can

  derive $\dfrac{\tau' \equiv \tau \qquad \tau \equiv \tau_1' \to \tau_2'}{\tau' \equiv \tau_1' \to \tau_2'}$, we have $\tau_1 \equiv \tau_1'$, $\gamma, x : \tau_1^s \vdash^s e : \tau_2'$, and $\gamma \vdash \tau_1 :: *$ by IH.

- Case $\dfrac{\gamma, x : \tau_1^s \vdash^s e : \tau_2}{\gamma \vdash^s (\lambda x : \tau_1. \, e) : \tau_1 \to \tau_2}$ TT-ABS: By Collorary 1 and $\tau_1 \to \tau_2 \equiv \tau_1' \to \tau_2'$, there exists τ'' such that $\tau_1 \to \tau_2 \Rrightarrow^* \tau''$ and $\tau_1' \to \tau_2' \Rrightarrow^* \tau''$. Then, by Lemma 10, there exist τ_1'' and τ_2'' such that $\tau'' = \tau_1'' \to \tau_2''$, $\tau_1 \Rrightarrow^* \tau_1''$, $\tau_2 \Rrightarrow^* \tau_2''$, $\tau_1' \Rrightarrow^* \tau_1''$, and $\tau_2' \Rrightarrow^* \tau_2''$. Thus, by Lemma 4, we have $\tau_2 \equiv \tau_2''$ and $\tau_2'' \equiv \tau_2'$. Since $\gamma \vdash \tau_2' :: *$ holds by tracing back the derivation of the assumption $\gamma \vdash \tau_1' \to \tau_2' :: *$, we can derive:

$$\dfrac{\gamma, x : \tau_1^s \vdash^s e : \tau_2 \qquad \dfrac{\tau_2 \equiv \tau_2'' \qquad \tau_2'' \equiv \tau_2'}{\tau_2 \equiv \tau_2'} \qquad \gamma \vdash \tau_2' :: *}{\gamma, x : \tau_1^s \vdash^s e : \tau_2'.} \text{TT-TEQ}$$

Lemma 12. $\gamma \vdash^s e : \tau$ implies $\vdash \gamma$ and $\gamma \vdash \tau :: *$.

Proof. By straightforward induction on the derivation of $\gamma \vdash^s e : \tau$.

Theorem 1 (Preservation). If $\gamma \vdash^n e : \tau$ and $e \xrightarrow{n} e'$, then $\gamma \vdash^n e' : \tau$.

Proof. By induction on the derivation of $\gamma \vdash^n e : \tau$. We implicitly use Lemma 12 in the proof below.

- Case $\dfrac{\gamma \vdash^{n+1} e_1 : \tau'}{\gamma' \vdash^n \langle e_1 \rangle : \langle \tau' \rangle}$ TT-BRKT: The last rule for deriving $\langle e_1 \rangle \xrightarrow{n} e'$ is TE-BRKT, and thus we have $e_1 \xrightarrow{n+1} e_1'$ and $e' = \langle e_1' \rangle$. By IH, we have $\gamma \vdash^{n+1} e_1' : \tau'$, and can thereby derive $\dfrac{\gamma \vdash^{n+1} e_1' : \tau'}{\gamma \vdash^n \langle e_1' \rangle : \tau'}$ TT-BRKT.

- Case $\dfrac{\gamma \vdash^{n-1} e_1 : \langle \tau \rangle}{\gamma \vdash^n \sim e_1 : \tau}$ TT-ESC: The last rule for deriving $\sim e_1 \xrightarrow{n} e'$ is either TE-ESC1 or TE-ESC2.
  - Case TE-ESC1 is straightforward by IH.
  - Case TE-ESC2: We have $n = 1$, $e_1 = \langle v^{(1)} \rangle$, and $e' = v^{(1)}$. By Lemma 11, we have $\gamma \vdash^1 v^{(1)} : \tau$.

- Case $\dfrac{\gamma \vdash^0 e_1 : \exists \alpha :: \kappa. \, \tau_1 \qquad \gamma, \alpha :: \kappa, x : \tau_1^0 \vdash^0 e_2 : \tau \qquad \gamma \vdash \tau :: *}{\gamma \vdash^0 \mathbf{unpack} \, (\alpha, x) = e_1 \, \mathbf{in} \, e_2 : \tau}$ TT-UNPACK: The last rule for deriving $(\mathbf{unpack} \, (\alpha, x) = e_1 \, \mathbf{in} \, e_2) \xrightarrow{n} e'$ is either TE-UNPACK1 or TE-UNPACK2.
  - Case TE-UNPACK1 is straightforward from IH.
  - Case TE-UNPACK2: We have $n = 0$, $e_1 = (\mathbf{pack} \, (\tau_1', v^{(0)}) \, \mathbf{as} \, \tau')$, and $e' = [v^{(0)}/x][\tau_1'/\alpha]e_2$. By Lemma 11, we have $\exists \alpha :: \kappa. \, \tau_1 \equiv \tau'$, $\gamma \vdash \tau_1' :: *$, and $\gamma \vdash^0 v^{(0)} : [\tau_1'/\alpha]\tau_1$. Then, by Lemma 2, from $\gamma, \alpha :: \kappa, x : \tau_1^0 \vdash^0 e_2 : \tau$ and $\gamma \vdash \tau_1' :: *$, we have $\gamma, x : [\tau_1'/\alpha]\tau_1^0 \vdash^0 [\tau_1'/\alpha]e_2 : [\tau_1'/\alpha]\tau$. Since $\alpha \notin ftv(\tau)$ holds by $\gamma \vdash \tau :: *$, we have $[\tau_1'/\alpha]\tau = \tau$. Therefore, by Lemma 1, we have $\gamma \vdash^0 [v^{(0)}/x][\tau_1'/\alpha]e_2 : \tau$.

- Case $\dfrac{\gamma \vdash^0 e_1 : \forall \sigma.\ \tau' \qquad \gamma \vdash s_2}{\gamma \vdash^0 e_1 \uparrow s_2 : [s_2/\sigma]\tau'}$ TT-STGAPP: The last rule for deriving $(e_1 \uparrow s_2) \xrightarrow{n} e'$ is either TE-STGAPP or TE-STGBETA.
  - Case TE-STGAPP is straightforward by IH.
  - Case TE-STGBETA: We have $n = 0$, $s_2 = n'$, $e = \Lambda\sigma.\ e_{11}$, and $e' = [n'/\sigma]e_{11}$. By Lemma 11, we have $\gamma, \sigma \vdash^0 e_{11} : \tau'$. Therefore, by Lemma 3, we have $\gamma \vdash^0 [n'/\sigma]e_{11} : [n'/\sigma]\tau'$.
- Cases TT-STGABS, TT-BRKTVAR, and TT-ESCVAR contradict the assumption $e \xrightarrow{n} e'$.

The other cases can be shown in similar ways by using IH and Lemma 11.

Lemma 13. *Suppose $\vdash^{\geq 1} \gamma$ and γ does not contain stage variables.*

1. *If $\gamma \vdash^0 v^{(0)} : \tau \to \tau'$, then $v^{(0)}$ is of the form $(\lambda x : \tau_1.\ e)$.*
2. *If $\gamma \vdash^0 v^{(0)} : \forall \alpha :: \kappa.\ \tau$, then $v^{(0)}$ is of the form $(\Lambda \alpha :: \kappa.\ e)$.*
3. *If $\gamma \vdash^0 v^{(0)} : \exists \alpha :: \kappa.\ \tau$, then $v^{(0)}$ is of the form $\mathbf{pack}\ (\tau_1, e)\ \mathbf{as}\ \tau_2$.*
4. *If $\gamma \vdash^0 v^{(0)} : \{l_1 : \tau_1, \ldots, l_m : \tau_m\}$, then $v^{(0)}$ is of the form $\{l_1 = v_1^{(0)}, \ldots, l_m = v_m^{(0)}\}$.*
5. *If $\gamma \vdash^0 v^{(0)} : \langle \tau \rangle$, then $v^{(0)}$ is of the form $\langle v_1^{(1)} \rangle$.*
6. *If $\gamma \vdash^0 v^{(0)} : \forall \sigma.\ \tau$, then $v^{(0)}$ is of the form $(\Lambda \sigma.\ e)$.*

Proof. Almost the same as Lemma 30.1.15 of [22]; by contradiction about the form of $v^{(0)}$ using Lemmata 1 and 10.

Theorem 2 (Progress). *If $\vdash^{\geq 1} \gamma$, $\gamma \vdash^n e : \tau$, and γ does not contain stage variables, then e is a value at stage n, or there exists e' such that $e \xrightarrow{n} e'$.*

Proof. By induction on the derivation of $\gamma \vdash^n e : \tau$.

- Case $\dfrac{\vdash \gamma \qquad \gamma(x) = \tau^n}{\gamma \vdash^n x : \tau}$ TT-VAR: By the assumption $\vdash^{\geq 1} \gamma$, we have $n \geq 1$. Thus, x is a value at stage $n \geq 1$.
- Case $\dfrac{\gamma, x : \tau_1^n \vdash^n e_2 : \tau_2}{\gamma \vdash^n (\lambda x : \tau_1.\ e_2) : \tau_1 \to \tau_2}$ TT-ABS:
  - Case $n = 0$: $\lambda x : \tau_1.\ e_2$ is a value at stage 0.
  - Case $n \geq 1$: Since $\vdash^{\geq 1} \gamma, x : \tau_1^n$ holds, we have either of the following by IH:
    * Case where e_2 is a value $v_2^{(n)}$: $\lambda x : \tau_1.\ v_2^{(n)}$ is a value at stage n.
    * Case where $e_2 \xrightarrow{n} e_2'$ for some e_2': We can derive:
      $$\dfrac{e_2 \xrightarrow{n} e_2'}{\lambda x : \tau_1.\ e_2 \xrightarrow{n} \lambda x : \tau_1.\ e_2'}\ \text{TE-ABS.}$$
- Case $\dfrac{\gamma \vdash^n e_1 : \tau_2 \to \tau \qquad \gamma \vdash^n e_2 : \tau_2}{\gamma \vdash^n e_1\ e_2 : \tau}$ TT-APP:
  - Case where $e_1 \xrightarrow{n} e_1'$ for some e_1': We can derive
    $$\dfrac{e_1 \xrightarrow{n} e_1'}{e_1\ e_2 \xrightarrow{n} e_1'\ e_2}\ \text{TE-APP1.}$$

- Case where e_1 is a value $v_1^{(n)}$ and $e_2 \xrightarrow{n} e_2'$ for some e_2': We can derive

$$\frac{e_2 \xrightarrow{n} e_2'}{v_1^{(n)}\, e_2 \xrightarrow{n} v_1^{(n)}\, e_2'}\ \text{TE-App2}.$$

- Case where both e_1 and e_2 are values $v_1^{(n)}$ and $v_2^{(n)}$, respectively:
  * Case $n \geq 1$: $(v_1^{(n)}\, v_2^{(n)})$ is a value at stage $n \geq 1$.
  * Case $n = 0$: By Lemma 13, $v_1^{(0)}$ is of the form $(\lambda x : \tau_{11}.\, e_{12})$. Thus, we can derive $\dfrac{}{(\lambda x : \tau_{11}.\, e_{12})\, v_2^{(0)} \xrightarrow{0} [v_2^{(0)}/x]e_{12}}\ \text{TE-Beta}.$

$\dfrac{\gamma \vdash^{n-1} e_1 : \langle \tau \rangle}{\gamma \vdash^n \sim e_1 : \tau}\ \text{TT-Esc}$: We have $n \geq 1$. By IH, one of the following holds:

- Case where $e_1 \xrightarrow{n-1} e_1'$ for some e_1': We can derive $\dfrac{e_1 \xrightarrow{n-1} e_1'}{\sim e_1 \xrightarrow{n} \sim e_1'}\ \text{TE-Esc1}.$

- Case where e_1 is a value $v_1^{(n-1)}$:
  * Case $n \geq 2$: $\sim v_1^{(n-1)}$ is a value at stage n.
  * Case $n = 1$: By Lemma 13, $v_1^{(0)}$ is of the form $\langle v^{(1)} \rangle$. Therefore, we can derive $\dfrac{}{\sim\langle v^{(1)} \rangle \xrightarrow{1} v^{(1)}}\ \text{TE-Esc2}.$

The other cases are similar.

D   Proofs for Soundness of Elaboration

Assumption 5. *1. If $\Gamma \vdash \tau \leqslant \tau' \rightsquigarrow e$, then $\mathrm{fsv}(\tau) = \mathrm{fsv}(\tau') = \varnothing$ (i.e., neither τ nor τ' contains free stage variables), $\mathrm{fv}(e) = \varnothing$ (i.e., e is a closed term), $\lfloor \Gamma \rfloor \vdash \tau :: *$, $\lfloor \Gamma \rfloor \vdash \tau' :: *$, and, for any stage s, we have $\lfloor \Gamma \rfloor \vdash^s e : \tau \to \tau'$.*

2. The constructs for source types T other than $T \to T$, $(T\ T)$, P, or $\langle T \rangle$ do not violate the property that $\Gamma \vdash T::\kappa \rightsquigarrow \tau$ implies $\lfloor \Gamma \rfloor \vdash \tau :: \kappa$.

3. The constructs for source expressions E other than x, $(\lambda x : T.\ E)$, $(E\ E)$, P, $\langle E \rangle$, or $\sim E$ do not violate the property that $\Gamma \vdash^s E : \tau \rightsquigarrow e$ implies $\lfloor \Gamma \rfloor \vdash^s e : \tau$ and $\mathrm{fsv}(\tau) = \varnothing$.

Theorem 3 (Soundness of Signature Subtyping).

1. If $\Gamma \vdash \Sigma \leqslant \exists \boldsymbol{b}.\ \Sigma' \uparrow (\tau_i)_{i=1}^m \rightsquigarrow e$ and $\lfloor \Gamma \rfloor, \boldsymbol{b} \vdash \lfloor \Sigma' \rfloor :: *$, then $\lfloor \Gamma \rfloor \vdash^0 e : \lfloor \Sigma \rfloor \to \lfloor [\tau_i/\alpha_i]_{i=1}^m \Sigma' \rfloor$, $\mathrm{fsv}(\Sigma) = \mathrm{fsv}(\Sigma') = \varnothing$, and $\lfloor \Gamma \rfloor \vdash \tau_i :: \kappa_i$ for each i, where $\boldsymbol{b} = (\alpha_i :: \kappa_i)_{i=1}^m$.

2. $\Gamma \vdash \Sigma \leqslant \Sigma' \rightsquigarrow e$ implies $\lfloor \Gamma \rfloor \vdash \lfloor \Sigma \rfloor :: *$, $\lfloor \Gamma \rfloor \vdash \lfloor \Sigma' \rfloor :: *$, $\mathrm{fsv}(\Sigma) = \mathrm{fsv}(\Sigma') = \varnothing$, and $\lfloor \Gamma \rfloor \vdash^0 e : \lfloor \Sigma \rfloor \to \lfloor \Sigma' \rfloor$.

3. $\Gamma \vdash \xi \leqslant \xi' \rightsquigarrow e$ implies $\lfloor \Gamma \rfloor \vdash \lfloor \xi \rfloor :: *$, $\lfloor \Gamma \rfloor \vdash \lfloor \xi' \rfloor :: *$, $\mathrm{fsv}(\xi) = \mathrm{fsv}(\xi') = \varnothing$, and $\lfloor \Gamma \rfloor \vdash^0 e : \lfloor \xi \rfloor \to \lfloor \xi' \rfloor$.

Proof. By mutual induction on the derivation. We only show the cases of U-Val, U-PersAsPers, and U-PersAsNonPers for 2; the others are almost the same as the corresponding proofs for F-ing Modules [24].

– Case
$$\dfrac{\Gamma \vdash \tau \leqslant \tau' \rightsquigarrow e'}{\Gamma \vdash [\![\tau]\!]^n \leqslant [\![\tau']\!]^n \rightsquigarrow \lambda x : \langle\!\langle \{\mathtt{val} : \tau\} \rangle\!\rangle^{\times n}. \langle\!\langle \{\mathtt{val} = e' \, ((\sim^{\times n} x)\#\mathtt{val})\} \rangle\!\rangle^{\times n}} \;\text{U-Val:}$$

By $\Gamma \vdash \tau \leqslant \tau' \rightsquigarrow e'$ and Assumption 5, we have $\lfloor \Gamma \rfloor \vdash^n e' : \tau \to \tau'$, $\lfloor \Gamma \rfloor \vdash \tau :: *$, $\lfloor \Gamma \rfloor \vdash \tau' :: *$, $\mathrm{fsv}(\tau) = \mathrm{fsv}(\tau') = \varnothing$, and $\mathrm{fv}(e') = \varnothing$. Since $\gamma \vdash^n e' : \tau \to \tau'$ holds by the evident weakening, we can derive the following, where $\gamma := \lfloor \Gamma \rfloor, x : \lfloor [\![\tau]\!]^n \rfloor^0$:

$$\dfrac{\gamma \vdash^n e' : \tau \to \tau' \qquad \dfrac{\dfrac{\dfrac{\gamma \vdash^0 x : \langle\!\langle \{\mathtt{val} : \tau\} \rangle\!\rangle^{\times n}}{\vdots}}{\dfrac{\gamma \vdash^n \sim^{\times n} x : \{\mathtt{val} : \tau\}}{\gamma \vdash^n (\sim^{\times n} x)\#\mathtt{val} : \tau}}}{\gamma \vdash^n e' \, ((\sim^{\times n} x)\#\mathtt{val}) : \tau'}}{\dfrac{\dfrac{\gamma \vdash^n \{\mathtt{val} = e' \, ((\sim^{\times n} x)\#\mathtt{val})\} : \{\mathtt{val} : \tau'\}}{\vdots}}{\dfrac{\gamma \vdash^0 \langle\!\langle \{\mathtt{val} = e' \, ((\sim^{\times n} x)\#\mathtt{val})\} \rangle\!\rangle^{\times n} : \lfloor [\![\tau']\!]^n \rfloor}{\lfloor \Gamma \rfloor \vdash^0 \lambda x : \langle\!\langle \{\mathtt{val} : \tau\} \rangle\!\rangle^{\times n}. \langle\!\langle \{\mathtt{val} = e' \, ((\sim^{\times n} x)\#\mathtt{val})\} \rangle\!\rangle^{\times n} : \lfloor [\![\tau]\!]^n \rfloor \to \lfloor [\![\tau']\!]^n \rfloor.}}}$$

We also have $\lfloor \Gamma \rfloor \vdash \lfloor [\![\tau]\!]^n \rfloor :: *$, $\lfloor \Gamma \rfloor \vdash \lfloor [\![\tau']\!]^n \rfloor :: *$, and $\mathrm{fsv}([\![\tau]\!]^n) = \mathrm{fsv}([\![\tau']\!]^n) = \varnothing$.

– Case
$$\dfrac{\Gamma \vdash \tau \leqslant \tau' \rightsquigarrow e' \qquad n \leq n' \qquad e'' = \sim^{\times n'} \sim^{\sigma'} (x \uparrow ((n'-n)+\sigma'))}{\Gamma \vdash [\![\tau]\!]^{\geq n} \leqslant [\![\tau']\!]^{\geq n'} \rightsquigarrow \lambda x : \lfloor [\![\tau]\!]^{\geq n} \rfloor. \Lambda \sigma'. \langle\!\langle \{\mathtt{val} = e' \, (e''\#\mathtt{val})\} \rangle\!\rangle^{\times n'})^{\sigma'}} \;\text{U-PersAsPers:}$$

Let $\gamma := (\lfloor \Gamma \rfloor, x : \lfloor [\![\tau]\!]^{\geq n} \rfloor^0, \sigma')$. Similarly to the previous case, we have $\gamma \vdash^{n'+\sigma'} e' : \tau \to \tau'$, $\mathrm{fsv}(\tau) = \mathrm{fsv}(\tau') = \varnothing$, and $\mathrm{fv}(e') = \varnothing$. Since $[(n'-n)+\sigma'/\sigma]\tau = \tau$, we can derive:

$$\dfrac{\gamma \vdash^{n'+\sigma'} e' : \tau \to \tau' \qquad \dfrac{\dfrac{\dfrac{\dfrac{\gamma \vdash^0 x : \forall \sigma. \langle\!\langle (\{\mathtt{val} : \tau\})^{\times n} \rangle\!\rangle^{\sigma}}{\gamma \vdash^0 x \uparrow ((n'-n)+\sigma') : \langle\!\langle (\{\mathtt{val} : \tau\})^{\times n'} \rangle\!\rangle^{\sigma'}}}{\gamma \vdash^{0+\sigma'} \sim^{\sigma'} (x \uparrow ((n'-n)+\sigma')) : \langle\!\langle \{\mathtt{val} : \tau\} \rangle\!\rangle^{\times n'}}}{\vdots}}{\dfrac{\gamma \vdash^{n'+\sigma'} e'' : \{\mathtt{val} : \tau\}}{\gamma \vdash^{n'+\sigma'} e''\#\mathtt{val} : \tau}}}{\gamma \vdash^{n'+\sigma'} e' \, (e''\#\mathtt{val}) : \tau'}}$$

$$\dfrac{\dfrac{\dfrac{\gamma \vdash^{n'+\sigma'} \{\mathtt{val} = e' \, (e''\#\mathtt{val})\} : \{\mathtt{val} : \tau'\}}{\vdots}}{\dfrac{\gamma \vdash^{0+\sigma'} \langle\!\langle \{\mathtt{val} = e' \, (e''\#\mathtt{val})\} \rangle\!\rangle^{\times n'} : \langle\!\langle \{\mathtt{val} : \tau'\} \rangle\!\rangle^{\times n'}}{\dfrac{\gamma \vdash^0 \langle\!\langle \langle\!\langle \{\mathtt{val} = e' \, (e''\#\mathtt{val})\} \rangle\!\rangle^{\times n'} \rangle\!\rangle^{\sigma'} : \langle\!\langle \langle\!\langle \{\mathtt{val} : \tau'\} \rangle\!\rangle^{\times n'} \rangle\!\rangle^{\sigma'}}{\dfrac{\lfloor \Gamma \rfloor, x : \lfloor [\![\tau]\!]^{\geq n} \rfloor^0 \vdash^0 \Lambda \sigma'. \langle\!\langle \langle\!\langle \{\mathtt{val} = e' \, (e''\#\mathtt{val})\} \rangle\!\rangle^{\times n'} \rangle\!\rangle^{\sigma'} : \lfloor [\![\tau']\!]^{\geq n'} \rfloor}{\lfloor \Gamma \rfloor \vdash^0 \lambda x : \lfloor [\![\tau]\!]^{\geq n} \rfloor. \Lambda \sigma'. \langle\!\langle \langle\!\langle \{\mathtt{val} = e' \, (e''\#\mathtt{val})\} \rangle\!\rangle^{\times n'} \rangle\!\rangle^{\sigma'} : \lfloor [\![\tau]\!]^{\geq n} \rfloor \to \lfloor [\![\tau']\!]^{\geq n'} \rfloor.}}}}}$$

– Case
$$\dfrac{\Gamma \vdash \tau \leqslant \tau' \rightsquigarrow e' \qquad n \leq n' \qquad e'' = \sim^{\times n'} (x \uparrow (n'-n))}{\Gamma \vdash [\![\tau]\!]^{\geq n} \leqslant [\![\tau']\!]^{n'} \rightsquigarrow \lambda x : \lfloor [\![\tau]\!]^{\geq n} \rfloor. \langle\!\langle \{\mathtt{val} = e' \, (e''\#\mathtt{val})\} \rangle\!\rangle^{\times n'}} \;\text{U-PersAsNonPers:}$$
We can derive the following in a manner similar to the previous case, where $\gamma := \lfloor \Gamma \rfloor, x : \lfloor [\![\tau]\!]^{\geq n} \rfloor^0$:

$$\frac{\gamma \vdash^0 x : \forall \sigma.\; \langle\!\langle\{\mathtt{val} : \tau\}\rangle\!\rangle^{\times n})^{\sigma}}{\gamma \vdash^0 x \uparrow (n' - n) : \langle\!\langle\{\mathtt{val} : \tau\}\rangle\!\rangle^{\times n'}}$$

$$\vdots$$

$$\frac{\gamma \vdash^{n'} e' : \tau \to \tau' \qquad \dfrac{\gamma \vdash^{n'} e'' : \{\mathtt{val} : \tau\}}{\gamma \vdash^{n'} e''\#\mathtt{val} : \tau}}{\dfrac{\gamma \vdash^{n'} e'\;(e''\#\mathtt{val}) : \tau'}{\gamma \vdash^{n'} \{\mathtt{val} = e'\;(e''\#\mathtt{val})\} : \{\mathtt{val} : \tau'\}}}$$

$$\vdots$$

$$\frac{\gamma \vdash^0 \langle\!\langle\{\mathtt{val} = e\;(e'\#\mathtt{val})\}\rangle\!\rangle^{\times n'} : \lfloor[\![\tau']\!]^{n'}\rfloor}{\lfloor \Gamma \rfloor \vdash^0 \lambda x : \lfloor[\![\tau]\!]^{\geq n}\rfloor.\; \langle\!\langle\{\mathtt{val} = e\;(e'\#\mathtt{val})\}\rangle\!\rangle^{\times n'} : \lfloor[\![\tau]\!]^{\geq n}\rfloor \to \lfloor[\![\tau']\!]^{n'}\rfloor.}$$

Theorem 4 (Soundness of Elaboration).

1. $\Gamma \vdash T :: \kappa \leadsto \tau$ *implies* $\lfloor \Gamma \rfloor \vdash \tau :: \kappa$ *and* $\mathrm{fsv}(\tau) = \varnothing$.
2. $\Gamma \vdash^s E : \tau \leadsto e$ *implies* $\lfloor \Gamma \rfloor \vdash^s e : \tau$ *and* $\mathrm{fsv}(\tau) = \varnothing$.
3. $\Gamma \vdash P : \Sigma \leadsto e$ *implies* $\lfloor \Gamma \rfloor \vdash^0 e : \lfloor \Sigma \rfloor$ *and* $\mathrm{fsv}(\Sigma) = \varnothing$.
4. $\Gamma \vdash D \leadsto \exists \boldsymbol{b}.\; R$ (*resp.* $\Gamma \vdash D \leadsto \exists \boldsymbol{b}.\; R$) *implies* $\lfloor \Gamma \rfloor \vdash \lfloor \exists \boldsymbol{b}.\; \{R\} \rfloor :: *$ *and* $\mathrm{fsv}(\exists \boldsymbol{b}.\; \{R\}) = \varnothing$.
5. $\Gamma \vdash B : \exists \boldsymbol{b}.\; R \leadsto e$ (*resp.* $\Gamma \vdash B : \exists \boldsymbol{b}.\; R \leadsto e$) *implies* $\lfloor \Gamma \rfloor \vdash^0 e : \lfloor \exists \boldsymbol{b}.\; \{R\} \rfloor$ *and* $\mathrm{fsv}(\exists \boldsymbol{b}.\; \{R\}) = \varnothing$.
6. $\Gamma \vdash S \leadsto \xi$ *implies* $\lfloor \Gamma \rfloor \vdash \lfloor \xi \rfloor :: *$ *and* $\mathrm{fsv}(\xi) = \varnothing$.
7. $\Gamma \vdash M : \xi \leadsto e$ *implies* $\lfloor \Gamma \rfloor \vdash^0 e : \lfloor \xi \rfloor$ *and* $\mathrm{fsv}(\xi) = \varnothing$.

Proof. By mutual induction on the derivation. We only show the proofs about E-Path, E-PersInPers, E-PersInNonPers, B-Val, and B-ValPers for 2 and 5; the rest of the proofs are quite straightforward or essentially the same as the corresponding ones for F-ing Modules [24].

2. – Case $\dfrac{\Gamma \vdash P : [\![\tau]\!]^n \leadsto e'}{\Gamma \vdash^n P : \tau \leadsto (\sim^{\times n} e')\#\mathtt{val}}$ E-Path: We have $\lfloor \Gamma \rfloor \vdash^0 e' : \langle\!\langle\{\mathtt{val} :$ $\tau\}\rangle\!\rangle^{\times n}$ and $\mathrm{fsv}([\![\tau]\!]^n) = \varnothing$ by IH. Thus, we can derive:

$$\lfloor \Gamma \rfloor \vdash^0 e' : \langle\!\langle\{\mathtt{val} : \tau\}\rangle\!\rangle^{\times n}$$

$$\vdots$$

$$\frac{\lfloor \Gamma \rfloor \vdash^n \sim^{\times n} e' : \{\mathtt{val} : \tau\}}{\lfloor \Gamma \rfloor \vdash^n (\sim^{\times n} e')\#\mathtt{val} : \tau.}$$

We also have $\mathrm{fsv}(\tau) = \varnothing$ by $\mathrm{fsv}([\![\tau]\!]^n) = \varnothing$.

– Case $\dfrac{\sigma \in \Gamma \qquad \Gamma \vdash P : [\![\tau]\!]^{\geq n'} \leadsto e' \qquad n \geq n'}{\Gamma \vdash^{n+\sigma} P : \tau \leadsto (\sim^{\times n} \sim^{\sigma}(e' \uparrow ((n - n') + \sigma)))\#\mathtt{val}}$ E-PersInPers: By IH, we have $\lfloor \Gamma \rfloor \vdash^0 e' : \forall \sigma'.\; \langle\!\langle\{\mathtt{val} : \tau\}\rangle\!\rangle^{\times n})^{\sigma'}$ and $\mathrm{fsv}([\![\tau]\!]^{\geq n'}) = \varnothing$. Then, we have $\mathrm{fsv}(\tau) = \varnothing$ and thereby $[(n - n') + \sigma/\sigma']\tau = \tau$. This enables us to derive:

$$\cfrac{\cfrac{\lfloor \Gamma \rfloor \vdash^0 e' : \forall \sigma'. \langle\!\langle\{\mathtt{val} : \tau\}\rangle^{\times n'}\rangle^{\sigma'} \qquad \cfrac{\sigma \in \lfloor \Gamma \rfloor}{\lfloor \Gamma \rfloor \vdash (n - n') \dotplus \sigma}}{\lfloor \Gamma \rfloor \vdash^0 e' \uparrow ((n - n') \dotplus \sigma) : \langle\!\langle\{\mathtt{val} : \tau\}\rangle^{\times n}\rangle^{\sigma}}}{\lfloor \Gamma \rfloor \vdash^{0 + \sigma} \sim^{\sigma}(e' \uparrow ((n - n') \dotplus \sigma)) : \langle\{\mathtt{val} : \tau\}\rangle^{\times n}}$$

$$\vdots$$

$$\cfrac{\lfloor \Gamma \rfloor \vdash^{n + \sigma} \sim^{\times n}\sim^{\sigma}(e' \uparrow ((n - n') \dotplus \sigma)) : \{\mathtt{val} : \tau\}}{\lfloor \Gamma \rfloor \vdash^{n + \sigma} (\sim^{\times n}\sim^{\sigma}(e' \uparrow ((n - n') \dotplus \sigma)))\#\mathtt{val} : \tau.}$$

- Case $\cfrac{\Gamma \vdash P : [\![\tau]\!]^{\geq n'} \rightsquigarrow e' \qquad n \geq n'}{\Gamma \vdash^n P : \tau \rightsquigarrow (\sim^{\times n}(e' \uparrow (n - n')))\#\mathtt{val}}$ E-PersInNonPers: Similarly

to the previous case, we have $\mathrm{fsv}(\tau) = \varnothing$ and can thereby derive:

$$\cfrac{\lfloor \Gamma \rfloor \vdash^0 e' : \forall \sigma'. \langle\!\langle\{\mathtt{val} : \tau\}\rangle^{\times n'}\rangle^{\sigma'} \qquad \lfloor \Gamma \rfloor \vdash n - n'}{\lfloor \Gamma \rfloor \vdash^0 e' \uparrow (n - n') : \langle\{\mathtt{val} : \tau\}\rangle^{\times n}}$$

$$\vdots$$

$$\cfrac{\lfloor \Gamma \rfloor \vdash^n \sim^{\times n}(e' \uparrow (n - n')) : \{\mathtt{val} : \tau\}}{\lfloor \Gamma \rfloor \vdash^n (\sim^{\times n}(e' \uparrow (n - n')))\#\mathtt{val} : \tau.}$$

5. - Case $\cfrac{\Gamma \vdash^n E : \tau \rightsquigarrow e'}{\Gamma \vdash \mathtt{val}^n X = E : \exists \varepsilon. \{l_X \mapsto [\![\tau]\!]^n\} \rightsquigarrow \{l_X = \langle\{\mathtt{val} = e'\}\rangle^{\times n}\}}$ B-Val: By IH,

we have $\lfloor \Gamma \rfloor \vdash^n e' : \tau$ and $\mathrm{fsv}(\tau) = \varnothing$. Thus, we can derive:

$$\cfrac{\lfloor \Gamma \rfloor \vdash^n e' : \tau}{\lfloor \Gamma \rfloor \vdash^n \{\mathtt{val} = e'\} : \{\mathtt{val} : \tau\}}$$

$$\vdots$$

$$\cfrac{\lfloor \Gamma \rfloor \vdash^0 \langle\{\mathtt{val} = e'\}\rangle^{\times n} : \langle\{\mathtt{val} : \tau\}\rangle^{\times n}}{\lfloor \Gamma \rfloor \vdash^0 \{l_X = \langle\{\mathtt{val} = e'\}\rangle^{\times n}\} : \{l_X : \lfloor [\![\tau]\!]^n \rfloor\}}$$

and have $\mathrm{fsv}(\lfloor \exists \varepsilon. \{R\} \rfloor) = \mathrm{fsv}(\tau) = \varnothing$.

- Case $\cfrac{\sigma \notin \Gamma \qquad \Gamma, \sigma \vdash^{n + \sigma} E : \tau \rightsquigarrow e'}{\Gamma \vdash \mathtt{val}^{\geq n} X = E : \exists \varepsilon. \{l_X \mapsto [\![\tau]\!]^{\geq n}\} \rightsquigarrow \{l_X = \Lambda\sigma. \langle\!\langle\{\mathtt{val} = e'\}\rangle^{\times n}\rangle^{\sigma}\}}$ B-ValPers:

By IH, we have $\lfloor \Gamma, \sigma \rfloor \vdash^{n + \sigma} e' : \tau$ and $\mathrm{fsv}(\tau) = \varnothing$. Therefore, we can derive:

$$\cfrac{\lfloor \Gamma \rfloor, \sigma \vdash^{n + \sigma} e' : \tau}{\lfloor \Gamma \rfloor, \sigma \vdash^{n + \sigma} \{\mathtt{val} = e'\} : \{\mathtt{val} : \tau\}}$$

$$\vdots$$

$$\cfrac{\cfrac{\cfrac{\lfloor \Gamma \rfloor, \sigma \vdash^{0 + \sigma} \{\mathtt{val} = e'\}^{\times n} : \langle\{\mathtt{val} : \tau\}\rangle^{\times n}}{\lfloor \Gamma \rfloor, \sigma \vdash^0 \langle\!\langle\{\mathtt{val} = e'\}\rangle^{\times n}\rangle^{\sigma} : \langle\!\langle\{\mathtt{val} : \tau\}\rangle^{\times n}\rangle^{\sigma}}}{\lfloor \Gamma \rfloor \vdash^0 \Lambda\sigma. \langle\!\langle\{\mathtt{val} = e'\}\rangle^{\times n}\rangle^{\sigma} : \forall \sigma. \langle\!\langle\{\mathtt{val} : \tau\}\rangle^{\times n}\rangle^{\sigma}}}{\lfloor \Gamma \rfloor \vdash^0 \{l_X = \Lambda\sigma. \langle\!\langle\{\mathtt{val} = e'\}\rangle^{\times n}\rangle^{\sigma}\} : \{l_X : \lfloor [\![\tau]\!]^{\geq n} \rfloor\}}$$

and have $\mathrm{fsv}(\lfloor \exists \varepsilon. \{R\} \rfloor) = \mathrm{fsv}(\tau) = \varnothing$.

References

1. Bochao, L., Ohori, A.: A flattening strategy for SML module compilation and its implementation. Inf. Media Technol. **5**(1), 58–76 (2010)
2. Calcagno, C., Moggi, E., Sheard, T.: Closed types for a safe imperative MetaML. J. Funct. Program. **13**(3), 545–571 (2003)
3. Crary, K.: Fully abstract module compilation. Proc. ACM Program. Lang. **3**(POPL), 1–29 (2019)
4. Crary, K.: A focused solution to the avoidance problem. J. Funct. Program. **30**, e24 (2020)
5. Davies, R.: A temporal-logic approach to binding-time analysis. In: Proceedings of the 11th Annual IEEE Symposium on Logic in Computer Science, LICS 1996, USA, p. 184. IEEE Computer Society (1996)
6. Davies, R.: A temporal logic approach to binding-time analysis. J. ACM **64**(1), 1–45 (2017)
7. Dreyer, D., Crary, K., Harper, R.: A type system for higher-order modules. In: Proceedings of the 30th ACM SIGPLAN-SIGACT Symposium on Principles of Programming Languages, POPL 2003, pp. 236–249. Association for Computing Machinery, New York (2003)
8. Elsman, M.: Static interpretation of modules. In: Proceedings of the Fourth ACM SIGPLAN International Conference on Functional Programming, ICFP 1999, pp. 208–219. Association for Computing Machinery, New York (1999)
9. Elsman, M., Henriksen, T., Annenkov, D., Oancea, C.E.: Static interpretation of higher-order modules in Futhark: functional GPU programming in the large. Proc. ACM Program. Lang. **2**(ICFP), 1–30 (2018)
10. Flatt, M.: Composable and compilable macros: you want it when? In: Proceedings of the Seventh ACM SIGPLAN International Conference on Functional Programming, ICFP 2002, pp. 72–83. Association for Computing Machinery, New York (2002)
11. Girard, J.Y.: Interprétation fonctionnelle et élimination des coupures de l'arithmétique d'ordre supérieur. Ph.D. thesis, Université Paris VII (1972)
12. Glück, R., Jørgensen, J.: Efficient multi-level generating extensions for program specialization. In: Hermenegildo, M., Swierstra, S.D. (eds.) PLILPS 1995. LNCS, vol. 982, pp. 259–278. Springer, Heidelberg (1995). https://doi.org/10.1007/BFb0026825
13. Hanada, Y., Igarashi, A.: On cross-stage persistence in multi-stage programming. In: Codish, M., Sumii, E. (eds.) FLOPS 2014. LNCS, vol. 8475, pp. 103–118. Springer, Cham (2014). https://doi.org/10.1007/978-3-319-07151-0_7
14. Harper, R., Lillibridge, M.: A type-theoretic approach to higher-order modules with sharing. In: Proceedings of the 21st ACM SIGPLAN-SIGACT Symposium on Principles of Programming Languages, POPL 1994, pp. 123–137. Association for Computing Machinery, New York (1994)
15. Harper, R., Stone, C.: A type-theoretic interpretation of standard ML, pp. 341–387. MIT Press, Cambridge (2000)
16. Inoue, J., Kiselyov, O., Kameyama, Y.: Staging beyond terms: prospects and challenges. In: Proceedings of the 2016 ACM SIGPLAN Workshop on Partial Evaluation and Program Manipulation, PEPM 2016, pp. 103–108. Association for Computing Machinery, New York (2016)
17. Kiselyov, O.: Let-insertion as a primitive (2017). https://okmij.org/ftp/ML/MetaOCaml.html#genlet. Accessed 10 Dec 2023

18. Kiselyov, O., Kameyama, Y., Sudo, Y.: Refined environment classifiers: type- and scope-safe code generation with mutable cells. In: Igarashi, A. (ed.) APLAS 2016. LNCS, vol. 10017, pp. 271–291. Springer, Cham (2016). https://doi.org/10.1007/978-3-319-47958-3_15

19. Leroy, X.: Manifest types, modules, and separate compilation. In: Proceedings of the 21st ACM SIGPLAN-SIGACT Symposium on Principles of Programming Languages, POPL 1994, pp. 109–122. Association for Computing Machinery, New York (1994)

20. Lillibridge, M.: Translucent sums: a foundation for higher-order module systems. Ph.D. thesis, Carnegie Mellon University (1997)

21. MacQueen, D.: Modules for standard ML. In: Proceedings of the 1984 ACM Symposium on LISP and Functional Programming, LFP 1984, pp. 198–207. Association for Computing Machinery, New York (1984)

22. Pierce, B.C.: Types and Programming Languages, 1st edn. The MIT Press, Cambridge (2002)

23. Rossberg, A., Russo, C., Dreyer, D.: F-ing modules. In: Proceedings of the 5th ACM SIGPLAN Workshop on Types in Language Design and Implementation, TLDI 2010, pp. 89–102. Association for Computing Machinery, New York (2010)

24. Rossberg, A., Russo, C., Dreyer, D.: F-ing modules. J. Funct. Program. **24**(5), 529–607 (2014)

25. Russo, C.V.: First-class structures for standard ML. In: Smolka, G. (ed.) ESOP 2000. LNCS, vol. 1782, pp. 336–350. Springer, Heidelberg (2000). https://doi.org/10.1007/3-540-46425-5_22

26. Sato, Y., Kameyama, Y., Watanabe, T.: Module generation without regret. In: Proceedings of the 2020 ACM SIGPLAN Workshop on Partial Evaluation and Program Manipulation, PEPM 2020, pp. 1–13. Association for Computing Machinery, New York (2020)

27. Shao, Z.: Transparent modules with fully syntatic signatures. In: Proceedings of the Fourth ACM SIGPLAN International Conference on Functional Programming, ICFP 1999, pp. 220–232. Association for Computing Machinery, New York (1999)

28. Suwa, T.: SATySFi (2017–2023). https://github.com/gfngfn/SATySFi. Accessed 10 Dec 2023

29. Suwa, T.: Develop SATySFi 0.1.0 (2021–2023). https://github.com/gfngfn/SATySFi/pull/294. Accessed 10 Dec 2023

30. Taha, W.: Multi-Stage Programming: Its Theory and Applications. Oregon Graduate Institute of Science and Technology (1999)

31. Taha, W., Nielsen, M.F.: Environment classifiers. In: Proceedings of the 30th ACM SIGPLAN-SIGACT Symposium on Principles of Programming Languages, POPL 2003, pp. 26–37. Association for Computing Machinery, New York (2003)

32. Taha, W., Sheard, T.: Multi-stage programming with explicit annotations. SIGPLAN Not. **32**(12), 203–217 (1997)

33. Taha, W., Sheard, T.: MetaML and multi-stage programming with explicit annotations. Theor. Comput. Sci. **248**(1), 211–242 (2000)

34. Tsukada, T., Igarashi, A.: A logical foundation for environment classifiers. In: Curien, P.L. (ed.) TLCA 2009. LNCS, vol. 5608, pp. 341–355. Springer, Heidelberg (2009). https://doi.org/10.1007/978-3-642-02273-9_25

35. Watanabe, T., Kameyama, Y.: Program generation for ML modules (short paper). In: Proceedings of the ACM SIGPLAN Workshop on Partial Evaluation and Program Manipulation, PEPM 2018, pp. 60–66. Association for Computing Machinery, New York (2017)

36. Xie, N., White, L., Nicole, O., Yallop, J.: MacoCaml: staging composable and compilable macros. Proc. ACM Program. Lang. **7**(ICFP), 604–648 (2023)
37. Yallop, J., White, L.: Modular macros. In: OCaml Users and Developers Workshop, vol. 6 (2015)
38. Yuse, Y., Igarashi, A.: A modal type system for multi-level generating extensions with persistent code. In: Proceedings of the 8th ACM SIGPLAN International Conference on Principles and Practice of Declarative Programming, PPDP 2006, pp. 201–212. Association for Computing Machinery, New York (2006)

Rhyme: A Data-Centric Multi-paradigm Query Language Based on Functional Logic Metaprogramming
System Description

Supun Abeysinghe[✉][iD] and Tiark Rompf[iD]

Purdue University, West Lafayette, IN 47906, USA
{tabeysin,tiark}@purdue.edu

Abstract. We present Rhyme, a declarative multi-paradigm query language designed for querying and transforming nested structures such as JSON, tensors, and beyond. Rhyme is designed to be multi-paradigm from ground-up allowing it to seamlessly accommodate typical data processing operations–ranging from aggregations and group-bys to joins–while also having the versatility to express diverse computations like tensor expressions (à la einops) and declaratively express visualizations (e.g., visualizing query outputs with tables, charts, and so on). Rhyme generates optimized JavaScript code for queries by constructing an intermediate representation that implicitly captures the program structure via dependencies. This paper presents a system description of Rhyme implementation while highlighting key design decisions and various use cases covered by Rhyme.

Keywords: Declarative query languages · Logic programming · Tensor expressions · Multi-paradigm languages · Rhyme

1 Introduction

This paper introduces the design of Rhyme, a new declarative multi-paradigm query language tailored for querying and transforming nested structures, encompassing formats such as JSON, tensors, and more. Rhyme draws inspiration from an array of existing approaches, including query languages such as GraphQL [18], JQ [3], XQuery [4], logic programming languages like Datalog [10], and recent functional logic programming languages like Verse [12]. Rhyme is implemented in JavaScript and currently available as an open source Node.js package[1]. Below are the main defining characteristics of Rhyme:

- **Data-centric query language:** Focused explicitly on extracting information and transforming data, not general-purpose programming.

---

[1] Available at https://rhyme-lang.github.io/.

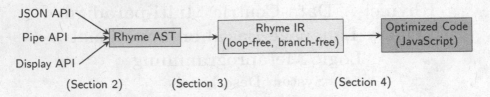

Fig. 1. The end-to-end workflow of Rhyme. Rhyme provides multiple APIs for different types of workloads that targets the common Rhyme AST which serves as an entry point. The AST gets transformed to an IR that implicitly captures program structure (i.e., no loops or branches). Optimized JavaScript code is then generated from this IR.

- **Multi-paradigm:** Still, flexible enough to support a wide range of typical data processing operations (e.g., SQL/DataFrames), tensor expressions, visualization, etc., in a single language.
- **Functional:** Not based on relations as the core abstraction but on functions, including representing data as materialized functions (i.e., objects mapping keys to values).
- **Logic:** Using logic variables and unification to express joins, aggregations, and other forms of iteration.
- **Metaprogramming:** Relying on an expressive host language to compose query fragments and run queries (using functional/Object-Oriented APIs, as well as quasiquotation syntax).

Rhyme is designed to be multi-paradigm from the ground up, seamlessly accommodating standard data processing operations like aggregations, group-bys, joins, and others, along with paradigms beyond conventional data-processing operations. These include the expression of various types of computations, such as tensor operations (akin to einops [24]), and the ability to declaratively express visualizations (e.g., a table summarizing query outputs).

This facilitates the expression of diverse workloads; for example, a complex data processing pipeline mixing tasks such as group-based aggregations intertwined with tensor computations (e.g., incorporating a pre-trained model), followed by the creation of visualizations, such as dashboards-all achieved through a unified query language. This bears significance on two fronts. Firstly, in terms of programmer productivity, end-users can leverage a single, unified query language to express the entirety of their workload logic, eliminating the need for multiple domain-specific languages. Secondly, concerning performance, the unified system seamlessly manages all workload paradigms, mitigating the performance overhead typically incurred at system boundaries when employing various domain-specific systems-a pressing problem in practical scenarios [9,23].

Figure 1 illustrates the end-to-end workflow of Rhyme. Queries can be expressed through different frontend APIs (as detailed in Sect. 2), where all these APIs target a common AST representation, serving as the entry point to the system. Subsequently, this AST representation serves as the basis for deriving an intermediate representation (IR) that encapsulates the query logic.

A key characteristic of this IR is that it does not explicitly capture the program structure corresponding to the query. Instead, the program structure is implicitly captured through dependencies, making it easier to perform optimizations (as detailed in Sect. 3). Then, the IR is transformed into optimized JavaScript code, incorporating various optimizations

The remainder of the paper is structured into sections that delve into each component of Rhyme, as depicted in Fig. 1. Section 2 outlines the various frontends provided by Rhyme, catering to the expression of diverse workload types. We offer several alternative APIs designed to express Rhyme queries, each tailored for specific use cases. Moving forward, Sect. 3 delves into the design of Rhyme AST, Rhyme IR, and the process of constructing the IR from the AST, how an optimized program structure is derived from this loop-free, branch-free representation and elucidate the generation of optimized JavaScript code for a given query.

The foundational concepts of Rhyme were initially introduced in [8]. This paper takes a more in-depth exploration to the design and implementation of Rhyme frontend, providing comprehensive discussions on recent advancements in some of the APIs, including surface syntax (e.g., quasiquotations, etc.), and offering extensive insights into the graphics API.

2   Rhyme Front End

As illustrated in Fig. 1, Rhyme offers users various frontends to express their queries. In this section, we will explore each of these APIs, demonstrating their utility across diverse use cases.

2.1   JSON API

Given the thorough discussion of this API in previous work [8], we refrain from offering an exhaustive discussion here. Nonetheless, we add a summary of key components for the sake of completeness.

Table 1 provides a summary of the primary operators in the JSON API. Most operators are self-explanatory and intuitive in nature. It is worth noting that Rhyme also supports user-defined functions (UDFs), joins, and various typical data processing operations, other than the ones mentioned in the table. One noteworthy aspect of Rhyme lies in its approach to expressing group-bys and the contextual evaluation semantics of expressions like `sum(data.*A.value)`. Specifically, when nested within a `{ data.*A.key : ... ,` the `sum(data.*A.value)` corresponds to a per-group sum; otherwise, it represents a total sum (note the use of the same `*A`).

The following code snippet illustrates the utilization of the Rhyme JSON API to query the DBLP REST API and compute various details about past FLOPS conference publications. This snippet is a fully executable JavaScript program, assuming the Rhyme library is appropriately set up and imported[2].

---

[2] As detailed in https://github.com/rhyme-lang/rhyme?tab=readme-ov-file#using-in-the-browserfrontend.

Table 1. Basic query operators of Rhyme JSON API. Full API documentation is available at https://rhyme-lang.github.io/docs/frontends/json/.

Operation	Query	Result
Sample Dataset	`[ {key: A, value: 10}, {key: B, value: 20},` `  {key: B, value: 15}, {key: A, value: 30} ]`	-

Simple Indexing	`// directly indexing into a sequence of data`
	`data.0.value`
	`data.2.key`
		10
		B

Creating structures	`// creating structures from queries`
	`// (can compose arbitrarily)`
	`{ first : data.0.key }`
		`{ first : 10}`

Iterating (using *)	`// iterating data and collecting into an array`
	`[data.*.value]`
	`// iterators are logic variables (named *A, *B, ...)`
	`[data.*A.key]`
		`[10,20,15,30]`
		
		`[A,B,B,A]`

Aggregations	`// computing aggregates`
	`sum(data.*.value)`
	`// creating a new object from a query`
	`{ total : sum(data.*.value) }`
		75
		
		`{ total: 75 }`

Group-bys, Joins	`// group-by: expressed by having *, *A, ... as key`
	`// compute per-key sum of values`
	`{ data.*.key : sum(data.*.value) }`
	`// compute per-key relative sum`
	`// sum(data.*A.value):`
	`//    nested within data.*A.key -> per-group sum`
	`// sum(data.*B.value):`
	`//    not nested within another *B key -> total sum`
	`{`
	`  data.*A.key :`
	`      sum(data.*A.value) / sum(data.*B.value)`
	`}`
		`{ A: 40, B: 35 }`
		
		`{`
		`  A: 0.53,`
		`  B: 0.47`
		`}`

```
let url =
    "https://dblp.org/search/publ/api?q=stream:streams/conf/flops:&h=1000&format=json"

// fetch the data from the REST endpoint and query
fetch(url).then(p => p.json()).then(data => {
  // Query1: produces all papers by year
  let query1 = {
    "data.result.hits.hit.*.info.year": ["data.result.hits.hit.*.info.title"]
  }
  let res = api.query(query1)
  display(res({data}))
  // result: {1998: [...FLOPS papers of 1998 ...], 1999: [ ... ], ...}

  // Query2: compute number of papers per year
  let query2 = {
    "data.result.hits.hit.*.info.year": api.count("data.result.hits.hit.*.info.title")
  }
  res = api.query(query2)
  display(res({data}))
  // result: {1998: 16, 1999: 24, 2001: 25, ...}

  // Query3: For all authors, list years they published
  let query3 = {
    // need to build union of single-author and
    // multi-author papers
```

```
    "data.result.hits.hit.*.info.authors.*A.*B.text": ["data.result.hits.hit.*.info.year"],
    "data.result.hits.hit.*.info.authors.*A.text": ["data.result.hits.hit.*.info.year"],
  }
  res = api.query(query3)
  display(res({data}))
  // result: {"author A": [2022, 2012, 2010, ...], "author B": [2016, 2012, ...], ...}
})
```

As depicted in Fig. 1, similar to the other APIs, the JSON API follows the process of constructing the Rhyme AST, which is subsequently transformed into Rhyme IR. Moreover, since all of these APIs are implemented in the same host language, JavaScript, they can be seamlessly mixed and matched as the users see fit. This IR is then further processed to generate optimized JavaScript code, as detailed in Sect. 3.

2.2 Pipe API

The JSON API enables expressing queries in a format resembling the expected output structure, akin to approaches like GraphQL. However, there are scenarios where it is more intuitive to formulate computations as a sequence of transformation steps on the input(s). Rhyme offers the Pipe API to accommodate such workloads.

Rhyme offers a textual API based on JavaScript's template literals for this purpose. Template literals enable string interpolation with embedded expressions and allow the addition of custom desugaring logic. Rhyme utilizes the rh'...' template to express queries through this API. To explain how this API functions, let us take a simple example that computes the sum of values expressed using the JSON API: `api.sum("data.*.value")`. This same query can be written using our surface syntax in the following ways:

```
rh`sum(data.*.value)`
rh`sum data.*.value`
rh`data | sum(.*.value)`
rh`data | .* | sum(.value)`
rh`data | .* | .value | sum`
```

All of the above queries are equivalent and are parsed into the same AST as the original query. This approach offers a more intuitive and straightforward means of expressing the query as a series of transformation steps applied to the inputs. Under the hood, each transformation step (i.e., operators appear sequentially after pipes) gets desugared to operators with holes. For a call expression like f(a) (e.g., `sum(.value)` above) or a|f (e.g., `.value|sum` above), we explicitly desugar 'f' with the expectation that it is a function. This process is akin to bidirectional typing [16], i.e., potentially transforming code to conform to an expected type.

In this process, we examine whether any expressions contain holes-e.g., '.value' is incomplete, conceptually featuring a hole on the left, and is desugared to □.value. Similarly, sum(.value) is parsed as sum(□.value). Moreover, if any intermediate operations in the sequence do not contain holes, such as when UDFs are applied as part of the transformation (e.g., `splitPipe` in the example query later in this section), the expression is treated as a reference to a function and is eta-expanded by inserting a hole on the right for application (e.g., `splitPipe(□)`). In our implementation, we treat these terms with holes as anonymous functions; for instance, `sum(□.value)` becomes `x => sum(x.value)`.

There may be situations where a single operator involves multiple holes. In such cases, we have a choice: whether to consider all of them as references to the same argument (`x => ...`) or treat them as arguments to a multi-argument function (`((x, y)=> ...`). Presently, Rhyme exclusively handles single-argument functions (which is the situation with pipes like `a | f`), but it does support currying, allowing for repeated applications (as in `b | f(a)`).

Moreover, this surface language provides a way of using quasi-quotations via `${...}` , for example to define and directly call user-defined functions. For instance, consider a case where we want to compute the average using a UDF. The average UDF can be expressed using `sum` and `count`.

```
let avg = x => rh`sum(${x}) / count(${x})`
// computing average of data.*.value (both queries compute the avg)
rh`${avg}(data.*.value)`
rh`data.*.value | ${avg}`
```

To demonstrate the effectiveness of this API, we take an example query from a previous work [8], which is originally taken from Advent of Code 2022 [1]. The input is a sequence of numbers separated by pipes into chunks where each chunk contains multiple comma-separated numbers. The task is to compute the sum of each chunk and find the maximum sum across all chunks.

```
let input = '100,200,300|400|500,600|700,800,900|1000' // sample input
// some UDFs for parsing the data
let udf = {
  'splitPipe'  : x => x.split('|'),
  'splitComma' : x => x.split(','),
  'toNum'      : x => Number(x)
}
```

As shown in [8], this query can be expressed using Rhyme's JSON API, as depicted on the left. Alternatively, the same query can be expressed in a nice, intuitive manner using the pipe-based surface language, as illustrated on the right.

```
// JSON API
let query = max(get({
'*chunk': sum(
  apply('udf.toNum',
    get(apply('udf.splitComma',
      get(apply('udf.splitPipe', '.input'),
        '*chunk')),
      '*line')))
},'*'))
```

```
// Pipe API
// Produce output by applying a sequence of
//   transformations to input
let query =
  rh`.input | udf.splitChunk | .*chunk
    | udf.splitComma | .*line | udf.toNum
    | sum | group *chunk | .* | max`
```

While both queries generate the same AST and yield the same expected result, the query on the right is better suited for these types of tasks. It offers a cleaner and more intuitive approach to expressing the query as a sequence of transformations on the input. This stands in contrast to the JSON API, which requires the query to be written in a way that mirrors the output structure.

2.3   Visualization API

Many data processing workloads demand some form of visualization as the final output. Traditionally, the implementation of these visualizations is separate from the data processing logic. However, Rhyme allows users to integrate the logic for visualization directly within the same language. Since Rhyme and all its existing APIs are implemented in JavaScript, end users can effortlessly import the corresponding JavaScript file into their browser/HTML and easily create visualizations.

Rhyme introduces the `"$display"` keyword for specifying visualizations. One type of visualization Rhyme supports is the declarative specification of SVG drawings. To create SVG drawings, users can employ `"$display": "dom"` and `"type": "svg:<svg_shape>"`, where `<svg_shape>` represents any available SVG shape, such as ellipse, polyline, rect, polygon, etc. The properties associated with each shape can be passed using the `props` key. For example, the query below draws a rectangle, incorporating features like colors, rounded edges, and additional attributes by passing the corresponding properties to `props` (visualization is shown on the right).

```
{
  "$display": "dom", type: "svg:rect",
  props: {
    x: 100, y: -50, width: 50, height: 50, rx: 10, ry: 10,
    fill: "lightblue", stroke: "hotpink", "stroke-width": 5,
    opacity: 0.7, transform: "rotate(45)"
  }
}
```

It is important to highlight that this graphical drawing capability seamlessly integrates with Rhyme's other APIs. To illustrate its utility, let us consider a scenario where we aim to visualize some sample data. While we currently use synthetic data for illustration purposes, it is crucial to note that this data could be sourced from another Rhyme query that processes and analyzes real-world data. Shown below is some sample data.

```
let data = [{x:20,y:70},{x:40,y:30},{x:60,y:50},{x:80,y:60},{x:100,y:40}]
```

Suppose we aim to represent this data through three distinct types of charts: line, bar, and points. Below, we show the queries for generating these three drawings, accompanied by their respective outputs.

```
let line = {
  "$display": "dom", type: "svg:polyline",
  props: {
    points: rh`${join}((data.*.x + ',' + data.*.y), ' ')`,
    stroke: "black", fill:"none" }
}
```

```
let bars = {
  "$display": "dom",
  "type": "svg:rect",
  "props": {
    "width": "16px",
    "height": rh`100 - data.*.y`,
    "x": rh`data.*.x - 8`,
    "y": rh`data.*.y`,
    "stroke": "black",
    "fill": "none" },
}
```

```
let points = {
  "$display": "dom",
  "type": "svg:ellipse",
  "props": {
    "rx": "3px", "ry": "3px",
    "cx": "data.*.x",
    "cy": "data.*.y",
    "stroke": "black",
    "fill": "#EEE" },
}
```

Multiple SVG graphics can be overlapped by using "type": "svg:svg" and providing the corresponding queries as an array to the "children" key. Shown below is a query that draws a data-dependent graphic by overlapping multiple "svg:elipse" drawings.

```
let data = []
for (let j = 0; j < 360; j += 20) data.push(j)
let query = {
  "$display": "dom",
  "type": "svg:svg",
  "props": { "width": "300px", "height": "200px" },
  "children": [{
    "$display": "dom",
    "type": "svg:ellipse",
    "props": {
      "rx": "40px",
      "ry": "15px",
      "cx": "200px",
      "cy": "100px",
      "fill": rh`'hsl(' + data.* + ' 90%`
      "fill-opacity": "70%"
      "transform": rh`'rotate(-' + data.* + ' 150 100)'` },
  }]
}
```

Another "$display" option available for Rhyme is "select". This option adds a set of buttons at the top to toggle between different sets of visualizations. For instance, suppose we want to visualize the above three graphics in both an overlapped and a side-by-side arrangement. This can be achieved using the select option. The corresponding query is shown below. The images on the right illustrate both scenarios, each activated by clicking the corresponding button.

```
{
  "$display": "select",
  data: {
    "All in one": {
      "$display": "dom", type: "svg:svg",
      props: { width: "300px", height: "100px" },
      children: [bars, line, points]
    },
    "Side by side": {
      "$display": "dom", type: "div",
      children: [{
        "$display": "dom", type: "svg:svg",
        props: { width: "120px", height: "100px" },
        children: [points]
      },{
        "$display": "dom", type: "svg:svg",
        props: { width: "120px", height: "100px" },
        children: [line]
      },{
        "$display": "dom", type: "svg:svg",
        props: { width: "120px", height: "100px" },
        children: [bars]
      }]
    },
  }
}
```

Rhyme offers additional display options beyond the ones discussed earlier. Two particularly useful options are "table" and "bar", designed for creating tables and bar charts from data, respectively. While the complete query is not included here, the following (excerpt) visualization shows a table mixed with bar charts. This visualization was generated by computing summary statistics from a sample warehouse dataset using a Rhyme query and specifying all the visualization-related logic entirely within Rhyme.

	Quantity	Bar Chart	Percent Total
Total	1210		100 %
San Jose	650		53 %
iPhone	300		24 %
7	50		4 %
6s	100		8 %
X	150		12 %
Samsung	350		28 %
Galaxy S	200		16 %
Note 8	150		12 %
San Francisco	560		46 %
iPhone	260		21 %
7	10		0 %
6s	50		4 %

3   Rhyme Backend

This section explores the end-to-end process of transforming queries into optimized JavaScript code. This translation happens in three steps. As we saw in Fig. 1, all the frontend API directly targets Rhyme AST, which serves as the entry point to the system. This AST representation is further transformed into Rhyme IR, which implicitly captures the program structure. Finally, this Rhyme IR is transformed into optimized JavaScript code. To enhance comprehension, we will employ the following query as a running example throughout this section. As we saw in Table 1 (second example query for group-by), this query computes per-key relative sum for all the keys.

```
{
  data.*A.key: sum(data.*A.value) / sum(data.*B.value)
}
```

3.1   AST

The Rhyme AST is represented using JSON objects and closely resembles the JSON API. The keys corresponding to implicit group-by clauses (for example `{ data.*.key: ...}`) remain unchanged in the AST representation. Other parts corresponding to query operators are transformed into nested JSON objects. For instance, reduction operators like `sum`, `max`, `min`, etc., are transformed into objects containing the aggregate name and the parameters passed to the aggregate. For example, `sum(data..value)` will be transformed into `{ agg: 'sum', param: 'data..value'}`. Similarly, for other operators that are not reductions (i.e., stateless ones), an object with the operator type (referred to as `path`) and parameters is created. The AST representation for the running example query is illustrated below.

```
{
  "data.*.key": {
    path: 'div',
    param: [
      {agg: 'sum', param: 'data.*A.val'},
      {agg: 'sum', param: 'data.*B.val'}
    ]
  }
}
```

The translation from different frontends to the AST representation is relatively straightforward and, therefore, not extensively discussed. For example, in the JSON API, we define functions for each stateless and stateful operator, such as `sum`, `max`, `min`, `plus`, and so on, to generate the corresponding AST fragment. Below, we provide the logic for `sum` and `plus`:

```
api["sum"] = (e) => ({          api["plus"] = (e1, e2) => ({
  agg: "sum",                     path: "plus",
  param: e                        param: [e1, e2]
})                              })
```

The same set of AST fragment building functions is utilized by the rest of the frontends. For example, in the template literals-based frontend discussed in Sect. 2.2, the corresponding operators are desugared by invoking the relevant `api` functions.

3.2   Structure of the Rhyme IR

The Rhyme IR is comprised of two types of operators: *generators* and *assignments*. As the name implies, generators are instructions responsible for iterating values from data sources, such as an array of JSON objects. In contrast, assignments correspond to instructions that execute computations and assign (partial) results to intermediate state variables. This approach, employing multiple intermediate state variables to compute the final result, draws inspiration from previous work on generating triggers for incremental execution [7,20].

In our ongoing example query, Rhyme generates three temporaries-tmp[0], tmp[1], and tmp[2]-which correspond to the final result object, per-key aggregate object, and total aggregate, respectively. The presence of *A and *B in the query signifies two generators. The IR for this query is presented below, where the assignment instructions on temporaries are self-explanatory.

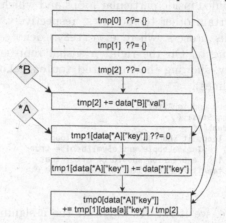

A defining feature of the Rhyme IR lies in its avoidance of explicitly storing the program structure (inspired by prior work [13,14]). Taking the ongoing query as an example, the query indicates that the *B generator should be nested within *A, forming a nested loop structure. However, rather than strictly enforcing this structure within the IR, Rhyme stores dependencies that implicitly capture the query's structure.

Specifically, the use of a generator within an assignment instruction gives rise to a generator-assignment dependency, while other assignment-assignment dependencies typically represent data dependencies. As we delve into Sect. 3.3, we will explore how this dependency-based representation facilitates certain optimizations, making tasks such as loop hoisting more straightforward.

In the current Rhyme implementation, dependencies are tracked at the level of temporaries, such as tmp[0], tmp[1], and so on. To achieve this, each assignment is assigned a write rank, ensuring a specific order during code generation. While this systematic approach guarantees a sequential order of writes, it may introduce imprecise dependencies in certain scenarios, potentially resulting in suboptimal code. This is because automatically enforcing a serial order for writes might not accurately capture their true dependencies. An alternative approach involves treating each write rank more like a static-single assignment (SSA)-style variable, allowing for a finer-grained tracking of dependencies. This approach provides a more nuanced representation of dependencies, potentially improving the precision of the generated code.

3.3   Code Generation

Following the construction of the IR, the next step involves generating the final optimized JavaScript code for the query based on this IR. Given that our IR does not store explicit program structure, reconstructing the program's architecture requires an analysis of dependencies. To accomplish this, we perform multiple analysis passes over the IR.

The initial analysis focuses on determining the placement of intermediate temporaries with respect to loops and other temporaries. Specifically, this pass computes `tmpInsideLoop` and `tmpAfterTmp`, which track which temporaries should be scheduled inside particular loops and which temporaries should be scheduled after certain other temporaries, respectively. The following code excerpt illustrates this process, where `e.writeSym` denotes the left-hand side temporary of assignments. On the right, a visual representation is provided for our example query, showing the computed `tmpInsideLoop` (solid lines) and `tmpAfterTmp` (dotted lines).

```
// compute tmpInsideLoop and tmpAfterTmp
for (let e of assignmentStms) {
    for (let dep of e.deps) {
        // depends on a loop, it should be inside the loop
        if (isloop(dep)) tmpInsideLoop[e.writeSym][dep] = true
        // depends on a tmp, expression should be after that
        if (istmp(dep)) tmpAfterTmp[e.writeSym][dep] = true
    }
}
```

In the above code, we iterate through all the assignment statements and examine all their dependencies. If a statement depends on a loop, it means the corresponding temporary variable must be scheduled inside the loop, thus updating the `tmpInsideLoop` variable. Furthermore, if an assignment depends on another temporary value, it means the corresponding temporary variable must be scheduled after that, consequently updating the `tmpAfterTmp` variable.

The next step involves determining which temporaries should be scheduled *after* a given loop has been fully scheduled. This analysis leverages the information obtained from the earlier computations of `tmpInsideLoop` and `tmpAfterTmp`. The outcomes of this analysis are then stored in the `tmpAfterLoop`. The following is an excerpt from the corresponding analysis code in Rhyme.

```
// compute tmpAfterLoop
for (let t2 in tmpAfterTmp) {
    // gather loop 'prior' tmps are in
    for (let t1 in tmpAfterTmp[t2]) {
        for (let l in tmpInsideLoop[t1])
            tmpAfterLoop[t2][l] = true
    }
    // remove own loops
    for (let l in tmpInsideLoop[t2])
        delete tmpAfterLoop[t2][l]
}
```

In essence, if our analysis indicates that a temporary variable `t2` should be scheduled after another temporary `t1` (i.e., `tmpAfterTmp[t2][t1]`), and `t1` is known to be inside a loop `l` (provided that `t2` itself is not part of loop `l`), it implies that t2 should be scheduled after the completion of loop l. For example, in our sample query tmp[0] is determined to be scheduled after *A.

The final step of the analysis involves figuring out the relationships between loops. Our objective is twofold: first, to discern which loops should be scheduled strictly after others (captured in loopAfterLoop), and second, to identify which loops should be scheduled within the same loop nest (recorded in loopInsideLoop). These essentially help identify how the loops should be scheduled. Specifically, if our previous analysis revealed that a given temporary variable t should be scheduled within both loops l1 and l2, it implies that l1 and l2 should form part of the same loop nest. Conversely, if we determine that for a specific temporary variable t, it should be scheduled inside a loop l2, and we also know that t should be scheduled after another loop l1, it implies that loop l2 should be scheduled after l1-provided they are not part of the same loop nest. The corresponding code illustrating these analyses is presented below.

```
// compute loopInsideLoop                      // compute loopAfterLoop
for (let t in tmpInsideLoop) {                 for (let t in tmpAfterLoop) {
   for (let l2 in tmpInsideLoop[t]) {             for (let l2 in tmpInsideLoop[t]) {
      for (let l1 in tmpInsideLoop[t]) {            for (!loopInsideLoop[l2] ||
         loopInsideLoop[l2][l1] = true                  !loopInsideLoop[l2][l1]) {
         loopInsideLoop[l1] ??= {}                   if (!loopInsideLoop[l2][l1])
         loopInsideLoop[l1][l2] = true                  loopAfterLoop[l2][l1] = true
      }                                            }
   }                                            }
}                                            }
```

After completing the analysis steps, we move on to the code generation process. The core driver of the code emitting logic is encapsulated within the emitConvergence function. This function relies on two additional helper functions: emitGenerators and emitAssignments. The former is responsible for emitting loop structures, while the latter deals with the generation of assignment instructions. These functions are invoked repeatedly until all generators and assignments are fully emitted. We present an excerpt from emitGenerators below:

```
function emitGenerators() {
   let (available, remaining) = getAvailable(generators) // identify current scope loops
   generators = remaining      // remaining generators that are not available yet
   for (let g of available) {
      emitLoopHeader(g)
      emitConvergence()        // emit loop body (nested generators and assignments)
      emitLoopFooter()
   }
}
```

Here, generators is a global variable that keeps track of the remaining generators that is yet to be scheduled. The emitGenerators function is responsible for orchestrating the generation of loops corresponding to these generators. It commences by identifying generators that become available in the current scope, leveraging information such as loopAfterLoop, tmpAfterTmp, and others we saw before. The getAvailable function checks the dependencies of pending generators and picks the ones where all dependencies are satisfied. Consequently, this function schedules loops that are available at the present scope and invokes emitConvergence recursively to schedule any inner loops and assignments that must be scheduled inside these loops. `emitAssignments` function follows a similar structure to that of the `emitGenerators`. It schedules assignment instructions as soon as they become available in the current context.

As program control structures were not enforced from the front end, our code scheduling mechanism freely moves assignments and generators during the code generation phase. For example, generators without dependencies on the 'other query' are hoisted and scheduled as separate queries. This approach prevents redundant computations within nested loops, enhancing efficiency. For instance, for our example query, the computation of the total aggregate (i.e. `sum(data.*B.value)`) is hoisted out of the `*A` loop into a completely independent loop, preventing the recomputation of the aggregate for each different key.

4   Related Work

This section provides a summary of the closely related works to Rhyme, as presented in [8].

Various efforts have aimed to address the challenge of efficiently handling multi-paradigm workloads by constructing common IR, as seen in prior work like Weld [23], Delite [25], and Flern [9]. In this landscape, Rhyme takes a different approach by introducing a *query language*-as opposed to a common low-level IR-that possesses the capability to express diverse multi-paradigm workloads at a higher level.

Numerous query languages have been crafted for working with semi-structured data like JSON, each exhibiting its unique focus and strengths. Notable among them is JSONiq [5,17], a query language explicitly tailored for JSON data and borrowing syntax from XQuery [4], featuring constructs such as FLWOR expressions. Engines like Zorba [6] and RumbleDB [21] support JSONiq, with RumbleDB utilizing Spark [26] as a backend to leverage its scalability for execution. In the realm of semi-structured data, AsterixDB adopts AQL [2] and SQL++ [22] as its query languages.

Rhyme draws inspiration from functional logic programming languages such as Verse [12], Curry [19], miniKanren [15], and Scalogno [11], adapting these ideas into a novel data-centric declarative language.

5   Conclusion

This system description outlined the design and implementation of Rhyme, a data-centric and multi-paradigm declarative query language rooted in functional logic and metaprogramming. Rhyme offers diverse front-end APIs tailored to various workloads, extending beyond conventional data processing to encompass applications like tensor expressions (not discussed in this paper but elaborated in [8]) and expressive visualizations. The system achieves performance efficiency by constructing a loop-free and branch-free IR, facilitating optimization before transforming it into optimized JavaScript code for the given query. Currently, Rhyme is accessible as an open-source Node.js package, adaptable for integration into other Node.js projects or as a script importable into HTML pages.

References

1. Advent of code 2022. https://adventofcode.com/2022/day/1. Accessed 27 Sep 2023
2. The asterix query language (AQL). https://asterixdb.apache.org/docs/0.9.8/aql/manual.html. Accessed 27 Sep 2023
3. jq manual. https://jqlang.github.io/jq/manual/. Accessed 27 Sep 2023
4. XQuery 3.1: An xml query language (2017). https://www.w3.org/TR/xquery-31/. Accessed 27 Sep 2023
5. Jsoniq (2018). https://www.jsoniq.org/. Accessed 27 Sep 2023
6. Zorba (2018). https://www.zorba.io/. Accessed 27 Sep 2023
7. Abeysinghe, S., He, Q., Rompf, T.: Efficient incrementialization of correlated nested aggregate queries using relative partial aggregate indexes (RPAI). In: SIGMOD Conference, pp. 136–149. ACM (2022)
8. Abeysinghe, S., Rompf, T.: Rhyme: a data-centric expressive query language for nested data structures. In: Gebser, M., Sergey, I. (eds.) Practical Aspects of Declarative Languages. PADL 2024. LNCS, vol. 14512, pp. 64–81. Springer, Cham (2023). https://doi.org/10.1007/978-3-031-52038-9_5
9. Abeysinghe, S., Wang, F., Essertel, G.M., Rompf, T.: Architecting intermediate layers for efficient composition of data management and machine learning systems. CoRR **abs/2311.02781** (2023)
10. Abeysinghe, S., Xhebraj, A., Rompf, T.: Flan: an expressive and efficient datalog compiler for program analysis. Proc. ACM Program. Lang. **8**(POPL) (2024)
11. Amin, N., Byrd, W.E., Rompf, T.: Lightweight functional logic meta-programming. In: Lin, A.W. (ed.) APLAS 2019. LNCS, vol. 11893, pp. 225–243. Springer, Cham (2019). https://doi.org/10.1007/978-3-030-34175-6_12
12. Augustsson, L., et al.: The verse calculus: a core calculus for deterministic functional logic programming. Proc. ACM Program. Lang. **7**(ICFP) (2023)
13. Bracevac, O., et al.: Graph irs for impure higher-order languages (technical report). CoRR **abs/2309.08118** (2023)
14. Bračevac, O., et al.: Graph irs for impure higher-order languages: making aggressive optimizations affordable with precise effect dependencies. Proc. ACM Program. Lang. **7**(OOPSLA2), 236:1–236:31 (2023)
15. Byrd, W.E.: Relational programming in miniKanren: techniques, applications, and implementations. Ph.D. thesis, Indiana University (2009)
16. Dunfield, J., Krishnaswami, N.: Bidirectional typing. ACM Comput. Surv. **54**(5), 98:1–98:38 (2022)
17. Florescu, D., Fourny, G.: JSONiq: the history of a query language. IEEE Internet Comput. **17**(5), 86–90 (2013)
18. GraphQL: a query language for your API. https://graphql.org/. Accessed 27 Sep 2023
19. Hanus, M.: Functional logic programming: from theory to curry. In: Voronkov, A., Weidenbach, C. (eds.) Programming Logics. LNCS, vol. 7797, pp. 123–168. Springer, Heidelberg (2013). https://doi.org/10.1007/978-3-642-37651-1_6
20. Koch, C., et al.: Dbtoaster: higher-order delta processing for dynamic, frequently fresh views. VLDB J. **23**(2), 253–278 (2014)
21. Müller, I., Fourny, G., Irimescu, S., Cikis, C.B., Alonso, G.: Rumble: data independence for large messy data sets. Proc. VLDB Endow. **14**(4), 498–506 (2020)
22. Ong, K.W., Papakonstantinou, Y., Vernoux, R.: The SQL++ semi-structured data model and query language: a capabilities survey of sql-on-hadoop, nosql and newsql databases. CoRR **abs/1405.3631** (2014)

23. Palkar, S., et al.: A common runtime for high performance data analysis. In: CIDR (2017). www.cidrdb.org
24. Rogozhnikov, A.: Einops: clear and reliable tensor manipulations with einstein-like notation. In: ICLR. OpenReview.net (2022)
25. Sujeeth, A.K., et al.: Delite: a compiler architecture for performance-oriented embedded domain-specific languages. ACM Trans. Embed. Comput. Syst. **13**(4s), 134:1–134:25 (2014)
26. Zaharia, M., et al.: Apache spark: a unified engine for big data processing. Commun. ACM **59**(11), 56–65 (2016)

Proofs

Language-parameterized Proofs
for Functional Languages with Subtyping

Seth Galasso$^{(\boxtimes)}$ and Matteo Cimini

University of Massachusetts Lowell, Lowell, MA 01854, USA
seth_galasso@student.uml.edu, matteo_cimini@uml.edu

Abstract. Language designers often strive to prove that their programming languages satisfy the properties that were intended at the time of design. LANG-N-PROVE is a DSL for expressing language-parametrized proofs, that is, proofs that apply to classes of languages rather than a single language. Prior work has used LANG-N-PROVE to express the language-parametrized proofs of type soundness (excluding the substitution lemmas) for a certain class of functional languages. In this paper, we address this class of languages when subtyping is added to them. We provide the language-parametrized proofs of their type soundness (excluding the substitution lemmas) and of the equivalence between algorithmic and declarative subtyping. To express these proofs naturally, we have extended LANG-N-PROVE with new operations. Our extension of LANG-N-PROVE generates Abella proofs that machine-check the type soundness of a nontrivial class of functional languages with declarative and algorithmic subtyping, when just a few simple lemmas are admitted.

Keywords: Type safety · Subtyping · Functional languages

1 Introduction

Language verification is an important aspect in the cycle of programming language development. After creating a programming language, it is often the case that language designers strive to determine whether the properties that were intended at the time of design actually hold for the language. It is especially desirable when these properties are established with mathematical proofs.

Proofs of language properties are often very involved and follow reasoning lines that are unique to the language at hand. Other times, these proofs follow a reasoning line that applies to many languages. To make an example, let us consider the canonical form lemmas for booleans (with if-then-else) and for the function type. The canonical form lemma of a type constructor establishes the syntactic forms of the values of that type.

Theorem *canonical-form-bool* :
$\forall e. \vdash e : \mathtt{Bool} \Rightarrow e\ is\ a\ value \Rightarrow (e = \mathtt{true} \vee e = \mathtt{false})$.
introduce the proviso of the theorem, and case analysis on $\vdash e : \mathtt{Bool}$.

© The Author(s), under exclusive license to Springer Nature Singapore Pte Ltd. 2024
J. Gibbons and D. Miller (Eds.): FLOPS 2024, LNCS 14659, pp. 291–310, 2024.
https://doi.org/10.1007/978-981-97-2300-3_15

this value is in the goal, conclude this proof case. $\#$ $e =$ `true`
this value is in the goal, conclude this proof case. $\#$ $e =$ `false`
contradiction with hypothesis "e is a value". $\#$ *case of* `if`
contradiction with hypothesis "e is a value". $\#$ *case of* `app`

Theorem *canonical-form-arrow* :

$\quad \forall e, T_1, T_2. \vdash e : T_1 \rightarrow T_2 \Rightarrow e$ *is a value* $\Rightarrow \exists e', T.$ $e = \lambda x : T.e'$
introduce the proviso of the theorem and case analysis on $\vdash e : T_1 \rightarrow T_2$.
this value is in the goal, conclude this proof case. $\#$ $e = \lambda x : T.e'$
contradiction with hypothesis "e is a value". $\#$ *case of* `if`
contradiction with hypothesis "e is a value". $\#$ *case of* `app`

The two proofs follow a well-defined schema that can be defined algorithmically. For example, their statement is built with or-formulae that contain all the productions of the grammar of values whose typing rule has output type `Bool` and the function type, respectively. Case analysis is also uniform. If the expression e is a value then it has the type being sought after because the statement specifically says $\vdash e : $ `Bool` and $\vdash e : T_1 \rightarrow T_2$, respectively. Values of other types are not even proposed by the case analysis. So, we can conclude these proof cases quickly. If the expression e is not a value then the case is proved by contradiction. A generalized proof could simply detect whether an expression that is not a value can be typed at the requested type (`Bool` or $T_1 \rightarrow T_2$ above) and appeal to a contradiction regardless of whether it is `if`, application, or whether it is `head`, `fst`, `snd`, and so on, in other languages.

In [8], Cimini has developed LANG-N-PROVE, a DSL that can express proofs based on the components of a language given as input. These proofs are *language-parametrized proofs* in that they apply to classes of languages rather than a single language. LANG-N-PROVE has been used in [8] to express type soundness proofs (canonical form lemmas, progress theorem, and type preservation theorem, except substitution lemmas). These language-parametrized proofs apply to a class of languages that is described in [8] as *pure harmonious functional languages with derived operators and error handlers*. (We describe these languages in Sect. 2.) This class includes common types and operators such as pairs, option types, sum types, universal and recursive types, exceptions, list operations such as map, filter, range and reverse, as well as others. LANG-N-PROVE generates machine-checked proofs in Abella [4] and [8] reports having generated the mechanized proof that fully machine checks the type soundness of the above-mentioned languages when the correct code for substitution lemmas is provided.

Our Contribution: Extension to Subtyping. In this paper, we extend the work of Cimini to include subtyping. Our first contribution is the LANG-N-PROVE language-parametrized proofs of type soundness for the languages captured in [8] when declarative subtyping is added to them. This endeavor entails both extending the proofs of [8] as well as modeling new proofs, namely for the subtyping and typing inversion lemmas, which were not needed in [8].

Our second contribution is the language-parametrized proofs of the equivalence between declarative and algorithmic subtyping for the above-mentioned languages. We have also extended LANG-N-PROVE with new operations for naturally expressing the language-parametrized proofs of this paper. To make an example, both inversion subtyping and typing lemmas are built from the components of inference rules. We therefore added operations to quickly retrieve premises and parts of the conclusions of rules. Furthermore, inversion typing lemmas simultaneously handle a typing rule and a subtyping rule, which then need to agree on the set of variables being used. We therefore added an operation called `align` to make the two rules use the same set of variables.

We have extended the implementation of Cimini [8] with the new operations that we describe in this paper. We have also added our language-parametrized proofs for subtyping to the tool. The repo of language definitions of [8] consists of 145 languages. (This is due to a base of several operations and types which are then combined and given in different evaluation strategies.) We have addressed the typical subtyping relation of the form $T <: T$, and therefore we have excluded from the repo languages such as System $F_{<:}$ and languages with recursive types, which make use of a relation $\Gamma \vdash T <: T$ with a context for type variables. In total, we have added subtyping to 132 languages of the repo of [8]. We did not contribute to the missing substitution lemmas of [8]. Therefore, those lemmas must be provided manually as in [8]. We confirm that our extension of LANG-N-PROVE generates the full machine-checked proof of type soundness for all these languages, when the substitution lemmas are manually added. We also confirm that our extension of LANG-N-PROVE generates the machine-checked proof of equivalence of declarative and algorithmic subtyping for all these languages, when subtyping reflexivity and a trivial lemma for the top type are admitted. (We discuss this issue in Sect. 5.)

The paper is organized as follows. Section 2 reviews operational semantics and LANG-N-PROVE. Section 3 provides our language-parametrized proofs of type soundness for declarative subtyping. Section 4 provides our language-parametrized proofs of the equivalence between declarative and algorithmic subtyping. Section 5 discusses our evaluation and the limitations of our work. Section 6 discusses related work and Sect. 7 concludes the paper.

2   Operational Semantics and Lang-n-Prove (Review)

We focus on languages defined with operational semantics. To review, Fig. 1 shows a λ-calculus with booleans, the `try` error handler, and subtyping with a top type $\top$. We call this language $\mathtt{fl}_{<:}$. (The reduction relation is standard and we do not show it in Fig. 1.)

A language has a grammar which consists of a series of *grammar rules*. A grammar rule defines a *syntactic category*, such as Type and Expression, by declaring a metavariable and its *grammar productions*, such as $\top$, Bool, and $T \rightarrow T$ of the syntactic category Type.

A language also has inference rules that define relations such as a typing and a subtyping relation. The formulae above the horizontal line are the *premises* of the rule, and the formula below is the *conclusion*. For example, $\Gamma \vdash e : T_1$

$$\text{Type} \qquad T ::= \top \mid \text{Bool} \mid T \to T$$
$$\text{Expression } e ::= \text{top} \mid \text{true} \mid \text{false} \mid \text{if } e \text{ then } e \text{ else } e$$
$$\mid x \mid \lambda x : T.e \mid (e\,e) \mid \text{raise } e \mid \text{try } e \text{ with } e$$

Declarative Type System $\boxed{\Gamma \vdash e : T}$

$$\Gamma \vdash \text{top} : \top$$

$$\Gamma \vdash \text{true} : \text{Bool} \qquad \Gamma, x : T \vdash x : T \qquad \dfrac{\Gamma, x : T_1 \vdash e : T_2}{\Gamma \vdash \lambda x : T_1.e : T_1 \to T_2}$$

$$\Gamma \vdash \text{false} : \text{Bool}$$

(T-APP)
$$\dfrac{\Gamma \vdash e_1 : T_1 \to T_2 \qquad \Gamma \vdash e_2 : T_1}{\Gamma \vdash (e_1\,e_2) : T_2}$$

(T-IF)
$$\dfrac{\Gamma \vdash e_1 : \text{Bool} \qquad \Gamma \vdash e_2 : T \qquad \Gamma \vdash e_3 : T}{\Gamma \vdash \text{if } e_1 \text{ then } e_2 \text{ else } e_3 : T}$$

(T-TRY)
$$\dfrac{\Gamma \vdash e : \text{Bool}}{\Gamma \vdash \text{raise } e : T} \qquad \dfrac{\Gamma \vdash e_1 : T \qquad \Gamma \vdash e_2 : \text{Bool} \to T}{\Gamma \vdash \text{try } e_1 \text{ with } e_2 : T}$$

(T-SUB)
$$\dfrac{\Gamma \vdash e : T_1 \qquad T_1 <: T_2}{\Gamma \vdash e : T_2}$$

Algorithmic Type System $\boxed{\Gamma \vdash\!\!\shortmid\, e : T}$

all rules of $\vdash$ except (T-APP), (T-IF), (T-TRY), and (T-SUB) but using $\vdash\!\!\shortmid$

(ALGO-T-APP)
$$\dfrac{\Gamma \vdash\!\!\shortmid\, e_1 : T_1 \to T_2 \qquad \Gamma \vdash\!\!\shortmid\, e_2 : T_3 \qquad T_3 <_a T_1}{\Gamma \vdash\!\!\shortmid\, (e_1\,e_2) : T_2}$$

(ALGO-T-IF)
$$\dfrac{\Gamma \vdash\!\!\shortmid\, e_1 : \text{Bool} \quad \Gamma \vdash\!\!\shortmid\, e_2 : T_1 \qquad \Gamma \vdash\!\!\shortmid\, e_3 : T_2 \qquad T_1 \vee T_2 = T_j}{\Gamma \vdash\!\!\shortmid\, \text{if } e_1 \text{ then } e_2 \text{ else } e_3 : T_j}$$

(ALGO-T-TRY)
$$\dfrac{\Gamma \vdash e_1 : T_1 \qquad \Gamma \vdash e_2 : T_3 \to T_2 \qquad \text{Bool} <_a T_3 \qquad T_1 \vee T_2 = T_j}{\Gamma \vdash \text{try } e_1 \text{ with } e_2 : T_j}$$

Declarative Subtyping $T <: T$, Algorithmic Subtyping $T <_a T$, and Join $T \vee T = T$

$$T <: \top \qquad T <: T \qquad \dfrac{T_1 <: T_2 \quad T_2 <: T_3}{T_1 <: T_3}$$

(S-ARROW)
$$\dfrac{T_3 <: T_1 \qquad T_2 <: T_4}{T_1 \to T_2 <: T_3 \to T_4}$$

$$T <_a \top \qquad \begin{array}{c} \text{Bool} <_a \top \\ (T_1 \to T_2) <_a \top \end{array} \qquad \text{Bool} <_a \text{Bool} \qquad \dfrac{T_3 <_a T_1 \qquad T_2 <_a T_4}{T_1 \to T_2 <_a T_3 \to T_4}$$

$$\top \vee T = \top \qquad \begin{array}{c} \text{Bool} \vee T = \top \\ T_1 \to T_2 \vee T = \top \\ \text{Bool} \vee \text{Bool} = \text{Bool} \end{array} \qquad \dfrac{T_1 \wedge T_1' = T_1'' \qquad T_2 \vee T_2' = T_2''}{\begin{array}{c} T_1 \to T_2 \\ \vee \\ T_1' \to T_2' \end{array} = T_1'' \to T_2''}$$

Fig. 1. Language definition of $\text{fl}_{<:}$ (typing and subtyping). We use notation $T <_a T$ for algorithmic subtyping rather than the more standard $\vdash\!\!\shortmid T <: T$ [21].

and $T_1 <: T_2$ are the premises of (T-SUB), and $\Gamma \vdash e : T_2$ is the conclusion of (T-SUB). Inference rules that derive $\vdash$-formulae are called *typing rules*, whereas those that derive $<:$-formulae are called *subtyping rules*. The latter rules in Fig. 1 equip $\texttt{fl}_{<:}$ with *declarative subtyping*. We refer to rules such as (S-ARROW) as *the specific* subtyping rule of the function type. It is well-known that declarative subtyping does not suggest an implementation [21], and implementations employ *algorithmic subtyping*. The inference rules of $\texttt{fl}_<$ whose conclusion can derive $\vdash$-formulae are called *algorithmic typing rules*, whereas those that derive $<a$-formulae are called *algorithmic subtyping rules*. Algorithmic typing rules do not include (T-SUB) and modify some existing typing rules to accommodate for different types where type equality is required instead. Those types are then related by subtyping means (subtyping or join, as we shall describe below). In Fig. 1, (ALGO-T-APP) replaces (T-APP), (ALGO-T-IF) replaces (T-IF), and (ALGO-T-TRY) replaces (T-TRY). (ALGO-T-APP) assigns two metavariables T_1 and T_3 to the metavariable T in (T-APP) and checks that $T_3 <: T_1$ because of parameter passing. (Following [21], (ALGO-T-APP) does not use premises $\vdash e_1 : T$ and $T <a\ T_1 \to T_2$, and neither do other rules.) Rule (T-IF) assigns T_1 and T_2 to T but these two types are peers and we compute the *join type* of them with the join operation $\vee$. The join type of T_1 and T_2 is the least common supertype of T_1 and T_2. Since the domain of functions is contravariant, the join type of two function types makes use of the meet type of their domains. The meet of T_1 and T_2 is their greatest common subtype.

LANG-N-PROVE provides a DSL for expressing proofs that apply to classes of languages, that is, language-parametrized proofs. The following provides a subset of the syntax of LANG-N-PROVE from [8], which gives the general structure of language-parametrized proofs (called *proof schemas* in the grammar below).

Proof Schema	$\hat{th}$	$::=$ **for each** Z **in** $\hat{t}$, **Theorem** $n\hat{ame} : \hat{f}$. **Proof** $\hat{p}$.
LNP Name	$n\hat{ame}$	$::= name \mid name\_(\hat{t})$
LNP Formula	$\hat{f}$	$::= n\hat{ame} : \hat{a} \mid \hat{f} \wedge \hat{f} \mid \hat{f} \vee \hat{f} \mid \hat{f} \Rightarrow \hat{f} \mid \forall X.\hat{f} \mid \exists X.\hat{f}$
		$\mid \bigwedge_{(Z \text{ in } \hat{t})} . \hat{f} \mid \bigvee_{(Z \text{ in } \hat{t})} . \hat{f} \mid \Rightarrow_{(Z \text{ in } \hat{t})} . \hat{f}$
LNP AFormula	$\hat{a}$	$::= (pname\ \hat{t}_1 \ldots \hat{t}_n)$
LNP Term	$\hat{t}$	$::= X \mid (opname\ \hat{t}_1 \cdots \hat{t}_n) \mid \texttt{ofType}(\hat{t})$
		$\mid \texttt{isEliminationForm}(\hat{t}) \mid several\ others,\ see\ [8]$
LNP Proof	$\hat{p}$	$::= \texttt{intros} \mid \texttt{search} \mid n\hat{ame} : \texttt{case}\ n\hat{ame} \mid \texttt{noOp}$
		$\mid n\hat{ame} : \texttt{induction on}\ n\hat{ame}$
		$\mid n\hat{ame}_0 : \texttt{apply}\ n\hat{ame}_1\ \texttt{to}\ n\hat{ame}_2, \ldots, n\hat{ame}_n$
		$\mid \texttt{backchain}\ n\hat{ame}$
		$\mid \hat{p}.\hat{p} \mid \texttt{for each}\ Z\ \texttt{in}\ \hat{t} : \hat{p} \mid \texttt{if}\ \hat{t}\ \texttt{then}\ \hat{p}\ \texttt{else}\ \hat{p}$

One proof has the form **Theorem** $n\hat{ame} : \hat{f}$. **Proof** $\hat{p}$ where $n\hat{ame}$ is the name of the theorem, $\hat{f}$ is its statement, and $\hat{p}$ is its proof. A proof schema $\hat{th}$ has the ability to replicate one proof for each element Z of a list $\hat{t}$. Names $n\hat{ame}$ are strings to which we can append terms. For example, *canonical-form-_(bool)*, where *bool* may come from the grammar of types, generates the lemma name

canonical-form-bool. Examples of atomic formulae $\hat{a}$ are $e \longrightarrow e$ and $\Gamma \vdash e : T$.
They are accommodated in AST style (with a top-level predicate name) but we
shall write them in their familiar shape. Formulae can use conjunction, disjunc-
tion, and implication, as well as their iterative form. For example, $\bigwedge_{(Z \text{ in } \hat{t})} \cdot \hat{f}$
generates a formula for each element Z of the list $\hat{t}$ and places these formu-
lae in conjunction. Terms can be the elements that may occur in grammars.
LANG-N-PROVE also provides operations that are specific to operational semantics. For example, ofType(*true*) looks at the typing rule of *true* and returns *bool*.
As another example, the test isEliminationForm(*app e e*) holds because function application is an elimination form while isEliminationForm(*true*) does not
hold. LANG-N-PROVE provides several of these operations. We cannot cover them
all and we refer the reader to [8]. (We shall describe operations as we encounter
them, and we shall clearly address the new operations that we added.) The proof
tactics of LANG-N-PROVE are based on Abella's tactics [4]. The tactic intros
introduces the proviso of the theorem. The search tactic denotes that we have
everything we need to prove the goal. We can do case analysis and induction
and we can apply lemmas or hypotheses. The backchain tactic applies a lemma
or hypotheses to conclude the proof case. (backchain is a bit more general, see
[4], but that is how we use it in this paper.) Proofs can be put in sequence with
$\hat{p}.\hat{p}$ and noOp has no effect. Furthermore, a for-each construct replicates a proof
for each element Z of the list $\hat{t}$, and we can use an if-then-else statement.

LANG-N-PROVE has been applied to a class of languages that [8] describes as
1) pure functional, i.e., reduction relation $e \longrightarrow e$, 2) harmonious [11,19], i.e.,
operators can be classified in introduction forms and elimination forms and 3)
to which we can add error handlers and derived operators (such as let, though
we have not added any in $\mathtt{fl}_{<:}$). Due to lack of space, we cannot review this
class in detail, and we refer the reader to Section 2 and 9 of [8].

3   Declarative Subtyping with Lang-n-Prove

3.1   Inversion Subtyping Lemmas

The proof of type safety uses an inversion subtyping lemma for each type constructor. The lemma establishes what information we can derive from a formula
$T_1 <: T_2$ when T_2 is built with such constructor applied to distinct metavariables. These lemmas are built from the subtyping rule of that type constructor.
Figure 2 shows the inversion subtyping lemma of the function type and list type
at the bottom of the figure. We use colors to show how the components of their
subtyping rules form such lemmas. For example, for the function type, the lemma
starts with a type $T_3 \rightarrow T_4$ obtained from the right argument of the subtyping
formula in the conclusion of the subtyping rule. The lemma derives the type T
that would be a subtype of that type according to the rule, which is the left
argument of the <:-conclusion. Furthermore, it also establishes the conditions
that must have held; These are the premises of the subtyping rule.

① for each ty in $(Type - \top)$, Theorem *inversion-subtyping-_(ty)* :
②   let $r = ty.\text{rule}[<:]$ in
③ $\forall *.$ Main: $T <: r.\text{right} \Rightarrow \exists *.\ T = \boxed{r.\text{left}}\ (\bigwedge_{(p\ \text{in}\ \boxed{r.\text{premises}})} \cdot\ \boxed{p}\ ).$
④ Proof. intros. *(PremiseAt _)* : induction on *Main*.
⑤ search. search.
⑥ apply *IH0* to *(PremiseAt 1)*. apply *IH0* to *(PremiseAt 0)*. search.

Example of statements:

$$\frac{T_3 <: T_1 \quad T_2 <: T_4}{\boxed{T_1 \to T_2} <: \ T_3 \to T_4} \qquad\qquad \frac{T_1 <: T_2}{\text{List } \boxed{T_1} \ <: \ \text{List } T_2} \qquad \begin{array}{l} \text{premises} \\ \text{left} \\ \text{right} \end{array}$$

Theorem *inversion-subtyping-arrow*:
$\forall T, T_3, T_4.\ T <: T_3 \to T_4 \Rightarrow \exists T_1, T_2.\ T = \boxed{T_1 \to T_2}\ \wedge T_3 <: T_1 \wedge T_2 <: T_4$

Theorem *inversion-subtyping-list* :
$\forall T, T_2.\ T <: \text{List } T_2 \Rightarrow \exists T_1.\ T = \boxed{\text{List } T_1}\ \wedge T_1 <: T_2$

Fig. 2. Language-parametrized proof for inversion subtyping lemmas

To use this approach, we extended LANG-N-PROVE with a dot-notation $t.\text{rule}[rel]$ to return the rule that defines the relation rel for the top-level constructor of the term t. This dot-notation is also used to retrieve parts of rules: $r.\text{left}$ retrieves the left argument of the conclusion of r, $r.\text{right}$ retrieves the right argument, and $r.\text{premises}$ retrieves the premises of the rule as a list. Our language-parametrized proof is in Fig. 2. Line 1 generates a lemma for each type ty in the grammar Type (except $\top$, which does not need one). The name of each lemma contains the top-level constructor name of ty, appended with "$\_(ty)$" at Line 1. Then, $ty.\text{rule}[<:]$ retrieves the subtyping rule of ty. Line 3 builds the statement of the lemma: If T is a subtype of $r.\text{right}$ then T must be $r.\text{left}$ and satisfy the (subtyping) premises of r. The latter part is realized with an and-quantification over $r.\text{premises}$. Notice that we have also extended LANG-N-PROVE with *automatic quantification* $\forall *$, used at Line 3. This operation universally quantifies the variables that are not already quantified in the formula that follows. (We have also added its existential counterpart $\exists *$.)

The proof is by induction on the main premise of the theorem. There are three cases. The first is for the specific subtyping rule of the type constructor and the second is for reflexivity and they both trivially hold. The third case is for transitivity, which offers premises $T_1 <: T_2$ and $T_2 <: T_3 \to T_4$. We apply the inductive hypothesis on the second premise to derive that T_2 is a function type, which makes the inductive hypothesis applicable to the first premise, as well. Afterwards, the goal trivially holds.

Line 4–6 generates the proof. We have extended LANG-N-PROVE with families of hypotheses $(NameOfHyp\ n_1\ n_2\ \dots\ n_k)$ for numbers $n_1, n_2, \dots n_k$, which simply creates the hypothesis name $NameOfHyp\text{-}n_1\text{-}n_2\text{-}\dots\text{-}n_k$. (The benefits

for each *ty* in *Type*, Theorem *canonical-form-__(ty)* : ... *see [8]*
Proof. *(TypingPremAt __)* : induction on *Main.*
    ... *see [8]*
apply *inversion-subtype-__(ty)* to *(TypingPremAt 0).* backchain *IH0*

Fig. 3. Language-parametrized proof for canonical form lemmas

Theorem *progress* : $\forall e, T.$ *Main* : $\vdash e : T \Rightarrow e$ *progresses.*
Proof. *Typ* : induction on *Main.*
    ... *see [8]*
backchain   .

for each *e* in *Expression*, Theorem *progress-__(e)* : ... *see [8]*
Proof. intros. *Typ* : induction on *Main.*
    ... *see [8]*
backchain *IH0.*

Fig. 4. Language-parametrized proofs for the progress theorem

of this feature are best seen in Sect. 4.3). Line 4 declares family *(PremiseAt __)*. The inductive hypothesis is applied to the second premise *(PremiseAt 1)* first and then to the first *(PremiseAt 0)* before concluding the proof.

3.2 Canonical Form Lemmas

Figure 3 highlights the modifications that we made to the proof of canonical form lemmas of [8]. The proof in [8] performs a case analysis on typing formulae, but our proof needs to handle the extra case for the subsumption rule (T-SUB), which is inductive. Therefore, the proof is by induction rather than case analysis. Rule (T-SUB) offers $\Gamma \vdash e : T_3$ and $T_3 <: T_1 \rightarrow T_2$ for some T_3. We apply the *inversion subtyping lemma* to discover that $T_3 = T'_1 \rightarrow T'_2$ for some T'_1 and T'_2, which derives $\Gamma \vdash e : T'_1 \rightarrow T'_2$. The inductive hypothesis concludes the proof. Appendix B shows an example of this proof for the function type.

3.3 Progress Theorem

The progress theorem is divided into two parts in [8]. The first part is the main theorem, which calls the operator-specific progress theorem of each expression constructor. An example of such theorem is *progress-app* for function application: $\forall T, e_1, e_2.$ $\Gamma \vdash (e_1 \ e_2) : T \Rightarrow e_1$ *progresses* $\Rightarrow e_2$ *progresses* $\Rightarrow (e_1 \ e_2)$ *progresses,* where "*e progresses*" holds whenever *e* is a value, *e* is an error, or $e \longrightarrow e'$. We refer the reader to [8] for their proofs. Figure 4 highlights the modifications that we made to them. They both need to handle the extra case of (T-SUB) with the inductive hypothesis. The operator-specific theorems use case analysis in [8] but they need induction here for the same reasons as in the canonical form lemmas.

① `for each` v `in` *Value*, `Theorem` *inversion-typing-_(v)* :
②   `let` *srule* = `ofType(`v`).rule[<:]` `in`
③   `let` *trule* = `align` v`.rule[⊢]` `to` *srule* `where` `outputType = left` `in`
④ $\forall*.$ `Main` $: \Gamma \vdash$ *trule*.`exp` $:$ *srule*.`right`
⑤ $\Rightarrow \exists*. (\bigwedge_{(p\ \text{in}\ \boxed{trule.\text{premises}})} \cdot \boxed{p}) \wedge (\bigwedge_{(p\ \text{in}\ \boxed{srule.\text{premises}})} \cdot \boxed{p}).$
⑥ `Proof.` *(SubtypingPremAt _)* : `induction on` *Main*.
⑦ `search.`
⑧ `apply` *inversion-subtyping-_(*`ofType(`v`))` `to` *(SubtypingPremAt 1)*.
⑨ `apply` *IH0* `to` *(SubtypingPremAt 0)*. `search.`

Example for λ-abstraction: *(More examples can be found in Appendix A)*

$$\frac{\Gamma, x : T' \vdash e : T''}{\Gamma \vdash \lambda x : T'.e : T' \to T''} \quad \Longrightarrow \quad \frac{\Gamma, x : T_1 \vdash e : T_2}{\Gamma \vdash \boxed{\lambda x : T_1.e} \; : \; T_1 \to T_2} \quad \begin{array}{l}\boxed{\text{premises}}\\[4pt]\boxed{\text{exp}}\\[4pt]\boxed{\text{outputType}}\end{array}$$

$$\frac{T_3 <: T_1 \quad T_2 <: T_4}{T_1 \to T_2 \; <: \; T_3 \to T_4} \quad \begin{array}{l}\boxed{\text{premises}}\\[4pt]\boxed{\text{left, must align with outputType}}\\[4pt]\text{right}\end{array}$$

`Theorem` *inversion-typing-abs* :
$\forall e, T_1, T_3, T_4.$
$\Gamma \vdash \boxed{\lambda x : T_1.e} \; : \; T_3 \to T_4 \Rightarrow \exists T_2. \; \boxed{\Gamma, x : T_1 \vdash e : T_2} \; \wedge T_3 <: T_1 \wedge T_2 <: T_4$

Fig. 5. Language-parametrized proof for inversion typing lemmas

3.4 Inversion Typing Lemmas

The proof of type safety uses an inversion typing lemma for each value. For a value v, this lemma establishes what information we can derive from $\Gamma \vdash v : T$ when T is built with a type constructor applied to distinct metavariables. As the value may have been typed using the subsumption rule, the information we derive is not from the premises of the typing rule alone but also from the premises of the subtyping rule of the type of the value. To combine both premises, however, they need to align w.r.t. the names of their metavariables.

Figure 5 shows an example lemma (and others can be found in Appendix A) and our language-parametrized proof. Line 1 generates a lemma for each value, and 2–5 generate one statement. Line 2 retrieves the type of the value with `ofType(`v`)` and binds its subtyping rule to *srule*. Line 3 also retrieves the typing rule of the value with v`.rule[⊢]`. We have added labels `exp` and `outputType` to our dot-notation to retrieve e and T of $\Gamma \vdash e : T$. We also added the operation `align` r_1 `to` r_2 `where` $\ell_1 = \ell_2$. This operation returns a rule that is α-equivalent to rule r_1 and is such that the argument in its conclusion that is denoted by the label ℓ_1 matches the argument in the conclusion of r_2 that is denoted by ℓ_2. Line 3 uses `align` to obtain a version of the typing rule where its output type makes use of the same variables as the left argument of the conclusion of *srule*. Lines 4–5 creates the lemma statement as described above.

(1) Theorem *type-preservation* : $\forall e, e', T.\ Main : \vdash e : T \Rightarrow Step : e \longrightarrow e' \Rightarrow \vdash e' : T$

(2) Proof *(PremAt __)* : induction on *Main*.

(3) for each e in *Expression* :

(4)   *StepOfArg* : case *Step*.

(5)   for each tg in stepsWithoutPM(e) : if containsSubst(tg) then □ else search.

(6)   if isEliminationForm(e)

(7)   for each v in valuesOf(getArgType(e, 0)) :

(8)   if containsSubst(targetOfElimForm(e, v)) then □

(9)   else apply *inversion-typing-__*(v) to *(PremAt 0)*. search.

(10)   else if isErrorHandler(e)

(11)   for each err in *Error* :

(12)   if containsSubst(targetOfErrorHandler(e, err)) then □

(13)   else apply *inversion-typing-__*(err) to *(PremAt 0)*. search.

(14)   else noOp

(15) for each i in contextualArgs(e) : apply *IH0* to *(PremAt i) StepOfArg*. search

(16) for each i in contextualArgs(e) : if isErrorHandler(e) and $i = 0$

(17)   then noOp else backchain *error-types-all*

(18) apply *IH0* to *(PremAt 0) Step*. search

apply substitution lemma at □

Fig. 6. Language-parametrized proof for the type preservation theorem

The proof is by induction on $\Gamma \vdash v : T$. There are two cases: 1) The typing rule of the value, which trivially holds (Line 7), and 2) rule (T-SUB), which is proved in the same way as for the canonical form lemmas (Lines 8–9).

Inversion lemmas for errors are simpler and can be found in Appendix C.

3.5   Type Preservation Theorem

Type preservation establishes that for each expression e such that $\vdash e : T$, for some T, if $e \longrightarrow e'$, then $\vdash e' : T$. The proof is by induction on $\vdash e : T$ and then by case analysis on the steps of e. Our proof differs from [8] only for elimination forms and error handlers, and for handling (T-SUB).

Consider the reduction rule head (cons $v_1\ v_2$) $\longrightarrow v_1$. In the corresponding proof case, the proof offers the premise of the typing rule of head: $\vdash$ cons $v_1\ v_2$: List T, for some T. With (T-SUB) absent, the proof of [8] retrieves the types of v_1 and v_2 with a case analysis on that typing formula. As we have (T-SUB), we must apply an inversion typing lemma. This means that, for a reduction rule, we need to know which value is handled so that we can call the correct inversion typing lemma and conclude the proof. Error handlers follow the same line.

Figure 6 shows our proof for the type preservation theorem. It is the one in [8] except for the parts that are highlighted. Lines 6–9 handle elimination forms in the way described above. Line 7 retrieves the type of the first argument (index 0)

① Theorem *subtyping-soundness* : $\forall*$. *Main* : $T_1 <a\ T_2 \Rightarrow T_1 <: T_2$.
② Proof. (*PremiseAt* __) : induction on *Main*.
③ search.
④ for each *ty* in (*Type* $-\ \top$) :
⑤   for each *p* in *ty*.rule[$<a$].premises[$<a$] : apply *IH0* to (*PremiseAt p*).
⑥   search. search.

⑦ Theorem *typing-soundness* : $\forall*$. *Main* : $\vdash\!\!\!\!\vdash e : T \Rightarrow\ \vdash e : T$.
⑧ Proof. (*Prem* __) : induction on *Main*.
⑨ for each *e* in *Expression* :
⑩   for each *p* in *e*.rule[$\vdash\!\!\!\!\vdash$].premises[$\vdash\!\!\!\!\vdash$] : apply *IH0* to (*Prem p*).
⑪   for each *p* in *e*.rule[$\vdash\!\!\!\!\vdash$].premises[$<a$] : apply *subtyping-soundness* to (*Prem p*).
⑫   for each *p* in *e*.rule[$\vdash\!\!\!\!\vdash$].premises[$\vee$] : apply *join-implies-subtyping* to (*Prem p*).
⑬ search.

Fig. 7. Language-parametrized proofs for subtyping and typing soundness

of *e* with `getArgType`$(e, 0)$. (Values are handled at argument 0 by convention.) We retrieve all the values of that type with `valuesOf` and, for each, we retrieve the target of the reduction rule of the elimination form (e) that handles that value (v). We do so with a new operation `targetOfElimForm`(e, v) that we have added to LANG-N-PROVE. If substitution is not used, we apply the inversion typing lemma and conclude the proof. If *tg* uses substitution (`containsSubst`(tg)), [8] leaves a hole $\Box$ in the proof because [8] does not provide substitution lemmas and we do not either. Lines 10–14 handle error handlers similarly. Line 18 handles the subsumption rule with the induction hypothesis.

4 Algorithmic Subtyping

4.1 Subtyping and Typing Soundness

Figure 7 shows the proofs for the soundness of algorithmic subtyping and typing. The former establishes that algorithmic subtyping implies declarative subtyping. Its proof is by induction on how to derive algorithmic subtyping formulae. The first case is for $\top <a\ \top$, which holds trivially (Line 3). For all other type constructors, we have two cases: 1) their specific subtyping rule and 2) the rule that declares them as a subtype of $\top$ (e.g., $T_1 \rightarrow T_2 <a\ \top$). For the former, we call the inductive hypothesis on the premises to turn them into $<:$-formulae and conclude the case. The latter case holds trivially (second `search` of Line 6).

Typing soundness establishes that if an expression has some algorithmic type T then it also has type T according to declarative subtyping. Its proof (bottom of Fig. 7) is similar to *subtyping-soundness*. This time around, algorithmic typing rules have three kinds of premises: 1) Algorithmic typing premises, to which we apply the inductive hypothesis to turn them into declarative typing formulae, 2) $<a$-premises, to which we apply soundness to turn them into $<:$-formulae, and 3) join premises, to which we apply the *join-implies-subtyping* lemma that derives that $T_1 \vee T_2 = T_3$ implies $T_1 <: T_3$ and $T_2 <: T_3$.

(1) Theorem *subtyping-completeness* : $\forall *.\ Main : T_1 <: T_2 \Rightarrow T_1 <a\ T_2.$
(2) Proof. (*PremiseAt i*) : induction on *Main*.
(3) backchain *subtype-algo-top*.
(4) for each *ty* in (*Type* − ⊤) :
(5)   for each *p* in *ty*.rule[<a].premises[<a] : apply *IH0* to (*PremiseAt p*).
(6)   search.
(7) backchain *subtype-algo-reflexivity*.
(8) apply *IH0* to (*PremiseAt 0*). apply *IH0* to (*PremiseAt 1*).
(9) backchain *subtype-algo-transitivity*.

Fig. 8. Language-parametrized proofs for subtyping completeness

4.2 Subtyping Completeness

Figure 8 shows the language-parametrized proof for the completeness of algorithmic subtyping, that is, declarative subtyping implies algorithmic subtyping. The proof is by induction and there are four cases. The first case is for the rule $T <: \top$, which is proved with lemma *subtype-algo-top*: $\forall T.T <a\ \top$ (Line 3). The second case is for all algorithmic subtyping rules of constructors other than ⊤. We apply the inductive hypothesis to their premises to turn them into $<a$-formulae and conclude (Lines 4–6). The third case is reflexivity, which is proved with lemma *subtype-algo-reflexivity* (Line 7). The fourth case is transitivity. We turn the two premises into $<a$-formulae and we conclude with lemma *subtype-algo-transitivity*: $\forall T_1, T_2, T_3.T_1 <a\ T_2 \Rightarrow T_2 <a\ T_3 \Rightarrow T_1 <a\ T_3$ (Lines 8–9).

4.3 Typing Completeness

Typing completeness establishes that if an expression has some type T_1 according to declarative typing, then it has algorithmic type T_2, for some type $T_2 <: T_1$ (We follow TAPL [21].) The proof is by induction on the typability of expressions. For each declarative typing rule, we seek its corresponding algorithmic rule. The proof is based on the premises in the algorithmic typing rule, as they must be satisfied: typing premises, subtyping premises, and join premises.

For typing premises, we apply the inductive hypothesis to derive its algorithmic version. Notice that the theorem needs to prove *algorithmic* typing of e and *declarative* subtyping $T_2 <: T_1$. Therefore, we always derive subtyping information in both declarative and algorithmic forms. There is another aspect to handle. We call a type *constructed* if it is built with a type constructor. If the output type of the premise is constructed, then the inductive hypothesis may derive a formula such as, say, $T <: T_1 \rightarrow (T_2 \rightarrow T_3)$. We then must use the inversion subtyping lemma to derive that T is $T_1' \rightarrow T2'$ with $T_1 <: T_1'$ and $T_2' <: (T_2 \rightarrow T_3)$. As we can see, we would also need to apply the inversion subtyping lemma for T_2' and, in general, for all the subterms that are constructed and appear in covariant position, as $T_2 \rightarrow T_3$ in $T_1 \rightarrow (T_2 \rightarrow T_3)$, because they end up at the right of a <:-formula with a metavariable on the left.

① Theorem *typing-completeness* : $\forall *$. *Main* : $\vdash e : T_1 \Rightarrow \exists *$. $\vdash e : T_2 \wedge T_2 <: T_1$.
② Proof. (*PremiseAt* __) : induction on *Main*.
③ for each *e* in *Expression* :
④   for each *p* in *e*.rule[↦].premises[↦] :
⑤   (*Ih p* __) : apply *IH0* to (*PremiseAt p*).
⑥   (*SubtypeA p*) : apply *subtyping-completeness* to (*Ih p 1*).
⑦   if constructed(*p*.out) then
⑧   (*Subtype p* __) : apply *inversion-subtyping__*(*p*.out) to (*Ih p 1*).
⑨   (*SubtypeA p* __) : apply *inversion-subtyping-algo__*(*p*.out) to (*SubtypeA p*).
⑩   for each *i* in range(arity(*p*.out)) :
⑪   if constructed(getArg(*p*.out, *i*)) and covariant(*p*.out, *i*) then
⑫   (*Subtype p i* __) : apply *inv-sub__*(getArg(*p*.out, *i*)) to (*Ih p 1*).
⑬   (*SubtypeA p i* __) : apply *inv-sub-alg__*(getArg(*p*.out, *i*)) to (*SubtypeA p*)
⑭   else noOp
⑮   else noOp (* below, "premises" is shorthand for rule[↦].premises[↦] *)
⑯   for each *p* in *e*.rule[↦].premises[<*a*] :
⑰   if varIsInPremises(*p*.left, *premises*)
⑱   and varIsInPremises(*p*.right, *premises*) then
⑲   apply *subtyping-algo-transitivity* to (*SubtypeA* ⇐ findVar *p*.left *premises*)
⑳   (*SubtypeA* ⇐ findVar *p*.right *premises*)
㉑   else noOp
㉒   for each *p* in *e*.rule[↦].premises[∨] :
㉓   if varIsInPremises(*p*.left, *premises*)
㉔   and varIsInPremises(*p*.right, *premises*) then
㉕   (*Join* __) : apply *existence-of-join* to (*SubtypeA* ⇐ findVar *p*.left *premises*)
㉖   (*SubtypeA* ⇐ findVar *p*.right *premises*)
㉗   apply *subtyping-soundness* to (*Join 1*).
㉘   else noOp
㉙   search.
㉚ apply *IH0* to (*PremiseAt 0*). search

Fig. 9. Language-parametrized proof for typing completeness. Above, *inv-sub* abbreviates *inversion-subtyping* and *inv-sub-alg* abbreviates *inversion-subtyping-algo*. The latter derives <*a*-formulae rather than <:-formulae.

For subtyping premises $T_1 <a\ T_2$, the inductive hypothesis or an inversion lemma of the previous step had produced one <*a*-formula for T_1 and one for T_2. We apply transitivity to derive $T_1 <a\ T_2$. For join premises $T_1 \vee T_2 = T_3$, we analogously have one <*a*-formula for T_1 and one for T_2 from induction or inversion. The *existence-of-join* lemma then derives the existence of a join T_3.

Figure 9 shows the proof for typing completeness. Lines 4–15 handle typing premises as described above. We implemented the operators `constructed` and `covariant` to test those properties on terms. Although an inversion subtyping lemma should be applied exhaustively for the output type, out of simplicity, we apply it only to the top-level (Lines 7–9) and its direct arguments (Lines 10–14).

We use families of hypotheses to model a coordinate system to locate formulae. We store <:-formulae within the *Subtyping* family and <*a*-formulae within the *SubtypingA* family. Consider $T_1 \to (T_2 \to T_3)$ from above, and assume it is from the third premise. We store the $<a$-formula of T_1 in *(SubtypeA 2 0)* because it is the first (0) argument of the top-level constructor from the third (2) premise. The $<a$-formula of T_2 is stored in *(SubtypeA 2 1 0)* because it is the first argument (0) of the second argument (1) of the constructor.

Lines 16–21 handle subtyping premises as described above. The transitivity lemma requires the $<a$-formulae of the two metavariables to be linked. These are stored according to the coordinate system just described. We extended LANG-N-PROVE with the operation *(Hyp $\Leftarrow$ findVar var premises)*, which finds the position of the metavariable *var* in the premises *premises* and builds a hypothesis based on that position. For example, for T_2 above, it finds the coordinate 2-1-0 and returns *(Hyp 2 1 0)*. Line 19 uses this operation with family *SubtypeA* to generate *(SubtypeA 2 1 0)*, exactly where the previous step would have placed the $<a$-formula for T_2. We also implemented `varIsInPremises` to check beforehand that metavariables can be found. Lines 22–28 handle join premises and find the hypotheses for *existence-of-join* with `findVar`.

After all this information has been derived, Line 29 concludes this case with `search`. Finally, Line 30 handles (T-SUB) with the inductive hypothesis.

5   Evaluation and Limitations of Our Work

We have extended the implementation of LANG-N-PROVE with the new operations described in this paper: dot-notation to retrieve rules and components of rules, automatic quantifications $\forall*$ and $\exists*$, and families of hypotheses (Sect. 3.1), `align` (Sect. 3.4), `targetOfElimForm` (Sect. 3.5), and `constructed`, `covariant`, `varIsInPremises`, and `findVar` (Sect. 4.3). LANG-N-PROVE accepts a textual representation of languages[1] similar to Ott [24]. The repo of language definitions of LANG-N-PROVE contains 145 functional languages with common types and operators. We do not handle subtyping à la System $F_<$ nor recursive subtyping (see paragraph "Limitations" below). Therefore, we could extend 132 of those languages with subtyping (and $\top$). (Appendix D shows examples of algorithmic typing rules that we have used.) We confirm that the language-parametrized proofs of Sects. 3 (type soundness) generate the Abella [4] code that machine-checks the type soundness of the languages above, except that, as in [8], substitution lemmas must be manually provided.

Other proofs rely on lemmas *join-implies-subtype*, *subtyping-algo-transitivity*, and others. We did not show their language-parametrized proofs but they can be found in the repo of the tool [12]. However, we admit two trivial lemmas, *subtype-algo-top* : $\forall T.T <a \top$ and *subtype-algo-reflexivity* : $\forall T.T <a T$ because Abella does not allow induction over T. We could solve this with a predicate, say `isType`, that establishes the structure of T. However, this changes the two lemmas and imposes other theorems to prove `isType` formulae. We did not include this reasoning in our proofs. We confirm that the language-parametrized

---

[1] See `.lan` files at https://github.com/mcimini/lang-n-prove/blob/main/repo-subDA.

proof of the equivalence between declarative and algorithmic subtyping generate the Abella proof code that machine-checks such equivalence for the 132 above-mentioned languages, except that reflexivity and *subtype-algo-top* are admitted.

Limitations. We do not handle languages with a state, dependent types, typestate, and many other sophisticated type systems. We also address a subtyping relation $T <: T$ whereas some languages such as System $F_{<:}$ and languages with recursive types use a context for type variables, and are therefore out of our scope. Also, our typing completeness proof of Sect. 4.3 does not support chained subtyping formulae as in premises $T_1 \vee T_2 = T_3$ and $T_3 <: T_4$ and $T_4 <: T_5$. This would require multiple applications of the transitivity lemma to follow such formulae. This situation did not occur in the many languages that we tested. The tool does not provide useful error messages, as it lacks a debugging system that links errors in the generated proofs back to the source code.

6 Related Work

The work of Pfenning and Schürmann with Twelf [20] demonstrates that the theorems of type safety can be automatically proved for some functional languages. Veritas [13–15] creates soundness theorems from language definitions, and these theorems are then checked with an automated prover. With intrinsic typing [6], the evaluator of a language is implemented using a type theory in such a way that if it type checks then the language is type sound [1–3,5,16,22,23,26]. Cimini et al. [10] proposes an extrinsic type system that classifies parts of a (functional) language definition and imposes a language organization [7,10].

These approaches differ from our work in that they do not *describe* proofs. Although some of these approaches can automate "prove lemma using induction and auxiliary lemma ℓ", they do not express statements and proofs based on the grammar, inference rules, and roles of operators (intro/elimination forms).

7 Conclusion

We presented language-parametrized proofs for the type soundness of the languages addressed in [8] when subtyping (and ⊤) is added and for establishing the equivalence of declarative and algorithmic subtyping.

We added subtyping (and ⊤) to 132 of the 145 languages in the repo of [8]. Our extension of LANG-N-PROVE has generated the Abella proofs that machine-check their type soundness, when the substitution lemmas are provided. Our proofs also mechanize the equivalence of declarative and algorithmic subtyping, though two trivial lemmas (reflexivity and *subtype-algo-top*) are admitted.

In the future, we plan to explore generating proofs for other theorem provers. There is work on automatically adding subtyping to languages [17,18] and we plan to integrate it with our tool. We would like to study the complexity of our proofs as illustrated in [9]. We also would like to develop a language-parametrized proof of strong normalization based on Tait's method [25].

Acknowledgments. This material is based upon work supported by the National Science Foundation under Grant No. 2317257.

A   Examples of Inversion Typing Lemmas

Figure 10 provides more examples of inversion typing lemmas produced by Fig. 5.

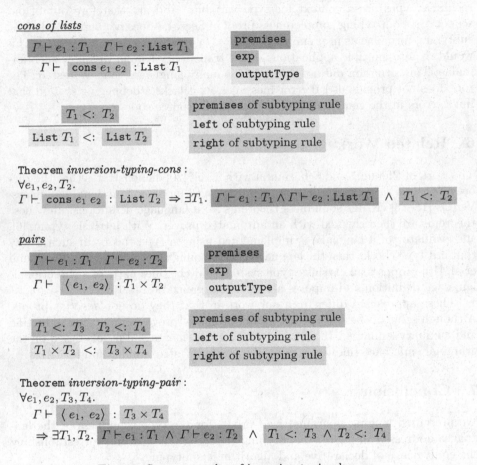

Fig. 10. Some examples of inversion typing lemmas

B   Examples of Generated Proofs

The following are the Abella proofs generated by our language-parametrized proofs of the inversion subtyping lemma and canonical form lemma for the function type in the simply typed λ-calculus. Language definition at:

https://github.com/mcimini/lang-n-prove/blob/main/repo-subD/stlc_cbv.lan

```
Theorem Inversion-subtype-arrow:
forall typ, forall T1', forall T2',
 {subtype typ (arrow T1' T2')} -> exists T1, exists T2,
      (typ = (arrow T1 T2))
      /\ (({subtype T1' T1}) /\ ({subtype T2 T2'})).
IH0 : induction on 1. intros Main.
PremiseAt0: case Main.
search.
search.
apply IH0 to PremiseAt1.
apply IH0 to PremiseAt0.
search.


Theorem Canonical-form-arrow:
forall e, forall T1, forall T2,
 {typeOf (empty) e (arrow T1 T2)} -> {value e} ->
      exists T1, exists R2, e = (abs T1 R2).
IH0 : induction on 1. intros Main ValHyp.
TypingPremAt0: case Main.
search.
case ValHyp.
apply Inversion-subtype-arrow to TypingPremAt1.
backchain IH0.
```

C Inversion Typing Lemmas for Errors

① for each *err* in *Error*, **Theorem** *inversion-typing-_(err)* :
②   let $r = err.\text{rule}[\vdash]$ in
② $\forall*.\ Main : \Gamma \vdash r.\text{exp} : r.\text{outputType} \Rightarrow \exists*.\ (\bigwedge_{(p\ \text{in}\ r.\text{premises})} \cdot p).$
⑤ **Proof.** *Subtype0* : induction on *Main*.
⑥ search. backchain *IH0*.

D Examples of Algorithmic Typing Rules

Below, we show some examples of algorithmic typing rules (other than those of
$fl_{<:}$) that we have used in our tested language definitions.

Our extension of LANG-N-PROVE uses |a- to denote the algorithmic typing
relation and <a to denote the algorithmic subtyping relation.

```
Gamma |a- (cons E1 E2) : (list T3)
<== Gamma |a- E1 : T1
    /\ Gamma |a- E2 : (list T2)
    /\ join T1 T2 T3.
```

```
Gamma |a- (append E1 E2) : (list T3)
<== Gamma |a- E1 : (list T1)
    /\ Gamma |a- E2 : (list T2)
    /\ join T1 T2 T3.

Gamma |a- (filter E1 E2) : (list T1)
<== Gamma |a- E1 : (list T1)
    /\ Gamma |a- E2 : (arrow T2 (bool))
    /\ T1 <a T2.

Gamma |a- (map E1 E2) : (list T3)
<== Gamma |a- E1 : (list T1)
    /\ Gamma |a- E2 : (arrow T2 T3)
    /\ T1 <a T2.

Gamma |a- (fix E) : T2 <== Gamma |a- E : (arrow T1 T2)
                          /\ T2 <a T1.
```

References

1. Altenkirch, T., Reus, B.: Monadic presentations of lambda terms using generalized inductive types. In: Flum, J., Rodriguez-Artalejo, M. (eds.) CSL 1999. LNCS, vol. 1683, pp. 453–468. Springer, Heidelberg (1999). https://doi.org/10.1007/3-540-48168-0_32
2. Appel, A.W., Leroy, X.: A list-machine benchmark for mechanized metatheory: (extended abstract). Electron. Notes Theor. Comput. Sci. **174**(5), 95–108 (2007). https://doi.org/10.1016/j.entcs.2007.01.020
3. Bach Poulsen, C., Rouvoet, A., Tolmach, A., Krebbers, R., Visser, E.: Intrinsically-typed definitional interpreters for imperative languages. In: Proceedings of the ACM on Programming Languages (PACMPL), vol. 2, no. POPL, December 2017. https://doi.org/10.1145/3158104
4. Baelde, D., et al.: Abella: a system for reasoning about relational specifications. J. Formaliz. Reason. **7**(2), 1–89 (2014). https://doi.org/10.6092/issn.1972-5787/4650
5. Benton, N., Hur, C., Kennedy, A., McBride, C.: Strongly typed term representations in Coq. J. Autom. Reason. **49**(2), 141–159 (2012). https://doi.org/10.1007/s10817-011-9219-0
6. Church, A.: A formulation of the simple theory of types. J. Symb. Log. **5**, 56–68 (1940). https://doi.org/10.2307/2266170
7. Cimini, M.: Early experience in teaching the basics of functional language design with a language type checker. In: Bowman, W.J., Garcia, R. (eds.) TFP 2019. LNCS, vol. 12053, pp. 21–37. Springer, Cham (2020). https://doi.org/10.1007/978-3-030-47147-7_2
8. Cimini, M.: Lang-n-prove: a DSL for language proofs. In: Proceedings of the 15th ACM SIGPLAN International Conference on Software Language Engineering, SLE 2022, New York, NY, USA, pp. 16–29. Association for Computing Machinery (2022). https://doi.org/10.1145/3567512.3567514

9. Cimini, M.: Towards the complexity analysis of programming language proof methods. In: Ábrahám, E., Dubslaff, C., Tarifa, S.L.T. (eds.) ICTAC 2023. LNCS, vol. 14446, pp. 100–118. Springer, Cham (2023). https://doi.org/10.1007/978-3-031-47963-2_8

10. Cimini, M., Miller, D., Siek, J.G.: Extrinsically typed operational semantics for functional languages. In: Lämmel, R., Tratt, L., de Lara, J. (eds.) Proceedings of the 13th ACM SIGPLAN International Conference on Software Language Engineering, SLE 2020, Virtual Event, USA, 16–17 November 2020, pp. 108–125. ACM (2020). https://doi.org/10.1145/3426425.3426936

11. Dummett, M.: Frege: Philosophy of Language, 2nd edn. Harvard University Press, Cambridge (1993)

12. Galasso, S., Cimini, M.: Extension of the lang-n-prove tool (2023). GitHub repo of the Lang-n-Prove tool at https://github.com/mcimini/lang-n-prove

13. Grewe, S., Erdweg, S., Mezini, M.: Using vampire in soundness proofs of type systems. In: Kovács, L., Voronkov, A. (eds.) Proceedings of the 1st and 2nd Vampire Workshops. EPiC Series in Computing, vol. 38, pp. 33–51. EasyChair (2016). https://doi.org/10.29007/22x6

14. Grewe, S., Erdweg, S., Mezini, M.: Automating proof steps of progress proofs: comparing Vampire and Dafny. In: Kovács, L., Voronkov, A. (eds.) Vampire 2016. Proceedings of the 3rd Vampire Workshop. EPiC Series in Computing, vol. 44, pp. 33–45. EasyChair (2017). https://doi.org/10.29007/5zjp

15. Grewe, S., Erdweg, S., Wittmann, P., Mezini, M.: Type systems for the masses: deriving soundness proofs and efficient checkers. In: Murphy, G.C., Steele, G.L., Jr. (eds.) 2015 ACM International Symposium on New Ideas, New Paradigms, and Reflections on Programming and Software (Onward!), Onward! 2015, New York, NY, USA, pp. 137–150. ACM (2015). https://doi.org/10.1145/2814228.2814239

16. Harper, R., Stone, C.: A type-theoretic interpretation of Standard ML. In: Plotkin, G., Stirling, C., Tofte, M. (eds.) Proof, Language, and Interaction: Essays in Honor of Robin Milner. MIT Press (2000). https://doi.org/10.5555/345868.345906

17. Mourad, B., Cimini, M.: A calculus for language transformations. In: Chatzigeorgiou, A., et al. (eds.) SOFSEM 2020. LNCS, vol. 12011, pp. 547–555. Springer, Cham (2020). https://doi.org/10.1007/978-3-030-38919-2_44

18. Mourad, B., Cimini, M.: System description: lang-n-change - a tool for transforming languages. In: Nakano, K., Sagonas, K. (eds.) FLOPS 2020. LNCS, vol. 12073, pp. 198–214. Springer, Cham (2020). https://doi.org/10.1007/978-3-030-59025-3_12

19. Pfenning, F.: Lecture notes on harmony (lecture 3) 15-317: constructive logic (2009). https://www.cs.cmu.edu/~fp/courses/15317-f09/lectures/03-harmony.pdf

20. Pfenning, F., Schürmann, C.: System description: Twelf — a meta-logical framework for deductive systems. In: CADE 1999. LNCS (LNAI), vol. 1632, pp. 202–206. Springer, Heidelberg (1999). https://doi.org/10.1007/3-540-48660-7_14

21. Pierce, B.C.: Types and Programming Languages. MIT Press, Cambridge (2002)

22. van der Rest, C., Poulsen, C.B., Rouvoet, A., Visser, E., Mosses, P.: Intrinsically-typed definitional interpreters à la carte. In: Proceedings of the ACM on Programming Languages (PACMPL), vol. 6, no. OOPSLA2, October 2022. https://doi.org/10.1145/3563355

23. Rouvoet, A., Bach Poulsen, C., Krebbers, R., Visser, E.: Intrinsically-typed definitional interpreters for·linear, session-typed languages. In: Blanchette, J., Hritcu, C. (eds.) Proceedings of the 9th ACM SIGPLAN International Conference on Certified Programs and Proofs, CPP 2020, New Orleans, LA, USA, 20–21 January 2020, pp. 284–298. ACM (2020). https://doi.org/10.1145/3372885.3373818

24. Sewell, P., et al.: Ott: effective tool support for the working semanticist. J. Funct. Program. **20**(1), 71–122 (2010). https://doi.org/10.1017/S0956796809990293
25. Tait, W.W.: Intensional interpretations of functionals of finite type I. J. Symb. Log. **32**(2), 198–212 (1967). https://doi.org/10.2307/2271658
26. Thiemann, P.: Intrinsically-typed mechanized semantics for session types. In: Komendantskaya, E. (ed.) Proceedings of the 21st International Symposium on Principles and Practice of Declarative Programming, PPDP 2019, New York, NY, USA, pp. 19:1–19:15. Association for Computing Machinery (2019). https://doi.org/10.1145/3354166.3354184

System Description: A Theorem-Prover for Subregular Systems: The Language Toolkit and Its Interpreter, Plebby

Dakotah Lambert[✉][iD]

Université Jean Monnet Saint-Étienne, CNRS, Institut d Optique Graduate School, Laboratoire Hubert Curien, UMR 5516, 42023 Saint-Étienne, France
dakotahlambert@acm.org

Abstract. We introduce here a domain-specific language, PLEB. The Piecewise-Local Expression Builder interpreter (plebby) is an interactive system for defining, manipulating, and classifying regular formal languages. The interactive theorem-proving environment provides a generalization of regular expressions with which one can intuitively construct languages via constraints. These constraints retain their semantics upon extension to larger alphabets. The system allows one to decide implications and equalities, either at the language level (with a specified alphabet) or at the logical level (across all possible alphabets). Additionally, one can decide membership in a number of predefined classes, or arbitrary algebraic varieties. With several views of a language, including multiple algebraic structures, the system provides ample opportunity to explore and understand properties of languages.

Keywords: Formal language theory · Subregular analysis · Semigroup classification · Interactive theorem proving · Mathematical library

1 Introduction

The study of formal languages is fundamental to the field of theoretical computer science. The regular languages in particular correspond to finite-state automata, which model stateful systems such as neural networks [21], text processing [43], robotics [33], and much more. So fundamental are these concepts that nearly any text on the theory of computation will include chapters on the regular languages including constructions of finite automata and operations under which they are closed, *cf.* [18,25,41]. Beyond theoretical computer science, finite-state methods form a basis for much of computational linguistics, *cf.* [7,15,19].

Initially developed as a study aid over the duration of an undergraduate course in the theory of computation, the Language Toolkit (LTK) is a Haskell library for working with constraint-based descriptions of languages. It is freely available under the MIT open-source license.[1] Of the many tools it ships with,

---

[1] At https://github.com/vvulpes0/Language-Toolkit-2/tree/develop one finds the latest unstable version of the software, and full stable releases can be found at https://hackage.haskell.org/package/language-toolkit.

© The Author(s), under exclusive license to Springer Nature Singapore Pte Ltd. 2024
J. Gibbons and D. Miller (Eds.): FLOPS 2024, LNCS 14659, pp. 311–328, 2024.
https://doi.org/10.1007/978-981-97-2300-3_16

we focus here on the domain-specific language it defines (PLEB) and its associated interpreter, plebby. This provides a practical and pedagogical system for manipulating regular languages and finite machines, essentially a Prolog for the regular languages. The primary features of the system are the ability to decide equivalences and implications, at the logical level or at the language level, and the ability to decide which subregular classes contain a given language.

The space of regular languages is rich. McNaughton and Papert [27] discuss several of these classes, and for each class they provide a description of what kind of information is relevant to its patterns. For instance, the languages locally testable in the strict sense (often called "strictly local") distinguish words by their substrings up to some fixed length k. Rogers and Lambert [36] discuss a broader collection of classes of formal languages, with a focus on those that correspond to quantifier-free first-order systems. The PLEB programming language is particularly optimized for expressing these quantifier-free formulae, but it is powerful enough to describe any regular language. The direct mapping between these logical languages and PLEB expressions allows students and researchers to better analyze and comprehend these patterns than with basic regular expressions alone. Because of this and other functionality, plebby has been used in teaching graduate courses in computational linguistics at Stony Brook University, as well as in projects such as the machine-learning benchmark, MLRegTest [31].

Like foma [20], Pyformlang [38], and OpenFST [1], the LTK provides mechanisms for defining regular languages via the equivalence between regular expressions and finite-state automata. The core Haskell library implements all of the operations that one would expect. It offers constructions for products, concatenations, complements, and reversals, among other things. It also provides mechanisms to determinize automata or to minimize them. The PLEB language allows one to incrementally define arbitrary regular languages by describing the interaction of constraints. The semantics of constraints are maintained through all manipulations, so they need only mention relevant symbols. The alphabet grows as new symbols are encountered. We offer some degree of compatibility with foma [20] and OpenFST [1] by means of the common AT&T-style textual format for interchange. Additionally we support visualizations via the AT&T GraphViz system.

Unlike these other systems, a distinguishing feature of the LTK is the inclusion of functions for algebraic analysis. As algebraic techniques provide a simple and uniform way to characterize classes of formal languages, they form the foundation for many of our classification algorithms. Caron [5] implements tests for some of the same classes in the LANGAGE package for Maple, but the algebraic lens provides much more power and flexibility. The Semigroups package for GAP [28] provides some tooling for this kind of classification (via semigroups), but offers no simple mechanism for constructing regular languages. And while both foma and OpenFST are excellent packages for constructing regular languages, they do not offer the same level of support for classification, for exploring logical implications between systems of constraints, nor for grammatical inference [17]. We provide all of these things, although we will not discuss grammatical inference further in this work.

In short, the Language Toolkit is not yet another automata library. Automata are a core internal representation, but the primary features of the system are as follows. First, it allows for definition of languages with an expression format built upon logical formulae involving precedence, adjacency, and relativized adjacency. This logic-based formalism replaces the more traditional regular-expression syntax. One can then use the system to prove or disprove logical claims regarding those languages. Next, languages can be classified with respect to several subregular hierarchies, indicating which kinds of logic suffice to describe them and which computational mechanisms suffice to recognize them or learn them. With the algebraic techniques, classification is extended to user-defined classes with no modification to the code. Finally, there are grammatical inference and constraint-extraction tools. These are the features that have made the Language Toolkit so useful during the past decade of its development. Not only does it provide clean implementations of textbook algorithms on automata for pedagogical use, it provides this wealth of utility for analysis of regular languages that one would not find in any other system.

We begin in Sect. 2 by detailing our generalized regular expression format, PLEB expressions. These include containment of factors, all of the operations which define regular expressions, the other Boolean operations, infiltration and shuffle products, upward and downward closures with respect to subsequences, neutral letters, and Brzozowski derivatives. Only Unicode (UTF-8) input is supported, but every operation can be expressed in pure ASCII if this is desired. The complete set of operations is listed in both forms in Table 2 on page 302.

Next in Sect. 3, we detail how one might use the system to explore relationships between languages or between systems of constraints. We describe how the `:cequal` and `:cimplies` commands query logical equivalence and implication, respectively, between systems of constraints. The `:equal` and `:implies` commands operate instead at the language level, restricted to the current universe of symbols. This separation is possible due to our use of what we call automata with constraint semantics. In Sect. 4, we give a brief overview of the algebraic theory of formal languages and demonstrate how one might classify languages. This allows for some exploration of the relationships between language classes, as one may construct a separating language and verify that it does, indeed, separate the classes. Finally, we conclude with directions for future extension. Throughout this work, lines prefixed by > are code that can be run in plebby. We also include an appendix, demonstrating how one might use plebby to help answer some questions from various textbooks.

2 Generalized Regular Expressions

In this section, we note some useful operations under which the regular languages are closed. Using these, we introduce a generalized regular expression format that adds no computational power yet vastly simplifies language definition.

Kleene [21] introduced the regular expressions to describe the patterns represented by the artificial neural networks of McCulloch and Pitts [26]. Let $[\![R]\!]$ denote the meaning of the expression R, and suppose A and B are regular expressions. A regular expression over a finite alphabet Σ is defined inductively:

- $\emptyset$ is a regular expression where $[\![\emptyset]\!] = \emptyset$
- For each $\sigma \in \Sigma$, there is an expression σ where $[\![\sigma]\!] = \{\sigma\}$.
- $[\![(A|B)]\!] = [\![A]\!] \cup [\![B]\!]$ is a **union**.
- $[\![(AB)]\!] = \{ab : a \in [\![A]\!], b \in [\![B]\!]\}$ is a **concatenation**.
- $[\![A*]\!] = \varepsilon \cup [\![A]\!] \cup [\![AA]\!] \cup [\![AAA]\!] \cup \cdots$ is the **iteration closure** of A, where ε denotes the empty string. It is the fixed point of $A* = \varepsilon \cup AA*$.

As union and concatenation are associative, bracketing is often omitted. As a matter of convention, iteration binds more tightly than concatenation, which in turn binds more tightly than union. Given a finite set $S = \{s_1, s_2 \ldots, s_n\}$, we denote by S the regular expression $(s_1 | s_2 | \cdots | s_n)$. Thus $\Sigma*$ is the set of all, possibly empty, finite words over letters in Σ.

2.1 Factors and Symbol Sets

Following Rogers and Lambert [37], we take factors to be the fundamental unit of expressions. If $w = \sigma_1 \sigma_2 \ldots \sigma_n$ for $\sigma_i \in \Sigma$, then the expression $\langle \sigma_1\ \sigma_2\ \cdots\ \sigma_n \rangle$, with whitespace between each symbol, represents the set of words which contain w as a substring. That is, it represents words of the form uwv where u and v are elements of $\Sigma*$. At any point between two symbols, a comma may be used to signify an arbitrary gap. Then $\langle \sigma_1, \sigma_2, \ldots, \sigma_n \rangle$ is the set of words which contain w as a subsequence, words of the form $u_0 \sigma_1 u_1 \sigma_2 u_2 \ldots \sigma_n u_n$. Two modifiers anchor the factor to word boundaries: $\rtimes$ fixes the first component to the left edge while $\ltimes$ fixes the last to the right edge. These may be used together: $\rtimes\ltimes \langle \sigma_1\ \sigma_2\ \cdots\ \sigma_n \rangle$ represents the singleton set $\{w\}$. Empty sequences are allowed: $\langle\rangle$ denotes the set of all words containing the empty string as a substring. In other words, $\langle\rangle$ denotes $\Sigma*$.[2]

The individual components of a factor are not actually mere symbols, but sets of symbols. Suppose a and b are symbol sets; a symbol set is defined inductively:

- For any valid name sym it holds that $[\![/sym]\!] = \{sym\}$.
- Named variables are permitted. $[\![s]\!]$ is the set that had been assigned to the variable s, if such a set exists.
- $[\![\{a, b\}]\!] = [\![a]\!] \cup [\![b]\!]$.
- $[\![[a, b]]\!] = [\![a]\!] \cap [\![b]\!]$.

Assignment is expressed by $= name\ value$. In order to save on typing slashes, it is good practice to begin a file or session with a header that declares the symbols to be used, such as:

---

[2] In ASCII, the word boundaries are %| (left) and |% (right), while angle-brackets are represented by less-than and greater-than signs. Other equivalences are given in Table 2 on page 302.

Table 1. Base cases and operations for regular expressions.

	Empty	Symbol	Union	Concatenate	Iterate
Reg	$\emptyset$	σ	$(e_1\|e_2)$	(e_1e_2)	$e*$
Gen	$\neg\langle\rangle$	$\rtimes\ltimes\langle\sigma\rangle$	$\bigvee\{e_1,e_2\}$	$\bullet\{e_1,e_2\}$	$*e$

> $=$a$\{$/a$\}$=b$\{$/b$\}$=c$\{$/c$\}$

This is three assignments collapsed onto a single line, binding the symbols a, b, and c to the variables a, b, and c, respectively. Except in close proximity to such definitions, we shall continue to use the slash notation throughout, so that all examples behave properly in a fresh environment.

2.2 Booleans, Concatenation, and Iteration

Any introductory text on finite automata, such as that of Hopcroft and Ullman [18], will contain a proof that regular languages are all and only those expressible by such machines. Using this equivalence, one easily finds that the class of regular languages is closed not only under (finitary) union but also under (finitary) **intersection** and under **complement**. If $e_1, e_2, \ldots, e_n$ are PLEB-expressions, then $\bigvee\{e_1, e_2, \ldots, e_n\}$ denotes their union, $\bigwedge\{e_1, e_2, \ldots, e_n\}$ their intersection, and $\neg e_1$ the complement of e_1. For empty sequences, the neutral element of the operation is chosen. An empty union is the empty set, equivalent to $\neg\langle\rangle$, while an empty intersection is the universal language that accepts every word, equivalent to $\langle\rangle$. Union and intersection are variadic operations, taking a sequence of arguments. Complement is a monadic operator, taking just one.

Concatenation, denoted $\bullet(e_1, e_2, \ldots, e_n)$, is another variadic operator. There is also gapped concatenation, denoted $\bullet\bullet(e_1, e_2, \ldots, e_n)$ and equivalent to concatenation interspersed with arbitrary content: $\bullet(e_1, \langle\rangle, e_2, \langle\rangle, \ldots, \langle\rangle, e_n)$. The Kleene star operator signifying the iteration closure is yet another monadic operator, denoted $*e_1$. We provide $+e_1$ as syntactic sugar for $\bullet(e_1, *e_1)$. All operators are prefixes; the monadic operators attach directly to the expression upon which they act, while variadic operators attach to braces (or, equivalently, parentheses) embracing a comma-separated sequence of operands. At this point, we can represent any regular expression. A summary of equivalences is provided in Table 1. The union and iteration operators would work identically if concatenation were right-to-left rather than left-to right. So regular languages are closed under reversal as well. We offer a monadic operator, $\rightleftarrows$, for this task.

2.3 Subsequences and Shuffle Ideals

In Sect. 2.1 we noted that if $w = \sigma_1\sigma_2\ldots\sigma_n$ then $\langle\sigma_1, \sigma_2, \ldots, \sigma_n\rangle$ is the set of all words that contain w as a subsequence. This is a **shuffle ideal**. In general, given an arbitrary expression e, we can define $\uparrow e$ as the set of all words which contain any word in $[\![e]\!]$ as a subsequence. That this **upward closure** is regular is a consequence of Higman's Lemma and the resulting language is in the one-half level of the Straubing hierarchy, *cf.* [30]. One constructs ↑*e* by adding self-loops on each symbol to each state of the automaton represented by *e*. This operation is idempotent.

We will see more on the `:cequal` command in the next section. Essentially, it indicates whether two constraints are logically equivalent. With it, we can verify the equivalence between an upward closure and a subsequence-factor:

> `:cequal` ↑⋈⋉⟨/a /b /b /a⟩ ⟨/a,/b,/b,/a⟩
True

We may also close in the other direction: the **downward closure** of *e*, denoted ↓*e*, is the set of all words which are contained as a subsequence by some word in *e*. That is, ↓*e* is the set of words obtained by beginning from some word in *e* and deleting zero or more instances of zero or more symbols. One constructs ↓*e* by adding edges consuming no input in parallel with all edges of the automaton represented by *e*. This operation is idempotent. Languages closed under subsequence, that is, languages L such that $\downarrow L \equiv L$, have been studied by Haines [14] for their interesting mathematical properties as well as by Rogers *et al.* [35] for their linguistic relevance.

Upward closure is a specific case of the shuffle product. The shuffle product of two words is defined inductively as follows, where *a* and *b* are symbols in Σ and *u* and *v* are words in $\Sigma*$ [24].

$$u \sqcup \varepsilon = u = \varepsilon \sqcup u$$
$$au \sqcup bv = a(u \sqcup bv) \cup b(au \sqcup v)$$

Given two languages A and B, their shuffle product is the set $A \sqcup B = \{a \sqcup b : a \in A, b \in B\}$. For a given expression *e*, it is the case that $\uparrow e$ is logically equivalent to $\sqcup\{e, \langle\rangle\}$. The infiltration product, denoted ⇑, is defined similarly [8].

$$u \Uparrow \varepsilon = u = \varepsilon \Uparrow u$$
$$au \Uparrow bv = \begin{cases} a(u \Uparrow bv) \cup b(au \Uparrow v) \cup a(u \Uparrow v) & \text{if } (a = b) \\ a(u \Uparrow bv) \cup b(au \Uparrow v) & \text{otherwise.} \end{cases}$$

We provide monadic ↑ and ↓ operators as well as variadic ⇑ and ⊔ operators. The variadic operators require some caution. As discussed in Sect. 3, subexpressions have their alphabets semantically extended when used in larger expressions. When computing shuffle products, it may be wise to fix the alphabet of each subexpression to a desired set T by intersecting with $*⋈⋉\langle\{T\}\rangle$.

2.4   Tiers and Neutral Letters

Subsequences provide a simple mechanism to describe long-distance dependencies, but they are not the only available mechanism. Another possibility, which has been useful in computational linguistics [16] and in robotic control [33] hinges on the notion of a **tier** of salient symbols. If symbols are not salient to the constraint, then they are ignored entirely. Neither inserting them nor deleting them can influence whether a word is accepted [23]. In other words, symbols not salient are **neutral**. Using this notion of salience and neutrality, one can describe long-distance constraints as if they were local.

Given a symbol set T, we provide two monadic operators. The first, $[T]e$, restricts the alphabet of e to the symbols in T, then adds self-loops on each other symbol to each state. This yields the inverse tier-projection from T of e, the words which satisfy e on the T-tier. The other operator, $|T|e$, makes each element of T neutral in e. Edges which consume no input are added in parallel to each edge labeled by an element of T, and then self-loops labeled by each such element are added to each state. $|T|e$ is equivalent to $\sqcup\{\bigwedge\{e, *\rtimes\ltimes\langle T\rangle\}, \neg\langle T\rangle\}$. For convenience, if T is a union of multiple symbol sets then the outermost braces may be omitted.

For example, the constraint $[/a, /b]\neg\langle/a\ /b\rangle$ over projected substrings is logically equivalent to the constraint $\neg\langle/a, /b\rangle$ over subsequences. As we will see in the next section, one can verify this:

```
> :cequal  [/a,/b]¬⟨/a /b⟩  ¬⟨/a,/b⟩
True
```

Both $[T]$ and $|T|$ are idempotent operations. Further, $\neg[T]e$ is equivalent to $[T]\neg e$ and $\neg|T|e$ is equivalent to $|T|\neg e$ [23].

2.5 Brzozowski Derivatives and Quotients

Given a language L and a prefix s, one might wish to know which strings t act as valid completions where $st \in L$. This **Brzozowski derivative** is sometimes denoted $s^{-1}L$, so named as Brzozowski used the operation in finding the derivatives of regular expressions [3]. A generalization of this is the **left-quotient** $A\backslash B$, the set of strings t that can be appended to a string in A to yield a string in B.

Similarly, the **right-quotient** B/A is the set of strings s that can be prepended to a string in A to yield a string in B. The expression B/A is clearly equivalent to $(A^R\backslash B^R)^R$, where x^R denotes the reversal of x.

Hopcroft and Ullman [18] provide a nonconstructive proof that if B is regular then B/A (and, of course, $A\backslash B$) is regular for any language A. For regular A, we may use a simple construction on automata. In order to compute $A\backslash B$, first compute the concatenation $C = A\Sigma*$. Then, compute the product $(A \times C) \times B$. The accepting states are those whose B- and C-components are both accepting, and the initial states are those whose A-components are accepting. This then begins computation at any state where A could end, and accepts only strings that would be valid continuations in B.

We provide variadic functions for both quotients. They are not associative operations, and so they are best used only dyadically: $[\![\backslash\backslash(A, B)]\!] = [\![A]\!]\backslash[\![B]\!]$ and $[\![//(B, A)]\!] = [\![B]\!]/[\![A]\!]$.

An example, suppose that B is the set of words that do not contain an ab substring and that A is a set of words such that every word in A ends on a.

Table 2. Monadic (left, $\oplus e$), and variadic (right, $\oplus\{e_1, e_2, \ldots, e_n\}$) operators.

Syntax	ASCII	Meaning		Syntax	ASCII	Empty	Meaning
¬	!	complement		⋁	\/	¬⟨⟩	union
*	*	iteration closure		⋀	/\	⟨⟩	intersection
+	+	iteration (nonempty)		•	@	⋈⋉⟨⟩	concatenation
⇌	-	reversal		••	@@	⋈⋉⟨⟩	gapped concatenation
↑	^	upward closure		⇑	.^.	⋈⋉⟨⟩	infiltration product
↓	$	downward closure		⊔	|_|_|	⋈⋉⟨⟩	shuffle product
[T]	[T]	salience restriction		\\	\\	⋈⋉⟨⟩	left-quotient
|T|	|T|	neutralizing		//	//	⋈⋉⟨⟩	right-quotient

Note that $A\backslash B$ is the set of all words that neither begin with b nor contain the ab substring. We shall see more on the `:cimplies` command in the next section, but for now we notice that in this quotient no word begins with b.

```
> :cimplies  \\(⋉⟨/a⟩,¬⟨/a /b⟩)  ¬⋈⟨/b⟩
True
```

We can also use these quotients to construct the prefix closure $//(e, \langle\rangle)$ or suffix closure $\backslash\backslash(\langle\rangle, e)$ of an expression e. Then the substring closure is $\backslash\backslash(\langle\rangle, //(e, \langle\rangle))$.

2.6 Summary

Table 2 lists the available operators, both in Unicode syntax and in ASCII syntax. They are listed in the order introduced in the text. Monadic operators are written directly before their operand. Variadic operators take zero or more comma-separated operands surrounded by either curly braces or parentheses and are written before the opening delimiter. Factors also have ASCII syntax: use less-than and greater-than signs in place of the angle-brackets, and replace the anchor symbols with %| (left) and |% (right).

Like with symbol sets, expressions may be assigned to variables using the syntax = *name value*. A bare expression acts as an assignment to the special variable *it*. And finally, all assignments of both symbol sets and expressions update a special variable *universe*, a symbol set containing all symbols used so far in bound variables.

With the tools discussed so far, one can easily define regular languages using generalized regular expressions known as PLEB expressions. In the next section we discuss how to check for equalities or implications and how one might minimize constraint-based descriptions.

We close this section with a final example. Krebs *et al.* [22] describe a language U_2 that has been instrumental to their work on characterizing classes of languages definable with fragments of first-order logic restricted to two variables. In their work, U_2 is defined over the alphabet $\Sigma = \{a, b, c\}$ as follows.

$$U_2 = (\Sigma* - (\Sigma*ac*a\Sigma*)) \cup (\Sigma* - (\Sigma*bc*b\Sigma*))ac*a\Sigma*$$

Already this expression is extended to include (relative) complements. In this language, c is a neutral letter. After ignoring c, U_2 is a language in which either no aa substring occurs, or there is an aa substring not preceded at any distance by a bb substring. An equivalent PLEB expression is as follows.

```
> =a{/a}=b{/b}=c{/c}
> = U2 [a,b] ⋁{¬⟨a a⟩,•(¬⟨b b⟩,⋈⟨a a⟩)}
```

3 Constraint Analysis

In the previous section, we briefly mentioned the `:cequal` and `:cimplies` commands. This section introduces the mechanism behind them and describes a few of the other commands available. We begin by distinguishing constraints from the languages they yield.

A (formal) language is merely a set of words. A constraint is a logical formula that might be satisfied by one or more words, or which might be unsatisfiable. For example $⟨/a\ /b⟩$ expresses a constraint that the ab substring appears somewhere, and $⟨/a,/b⟩$ expresses a constraint that the ab subsequence appears somewhere. These are not logically equivalent, but the first does logically imply the second. And if the alphabet is merely $\{a, b\}$, then the language they express is the same.

```
> = substr ⟨/a /b⟩
> = subseq ⟨/a,/b⟩
> :cequal substr subseq
False
> :cimplies substr subseq
True
> :cimplies subseq substr
False
> :equal substr subseq
True
> =c{/c}
> :equal substr subseq
False
```

This example demonstrates the above observations. The presence of an ab substring logically implies the presence of an ab subsequence, but the reverse does not hold. The `:cequal` and `:cimplies` commands operate at the constraint level, comparing logical semantics. However, the `:equal` and `:implies` commands operate at the language level, restricting the domain to the current universe of symbols. If the alphabet is exactly the set $\{a, b\}$, then the two expressions yield the same language, but if instead it were $\{a, b, c\}$ then they would not.

This works because factors are constructed in such a way that their semantics are preserved. Expressions are compiled to finite-state automata using not only the symbols they mention, but also a special symbol, ⟨?⟩, which represents all others. This acts as the @ of [19]. When combining expressions, their alphabets

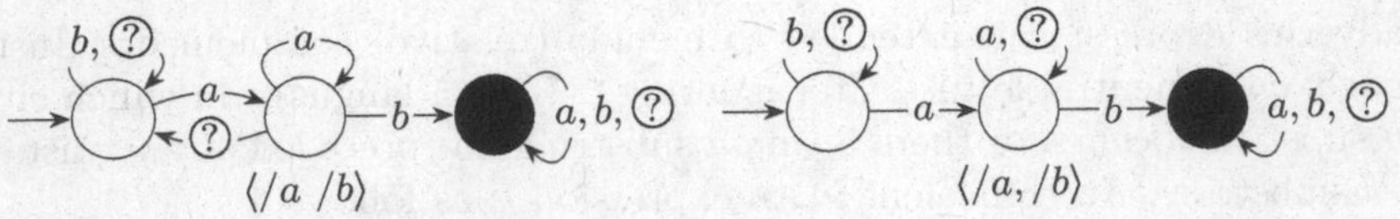

Fig. 1. Automata with constraint semantics.

must be **semantically extended** by inserting edges on any new symbols in parallel with these ⑦-edges. We designate these as automata with **constraint semantics**. Figure 1 depicts our example substring and subsequence constraints. When displaying automata with the `:display` command, they are first **desemantified** by stripping the wildcard symbols and normalizing the result.

One might use these tools to construct expressions that recreate a given pattern. Given a language, be that one constructed from a PLEB expression, one read from an OpenFST-compatible automaton file using `:readATT`, or one imported using the grammatical inference commands (not described in this work), one can hypothesize constraints and ask if the language `:implies` those constraints. Keeping any that are successfully implied, eventually one reaches a point where the cooccurrence (intersection) of the proposed constraints is `:equal` to the language. The set may be large. Removing one constraint at a time, one may ask if the cooccurrence of the remaining constraints `:implies` the removed constraint. If this implication holds, then the constraint is redundant and need not be included. At times, it may be useful to `:display` the difference between systems of constraints, in order to see what is accepted that should not be or vice versa. Finally one is left with a minimal set of constraints that describes the language. There may well be other such sets.

This has been a sampling of ways in which plebby can help explore formal languages through verifying accurate factorization and minimizing systems of constraints. The next section describes classification techniques. Different classes of languages correspond to different kinds of constraints, so the techniques presented ahead may also be useful for such analysis.

4   Algebra and Complexity Analysis

Chomsky's [9] hierarchy includes no classes more restrictive than the regular languages. However, there are several well-motivated subclasses of this class. Every language is associated with a semigroup called its **syntactic semigroup**, and the regular languages are all and only those whose syntactic semigroups are finite [32]. We offer commands to display the algebraic structure of a language in various ways. One can view a Cayley graph using `:synmon`, or an egg-box diagram in the sense of [10] using `:eggbox`. Additionally, a Hasse diagram of the syntactic order in the sense of Pin [29] can be displayed with `:synord`.

Eilenberg's theorem established a formal correspondence between classes of regular languages and classes defined by collections of equations, called pseudovarieties, of finite semigroups [12,13]. A **pseudovariety**, henceforth simply called a **variety,** is a class of semigroups closed under division and finitary products, where a semigroup S is said to divide another semigroup T if S is a quotient of a subsemigroup of T. Varieties of (finite) semigroups are called +-varieties, while varieties of (finite) monoids are *-varieties. We provide three commands: `:isVarietyM` for *-varieties, `:isVarietyS` for +-varieties, and `:isVarietyT` for what would be +-varieties after removing any neutral letters.

These commands take two arguments. The first is a description of the variety, and the second is the expression to test. A variety is a semicolon-separated collection of universally-quantified weak inequalities, all wrapped in square brackets. Inequalities are over the syntactic order of Pin [29]. All variables in these relations are a single letter, and concatenation (multiplication in the semigroup) is denoted by adjacency. Reiterman describes another operator, denoted $\pi(x)$, which maps x to the unique idempotent element in the subsemigroup generated by x [34]. Since then, this has more typically been denoted x^ω, cf. [29], although in plebby we denote it $x*$ for ease of entry. This operator allows varieties to be defined by a single conjunction of equations rather than being ultimately defined by a series of such conjunctions [34].

For example we might ask whether a language has a syntactic semigroup which is both commutative ($ab = ba$) and idempotent ($xx = x$). For concreteness, we will perform this test against two languages: the language which contains an ab substring, and the language which contains both a and b. In both cases, the alphabet shall be $\Sigma = \{a, b, c\}$.

```
> =a{/a}=b{/b}=c{/c}
> :isVarietyS [ab=ba;xx=x] ⟨a b⟩
False
> :isVarietyS [ab=ba;xx=x] ⋀{⟨a⟩,⟨b⟩}
True
```

This particular class is well-studied and so there is a shortcut, `:isCB` (for "commutative band"), which performs the same operation. In many cases, the shortcut commands employ faster algorithms than the general variety check.

Because a language and its complement share the same syntactic semigroup, a class not closed under complement cannot be a variety. Pin uses the concept of a syntactic order to capture some such classes as varieties of ordered semigroups [29]. It is for this reason that our variety-testing commands also allow the use of the weak inequalities, $\leq$ and $\geq$, under the syntactic order. As all variables are universally-quantified, strict inequalities are meaningless. Thus $<$ and $>$ are synonyms for $\leq$ and $\geq$, respectively.

4.1   Some Varieties with Shortcuts

As one might imagine, there are boundless varieties of interest. We provide shortcut commands for many of them. In this section we list a few of them by name alongside their equivalent commands and their language-theoretic characterizations. There are several others; for a full list, see the `:help` in the interpreter.

Locally Testable. See [27] or [4]. A language is locally testable iff there is some integer k such that the set of substrings of length k of a word is sufficient information to determine whether the word is accepted. The commands for deciding this class are :isLT and :isVarietyS [a*xa*ya*=a*ya*xa*;(a*xa*)*=a*xa*].

Tier-Based Locally Testable. See [23]. A language is tier-based locally testable iff after removing its neutral letters it is locally testable. This class is decided by :isTLT and :isVarietyT [a*xa*ya*=a*ya*xa*;(a*xa*)*=a*xa*]. In either case, the set, T, of nonneutral letters is reported.

Piecewise Testable. See [40]. The subsequence analogue of locally testable, a language is piecewise testable iff there is some integer k such that the set of subsequences of length k of a word is sufficient information to determine whether the word is accepted. The commands for deciding this class are :isPT and :isVarietyM [y(xy)*=(xy)*=(xy)*x].

Strictly Piecewise. See [14] or [35]. A restriction of the piecewise testable languages, the strictly piecewise languages are those definable by a finite set of forbidden subsequences. This class is decided by the :isSP or :isVarietyM [1≤x] commands. The size, k, of forbidden subsequences is reported when using :isSP. Equivalently, given an expression e, one can decide whether e is strictly piecewise using :equal e ↓e. The complements of strictly piecewise languages correspond precisely to the one-half level of the Straubing hierarchy [30].

Locally Threshold Testable. See [27] or [2]. A language is locally threshold testable iff it is definable by Boolean combinations of constraints that a particular substring occurs at least some fixed finite number n of times. These are the languages first-order definable with successor but without general precedence [42]. The commands for deciding this class are :isLTT and :isVarietyS [e*af*be*cf*=e*cf*be*af*;xx*=x*].

Tier-Based Locally Threshold Testable. See [23]. A language is tier-based locally testable iff after removing its neutral letters it is locally threshold testable. The commands for deciding this class are :isTLTT or :isVarietyT [e*af*be*cf*=e*cf*be*af*;xx*=x*]. In either case, the set, T, of nonneutral letters is reported.

Star-Free. See [39]. A language is star-free if and only if it is definable by a regular expression generalized to allow intersection and complement but restricted by disallowing the use of the iteration operator. These are the languages first-order definable with general precedence [27]. The commands for deciding this class are :isSF and :isVarietyM [xx*=x*]. Notice that this equation is one of the equations for locally threshold testable. This is in general an easy way to construct sub- and supervarieties of a variety: simply add or remove equations, add or remove constraints.

4.2   Some Other Well-Studied Classes

While a number of language classes correspond precisely to varieties of semi-groups or monoids, this is not always the case. As noted in the previous section, inequalities allow for the capture of classes that are not closed under comple-ment. However, even these ordered varieties cannot capture classes not closed under both union and intersection. This section discusses two such classes which see wide application.

Strictly Local. See [27]. A restriction of the locally testable languages, analo-gous to that which derives strictly piecewise from piecewise testable, a language is strictly local if and only if it is definable by a finite set of forbidden substrings. These are decided by :isSL using an algorithm implied by the work of Caron [5] and by Edlefsen *et al.* [11]. The size, k, of forbidden substrings is reported.

Tier-Based Strictly Local. See [16] or [23]. A language is tier-based strictly local if and only if after removing its neutral letters it is strictly local. This class is decided by :isTSL. The size, k, of forbidden substrings is reported, as is the set T of nonneutral letters.

4.3   Summary

This section has discussed a sampler of the classification algorithms offered by plebby and, in general, by the Language Toolkit. A full list is available in the interpreter's help system (see :help classification), or arbitrary varieties may be tested. (Note that all of these decision problems operate at the language level, not at the constraint level.) Knowing which set of classes contain a given language can offer insight regarding the properties of the language. This can assist in factoring the language, as one knows what types of constraints to try to find.

This system is also useful in exploring relationships between classes. While it cannot at this moment automatically determine whether a subclass relationship exists, one can manually construct a separating example language and verify that the separation holds. If a language is in class C but not in class C', then C is not a subclass of C'.

5   Conclusion

We have introduced plebby, the interactive theorem-prover built atop and pack-aged with the Language Toolkit, and demonstrated its use in defining, manipu-lating, and classifying regular languages. The project is freely available under the

MIT open-source license. Functionality goes well beyond what has been discussed here; all available commands are documented in the included manual pages or the interpreter's `:help` system. We only briefly touched on the visualization capabilities, and did not even mention the file I/O or grammatical inference capabilities. There are additionally stand-alone programs to `classify`, `display`, or automatically `factorize` regular languages.

As these tools were created for the purposes of education and research in mathematical and computational linguistics, performance was never the greatest concern. However, in order to be more widely useful, one key area of future work will be to improve performance to scale to industrial operations, where the automata under consideration might have large alphabets and several thousand states. Part of this work will involve changing the underlying representation of some of the core data structures; this work has already begun through splitting off some of the algebraic procedures into a separate `finite-semigroups` package.[3] The tradeoff is that the representation in this package strips much of the information that is pedagogically useful, such as which elements correspond to which strings. Thus care must be taken to avoid diminishing pedagogical utility when constructing representations for speed. For the classification task alone, we have also created AMALGAM[4] in the C programming language, which similarly discards information for better performance.

Other directions for future work are numerous. Some of our classification procedures return a description of the class parameters in addition to the Boolean response. We would like to provide such parameterizations for more classes in the future. For nonmembership, in some cases it might be nice to generate parameterized words as evidence. For some classes, this would be easy and would add to the utility as a theorem-prover. We would also like to be able to automatically generate semigroups satisfying given conditions, which may help in disproving a subset relationship between two varieties. Extending our current system, or perhaps creating a companion system, for similar analysis of finite-state transducers is a more involved goal. Using symbolic predicate-based symbols like the Microsoft Automata toolkit would increase utility in computational linguistics, especially with Carpenter-style feature systems [6]. Finally, we would like to add the capacity to translate foma scripts into PLEB expressions, or otherwise import automata with constraint semantics from such files.

We hope that this system will continue to enlighten all who study formal languages and their connections to algebra and logic.

Acknowledgments. The system described in this work owes its creation to the wonderful Theory of Computation course taught by Jim Rogers at Earlham College. Further enhancements arose from work with Jeffrey Heinz at Stony Brook University. And much gratitude is extended to the anonymous reviewers for their helpful suggestions.

Disclosure of Interests. The authors have no competing interests to declare that are relevant to the content of this article.

---

[3] Available at https://hackage.haskell.org/package/finite-semigroups.
[4] Available at https://github.com/vvulpes0/amalgam.

Appendix

This appendix contains selected worked exercises from various textbooks.

Exercise 2.1 from McNaughton and Papert [27]

"Decide whether each of the Figures 2.2–2.8 represents a locally testable event. Decide further whether it is locally testable in the strict sense." We cover only figures 2.4, 2.7 and 2.8. These figures are represented by the following AT&T files, named mp-2-1-4.att, mp-2-1-7.att and mp-2-1-8.att, respectively.

mp-2-1-4.att			mp-2-1-7.att			mp-2-1-8.att		
1	4	a	1	2	a	1	2	a
1	2	b	1	1	b	1	5	b
1			1			2	2	a
2	6	a	2	3	a	2	3	b
2	3	b	2	1	b	3	2	a
3	1	a	2			3	4	b
3	6	b	3	3	a	4	2	a
4	5	a	3	4	b	4	4	b
4	6	b	4	3	a	4		
5	6	a	4	5	b	5	6	a
5	1	b	5	6	a	5	5	b
6	6	a	5	7	b	6	7	a
6	6	b	6	3	a	6	5	b
			6	7	b	7	7	a
			7	6	a	7	5	b
			7	1	b	7		

```
> :readATT mp-2-1-4.att _ _
> :isLT it
True
> :isSL it
True: k=5
> :readATT mp-2-1-7.att _ _
> :isLT it
False
> :isSL it
False
> :readATT mp-2-1-8.att _ _
> :isLT it
True
> :isSL it
False
```

Here, the tool directly answers the exercises, even providing additional information regarding the factor size k for the language locally testable in the strict sense.

5.1 Exercises from Sipser [41]

In the third edition of "Introduction to the Theory of Computation", Sipser [41] asks students to construct state diagrams for various regular languages. Exercise 1.4 focuses on intersections, 1.5 on complements, and 1.6 has assorted other languages. We select a small sample to cover here, all over the alphabet $\Sigma = \{a, b\}$:

1.4e $\{w | w$ starts with an a and has at most one b$\}$

1.5c $\{w | w$ contains neither the substrings ab nor ba$\}$

1.6n All strings except the empty string

As an aside, exercise 1.6 uses $\Sigma = \{0, 1\}$ in the original.

```
> =a{/a}=b{/b}
> :display  ⋀{⋈⟨a⟩,¬⟨b,b⟩}        # 1.4e
> :display  ¬⋁{⟨a b⟩,⟨b a⟩}       # 1.5c
> :display  ¬⋈⋈⟨⟩                  # 1.6n
```

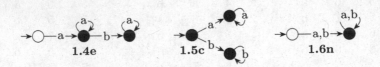

1.4e   **1.5c**   **1.6n**

Fig. 2. State diagrams for Sipser, with node labels omitted.

Figure 2 depicts the results. Rejecting sink states are omitted from the display and must be filled in by hand.

References

1. Allauzen, C., Riley, M., Schalkwyk, J., Skut, W., Mohri, M.: OpenFst: a general and efficient weighted finite-state transducer library. In: Holub, J., Žd'árek, J. (eds.) CIAA 2007. LNCS, vol. 4783, pp. 11–23. Springer, Heidelberg (2007). https://doi.org/10.1007/978-3-540-76336-9_3
2. Beauquier, D., Pin, J.-E.: Factors of words. In: Ausiello, G., Dezani-Ciancaglini, M., Della Rocca, S.R. (eds.) ICALP 1989. LNCS, vol. 372, pp. 63–79. Springer, Heidelberg (1989). https://doi.org/10.1007/BFb0035752
3. Brzozowski, J.A.: Derivatives of regular expressions. J. ACM **11**(4), 481–494 (1964). https://doi.org/10.1145/321239.321249
4. Brzozowski, J.A., Simon, I.: Characterizations of locally testable events. Discret. Math. 4(3), 243–271 (1973). https://doi.org/10.1016/S0012-365X(73)80005-6
5. Caron, P.: LANGAGE: a maple package for automaton characterization of regular languages. In: Wood, D., Yu, S. (eds.) WIA 1997. LNCS, vol. 1436, pp. 46–55. Springer, Heidelberg (1998). https://doi.org/10.1007/BFb0031380

6. Carpenter, B.: The Logic of Typed Feature Structures. Cambridge Tracts in Theoretical Computer Science, vol. 32. Cambridge University Press (1992). https://doi.org/10.1017/CBO9780511530098

7. Chandlee, J.: Strictly local phonological processes. Ph.D. thesis, University of Delaware (2014). https://chandlee.sites.haverford.edu/wp-content/uploads/2015/05/Chandlee_dissertation_2014.pdf

8. Chen, K.T., Fox, R.H., Lyndon, R.C.: Free differential calculus IV. The quotient groups of the lower central series. Ann. Math. **68**(1), 81–95 (1958). https://doi.org/10.2307/1970044

9. Chomsky, N.: On certain formal properties of grammars. Inf. Control **2**(2), 137–167 (1959). https://doi.org/10.1016/S0019-9958(59)90362-6

10. Clifford, A.H., Preston, G.B.: The Algebraic Theory of Semigroups, Mathematical Surveys and Monographs, vol. 7. American Mathematical Society, Providence (1961)

11. Edlefsen, M., Leeman, D., Myers, N., Smith, N., Visscher, M., Wellcome, D.: Deciding strictly local (SL) languages. In: Breitenbucher, J. (ed.) Proceedings of the 2008 Midstates Conference for Undergraduate Research in Computer Science and Mathematics, pp. 66–73 (2008)

12. Eilenberg, S.: Automata, Languages, and Machines, vol. B. Academic Press, New York (1976)

13. Eilenberg, S., Schützenberger, M.P.: On pseudovarieties. Adv. Math. **19**(3), 413–418 (1976). https://doi.org/10.1016/0001-8708(76)90029-3

14. Haines, L.H.: On free monoids partially ordered by embedding. J. Comb. Theory **6**(1), 94–98 (1969). https://doi.org/10.1016/s0021-9800(69)80111-0

15. Heinz, J.: Inductive learning of phonotactic patterns. Ph.D. thesis, University of California, Los Angeles (2007)

16. Heinz, J., Rawal, C., Tanner, H.G.: Tier-based strictly local constraints for phonology. In: Proceedings of the 49th Annual Meeting of the Association for Computational Linguistics: Short Papers, Portland, Oregon, vol. 2, pp. 58–64. Association for Computational Linguistics (2011). https://aclanthology.org/P11-2011

17. de la Higuera, C.: Grammatical Inference: Learning Automata and Grammars. Cambridge University Press (2010). https://doi.org/10.1017/CBO9781139194655

18. Hopcroft, J.E., Ullman, J.D.: Introduction to Automata Theory, Languages, and Computation. Addison-Wesley (1979)

19. Hulden, M.: Finite-state machine construction methods and algorithms for phonology and morphology. Ph.D. thesis, The University of Arizona (2009). https://hdl.handle.net/10150/196112

20. Hulden, M.: Foma: a finite-state compiler and library. In: Proceedings of the Demonstrations Session at EACL 2009, Athens, Greece, pp. 29–32. Association for Computational Linguistics (2009). https://aclanthology.org/E09-2008

21. Kleene, S.C.: Representation of events in nerve nets and finite automata. In: Shannon, C.E., McCarthy, J. (eds.) Automata Studies, Annals of Mathematics Studies, vol. 34, pp. 3–42. Princeton University Press (1956). https://doi.org/10.1515/9781400882618-002

22. Krebs, A., Lodaya, K., Pandya, P.K., Straubing, H.: Two-variable logics with some betweenness relations: expressiveness, satisfiability, and membership. Logical Methods Comput. Sci. **16**(3), 1–41 (2020). https://doi.org/10.23638/LMCS-16(3:16)2020

23. Lambert, D.: Relativized adjacency. J. Logic Lang. Inform. **32**(4), 707–731 (2023). https://doi.org/10.1007/s10849-023-09398-x

24. Lothaire, M.: Combinatorics on Words. Cambridge University Press, New York (1983)

25. MacCormick, J.: What Can Be Computed? A Practical Guide to the Theory of Computation. Princeton University Press (2018)

26. McCulloch, W.S., Pitts, W.: A logical calculus of the ideas immanent in nervous activity. Bull. Math. Biol. **5**, 115–133 (1943). https://doi.org/10.1007/bf02478259

27. McNaughton, R., Papert, S.A.: Counter-Free Automata. MIT Press, Cambridge (1971)

28. Mitchell, J., et al.: Semigroups – GAP Package, 5.1.0 edn. (2022). https://doi.org/10.5281/zenodo.592893

29. Pin, J.-E.: Syntactic semigroups. In: Rozenberg, G., Salomaa, A. (eds.) Handbook of Formal Languages, pp. 679–746. Springer, Heidelberg (1997). https://doi.org/10.1007/978-3-642-59136-5_10

30. Pin, J.E., Weil, P.: Polynomial closure and unambiguous product. Theory Comput. Syst. **30**(4), 383–422 (1997). https://doi.org/10.1007/bf02679467

31. van der Poel, S., et al.: MLRegTest: a benchmark for the machine learning of regular languages (2023). https://doi.org/10.48550/arXiv.2304.07687

32. Rabin, M.O., Scott, D.: Finite automata and their decision problems. IBM J. Res. Dev. **3**(2), 114–125 (1959). https://doi.org/10.1147/rd.32.0114

33. Rawal, C., Tanner, H.G., Heinz, J.: (Sub)regular robotic languages. In: 2011 19th Mediterranean Conference on Control & Automation (MED), pp. 321–326 (2011). https://doi.org/10.1109/MED.2011.5983140

34. Reiterman, J.: The Birkhoff theorem for finite algebras. Algebra Universalis **14**, 1–10 (1982). https://doi.org/10.1007/BF02483902

35. Rogers, J., et al.: On languages piecewise testable in the strict sense. In: Ebert, C., Jäger, G., Michaelis, J. (eds.) MOL 2007/2009. LNCS (LNAI), vol. 6149, pp. 255–265. Springer, Heidelberg (2010). https://doi.org/10.1007/978-3-642-14322-9_19

36. Rogers, J., Lambert, D.: Extracting subregular constraints from regular stringsets. J. Lang. Model. **7**(2), 143–176 (2019). https://doi.org/10.15398/jlm.v7i2.209

37. Rogers, J., Lambert, D.: Some classes of sets of structures definable without quantifiers. In: Proceedings of the 16th Meeting on the Mathematics of Language, Toronto, Canada, pp. 63–77. Association for Computational Linguistics (2019). https://doi.org/10.18653/v1/W19-5706

38. Romero, J.: Pyformlang: an educational library for formal language manipulation. In: Proceedings of the 52nd ACM Technical Symposium on Computer Science Education, pp. 576–582. Association for Computing Machinery, New York (2021). https://doi.org/10.1145/3408877.3432464

39. Schützenberger, M.P.: On finite monoids having only trivial subgroups. Inf. Control **8**(2), 190–194 (1965). https://doi.org/10.1016/s0019-9958(65)90108-7

40. Simon, I.: Piecewise testable events. In: Brakhage, H. (ed.) GI-Fachtagung 1975. LNCS, vol. 33, pp. 214–222. Springer, Heidelberg (1975). https://doi.org/10.1007/3-540-07407-4_23

41. Sipser, M.: Introduction to the Theory of Computation, 3rd edn. Cengage Learning, Boston (2013)

42. Thomas, W.: Classifying regular events in symbolic logic. J. Comput. Syst. Sci. **25**, 360–376 (1982). https://doi.org/10.1016/0022-0000(82)90016-2

43. Thompson, K.: Programming techniques: regular expression search algorithm. Commun. ACM **11**(6), 419–422 (1968). https://doi.org/10.1145/363347.363387

Author Index

J. Gibbons and D. Miller (Eds.): FLOPS 2024, LNCS 14659, p. 329, 2024.
https://doi.org/10.1007/978-981-97-2300-3

Printed in the United States
by Baker & Taylor Publisher Services